Sociology of
Deviant Behavior
fifth edition

Marshall B. Clinard
University of Wisconsin—Madison

Robert F. Meier
Washington State University

HOLT, RINEHART AND WINSTON
New York   Chicago   San Francisco   Dallas
Montreal   Toronto   London   Sydney

Senior Acquisitions Editor	*Frank Graham*
Senior Developmental Editor	*Rosalind Sackoff*
Managing Editor	*Jeanette Ninas Johnson*
Senior Project Editor	*Françoise Bartlett*
Project Editor	*Robin M. Gross*
Production Manager	*Annette Wentz*

Library of Congress Cataloging in Publication Data

Clinard, Marshall Barron, 1911—
  Sociology of deviant behavior.

  Includes bibliographies and indexes.
  1. Deviant behavior.   2. Criminal psychology.
 I. Meier, Robert Frank, 1944– , joint author.
 II. Title.

HM291.C58   1979   301.6′2   78-10495
ISBN 0-03-045026-8

To my children, from whom I have learned a great deal:

Marsha
Stephen
Lawrence

—Marshall B. Clinard

To my parents, who made my learning possible:

Eileen
Frank

—Robert F. Meier

Preface

THIS text is written for undergraduate sociology students of deviance. It provides both a conceptual and a theoretical overview and an analysis of a large number of specific forms of deviance. The emphasis throughout is on the sociological understanding of the meaning, the process, and the control of deviant behavior. Socialization is a unifying theme throughout the text, in addition to the wide array of other theories and studies discussed.

As in the previous editions, we have taken the position that deviant behavior is social behavior, and that if one is to understand what constitutes deviance one must have a knowledge of basic social behavior. Any sociological understanding of deviance requires knowledge of fundamental social processes such as social relationships, social situations, interpersonal influences, and position in the social structure. Basic sociological theory and concepts have been incorporated into the text; thus, an extensive background in sociology is not a prerequisite. Special emphasis has been given such concepts as social norms, social differentiation, subcultural norms, societal reaction, social control, socialization, social roles, deviant acts, and primary and secondary deviation.

The first edition of this book appeared some twenty years ago. It represented a shift from the former conceptual frame of reference of social disorganization and social problems to a more *sociological* orientation built around the concept of deviance from social norms. This first edition moved away from the often eclectic, nonsociological perspective of social problems that characterized writing and teaching in this area, both in the past and even today. Rubington and Weinberg have pointed out that

> the first textbook in deviant behavior appeared in 1957. This book, *Sociology of Deviant Behavior* by Marshall Clinard, provided the first codification of the deviant behavior perspective. . . . Soon after this book appeared, social problems courses began to be redefined. Numerous courses, once called either Social Problems or Social Disorganization, were renamed Sociology of Deviant Behavior (Earl Rubington and Martin S. Weinberg, *The Study of Social Problems: Five Perspectives,* 2d ed., New York: Oxford University Press, 1977, p. 148).

The excellent reception of subsequent editions of this book has probably been due to the fact that each revision has been a substantial revision, demonstrating that a science such as sociology is not static but continues to grow and to change. As a result, each revision has incorporated the changes in sociological approaches to deviance, new concepts, new research, and new literature. Areas of deviance have been added; likewise, others have been dropped to maintain a more contemporary orientation.

Similarly, throughout the various editions, the original author's views have altered, such as changes in the definition of deviance itself. A co-author has been added to the fifth edition, and this has meant the addition of new perspectives in theory and in organization.

As in the past, this new edition is a complete revision. In addition to including pertinent recent deviance literature and reorganizing the book, we have added two new chapters. A new Chapter 3 reviews the main sociological theories of deviance, and a concluding chapter has been added that ends on a more optimistic note, with some new ideas and conclusions rather than the final chapter of suicide as in the previous edition! The new chapter on sociological theories of deviance brings better balance and a contrast with the chapter on individualistic theories, for example, psychiatry and psychoanalysis. In a single chapter it presents and evaluates the sociological approaches of social pathology, social disorganization, anomie, labeling, conflict, control theory, and socialization. It is thus unnecessary for the instructor to add one of the many present-day books that deal with theories of deviance. This book can still be used, however, in social problems courses that emphasize the forms of deviance in our society discussed here.

We have tried to see that the theoretical orientation discussed in the first five chapters is incorporated into the later chapters where various forms of deviance are discussed. The importance of socialization and learning in the acquisition and mainte-nance of deviance, for example, is more explicit in the chapters that deal with crime, drug use, problem drinking, sexual deviance, mental disorders, suicide, and physical disabilities.

In keeping with the earlier editions, most chapters contain a lengthy discussion and an evaluation of various social control measures to deal with specific forms of deviance. These sections combine both theory and social action. Discussions are presented of the role of social control both in inhibiting and intensifying deviance, of such agencies as the police and institutions for deviants, of various alternatives to prisons and mental hospitals, and of methods to deal with illegal behavior of corpora-tions. The issue of the decriminalization of many criminal laws that affect personal morality, such as drug use, public drunkenness, and sexual behavior, is also discussed.

This edition, as did previous editions, emphasizes that almost no behavior can be regarded as being universally deviant in our modern, highly differentiated, urban-ized society. When such unanimity does appear to occur, as in the legal systems of the political state, this may reflect not unanimous accord in a society but the result of the political, social, and economic power of interest groups that try to impose their own views of what constitutes deviance on others who do not view the behavior from the same perspective.

Consequently, while critically examining the absolutist, the statistical, and the labeling definitions of deviance, we have generally adopted a modified relative definition. This relativistic emphasis affords the opportunity for greater balance between an examination, for example, of ordinary property crime such as theft and burglary as well as white-collar and corporate crime. The deviance of persons in high places, whether it relates to a large corporation or to government, is the subject of particular analysis in this fifth edition. In so doing, we have tried to eliminate any bias in studying exclusively the deviance of the lower and the working classes that frequently characterizes much of the writing in this area even today. In fact, the conclusion of the book includes the implications of Watergate for much deviant behavior in general.

Each chapter of this new edition has been revised extensively, dated material has been deleted, and new material has been added. Wherever possible or feasible, lengthy quotations have been greatly shortened and often paraphrased, producing not only a more readable text but one less confusing to the student. Most chapters contain illustrative material from personal documents and case material. Photographs have been included for the first time since the original edition, in keeping with the general interest of students today in visual presentation. Selected readings appear at the end of each chapter. Wherever possible the importance of viewing deviance from the deviant's own perspective has been stressed. Although we recognize the concern for identifying male and female persons in general references, in lieu of a smooth solution we have used the convention of a masculine pronoun when both male and female persons are included in a reference.

The prior editions have acknowledged those persons who have been helpful in the development of this book throughout the years. In this fifth edition we would like particularly to express our appreciation to Barry M. Dank and to Richard S. Stephens for their assistance in their specialized areas of deviance. Gilbert Geis offered a number of useful bibliographical suggestions and criticisms. The contribution of those persons who have made this book possible through their publications on theory and research on deviance is recognized in the footnote citations. To Ruth Clinard we acknowledge the invaluable editorial assistance and the astute criticisms she provided in developing this edition. As in all previous editions, many long hours have gone into her careful editing of the various drafts of the manuscript. We should also like to thank Françoise Bartlett who, as in the previous edition, did the final editing, and Robin M. Gross, who saw the book through to publication.

Madison, Wisconsin   M. B. C.
Pullman, Washington   R. F. M.
October 1978

Contents

PART TWO   **DEVIANT BEHAVIOR** 163

PART ONE

DEVIANCE

One says odd.
Another claims different.
One says strange.
Another claims misfit.
Mighty peculiar how one
and the another
see each one
and one another.
—Bettie N. Holmes

CHAPTER 1

The Concept of Deviance

T HE sociological investigation of deviance as an area of scientific study is little more than a century old. Before that, deviant behavior, whether individual or group in nature, was largely in the realm of philosophical speculation and reasoning or was a subject for moralists. The scientific study of such human behavior as deviance has progressed only as concepts of human behavior—particularly deviant behavior— have developed in the social sciences, along with the tools that make such research possible. Before one can study, or even understand, the nature of deviance, an understanding of society and social norms, social differentiation and subcultural norms, and social sanctions and the process of social control is essential.

SOCIETY AND SOCIAL NORMS

The term "society," or "social group," can be applied to no animals other than humans, for the ties that bind a human group are abstract social relations and not merely biological needs. Human beings depend upon each other from birth, not only for physical and economic survival; they rely on each other socially and for personal development. Human beings alone live in true social groups. Although most animals, like humans, form groups, with even prolonged association, mutual dependence, and cooperation toward biologically common goals, only human social groups share sets of common meanings or symbols and social systems of mutual obligation. Although some people may say that certain human counterparts characterize the lives of other animals, human beings alone have such social institutions as a political state, an economic system, and a religion. Only humans have laws and moral judgments, and only humans experience recurring and repeated social interaction leading to complex social relations. In this process of *social interaction* each individual, by his actions, takes into account what he considers to be the expectation of others; in turn, his behavior shows that he expects others to act toward him in a certain manner.

As a result of group experiences, a human being becomes dependent upon others for human associations, conversation, and social interaction. The importance of this dependence on groups can be demonstrated in situations where group contacts are removed. For example, prison officials have learned that solitary confinement, with its almost complete isolation from human associations, is one of the most severe forms of punishment for any human being. A few days of this type of treatment will usually render the most defiant prisoner tractable. Admiral Byrd, the famous explorer of the Antarctic, voluntarily isolated himself for several months in uninhabited polar regions more than a hundred miles from the nearest human being of his expedition. He described his experiences of being alone and vividly showed how dependent the individual is on social groups when such contacts are removed.

10 P.M. Solitude is an excellent laboratory in which to observe the extent to which manners and habits are conditioned by others. My table manners are atrocious—in this respect I've slipped back hundreds of years; in fact, I have no manners whatsoever. If I feel like it, I eat with my fingers, or out of a can, or standing up—in other words, whichever is easiest. What's left over, I just heave into the slop pail, close to my feet. Come to think of it, no reason why I shouldn't. It's rather a convenient way to eat; I seem to remember reading in Epicurus that a man living alone lives the life of a wolf.

A life alone makes the need for external demonstration almost disappear. Now I seldom cuss, although at first I was quick to open fire at everything that tried my patience. Attending to the electrical circuit on the anemometer pole is no less cold than it was in the beginning; but I work in soundless torment, knowing that the night is vast and profanity can shock no one but myself.

My sense of humor remains, but the only sources of it are my books and myself, and, after all, my time to read is limited. Earlier today, when I came into the hut with my water bucket in one hand and the lantern in the other, I put the lantern on the stove and hung up the bucket. I laughed at this; but, now, when I laugh, I laugh inside; for I seem to have forgotten how to do it aloud. This leads me to think that audible laughter is principally a mechanism for sharing pleasure. . . . My hair hasn't been cut in months. I've let it grow because it comes down around my neck and keeps it warm. I still shave once a week—and that only because I found that a beard is an infernal nuisance outside on account of its tendency to ice up from the breath and freeze the face. Looking in the mirror this morning, I decided that a man without women around him is a man without vanity; my cheeks are blistered and my nose is red and bulbous from a hundred frostbites. How I look is no longer of the least importance; all that matters is how I feel. However, I have kept clean, as clean as I would keep myself at home. But cleanliness has nothing to do with etiquette or coquetry. It is comfort. My senses enjoy the evening bath and are uncomfortable at the touch of underwear that is too dirty.[1]

Norms

Human social relations and behavior are regulated through *social norms.* These social norms are often referred to as standardized ways of acting, or expectations that govern limits of variation in social behavior. A social norm is "any standard rule that states what human beings should or should not think, say, or do under given circumstances."[2] This implies, first, that behavior may differ from the norm, and, second, that it will differ from the norm unless some force, usually termed a *sanction,* is used to bring about conformity. Norms are basic to the definition and to the study of deviance because the potentiality for deviance exists in every norm or rule.[3] The line of how and when behavior is to be interpreted as deviant or to be tolerated is constantly shifting according to public views and the views of various groups. Criminal laws, which also respond to these shifting forces, are simply legal norms that regulate various types of behavior and which the political state enforces by coercive means.

Norms may be classified according to the degree of their acceptance, the mode of any given norm's enforcement, the way any norm is transmitted, and the amount of conformity required by the norm. Some norms are fairly stable in nature; others are more localized.[4] Some social norms may require considerable force to ensure compliance; others may require little or none. Rarely are individuals in a society consciously

---

[1] Reprinted by permission of G. P. Putnam's Sons from *Alone* by Richard E. Byrd. Copyright 1938 by Richard E. Byrd; 1966 by Marie A. Byrd.

[2] Judith Blake and Kingsley Davis, "Norms, Values, and Sanctions," in Robert E. L. Faris, ed., *Handbook of Modern Sociology* (Chicago: Rand McNally, 1964), p. 456. For a discussion of the role of norms, see Arnold Birenbaum and Edward Sagarin, *Norms and Human Behavior* (New York: Holt, Rinehart and Winston, 1976).

[3] Albert K. Cohen, *Deviance and Control* (Englewood Cliffs, N.J.: Prentice-Hall, 1966), p. 4.

[4] Richard T. Morris, "A Typology of Norms," *American Sociological Review,* 21 (1956), 610–613; and Jack P. Gibbs, "Norms: The Problem of Definition and Classification," *American Journal of Sociology,* 70 (1965), 586–594.

aware of the often arbitrary nature of the social norms of a culture or subculture, since they have been introduced to them in the ongoing process of living. They have been learned in this process and transmitted through groups from generation to generation; in this way each individual has incorporated into his own life organization the language, the ideas, and the beliefs of the groups to which he belongs. Human beings thus see the world not with the eyes alone, for if they saw only with the eyes, each would see the same thing; rather, they see the world through their cultural and other group experiences. Even moral judgments are generally not those of the individual alone but of the group or groups to which the individual belongs.[5] The significance of the group nature of norms and of understanding the world through norms has probably never been stated more cogently, even poignantly, than by Faris many years ago when he stated: "For we live in a world or 'cultural reality,' and the whole furniture of earth and choir of heaven are to be described and discussed as they are conceived by men. Caviar is not a delicacy to the general [population]. Cows are not food to the Hindu. Mohammed is not the prophet of God to me. To an atheist, God is not God at all."[6]

In the maintenance of order, norms are crucial. They may be regarded as cultural ideals, or they may be considered in terms of actual behavior in a statistical sense: for example, sexual norms can be examined as cultural ideals or in terms of actual practices. Ideal cultural norms can be inferred from what people say or by observing what they support through their sanctions in the form of rewards or penalties. "Cultural norms, as discovered by research, are statistical entities; that is, there is not a sharp line between normative and not normative, but a gradual shading from norms intensely supported by nearly everyone, to those only casually accepted by relatively few."[7] In any society the qualities of norms are important; some have qualities of "ought" or "should" while others have a more permissive quality. Some are *proscriptive norms:* a person is supposed "not to do this," because certain forms of behavior, such as those contained in the Ten Commandments, must be avoided. *Prescriptive norms* outline what the person must do, indicating this and that form of behavior to which the individual must conform. In one study, it was shown that the predominantly proscriptive norms are more likely to lead to extreme forms of reactions, or sanctions, than when deviations occur from prescriptive norms.[8]

SOCIAL DIFFERENTIATION AND SUBCULTURAL NORMS

An understanding of the underlying nature of highly differentiated, often conflicting norms as an integral part of the organization of modern industrial societies is essential to a meaningful analysis of social deviation. In complex modern societies, group

---

[5]See Leonard Berkowitz and Nigel Walker, "Laws and Moral Judgments," *Sociometry,* 30 (1967), 410–422.
[6]Ellsworth Faris, *The Nature of Human Nature* (New York: McGraw-Hill, 1937), pp. 150–151.
[7]Robin M. Williams, Jr., *American Society* (New York: Knopf, 1960), p. 32.
[8]Ephriam H. Mizruchi and Robert Perrucci, "Norm Qualities and Differential Effects of Deviant Behavior," *American Sociological Review,* 27 (1962), 391–399.

norms may differ radically or only slightly from one another; in other cases, the norms simply differ in emphasis. As a result persons who belong to a number of groups, with each group having either different norms or emphasizing them differently, may experience much personal conflict. The norms and social roles a person acquires from the family group do not necessarily always agree with the norms and social roles of the play group, the age or peer group, work group, or political group. Certain groups may become more important to an individual's life organization than others, and he may, as a result, tend to conform more closely to the norms of the groups with which he feels more closely identified. Although the family group is important, it is only one of many groups related to a person's behavior, whether deviant or nondeviant. Many other sources of norms and social relationships in modern societies are important: social class, occupation, neighborhood, school, church, and the gang or clique. Among more homogeneous peoples, such as primitive or folk societies, most norms and values are perceived in a like fashion by group members, although certainly not entirely so.[9] Members of such societies thus come to share many common objectives and meanings, in contrast to the far more complex modern societies. Relatively distinct groups of persons develop in these complex societies. Here social groups arise out of many attributes such as race, occupation, ethnic background, religion, political party, residence, and many more. Particularly significant in the development of this differentiation are social-class and age or peer groups, as well as a myriad of different occupational groups. Williams points out that "within such complex aggregates as modern nations, many norms are effective only within limited subcultures, and there are wide differences in individual conformity and conceptions of normative structure."[10]

Subcultures

The subcultural norms of most large societies, because of the degree of social differentiation, are so diverse that in all probability only a few norms are accepted as binding on all persons. Sometimes the social groups that have arisen in the manner described here may develop and share a set of values and meanings shared by society of which they are a part. When this occurs such a group may be called a subculture. Simply speaking, a *subculture* is a "culture within a culture." More specifically, a subculture is a collection of norms, values, and beliefs whose content is distinguishable from those of the dominant culture. This implies that the subcultural group participates in and shares the "larger" culture of which it is a part, while at the same time, it has some meanings and values that are unique to it. A subculture is not necessarily in opposition to the larger culture, although if it is the term *counterculture* is more appropriate.[11] Some groups represent countercultures, as in the case of a criminal youth gang.

---

[9]Robert Edgerton, *Deviance: A Cross-Cultural Perspective* (Menlo Park, Calif.: Cummings Publishers, 1976).

[10]Williams, p. 30.

[11]See J. Milton Yinger, "Countercultures and Social Change," *American Sociological Review,* 42 (1977), 833–853. For a critical discussion and review of these concepts, see Marvin E. Wolfgang and Franco Ferracuti, *The Subculture of Violence: Towards an Integrated Theory in Criminology* (London: Tavistock, 1967); and David O. Arnold, ed., *The Sociology of Subcultures* (Berkeley, Calif.: Glendassary Press, 1970).

A variety of subcultures and countercultures, then, characterize large modern societies; often each has its own set of norms and values not only concerning what constitutes proper conduct but also even having to do with what the goals are of life itself. Cohen suggests that subcultures arise in a highly differentiated society when, in the process of effective interaction with one another, a number of persons have similar problems.[12] Sociological research has shown the existence of pronounced differences in normative structures of subcultures or countercultures involving persons of different age groups, social classes, occupations, racial, ethnic, and religious groups, neighborhoods, and regions. Certain businesses, corporations, or political machines may practice unethical norms quite antithetical to those of other groups or contrary to the laws of the political state. In addition, certain even more limited deviant countercultures develop, such as those among teenage gangs, prostitutes, alcoholics, drug addicts, homosexuals, and professional and organized criminals. Even institutions for deviants, such as prisons and mental hospitals, may have subcultures within their own subculture.[13] Groups of deviants themselves have their own sets of norms as to what constitutes moral or "acceptable" behavior and deviations within their own groups. Rule violations can result in "deviant deviants," for example, among professional thieves, who must live up to commitments to one another and not inform on others;[14] among members of Alcoholics Anonymous, who must obey the rules of the group;[15] and among drug addicts, who must protect their sources of drugs from the danger of police informers.

Subcultural Norms

The social norms and behavior of social classes in the United States vary greatly with respect to many attitudes and values. The norms of longshoremen differ from those of doctors or professors; construction workers display markedly different attitudes than do college students. Child-rearing patterns have been shown to differ significantly. Lower-class parents, for example, tend to use corporal punishment more often as a disciplinary measure than do middle-class parents, although not as much as some expect.[16] Nearly all crimes of violence, such as murder and forcible rape, are committed by lower-class persons, and the presence of a lower-class "subculture of violence," as will be discussed later (see page 195), may offer a partial explanation. Prostitution appears to be consistently more prevalent among the lower classes. The more ordinary, overt types of crime, such as burglary, are rare among members of the middle and upper classes; members of these groups are more involved in types of

---

[12]See Albert K. Cohen, *Delinquent Boys: The Culture of the Gang* (New York: Free Press, 1955), p. 14. Also see Louis Schneider, *The Sociological Way of Looking at the World* (New York: McGraw-Hill, 1975), Chapter 6, "Cultural Change and Cultural Criticism: A Study of the Counterculture."

[13]See, for example, Charles W. Thomas and David M. Petersen, *Prison Organization and Inmate Subcultures* (Indianapolis: Bobbs Merrill, 1977).

[14]See Andrew Walker, "Sociology and the Professional Criminal," in Abraham S. Blumberg, ed., *Current Perspective on Criminal Behavior* (New York: Knopf, 1974), pp. 87–113.

[15]Fred Montanino, "Alcohol: Use and Abuse," in Edward Sagarin and Fred Montanino, eds., *Deviants: Voluntary Actors in a Hostile World* (Morristown, N.J.: General Learning Press, 1977), pp. 356–360.

[16]See Howard S. Erlanger, "Social Class and Corporal Punishment in Childrearing: A Reassessment," *American Sociological Review*, 39 (1974), 68–85.

crimes termed white-collar crimes. Such crimes of a different type, involving more sophisticated fraud and deception, are committed by white-collar persons in the middle and upper classes, such as government officials, people in business, labor union leaders, doctors, and lawyers.[17] Largely because of greater family and neighborhood stress situations, probably no area reflects social-class differences as dramatically as do certain mental disorders. Schizophrenia, a common form of mental disorder, for example, has been reported in one study as nine times more prevalent among persons of the lowest social class.[18]

Neighborhoods in large U.S. cities are often characterized by distinct behavioral norms and values. Those of one neighborhood may contribute to the development of stealing among teenaged boys who regard it as a form of recreation or the means to gain social status; in another neighborhood the social norms and values may encourage teenage participation in scouting programs or other community-directed activities more conducive to nondelinquent behavior. The neighborhood norms of one area may define policemen as "enemies," while in another they are defined as symbols of respect for law.

To summarize the significance and the importance of group norms in modern complex societies the following generalizations may be helpful. (1) In modern societies there may be almost as pronounced differences among the groups within the society in respect to the norms of accepted behavior as there are differences between large cultures themselves. (2) Any logical explanation of how members of certain deviant subgroups within a society act as they do must trace the development of the behavior in the same way that any member of any cultural group learns how to act, for example, how an Eskimo learns through his culture to become an Eskimo. (3) Finally, it must be remembered that even when the norms of any given family are discussed, it is probable that one is discussing actually the social class, the occupational group, or some specific subcultural group to which the family happens to belong.

SOCIETAL REACTION

A definition of deviance presents problems, not the least of which is the fact that norms are abstract entities that are seldom directly observable.[19] For this reason, it is sometimes difficult to discern precisely which norm, if any, is being violated. Some

---

[17]Gilbert Geis and Robert F. Meier, eds., *White-Collar Crime: Offenses in Business, Politics and the Professions* (New York: Free Press, 1977); and John E. Conklin, *Illegal But Not Criminal* (Englewood Cliffs, N.J.: Prentice-Hall, 1977).

[18]August B. Hollingshead and Frederick Redlich, *Social Class and Mental Illness* (New York: Wiley, 1958). See also Bruce P. Dohrenwend and Barbara Snell Dohrenwend, *Social Status and Psychological Disorder* (New York: Wiley, 1969); and H. Harvey Brenner, *Mental Health and the Economy* (Cambridge, Mass.: Harvard University Press, 1974).

[19]Jack P. Gibbs, "Issues in Defining Deviant Behavior," in Robert A. Scott and Jack D. Douglas, eds., *Theoretical Perspectives on Deviance* (New York: Basic Books, 1972), pp. 39–68. Also see John I. Kitsuse, "Deviance, Deviant Behavior, and Deviants: Some Conceptual Problems," in William J. Filstead, ed., *An Introduction to Deviance: Readings in the Process of Making Deviance* (Chicago: Markham, 1972), pp. 237–238. Kitsuse expands on this observation in his "New Conception of Deviance and Its Critics," in Walter R. Gove, ed., *The Labelling of Deviance: Evaluating a Perspective* (New York: Halsted/Sage, 1975), pp. 276–280.

norms are easily determined, such as those defined in the written statutes; others are detectable only indirectly through observation of behavior that can be inferred as either conforming or deviating from the norm. The normative structure of a group can be inferred from the behavior and actions of the members of that group. Thus the societal reaction and the social control process, which are much more visible than the existence of nondiscernible norms and rules, provide evidence that one or another norm has been violated, and to a degree sufficient to warrant reaction in the form of either correcting or punishing the person whose behavior brought about the reaction.

The objective determination of norms and their strength are probably best accomplished by observing the application of sanctions, or the social control measures, utilized for behavior that constitutes norm violations. Great variations can occur in these social control measures; reactions can vary in the direction of approval, tolerance, or disapproval. Most members of modern societies encourage a certain extent of nonconformity provided it is in an approved direction. Deviations of which groups approve may be rewarded by admiration, prestige, money, or other symbols. Some deviations, for example, in the form of new mechanical inventions or architectural styles, painting, literature, music, and fashion may meet with general approval. Approved deviations may also include behavior thought to be more industrious, ambitious, pious, patriotic, brave, or honest than called for by the norms of a particular situation. A certain degree of heroism is expected of everyone, civilian as well as soldier, but medals or other forms of recognition are given to soldiers, and occasionally to civilians, who have been particularly brave and who have risked their own lives. Although everyone is supposed to be a careful driver, as a further example, rewards are sometimes given to the driver who has had no accidents over a prolonged period of time.

Generally, however, most segments in a society appear to be concerned more with punishing disapproved deviations from norms than with rewarding compliance with them.[20] Deviations may encounter societal reactions involving varying degrees of disapproval. Groups may react with disgust, anger, hate, gossip, isolation, and ostracism or with physical punishment, arrest, fines, or confinement within an institution. What constitutes social deviation is not something that is universal or "natural." It varies according to what particular groups with power in a society wish to make into rules.[21] Furthermore, behavior that is disapproved at one time may later become approved as ideas of what is proper or improper normative behavior change. Over the years, for example, scientists who have challenged traditional beliefs have been scorned, ridiculed, ostracized, and even punished. Copernicus, Galileo, and many others who were regarded as deviants in their day would undoubtedly be regarded today with the same approval accorded Einstein. Within comparatively recent times strong disapproval was expressed for women who drank alcoholic beverages, smoked, used make-up, wore short bathing suits, or engaged in political activities. Many religious offenses, such as engaging in recreation on the Sabbath, were formerly considered crimes. Professional boxing matches or "prize fights" were generally

[20]Jack P. Gibbs, "Sanctions," *Social Problems,* 14 (1966), 147–159.
[21]See Valery Chalidze, *Criminal Russia: Essays on Crime in the Soviet Union* (New York: Random House, 1977).

criminal offenses in the United States during most of the nineteenth century. New York did not legalize professional boxing until 1896, and the laws were subsequently changed several times.

> During Iceland's Viking era, it was a crime for a person to write verses about another, even if the sentiment was complimentary, if the verses exceeded four stanzas in length. A Prussian law of 1784 prohibited mothers and nurses from taking children under two years of age into their beds. The English villein (freecommon villager) in the fourteenth century was not allowed to send his son to school, and no one lower than a freeholder was permitted by law to keep a dog. The following have at different times and in different places been crimes: printing a book, professing the medical doctrine of circulation of the blood, driving with reins, selling coins to foreigners, having gold in the house, buying goods on the way to market or in the market for the purpose of selling them at a higher price, writing a check for less than one dollar. On the other hand, many of our present laws were not known to earlier generations—quarantine laws, traffic laws, sanitation laws, factory laws.[22]

The intensity of the reaction to the deviation also varies, as does the direction of approval or disapproval. Some deviations from norms in a society are not only approved but encouraged. Likewise, disapproved deviations may encounter various degrees of sanction, varying from a limited degree of tolerance to mild and even strong disapproval. Certain behavior of the "idle rich," of actors, musicians, and artists, or of extreme religious sects, although not approved, may be tolerated. Deviations from norms of politeness, dress, table manners, and cleanliness, as well as the telling of risqué stories in public, may encounter mild disapproval in the form of ridicule or scorn. Lying and malicious gossip may be more strongly disapproved, while certain behavior, such as murder, burglary, and robbery, may be severely punished by the political state through a fine, imprisonment, or even death.

Norms have varying degrees of strength, or "resistance potential," in the event of a disapproved deviation from them, "a power which may be measured in degrees of what the group regards as the severity of the sanction."[23] Each norm can be thought of as having a *tolerance limit,* that is, the ratio between violations of the norm and the willingness of a group to tolerate or suppress it.[24] Deviations from sexual norms, for example, have different tolerance limits, depending upon the society. Over the centuries prostitution has been approved, tolerated, or disapproved, all depending upon cultural norms. Today prostitution may be illegal in many European, Latin American, African, and Asian countries, but it is not actively suppressed. Some communities in the United States tolerate prostitution by ignoring its presence and by not fully enforcing laws against it. Other communities take strong positions and attempt to eradicate it. In some respects, however, the concept of "tolerance limit" is misleading, as it implies a definite point at which norm violations will evoke a reaction.

---

[22]Edwin H. Sutherland and Donald R. Cressey, *Criminology,* 10th ed. (Philadelphia: Lippincott, 1978), p. 17.

[23]Thorsten Sellin, *Culture Conflict and Crime* (New York: Social Science Research Council, 1938), p. 34.

[24]Courtland C. Van Vechten, "The Tolerance Quotient as a Device for Defining Certain Social Concepts," *American Journal of Sociology,* 46 (1940), 35–44; Edwin M. Lemert, *Social Pathology* (New York: McGraw-Hill, 1951), pp. 57–58; and Elmer H. Johnson, *Social Problems of Urban Man* (Homewood, Ill.: Dorsey Press, 1973), p. 37.

Actually, the relation between norm violation and societal reaction is not this simple, and it may depend upon other factors such as the nature of the situation or the social status of the deviant person.

DEFINING DEVIANCE

Deviance, then, constitutes norm violations; but the precise nature of the norms violated, who supports them, and the degree of societal reaction to their violation represent major concerns in the definition of deviance. Some people regard certain behavior as deviant; others do not. Deviance may be defined in four ways—absolutist, statistical, labeling, and relativistic.

Absolutist

Probably until the early 1950s most sociologists, psychiatrists, and psychologists had comparatively little difficulty with the concept of deviance because they considered it an absolute. Deviance was taken for granted, as though everyone agreed that certain violations of norms were abnormal and others were not. Among sociologists, for example, violations of the criminal law, regardless of types or how they had become crimes or the degree of support they had, were considered deviations simply because the law said they were. At the same time certain other legal and ethical violations by businessmen, corporations, and professional persons were not often considered within the scope of deviance. Likewise, premarital sexual relations and homosexual behavior were considered obvious deviance. In other words, the definition of deviance has reflected the values of the society as determined by sociologists or other social scientists. For the most part, sociologists generally viewed social rules as "absolute, clear, and obvious to all members of a society in all situations."[25] This absolutist, or arbitrary, conception of deviance assumed that the basic norms of a society are obvious and that its members are in general agreement on what constitutes deviance, because the norms and values of society are laid out in advance. Everyone is presumed to know how to act according to universally held values; violations of these norms constitute deviance, and the possibility of some type of sanction is incurred. The sources of these universal norms have usually been the moral values of the middle class and the personal biases of some writers who, coming from rural, traditional, and religious backgrounds, have viewed many forms of behavior related to urban life and industrial society as being destructive to what they thought was moral.[26]

The absolutist definition of deviance is widely supported today, particularly by psychiatrists and psychologists who regard deviance in terms of a "medical model," as a form of "sickness." Crime, mental disorder, suicide, alcoholism, drug addiction, and

---

[25]Scott and Douglas, p. 4. Also see Richard Hawkins and Gary Tiedeman, *The Creation of Deviance: Interpersonal and Organizational Determinants* (Columbus, O.: Charles E. Merrill, 1975), pp. 20–41.
[26]See Svend Ranulf, *Moral Indignation and Middle Class Psychology: A Sociological Study* (New York: Shocken Books, 1964; first published in 1938 in Denmark); and C. Wright Mills, "The Professional Ideology of Social Pathologists," *American Journal of Sociology,* 49 (1943), 165–180.

so on, become absolutes much as diseases such as cancer, and they are universal expressions of individual maladjustment regardless of differences in cultural and subcultural norms. Social differentiation, cultural differences, and changes in norms are generally ignored.[27]

> The absolutist asserts that, regardless of time and social context, certain culture-free standards, such as how fully persons develop their innate potential or how closely they approach the fulfillment of the highest human values, enable one to detect deviance. Thus suicide or alcoholism destroys or inhibits the possibility of the actor's developing his full human potential and is therefore always deviant. . . . The absolutist believes that he knows what reality *is,* what people *should be* and what constitutes full and appropriate development. In the case of suicide, for example, he believes that life is obviously and almost always better than death.[28]

In actuality, deviant behavior is, in part, the normal consequence of social definitions that are imposed by others, and the nature and function of deviance must be sought in the society and in the culture.[29] Like deviance, morality is not absolute; rather than being absolute, morality tends to be abstracted, situated, made to fit our everyday experiences. Moral meanings are constructed, negotiated, and shaped through an interaction process. The conception of persons as "deviants" implicitly raises questions about "normals."[30]

Statistical

Another way to define deviance is a statistical process that views deviance as variations or departures from "average" norms of behavior. This approach assumes that whatever it is that "most" people do is the "correct" way. This definition faces some immediate difficulties because it can lead to some confusing conclusions if, for example, the minority could always be defined as deviants. With a statistical definition of deviance, those who have never stolen anything or never violated any law, those who have never used marijuana, those who do not drink alcoholic beverages or coffee, those who have never had premarital sex relations might be considered deviant.[31] It appears that the meaning of deviance is not to be found in the statistical regularities of behavior, but rather in the fact that deviance connotes some difference or departure from some norm. In other words, a statistical definition would tell us

---

[27]Even Merton's well-known deviance model of *anomie* (see page 67) seems to assume that certain behavior could be considered deviant by everyone. See Robert K. Merton, *Social Theory and Social Structure,* enlarged edition (New York: Free Press, 1968), pp. 185–248. Also see Marshall B. Clinard, "The Theoretical Implications of Anomie and Deviant Behavior," in Marshall B. Clinard, ed., *Anomie and Deviant Behavior* (New York: Free Press, 1964), pp. 1–56.

[28]John Lofland, *Deviance and Identity* (Englewood Cliffs, N.J.: Prentice-Hall, 1969), pp. 23–24.

[29]It is erroneous to view deviance, such as crime, mental disorder, and prostitution, as "soft spots" that have developed naturally on the surface of society but have had little to do with its "core" values, structures, and processes. See Robert A. Scott, "A Proposed Framework for Analyzing Deviance as a Property of Social Order," in Scott and Douglas, p. 9.

[30]Jack D. Douglas, ed., *Deviance and Respectability: The Social Construction of Moral Meanings* (New York: Basic Books, 1970), p. 28.

[31]See William A. Rushing, ed., *Deviant Behavior and Social Process,* 2d ed. (Chicago: Rand McNally, 1975), pp. 3–4.

"what is," while the concept of deviance implies that the crucial meaning is "what should or should not be" according to the views of certain groups.

Labeling

A well-known definition of deviance is that of Howard Becker, who terms it the consequence of the application of rules and sanctions by others to an "offender." The deviant is the person to whom the label "deviant" has been successfully applied, and the "deviant" behavior is the behavior that people so label.[32] In Becker's definition acts can be identified as deviant *only* in reference to the reaction to the acts through the labeling of a person as deviant by society and its agents of social control. An act that constitutes deviant behavior must first be known to others and then be reacted to by the formal agencies of social control. This labeling position has attracted a wide following because it has furnished what at least appeared to be a way of getting around the persistent difficulty of defining deviance in the face of a reality where deviance in terms of norms is highly relative. As time has passed, however, Becker's definition has been increasingly subjected to much criticism, and one can now conclude that, since it is an overstatement, it represents an inadequate definition of deviance. The labeling definition rejects, expressly or tacitly, a normative definition of deviance, even if it is broad and relative in its scope: it is not the normative violation that is the heart of the definition but only the labeling of the violation. An act would not be deviant, therefore, unless it is detected and there is a particular kind of reaction to it. The illogical nature of this view can be illustrated in a case in which a man engaging in burglary was not discovered; because he is not discovered he is not reacted to and thus not regarded as deviant.

Relative

Deviance may be regarded as a sensitizing concept rather than something absolute or statistical. Blumer suggests that this concept provides for the user a general sense of reference and guidance in approaching empirical instances. "Whereas definitive concepts provide prescriptions of what to see, sensitizing concepts merely suggest a direction along which to look."[33] In these relative terms deviance is defined in terms of the variations and the relativity of modern social life. Consequently, for our purposes, the definition will be adopted that deviance constitutes *only those deviations from norms which are in a disapproved direction and of sufficient degree to exceed the tolerance limits of a social group such that the deviation elicits, or is likely to elicit if detected, a negative sanction.*[34]

---

[32]Howard S. Becker, *Outsiders: Studies in the Sociology of Deviance,* enlarged edition (New York: Free Press, 1973), p. 9.

[33]Herbert Blumer, *Symbolic Interactionism* (Englewood Cliffs, N.J.: Prentice-Hall, 1969), p. 148.

[34]Similar definitions can be found in Albert K. Cohen, "The Study of Social Disorganization and Deviant Behavior," in Robert K. Merton, Leonard Broom, and Leonard S. Cottrell, eds., *Sociology Today: Problems and Prospects* (New York: Basic Books, 1959), p. 462; Robert W. Winslow and Virginia Winslow, *Deviant Reality: Alternative World Views* (Boston: Allyn and Bacon, 1974), p. 18; Armand L. Mauss, *Social Problems as Social Movements* (Philadelphia: Lippincott, 1974), p. 37; Rushing, pp. 1–9; and Birenbaum and Sagarin, p. 37.

Meaning of Relative Deviance Deviance may thus take many forms far beyond the conventional ones customarily alluded to by most people, for example, burglary, robbery, mental disorder, and prostitution. An almost endless variety of behaviors and characteristics are considered to be deviant by some people at least and encounter pronounced stigma in certain groups, depending upon the conditions and situations. They include, for example, physical disabilities and impairments such as crippling, blindness, mental retardation, obesity, and stuttering; violations of rules of etiquette; lying; cheating; nudism; window peeping; exhibitionism; smoking marijuana; illegitimacy; nonsupport of minor children; violations of safety regulations; hijacking; health care quackery; and violations of certain amateur and professional sports rules. Social types perceived by some as deviants include reckless drivers, pacifists, racists, "hippies," radicals, "squares" and conservatives, the very rich and the very poor, old people, drinkers and nondrinkers, and motorcycle gangs. Deviance may be imputed to more respectable higher-status persons and may include violations of laws and ethics by business people, doctors, and lawyers, such as fraud, false income tax reports, false advertising, fee splitting, and the sale of impure drugs. When we ask ourselves what deviance is and who is a deviant, we are faced with specifying which groups within society define certain behavior as deviant and which groups do not. Deviance must be viewed from the perspective of the viewing audience. One writer has expressed this important aspect of deviance:

> *So deviance, like beauty, is in the eyes of the beholder* . . . almost every conceivable human characteristic of activity is pariah in somebody's eyes. This means that most people (you and I included) would be labeled deviant by some existing persons and groups. Anyone who moves around much from place to place or social world to social world has probably run into this. There is nothing inherently *deviant* in any human act; something is deviant only because some people have been successful in labeling it so. The labeling is a local matter that changes from place to place and even from time to time in the same place. To understand deviance, we have to understand its environmental context. So we have to look at the people doing the labeling as much as at the deviant himself.[35]

Power Deviance is a created situation, created by audiences or groups within a society which makes the rules and which imposes negative sanctions upon certain behavior, for "actions are not in themselves moral or immoral, deviant or nondeviant. It is the judgment that is passed on the behavior by others, and not the behavior itself, that determines and defines deviance."[36]

Another sociologist has said that "Deviance is not a property *inherent* in certain forms of behavior; it is a property *conferred upon* these forms by the audiences which directly or indirectly witness them. Sociologically, then, the critical variable is the social *audience* . . . since it is the audience which eventually decides whether or not any given action or actions will become a visible case of deviation."[37]

The element of power to control the behavior of others is important. Thus, as

[35]J. L. Simmons, *Deviants* (Berkeley, Calif.: Glendassary Press, 1969), p. 4. Italics are the author's.
[36]Alfred R. Lindesmith, Anselm L. Strauss, and Norman K. Denzin, *Social Psychology,* 4th ed. (Hinsdale, Ill.: Dryden Press, 1975), p. 529.
[37]Edwin M. Schur, *Labeling Deviant Behavior: Its Sociological Implications* (New York: Harper & Row, 1971), p. 12.

will be shown later, strong negative attitudes toward the taking of one's own life through suicide, the practice of prostitution, homosexuality, drunkenness, and other means of expressing personal choice have stemmed for the most part from certain church groups. Opposition to the use of marijuana, nudity, and the distribution of pornographic materials rests with other moral entrepreneurs who attempt to impose their views on others.[38] What constitutes a large part of crime, as Quinney points out, is really behavior that conflicts with the interests of the segments of society that have the power to shape criminal policy.[39] In no area has the element of power been more clearly demonstrated until recently in certain areas of the United States than in the segregation laws imposed by whites on blacks and other minorities in some cases. Blacks were denied by law the right to vote and to attend schools with whites. It was a crime to intermarry with whites, to use certain public facilities used by whites such as hotels, motels, restaurants, theaters, parks, playgrounds, swimming pools, and even beaches, toilets, and drinking fountains. These discriminations and many others far more rigorous are now imposed under the criminal laws of South Africa on 15 million Africans, colored, and Asians by 3 million whites who have the political power to make and to enforce the segregation or apartheid laws.

Moreover, those segments of society that have the power to shape the enforcement and administration of the criminal law through agents like the police and the courts determine what criminal laws are actually enforced. The political criminal who takes as a goal the improvement of society, for example, and who is supported by certain groups may suffer torture, imprisonment, and even death because certain power groups do not approve of his means, nor of his ends; the improvement of society to the political criminal is seen as the destruction of society by others. Laws regulating personal morality, such as public drunkenness, the use of marijuana, pornography, and obscenity, all become relative to the values of the viewers. In the Soviet Union, where the state and the party determine which behavior is "good" and which is "bad," the result is a great deal of dissension about deviance between the public and the state.[40] Some forms of deviance, such as theft of state property and excessive drinking, are important to the state, but on both scores, according to a recent study, large segments of the public could not care less.[41] In fact, what is a major form of deviance to the political state of the Soviet Union is probably of little concern to the people themselves—unauthorized creative writing, the circulation of dissident manifestos, and open protests by students and intellectuals against the regime.

Determining Norms

A difficult sociological problem in the study of deviance in these terms is determining how strongly certain norms are opposed by various groups within a society.[42] Some norms are more easily determined than others. The criminal law contains a body of

---

[38]Becker, pp. 147–163.
[39]Richard Quinney, *Crime, Class and State* (New York: David McKay, 1977).
[40]See Chalidze. See also Francis T. Cullen, Jr., and John B. Cullen, "The Soviet Model of Soviet Deviance," *Pacific Sociological Review*, 20 (1977), 389–410.
[41]See Walter D. Connor, *Deviance in the Soviet Society: Crime, Delinquency, and Alcoholism* (New York: Columbia University Press, 1972).
[42]Edward Sagarin, *Deviants and Deviance: An Introduction to the Study of Disvalued People and Behavior* (New York: Holt, Rinehart and Winston, 1975), p. 222.

legal norms that all can see and that are made applicable within a political jurisdiction. Norms regulating sexual behavior, on the other hand, are often ambiguous, changing from group to group and over a period of time. The problem is made even more difficult by the fact that many norms do change. Cigarette smoking, for example, has undergone a number of changes in acceptability in the United States since the 1880s. In the 1870s it was strongly condemned by many groups and by many individuals, in part because it was most common among urban immigrants who had low social status and who were often also characterized by heavy drinking. At that time, too, smoking by women was considered to be particularly deviant, being associated with prostitution. In spite of its being considered deviant, cigarette smoking increased in the United States, and attitudes began to change following World War I. By the end of World War II, it was considered acceptable behavior, socially desirable, and in some subcultures, even necessary.[43] Attitudes again began to change in the 1960s as evidence began to accumulate that tobacco smoking is linked to a number of serious physical illnesses. In the 1970s, cigarette advertising on television and radio was legally prohibited. Smoking is increasingly banned in public places because nonsmokers inhale the fumes and because many people find the odor objectionable. Indeed, a number of citizen groups today are campaigning for even stronger measures to end all smoking. Thus, cigarette smoking has again become deviant as norms regulating this behavior have changed. Changing attitudes toward tobacco smoking by juveniles also indicate how normative standards can be redefined in time. Formerly there was great concern about cigarette smoking among juveniles—laws were passed to forbid it, and they were often strictly enforced. Smoking was thought to be related to a variety of other problems such as juvenile delinquency. Today there is more preoccupation with the smoking of marijuana, particularly by juveniles and youth, as a result of increasingly strong attitudes favorable to the smoking of marijuana in teenaged peer-group subcultures. Cigarette smoking is of far less concern.

Deviance is relative to the tolerance limits of social groups. Despite this relativism some limited behavior is viewed as deviance even by large societies with exceptionally high degrees of unanimity. Cannibalism is regarded as a deviant act in all societies today. Armed robbery and the theft of personal property are almost universally viewed as deviance, as is sexual intercourse with a child under the approximate age of 10, or the beating of an octogenarian by a young person.

Obviously a book such as this one cannot analyze all forms of social behavior that might possibly be termed deviant: one must be selective.[44] Consequently, the

---

[43]Elane Nuehring and Gerald E. Markle, "Nicotine and Norms: The Re-Emerging of a Deviant Behavior," *Social Problems,* 21 (1974), 513–526.
[44]Deviance related to social behavior and deviance related to social problems are not necessarily the same, even though the two kinds of deviance may overlap. Not all social problems are instances of deviance. For example, soil erosion, flood damage, and forest destruction have been considered to be social problems for decades. Infant mortality, population control, and problems of mass communication are also matters of great concern as problems of society; yet they can hardly be considered instances of deviant behavior. The same could be said about other social problems such as pollution, urban smog, and traffic congestion. When these conditions are dealt with in "social problems" textbooks they are completely in order: it is suggested only that they do not constitute deviance within the framework presented here. For a discussion of the issues in the distinction between social problems and social deviance see Jerome G. Manis, "The Concept of Social Problems: Vox Populi and Sociological Analysis," *Social Problems,* 21 (1974), 305–315; Jerome G. Manis, *Analyzing Social Problems* (New York: Holt, Rinehart and Winston, 1976); and John I. Kitsuse and Malcolm Spector, "Social Problems and Deviance," *Social Problems,* 22 (1975), 584–594.

forms of deviant behavior selected for study here are those over which there is, for the most part, much contemporary interest, debate, and concern, particularly as they relate to measures of social control. Some represent the efforts of certain groups which have social and political power to impose their own conceptions on others or to avoid the categorization of deviance for their own behavior. In the past different types of behavior might well have been discussed as being deviant: 300 years ago, or even less, blasphemy and heresy might have been included, because they were then regarded as serious forms of deviance; in the future some forms of behavior regarded today as deviance may well disappear as major new issues arise.

Those forms of behavior designated here as deviance in terms of the criteria stated are certain types of crimes, including those of personal violence and those against property, crimes against the political state, and those committed in connection with an occupation such as white-collar and corporate crime; illegal drug use; deviant alcohol use and alcoholism; prostitution; nudity; co-marital sexual relations; illegal distribution of pornographic materials; homosexual acts; mental disorders; suicide; and severe physical disabilities such as those experienced by the crippled, the obese, the mentally retarded, and stutterers. Considerable consensus exists about the deviant nature of some of these behaviors, as in the case of theft of private personal property or alcoholism. In others, such as homosexual behavior, the use of marijuana, and white-collar and corporate crime, less agreement is seen, accompanied by more controversy. Even when some measure of agreement exists that certain behavior constitutes deviance, there may be strong disagreement regarding approaches to its social control.[45] Most persons would agree that burglarizing a home is deviant behavior, yet some believe that the excessive sanctions applied in the form of 5 to 10 years of imprisonment typify the power of the upper-class interest groups, which punish much more leniently the more socially disruptive and more costly violations such as fraud, political corruption, and corporate crime that are committed by higher-status persons.

SOCIAL CONTROL

All societies and all social groups have developed means to deal with behavior that is beyond the range of tolerance of their societal and group norms. These methods are collectively called *social control*. They insure, or at least attempt to insure, conformity to norms.[46] In this sense social control refers to the processes whereby members of a society keep each other in line.[47] Societal reactions have the hoped-for effect of manipulating behavior in such a way that conformity to norms will be guaranteed.

---

[45]This point has been made by Fuller in his distinction between moral and ameliorative social problems. See Richard Fuller and Richard R. Myers, "Some Aspects of a Theory of Social Problems," *American Sociological Review,* 6 (1941), 24–32.

[46]George C. Homans, *Social Behavior: Its Elementary Forms,* rev. ed. (Boston: Houghton Mifflin, 1974).

[47]Birenbaum and Sagarin, p. 49.

Processes of Social Control

Two basic social control processes are normally distinguished by sociologists: (1) the *internationalization of group norms* wherein conformity to norms comes about through the socialization of both knowing what is expected and being desirous and able to conform to that expectation;[48] and (2) social reaction through *external pressures in the form of sanctions from others* in the event of anticipated or actual nonconformity to norms. In the first process social control is the result of the socialization whereby persons acquire a motivation to conform regardless of other external pressures. No conscious effort is required on the part of the society to secure compliance with most group norms, for they are the spontaneous and unconscious ways of acting that characterize the bulk of the customs of any culture. Mechanisms of social control, like customs, traditions, beliefs, attitudes, and values, are generally taught through prolonged interaction between persons. The fact that most wives do not murder their husbands is due not entirely, or even mostly, to the severe legal penalties for criminal homicide; most automobile drivers stay on the correct side of the road not entirely because others will regard their driving as deviant and even illegal; and drinkers of alcoholic beverages do not all become drunks simply because the neighbors will gossip. Rather, most persons conform to most norms most of the time because, first, they have been taught the content of the norms of their society, and, second, because they have accepted these norms as their own norms and operate as though they were taken for granted. There is conformity to norms because persons have been socialized to believe they should conform, regardless of and independent of any anticipated reaction of other persons. In this sense socialization can be referred to as "self-control," which is developed through social processes. Parsons has explained the process in this way: "The preventing or forestalling aspects of social control consist in a sense of processes which teach the actor not to embark on processes of deviance. They consist in his learning how not to rather than how to in the positive sense of socialization."[49]

Social controls through external pressures include both negative and positive sanctions. Such sanctions may be classified as informal or formal. *Informal controls,* such as gossip or ostracism, are unofficial group actions (see Table 1.1.). Official actions or *formal controls* such as the use of the criminal law are derived from the official group machinery set up to carry out the functions of the group or agency. These controls, in effect, are imbedded in the formal structure of the group, but they are supported by certain beliefs, ideals, customs, convictions, attitudes, and opinions that, in themselves, are actually informal controls. In this sense informal and formal controls cannot be considered completely separate categories. In one study, for example, it was found that among a sample of more than 800 teenage boys more concern was indicated for what their families would think of them than about having

---

[48]John Finley Scott, *The Internalization of Norms* (Englewood Cliffs, N.J.: Prentice-Hall, 1971).
[49]Talcott Parsons, *The Social System* (New York: Free Press, 1951), p. 298.

TABLE 1.1   Examples of Types of Sanctions

		Content of Sanction	
		Positive	Negative
Source of Sanction	Formal	Bonuses Medals Citations Promotions	Imprisonment Fines Dismissal from job Excommunication from church
	Informal	Praise Encouragement Pats on back Signs of approval	Criticism Ridicule Gossip Ostracism

been arrested by the police and having been subjected to formal penalties.[50] This suggests that while formal sanctions may have an independent effect on the behavior of persons, the element of informal sanctions combined with the formal sanctions is of great importance.

Informal Social Controls

Simply stated, "informal social sanctions consist of the techniques whereby people who know one another on a personal basis accord praise to those who comply with their expectations and show displeasure to those who do not."[51] They may be observed in specific behaviors such as gossip, ridicule, reprimands, praise, criticism, gestural cues, glances of approval or disapproval, denial or bestowal of affection, ostracism, or verbal rationalizations and expressions of opinion. Gossip, or the fear of gossip, is undoubtedly one of the most effective instruments yet devised in any society for bringing people into conformity with norms. Unlike formal controls, these informal social controls are not exercised through official group mechanisms.

Informal sanctions may be more effective in smaller social groups where everyone knows everyone else and the same people are brought into continual face-to-face contact with each other. One example of an informal sanction, in this case gossip, has been reported in such a society.

> Early this morning, when everyone was still around the village, Fokanti began loudly complaining to an affine (who was several huts away and was probably chosen for that reason) that someone was "killing her with broken promises." Who? Asibi. He promised to help Fokanti with her rice planting today and now he's reneged. At this point Asibi

[50]H. D. Willcock and J. Stokes, *Deterrents and Incentives to Crime among Youths Aged 15–21 Years* (London: Home Office, Government Social Survey, 1968), as cited in Nigel Walker, *Crimes, Courts and Figures: An Introduction to Criminal Statistics* (Baltimore: Penguin Books, 1971), pp. 98–103.
[51]Tamotsu Shibutani, *Society and Personality: An Interactionist Approach to Social Psychology* (Englewood Cliffs, N.J.: Prentice-Hall, 1961), p. 426.

appeared and tried to explain how something else had come up which required his attention. This cut no ice with the woman, who proceeded—her voice still at high volume—to attribute Asibi's unreliability to his "just wanting to go to dances all the time, like last night!" None of this public broadcasting was helping Asibi's reputation any, so he promised to change his plans and make good his original promise.[52]

Formal Social Controls

Formal controls arise when the socialization process that gives rise to self-control, and is thus informal, is insufficient to maintain conformity to certain norms.[53] These controls involve organized systems of specialized agencies and standard techniques. The two main types are those instituted by the political state and those imposed by agencies other than the state. They include the church, business and labor groups, educational institutions, clubs and other organizations, and the political state.

Because formal sanctions are incorporated in the institutional systems of society, they are administered by persons who occupy positions, or roles, within those institutions. These persons are commonly known as agents of social control since the administration of these sanctions is part of their duties. In the most general sense, anyone who attempts to manipulate the behavior of others through the use of formal sanctions can be considered an agent of social control. The police, prosecutors and judges of the criminal justice system, employers, teachers, and ministers and priests who promise heaven and threaten hell to believers, all are examples of agents of social control.

Nonpolitical groups impose penalties, some of which may be more severe than punishments imposed by the political state for crimes (see Table 1.2.). A business concern may fire a person, even after long years of employment.[54] A professional group or union may suspend a member or even expel the individual from the group, which may mean loss of livelihood. Professional athletes who do not obey the rules of the club or league may be fined several hundred or several thousand dollars for an infraction and may even be suspended. Religious organizations may demand penance or withhold certain religious services, such as the wedding privilege or a religious service at death. They may even use what is, to members of a particular faith, the most drastic punishment of all—excommunication from the church. Clubs and similar groups generally utilize a scale of fines, temporary suspension of membership privileges, or even expulsion as a formal means of controlling their members.

A series of specific actions are established to punish the transgressor and to reward those whose compliance with the norms equals or goes beyond the expectations of the group. Curiously, nonpolitical agencies, such as business concerns and professional, religious, or social groups, probably use more rewards than penalties.[55]

---

[52]Edward C. Green, "Social Control in Tribal Afro-America," *Anthropological Quarterly,* 50 (1977), p. 110.
[53]Michael Schwartz and Sheldon Stryker, *Deviance, Selves and Others* (Washington, D.C.: American Sociological Association, Rose Monograph Series, 1970), p. 15.
[54]Joseph Bensman and Israel Gerver, "Crime and Punishment in the Factory: The Function of Deviance in Maintaining the Social System," *American Sociological Review,* 28 (1963), 588–598.
[55]See Richard T. Santee and Jay Jackson, "Cultural Values as a Source of Normative Sanctions," *Pacific Sociological Review,* 20 (1977), 439–454.

TABLE 1.2

Examples of Institutions of Social Control			
Institution	*Agent*	*Deviance*	*Sanction*
Religion	Minister, priest	Sin	Penance, withholding rites, excommunication
Business	Employer	Absence, laziness, violation of work rules	Dismissal, suspension, fine
Labor union	Labor representative	Failure to obey union rules	Expulsion from union, fine
Professional group	Officer	Ethical violations	License revocation, expulsion from group
Political state	Police, prosecutor, judge	Violations of administrative, civil, or criminal law	Fine, probation, imprisonment, damage suit
Clubs and social organizations	Officers	Violations of club rules	Fines, suspension of privileges, expulsion
Family	Parents	Youthful disobedience	Spanking, "grounding," withholding privileges

Through promotions, bonuses, or some token of merit, business organizations frequently reward those who have made an outstanding contribution to the firm, who have rarely been absent, or who have had an unusual safety record. Professional groups often reward outstanding service with election to office or a special citation. Religious groups reward faithful adherents by promises of a future state of euphoria, by positions of leadership, and by pins or scrolls for exemplary service and commitment. Clubs, lodges, fraternities, and sororities likewise offer a large number of prestige symbols for those who walk the path from neophyte to full-fledged member without reflecting dishonor on the group. Recognition of a type similar to military rewards is given to a small number of civilians each year in the United States through the Carnegie awards for outstanding heroism.

The state exercises another type of formal control through its political and legal institutions. The control of the political state is seldom exercised through positive sanctions or rewards, however, and the citizen who goes through life obeying most requirements put upon him by law seldom receives rewards or commendations. Although a person's good reputation may be a benefit in connection with certain occupational or community responsibilities, and good past conduct might mitigate punishment if an individual should be apprehended for a law violation, special commendations are not anticipated or expected. Some states or cities occasionally give publicity to long-term safe and courteous drivers, but this is one of the few exceptions.

The state can impose a variety of punishments to control the behavior of civilians. Law violators below the legal age of adulthood come under the jurisdiction of juvenile courts; those who have attained adulthood are subject to punishment under the criminal law. Offenders can be fined, imprisoned, put on probation or in some countries even condemned to death. In the past the political state has imposed various cruel and inhumane methods of punishing criminal offenders. The state also has as a means of controlling law violations certain penalties in addition to the criminal law. It can use administrative and civil sanctions to compel adherence to law, including monetary payments, court injunctions, and license revocations. For the most part penalties of these types are used in cases of business and professional law violations. In the settlement of claims for payment of past-due taxes or fraudulent tax returns, for example, the government, under administrative law, may require additional monetary penalties.

THE FUNCTION OF DEVIANCE

The layman considers that social deviation is "bad" by nature; social deviation weakens the social system and has no positive values. Although deviation often interferes with the willingness of persons to take part in an ongoing activity, and may seriously interfere with the continued dedication to the "rules" of society among its members, it is incorrect to assume that deviation is naturally bad and that it has no positive functions.[56] Several functions of deviance may be cited.

1. Many deviations develop from, and are the consequences of, legitimate and conventional controls.[57] The rules and functioning of the social systems of a society create both deviations and nondeviations: both are normal in a society. Many years ago, Durkheim pointed out that deviations are not necessarily "bad" or at least "abnormal." Rather, they are *normal* within the context of society.[58] Durkheim remarked that crime is an integral part of all "healthy societies" since society makes the laws that constitute crimes.[59] Thus, the conformist and the deviant are creations of the same culture, inventions of the same imaginations. Men who feared witches found them and burned them. Witchcraft in Puritan New England was normal in view of the beliefs many had of religious heresy and the predestination of a religious value.[60] Persons who sanctify the value of property find everywhere those who try to take it away from them.

2. Deviations alert people to a greater awareness of their common interests; it gives them a sense of common morality. A certain amount of deviance within a group can increase the sense of community among conforming members and thus enhance the importance of group conformity which might otherwise have been taken for

---

[56]See Cohen, *Deviance and Control,* pp. 4–5 and 11.
[57]Cohen, "The Study of Social Disorganization and Deviant Behavior," p. 474.
[58]Emile Durkheim, *The Rules of Sociological Method,* translated by S. A. Solvaay and G. H. Mueller (New York: Free Press, 1958).
[59]Durkheim, p. 67.
[60]Kai T. Erikson, *Wayward Puritans: A Study in the Sociology of Deviance* (New York: Wiley, 1966), pp. 21–23.

granted.[61] "The criminal," "the armed robber," "the rapist," and "the hard drug addict," for example, become the "enemy" to many, and this tends to solidify others in comon defense.

3. The recognition of "deviations" sets the outer *limits* of rules or norms, limits beyond which the group will not tolerate violations. This might best be illustrated in the case of the sexual molestation of a child or the use of hard drugs like heroin, both of which are beyond the limits of any group norms. The recognition of deviations indicates how much diversity can be permitted before a group loses its identity. Agents of social control help to define these limits, as in criminal trials and in psychiatric counseling. Each time that groups in power move to censure a deviant in the form of what has been called "degradation ceremonies," as in a criminal trial, the norms that have been violated are sharpened and the limits of rule toleration reinstated.[62]

4. A certain amount of deviance can well serve as a "safety valve" for persons and thus prevents excessive discontent and alleviates some of the strain on social institutions. It might be argued, for example, that prostitution serves as a safety valve without threatening the institution of the family and without involving emotional attachments outside of marriage that might result from premarital or extramarital relations.[63]

5. Deviance may well serve as a signal or warning of some basic defect within the social organization. Through the commission of a deviant act, the deviant helps to expose the inadequacies or defects of the system. Examples such as school truants, runaways, and disturbances within correctional institutions "reveal unsuspected causes of discontent, and lead to changes that enhance efficiency and morale."[64]

6. Changes in rates of deviance may also serve as warnings of impending social or legal changes. Increased use of certain drugs, particularly possession and use of marijuana in the 1960s and 1970s, for example, foreshadowed changes both in the legal structure and in social attitudes toward their use.[65]

SOME DEFINITIONS

A number of types of deviant behavior are examined in the chapters that follow. The discussion here briefly defines some important terms that will be used often throughout the book.

---

[61]Lewis A. Coser, "Some Functions of Deviant Behavior and Normative Flexibility," *American Journal of Sociology,* 68 (1962), 172–179. In some situations, as was shown in a study of Quaker work camps, common concerns over a group's deviants, together with a degree of tolerance and acceptance, can even strengthen a group. See Robert A. Dentler and Kai T. Erikson, "The Functions of Deviance in Groups," *Social Problems,* 7 (1959), 98–107.

[62]Harold Garfinkel, "Conditions of Successful Degradation Ceremonies," *American Journal of Sociology,* 61 (1956), 420–424. The importance of these boundaries in terms of their implications for social control is discussed in James M. Inverarity, "Populism and Lynching in Louisiana, 1889–1896: A Test of the Relationship between Boundary Crisis and Repressive Justice," *American Sociological Review,* 41 (1976), 262–280.

[63]Cohen, *Deviance and Control,* pp. 7–8.

[64]Cohen, *Deviance and Control,* p. 10.

[65]See John Kaplan, *Marijuana—The New Prohibition* (Cleveland: New World, 1970); and National Commission on Marijuana and Drug Abuse, *Marijuana: A Signal of Misunderstanding* (Washington, D.C.: Government Printing Office, 1972).

Conventional crimes are those ordinarily regarded as crimes—larceny, burglary, auto theft, robbery, and the like. *Occupational crimes* are violations of laws committed in connection with a legitimate occupation, whether or not they are in connection with a higher- or lower-status occupation. They range from law violations by auto and television repairmen to those by physicians and lawyers. *White-collar crimes* belong to a subtype of occupational crime and include violations of laws by persons with particularly high status, such as persons in business, professionals, and politicians in connection with their occupations. These violations are often not regarded as "crimes," although the effect they have on society may be as great or greater than that of conventional crimes. These offenses include embezzlement and other trust violations, falsification of income tax returns, political corruption, fee splitting among doctors, and violations of countless other regulations affecting persons of the white-collar classes. *Corporate crime* is a subtype of white-collar crime, and it includes violations of the law by corporations such as antitrust laws regulating monopoly control, banking and security laws, food and drug regulations, environmental protection laws, and so on.

The practice of consuming alcohol mainly for purposes of conviviality or ceremony is termed *social* or *controlled drinking*. *Social drinkers* are able to control their drinking and rarely become intoxicated. Excessive drinkers, on the other hand, use alcohol for the purpose of intoxication, and some may become dependent upon it. The *heavy drinker* uses alcohol more frequently than the social drinker and has occasional drunken sprees, but generally the drinking does not seriously deviate from the drinking norms. *Alcoholics* or *problem drinkers* are excessive drinkers who deviate markedly from the drinking norms in the frequency and quantity of the alcohol consumed and in the unconventional aspects of this consumption. Their excessive consumption of alcohol disturbs their interpersonal relationships within family, occupational, and social groups.[66] The alcoholic is neither able consistently to control the start of drinking nor its termination once it has started.

Every society tolerates a range of behavior and a certain amount of eccentricity; others it does not tolerate. *Mental disorders* will be regarded here in terms of the norms violated and the social context in which they occur. Normative violations in mental disorder have been termed "residual rule breaking" as distinguished from other types of norm violations.[67] According to the view presented here, definite norms cover crime, sexual deviations, drunkenness, and even bad manners; what is left is "residual" without a specific label. Norm violations termed mental disorder would include significant withdrawal from contact with others, hallucinations, delusions, peculiar language constructions, excessive aggressiveness, muttering, posturing, compulsive behavior, inappropriate affect, and hypochondria. Some mentally disordered persons have difficulties in relating to other persons and in appreciating the norms and objectives of others in given situations.

The *neuroses* and the *psychoses* are the broad general categories of mental disorders traditionally used by psychiatrists and others. Neurotic conditions are not as noticeable to other persons as psychotic behavior generally is. They may be of a mild

[66]Peter Wuthrich, "Social Problems of Alcoholics," *Journal of Studies on Alcohol,* 38 (1977), 881–890.
[67]Thomas J. Scheff, *Being Mentally Ill: A Sociological Theory* (Chicago: Aldine, 1966).

form recognized as a problem only by the person or by his or her immediate family or friends. These neurotic conditions include compulsions, phobias, and hypochondria. Compulsive neurotic disorders comprise repetitive or ritualistic behavior like washing of the hands or dressing in a particular set manner. Phobias represent obsessive fears of something, including preoccupation with death, fear of being in high places, fear of illness, or fear of "losing one's mind." Hypochondriacs are unduly, and usually needlessly, concerned about their physical health.

Psychotic individuals often cannot interact with other persons, and a person with a severe disorder may experience increased difficulties in participating in the general society. The psychoses are generally classed in broad general terms associated with their origins. The *organic psychoses* presumably are associated with disturbances in the physical condition of the person: they include the senile psychoses or disorders of old persons; the psychoses resulting from alcoholism; and paresis which results from a prolonged syphilitic condition. The *functional psychoses* constitute the bulk of mental disorders: they include schizophrenia, which is characterized by withdrawal from reality, hallucinations, and delusions; the manic-depressive psychoses, the symptoms of which include extreme elation or deep depression, or both; and paranoia, which is usually indicated by illusions of grandeur and extreme beliefs of persecution. The basic functional, or nonorganic, origin of these psychotic disorders has been shown in the tremendous variations that have been found among the diagnostic conclusions of psychiatrists themselves.

The other forms of deviance to be presented and analyzed here are probably self-explanatory, but certain definitions may be helpful. *Prostitution* is the act of engaging in sexual intercourse for money. *Homosexual behavior* involves specific acts such as sodomy and fellatio in the case of males and cunnilingus and other means of sexual intimacy in the case of females. It is the act of homosexuality, primarily in the case of males, that makes it illegal, not the state of mind. *Drug addiction* includes legal drugs, alcohol, and cigarettes, as well as the use of illegal drugs like marijuana, heroin, and cocaine. Although *suicide* may seem obvious, the definition of suicide is more technical because it involves not only the taking of one's own life but also the failure to try to prevent death when it is threatened. *Physical disabilities* as deviance include blindness, mental retardation, visible physical handicaps, obesity, and stuttering.

SELECTED REFERENCES

Birenbaum, Arnold, and Edward Sagarin. *Norms and Human Behavior.* New York: Holt, Rinehart and Winston, 1976.

Campbell, Ernest Q. *Socialization: Culture and Personality.* Dubuque, Ia: William C. Brown, 1975.

Cohen, Albert K. *Deviance and Control.* Englewood Cliffs, N.J.: Prentice-Hall, 1966.

Edgerton, Robert. *Deviance: A Cross-Cultural Perspective.* Menlo Park, Calif.: Cummings Publishers, 1976.

Gibbs, Jack P. "Issues in Defining Deviant Behavior," in Robert A. Scott and Jack D. Douglas, eds., *Theoretical Perspectives on Deviance.* New York: Basic Books, 1972.

Gibbs, Jack P., and Maynard L. Erickson. "Recent Developments in the Study of Deviance," *Annual Review of Sociology,* 1 (1975), 29–43.

Hawkins, Richard, and Gary Tiedeman. *The Creation of Deviance: Interpersonal and Organizational Determinants.* Columbus, O: Charles E. Merrill, 1975.

Homans, George C. *Social Behavior,* rev. ed. Boston: Houghton Mifflin, 1974.

Janowitz, Morris. "Sociological Theory and Social Control," *American Journal of Sociology,* 81 (1975), 82–108.

Kitsuse, John I. "Deviance, Deviant Behavior, and Deviants: Some Conceptual Problems," in William J. Filstead, ed., *An Introduction to Deviance: Readings in the Process of Making Deviants.* Chicago: Markham, 1972.

Kitsuse, John I., and Malcolm Spector. "Social Problems and Deviance," *Social Problems,* 22 (1975), 584–594.

Lemert, Edwin M. *Social Pathology.* New York: McGraw-Hill, 1951.

McCaghy, Charles H. *Deviant Behavior: Crime, Conflict and Interest Groups.* New York: Macmillan, 1976.

Meier, Robert F., and Weldon T. Johnson. "Deterrence as Social Control: Legal and Extralegal Factors in the Production of Conformity," *American Sociological Review,* 42 (1977), 293–304.

Newman, Graeme. *Comparative Deviance: Perception and Law in Six Cultures.* New York: Elsevier, 1976.

Sagarin, Edward. *Deviants and Deviance: An Introduction to the Study of Disvalued People and Behavior.* New York: Holt, Rinehart and Winston, 1975.

Scott, John Finley. *The Internalization of Norms.* Englewood Cliffs, N.J.: Prentice-Hall, 1971.

Watkins, C. Ken. *Social Control.* New York: Longmans, 1975.

CHAPTER 2

Much social behavior is shaped through participation in subcultures, such as this motorcycle gang, from whom a person learns appropriate social roles and norms.

Becoming Deviant

U P to this point, we have dealt with norms, the definition of deviance, and considerations of social control. In this chapter the emphasis will be on how the individual becomes deviant. If the sociological criterion for being a "deviant" were simply the commission of a deviant act, we would all be deviants and the term would have little meaning. In the sociological discussion of the deviant that follows we shall critically analyze the relation of biological factors to deviant behavior. We shall also examine the social nature of human beings, including the self and identity of deviants, the process of socialization into a deviant role, the important distinction between a primary and secondary deviant, and the need to recognize the deviant's own perspective on his behavior.

In various ways, our mode of perceiving and interpreting the world and the things about us is conditioned by meanings and categories with which our culture has provided us. We see our world through a cultural mesh; nowhere is this truer than in our perception of the implied real nature of social deviants. The difference between conforming and deviant behavior does not mean different physical or psychological qualities which the deviant possesses as compared to the conformist. This assertion is alien to the thinking of many persons. We often learn to look upon those who behave differently from the way "we" behave as possessing individual qualities and characteristics unlike our own. We tend to believe, furthermore, that these qualities are the "causes" of the behavior involved. Thus we say a person is an alcoholic, or drinks excessively, because that individual is "weak," "has no character," "has no will power," or "has bad heredity." We say that ordinary criminals, but not white-collar ones, have "a need to rebel," or that they are "releasing aggressive drives which they have been suppressing."

The belief that deviants are inherently different is built upon a series of false assumptions, for *all deviant behavior is human behavior,* and the basic processes which produce behavior are the same for the deviant and the nondeviant. The subprocesses affecting deviants operate within the general framework of a theory of human nature. The units of analysis, as well as the fundamental social processes in all human conduct, are the same whether the end products are inmates of correctional institutions or wardens, mental patients or psychiatrists, corrupt businessmen or ministers. Moreover, deviance, as we have shown, is a highly relative concept, and, therefore, the direction of behavior is relative. One sociologist has elaborated this view:

> Men are rarely isolated and acting purely as independent agents. . . . This means that what a man does cannot be explained exclusively in terms of his personality traits, his attitudes, or his motives. People frequently do things they do not want to do. Human behavior is something that is constructed in the course of interaction with other people, and the direction it takes depends upon the inclinations of others as well as those of the actor.[1]

Moreover, there does not appear to be any general personality pattern of conformity and nonconformity with social norms or values, although there might be

---

[1]Tamotsu Shibutani, *Society and Personality: An Interactionist Approach to Social Psychology,* © 1961, p. 60. Reprinted by permission of Prentice-Hall, Inc., Englewood Cliffs, New Jersey.

general nonconformity to a given class or set of norms.[2] Persons may deviate from certain norms and comply with others.[3] Those who deviate from sexual norms may not steal, for example, and many white-collar criminals may have a rigid sexual code. In most cases, strongly disapproved deviations may be but a small proportion of a person's total life activities. Even where the deviations constitute a more organized subculture, as in professional crime, accepted conduct may coincide at many points with norms and values of the larger community.[4] In the case of professional crime, for example, personal honor and "honesty among thieves" are generally the norm because it would be inappropriate to depend on the police for support.

With this statement of the thesis that both deviant and nondeviant persons have fundamentally the same essential components of human nature, some further consideration of these components is necessary. Here the interest is not so much in norms, society, or group as it is in the individual. First, we must understand the relation between human biological structure and behavior, deviant or otherwise, as well as the differences between the biological nature of humans and that of other animals.

BIOLOGY AND SOCIAL BEHAVIOR

Human beings possess a biological nature and a social nature, and it is obvious that without a biological nature there could be no human nature. There is an interplay between the two rather than opposition. Humans are animals who must breathe, eat, rest, and eliminate wastes. Like any other animals, they require calories, salt and other chemicals, and a particular temperature range and oxygen balance. Humans are animals that are dependent on their environment and limited by certain biological capacities.

Biology is of little relevance, however, to the social or symbolic behavior of humans or to deviant behavior. There are no physical functions or structures, no combination of genes, and no glandular secretions that contain within themselves the power to direct, guide, or determine the type, form, and course of the social behavior of human beings. Physical structures or properties set physical limits on the activities of persons, but whether such structures also set *social* limits depends on the way in which cultures or subcultures symbolize or interpret these physical properties. Despite this, there are still some scientists and practitioners who claim that certain forms of deviant behavior can be traced to certain physical anomalies, body chemistry, or heredity. These beliefs, in turn, have important consequences for the nature of some suggested preventive and "treatment" programs. Those, for example, who believe in the sterilization of certain types of deviants are advocating a biological view of human nature.

---

[2]Talcott Parsons has suggested, without supporting evidence, that there is a relation between a nonconformist personality pattern and deviant behavior. See *The Social System* (New York: Free Press, 1951), Chapters 7–9, particularly pp. 256–267.

[3]Robert Harper, "Is Conformity a General or Specific Trait?" *American Sociological Review,* 12 (1947), 81–86.

[4]See Edwin M. Lemert, *Social Pathology* (New York: McGraw-Hill, 1951), p. 49.

From time to time various explanations of certain forms of deviance in terms of certain biological characteristics arise, but sooner or later all of them disappear as valid theories. Explanations have been offered in terms of body type, glandular disturbances, brain pathology, and, more recently, in the 1960s and 1970s, the relation of chromosomes to deviant behavior, particularly crime. Here the explanation for aggressive male crime has been sought in terms of the presence of XYY chromosomes, the normal male having only XY chromosomes.[5] A conference of experts in various scientific disciplines sponsored by the National Institute of Mental Health, however, concluded that no definite conclusions could be drawn about the relation between the presence of XYY chromosomes and deviant, criminal, and violent behavior.[6] All of these explanations fail to take into consideration the relativity of "deviance" and the essentially socially acquired nature of human behavior.

Inherited Deviance

Some biologists still believe that crime, alcoholism, certain types of mental illness, and certain sexual deviations can be carried as a specific unit in biological inheritance. The evidence has been overwhelmingly against such a view. In order to prove that deviant behavior is inherited, one would have to state the nature of the inheritance in such precise terms as to suggest the part of the human organism that is involved in the inheritance—tissues in the brain, the blood, or the central nervous system. Moreover, one would have to prove the presence of specific factors at the time the ovum is fertilized by the spermatozoon. An inherited quality would have to be reasonably specific, and it would have to be stable enough to be able to affect all members of the species. None of this proof has been forthcoming. Deviant behavior cannot be hereditary, as will be shown later, since social norms that are directly related to deviant behavior cannot be inherited. Such a theory of inheritance would assume that what constitutes disapproved behavior is the same in all societies and throughout time. This is an erroneous assumption. Morality varies by generation, an easily demonstrable fact clearly illustrated by the norms designated in the criminal code each year. Two leading authorities in the field of criminology stated that it is "obviously impossible for criminality to be inherited as such, for crime is defined by acts of legislature and these vary independently of the biological inheritance of the violators of law."[7]

Few persons today support the view of the direct inheritance of deviance. Instead, some have substituted the "inherited tendency" for such behavior. In many ways, this is an even more unscientific approach, since the nature and physiological location of the tendency is left unspecified. Sagarin has replied as follows to this approach:

---

[5]For a review of the literature see W. H. Price and P. B. Whatmore, "Behavior Disorders and Patterns of Crime among XYY Males Identified at a Maximum Security Hospital," *British Medical Journal,* 1 (1967), 533–537; M. D. Casey et al., "YY Chromosome and Anti-Social Behavior," *Lancet,* 2 (1966), p. 859; and Saleem A. Shah and Loren H. Roth, "Biological and Psychophysiological Factors in Criminality," in Daniel Glaser, ed., *Handbook of Criminology* (Chicago: Rand McNally, 1974), pp. 101–173.

[6]See *Report of the XYY Chromosomal Abnormality,* Public Health Service Publication No. 2103 (Washington, D.C.: Government Printing Office, 1970).

[7]Edwin H. Sutherland and Donald R. Cressey, *Criminology,* 10th ed. (Philadelphia: Lippincott, 1978), p. 123.

For a time, various forms of sex deviance, particularly homosexuality, were thought of as inborn, as were problems of gender disorientation. The so-called true homosexual was contrasted with the perverse, the former a constitutionally conditioned and the latter a learned behavior. The language remains, but the concept is now almost dead: It survives only in the form of predilections and tendencies, not for homosexuality (or for murder, rape, check forgery, alcoholism, or drug use), but for greater or lesser self-control, ego strength, proneness to violence, and the like. . . . The most serious argument against biological theory in this area of human behavior may be its inability to account for fluctuations in deviance in a single gene pool from one period to the next.[8]

What many persons may confuse as inheritance in behavior is the social transmission of somewhat similar ways of behaving from one generation to another in a culture, or from one family to another. Actually, none of this is heredity, for there is no way in which so-called family traits or culture can be inherited through the genes. The complexity of gene structure which would be required to transmit a culture or family attitudes and values as part of the biological heritage would be inconceivable. One reason for the belief in constitutional differences was the error in perceiving the bases for resemblances and differences in the social behavior of father and son, mother and daughter, and brother and sister. No two children have exactly the same experiences, even for an hour or a day, let alone a month, a year, or longer. The child learns to adapt to the world and to the people in the world. Thus, the experiences of two brothers, one deviant and the other not, particularly if there is a considerable age disparity, may be even more dissimilar than the experiences of the friends of either brother. Among these differences in experiences are, obviously, the addition of a sibling, different associates, different school classes, different teachers. If the family has moved during the childhood of two brothers, as a great many families do, the neighbors and the general environment may be quite different for each brother. What is probably even more important is the change in attitudes of the father and mother with additional children, as well as changes in social status and possibly a change in occupation. The method of treating an older and a young child may be quite different because of changes in the parents' social situation. It is quite obvious, however, that behavioral traits can be passed on in a family through the sharing of common experiences and attitudes.

Physical defects like crossed eyes, facial deformities, severe acne, and so on, may contribute to deviance (see Chapter 15) and are thought by some to be related to such forms of deviance as delinquency and crime. There is no one-to-one causal relation between such situations. Due to a negative societal reaction, persons with physical defects of these types are often more likely to be processed and labeled, however, as deviants by authorities, particularly if their condition is deemed threatening. All this is to say that one should not exclude all biological factors from the study of deviance. In certain situations, brain tumors, an illness, or similar factors may be related to deviant episodes. But these are rare instances and do not comprise the usual

---

[8]Edward Sagarin, *Deviants and Deviance: An Introduction to the Study of Disvalued People and Behavior* (New York: Holt, Rinehart and Winston, 1975). p. 88. But see Sarnoff Mednick and Karl O. Christiansen, eds., *Biosocial Bases of Criminal Behavior* (New York: Gardner Press, 1977).

deviant situation. We are here concerned with normative behavior and the acquisition of deviant norms from a social perspective.

SOCIAL NATURE OF HUMAN BEINGS

Despite the fact that humans are animals, among all animals humans alone possess language; with language they can convey abstract meanings. They alone have the language and the intelligence needed to convey highly technical ideas, such as mathematical concepts. They alone have a self, play a variety of social roles, and make moral distinctions. The limitations on the possibility that animals can approach human beings in their behavior far outweigh the few similarities. It is largely a fallacy to try to derive much valid knowledge about the social behavior of human beings from experiments on animals, for experimentation with animals neglects the fact that human subjects are more intelligent, are able to use language, and possess a self.

Without human communication through language there can be no abstract reasoning, no social interaction, no self or conception of the self; without language the human animal cannot play social roles. The possession of language is the most important distinguishing characteristic separating humans from other animals.[9] Language enables the human being to deal with norms and values. Scientific, moral, and religious ideas are carried and expressed through language. The absence of morality, religion, conscience, and so on, among adult apes and human infants is based upon the same inability to represent to oneself in terms of a human language one's own goals, purposes, or principles.[10] Terms like "criminal," "drunk," "mugger," "addict," "queer," "hippie," "pusher," and "square" take on abstract or stereotyped meanings in common language. One does not hear a phrase like "He's a kind murderer." Such a phrase has a peculiar sound; the adjective "kind" is incongruent with the image portrayed by the noun "murderer."

Socialization

The socialization of a child takes place through language. In communication with others through language throughout a long infancy, childhood, and young adulthood, the human being interacts with others, and through this interaction both the individual's own and other personalities become modified. Most attitudes are developed through group associations rather than as a result of individual experience. Inasmuch as people are all, in one way or another, members of groups, attitudes generally represent shared meanings. Hence most attitudes are derived from cultural norms. Groups to which an individual belongs serve as a frame of reference and undoubtedly influence his attitudes. A group in terms of whose norms a person orients his behavior

---

[9]Alfred R. Lindesmith, Anselm L. Strauss, and Norman K. Denzin, *Social Psychology,* 4th ed. (Hinsdale, Ill.: Dryden Press, 1975).
[10]Lindesmith, Strauss, and Denzin, p. 83.

to is a *reference group*. Such groups are not necessarily the same as *membership groups* to which a person is recognized as belonging. A delinquent gang may be the reference group of a delinquent rather than such membership groups as family, church, and similar groups.

Attitudes

Although persons secure most of their attitudes from the general culture and from subcultural situations that differ according to region, neighborhood, class, occupation, religion, and education, occasionally attitudes result from some unique personal experience. Most attitudes involving disrespect for law are acquired through group experiences, but some persons who have had particularly brutal experiences in a correctional institution or in a so-called reformatory may have attitudes of disrespect turn into hatred for law and law officers.

Research on attitudes has brought out the fact that, while they may be relatively stabilized definitions of situations, they can and do change. It is important, however, to distinguish between compliance as behavior change and attitude change. Outward behavior is generally more often altered than internally held attitudes. Whereas a prisoner may be induced to comply with prison rules under the surveillance of guards in order to obtain a reward, that is, to be released, there is no guarantee that the individual's preprison attitudes favorable to criminal activity have changed. In fact, experimental research has concluded that the greater the reward for a behavior, the less the resultant attitude change.[11] The nature of the link between attitude and behavior change is still being discussed.[12]

Among the more important variables which change attitudes appear to be such factors as the strength of a particular attitude in the presence of external influences; increased familiarity due to firsthand experience; and the prestige of the model presenting a given attitude. These three ideas can be illustrated by the resistance to the use of drugs on the part of a middle-class boy who has attended a high school where there is little drug use and who has been active in conventional groups. Suppose that a boy who has been taking drugs moves into his neighborhood. Under the personal influence of this boy the nondrug user may tend to alter his attitudes. If the new boy is someone with considerable prestige and one whom he admires, there is an increased possibility that he himself may engage in drug use. If the prestige model in this example were reversed, the boy taking drugs might become a nonuser.

Even so-called *motives* are acquired as the result of social experience.[13] They are socially molded, usually in accord with the prevailing norms of particular groups to which the individual belongs. Persons appear to vary in their emphasis on given

[11]For a classic statement of this finding see L. Festinger and J. M. Carlsmith, "Cognitive Consequences of Forced Compliance," *Journal of Abnormal and Social Psychology,* 58 (1959), 203–210.

[12]Herbert Blumer has challenged the utility of the concept of attitude in explaining human behavior in "Attitudes and the Social Act," *Social Problems,* 3 (1955), 59–65. See also Allen E. Liska, ed., *The Consistency Controversy* (Cambridge: Schenkman, 1975).

[13]For various theories of motivation see Charles N. Cofer and Mortimer H. Appley, *Motivation: Theory and Research* (New York: Wiley, 1964). See also Stanford M. Lyman and Marvin B. Scott, "Accounts," *American Sociological Review,* 33 (1968), 46–62.

motives, depending on cultural and subcultural norms, the definition of the situation, and the life organization of the individual. In the process of reaching goals, deviants and nondeviants may adopt what might appear to be different patterns of behavior, but in reality they may be achieving similar goals in their own way. Some boys may have fun playing baseball or indulging in other sports, whereas others may find even more fun stealing automobiles, slashing tires, wrecking a school, beating up a stranger, or taking drugs. Some may find companionship in a delinquent gang rather than in a boy scout troop; some people may prefer the fellowship of drinking companions in a tavern to the fellowship offered by a church. A young "punk" in the city slum may seek to gain a status of a far different kind from that sought by a college student. Some men would probably prefer to have the prestige and acclaim accorded them in an organized criminal syndicate or in professional crime than be president of a university. Businessmen and politicians may often engage in illegal behavior in order to secure funds with which to buy material goods, which, in turn, bring them greater recognition in society.

Self and Identity

Human beings are the only animals with a self and identity in the sense that they conceive of themselves as separate beings, have an understanding of who and what they are, and are even able to evaluate themselves in ways that are sometimes laudatory and others reproving.[14] The human being is not born with a self: it is acquired through social interaction with others.[15] Symbolic interactionists view the self as being an object to itself; they see the development of the self as reflecting a process of role-taking whereby the child learns to take the attitudes held by significant others toward himself as his own self attitude. In addition, the child develops his own self as he learns of the existence of other social categories and how these relate to each other and to his own self. This acquisition of a self identity has great consequences for the behavior of human beings, since what an individual does or does not do depends in large measure upon the person's self conception.

> Many of the distinctive features of human behavior arise from the fact that men orient themselves within a symbolic environment and strive to come to terms with what they believe themselves to be. Men give their lives willingly for a variety of worthy causes; they deny themselves many joys in order to build gigantic political or industrial empires; they build up social barriers to protect their progeny against miscegenation; they plot vengeance for a wrong suffered long ago by their ancestors; they create monuments in their own honor; they push their children to "make a name" for themselves; lovers commit suicide when they are denied the right to marry; artists paint happily for "posterity," serenely indifferent to the fact that their contemporaries regard them as mad. Although men take these activities for granted as a part of human life, no other animal is known to engage in such conduct. It is unlikely that any creature without self-conceptions would do

---

[14]Perhaps some person would rush to defend a pet dog and say that the animal not only conceives of itself as a separate being but when punished has been observed to sulk. We would be the last to disturb such a pleasant fantasy, but it might be well to suggest that two elements make this improbable: a dog has no way to refer to itself and possesses no words with which to talk to itself about the errors of its ways.

[15]See Chad Gordon and Kenneth J. Gergen, eds., *The Self in Social Interaction* (New York: Wiley, 1968).

any of these things. Human behavior consists of a succession of adjustments to life conditions, but each man must come to terms with himself as well as with other features of his world. To understand what men do we must know something about what each person means to himself.[16]

The symbolic interaction approach is concerned with the processes involved in the creation of meaning; that is, how actors create meaning for human and nonhuman subjects.[17] George Herbert Mead wrote that no "hard-and-fast line can be drawn between our own selves and the selves of others, since our own selves exist . . . only insofar as the selves of others exist."[18] This symbolic interactionist perspective of the self as a social object has particular importance in relation to the development and continuation of certain types of deviant behavior.[19] The dynamics involved in the continuance of deviant behavior cannot be understood without understanding the relation between deviance and self-identity.

An organized and integrated self permits a person to put himself in the place of another while still maintaining his own identity. This growth of self-realization can be illustrated by the development of children's moral ideas. Since individuals are not born with "natural" moral judgment, children in the early years have abstract conceptions of justice and "fairness" which are not yet specific. In a study of lower-class children in Switzerland, Piaget showed that the child's ideas of fair play move from self-centered judgments to seeing them through the eyes of others.[20] Until about the age of five, a child has an absolute idea of right and wrong, and from then until about the age of ten, the child comes to realize that moral ideas are not real in themselves but are related to numerous group ideas. Finally, the child learns that the group can make exceptions to rules and that new rules can be made by the group. In this way, he learns to acquire abstract, generalized ideals.

To the symbolic interactionist, the self is not an immutable and unchanging social object. This perspective sees the social world of reality, and the self "a thing to be debated, compromised, and legislated."[21] This self changes as the others with whom one identifies change, or as the expectations of these others are altered. The concept of self which one has as a child is likely to be decidedly different from one's concept of self as an aged person.[22]

---

[16]Shibutani, *Society and Personality: An Interactionist Approach to Social Psychology,* © 1961, pp. 247–248. Reprinted by permission of Prentice-Hall, Inc., Englewood Cliffs, New Jersey.

[17]Herbert Blumer, *Symbolic Interactionism: Perspective and Method* (Englewood Cliffs, N.J.: Prentice-Hall, 1969). David Matza has discussed the development of a deviant career in the concept of "signification"; see his *Becoming Deviant* (Englewood Cliffs, N.J.: Prentice-Hall, 1969). Also see John Lofland, *Deviance and Identity* (Englewood Cliffs, N.J.: Prentice-Hall, 1969).

[18]George H. Mead, *Mind, Self and Society* (Chicago: University of Chicago Press, 1934), p. 164.

[19]Norman K. Denzin, "The Methodological Implications of Symbolic Interactionism for the Study of Deviance," *British Journal of Sociology,* 3 (1974), 269–282. Also see Norman K. Denzin, *Socialization and Social Relationships* (Chicago: Aldine, 1973).

[20]Jean Piaget, *Moral Judgment of the Child* (London: Routledge & Kegan Paul, 1932). Also see Lawrence Kohlberg, "Stage and Sequence: The Cognitive-Developmental Approach to Socialization," in David A. Goslin, ed., *Handbook of Socialization Theory and Research* (Chicago: Rand McNally, 1969), pp. 347–480.

[21]George McCall and J. L. Simmons, *Identities and Interactions* (New York: Free Press, 1966), p. 42.

[22]See, for example, Zena S. Blau, "Changes in Status and Age Identification," *American Sociological Review,* 21 (1956), 198–203.

The self, then, in interactionist terms, is a set of discrete roles and identities that requires both the responses of others and the acceptance of such designations by the actor himself. Thus movement from a nondeviant to a deviant sense of self involves the active participation of the person as well as societal reaction. He must sort out the meaning of what is happening to him in terms of his conception of who he really is. This requires an ability to distinguish between doing and being, for the self-motivated deviant does deviant acts as part of the conscious process of becoming deviant.[23] The person is likely to be actively involved in the creation of his self-concept. He builds his identity in an interactive context, mediating his experiences with significant others. He is not a passive recipient of labeling reactions of others. Consequently, a person may choose to reject the judgments of others which are discrepant with his own sense of self. For example, some researchers on delinquency feel that the self-concept of nondelinquent boys who live in high delinquency areas serves as an insulating factor in the "function of the acquisition and maintenance of a socially acceptable or appropriate self-concept."[24] Another study, however, showed that teachers and administrators may judge a boy to be delinquent when, in fact, this is not how he views himself.[25] When teachers and administrators in an all-black, inner-city, lower-class school were asked to name those boys who, in their opinions, would come into official contact with the law, as well as those who would not, it was found that both "bad" and "good" boys perceived others—mothers, friends, teachers—as having views of them which they themselves did not share. Thus not all perceptions of what others think are incorporated into one's sense of self. The person chooses among varied interaction experiences in developing his sense of who he really is.

SOCIALIZATION AND SOCIAL ROLES

This leads now to a further discussion of the socialization process and the significance of social roles. Social behavior has to be acquired. It is not there at birth; it develops through socialization.[26] Behavior becomes modified in response to the demands and expectations of others. Practically all behavior is a product of social interaction and is seen only in relation to other people. Words like "honesty," "friendliness," "shyness" have meaning only in relation to other people. Even expressions of emotionality, such as anger or depression, although they have physiological concomitants, are mostly the

---

[23]See Matza.
[24]Walter C. Reckless, Simon Dinitz, and Barbara Kay, "The Self-Component in Potential Delinquency and Potential Non-Delinquency," *American Sociological Review*, 22 (1957), p. 566.
[25]Sandra S. Tangri and Michael Schwartz, "Delinquency Research and the Self-Concept Variable," *Journal of Criminal Law, Criminology and Police Science*, 58 (1967), 182–191. Also see James D. Orcutt, "Self-Concept and Insulation against Delinquency: Some Critical Notes," *The Sociological Quarterly*, 11 (1970), 381–391.
[26]For discussions of the socialization process, see John A. Clausen, ed., *Socialization and Society* (Boston: Little, Brown, 1968); Orville G. Brim, Jr., and Stanton Wheeler, *Socialization after Childhood* (New York: Wiley, 1966); and Ernest Q. Campbell, *Socialization: Culture and Personality* (Dubuque, Ia.: William C. Brown, 1975).

expressions of social reactions. They can be expressed, controlled, or accentuated to a variety of social and cultural definitions.

Social Roles

Deviants and nondeviants play a variety of *social roles* which represent the behavior that is expected of a person in a given position or status with reference to a particular group.[27] The activities of a human being in the course of daily life can be regarded as the performance of a series of roles which have been learned and which others expect the person to fulfill. It is through the expectations of others that persons are assigned roles and statuses, such as the roles played in a marital or family situation. Like the actor who plays some stage parts, even though they are exaggerated, persons fill numerous roles. Some of them are general, others specific; some are idealized, others actual. One's social roles are linked with one's position or status in society, and each of these has role prescriptions. There are age roles, sex roles, social-class roles, occupation roles, and family roles. Such roles are, for example, those of an old or young person, a man or a woman, a husband or a wife, a parent or a child, a private or a general, a doctor or a patient, a salesperson or a consumer. "Each of them, taken as a system of roles, presupposes that its members can indeed manage to engage in behaviors appropriate to that particular system when the situation warrants."[28]

Although a great deal of socialization in role-playing and role-taking occurs in childhood, it also continues into later life. This fact is often not adequately recognized by psychiatrists, for example, as will be shown in Chapter 4. Individuals learn new roles and abandon old ones as they pass through the life cycle and encounter new situations. Adolescence represents a period of adjustment to new roles: marriage represents the acquisition of new roles, entrance into professions or occupations requires new roles, and old age often becomes a major role adjustment.

Social behavior develops not only as we respond in relation to other people but also through social interaction as we anticipate the responses of other people to us and incorporate them into our conduct. When two or more persons interact, for example, all are more or less aware of the fact that each is evaluating the behavior of the others. In this process, each person also evaluates his own behavior. A social role more specifically involves four parts: "(1) an identification of self, (2) behavior in given situations appropriate to this identification, (3) a background of related acts by others (counter-roles) which serve as cues to guide specific performance, and (4) an evaluation by the individual and by others of the role enactment."[29] One's behavior, based on one's estimate of how one should act, is called role-playing, and one's idea of the other person's behavior is role-taking. A role set is a complement of role relations which persons have by occupying a particular social status, such as the role of a teacher to her pupils and to all the others connected with the school.[30] Social control

---

[27]See Bruce J. Biddle and Edwin J. Thomas, eds., *Role Theory: Concepts and Research* (New York: Wiley, 1966), particularly Chapter 1, "The Nature and History of Role Theory."
[28]Theodore M. Newcomb, Ralph H. Turner, and Philip E. Converse, *Social Psychology: The Study of Human Interaction* (New York: Holt, Rinehart and Winston, 1965), p. 393.
[29]Lindesmith, Strauss, and Denzin, p. 400.
[30]Robert K. Merton, "Instability and Articulation in the Role Set," in Biddle and Thomas, pp. 282–287.

becomes possible through the fact that persons acquire the ability to behave in a manner consistent with the expectations of others.[31] Self-control is social control, for the person sees himself from the standpoint of the group and thus tries to maintain self-respect by meeting group expectations.

Socialization as Role Taking

Socialization largely represents the learning of roles; that is, it refers to the "process by which the individual acquires the skills, knowledge, attitudes, values, and motives necessary for performance of social roles.[32] It involves a process of learning in which an individual is prepared in larger and smaller groups to meet the status requirements that society expects in a variety of social situations. The required behavior (habits, beliefs, attitudes, and motives) are an individual's *prescribed roles:* the requirements themselves are the *role prescriptions.*[33] The role prescriptions or norm requirements are learned in interaction with others. What roles the child learns in the family and elsewhere, such as the male or female sex role, are largely dictated by the social structure or the society itself. Groups, then, are multidimensional *systems of roles;* a group is what its role relations are. In the interaction of any group, there are various role relations involving mutual attitudinal and behavioral responses to one another. The individual members of a group may change, but the group may continue, as in the case of a delinquent gang, where the roles of the leader and other required roles in the gang may continue to be played despite changes in the gang membership.

Much deviant behavior is, then, directly expressive of roles.

> A tough and bellicose posture, the use of obscene language, participation in illicit sexual activity, the immoderate consumption of alcohol, the deliberate flouting of legality and authority, a generalized disrespect for the sacred symbols of the "square" world, a taste for marijuana, even suicide—all of these may have the primary function of affirming, in the language of gesture and deed, that one is a certain kind of person.[34]

Professional thieves, for example, play a variety of roles. Punctuality in keeping appointments with partners and the code of not "squealing" on another thief are of particular importance in their profession. Social status or position among thieves is based on their technical skill, connections, financial standing, influence, dress, manners, and wide knowledge. Their status is also reflected in the attitudes of lawyers, the police, court officials, and newspaper reporters. The professional criminal may play different roles toward victim, friend, wife, children, father, mother, grocer, or minister.

Persons occupying a given status position are influenced in their *role behavior* by the role prescriptions, or the "script," they are supposed to play. Most of the script

---

[31]Shibutani, pp. 118–121, 197.

[32]William H. Sewell, "Recent Developments in Socialization Theory and Research," *The Annals,* 349 (1963), 163–181. Also see David R. Heise, ed., *Personality and Socialization* (Chicago: Rand McNally, 1972).

[33]Orville G. Brim, Jr., David C. Glass, David E. Lavin, and Norman Goodman, *Personality and Decision Processes: Studies in the Social Psychology of Thinking* (Stanford, Calif.: Stanford University Press, 1962).

[34]Albert K. Cohen, "The Sociology of the Deviant Act: Anomie Theory and Beyond," *American Sociological Review,* 30 (1965), p. 13.

for these roles, both deviant and nondeviant, is derived from group experience and cultural or subcultural situations. A changed social position, for example, belonging to a delinquent gang or to a group taking drugs, may mean a changed social role. Actual role behavior may be somewhat different from the role prescriptions, however, for it is affected by a variety of influences, such as the behavior of others in the situation, belonging to groups whose role prescriptions are different, and so forth. In fact, some role prescriptions are highly structured and clear. On occasions, however, where appropriate roles are not provided, they may be unique to the individual's own life experience. Some persons play more roles than do others, and *role strain* may arise in situations requiring complex role demands and where a person is required to fulfill multiple roles.[35] Many of the problems arising in systems of roles are due to the fact that (1) the role prescriptions are unclear and the person has difficulty in knowing what is expected of him, (2) the roles are too numerous for the individual to fulfill adequately, with a resulting "role overload," and (3) they may conflict or be mutually contradictory, so that the individual must play a role he does not wish to play. The diversity of social roles in modern urban society is an important factor in the extent of social deviation in society.

Deviant Role Taking

One can speak of deviant roles in the same way one can speak of any other social roles. Criminals play roles, as do deviants who have physical disabilities—the obese, the crippled, the blind, the retarded. In fact, they often come to play social roles that cannot be explained entirely by the physical disability itself. The behavior of much mental disorder is a social role, as will be shown, as is also the behavior of the homosexual or the organized criminal offender. Even suicide is often the enactment of a social role to its final and ultimate conclusion. It has been stated that much deviance that seems to be "irrational" or "senseless" does make some sense when seen as an effort to proclaim or test a certain kind of self.

> The use of marijuana and heroin, especially the early experimental stages; driving at dangerous speeds and "playing chicken" on the highway; illegal consumption of alcoholic beverages; participation in illegal forms of social protest and civil disobedience; taking part in "rumbles"—all these are likely to be role-expressive behavior. In order to recognize this motivation, however, one must know the roles that are at stake, and what kinds of behavior carry what kinds of "role-messages" in the actor's social world.[36]

The following are several significant reasons for viewing deviant behavior in terms of roles:

1. It brings diverse actions together into a particular category or style of life such as the "homosexual," "drug addict," or "criminal."

---

[35]Newcomb, Turner, and Converse, pp. 393–427. Also see Biddle and Thomas, Part II, "The Conceptual Structure," p. 62. Parsons believes role conflict to be the basis of deviant behavior; such behaviors are responses to a strain or conflict in institutional role expectations which the individual faces. See Parsons, pp. 280–283.

[36]Albert K. Cohen, *Deviance and Control* (Englewood Cliffs, N.J.: Prentice-Hall, 1966), p. 99.

[37]See Ralph H. Turner, "Deviance Avowal as Neutralization of Commitment," *Social Problems,* 19 (1972), 308–322.

2. A deviant role provides a meaningfulness to interactive situations, the meanings being assigned on the basis of imputed self and other roles. "For an observer of another's behavior, the fact that deviance is a role means that he cannot interpret and react sensibly to a deviant action without first deciding whether it is a manifestation of a deviant role or not."[38] Lofland has similarly noted that if the significant others of the actor do not know of the existence of a deviant category or role, the subject's experience cannot be interpreted in terms of that category.[39] Lemert has also pointed out the importance of learned deviant categories, in that the individual with no prior awareness that the actions are defined or definable as deviant "must learn or must apply the definition either to his attributes or actions."[40]

3. Deviant social roles enable the observer or the public to reduce diverse behavior to a simplistic stereotyped version of the role, thus such things as "unruly hair, wearing a knapsack, using key words and phrases in speech, are then capable of eliciting proportionately acute fear and repression."[41]

4. The deviant individual develops a self-conception through selective identification with the deviant role out of the many roles he plays. When other people come to stress a particular deviant role a person plays, it is difficult for this person not to regard his deviance as central to his identity, as in the case of the physically handicapped. In fact, the status and role (or roles) which a person is assigned cannot be easily changed by his own desires; whether a person plays the role which society has assigned him or not, his behavior is still often interpreted by society as consistent with this role and its corresponding status. For example, the behavior of the former inmate of a prison in his home community may be interpreted in a manner consistent with real or imagined criminal "tendencies," even if he is making a determined effort to "go straight." The power of community interpretations in perpetuating a person's occupancy of a criminal status and role may have several consequences. Sometimes such persons will "give in" to the societal definition and actively play the role expected of them. The treatment of a person as if he were generally rather than specifically deviant produces a "self-fulfilling prophecy," setting in motion several mechanisms that "conspire to shape the person in the image people have of him."[42]

PRIMARY AND SECONDARY DEVIANTS

Some deviant acts result in a person's being termed immediately by others as a deviant. In other cases the deviant status arises only as a result of a variety or a combination of acts and status. They include:

---

[38]Turner, p. 311.
[39]Lofland, pp. 131–134.
[40]Edwin M. Lemert, *Human Deviance, Social Problems and Social Control,* 2d ed. (Englewood Cliffs, N.J.: Prentice-Hall, 1972), p. 80.
[41]Turner, p. 312.
[42]Howard S. Becker, *Outsiders: Studies in the Sociology of Deviance,* enlarged ed. (New York: Free Press, 1973), p. 34. Also see Marsh Ray, "The Cycle of Abstinence and Relapse among Heroin Addicts," *Social Problems,* 9 (1961), 132–140.

(1) that the action is regarded as serious, threatening to other persons or to the society; (2) that there is an official governmental reaction in the form of penal sanctions for the act's commission; (3) that it is repeated with some consistency or frequency, or that it is seen as a threat if repeated; (4) that it involves the entire "moral character" of the person, not just a phase of his being; (5) that it is sometimes biographical and hence ineffaceable; (6) that it is unlikely to be committed under conditions of anonymity or, if it is so committed, is so serious that, if discovered, the person would be fully and not merely slightly discredited; (7) that the act is not impermanent and ephemeral; and finally (8) that the language accommodates the identification of the individual as one who commits or has committed certain acts or classes of acts.[43]

Primary Deviants

On the basis of social roles, deviants can be distinguished as to their being primary or secondary (or career) deviants.[44] Persons may engage in deviant acts, but continue to occupy a conventional status and role. Such deviant behavior constitutes *primary deviance* when it is rationalized and considered as a function of a socially acceptable role. Thus, general physicians may unethically and illegally split fees with a surgeon, a politician may take a bribe, or a professor may have neurotic quirks, and in all cases the individual does not consider himself nor do others consider him to be far outside the conventional role. If deviant acts do not materially affect the person's self-concept or give him a deviant role, they remain primary; for example, a homosexual act or the taking of drugs may have few consequences for the individual's self-image or that of others toward him.

Secondary Deviants

On the other hand, *secondary or career deviance* develops when the deviant role is reinforced through further participation with other more pronounced deviants with whom the individual comes to associate, and often through the effects of labeling.[45] Primary deviant blind individuals, for example, may come to associate with other blind persons or come into contact with the activities of agencies for the blind; a homosexual may start to frequent gay bars; a drug addict may become immersed in a drug subculture; and an individual who accepts a bribe may become further involved in a corrupt political machine. Deviant actions may also be reacted to by arrest, imprisonment, confinement in a mental hospital, or other formal and informal sanctions which stigmatize the person and force him into deviant groups. With the individual whose initial socialization was largely conventional, the social costs of labeling are probably higher than for those whose early socialization was based more on deviant norms and values.[46] Becker points out some of the consequences for the career of the deviant when he moves into an organized deviant group:

---

[43]Sagarin, p. 49. Numbers have been inserted by the authors.
[44]Lemert, *Social Pathology*, pp. 75–76.
[45]Lemert, *Social Pathology*, pp. 75–76; and Becker. We consider the labeling perspective in more detail in Chapter 3.
[46]John DeLamater, "On the Nature of Deviance," *Social Forces*, 46 (1968), 445–455.

First of all, deviant groups tend, more than deviant individuals, to be pushed into rationalizing their position. . . . The second thing that happens when one moves into a deviant group is that he learns how to carry on his deviant activity with a minimum of trouble. All the problems he faces in evading enforcement of the rule he is breaking have been faced before by others. . . . Thus, the deviant who enters an organized and institutional deviant group is more likely than ever before to continue in his ways. He has learned, on the one hand, how to avoid trouble and, on the other hand, a rationale for continuing.[47]

Thus, persons may commit delinquencies and crimes without becoming secondary deviants and without being regarded as "delinquents" and "criminals." Women may engage in sex acts under conditions similar to those in which the prostitute operates, yet not consider themselves prostitutes. There are persons who engage in homosexual acts, but who are not homosexuals in the sense of secondary deviant roles. A person may be a heavy drinker and not play an alcoholic role. Once the person becomes a secondary deviant, it has important consequences for further deviant behavior. *The secondary deviant develops a deviant role which involves greater participation in a deviant subculture, the acquisition of more knowledge and rationalizations for the behavior, and skill in avoiding detection and sanctioning.* The process of self-evaluation in secondary deviation also has several effects, including a tendency to minimize the stigma of deviation. "Experiences at one time evaluated as degrading may shift full arc to become rewarding. The alcoholic is an example; deeply ashamed by his first stay in jail, he may as years go by come to look upon arrest as a means of getting food, shelter, and a chance to sober up."[48] In the perception of a deviant self, in secondary deviance "the person already has learned the definitions but progressively rationalizes or dissociates them from his actions."[49]

The secondary or career deviant becomes committed to deviance, as takes place in the case of certain criminal offenders. "Commitment is the belief on the part of the committed individual that he is trapped in his deviant role by the force of penalties that appear when he tries to establish himself in nondeviant circles. Recognition of these penalties marks a major turning point in his deviant career; one where his realization of the forces both for and against continued deviance is especially acute."[50]

The adoption of a secondary deviant identity may, however, have a number of positive aspects for the person involved. For a "closet" homosexual, "coming out," or acknowledging his homosexuality openly, may endanger his livelihood or his professional career, but it also absolves him from failure to assume the heavy responsibilities of marriage and parenthood. It becomes a way to avoid some painful heterosexual involvements and a possible means to initiate new homosexual acquaintances.[51] For some secondary deviants, the public affirmation of their deviant status is a particularly desirable instrumental process in itself. Through a combination of socialization into the role and the development of appropriate rationalizations, they positively value their

[47]Becker, *Outsiders: Studies in the Sociology of Deviance*, p. 40. Copyright © 1973, The Free Press.
[48]Lemert, *Human Deviance, Social Problems, and Social Control*, p. 84.
[49]Lemert, *Human Deviance, Social Problems, and Social Control*, p. 80.
[50]Robert Stebbins, *Commitment to Deviance* (Westport, Conn.: Greenwood Press, 1971), p. xvi.
[51]Lemert, *Human Deviance, Social Problems, and Social Control*, pp. 74–75.

deviant role and status. One criminal, a secondary career deviant, has remarked about the interest he has in others like himself.

> To me, it's much more interesting to be with a group of criminals than a group of suburbanites, because there's nothing about those people at all . . . they're so stereotyped they're dead. And, their talk . . . the man, if you can get down to it, he always "fancies" the woman next door but of course he never gets around to actually doing her. It's frightening. It's chronic. At least criminals have something interesting to talk about, their talk is deeper and more real, the life they lead goes at a much faster tempo and has got some excitement in it.[52]

The concept of secondary deviance is an important one, and it will be used at appropriate points in the analysis of various forms of deviant behavior throughout this book. It will be shown that some secondary deviance develops from subcultural and group participation, some through labeling by informal associations and formal agencies, and often as a result of the interaction of both.

DEVIANT ACTS

The social nature of deviance is evident in a consideration of deviant acts. Most deviant acts do not just happen; they develop over a period of time, out of a process or series of stages. Some deviant acts, such as vandalism or crimes of personal violence, often begin without the person's intending to commit the act; the act develops through interaction with others. "Each action of each party is in some measure dependent upon the previous action of the other party. The outcome of such an interaction process is a joint product of both."[53]

In some acts the person may choose among two or more alternatives, depending on the situation presented. A deviant act, such as an act of car theft, is often a "tentative, groping, feeling-out process, never fully determined by the past alone but always capable of changing its course in response to changes in the current scene."[54] One stage in a deviant act may not be necessarily determined by an antecedent stage. In defining a situation for appropriate deviant or nondeviant actions, one assumes the standpoint of real or imagined others and imaginatively rehearses the action expected by these others of oneself. Blumer has stated that action is built up "in coping with the world instead of merely being released from a pre-existing psychological structure by factors playing upon that structure. By making indications to himself and by interpreting what he indicates, the human being has to forge or piece together a line of action."[55] If a teenager, for example, perceives a set of keys left in a car, he may interpret the situation as an opportunity to steal it; another may pay no attention to the same situation. The presence of drugs in a pharmacy or in a doctor's office may be

---

[52]Tony Parker and Robert Allerton, "On Being a Criminal," in Charles H. McCaghy, James K. Skipper, Jr., and Mark Lefton, eds., *In Their Own Behalf* (New York: Appleton, 1968), p. 194.
[53]Lofland, p. 146.
[54]Cohen, *Deviance and Control,* p. 45.
[55]Herbert Blumer, "Sociological Implications of the Theory of George Herbert Mead," *American Journal of Sociology,* 71 (1966), p. 536.

perceived by a drug addict as a possible supply to be obtained by burglarizing the premises. A difficult situation may be perceived in one way by a person contemplating suicide and in a completely different way by someone else.

Deviance as an interactive process can be seen in at least three ways: (1) the deviant act over time, resulting from prior learning opportunities and past experiences; (2) the deviant act that comes about through interaction with a victim; and (3) deviant acts that, at least in part, result from contact with social control agencies. In each instance, the act must be seen in its social context as the outcome of a particular process.

The Deviant Act Over Time

Deviant acts cannot be studied in isolation from the total context, including the temporal relation of one to another. Persons may learn to commit deviant acts over a long period of time through a process of realizing that committing the deviant act is sometimes both adventurous and rewarding. The adult burglar, for example, may have begun his criminal career in adolescence with minor youth gang delinquencies and other risk-taking activities.[56] A member of a gay community may have engaged in homosexual activities sporadically at a younger age but did not acquire a homosexual identity until later participation in the gay community.[57] Risk-taking behavior, in the form of drug experimentation or gambling, may be both individually and socially rewarding to some persons. A study of gamblers has suggested that the lower-class regular gambler may begin his career by first being interested in acquiring a reputation for "seeking action." The person gambles because it is exciting and confirms a self-image of a lively, interesting person.[58] As gambling activities increase, some persons appear to fall into a continuing spiral of gambling involvement. As debts become heavier the compulsive gambler increasingly views gambling as the only way out, using up other, legitimate options (cutting expenses, loans from family and others) and relying on gambling to provide financial relief.[59] What began as a socially condoned activity has thus become a way of life for the individual. In some circumstances many "penny ante" poker games may eventually escalate into contacts with established gamblers, high stake games, and a long list of creditors.

Deviant Acts and Victims

The direction of a deviant act depends not only on past experiences and learning but also on the responses of others in the immediate situation, for it is these responses of

---

[56]See D. H. Stott and D. M. Wilson, "The Adult Criminal as Juvenile," *British Journal of Criminology,* 17 (1977), 47–57.
[57]See Barry Dank, "The Homosexual," in Don Spiegel and Patricia Keith-Spiegel, eds., *Outsiders USA* (San Francisco: Rinehart Press, 1973), pp. 269–297.
[58]Jay Livingston, *Compulsive Gamblers: Observations on Action and Abstinence* (New York: Harper & Row, 1974), pp. 53–70.
[59]Henry R. Lesieur, *The Chase: Career of the Compulsive Gambler* (New York: Doubleday Anchor Books, 1977).

others that the individual takes into account in defining the situation and that he organizes into his own behavior. In many cases unanticipated consequences arise from events which were not even considered in the earlier stages of the deviant act, as often occurs in cases of criminal homicide.

> For example, a person might set out to burglarize a house. Quite unexpectedly, the householder may come home and attack the burglar with a deadly weapon. The burglar, to save his own life, kills the attacker. What started out as a burglary might end up as murder, due to a circumstance that was not necessarily implicit in the earlier stage of the act. However, although the arrival of the householder was a separately determined event, unforeseen and perhaps unforeseeable, the situation as a whole is partly a product of the actor's own doing.[60]

A deviant act such as homicide involves victims, and on occasion these victims may actually contribute to their own deaths by provoking the offender to violent action. Three categories of offender-victim relationship have been identified in a study of homicide in Houston: (1) relatives; (2) friends and associates; and (3) strangers.[61] The most common pattern with respect to offenders and victims who were either related or friends is one in which each party had engaged in verbal abuse of the other, the level of emotion had escalated, and eventually the situation had been defined by at least one of the parties as one necessitating violence. Parents who abuse their children seriously in a physical manner may have been much abused themselves as children, and they may have learned to regard physical force as an acceptable form of discipline and punishment for certain acts of their children.

Not all deviant acts, however, have victims, at least in the form of a person or item of property. Mental disorders, for example, generally do not involve victims, although the effect of the disorders on marital and familial relationships may be severe. Similarly, homosexuality, drug addiction, and alcoholism are not acts directed toward harming other persons, although they too may have a great effect on persons associated closely with the deviant.

Deviant Contacts with Defining Agencies

The application of social control measures, under certain circumstances, may intensify or reinforce deviant acts in ways that had not been intended. Participation in a drug treatment program, for example, may intensify the drug user's self-conception or identity as an addict. The person may develop the feeling that continued association with other addicts and participation in the addict subculture is necessary or even "natural" in light of this self-conception. With the information now available, it is not clear why some deviants continue their deviance once they have been labeled while others do not. Some offenders may continue their criminal behavior after contact with the criminal justice system, while others may terminate completely their criminal

---

[60]Cohen, *Deviance and Control,* p. 103.
[61]Henry P. Lundsgaarde, *Murder in Space City: A Cultural Analysis of Houston Homicide Patterns* (New York: Oxford University Press, 1977).

activities. Similarly, some mentally disturbed persons may react to hospitalization by intensifying their symptoms while the symptoms of others may be terminated.

Deviant Acts and Social Organization

Various acts may be considered deviant because they are inappropriate to the social context in which they occur; that is, they violate the norms implied in social situations. Breeches of etiquette are typically such acts, although they are seldom regarded as serious instances of deviance, perhaps because they are thought to be unintentional. Sometimes, however, deviant acts are more serious and may lead others who witness the act to severely sanction the deviant, such as considering both the act and the actor as mentally ill. The guest who appears at a formal dinner in blue jeans and who then throws food at other guests may incur such a reaction. Although disruptive to the immediate situation, such acts may affirm the importance of social situations and contribute to ongoing soial organization by incurring such sanctions. As Goffmany says: "Just as we fill our jails with those who transgress the legal order, so we partly fill our asylums with those who act unsuitably—the first kind of institution being used to protect our lives and property; the second, to protect our gatherings and occasions."[62]

Deviant Acts and Physical Objects

The actual occurrence of a deviant act is often associated with factors in addition to the individual and the interaction between the individual and other persons. Lofland points out, for example, that the act may also depend upon the situation surrounding the act, the physical setting, and the presence of such nonhuman objects as "hardware."[63] Although technically "hardware" is unnecessary in many deviant acts such as homosexual behavior, adultery, prostitution, exhibitionism, and child beating, many deviant acts do require some type of physical artifacts. This availability of objects heightens the possibility of the commission of the deviant act. "Various kinds of violent assaults, some of which eventuate in homicide, often involve quite prosaic household implements and other common objects, among which are knives, bottles, meat cleavers, hammers, bricks, decorative statuary, etc."[64] Assault upon the self resulting in suicide is facilitated by many substances invariably available such as sleeping pills, ropes, knives, and the carbon monoxide gas produced by all automobiles. For the naive check forger who formerly made use of bank counter checks, the widely used credit cards now serve this purpose. "On a somewhat different level, the marked modern increase in the sheer *amount* of portable property, brought about by mass production, increases the number of things that can possibly be stolen, vandalized, pilfered or otherwise trifled with."[65] It has been observed that one of the best

---

[62]Erving Goffman, *Behavior in Public Places* (New YOrk: Free Press, 1963), p. 248.
[63]Lofland, pp. 69–70.
[64]Lofland, p. 69.
[65]Lofland, p. 70.

predictors of the auto-theft rate, which is usually a youth crime, is more a reflection of the number of automobiles available in an area rather than of some characteristic of the youths in question.[66] Cressey has written about the "hardware" in the case of embezzlers: "Accountants use checks which they have been entrusted to dispose of, salesclerks withhold receipts, bankers manipulate seldom-used accounts or withhold deposits, real estate men use deposits entrusted to them and so on."[67] In the case of drugs, certainly illegal drugs such as marijuana, LSD, cocaine, or heroin are not accessible to all, but they do circulate rather freely in certain social situations or areas. Medical doctors automatically possess the "hardware" needed for a variety of illegal activities, particularly their own drug use and illegal abortions. The use of computers has resulted in an increasing amount of serious computer crime. Over 2 million persons in the United States operate over 90,000 computers in banks, businesses, and large corporations. Computers can be employed to create false assets, to obtain illegally large sums of money, and to hide certain illegal and other accounting practices.

SEEING THE DEVIANT'S PERSPECTIVE

Ultimately, one must try to comprehend the world of the deviant as that individual experiences it, at the same time remaining sufficiently detached to understand and analyze the interrelations of the deviant world with the larger moral and social order. In previous social science research and even somewhat today, deviant actions have been largely viewed from the perspective of the observer, his norms and values, and his self-conception. Categorizations of "senseless," "immoral," "debauched," "brutal," and so on, were often bestowed on the deviant by outside observers, with no recognition that deviant actions might possibly have a different meaning to the actor. Moreover, only "bad things" were thought to result from the "bad conditions" of poverty or prostitution, for example. Matza has said that deviants are not "appreciated"as part of the world of naturalism which is to be felt and comprehended.[68] This "appreciation" of the deviant has, of course, often been difficult when the behavior has shocked the norms or the everyday moral scheme of the observer.

> Paupers occasionally fleece the welfare system, robbers often brutalize or otherwise molest their victims, motorcycle gangs are a terrible nuisance to policemen, prostitutes sometimes roll their customers, drug addicts are engaged in a great deal of petty and grand theft, homosexuals are relatively promiscuous. . . . These features—detestable by conventional standards—can hardly be denied or suppressed; they are part of what must

---

[66]Stanton Wheeler, "Deviant Behavior," in Neil J. Smelser, ed., *Sociology: An Introduction* (New York: Wiley, 1973), p. 679.

[67]Donald R. Cressey, *Other People's Money* (Belmont, Calif.: Wadsworth, 1971; originally published in 1953), p. 84. For a discussion of computer crime see August Bequai, *Computer Crime* (Lexington, Mass.: Lexington Bc

[68]Matza, p. 15. Also see David Sudnow, ed., *Studies in Social Interaction* (New York: Free Press, 1972); and Harold Garfinkel, *Studies in Ethnomethodology* (Englewood Cliffs, N.J.: Prentice-Hall, 1967).

be appreciated if one adheres to a naturalistic perspective, for they are a part of various deviant enterprises.[69]

On the other hand, an excessive "appreciation" of the deviant's world by romanticizing it obscures a meaningful, honest appraisal of deviant life-styles. Such reports give a view that the life of deviants is "worthwhile" and often "exciting." Generally they are written by romantic "hangers-on" who are not actually deviant themselves.

Part of the difficulty has been that most observers had little firsthand meaningful contact with the deviant world, and therefore the integrity of the phenomenon was violated. To share the perspective and the definition of the situation of the deviant does not mean the observer "always concurs with the subject's definition of the situation; rather, that his aim is to comprehend and to illuminate the subject's view and to interpret the world as it *appears to him*."[70] The deviant world has its own intrinsic satisfactions and meanings which must be inferred by the observer. This point has been nicely made in Howard Becker's book on deviance, *Outsiders,* whose title aptly signifies both that deviants are "outsiders" and that conventional persons are actually "outsiders" from the perspective of those involved in deviant acts. It is this latter interpretation that must be achieved. In any deviant behavior the complex and manifold character of the deviant activity must be observed; "once the subject is fully appreciated, the deviant person comes into proper human forms."[71]

Much material on deviant perspectives is now being obtained by sociologists and others through in-depth interviewing and by actual insider reports of deviants and by insider participant observation. Other information has come from participant observation, as has been carried out in studies, for example, of nudist camps, drug users, call girls, homosexuals, hippies, youth gangs, pool hall hustlers, Hell's Angels, white-collar adult drug users, or topless bar maids.[72] About the distinction between insider participant observation and simply participant observation, Douglas has pointed out that insider participant-observer reports come about by becoming a member of a group. Some of this research is done secretly: that is, the persons being studied do not know they are being studied. The members of the group treat the researcher as one of their own. Slightly different is the case of what Douglas calls *fictitious membership,* where the group knows who the researcher is, but they also know that the researcher will not report them to the police or other officials.[73]

Other material can be obtained from the life histories, diaries, and letters of deviant persons. In the chapters that follow, much use is made of such material from the perspective of the deviant—for example, the analysis of suicide notes to understand the meaning of suicide.

The sociologist wishing to comprehend the world of the deviant—or even to gain access to those who are deviant—need not, of course, be a deviant. In fact, there are severe disadvantages to being "coopted" into the deviant life-style and becoming

---

[69]Matza, p. 16.

[70]Matza, p. 25.

[71]Matza, p. 40.

[72]See Jack D. Douglas, ed., *Observations on Deviance* (New York: Random House, 1970). Also see Jack D. Douglas, ed., *Research on Deviance* (New York: Random House, 1972).

[73]Douglas, *Observations on Deviance,* pp. 6–8.

"one of them." Deviants do not have an exclusive claim to knowledge of "things deviant." Drug addicts are not experts on the addiction process, though they have experienced it personally. Homosexuals are not experts on the social dynamics of homosexuality, though they must "manage" (a term to be explained shortly) their identities and must have gone through the process of becoming homosexuals. No one would claim that only schizophrenics can understand that condition, although they have intimate knowledge of what it is to be a schizophrenic. Thus being an "insider" does not mean that the knowledge one has acquired in this manner is reliable for others who have undergone roughly the same experience, or that it is the type of information that is valuable to have about deviance. No one but a heroin addict can know personally what it feels like to experience the severe pains resulting from withdrawal from that drug. The important questions about heroin addiction and the withdrawal process are not what it feels like, but rather the role of the withdrawal process in continued addiction and the importance of the drug subculture in defining that experience.

Deviants, naturally, see the world differently from those who are not "insiders." One must balance a sensitivity to the perspective of the deviant and a concern with objectivity. Drug addicts know where to obtain their supply of drugs and from whom; they do not know, as addicts, the process whereby they came to be addicts. They know which of their acquaintances are "for" or "against" them; they do not necessarily know the extent and types of influences each exerts on them or their deviance. In other words, insiders do not know all that is known or should be known about deviance; in fact, what they know often does not provide reliable bases for generalized knowledge about one type of deviance or another.[74] Deviants cannot be expected to provide all worthwhile information about deviance merely because they are deviants. The virtue of being an insider is that one has certain kinds of information. The limitation of being an insider is that the person has knowledge only within narrowly prescribed boundaries. An alcoholic is a good source of information about that person's experiences (perhaps), but if the issue is the nature and extent of alcoholism in the United States, the social processes that generate and inhibit alcoholism, or the most effective means of treatment for the widest variety of alcoholics, one of the most unreliable sources of information would be the minute questioning of local skid row alcoholics.

The Management of Deviance

One of the most valuable aspects of seeing the deviant's perspective is that we become sensitive to some of the problems deviants face. The imposition of negative sanctions from others poses obvious difficulties that the deviant would like to avoid. Through the use of a number of techniques, the deviant is able either to manage (or cope with) the stigma, prevent the stigma altogether, or lessen what stigma may be present. Through

---

[74]See the excellent discussion of this and other related points in Robert K. Merton, "Insiders and Outsiders: A Chapter in the Sociology of Knowledge," *American Journal of Sociology*, 78 (1972), 9–47.

such techniques, the deviant is able to "save face," ward off social rejection, and cope with the situation. Management techniques are used that suit the particular form of rejection the deviant encounters, but a number of techniques may be common to a number of different forms of deviance.

1. Secrecy If others are not aware that an act of deviance has been committed or that a person occupies a deviant status, there will be no negative sanction. Homosexuals may hide this fact from their families and employers; obese persons may avoid social gatherings and maintain an isolated existence; heroin addicts may wear clothing that hides the needle marks on their arms and legs. "Secrecy is [often] urged upon deviants by their in-the-know friends and family among the normals: 'That's what you want to do, okay, but why advertise it?' "[75]

2. Rationalizations A deviant may "explain away" the deviance by justifying it in terms of the situation, the victim (if there is one), or some other factor usually beyond the deviant's control. Cheating on one's income taxes may be justified to the offender in terms of the already excessive taxes one pays; shoplifting may become acceptable because "the store can afford the loss and insurance will cover it anyway"; obese persons may unduly attribute their problem to a physiological condition. The use of rationalizations weakens the strength of the norm by placing the deviant act in a more acceptable framework. They also provide an effective means by which persons can maintain "face" when confronted with a troublesome situation. Singles dances, which are often seen by both participants and others as lacking full respectability, generate pressures toward the use of rationalizations either to account for one's presence at the dance ("A friend made me come because she/he was recently divorced") or rejection at the dance ("I haven't danced yet because I had a tiring day at work and want only to stand around for a while").[76]

3. Change to Nondeviance Another technique involves the movement from deviant to nondeviant status. For some criminals this technique is usually referred to as "going straight" or being rehabilitated; the obese person loses weight; the prostitute settles down with a family; and the problem drinker shuns alcohol. It is often difficult to determine whether or not someone has terminated deviance since this judgment is often a social one. The heroin addict who no longer uses heroin may take methadone, itself an addicting drug though a more socially acceptable one. Some deviants are unable to use this technique, such as the physically handicapped. There are also some deviants who have no motivation, even if they could, to change, such as the homosexual who prefers persons of the same sex. The change to nondeviance can also be seen on a group level with the affirmation of deviance by militants. Homosexuals, for example, in some communities have publicly proclaimed their status and have pressured legislatures to change the laws concerning this behavior. Similarly, militant prostitutes have taken like public stands advocating the decriminalization of this offense. In each

---

[75]Sagarin, p. 268.
[76]Bernard Berk, "Face-Saving at the Singles Dance," *Social Problems,* 24 (1977), 530–544.

instance, the idea is to change to nondeviance by redefining the behavior itself rather than changing individuals.

4. Deviant Subcultures Participation in a subculture is helpful for deviants in managing their deviance; it lessens the chances of receiving a negative sanction from others by protecting them from contact with "normals." Homosexuals who frequent gay bars and maintain interaction with other homosexuals, at least during that time, decrease the chance that outsiders will detect them. Subcultures offer the deviant sympathy, support, and association with other deviants; they help the deviant cope with social rejection while, at the same time, providing the opportunity to commit deviant acts.

Nonapplication of Sanctions

Every deviant act may be potentially subject to some type of sanctioning, but many deviant acts receive none. A number of reasons may be cited for this nonapplication of a sanction to a deviant act.

1. The deviant act may be anonymous; the audience to the act, either present or absent, may not be able to identify the deviant. In the case of a successful burglary, the guilty person escapes detection and thus avoids sanctioning. The manipulation of certain management techniques during business or occupational offenses shields the deviant from sanctioning. Many female alcoholics avoid sanctioning simply because they avoid detection by drinking at home when they are alone; even when their drinking becomes more public in nature, they are much less likely to be arrested for public drunkenness and thus become subjected to formal sanctioning.[77]

2. Often the deviant act is considered to be of a minor nature or "out of character" of the persons committing the act, and no sanctioning is invoked. Minor violations of norms may be excused as "accidental" or unavoidable under the circumstances. A man apprehended for speeding when he is taking his wife to the hospital for delivery is more likely to be given a police escort than a ticket for speeding. In a study of shoplifting, it was found that witnesses to acts of shoplifting more often referred to the police when the value of the goods taken was above a certain value.[78]

3. The single deviant act may not be associated with the person's identity. Although the act may be visible and the person clearly identified, the fact that it occurred only once may lead to the conclusion that a sanction is unnecessary. In situations where informal sanctioning suffices, such deviance as the inappropriate use of obscenities in situations where taboos are strong against them, or the lack of proper table manners, are usually simply excused if the general behavior of the person does not fit the actions.

---

[77]See Linda J. Beckman, "Women Alcoholics: A Review of Social and Psychological Studies," *Journal of Studies on Alcohol,* 36 (1975), 797–824; and Milton Argeriow and Donna Paulino, "Women Arrested for Drunken Driving in Boston: Social Characteristics and Circumstances of Arrest," *Journal of Studies on Alcohol,* 37 (1976), 648–658.

[78]Michael J. Hindelang, "Decisions of Shoplifting Victims to Invoke the Criminal Justice Process," *Social Problems,* 21 (1974), 580–595.

THE SOCIAL VISIBILITY OF DEVIANCE

Deviant acts do not necessarily become known to society. Wide variations exist in the "social visibility" of negatively regarded acts of deviance, that is, the extent to which behavior comes to the attention of people within a society and the acts are defined socially as "deviant." Wilkins has pointed out that the definition of what is deviant is considerably modified by the content of available information about certain behavior, the amount, and the channel of information.[79] The social visibility of events in a society such as the number arrested or imprisoned for offenses will have much to do with public definitions of acts as crimes.

Certain crimes, such as kidnapping, violent sex offenses, murder, lynching, and armed robbery, for example, are highly visible and create much comment and action. Offenses such as occupational and white-collar crime, illegal abortions, blackmail, homosexuality, and petty theft are not as socially visible. Symptoms of mental disorder are not always interpreted as such and so do not become visible to members of a society. In some instances the person is simply considered "eccentric," "odd," or "difficult." Generally, the physical symptoms of intoxication tend to be visible, as the intoxicated person usually displays such physical symptoms as thickened speech, flushed face, and unsteady gait, although certain physical illnesses may produce similar symptoms. It is the social behavior of the intoxicated person, however, that attracts the most attention from others and brings about the strongest reaction. Some persons can actually be quite intoxicated without exhibiting noticeable behavior patterns, but others may become quarrelsome, noisy, loquacious, silly, depressed, or otherwise annoying to other people so that the drunken behavior becomes even more conspicuous than the physical symptoms.

The social visibility of many forms of deviant behavior varies by social class and by racial characteristics. Among the lower and upper classes, for example, drunkenness may provoke less comment than drunkenness in a conservative, middle-class group where it may stand out like a fire on a hillside.

Not all deviant behavior becomes known by public agencies; hence official statistics are not an accurate picture of the amount of deviant behavior. Criminal statistics, for example, are based on recorded criminality, that is, offenses reported by individual citizens or through the action of police patrols. Whatever is recorded is only a sample of delinquency and crime in the total criminality.[80] The amount of crime recorded varies according to the visibility of the offense, the type of offense, the circumstances surrounding it, and the attitude of the victim. Robberies are most likely to be reported because the victim gives up his possessions by the threat of force. Similarly, murders, robberies of banks or business establishments, purse snatching,

[79]Leslie T. Wilkins, *Social Deviance: Social Policy, Action, and Research* (Englewood Cliffs, N.J.: Prentice-Hall, 1965), pp. 45–104.
[80]Thorsten Sellin, "The Significance of Records of Crime," in Marvin E. Wolfgang, Leonard Savitz, and Norman Johnston, eds., *Sociology of Crime and Delinquency* (New York: Wiley, 1962), p. 59. Also see Thorsten Sellin and Marvin E. Wolfgang, *The Measurement of Delinquency* (New York: Wiley, 1964).

check forgeries, and the theft of articles of considerable value are likely to be reported. On the other hand, small larcenies, fights and assaults where injury was not serious, and certain sex offenses are not as likely to be reported. Where only the general public or the government is a victim private citizens are less likely to report the offenses. These include violation of traffic or motor vehicle laws, gambling, or prostitution. Sometimes offenses are known only to the participants, as in cases of homosexuality, illegal abortion, illegal heterosexual behavior, and the use of drugs, and therefore may not become publicly known. Official crime statistics include but a small proportion of the cases of fraud, political corruption, and similar violations of law that are perpetrated by middle- and upper-class persons.

Official Records

Measures of deviant behavior vary according to the source. Police statistics on arrested persons, for example, are not as satisfactory as those based on crimes reported to them by citizens. Many persons are not arrested, police departments vary in efficiency, and arrest policies change, as they do for prosecutions. The number of persons arrested for given types of crimes varies a great deal: in 1975, for example, some 78 percent of all reported cases of murder and nonnegligent homicide in U.S. cities were "cleared" (solved by an arrest), but only 27 percent of the robberies and 18 percent of the burglaries were cleared (see Table 2.1.).

In calculating rates based on statistics of various forms of deviant behavior one must be careful to compute them on the population affected. For example, the well-known *Uniform Crime Reports (UCR)* of the U.S. Federal Bureau of Investigation (which cover national statistics on crimes reported to the police) is still the main source for public judgments about crime rate increases and decreases; yet their rates are based on the total population rather than on the composition of the crime-committing population.[81] Using a "standard population," one might more accurately compute rates based primarily on males aged 14–35, which is the greatest crime-committing

TABLE 2.1	**Percentage of Offenses Known to the Police Which Were Cleared by an Arrest, United States, 1977**

Offense	Percent Cleared
Murder and nonnegligent manslaughter	78
Aggravated assault	64
Forcible rape	51
Robbery	27
Larceny-theft	20
Burglary	18
Auto theft	14

Source: Federal Bureau of Investigation, *Uniform Crime Reports—1975* (Washington, D.C.: Government Printing Office, 1976), p. 166.

[81]Sellin, p. 65.

age. What has been said here also applies to the adequacy of rates for drug addiction, alcoholism, mental disorder, and suicide. Moreover, rates for many crimes should not be computed on the basis of the general population. Forcible rapes, for example, should be computed on women largely between the ages of 15 and 40, burglaries on the number of houses and stores, and auto thefts on the number of automobiles registered.[82]

Even more serious errors are committed in the *UCR* and similar reports which claim great increases in crime over a period of five to ten years, or from one year to another. The President's Commission on Law Enforcement and Administration of Justice in a 1967 report concluded that it was unable to decide whether the individual U.S. citizen today is more criminal than a citizen of 5, 10, 25, or more years ago.[83] It further stated that no data exist to make even simple comparisons of the incidence of crime among persons of the same age, sex, race, and place of residence for long periods of time. The *UCR* also fail to take into account the fact that a substantial proportion of crime—over 50 percent in some crimes—is never reported to the police, and much of this nonreporting is in lower-class urban areas. Changing definitions and classifications of offenses can also increase crime. "Citizens are probably reporting more to police as a reflection of higher expectations; and the police, in turn, because of this, are reporting more crimes in their statistics. More efficient law enforcement leads to higher rates of reported crime."[84]

Victimization Surveys

A new technique of crime victimization surveys has been developed over the past decade to meet these objections to, and partially to replace, official statistics, as well as to check on their reliability. The first major pilot surveys of this type were done in Boston, Chicago, and Washington, D.C., by the President's Commission on Law Enforcement and the Administration of Justice in 1966. This Commission also arranged for the National Opinion Research Center to interview a national sample of 10,000 households about their experiences as victims of crime during a previous time span, in this case 12 months.[85] Initial surveys showed three to ten times more crimes than the official statistics; burglaries, for example, were three and a half times as frequent as the number reported by the police. As a result of these initial surveys, and a limited number of other studies, the technique developed rapidly, and many such surveys have been carried out in the United States. Similar victimization surveys have subsequently been conducted in Europe and elsewhere. While practically all of these surveys have dealt with individuals and households, a few have studied the extent of crimes committed against business concerns.

---

[82]Albert J. Reiss, Jr., "Assessing the Current Crime Wave," in Barbara N. McLennan, ed., *Crime in Urban Society* (New York: Dunellen, 1970).

[83]President's Commission on Law Enforcement and Administration of Justice, *Criminal Victimization in the United States: A Report of a National Survey* (Washington, D.C.: Government Printing Office, 1967).

[84]Eugene Doleschal, *Criminal Statistics* (Rockville, Md.: Center for Studies of Crime and Delinquency, National Institute of Mental Health, 1972). p. 12.

[85]Philip H. Ennis, *Criminal Victimization in the United States: A Report of a National Survey,* President's Commission on Law Enforcement and Administration of Justice, Field Surveys II (Washington, D.C.: Government Printing Office, May 1967).

Victimization surveys have been carried out by the Bureau of the Census since 1972, under authorization by the Law Enforcement Assistance Administration (LEAA) of the U.S. Department of Justice.[86] Most criminologists hope that periodic surveys will become a permanent procedure to determine the extent of crime and crime trends, reflecting the actual situation more adequately than official statistics generally do. As it is now being carried out, the survey involves periodic interviewing of a national probability sample of 75,000 households and 15,000 business establishments. Termed the National Crime Panel, it provides data for the United States as a whole and also a subnational grouping of metropolitan areas by size. In addition, surveys of representative samples are being made in 16 major cities, and it is hoped that eventually data will be made available for 35 cities. In each of the five largest cities about 10,000 households have been covered in interviews, and approximately 2,500 commercial establishments have been included in the sample.

These surveys present certain problems, however. Interview questions must be carefully phrased to discover whether a "crime" was actually committed against the household or the person during the previous six months. Legal terms like "assault" have little meaning to most persons; instead the question is usually phrased as, "Did anyone beat you up, attack you or hit you with anything, say a rock or a bottle?" Moreover, some persons regard minor law infractions as crimes while others do not: some do not consider the taking of an object of little value or of a small sum of money as a "theft," while others do. Similarly, one may recall a minor assault involving a slight hit or threat with an object, while another may not define this act as a "crime" serious enough to be reported as such. Consequently, some persons have criticized these surveys on the basis that they tend to overreport real crime.[87]

The *Uniform Crime Reports'* index of crime, like most "crime" statistics, contains only conventional crimes, such as burglary and robbery, crimes largely committed by the lower class. A different, and perhaps more accurate, index of crime, as well as its direction, might be presented if we included violations of law by persons in business, corporations, politicians, and other upper-status groups in such acts as fraud, false advertising, and tax violations. Perhaps the trend in honesty of the people who pay income taxes might be a better index of increase or decrease of law violations in a nation.

Selecting Deviants

Official action against deviants seems to have elements of contingency, chance, or categoric risk.[88] Despite their similar behavior, arrest defines some persons as crimi-

---

[86]See Marie G. Argana, "Development of a National Victimization Survey," in Israel Drapkin and Emilio Viano, eds., *Victimology: A New Focus* (Lexington, Mass.: D. C. Heath, 1973), Vol III, *Crimes, Victims, and Justice,* pp. 171–179. Also see Michael J. Hindelang, *Criminal Victimization in Eight American Cities* (Cambridge, Mass.: Ballinger Publishing Company, 1976); and *Criminal Victimization in the United States 1973,* a National Crime Survey Report, U.S. Department of Justice, Law Enforcement Assistance Administration (Washington, D.C.: Government Printing Office, 1976).

[87]See James P. Levine, "The Potential for Crime Overreporting in Criminal Victimization Surveys," *Criminology,* 14 (1976), 307–330.

[88]Walter Reckless developed this concept of categoric risk in 1950. See Walter C. Reckless, *The Crime Problem* (New York: Appleton, 1950), pp. 56–74. For further elaboration see Lemert, *Social Pathology,* Chapters 2, 3, and 4.

nals, whereas others who are not arrested are not so defined. Similarly, some persons who exhibit deviant behavior involving mental disorder, criminal behavior, drug addiction, and prostitution may be committed to an institution such as a mental hospital or prison while others who exhibit similar behavior are not sent to an institution.

A person's selection and labeling as a deviant depends on several factors: the nature and seriousness of the deviance; the individual's social class, occupation, racial and ethnic background, age, and past record of deviation; the situation out of which the behavior has arisen; the pressures of public reaction; and the resources available to apprehend and to deal with the deviant.[89] It has been suggested that the number of deviants a society can afford to recognize in a community is likely to remain relatively stable because the problem of identifying them is limited by the available resources and by the difficulties society has in dealing with them once they have been recognized and apprehended. Consequently, most agencies of social control merely operate to keep certain deviance within bounds; a sufficient number of prostitutes, for example, may be arrested to show that there is some enforcement.

> A community's capacity for handling deviance, let us say, can be roughly estimated by counting its prison cells and hospital beds, its policemen and psychiatrists, its courts and clinics—and while this total cannot tell us anything important about the underlying psychological motives involved, it does say something about the manner in which the community views the problem. Most communities, it would seem, operate with the expectation that a relatively constant number of control agents is necessary to cope with a relatively constant number of offenders. The amount of men, money, and material assigned by society to "do something" about deviant behavior does not vary appreciably over time, and the implicit logic which governs the community's efforts to man a police force or maintain suitable facilities for the mentally ill seems to be that there is a fairly stable quota of trouble which should be anticipated.[90]

Whether or not, then, an offender is arrested, prosecuted, convicted, or imprisoned depends on available manpower. The resources are limited; all police departments have insufficient personnel to arrest, jails are limited in size, prosecutors and judges are few, prisons are small in comparison to the total offender population. Consequently, some laws are more strictly enforced than others; some persons or groups are selected out for arrest while others are less likely to be apprehended and processed.

Although heavy drinking is often found in the higher socioeconomic groups, arrests for public intoxication tend to concentrate in the lower groups, whose members are then labeled "drunks." A Rochester study found a significant negative relation between education and family income and the rate of arrests.[91] Moreover, nonwhites had a higher rate of arrests than whites.

Whether a person is committed for mental treatment depends on attitudes toward his behavior entertained by the next of kin, by a complainant, such as a

---

[89]For example, relatively few of the many cases of nonsupport of minor children are ever dealt with by legal authorities. See Kenneth W. Eckhardt, "Deviance, Visibility and Legal Action: The Duty to Support," *Social Problems,* 15 (1968), 470–478.
[90]Kai Erikson, *Wayward Puritans: A Study in the Sociology of Deviance* (New York: Wiley, 1966), p. 24.
[91]Melvin Zax, Elmer A. Gardner, and William T. Hart, "Public Intoxication in Rochester: A Survey of Individuals Charged in 1961," *Quarterly Journal of Studies on Alcohol,* 25 (1964), 669–678.

neighbor or an employer, or by a mediator, such as the family doctor, a psychiatrist, the police, or a clergyman.[92] Many persons never encounter a complainant face-to-face living in either the domestic establishment, the work place, or a public area such as a store, street, or park. Other factors affecting commitment include a person's social status, the visibility of the offense, the proximity of a mental hospital, and alternative community treatment facilities. The police have considerable discretion, on an emergency basis, in apprehending and conveying to hospitals those whom they perceive to be mentally ill.[93] Those admitted to a mental hospital are disproportionately those referred by a physician, those who are males, and those with a record of previous hospitalization.[94] Prostitutes, homosexuals, and drug addicts may be arrested when their behavior becomes unusually conspicuous or when public pressure for their arrest is increased.

All this means that official statistics of deviant behavior are not accurate measures of the number and characteristics of deviants, regardless of whether the statistics deal with delinquency, crime, mental hospitals, or arrests for drunkenness or drug use.[95] Such records are obviously not complete records, not only because of the selective processing of deviants but because of the changes in administrative recording procedures. This does not mean that these statistics have no use. In general, they give us an approximation of the volume of deviation; moreover, the rates of deviant behavior indicate who is selected out of a total population of deviants for specific actions by agencies of social control, that is, the social processing of deviants.[96] For example, for some forms of deviant behavior members of the lower class or minority groups may be more likely than other groups to come to the attention of authorities; for other cases, it may be largely males or young persons whose behavior is more visible and likely to be regarded as deviant.[97]

Some of the problems we have discussed with respect to official statistics on crime may be corrected in the future. In 1977, there was a long-awaited consolidation of federal statistics concerning criminality with the creation of a National Bureau of Criminal Statistics. This new agency will serve as a central collection point for criminal statistics from a number of sources and will function to reduce duplication and error from individual agencies who previously had performed this function.

SELECTED REFERENCES

Becker, Howard S. *Outsiders: Studies in the Sociology of Deviance,* enlarged ed. New York: Free Press, 1973.

---

[92]Erving Goffman, *Asylums* (New York: Doubleday, 1961), pp. 134–137.

[93]Egon Bittner, "Police Discretion in Emergency Apprehension of Mentally Ill Persons," *Social Problems,* 14 (1967), 287–292.

[94]Elliott G. Mishler and Nancy E. Waxler, "Decision Processes in Psychiatric Hospitalization: Patients Referred, Accepted and Admitted to a Psychiatric Hospital," *American Sociological Review,* 28 (1963), 576–587.

[95]Sellin; and James E. Price, "Testing the Accuracy of Crime Statistics," *Social Problems,* 14 (1966), 214–222.

[96]John I. Kitsuse and Aaron V. Cicourel, "A Note on the Uses of Official Statistics," *Social Problems,* 11 (1963), 131–139.

[97]For a discussion of these issues with respect to suicide statistics, see M. Ellen Warshauer and Mary Monk, "Problems in Suicide Statistics for Whites and Blacks," *American Journal of Public Health,* 68 (1978), pp. 383–388.

Biddle, Bruce J., and Edwin J. Thomas. *Role Theory: Concepts and Research.* New York: Wiley, 1966.

Blumer, Herbert. *Symbolic Interactionism: Perspective and Method.* Englewood Cliffs, N.J.: Prentice-Hall, 1969.

Brim, Orville G., Jr., and Stanton Wheeler. *Socialization after Childhood: Two Essays.* New York: Wiley, 1966.

Campbell, Ernest Q. *Socialization: Culture and Personality.* Dubuque, Ia.: William C. Brown, 1975.

Clausen, John A., ed. *Socialization and Society.* Boston: Little, Brown, 1968.

Cohen, Albert K. *Deviance and Control.* Englewood Cliffs, N.J.: Prentice-Hall, 1966.

Cohen, Albert K. "The Sociology of the Deviant Act: Anomie Theory and Beyond," *American Sociological Review,* 30 (1965), 5–14.

Davis, Nanette J. *Sociological Constructions of Deviance: Perspectives and Issues in the Field.* Dubuque, Ia.: William C. Brown, 1975.

DeLamater, John "On the Nature of Deviance," *Social Forces,* 46 (1968), 445–455.

Denzin, Norman K. "The Methodological Implications of Symbolic Interactionism for the Study of Deviance," *British Journal of Sociology,* 3 (1974), 269–282.

Douglas, Jack D., ed. *Observations of Deviance.* New York: Random House, 1970.

Douglas, Jack D., ed. *Research on Deviance.* New York: Random House, 1972.

Goffman, Erving. *Stigma: Notes on the Management of Spoiled Identity.* Englewood Cliffs, N.J.: Prentice-Hall, 1963.

Lemert, Edwin M. *Social Pathology.* New York: McGraw-Hill, 1951.

Lemert, Edwin M. *Human Deviance, Social Problems and Social Control,* 2d ed. Englewood Cliffs, N.J.: Prentice-Hall, 1972.

Lindesmith, Alfred R., Anselm L. Strauss, and Norman K. Denzin. *Social Psychology,* 4th ed. Hinsdale, Ill.: Dryden Press, 1975.

Lofland, John. *Deviance and Identity.* Englewood Cliffs, N.J.: Prentice-Hall, 1969.

Matza, David. *Becoming Deviant.* Englewood Cliffs, N.J.: Prentice-Hall, 1969.

McCall, George, and J. L. Simmons. *Identities and Interactions.* New York: Free Press, 1966.

Merton, Robert K. "Insiders and Outsiders: A Chapter in the Sociology of Knowledge," *American Journal of Sociology,* 78 (1972) 9–47.

Sagarin, Edward. *Deviants and Deviance: An Introduction to the Study of Disvalued People and Behavior.* New York: Holt, Rinehart and Winston, 1975.

Socialization
(Differential Association)

Edwin H. Sutherland

Anomie

Robert K. Merton

Conflict (Marxist)

Richard Quinney

Labeling
(Societal Reaction)

Edwin M. Lemert

Control Theory

Travis W. Hirschi

Labeling

Howard S. Becker

CHAPTER 3

Sociological Theories of Deviance

I T would indeed be simple if there were a single, agreed-upon sociological theory to explain deviance; unfortunately, this is not the case. Several controversial theories have been developed, in fact, and it is important to understand the various approaches that have been used in studying deviance. It is also important to recognize other theories relating to deviance in order to better understand the theoretical orientation that has been adopted here. Two earlier theoretical approaches that are examined here—social pathology and social disorganization—no longer have much of a sociological following, yet they have set the stage for establishing a meaningful context for the more contemporary theories—anomie, labeling, conflict, socialization, and control theories.

DEVIANCE AS A SOCIAL PATHOLOGY

One of the earliest sociological approaches to deviance was the concept of "social pathology." This concept was developed in the latter part of the nineteenth century and continued in use until the end of the 1930s. Its *organic analogy* base likened society to the functioning of a biological organism. The most sophisticated use of the organic analogy was made by Herbert Spencer, who believed that society is like an organism because it has interdependent parts, mass, a complexity of structures that increases with its growth, and a life longer than any sum of its parts. A sociology textbook published in 1930 was explicit: "Since society is made up of individuals bound together in social relationships, social pathology refers to the maladjustment in social relationships. The phrase is based on the analogy of bodily maladjustment of function in the organ."[1]

Social pathology attempted to apply a biological model, what might now be called a "medical model," to deviance in a society. Social pathologists believed that in a society some universal criteria were to be found for a healthy society, but that at the same time societies could develop pathologies or abnormalities such as crime. The conditions considered to be deviant were those that interfered with the "normal" or the "desirable" workings of society. Conditions like crime, suicide, drunkenness, poverty, mental illness, prostitution, and so forth, were deviant because they were known to be "bad."[2] Even today, it is not uncommon to hear such phrases as a "sick society" or "society is suffering from a sickness." Within this frame of reference, deviance was somewhat on the order of a universal disease or an "unhealthy" deviation from some assumed universally accepted norm of behavior. In other words, what does exist is defined according to what ought to be. With the conception of society as an organism, it is important that it be healthy, thus good, while sickness is undesirable and therefore bad. Persons or situations diverging from expectations that

---

[1]John L. Gillin and Frank W. Blackmar, *Outlines of Sociology* (New York: Macmillan, 1930), p. 527.
[2]See Don C. Gibbons and Joseph W. Jones, *The Study of Deviance: Perspectives and Problems* (Englewood Cliffs, N.J.: Prentice-Hall, 1975), p. 15. See also Earl Rubington and Martin S. Weinberg, *The Study of Social Problems: Five Perspectives,* 2d ed. (New York: Oxford University Press, 1977).

have been formulated in these terms are "sick." For social pathologists, a social problem was, in the end, a violation of *moral* expectations.[3]

Social pathologists worked from two perspectives—first, that there was a certain "sickness" in society, and, second, that certain individuals were also "sick." Increasingly, sociologists developed the view that personal maladjustments or "sicknesses" such as bad heredity, physical illnesses, mental deficiency, mental disorder, drunkenness, lack of education, and personal immorality due to poverty lay at the heart of what they then termed social pathology, later becoming known as deviance. All this was the forerunner somewhat later of the "medical model" approach of the psychiatrists. One writer just after the turn of the century wrote graphically about this organic analogy to social science.

> Pathology in social science has a certain parallel to pathology in medical science. As the study of physical disease is essential to the maintenance of physical health, social health can never be securely grounded without a wider and more definite knowledge of social disease. General pathology in medicine teaches that many diseases have much in common and there are morbid processes which may be discussed, as well as particular diseases. In social pathology the interrelation of the abnormal classes is one of the most impressive facts. Paupers often beget criminals; the offspring of criminals become insane; and to such an extent is the kinship of the defective, dependent, and delinquent classes exhibited, that some have gone so far as to hold that under all the various forms of social pathology there is a common ground in the morbid nervous condition of individuals.[4]

The social pathology approach was largely consistent with the personal ideologies and social backgrounds of its advocates. Many early U.S. sociologists interested in social pathology were recruited from small mid-western rural communities where they had been raised with a sense of the importance of traditional religion as well as a general distrust of social change and city life.[5] As a result they had developed an attitude, which one might describe as "sacred provincialism," that displayed a moralistic approach to deviance and to social problems. The first task of the social pathologists was to identify and call attention to the existence of social "evils" in society, and the second was to provide measures for their speedy correction. In the United States this approach to deviance, combining traditional middle-class and rural values, came at a time of relatively rapid urbanization and increasing social differentiation as a result of extensive immigration. From their own points of view, of course, the social pathologists had no need to understand the relative nature of the behavior they condemned because it was obviously wrong and must be changed. One observer wryly noted: "Like General Custer's, their [the social pathologists] tactics were simple; they 'rode to the sound of the guns.'"[6] Rather than a normative standard, the social pathologists employed a universal moral standard against which all behavior and persons could be judged: and it was against this standard that the determination was made of which

---

[3]Rubington and Weinberg, p. 19.
[4]Samuel Smith, *Social Pathology* (New York: Macmillan, 1911), pp. 8–9.
[5]C. Wright Mills, "The Professional Ideology of Social Pathologists," *American Journal of Sociology,* 49 (1943), 165–180; Herman Schwendinger and Julia Schwendinger, *Sociologists of the Chair* (New York: Basic Books, 1974).
[6]Edwin M. Lemert, *Social Pathology* (New York: McGraw-Hill, 1951), p. 3.

behavior was to be considered deviant and which acceptable.[7] The social pathologists were social reformers who wished to remove the "evils" of society and to "salvage" it for the middle class.[8] Their reform efforts dealt principally with such issues as poverty, child labor, divorce, ordinary crime, and assorted "vices" such as drinking alcoholic beverages and prostitution. It is difficult today to take the views of the social pathologists seriously for a number of reasons.

Norms Not Universal in Content

The norms were actually what the social pathologists thought they should be, or universal judgments of what should be right for society. This idea was incorrect, however, as "the idea of diversity contested pathology."[9] Social pathologists failed to recognize the important issue that deviance varies by time and place as norms change, and that it cannot be compared to a disease like cancer, which is universally designated as an illness. Becker, for example, pointed out that while there was little disagreement about what constitutes a healthy state of the organism, much less agreement is seen when one uses the idea of pathology analogically to describe the kinds of behavior regarded as deviant. In other words, people who agree on what constitutes a healthy organism do not similarly agree on what constitutes healthy behavior. In fact, "it is impossible to find one [a criterion] that people generally accept as they accept criteria of health for the organism."[10]

Deviance Is Not Illness

Deviance is not an individual "sickness" in the physiological sense but rather a violation of norms. Individuals, in the social pathology model, cannot be divided into the normal and pathological.[11]

SOCIAL DISORGANIZATION

The growth of cultural relativity in sociology and the questioning of the validity of certain "universal" values brought to an end the social pathology perspective. The pronounced social changes following World War I and the Great Depression, along with extensive immigration, urbanization, and industrialization in the United States, accompanied by the crowding of large numbers of newly arrived people from a

---

[7]See Robert F. Meier, "The New Criminology: Continuity in Criminological Theory," *Journal of Criminal Law and Criminology,* 67 (1976), 461–469.

[8]Nanette J. Davis, *Sociological Constructions of Deviance: Perspectives and Issues in the Field* (Dubuque, Ia.: William C. Brown, 1975), p. 31.

[9]David Matza, *Becoming Deviant* (Englewood Cliffs, N.J.: Prentice-Hall, 1969), p. 43.

[10]Howard S. Becker, *Outsiders: Studies in the Sociology of Deviance,* enlarged ed. (New York: Free Press, 1973), p. 5.

[11]See Matza, pp. 41–46.

diversity of cultures into urban areas and the rapid development of conditions conducive to deviance, necessitated some sort of different explanation with new concepts.

This need for a new framework resulted in the evolution of the concept of "social disorganization,"[12] developed originally in about 1920 by Thomas and Znaniecki, and by Charles Cooley, and continuing into the 1950s.[13] The concept of social disorganization is associated the "Chicago school" of sociology because most of the persons originally using the concept came from there.[14] Social disorganization was the result of great development that had taken place in sociology since about 1910 in both theory and method. Social pathology had borrowed from established disciplines, notably medicine; in method it was more philosophical than scientific, and there was much concern with social action and morals. Social disorganization "rooted" the problem in the social rules and norms that had made sociology a focus of scientific interest. Moreover, the increasing interest in "scientific precision" had created a greater interest in methodology and theory, and the result was that sociological study was no longer largely confined to the practical solutions of social problems. "Since disorganization writers stressed the development of theory over practical application, it followed that for them the acquisition of knowledge had to precede its application to social problems."[15]

According to the new view, deviance was a product in society of uneven development, with much social change and conflict affecting the behavior of individuals. Social disorganization theory emphasized that society was organized when people are presumed to have developed a common agreement about fundamental values and norms, as reflected in a high degree of behavioral regularity. In other words, social organization (social order) exists when there is a high degree of internal cohesion binding together individuals and institutions in a society. This cohesion consists largely of consensus about goals worth striving for (values) and how or how not to behave. When consensus concerning values and norms is upset and traditional rules no longer appear to apply, social disorganization results. The basic premise of this approach was that "conflict and disorganization are most apt to increase when the equilibrium of a social system is disturbed during periods of rapid social change, and as conflict and social disorganization increase, so will rates of deviance."[16]

In contrast to social disorganization, successful social organization, it was thought, involved an integration of customs, effective teamwork and morale, and harmonious social relationships. A well-integrated social group showed group solidarity, and modes of behavior were more homogeneous and traditional. There was little

---

[12]The term "social disorganization" is used to refer to an explanation of deviance and a state of society that produces deviance.

[13]W. I. Thomas and Florian Znaniecki, *The Polish Peasant in Europe and America,* 2d ed., 2 vols. (New York: Dover Press, 1958); and Charles H. Cooley, *Social Process* (New York: Scribner, 1918).

[14]The University of Chicago is credited with having the first department of sociology in the United States. Its first members were influential in shaping this perspective. See Robert E. L. Faris, *Chicago Sociology, 1920– 1932* (Chicago: University of Chicago Press, 1967); and James T. Carey, *Sociology and Public Affairs: The Chicago School* (Beverly Hills, Calif.: Sage Publications, 1975).

[15]Rubington and Weinberg, p. 50.

[16]Stuart H. Traub and Craig B. Little, eds., *Theories of Deviance* (Itasca, Ill.: F. E. Peacock, 1975), pp. 31– 32.

unconventional behavior and deviance, and informal social controls usually sufficed to regulate behavior.[17] The United States, particularly the urban areas, did not fit well into this idyllic set of characteristics, which made it clear to social disorganization theorists that a state of social disorganization existed in much of city life. It was in the cities, then, where they concentrated their research, on what they termed "disorganized local areas," generally slum areas of high crime, prostitution, mental disorder, suicide, and other forms of deviant behavior. It was assumed that changes were taking place in the ecological or spatial growth of the city and that these changes resulted in the general deterioration of group solidarity in certain areas.[18]

One can well understand why the social disorganization theorists singled out the city to study what they saw as the "disorganizing" aspects of life there, and particularly the effects on rates of deviant behavior in urban areas. In their own theoretical framework, the social patterns of the urban environment were conducive to social disorganization, which then led to the deviant behavior. Social disorganization theorists were aware of the great heterogeneity of people living in the same geographical area or in contiguous areas and of the vast differences in the values and norms of these persons; in addition, they noted that people moved into and out of the areas without ever developing a sense of neighborhood social organization. Lacking a real social organization, certain neighborhoods were, they considered, "socially disorganized," and this condition itself resulted in high rates of deviance, particularly when examined in terms of the more organized suburban and rural neighborhoods. Within these "disorganized" parts of the city, certain areas, particularly slum neighborhoods, appeared to have even more deviant behavior. "Thus for social disorganization theorists the city and its lower-class inhabitants became the primary objects of study."[19] Of special interest to these theorists, particularly in Chicago, was the problem of delinquency. It was generally felt that the highest rates of this type of deviance were to be found in the central inner-city core where basic social solidarity was particularly lacking.[20] By this they meant that the original group norms that had been brought to the United States from the old country had collapsed in the new land and that no new effective standards or controls over behavior had become solidified; in sum, a true situation of "social disorganization" existed. Because of the social disruption typical of this situation, alternative norms and modes of behavior arose, in the form of deviance.

An important implication of this view for the control of deviance was that

---

[17]This may be the situation with respect to Communist China, which fits more closely the pattern of social organization described here. See Amy Auerbacher Wilson, Sidney Leonard Greenblatt, and Richard Whittingham Wilson, eds., *Deviance and Social Control in Chinese Society* (New York: Holt, Rinehart and Winston, 1977).

[18]In their studies on these social changes, the social disorganization theorists, not unlike the social pathologists, used an analogy. While the important analogy for the social pathologists had been between physical illness and deviant behavior, the social disorganization advocates used a spatial-distribution analogy in which the city was likened to the ecological system of plants and animals. These theorists stressed the competition and selection of city dynamics, with city life adapting to physical surroundings and to economic realities. The problems of city life were termed social disorganization to denote a disruption in life-styles and in attitudes in these areas. See the discussion in Davis, pp. 41–46.

[19]Traub and Little, p. 33.

[20]Clifford Shaw and Henry D. McKay, "Report on Social Factors in Juvenile Delinquency," in *Report on the Causes of Crime*, II (Washington, D.C.: Government Printing Office, 1937), p. 110.

deviants should be integrated into conventional groups and that the integration process should focus on the local community, inasmuch as the local community was the prime producer of the deviance. The most typical example of a large-scale program designed to implement these ideas was the Chicago Area Projects, initiated in the 1930s. This series of neighborhood programs was organized to integrate and thereafter to change local communities with high rates of crime and delinquency.

A number of problems became evident in the social disorganization concept to explain deviance, and these problems contributed to the decline of the concept.

Subjectivity

A fundamental problem is that it is subjective and judgmental while it masquerades as an objective conceptual framework.[21] As a concept, social disorganization was almost as subjective as social pathology. In the social disorganization perspective, the concept of pathology was simply applied to the group instead of to the individual; no longer were persons pathological, communities were now disorganized. The designation of phenomena as deviant and the equation of deviance with disorganization were the focus of the sociological analyst or observer rather than findings derived from actual studies of what some people would term a state of social disorganization. Social disorganization was usually thought of as something "bad," and what was bad was often the value judgment of the observer and the members of his social class or other social groups.

The Only Deviants Are Lower-Class Persons

Concentrating as it did on slum areas, the concept tried to explain deviance almost entirely as a lower-class phenomenon, to the exclusion of middle- and upper-class deviance. In other words, it was biased in favor of middle-class values and norms. The lower class was assumed to have higher deviance rates because its members lived in the most disorganized areas of the city. "Thus, by circular reasoning, the lower class was most deviant because it was the most disorganized and it was, at the same time, the most disorganized because it contained the most deviants."[22]

Deviance or Change?

Social disorganization implies the disruption of a previously existing condition of organization, a situation that generally cannot be established. Social change was often confused with social disorganization, and little attention was paid to explaining why some social changes are disorganizing and others are, in fact, organized.

What Is Disorganized?

Although deviation is referred to as "social disorganization" and the society "disorganized," often what may seem like disorganization may actually be quite highly

---

[21]Gibbons and Jones, p. 19.
[22]Traub and Little, pp. 33–34.

organized systems of competing norms. Many subcultures of deviant behavior, such as youth gangs, organized crime, homosexuality, prostitution, and white-collar crime, including political corruption as well as corporate crime, are highly organized. Even the norms and values of the slums are highly organized, as Whyte clearly showed in his study of a slum area, *Street Corner Society*.[23]

Function of Deviance

Finally, deviance itself, as has been pointed out in the previous chapters, may contribute to social organization rather than to social disorganization.

ANOMIE

Today a widely held explanation for deviance is that it arises from the "anomic" state of contemporary society. This view was originally proposed by Robert Merton in the late 1930s.[24] Modern urban industrialized societies, like the United States, emphasize the acquisition of material success in the form of wealth and education as accepted status goals while simultaneously limiting institutional means or norms to certain segments of society who are able to use them legitimately. The segments of society that are denied access to legitimate means are generally the poor, those who belong to the lower class, and particularly persons of certain racial and ethnic groups who are discriminated against, such as blacks and Chicanos. As a result, a situation of *anomie* takes place when there is an acute disjunction between the cultural goals and the legitimate means available to certain groups in society to achieve them. Anomie represents a breakdown in the social structure, and the consequences for the individual are often referred to as anomia, anomy, or alienation.[25]

Success goals in cultural terms are generally presumed to be achieved by *legitimate means* through regular employment, in higher paid occupations, and through access to further education. These channels, however, are not as available to certain persons, such as the lower class. Although the goals of success are held out so

---

[23]William F. Whyte, *Street Corner Society* (Chicago: University of Chicago Press, 1943). Also see Marshall B. Clinard, *Slums and Community Development: Experiments in Self-Help* (New York: Free Press, 1967).
[24]Robert K. Merton, *Social Theory and Social Structure*, enlarged edition (New York: Free Press, 1968), pp. 185–248. Also see Marshall B. Clinard, "The Theoretical Implications of Anomie and Deviant Behavior," in Marshall B. Clinard, ed., *Anomie and Deviant Behavior* (New York: Free Press, 1964), pp. 1–56. Durkheim in 1897 used "anomie" in the slightly different sense of "normlessness" in connection with his classic discussion of anomic suicide. See Emile Durkheim, *Suicide*, John A. Spaulding, trans. (New York: Free Press, 1951). Actually, it would appear that Durkheim developed the concept of anomie in his work on *Moral Education*, a book written later than *Suicide*. See Stephen R. Marks, "Durkheim's Theory of Anomie," *American Journal of Sociology*, 80 (1974), 329–363.
[25]Another similar term is "alienation" in the sense of a feeling of powerlessness, estrangement, marginality, and isolation from the society. To some the "alienated" person is one "who has been estranged from, made unfriendly toward his society and the culture it carries" (Gwynn Nettler, "A Measure of Alienation," *American Sociological Review*, 22 [1957], p. 672). It is, of course, important to recognize that alienation from society has other origins besides poverty, although this is probably the dominant one, as Schacht has pointed out. See Richard L. Schacht, *Alienation* (New York: Doubleday, 1970). Also see Melvin Seeman, "On the Meaning of Alienation," *American Sociological Review*, 24 (1959), 783–791; and Seeman, "Alienation and Engagement," in Angus Campbell and Philip Converse, eds., *The Human Meaning of Social Change* (New York: Russell Sage, 1972), pp. 467–527.

that all can strive for them, the means for achieving them are restricted. Consequently, some persons are forced to achieve them through *illegitimate means,* through such forms of deviance as crime, prostitution, drug use, alcoholism, and mental disorder. In attempting to explain these forms of deviant behavior, the anomie theory has assumed that official rates of deviance are highest among the poor and among the lower class, where the greatest pressures for deviation occur and where opportunities to acquire both material goods and a higher level of education are limited. Schematically, the relation of anomie to social structure may be summarized in this manner:

1. *Exposure* to the cultural goal and norms regulating behavior oriented toward the goal.
2. *Acceptance* of the goal or norm as moral mandates and internalized values.
3. *Relative accessibility to the goal:* life chances in the opportunity structure.
4. *The degree of discrepancy* between the accepted goal and its accessibility.
5. *The degree of anomie.*
6. *The rates of deviant behavior* of the various types set out in typology of modes of adaptation.[26]

According to the anomie explanation, several *illegitimate adaptations* can be used by poor lower-class persons where legitimate means to achieve the culturally prescribed goals of success have been blocked. These adaptations are, chiefly, rebellion, innovation, and retreatism.[27] The particular adaptation is dependent on the individual's acceptance or rejection of cultural goals and the adherence to, or the violation of, accepted norms. Persons may turn away from conventional cultural goals and rebel against them. Through this *rebellion* they may seek to establish a new or greatly modified social structure. They try to set up new goals and procedures to change the existing social structure instead of trying to achieve the goals traditionally established by society. This type of deviant adaptation is represented by "hippies," political radicals, and revolutionaries.[28] *Innovation* is an adaptation involving the use of illegitimate means such as theft, burglary, robbery, organized crime, or prostitution to achieve culturally prescribed goals of success. This response is "normal" where access to success through conventional means is limited.[29] As evidence, Merton has maintained that unlawful behavior such as crime and delinquency are most common in the lower strata of society. The poor are largely restricted to manual labor, which is often stigmatizing; as a result of the low status and the low income, they cannot readily compete in terms of established standards of worth, and therefore they are more likely

---

[26]Clinard, "The Theoretical Implications of Anomie and Deviant Behavior," p. 14.
[27]Merton also includes conformity to goals and legitimate means as an adaptation as well as ritualism, but since they hardly result in deviant behavior under most circumstances, they will not be discussed here. Ritualism is the abandonment or the downward scaling of goals of wealth and social mobility to a point where aspirations are solved by ritualistic behavior and routine that avoids the frustrations of ambition.
[28]In another context, Merton similarly distinguishes between *nonconformists,* who challenge publicly the legitimacy of social norms, and *aberrant* persons, such as delinquents and criminals, who acknowledge the legitimacy of the norms they violate. The nonconformist, like the radical, the marijuana user, and the "hippie," makes known his dissent publicly; the aberrant hides behind his departure from norms. The nonconformist wishes to change the norms he challenges, the aberrant only wishes to escape sanction by society. See Robert K. Merton, "The Sociology of Social Problems," in Robert K. Merton and Robert Nisbet, eds., *Contemporary Social Problems,* 4th ed. (New York: Harcourt Brace Jovanovich, 1976).
[29]Merton, *Social Theory and Social Structure,* p. 199.

to engage in crime. *Retreatism,* according to Merton, represents the substantial abandonment of the cultural goals that society esteems and of the practices that had become institutionalized to achieve these goals.[30] The individual has fully internalized the cultural goals of success, but has not found them available through the institutional means of obtaining them. Being held from achieving the goal, through internalized pressures which prevent innovative practices, the individual becomes frustrated and handicapped, becoming defeated and even withdrawn. Retreating from cultural goals, the person becomes addicted to drugs, becomes an alcoholic, or may completely "escape" through a mental disorder or even suicide. Retreatism tends to be a private rather than a group or subcultural form of adaptation, even though the person may have contact with others in a similar position.

Cloward has reformulated Merton's theory to include not only differentials in the *availability of legitimate means* but variations in the access or *opportunity for illegitimate means,* such as are provided the person in the poor slum areas of cities.[31] According to Merton's theoretical statement, deviant behavior is a product of differentials in the access to goals of success through legitimate means. Cloward points out, however, that differentials are also seen in the access to illegitimate means and that this *differential opportunity* plays a large part in the distribution of deviant adaptations. Actually, the individual, whatever his position in the social structure, does not have illegitimate means equally available, for much the same reason that legitimate means vary by social strata.[32] The lower-class poor are provided greater opportunities for the acquisition of deviant roles, largely through access in slum areas to deviant subcultures and the opportunity for carrying out such deviant social roles once they have been acquired. Within this context, Cloward has sought to explain delinquency, crime, alcoholism, drug addiction, mental illness, and suicide. His view about some "retreatists," however, is different from Merton's. To the latter, retreatists, say drug addicts, are persons who do not wish to use illegitimate means such as innovation; to Cloward, they are "double failures" in that they have failed in the use of both legitimate and illegitimate means. Many have failed in the conventional as well as the unconventional world. Delinquency arises from the disparity between what lower-class youth are led to want and what is actually available to them. Desirous of such conventional goals as economic and educational success, they are faced with limitations on the legitimate avenues to success: unable to revise their goals downward, they become frustrated and turn to delinquency if the norms and opportunities are available to them.[33]

---

[30]Merton, *Social Theory and Social Structure,* pp. 203–204.
[31]Richard A. Cloward, "Illegitimate Means, Anomie and Deviant Behavior," *American Sociological Review,* 24 (1959), 164–176.
[32]Cloward, p. 168. Two things are implied here when we refer to "means," whether legitimate or illegitimate. First, there are appropriate learning environments for the acquisition of the values and skills associated with the performance of a particular role; and, second, the individual has opportunities to discharge the role once he has been prepared. The term subsumes both learning and opportunity structures.
[33]Richard A. Cloward and Lloyd E. Ohlin, *Delinquency and Opportunity: A Theory of Delinquent Gangs* (New York: Free Press, 1960). This theory of gang behavior has been applied to a number of practical attempts to control delinquency, such as the Mobilization for Youth program in the Lower East Side of New York City, which largely ended in failure. See Daniel P. Moynihan, *Maximum Feasible Misunderstanding: Community Action in the War on Poverty* (New York: Free Press, 1969).

A more recent reformulation of the anomie theory has been proposed by Simon and Gagnon.[34] They point out that Merton had originally formulated his theory in the 1930s, during a period of chronic economic depression, but that the affluence of the 1970s has had a substantially different impact on deviance than had been the case several decades earlier. Simon and Gagnon expand the number of adaptive responses to deviance to nine, based on (a) commitment to approach cultural goals and (b) the degree to which progress is achieved toward the realization of these goals.[35] These responses are optimal conformist, detached conformist, compulsive achiever, conforming deviant, detached person, escapist, conventional reformer, missionary, and total rebel. With their added adaptations, Simon and Gagnon argue that the revised model appears to account more adequately for deviance at the higher socioeconomic levels than does Merton's original model. Such a claim will require substantial empirical support before it can be accepted.

Explanations of deviance in terms of anomie tend to oversimplify what is a far more complex problem. Only a few of the more important inadequacies can be pointed out here.[36]

Assumption of Universality

Anomie assumes a universality of what constitutes "illegitimate means" that is not the case, because delinquent and criminal acts vary in time and in place. Deviance is a relative concept; it is not the same in all groups. The use of drugs, for example, such as marijuana and even cocaine and opium, are not deviations in many parts of the world today. It was largely not a century ago in Western societies generally, including the United States, that the use of opiates was made illegal.

> During the nineteenth century, opiates were generally available to anyone who wished to buy them, without a doctor's prescription. They were also liberally and carelessly used in medical practice, and countless patent medicines which contained them were widely advertised and sold as cures for most of the ills of the flesh. Since the drug was readily available through legal channels there was no significant illicit traffic and the habit was inexpensive.[37]

Class Bias

Anomie theory rests on the assumption that deviant behavior is disproportionately more common in the lower class, and it neglects the important role of social control agents in defining who is deviant. Considerable evidence can be cited that lower-class

---

[34]William Simon and John G. Gagnon, "The Anomie of Affluence: A Post-Mertonian Conception," *American Journal of Sociology,* 82, (1976), 356–378.

[35]Simon and Gagnon, p. 370.

[36]For more detailed criticism see Marshall B. Clinard, "The Theoretical Implications of Anomie and Deviant Behavior"; Edwin M. Lemert, "Social Structure, Social Control and Deviation"; James F. Short, Jr., "Gang Delinquency and Anomie"; H. Warren Dunham, "Anomie and Mental Disorder"; Alfred R. Lindesmith and John Gagnon, "Anomie and Drug Addiction"; and Charles R. Snyder, "Inebriety, Alcoholism, and Anomie," all in Clinard, *Anomie and Deviant Behavior.* See also Albert K. Cohen, "The Sociology of the Deviant Act: Anomie Theory and Beyond," *American Sociological Review,* 30 (1965), 5–14.

[37]Lindesmith and Gagnon, pp. 165–166.

persons and members of minority groups are more likely to be detected, and labeled, as delinquents, criminals, alcoholics, drug addicts, and mental patients than persons who belong to the middle and upper classes. Furthermore, studies of occupational, white-collar, and corporate crime have shown that crime occurs in the highest social strata, and delinquency is found among the middle as well as the lower classes.[38] Sykes points out, for example, that in contradiction to the Mertonian theory, many criminal offenders today, such as middle-class persons and college students apprehended for shoplifting, do not fit the "poverty syndrome," where crime is a means of breaking free from material deprivation.[39] Alcoholism may actually be as prevalent in the upper classes as in the lower, but members of the upper class are less likely to be arrested as chronic inebriates or to use public treatment facilities. The distribution rates of drug addiction are so varied among all classes, even though higher in the lower class, that it is difficult to reach definite conclusions; middle- and upper-class persons may use different drugs and be less visible than lower-class persons. The explanation of the high rate of drug addiction in black areas of large cities today may lie primarily in the concentration there of the drug traffic.

> If anomie is pronounced in the urban Negro [black] slums so also are the drugs easily obtained there. . . . If drug use occurred only in this situation, the theory of anomie would be a rather impressive one. But one still needs to keep in mind that however much the Negro [black] residents of slums may be influenced by anomie and however available illicit drugs may be for them, the vast majority do not become addicted.[40]

Although schizophrenia appears to be more common in the lower class, mental disorder occurs in all social classes, and the degree of differences is as yet unclear. The rates may be in part a reflection of differentials in societal reaction. Suicides occur among all social classes, and although the suicide rate is quite high in the lower class, there are a significant number of suicides at the upper ranges of the social structure as well.

Simplicity of Explanation

Anomie theory is too simple. While it is possible for an individual to be subject in some cases to something that resembles the strain of anomie, he is more likely to be "affected by role models, peer pressures, his self-image, his perceptions of other people's reaction to his behavior, and his power to defend the norms of his group(s) and his own behavior."[41]

Although the lower-class deviant, according to the anomie theory, makes individual illegal adaptations in the system because of "pressures" that develop due to failure to achieve certain goals, most deviant acts actually arise out of a process of

---

[38]See Gilbert Geis and Robert F. Meier, eds., *White-Collar Crime: Offenses in Business, Politics and the Professions* (New York: Free Press, 1977); Jack D. Douglas and John M. Johnson, eds., *Official Deviance: Readings in Malfeasance, Misfeasance and Other Forms of Corruption* (Philadelphia: Lippincott, 1977); and Edmund W. Vaz, ed., *Middle-Class Juvenile Delinquency* (New York: Harper & Row, 1967).
[39]Gresham M. Sykes, "New Crimes for Old," *American Scholar*, Autumn 1971, 592–598.
[40]Lindesmith and Gagnon, p. 165.
[41]Traub and Little, p. 61.

interaction with others who may serve as a reference group for the individual. Often the individual deviant is not a free agent in his choice, as he is restricted by the pressures of the groups to which he belongs. Many deviant acts, in fact, are a part of role expectations rather than representing a disjunction between goals and means.[42] The theory of anomie does not recognize the demonstrated importance of deviant subcultures, deviant groups, and the important role of the characteristics of urban life, along with the role of the slum in behavior. Many forms of deviant behavior, such as drug addiction, professional crime, occupational prostitution, homosexuality, and white-collar criminal behavior, are collective acts in which association with group-maintained values explains the behavior. In a test of anomie theory, delinquent gang behavior by lower-class boys, for example, was found more likely to be linked with status considerations that involve position in the peer group than with achievement of the status goals of society.[43]

The Trouble with Retreatism

The theory of the adaptation of means to goals through "retreatism" lacks precision, and it is also an oversimplification of what will later be shown to be actually a much more complex process of how alcoholism, drug addiction, mental disorder, and suicide develop. For example, an alcoholic looks upon obtaining alcohol as an end or goal; drug addicts are not retreatists, because their difficulties in securing their goals of drugs make them "active" rather than retreatist persons. In fact, a substantial number of addicts carry on other occupations as, for example, medical doctors who are responsible members of society. They have not abandoned their quest for success, nor are they "immune to the frustrations involved in seeking it."[44] Little evidence can be found to support the "double failure" explanation of drug addiction. In fact, the addict who is able to secure an adequate supply of drugs and thus maintain his habit is a "double success" rather than a double failure. The explanation of mental disorder, as will be shown later, is much more than a process of retreating from success goals; it involves normative actions and role-playing. Moreover, a major criticism of retreatism as an adaptation is that it fails to distinguish the origins of the deviance from the actual effects produced. Long periods of excessive drinking or drug use may impair a person's social relations and ability to achieve certain goals in society; in this way anomie confuses cause and effect.

Alternative Perspectives

The anomie theory uses a broad, social structural perspective within which deviance is analyzed. Different conclusions might be reached, however, if a situational viewpoint were taken. Drug use, for example, is alleged to represent an escape from economic

---

[42]Cohen.

[43]James J. Short, Jr., and Fred L. Strodtbeck, *Group Process and Gang Delinquency* (Chicago: University of Chicago Press, 1965).

[44]Lindesmith and Gagnon, p. 178.

failure, yet it may actually serve quite a different purpose. Drug use may be a form of innovative behavior, such as getting "kicks" from it, using it as a ritual act, as in the case of some American Indian usage of peyote, an act of peer conformity among adolescents, or an expression of rebellion against conformity in a society.[45]

DEVIANCE AND LABELING

A major contribution to the theory of deviance within recent years has been the labeling perspective. This perspective emphasizes the important consequences for individuals who have been sanctioned or "labeled" by official agencies and by other persons because of their deviant behavior. The major conceptualizations of this perspective are based on the writings of Lemert some 25 years ago, although a similar idea had previously been expressed by others, particularly George Herbert Mead, Frank Tannenbaum, and Alfred Schutz.[46] More recently, Howard Becker, Harold Garfinkel, Erving Goffman, Thomas Scheff, Kai Erikson, John Kitsuse, Edwin Schur, and others, have elaborated the labeling approach.[47] Such sociologists contributed to the development of the labeling perspective when they asked "when violations were sanctioned, by whom, against whom and with what social consequences."[48]

In the labeling approach, no attempt is made to try to explain why certain individuals engage initially in certain actions defined as deviant; instead, the labeling theorists stress the importance of both the social definitions and the negative social sanctions as they relate to the pressuring of an individual to engage in more deviant acts.[49] Attention is shifted from the individual and his actions to the dynamics involved in socially defining particular activities or persons as deviant. The developmental process in which deviance results is emphasized, a process with "varying stages of initiation, acceptance, commitment, and imprisonment in a deviant role because of the actions of others."[50] This analysis of the process is centered on the reaction of others (termed the "definers") to individuals or acts which these "evaluating others" per-

---

[45]Davis, p. 113.

[46]See Lemert, *Social Pathology,* and Edwin M. Lemert, *Human Deviance, Social Problems and Social Control,* 2d ed. (Englewood Cliffs, N.J.: Prentice-Hall, 1972). Also see Herbert Blumer, "Sociological Implications of the Thought of George Herbert Mead," in Herbert Blumer, ed., *Symbolic Interactionism* (Englewood Cliffs, N.J.: Prentice-Hall, 1969), pp. 62, 65, 66; Frank Tannenbaum, *Crime and the Community* (Boston: Ginn, 1938); and Alfred Schutz, *The Phenomenology of the Social World* (Evanston, Ill.: Northwestern University Press, 1967).

[47]Becker; Harold Garfinkel, *Studies in Ethnomethodology* (Englewood Cliffs, N.J.: Prentice-Hall, 1967); Erving Goffman, *Asylums* (New York: Doubleday Anchor Books, 1963); Thomas J. Scheff, *Being Mentally Ill* (Chicago: Aldine, 1966); Scheff, "The Labeling Theory of Mental Illness," *American Sociological Review,* 39 (1974), 444–452; Kai T. Erikson, "Notes on the Sociology of Deviance," *Social Problems,* 9 (1962), 307–314; John I. Kitsuse, "Societal Reaction to Deviant Behavior: Problems of Theory and Method," *Social Problems,* 9 (1962), 247–256; Edwin M. Schur, *Labeling Deviant Behavior: Its Sociological Implications* (New York: Harper & Row, 1971). Also see Prudence Rains, "Imputations of Deviance: A Retrospective Essay on the Labeling Perspective," *Social Problems,* 23 (1975), 1–11; and Erich Goode, "On Behalf of Labeling Theory," *Social Problems,* 22 (1975), 570–583.

[48]Rubington and Weinberg, pp. 193–194.

[49]Traub and Little, pp. 159–160.

[50]Traub and Little, p. 159.

ceive negatively. Labeling theorists, through focusing their attention on subjective definitions of behavior and on the consequences for the persons so labeled as a result of these definitions, shift the emphasis even further away from the person's actions to the "ways in which institutionalized processes of social control and social definitions define what (and who) is deviant."[51]

Deviance as Reaction

The labeling theorists claim that since the concept of deviance is exceedingly relative and ambiguous, the only way one can understand what is meant by it is to examine the reactions of others to the behavior. Perhaps Becker's definition of deviance is the most well known in terms of the labeling perspective. He claims that deviance is a "consequence of the application by others of rules and sanctions to an 'offender.' The deviant is one to whom the label has successfully been applied; deviant behavior is behavior that people label."[52] Thus the crucial dimension is the societal reaction to an act and not the deviant act itself. This reaction, in the form of sanctions, serves to label not only the behavior as deviant, but also the person whose behavior elicited the label in the first place. Deviance is not an attribute of acts or of actors, but is something imposed on them by others, the nondeviants. It is indeed ironic, however, that the labeling perspective of deviance is based upon the effects of the very measures that have been applied for the social control of the behavior.

As the emphasis is put on the label, interest shifts from the origin of the deviant behavior to the social reaction that becomes attached to persons and to the consequences of this "labeling" attachment for the individual's subsequent deviation. The official labeling of a person as delinquent, criminal, homosexual, drug addict, prostitute, or "insane" may have serious consequences for further deviation. Once it has been attached, the label initiates a further sequence of events leading to continued deviance. Schur believes that the emphasis on labeling signifies a shift from efforts to distinguish what "caused" individuals to be offenders to a more intensive study of the processes that have produced the deviant outcomes.[53] Lemert has particularly stressed this social control viewpoint and its consequences for deviance. He believes that this is a big step away from older sociology, which tended to rely heavily upon the idea that deviance leads to social control. "I have come to believe that the reverse idea (that is, social control leads to deviance) is equally tenable and the potentially richer premise for studying deviance in modern society."[54]

The labeling perspective has grown out of the current widespread recognition that sanctioning deviance is not randomly applied throughout the population of rule breakers. Discretionary or contingency factors operate in the selection of who becomes officially designated as a deviant. Official actions against deviants are affected by elements of contingency, chance, or categoric risks. This process of selection and the labeling of a deviant depend upon such factors as social class, occupation, racial

---

[51]Traub and Little, p. 160.
[52]Becker, p. 9.
[53]Schur, p. 27.
[54]Lemert, *Human Deviance, Social Problems and Social Control,* p. ix.

and ethnic background, age, past record of deviance, the situation out of which the behavior has arisen, the pressure of public reaction, and the resources available to apprehend and to deal with deviants.

In many cases official labeling does affect subsequent behavior. A person is often stigmatized by society not because a crime has been committed but because the person has been convicted or imprisoned. To illustrate the effect of societal reaction in giving the deviant a label, imagine a possible classroom situation. Consider the reaction of others if a student admitted publicly that he had stolen a car or committed a burglary but that nothing happened or the act was never known. The reaction of others would be different if the student admitted the act and then added that he had been placed on probation for two years or sent to prison. Although the act would have been the same, others would be reacting to the official labeling of deviance by society. In fact, official apprehension for one deviant act may mean that the individual will be regarded as deviant or will be thought to have undesirable characteristics. Much of what has been said applies as well to becoming known as one who has been committed to a mental hospital, arrested for the use of drugs or committed to a drug treatment center, or arrested or "known" as a homosexual. The consequences of labeling are not always the same, but in general they can make the deviant act assume a greater importance to the individual than the mere act itself. A youth who has been imprisoned for theft and labeled a "criminal" by the police and the courts, and is so regarded by neighbors and others, may find it difficult to go straight. Having commented in a positive way about the possible effect in some cases of labeling, however, it will later be pointed out that labelists have greatly overemphasized this factor.

Types of Deviants

According to the labeling theorists, the deviant label may produce a basic change in the nature and the meaning of deviance for the individual who is labeled. They distinguish between *primary deviance,* or behavior that has arisen for a number of reasons, including risk-taking, chance, and situational factors, and *secondary deviance,* which Lemert has described as the behavior of a person when beginning to "employ his deviant behavior or a role based upon it as a means of defense, attack, or adjustment to the overt and covert problems created by the consequent societal reaction to him."[55] The deviant label produces a deviant social role and is the basis upon which further social status may be conferred on the deviant; moreover, the deviance becomes part of that role and is thus perpetuated. The individual who engages in a homosexual act may adopt a homosexual identity if others react toward him as though he were a homosexual; an individual who performs an "eccentric" act may enact the role of a mentally disturbed person if he is formally treated by a psychiatrist or admitted to a mental hospital; and a drinker who has been labeled a "drunk" by his family may drink excessively to cope with the rejection he finds at home.

Once a label has been attached by an arrest, confinement in a mental hospital,

---

[55]Lemert, *Social Pathology,* p. 76. Italics in original omitted.

or other action through an official agency, it is claimed, a spiraling action is initiated which sets off a sequence of events leading to further deviation because of the stigmatizing effect of the societal reaction. In a sense the labeling of a person as a deviant may result in a self-fulfilling prophecy. Persons labeled as deviants continue acts of deviance, developing deviant careers or becoming secondary deviants. Labeling sets in motion a process that tends to shape the individual into the image people have of him. The person tends to be cut off from participation in conventional groups and thus moves into an organized deviant group. Lemert has presented an often quoted schematic version of this process, indicating the several specific steps in which one is led by official labeling and relabeling from primary to secondary deviance:

> (1) primary deviation; (2) social penalties; (3) further primary deviation; (4) stronger penalties and rejections; (5) further deviation, perhaps with hostilities and resentment beginning to focus upon those doing the penalizing; (6) crisis reached in the tolerance quotient, expressed in formal action by the community stigmatizing of the deviant; (7) strengthening of the deviant conduct as a reaction to the stigmatizing and penalties; (8) ultimate acceptance of deviant social status and efforts at adjustment on the basis of the associated role.[56]

Labeling may be a useful framework within which to explain *some* career deviance. The labeling perspective has also correctly focused on the significant role played by social conflict and social power considerations in a society's determination of what is to be enforced as deviance. Certain groups may influence the enforcement and administration of the criminal law, for example, through agents such as the police and the courts. The purposeful actions of other agents of social control have been influential in determining which persons are to be considered mentally ill and the appropriate manner in which they are to be dealt with, either in an institution or in the community.[57]

The labeling approach has been subjected to a number of criticisms, however, which we will now consider.

Where Is the Behavior?

The label does not create the behavior in the first place. The labeling perspective thus denies the reality of the deviant act and the basis on which the societal reaction is made—that is, a violation of some normative standard or expectation.[58] "People can, and do, commit deviant acts because of the particular contingencies and circumstances in their lives, quite apart from or in combination with labels others apply to them."[59] The majority of persons who are deviant are not officially labeled, whether

---

[56]From *Social Pathology* by Edwin Lemert. Copyright© 1951 by McGraw-Hill, Inc. Used with permission of McGraw-Hill Book Company.

[57]For a broader discussion of this point, see Andrew T. Scull, "The Decarceration of the Mentally Ill: A Critical View," *Politics and Society,* 6 (1976), 173–211.

[58]The term most often used in this respect is "putative." For a discussion of this term and its importance to labeling theory, see Rains.

[59]Ronald L. Akers, "Problems in the Sociology of Deviance: Social Definitions and Behavior," *Social Forces,* 46 (1968), 463.

their acts have involved stealing, homosexual behavior, marijuana use, drunken driving, or crimes committed by persons in business, corporations, or politics. Likewise, many persons who might be termed mentally disordered have not necessarily been officially labeled as mentally ill. Moreover, this reactive definition of deviance presents certain dilemmas: The reaction occurs because the act is deviant, and not the reverse. As one critic of labeling theory has stated, "Imagine a police officer saying or even thinking: 'This individual has committed a crime because I arrested him.' "[60]

The consequences of viewing deviance as a normative behavior rather than as labeling reaction have been well indicated:

> If an act is deviant only because of a certain kind of reaction to it, then the relation between deviation and reaction is fixed by definition. That point has some inconspicuous implications. The reactive definition leads to a declaration that an act is not a crime unless it is so labeled by officials. Accordingly, the notion of "unreported crimes" becomes meaningless, and along with it, a vast amount of research to determine the extent of criminality (or juvenile delinquency) apart from official records. Indeed, even speculation on the reliability of the crime rate as reported by the police is pointless. If an act is criminal only when labeled as such by the police, then the crime rate reported by the police is absolutely reliable. In other words, the crime rate is what the police report.[61]

Who or What Labels?

Three groups can affect labeling—official agents of social control, the society at large, and the immediate group one participates in, the significant others for whom one receives cues as to role performance. If empirical research cannot show that these three groups work as a whole, then it is difficult to speak of the effects of labeling as a whole. Rather, one must define specifically what group is doing the labeling. Those who define deviant behavior in terms of labeling, however, are not clear as to whether the labeling reaction involves social control through formal or informal sanctions, or both. In general, the labeling perspective has emphasized almost exclusively formal agency sanctioning, with minor importance being accorded informal sanctioning from family, friends, employers, and others. In fact, formal sanctions are regarded as the most effective in producing an increase or persistence in deviant conduct, because they represent more generalized stigma and have greater labeling implications than any informal expression of disapproval. In this connection, Stephens carried out an empirical test of the two facets of labeling in a study of relapse among 236 male narcotic addicts.[62] He found no relation between the extent of prior formal or official labeling and relapse; in fact, the data indicated greater chances of drug abstinence in cases where there had been prior formal labeling. On the other hand, informal labeling by family and addict friends was very important and related to relapse.

---

[60]Jack P. Gibbs, "Issues in Defining Deviant Behavior," in Robert A. Scott and Jack D. Douglas, eds., *Theoretical Perspectives on Deviance* (New York: Basic Books, 1972), pp. 43–44. Becker (p. 20) curiously allowed for the possibility of "secret deviance," where "an improper act is committed yet no one notices it or reacts to it as a violation of the rules."
[61]Gibbs, p. 44.
[62]Richard C. Stephens, "Relapse among Narcotic Addicts: An Empirical Test of Labeling Theory," unpublished Ph.d. dissertation, University of Wisconsin, Madison, 1970.

How Much of a Label?

Writers who have adopted the labeling definition of deviance are vague about how societal reaction constitutes effective labeling; in other words, how harsh must the reaction be to result in the person's being labeled or defined as a deviant? One might ask if labeling is to be only by formal social control agencies and, if this is the case, how severe is the penalty to be? Is it to be arrest, imprisonment, mental hospitalization, and so on, and what effect, on the other hand, will result from informal social control sanctions such as those exercised by family and neighborhood? Those who define deviance by the labeling perspective have not, according to one critic, been specific in the kinds of reactions that identify behavior as deviant.[63] If the reaction to homosexuals, for example, is quite mild, are they deviants? A further problem relates to the differential effects of labeling. One study found that blacks are far less susceptible than whites to adverse labels with regard to criminal behavior.[64] Thus, even when the degree of reaction is held constant, differential effects of the negative label are seen.

Who Is Deviant?

A major consequence of a labeling definition of deviance is that it largely restricts the concept of deviance to the lower classes, since the acts for which one is labeled are far more numerous in this group. Persons who engage in acts that are largely not labeled, because of social and economic position, escape the appellation of deviant.

> Because of these biases, there is an implicit, but very clear, acceptance by these authors [labeling theorists] of the current definitions of "deviance." It comes about because they concentrate their attention on those who have been successfully labeled as "deviant" and not those who break laws, fix laws, violate ethical standards, harm individuals and groups, etc., but who either are able to hide their actions, or, when known, can deflect criticism, labeling and punishment.[65]

What Are the Effects of Labels?

The evidence contradicts the claims that the application of formal sanctions, particularly when severe and frequent, always strengthens deviant conduct patterns; the argument is that persons assume deviant roles primarily because they have been labeled by others as deviants, and because they are excluded from resuming nondeviant roles in the community. In spite of contrary claims, labeling is not a necessary and sufficient condition for all secondary or career deviance even though this is more likely

---

[63]Jack P. Gibbs, "Conceptions of Deviant Behavior: The Old and the New," *Pacific Sociological Review*, 9 (1966), 12.

[64]Anthony R. Harris, "Race, Commitment to Deviance, and Spoiled Identity," *American Sociological Review*, 41 (1976), 432–442. Also see Harris, "Imprisonment and the Expected Value of Criminal Choice: A Specification and Test of Aspects of the Labeling Perspective," *American Sociological Review*, 40 (1975), 71–87.

[65]Alexander Liazos, "The Poverty of the Sociology of Deviance: Nuts, Sluts, and Preverts," *Social Problems*, 20 (1972), 109. See also Bob Fine, "Labeling Theory: An Investigation into the Sociological Critique of Deviance," *Economy and Society*, 6 (1977), 166–193.

to be the case in certain instances. In this connection, one can distinguish between achieved and ascribed rule-breaking.[66] In ascribed deviance, the rule-breaking is characterized by particular visible physical disabilities such as mental retardation; achieved deviance involves activities, such as those of a professional criminal, on the part of the rule-breaker.[67] The severely crippled, the blind, the obese, the spastic, the mentally retarded, stutterers, and those with severe facial disfigurements may encounter labeling because of imputed undesirable differences from what other persons believe is normal or appropriate. As a result of their being stigmatized, the social identity of the person is affected.[68] For these persons the physical condition constitutes a necessary condition for labeling and career deviance.

On the other hand, labeling does not appear to be necessary for achieved deviance. The achieved types of deviants can have deviant careers without ever having been "forced" into them by formal or informal agents of social control.[69] Many choose deviance as a way of life and are not forced to remain deviants because of the effects of any stigma; simply, they do not wish to conform. Ample empirical evidence supports the conclusion that a deviant career can develop without arrest or other official sanctions, as has been supported in studies, for example, of systematic check forgery,[70] embezzlement,[71] use of marijuana,[72] and homosexuality. In a study of three groups of homosexuals, it was found that the group never arrested or seen by a psychiatrist played a more confirmed homosexual role than the group who had.[73] Delinquent gang behavior may occasionally become highly sophisticated, yet with minimal or no contacts with the law, and offenders who have legitimate occupations, such as white-collar criminals, may pursue careers in deviance without ever having been sanctioned and often even without the fear of sanctioning.[74] Women alcoholics often are "secret" drinkers who have never been arrested and whose alcoholism has not been known to many persons. Physicians have one of the highest narcotic addiction rates, yet they are seldom detected and labeled by the authorities as drug addicts. More than half a million persons may presently be regular and frequent users of marijuana and presumably part of the marijuana subculture, but few of them have been arrested or otherwise labeled.[75]

---

[66]Milton Mankoff, "Societal Reaction and Career Deviance: A Critical Analysis," *The Sociological Quarterly,* 12 (1971), 204–218.

[67]Mankoff (p. 207) says: "Ascribed deviance is based upon rule-breaking phenomena that fulfill all the requirements of the labeling paradigm: highly 'visible' rule-breaking that is totally *dependent* upon the societal reaction of community members while being totally *independent* of the actions and intentions of rule-breakers".

[68]Eliot Freidson, "Disability as Social Deviance," in Marvin B. Sussman, ed., *Sociology and Rehabilitation* (Washington, D.C.: American Sociological Association, 1966).

[69]Mankoff, p. 211.

[70]Edwin M. Lemert, "An Isolation Closure Theory of Naive Check Forgery," *Journal of Criminal Law, Criminology and Police Science,* 44 (1953), 296–307.

[71]Donald R. Cressey, *Other People's Money* (Belmont, Calif.: Wadsworth, 1973), originally published in 1953.

[72]Becker, Chapter 3, "Becoming a Marijuana User."

[73]Michael Schofield, *Sociological Aspects of Homosexuality: A Comparative Study of Three Types of Homosexuals* (Boston: Little, Brown, 1965).

[74]Marshall B. Clinard and Richard Quinney, *Criminal Behavior Systems: A Typology* (New York: Holt, Rinehart and Winston, 1967), pp. 130–139, and Geis and Meier.

[75]See *Marijuana: A Signal of Misunderstanding.* First report of the National Commission on Marijuana and Drug Abuse (Washington, D.C.: Government Printing Office, 1972).

One of the most careful large-scale studies of the effects of imprisonment concluded that two thirds of the parolees were not recidivists (repeaters) two to five years later.[76] Although the subjective nature of the responses may be questioned, Glaser found that the postprison adjustment of inmates was due more to their unrealistic aspirations and lack of skills than to the stigma of imprisonment. It was concluded, in a more recent study, that the recidivism rate for released inmates may be decreasing below the one-third figure indicated above, actually closer to one quarter, in spite of the fact that penalties for crimes have generally increased in the past two decades, thereby increasing the stigma.[77] This appears to indicate that something other than labeling is involved in recidivism.

It has also been claimed that once a person is labeled by commitment to a mental hospital, breaking out of the deviant status is difficult. Unfortunately, these conclusions are often based on unrepresentative samples of long-term mental hospital commitments where social isolation and apathy were as important, or more so, than labeling. Studies indicate that the extent of rehospitalization is not as great as the labeling position has assumed; in one study, two thirds of the patients had not been hospitalized after seven years, and even in those cases few of the readmissions had been urged by relatives.[78] Most hospitalization is actually positive in the sense that it improves family relationships. The label "illness" may remove alienation of others, help erase the effects of long-term personal quarrels, and give the patient an opportunity to make new adjustments. In fact, one researcher maintains that the behavior in much mental disorder determines the expectations of others to a much greater degree than does the reverse situation.[79] The expectations of others may play some labeling role, but that role is more likely to be in terms of previous patterns of eccentric or unusual behavior.

Is Labeling a Theory?

Finally, subsequent labeling studies must ultimately rely upon making the approach more theoretical and rigorous in order to derive testable propositions that can be compared with empirical evidence.[80] Labeling "theory" has not yet attained this state of development, as has been amply demonstrated by the fact that there is considerable confusion concerning what constitutes supportive and negative evidence and what the overall conclusion from that evidence is. One study may be interpreted as negative by one investigator while another interprets it as supportive.[81] Propositions derived

---

[76]Daniel Glaser, *The Effectiveness of a Prison and Parole System* (Indianapolis: Bobbs-Merrill, 1964).

[77]Robert Martinson and Judith Wilks, reported in *Criminal Justice Newsletter,* 7 (October 25, 1976), 1–2.

[78]Walter R. Gove, "Societal Reaction as an Explanation of Mental Illness: An Investigation," *American Sociological Review,* 35 (1970), 873–884.

[79]See Walter R. Gove, "Labeling and Mental Illness: A Critique," in Walter R. Gove, ed., *The Labeling of Deviance: Evaluating a Perspective* (New York: Sage/Halsted, 1975), pp. 35–81.

[80]See Jack P. Gibbs and Maynard L. Erickson, "Major Developments in the Sociological Study of Deviance," *Annual Review of Sociology,* 1 (1975), 21–42.

[81]Compare, for example, Walter R. Gove, "Deviant Behavior, Social Intervention, and Labeling Theory," in Lewis A. Coser and Otto N. Larson, eds., *The Uses of Controversy in Sociology* (New York: Free Press, 1976), pp. 219–227; and Patrick W. Conover, "A Reassessment of Labeling Theory: A Constructive Response to Criticism," in Coser and Larson, pp. 228–243.

from a labeling perspective have not found adequate support, for example, in the empirical literature about crime and other forms of deviance.[82]

DEVIANCE AS CONFLICT

The conflict approach to deviance has been implicit in several of the theories previously examined here. Elements of a conflictlike explanation can be seen, for example, in the anomie tradition, where conflict is apparent between the haves and the have-nots. "Anomie is not simply a theory of the conflict between means and ends, but between those who are able to utilize legitimate means to gain access to socially approved goals, and those who resort to other mechanisms because opportunities to reach these goals by normative paths are blocked."[83] The labeling perspective emphasizes more strongly group conflict in the rule-making process, which forms the basis for the labeling of others.[84] To labelists, it is essential to look at the rule-creation process in order to discover whose rules are being violated and who has the power to label behavior as deviant. These rules constitute the "object of conflict and disagreement, part of the political process of society."[85] In the labeling perspective the origin of rules must be examined, because "people are always *forcing* their rules on others, applying them more or less against the will and without the consent of those others."[86]

Sociological conflict theory relies heavily on these ideas, while at the same time making much more explicit the political conditions under which certain kinds of rules are likely to arise.[87] Most writings within the conflict perspective pertaining to deviance have been related to criminality, but this approach also appears to be relevant to other forms of deviance.[88] The conflict view stresses the pluralistic nature of society and the differential distribution of political and social power among these groups. Because of the power they possess, some groups can create rules, particularly laws, that serve their own interests, often to the exclusion of the interests of others. In this respect, one has a view of society that recognizes differences in interests which groups consider essential, that the different groups will conflict with one another over interests that are not compatible with one another, and that those groups with sufficient power will create rules and laws to guarantee that their interests will be served.[89] Strong negative attitudes toward suicide, prostitution, homosexuality, drunkenness, and other forms of

---

[82]See Charles Wellford, "Labeling Theory and Criminology: An Assessment," *Social Problems,* 22 (1975), 323–345. See also Gove.

[83]Edward Sagarin, *Deviants and Deviance: An Introduction to the Study of Disvalued People and Behavior* (New York: Holt, Rinehart and Winston, 1975), p. 158.

[84]Meier.

[85]Becker, p. 19.

[86]Becker, pp. 17–18. Emphasis Becker's.

[87] See William J. Chambliss, ed., *Sociological Readings in the Conflict Perspective* (Reading, Mass.: Addison-Wesley, 1973).

[88]See Steven Spitzer, "Toward a Marxian Theory of Deviance," *Social Problems,* 22 (1975), 638–651.

[89]See, especially, Richard Quinney, *Criminology: Analysis and Critique of Crime in America* (Boston: Little, Brown, 1975), pp. 37–41; and Richard Quinney and John Wildeman, *The Problem of Crime: A Critical Introduction to Criminology* (New York: Harper & Row, 1977), pp. 2–35.

behavior have stemmed, for the most part, from certain church groups who regard such behavior as immoral. Opposition to the use of marijuana, nudity, and the distribution of pornographic materials rests with other "moral entrepreneurs" who attempt to impose their views on others. According to the conflict view, most crime represents behavior that conflicts sharply with the interests of the segments of society with the power to shape criminal policy. Moreover, these groups control the enforcement and the administration of the criminal law through such agents as the police and the courts.[90]

Deviance and Marx

Many of these contemporary ideas on the importance of social conflict in society generally can be traced to such older sociological theorists as Karl Marx, George Simmel, and more recently Louis Coser and Ralf Dahrendorf, to whom society is not a consensus but a struggle between social classes and class conflict, between powerful and less powerful groups. In fact, today most conflict writers in deviance and in crime identify themselves as "Marxists." Marx, for example, viewed society as composed primarily of two groups with incompatible economic interests: the bourgeois and the proletariat. The bourgeois are the ruling class—they are the wealthy, they control the means of economic production, have inordinate influence over the society's political and economic institutions, and have at their disposal great power to serve their interests. The proletariat, on the other hand, are the ruled—they are the workers whose labor the bourgeois exploits. The state is not a neutral party to the inevitable conflicts that arise between the two groups; it serves mainly to cushion the threats of the ruled against the rulers, and to foster the interests of the rulers. Marx foretold that as capitalism developed there would be a proliferation of criminal laws, since laws are considered important mechanisms by which the rulers maintain order. First, the laws can define certain conduct as illegal, particularly conduct that might pose a threat to the rulers' interests. Second, a law legitimizes the intervention of society's social control apparatus through the police, the courts, and correctional systems, all forces to be used against the ruled, whose behavior is most likely to be in violation of the law. In this sense, the criminal law comes to "side" with the upper classes against the lower classes. Marx's conception of conflict is ultimately tied to a particular economic system, capitalism; in this system it is inevitable that a major division will develop based on the means of production and the economic interests of persons, depending upon whether they own these means or work for those who do own them.

Recent Conflict Theorists

The conflict approach to crime is generally identified with the works of George Vold, Richard Quinney, Austin Turk, Ian Taylor, Paul Walton, Jock Young, Anthony Platt,

---

[90]See Richard Quinney, *Critique of Legal Order: Crime Control in Capitalist Society* (Boston: Little, Brown, 1974), especially pp. 51–135.

Paul Takagi, and William Chambliss, along with others.[91] These writers view criminal behavior as a reflection of power differentials in the sense that crime comes to be defined as a function of social-class position. Since the elite and the powerless have different interests, whatever benefits the elite will work against the interests of the powerless. It is not surprising, therefore, that the officially recorded crime rates are substantially higher in the lower classes than in the more privileged classes from which the elite are recruited. Since the elite also control the law-making as well as the law-enforcement process, the nature and content of criminal laws will coincide with their interests.[92] Laws relating to theft, for example, are said to have been enacted by persons in positions of power who have more to lose from stealing. It is no social accident, moreover, that these particular laws are invariably broken by persons in the lower, less powerful classes whose temptation toward theft is greater.

Conflict theorists regard crime as a rational act.[93] Persons who steal and rob have been forced into these acts by social conditions brought about by the inequitable distribution of wealth, while corporate crime is directed at protecting and augmenting the capital of its owners.[94] Organized crime is a rational way of supplying illegal needs in a capitalist society.

Law has also become the tool by which the ruling class exercises its control of the ruled. In addition to protecting the property of the elite, it serves to repress other political threats to the position of the elite through the coercive response of the criminal justice system. Quinney writes that while the state is the instrument of the ruling class, contrary to conventional wisdom, "law is the state's coercive weapon, with which it maintains the social and economic order. Criminal law in particular is established and enforced to secure domestic order. We understand crime in society as part of the capitalist state's political reality and that of its dominant class."[95]

---

[91]George B. Vold, *Theoretical Criminology* (New York: Oxford University Press, 1958); Quinney, *Criminology;* Quinney, *Critique of Legal Order;* Quinney and Wildeman, *The Problem of Crime;* Austin Turk, *Criminality and Legal Order* (Chicago: Rand McNally, 1969); Austin T. Turk, "Conflict and Criminality," *American Sociological Review,* 31 (1966), 338–352; Ian Taylor, Paul Walton, and Jock Young, *The New Criminology: For a Social Theory of Deviance* (London: Routledge & Kegan Paul, 1973); Ian Taylor, Paul Walton and Jock Young, eds., *Critical Criminology* (London: Routledge & Kegan Paul, 1975); Tony Platt, "Prospects for a Radical Criminology in the United States," *Crime and Social Justice,* 1 (1974), 2–10; Paul Takagi, "A Garrison State in a 'Democratic' Society," *Crime and Social Justice,* 1 (1974), 27–33; William J. Chambliss, "Functional and Conflict Theories of Crime: The Heritage of Emile Durkheim and Karl Marx," in William J. Chambliss and Milton Mankoff, eds., *Whose Law? Whose Order? A Conflict Approach to Criminology* (New York: Wiley, 1976), pp. 1–28; William J. Chambliss, "The State, the Law, and the Definition of Behavior as Criminal or Delinquent," in Daniel Glaser, ed., *Handbook of Criminology* (Chicago: Rand McNally, 1974), pp. 7–44; and William J. Chambliss, ed., *Sociological Readings in the Conflict Perspective* (Reading, Mass.: Addison-Wesley, 1973).
[92]Barry Krisberg, *Crime and Privilege: Toward a New Criminology* (Englewood Cliffs, N.J.: Prentice-Hall, 1975); and Taylor, Walton and Young, *The New Criminology.*
[93]Taylor, Walton and Young, *The New Criminology,* p. 221.
[94]David M. Gordon, "Capitalism, Class and Crime in America," *Crime and Delinquency,* 19 (1973), 163–186.
[95]Quinney, *Criminology,* p. 285. For a discussion of the role of law in settling or instigating conflicts see Austin T. Turk, "Law as a Weapon of Social Conflict," *Social Problems,* 23 (1976), 276–291. While older conceptions of the law saw it as a mechanism for settling disputes, the conflict theorists perceive the law as a mechanism for class conflict; it creates conflicts between disputing parties. Also see Richard Quinney, *Class, State and Crime: On the Theory and Practice of Criminal Justice* (New York: David McKay, 1977).

The conflict theorists perceive crime as an unchangeable feature of capitalist society. The United States is one of the most advanced capitalist societies, and its crime rates are among the highest in the world today. Since the country is organized to promote capitalism, it is organized to serve the interests of the dominant economic class, the capitalist ruling class. In this way the state, law, and criminal justice systems are organized to promote the interests of a few, because under capitalism "the system of coercion and punishment is intimately connected with the inequitable distribution of wealth."[96] Access to criminal opportunities vary by class; the poor can hardly engage in embezzlement or corporate crime, so they must instead choose burglary and mugging.

Capitalism is directed at maintaining conditions for profit accumulation and social harmony.[97] During times of social disorder, as during economic depressions, urban riots, labor disputes, and outbreaks of racial violence, the state uses the mechanisms of social control, particularly the criminal justice system, to establish order through coercion or the threat of coercion.[98] In this sense, a system of unequal power, a self-motivated elite and a coercive and repressive society based on capitalist economic principles, will perpetuate crime by defining as criminal those acts that are not consistent with the interests of the elite. The root cause of crime is the domination of one class over another, which is a characteristic of capitalistic societies. The implications of this view for the eradication of crime are clear: "Only with the collapse of capitalistic society, based on socialist principles, will there be a solution to the crime problem."[99]

The conflict model has made an important contribution to the study of deviance. It has focused attention dramatically on the role of the political, economic, and social structure in the definition of deviance, particularly through laws of the political state. The conflict theorists point out basic problems and contradictions of contemporary capitalism in their sharply worded analyses. They note that much of crime is a reflection of societal values and not merely a violation of those values.[100] The basic issue is how values are translated into crimes and other rules, and it is on this that conflict theory focuses. Several problems are associated with the conflict view, however, even though much of the general perspective is valid if overstated. More specifically, the following limitations of the theory are noted.

Explanation of Rules or Behavior?

The conflict theory does little to inform us about the process whereby a person comes to commit crimes or to develop deviance. It does raise pertinent questions about the origin of laws and norms, but it is less an explanation of deviance than it is an

---

[96]Takagi, p. 32.

[97]See James O'Connor, *The Fiscal Crisis of the State* (New York: St. Martin's Press, 1973); and Ralph Miliband, *The State in Capitalist Society* (New York: Basic Books, 1966).

[98]See, for example, the discussion in Spitzer.

[99]Quinney, *Criminology,* p. 291.

[100]Paul C. Friday, "Changing Theory and Research in Criminology," *International Journal of Criminology and Penology,* 5 (1977), 159–170.

explanation for the formation and enforcement of certain rules and laws.[101] To the conflict theorists, the basic structure of a society, both economic and social, shapes the behavior of individuals and not socialization processes or peer-group and subcultural patterns.[102] When the conflict approach does deal with the individual, it is assumed that deviance is a rational and purposive activity. Because the socialization process is ignored, it is assumed that deviance is a rational process in which behavior is selected from available norms, values, and roles.

Other Sources of Conflict

This approach, unfortunately, is overly restricted to the relation of social class and economic power interests to rules regulating deviance and crime. Greater merit would be seen in the approach if deviance and crime were assumed to be outgrowths of much broader conflicts of interest groups that include not only social class and economic interests but other power conflicts based, for example, on religion, sex, age, occupation, race and ethnicity, and those attempting to regulate morality or to protect the environment.[103]

Who Benefits?

Not all laws are necessarily devised by and operated for the advantage of the interest of one particular group. The conflict approach may be more applicable to those acts that generate disagreement about their deviant nature, such as political crime, prostitution, the use of certain drugs, and homosexuality, rather than acts that reveal no such disagreement. In fact, it would appear that most acts presently defined in the United States as conventional or ordinary crime have general consensus in regard to both the illegal nature of the behavior and the seriousness of the act.[104] Laws against homicide, robbery, burglary, and assault benefit all members of society, regardless of economic position. Any statement that the elite alone benefit from such laws neglects the fact that most victims of these offenses are other poor, lower-class urban residents and not members of any elite, however broadly defined. Although certainly the elite may have more property to lose from a theft or robbery, persons who actually lose the most are those who are the least able to afford it. If, on the other hand, one regards the operations of the criminal justice system, one sees considerable validity in the conflict perspective. Persons who commit conventional crimes, generally from the lower class, are much more likely to be arrested, convicted, and sentenced to longer prison terms than persons who commit white-collar and corporate crimes.

---

[101]Ronald L. Akers, *Deviant Behavior: A Social Learning Approach,* 2d ed. (Belmont, Calif.: Wadsworth, 1977), p. 29.

[102]Alex Thio, "Class Bias in the Sociology of Deviance," *American Sociologist,* 8 (1973), 1–12.

[103]In his first book on conflict and crime, Quinney adopted a much broader approach than social class, particularly in his discussion of the conflict of religious interests. See Richard Quinney, *The Social Reality of Crime* (Boston: Little, Brown, 1970), pp. 37–39 and 60–72.

[104]See Peter H. Rossi. Emily Waite, Christine E. Bose, and Richard E. Berk, "The Seriousness of Crime: Normative Structure and Individual Differences," *American Sociological Review,* 39 (1974), 224–237.

The Powerful Make Rules Everywhere

The assumption that powerful groups dictate the content of the criminal law, as well as other rule-making processes, and their enforcement for the protection of their own interests is too broad an assumption. All types of groups are involved in law-making; in fact, "who can conceive of a disinterested party enacting criminal laws?"[105] Powerful groups do have substantial input into the legal structure, but this would appear to be the case in any social system, whether capitalist, socialist, or communist. By penalizing those who violate it, the criminal law always defends the existing order and those holding power in it; "and the legal order never can do less than articulate the 'social and economic order,' capitalist or socialist. How could it be otherwise?"[106] It means little to say that the rules are made by those who have something to gain from those rules. This leaves unanswered important questions that relate to the characteristics of the "powerful," the process whereby some norms are made into law and others are not, the selective enforcement of some laws, and differences in law-making and enforcement processes in different economic and political systems.

Law Does Not "Cause" Behavior

Although the conflict perspective points to the criminal law, supported by certain interest groups, as the ultimate "cause" of criminal behavior, it does not follow logically that the law is responsible for the behavior. In referring to the labeling perspective, which generates similar confusion with its emphasis on rule-making and deviance by interest groups, Sagarin observes that "without schools, there would be no truancy; without marriage, there would be no divorce; without art, there would be no art forgeries; without death, there would be neither body-snatching nor necrophilia. Those are not causes, they are necessary conditions. Just the fact that you are alive is a condition for your reading this book, but it is not a cause of it."[107] There could be no crime if there were no laws to prohibit some behavior, but the existence of a law is not sufficient to account for the behavior.

Empirical Evidence

The empirical evidence supporting the conflict perspective tends to be broad and selective. General statements are made, but substantiating empirical evidence in terms of objective scientific evidence is often lacking, or existing contradictory evidence is usually omitted.

> From the conflict perspective, there is really no research in the traditional sense. There is, in fact, a rejection of [scientific] positivism and empiricism. Conclusions of research on the social control agencies is used as theoretical support in addition to journalistic and

---

[105]Gibbs and Erickson, pp. 37–38.
[106]Ernest van den Haag, "No Excuse for Crime," *The Annals,* 423 (1976), 137.
[107]Sagarin, pp. 143–144.

"muckraking" techniques drawing major conclusions from isolated case studies. The opinion of most conflict oriented criminologists is that traditional "scientific" methodology *cannot* effectively be used to uncover social structural inconsistencies. Only the dialectical methodology can do this.[108]

Few well-designed and operationalized research studies have been made to support the conflict ideology; in fact, most have been designed to support their viewpoint and largely have not looked for negative findings. Three examples may be cited. First, most evidence offered is from an analysis of capitalist U.S. society as a whole, with little recognition of variations in the evidence by states or differences between the United States and many Western European countries. Second, it is true that conventional criminal laws are directed primarily at the lower class, but there is no recognition of the fact that even the largest corporations are increasingly being subjected to severe restrictions, heavier penalties, and stronger governmental control, largely through the activities of consumer, environmental, and other groups. This is shown in an examination of the recent reports, for example, of the Securities and Exchange Commission, the Federal Trade Commission, particularly the antitrust actions and advertising, the Food and Drug Administration, the Environmental Protection Agency, the Consumer Products Safety Division, and others, along with their numerous state counterparts. The penalties imposed by the government through these agencies are not in any way proportionate to those imposed on lower-class crimes, but it is a recognition that even the enormous corporate power in this country is subject to the control of the state. Third, variations in the sentencing of conventional offenders frequently seem to rest on factors other than class bias and political power of elite groups.[109]

Theory as Ideology

The ultimate acceptance of the conflict view depends only partially, however, on the availability of a body of empirical evidence supporting the claim of the perspective. Perhaps more than any other approach to deviance, this theory has an ideological base that will either hasten or retard its acceptance, depending upon one's political and social viewpoint. Other sociological perspectives are not completely free from ideology,[110] but the conflict theory's emphasis on combining theory and practice in a socialist framework makes more obvious and explicit the political connotations of its explanatory scheme. As one recognized conflict worker in criminology stated: "The

---

[108]Friday, p. 165.
[109]These kinds of issues are raised, if not resolved, in Theodore G. Chiricos and Gordon P. Waldo, "Socioeconomic Status and Criminal Sentencing: An Empirical Assessment of a Conflict Proposition," *American Sociological Review,* 40 (1975), 753–772; David F. Greenberg, "Socioeconomic Status and Criminal Sentences: Is There an Association?" *American Sociological Review,* 42 (1977), 174–176; Andrew Hopkins, "Is There a Class Bias in Criminal Sentencing?" *American Sociological Review,* 42 (1977), 176–177; Charles E. Reasons, "On Methodology, Theory and Ideology," *American Sociological Review,* 42 (1977), 177–181; and the rejoinder by Theodore G. Chiricos and Gordon P. Waldo, "Reply to Greenberg, Hopkins and Reasons," *American Sociological Review,* 42 (1977), 181–185.
[110]See Scott G. McNall and James C. M. Johnson, "The New Conservatives: Ethnomethodologists, Phenomenologists, and Symbolic Interactionists," *Insurgent Sociologist,* 5(1975), 49–65.

retreat from theory is over and the politicalization of crime and criminality is imminent.''[111] In fact, movement toward socialism is the end product of a fully developed conflict theory. Quinney summarizes: "The underclass, the class that must remain oppressed for the triumph of the dominant economic class, will continue to be the object of crime control as long as the dominant class seeks to perpetuate itself, that is, as long as capitalism exists.''[112] If the elimination of deviation and crime through the dissolution of capitalism and the transition to socialism are perceived to be too costly, however, the appeal of the conflict view diminishes appreciably. It is insufficient merely to analyze the conditions under which deviance develops; one must also be willing to change those conditions in a political sense. We are, thus, talking about someone who is not only committed to science as a means to discover the "real world," but who is also a political being committed to a political ideology, an ideology that, it is believed, would eradicate deviance. Appeals to these issues as testable propositions, empirical evidence, and the putting into operation of key concepts and variables will only question the scientific status of the perspective, leaving untouched the ideological.[113] Any future evaluations of the conflict view must recognize that scientific criteria must be used to test it if it is to be acceptable as a sociological theory, particularly of deviance and crime.

DEVIANCE AND CONTROL THEORY

Control theory is an approach that has been more concerned with socialization to conformity than with socialization to deviance. In most theories conformity is assumed to be nonproblematic; that is, conformity is the "natural" order of things and needs no explanation. Control theory, on the other hand, reverses the approach, because it is conformity and not deviance that requires an explanation. "The important question is not 'Why do men *not* obey the rules of society,' but rather, 'Why *do* men obey the rules of society?'"[114] The control theory attempts to integrate theories of conformity with theories of deviance, and in this context control theorists assert that deviance is not caused as much by forces that motivate persons to deviate as it is simply by the fact that deviance is not prevented.[115] The focus of this prevention is social control, the most effective component of which is the social bond between an individual and society. The social control process "motivates" one to conform through the socialization process, which leads to a commitment on the part of the person to conform.[116]

---

[111]Taylor, Walton, and Young, *The New Criminology,* p. 28.

[112]Quinney, *Critique of the Legal Order,* p. 16.

[113]The political dimensions of the conflict view are apparent in most writings and are perhaps best exemplified in the work of Richard Quinney. He has provided the most explicit statement to date of the relationship between theory and practice, and deviance and capitalism. His work also makes clear the political course of action that must be taken if there is a commitment to the conflict perspective. See especially Quinney, *Class, State and Crime.*

[114]Travis Hirschi, *Causes of Delinquency* (Berkeley: University of California Press, 1969), p. 10.

[115]See F. Ivan Nye, *Family Relationships and Delinquent Behavior* (New York: Wiley, 1958), pp. 3–9.

[116]Walter Reckless, *The Crime Problem,* 4th ed. (New York: Appleton, 1973), pp. 55–57.

Control theory has its origins in the emphasis on social integration in the pioneer work of the famed sociologist of deviance Emile Durkheim. The theoretical problem that concerned Durkheim was the nature of the social order in complex societies. He asked how the social order can be maintained in view of the increased division of labor and the social differentiation, both of which, it would appear, are more conducive to social disorder. Durkheim sought the answer in the concept of "integration" and the bond of commitment that develops between the person and his larger social group.[117] He ambitiously studied what was thought to be a highly individualistic behavior, suicide, trying to explain it exclusively in social and group terms. His analysis indicated that, as predicted, suicide rates vary inversely with the degree of a person's social integration into society; for example, rates among Catholics were found to be lower than among Protestants, the Catholic Church providing its members with a greater sense of group belonging and participation.

Hirschi has provided what is probably the most explicit statement of control theory, identifying four components of the person's bond with society that tend to prevent deviance.[118] *Attachment,* the first element of the bond, refers to the extent to which the person is bound to the norms of his group through the socialization process. The term "internalization" describes the process by which norms become part of an individual and are incorporated into the person's cognitive and behavioral repertoire. *Commitment* is that element which describes the degree to which the person develops a "stake" in conforming behavior so that acts of deviance jeopardize other, more valued, conditions and activities.[119] Concern over one's reputation or being expelled from school or losing one's job are examples of commitment. *Involvement* refers to physical activity of a nondeviant nature: at the simplest level, little time is left for delinquency if one spends much time playing basketball, for example. Continued involvement in conventional activities also leads to strengthening of commitment. *Belief* refers to a person's allegiance to the dominant value system of his group. These values may assume the nature of moral imperatives for the individual, and it would be unthinkable to violate them.

Some forms of deviance are claimed to arise as a result of a lack of control. Delinquency and youth crime result from the failure of youth to have sufficient commitment to the traditional goals and values of society. The use of certain drugs, for example, depends upon one's own attitude toward using them as well as upon a perception of the strength of the norm regulating drug use and the influence other people have on one's sense of morality regarding their use.[120] Presumably, if the norm were strong enough and one's sense of morality makes one feel that taking drugs is wrong, the act will not occur. Problem drinking may also be prevented through a socialization process that stresses antialcohol attitudes over a long period of time.

---

[117]Emile Durkheim, *The Division of Labor in Society* (New York: Free Press, 1960).

[118]Hirschi, pp. 16–26.

[119]See Jackson Toby, "Social Disorganization and Stake in Conformity: Complementary Factors in the Predatory Behavior of Hoodlums," *Journal of Criminal Law, Criminology and Police Science,* 48 (1957), 12–17.

[120]Richard J. Pomazal and James D. Brown, "Understanding Drug Use Motivation: A New Look at a Current Problem," *Journal of Health and Social Behavior,* 18 (1977), 212–222.

The control approach has largely been applied only to delinquency and to youth crime.[121] It seems to have some merit in explaining, in part, some types of youth crime, certain drug use, and even suicide, but for most forms of deviance it is far too simplistic in theoretical design and in application. Moreover, the core of the problem is the meaning of conformity. What actually is conformity? What power segments define and support the conformist position? All of this presents the same difficulties of defining deviance, which is merely the reverse mirror of conformity. Control theory places great stress on the socialization process to explain conforming behavior. One of the products of effective socialization, however, is that persons learn that, under certain circumstances, deviance can lead to quicker and at times easier goal attainment than can conforming behavior.

SOCIALIZATION

The last theory of deviance to be presented will be described as socialization, adopted as the central frame of reference for this book. Incorporated into this approach at the same time will be certain aspects of the effects of labeling and the role of power in social conflict. The socialization approach has certain weaknesses, to be pointed out from time to time, but it seems best fitted in relation to the facts about deviance. Deviance, as it is presented by normative violations, is here approached as a learned phenomenon according to the same basic processes through which conformity is learned. Although the basic processes are the same, the direction and content of the learning may differ. The process of how acquiring norms, social roles, and self-conception represent socialization has been discussed in some detail in Chapter 2, and thus the details are omitted here. Participation in subcultures and countercultures plays a major part in this socialization process and thus has been emphasized in Chapter 1.

Sutherland's Theory

Deviance is the consequence of the learned acquisition of deviant norms and values, particularly those learned within the framework of subcultures and countercultures. The best-known socialization or general learning theory in these terms is Edwin H. Sutherland's theory of *differential association,* one of the most widely known theories in sociology. (see p. 171). Sutherland's theory was developed to account for crime, but actually it is a perspective that accounts as well for both the etiology, or the "cause" of an individual's deviance, and the epidemiology, or the "distribution," of deviance in terms of various rates. This combination requires an analysis of conflicting deviant and nondeviant social organizations or subcultures (differential organizations) and a social psychological approach to deviation at the individual level in terms of conflicting deviant and nondeviant associations (differential associations). In propositional form Sutherland's theory is stated in terms of its application to crime and the

---

[121]An application of various theories to the study of cases of deviance found the control theory to be the most satisfactory explanation of the behavior. See Charles E. Frazier, *Theoretical Approaches to Deviance: An Evaluation* (Columbus, O.: Charles E. Merrill, 1976), p. 210.

criminal, but the concept is modified here to apply to other forms of deviant behavior such as prostitution, drug addiction, alcoholism, and homosexual behavior, along with other forms of deviance. Certain modifications in the propositions to apply to drug addiction have already been done in one study.[122] These propositions of Sutherland's theory of differential association, with the modifications, are as follows:

1. Deviant behavior is learned.[123] This means that deviance is not inherited; nor is it the result of low intelligence, brain damage, and so on.

2. Deviant behavior is learned in interaction with other persons in a process of communication.

3. The principal part of the learning of deviant behavior occurs within intimate, personal groups. At most, communications such as the mass media of television, magazines, and newspapers play only a secondary role in the learning of deviance.

4. When deviant behavior is learned, the learning includes (a) techniques of deviance, which are sometimes very complicated, sometimes quite simple; and (b) the specific direction of motives, drives, rationalizations, and attitudes.

5. The specific direction of motives and drives is learned from definitions of norms as favorable or unfavorable. This proposition acknowledges the existence of conflicting norms. An individual may learn reasons for both adhering to and violating a given rule. For example, stealing is wrong—that is, unless the goods are insured and, of course, nobody really gets hurt.

6. A person becomes deviant because of an excess of definitions favorable to violation of norms over definitions unfavorable to violation of norms. This is the key proposition of the theory. An individual's behavior is affected by contradictory learning experiences, but the predominance of deviant definitions leads to deviant behavior. It is important to note that the associations are not necessarily only deviant *persons* but also definitions, norms, or patterns of behavior. Furthermore, in keeping with the notion of a learning theory, the proposition can be phrased: A person becomes nondeviant because of an excess of definitions unfavorable to violation of norms.

7. Differential associations may vary in frequency, duration, priority, and intensity. Frequency and duration are self-explanatory. Priority refers to the time in one's life when exposed to the association. Intensity concerns the prestige of the source of the behavior pattern.

8. The process of learning deviant behavior by association with deviant and nondeviant patterns involves all of the mechanisms that are involved in any other learning. Again, there is no unique learning process associated with acquiring deviant ways of behaving.

9. While deviant behavior is an expression of general needs and values, it is not

---

[122]See Rita Volkman and Donald R. Cressey, "Differential Association and the Rehabilitation of Drug Addicts," in John A. O'Donnell and John C. Ball, eds., *Narcotic Addiction* (New York: Harper & Row, 1966).

[123]The propositions are from Edwin H. Sutherland and Donald R. Cressey, *Criminology*, 10th ed. (Philadelphia: Lippincott, 1978), derived from pp. 80–82. Substitution of the term "deviant" for the original "crime" has been made by the authors. The amplification of each proposition is adapted from Charles H. McCaghy, *Deviant Behavior: Crime, Conflict and Interest Groups* (New York: Macmillan, 1976), pp. 66–67.

explained by those general needs and values, since nondeviant behavior is an expression of the same needs and values. A "need for recognition" can be used to explain mass murder, running for President, or a .320 batting average, but it really explains nothing since it apparently accounts for both deviant and nondeviant actions.

Some Evidence

In spite of its shortcomings, no other theory of deviance has generated such a favorable long-term acceptance as this socialization or differential association theory first presented by Sutherland in 1939. Its appeal has largely been based upon its flexibility in meeting simultaneously both the sociological and social psychological aspects of deviance. At the social-psychological level, the theory can account in a large part for the processes by which one individual, not a deviant at time A, becomes one at time B as a result of the learning process described in Sutherland's nine propositions. The theory is equally explanatory at the sociological or group level, thus accounting for the differential rates of deviance among groups, some of whom contain or exhibit higher rates of deviance than others. Arrest and conviction statistics reveal, for example, a ratio of males, urban residents, persons of lower socioeconomic status, and some minorities disproportionately higher than their distribution in the general population.[124] Sutherland's theory explains this disequilibrium on the basis that these groups are more exposed to deviant norms and thus have a higher probability of learning, internalizing, and acting on these norms. Even changes in the official rates of deviance for one group, females, would tend to support the differential theory. Official crime rates for females have traditionally remained low, except for a short period of increased rates during World War II. Even with this increase, however, rates of female criminality generally declined after the war, only to increase again in recent years.[125] In terms of differential association theory this can be explained by the increased opportunities for women during World War II to participate more fully in the general society and thus be more exposed to deviant norms. The more recent rate increases have been due to increased learning opportunities for women, together with changes in traditional sex roles, which had previously often placed a high premium on female submissiveness and a "stay-at-home" attitude.

The socialization theory may also describe in general terms any learning process that ultimately leads to deviance. Forcible rape, for example, may result from the separate and unequal socialization process for both males and females through which traditional masculine qualities (for example, aggressiveness, power, strength, dominance, and competitiveness) may be translated into aggressive sexual behavior.[126] Similarly, the role of peers and drinking companions may greatly influence attitudes

[124]See Federal Bureau of Investigation, *Uniform Crime Reports—1975* (Washington, D.C.: Government Printing Office, 1976). See also Michael J. Hindelang, "Race and Involvement in Common Law Personal Crimes," *American Sociological Review*, 43 (1978), pp. 93–109.
[125]See Freda Adler, *Sisters in Crime: The Rise of the New Female Criminal* (New York: McGraw-Hill, 1975); and Rita James Simon, *Women and Crime* (Lexington, Mass.: Heath, 1975).
[126]Diana Russell, *The Politics of Rape: The Victim's Perspective* (New York: Stein and Day, 1975). Also see Anne Vinsel, "Rape: A Review Essay," *Personality and Social Psychology Bulletin*, 3 (1977), 183–189.

toward, and behavior with, alcohol; patronage of particular taverns may increase the amount consumed, not because the alcohol is available but because it is a socially approved, integral part of the social interaction in these settings.[127]

Contrary Evidence

Socialization theory, as well as the more specific applications, as in differential association, has been the subject of some criticism. The most common criticism is that the theory tends to present an oversocialized conception of human beings in which the differential response in the form of individual motivation and rational actions are not sufficiently considered.[128] Dennis Wrong has argued, for example, that it is common in socialization theory to claim that people internalize social norms and seek a favorable self-image by conforming to the expectations of others.[129]

The learning of deviant norms and behavior patterns parallels the learning of nondeviant norms and behavior patterns; what differs, of course, is the content of the learning. The oversocialized conception of human beings sensitizes us to the dangers of claiming that all deviant acts are the result of learning. This is not the case, and we have included (see Chapter 15) a discussion of one form of deviance that does not require learning: physical disabilities. In spite of criticisms, however, socialization theory seems to offer the most adequate perspective to explain deviance. It has been elaborated in Chapter 2, and it will be used as a frame of reference later in an examination of various forms of deviant behavior.

SELECTED REFERENCES

Becker, Howard S. *Outsiders: Studies in the Sociology of Deviance*, enl. ed. New York: Free Press, 1973.

Chambliss, William J., and Milton Mankoff, eds. *Whose Law? Whose Order? A Conflict Approach to Criminology*. New York: Wiley, 1976.

Clinard, Marshall B., ed. *Anomie and Deviant Behavior*. New York: Free Press, 1964.

Davis, F. James, and Richard Stivers, eds. *The Collective Definition of Deviance*. New York: Free Press, 1975.

Davis, Nanette J. *Sociological Constructions of Deviance: Perspectives and Issues in the Field*. Dubuque, Ia.: William C. Brown, 1975.

Gibbons, Don C., and Joseph F. Jones. *The Study of Deviance: Perspectives and Problems*. Englewood Cliffs, N.J.: Prentice-Hall, 1975.

Gibbs, Jack P., and Maynard L. Erickson. "Major Developments in the Sociology of Deviance," *Annual Review of Sociology*, 1 (1975), 21–45.

Gove, Walter R., ed. *The Labelling of Deviance: Evaluating a Perspective*. New York: Sage/Halstead, 1975.

---

[127]See, for example, E. E. LeMasters, *Blue-Collar Aristocrats: Life-Styles in a Working-Class Tavern* (Madison: University of Wisconsin Press, 1975).

[128]For specific criticisms of differential association and a reply to them, see Sutherland and Cressey, pp. 83–95.

[129]Dennis Wrong, "The Oversocialized Conception of Man in Modern Sociology," *American Sociological Review*, 26 (1961), 183–193.

Hirschi, Travis. *Causes of Delinquency.* Berkeley: University of California Press, 1969.

Krisberg, Barry. *Crime and Privilege: Toward a New Criminology.* Englewood Cliffs, N.J.: Prentice-Hall, 1975.

Lemert, Edwin M. *Human Deviance, Social Problems, and Social Control,* 2d ed. Englewood Cliffs, N.J.: Prentice-Hall, 1972.

McCaghy, Charles H. *Deviant Behavior: Crime, Conflict, and Interest Groups.* New York: Macmillan, 1976.

Meier, Robert F. "The New Criminology: Continuity in Criminological Theory," *Journal of Criminal Law and Criminology,* 67 (1976), 461–469.

Merton, Robert K. *Social Theory and Social Structure,* enlarged ed. New York: Free Press, 1968.

Quinney, Richard. *Criminology: Analysis and Critique of Crime in America.* Boston: Little, Brown, 1975.

Rubington, Earl, and Martin S. Weinberg. *The Study of Social Problems,* 2d ed. New York: Oxford University Press, 1977.

Schur, Edwin M. *Labeling Deviant Behavior.* New York: Harper & Row, 1971.

Sutherland, Edwin H., and Donald R. Cressey. *Criminology,* 10th ed. Philadelphia: Lippincott, 1978, Chap. 4.

Taylor, Ian, Paul Walton, and Jock Young. *The New Criminology: For a Social Theory of Deviance.* London: Routledge & Kegan Paul, 1973.

Traub, Stuart H., and Craig B. Little, eds. *Theories of Deviance* Itasca, Ill.: F. E. Peacock, 1975.

CHAPTER 4

Sigmund Freud, founder of psychoanalysis, spent most of his career in Vienna. His theory can be considered the leading example of the individualistic approach to deviant behavior and the application of the "medical model" to human behavior.

Individualistic Theories of Deviance

S OCIOLOGICAL theories of deviance explore the social conditions that underlie deviance—how it is defined, how group and subcultural factors are related, and what the reactions toward deviance are. Individualistic theories of deviance, on the other hand, tend to try to explain the specific circumstances surrounding a person's deviance—the motivations, early family experiences, and the like—largely disregarding both problems of definitions and group and cultural factors. In this chapter, several individualistic approaches will be examined: the psychiatric, psychoanalytic, personality traits, behavior modification, and the medical mode.

Although it is necessary to refer to the "psychiatric," "psychoanalytic," "psychological," and "sociological" theories of deviant behavior, one must remember that these disciplines undergo constant modifications in theoretical orientations. It must also be kept in mind that not everyone in a given field accepts the general approach of his special area. Some psychologists and psychiatrists have a sociological approach; some sociologists have a psychological or behavior modification approach. Consequently, it might have been more practical to use neutral terms such as "position A," "position B," "position C," and so on, but this would have presented even more difficult problems. There are now indications that traditional, specialized approaches are slowly being abandoned and that research derived from the study of broad cultural and social factors is not only being increasingly utilized by psychologists and psychiatrists but is also gaining recognition among biologists. If this trend continues, the distinctions in the theoretical positions of psychiatry, clinical psychology, biology, and sociology may diminish, and a psychiatrist, for example, may apply, as a psychiatrist, a sociological approach to deviant behavior.[1] A multidisciplinary approach, which utilizes several traditional disciplines, may eventually afford a more complete understanding of contemporary problems of deviance.[2] Several universities at present have institutes of criminology on whose staffs are psychologists, sociologists, urban planners, criminologists, and lawyers.

THE PSYCHIATRIC THEORY OF DEVIANT BEHAVIOR

The psychiatric theory that deviant conduct is largely the result of childhood experiences in the family, while declining, still is popular. Psychiatry has a large following in present-day society, and literature in this field is extensive. This theory is largely supported by over 24,000 psychiatrists in the United States alone, by some clinical psychologists, and by many laymen. It is this view of deviation that is of frequent concern in popular magazines, the press, and other communications media.

---

[1]For a general discussion of this issue, see Marshall B. Clinard, "Contributions of Sociology to the Study of Deviant Behavior," British Journal of Criminology, 3 (1962), 110–129. For a recent attempt to integrate biology with the social sciences, see Edward O. Wilson, Sociobiology (Cambridge, Mass: Harvard University Press, 1975). For a rather despairing reaction to the present state of sociology and the biological alternative, see Lee Ellis, "The Decline and Fall of Sociology, 1975–2000," American Sociologist, 12 (1977), 56–66.

[2]For a description of such a program, see Arnold Binder, Daniel Stokols, and Ralph Catalano, "Social Ecology: An Emerging Multidiscipline," Journal of Environmental Education, 7 (1975), 32–44.

To a great extent this theory owes its ascendancy to the dissemination of psychiatric and psychoanalytic thought over the past decades.[3] Yet it could be said that both this idea, and indeed psychiatric thought in general, derive from more fundamental values which are rooted in the traditions of our culture. Prominent among these values are the beliefs that parents are responsible for preparing their children for adult life and that there is a relation between early childhood training and behavior in adulthood. The psychiatric position, however, implies that *certain childhood experiences have effects that transcend all other social and cultural experiences.* These proponents suggest that certain childhood incidents or family relationships lead to the formation of certain types of personalities which contain within themselves seeds of deviant or conforming behavior, irrespective of culture. Thus, childhood is the arena in which personality traits toward or away from deviance are developed, and a person's behavior after the childhood years is fundamentally the acting out of tendencies formed at that time. Essentially, these proponents offer the following psychiatric model for explaining deviant behavior.

A Psychiatric Model

1. All deviant behavior is a product of something within the individual, such as personal disorganization or "maladjusted" personality. Deviants are individuals who are psychologically "sick" persons. Culture is seen not as a determinant of deviant and conforming behavior but rather as the context within which these tendencies are expressed.

2. All persons at birth have certain inherent basic needs, in particular the need for emotional security.

3. Deprivation of universal needs during early childhood leads to the formation of particular personality patterns. Childhood experiences such as emotional conflicts largely but not exclusively determine personality structure and thus the pattern of behavior in later life. The degree of conflict, disorder, retardation, or injury to the personality will vary directly with the degree of deprivation.

4. By affecting his personality structure, a child's family experiences largely determine his behavior pattern in later life, whether deviant or nondeviant. The need for the mother to provide maternal affection is particularly stressed.

5. A high degree of certain so-called general personality traits, such as emotional insecurity, immaturity, feelings of inadequacy, inability to display affection, and aggression, characterize the deviant, but not the nondeviant. These traits are the products of early childhood experiences in the family. It is argued that because a child's first experiences with others are within the family group, traits arising there form the basis for the entire structure of personality. Deviant behavior is often a way of dealing successfully with such personality traits; for example, so-called immature or

---

[3]See Franz G. Alexander and Sheldon T. Selesnick, *The History of Psychiatry: An Evaluation of Psychiatric Thought from Prehistoric Times to the Present* (New York: Harper & Row, 1966). Psychiatrists are medical doctors who have had specialized training beyond their M.D. degree in a three-year psychiatric residency, usually from other psychiatrists. Psychoanalysts are nearly always medically trained persons who have received specialized training, usually in a psychoanalytic institute. The differences in psychiatric thinking are great, and the discussion here does not deal with those psychiatrists who take a nearly biochemical or organic approach to human behavior.

emotionally insecure persons may commit crimes, or emotionally insecure persons may drink excessively and become alcoholics.

This, then, is the basic theoretical framework on which psychiatry largely builds its explanation of deviant behavior. Each year many books and articles by psychiatrists attempt to explain such diverse forms of deviance as stealing, murder, sex offenses, delinquency, alcoholism, drug addiction, homosexuality, suicide, and mental disorders. For example, psychiatrists tend mainly to explain crime as resulting from displaced emotional aggression, mental disorder, and poor childhood environment, according to a survey of the 39 articles dealing with crime in psychiatric journals between 1966 and 1971.[4] Moreover, their interest tends to center on the more violent or bizarre types of crime rather than on property crime, including white-collar and corporate crime, which accounts by far for the major part of crime. In the 1966—1971 survey, 41 percent of published articles dealt with homicide, child murder or filicide, and child abuse.[5]

Evaluation of the Psychiatric Explanation

Criticisms of the psychiatric explanation largely involve a confusion about "sickness" and norms, the lack of objective criteria for assessing mental health, an overstatement of early childhood influences, the lack of scientific verification of their claims, and the assumption by psychiatrists that their theory is correct because of the effectiveness of psychotherapy. Psychotherapy does not necessarily follow the theory, because often it is improvised to fit individual cases. Too, the results achieved by therapy may be due to other factors, such as the intimate social relation between practitioner and patient. Certainly some favorable therapeutic results are achieved by psychiatrists working with deviants, but more and more skepticism is being expressed about the effects of psychotherapeutic methods in the treatment of severe forms of deviant behavior.

Deviance as Illness   *Psychiatric explanations of deviant behavior exemplify a blurring of the line between "sickness" and simply deviations from other norms.* According to these explanations, the presence of mental aberrations explains the occurrence of certain antisocial actions such as crime. Thus criminal or socially deviant behavior is itself made the criterion for the diagnosis of mental abnormality. In this sense, deviations from norms, or illegal behavior such as delinquency and crime, are used as the basis for inferring the presence of "sickness" or mental aberration. This tendency is similar to older attempts to link behavioral deviations with "possession by devils."[6] Moreover,

---

[4]Jan Hankin, "A Sociological Critique of Psychiatric Theories of Crime," unpublished paper, University of Wisconsin, Madison, 1972. Also see Seymour Halleck, *Psychiatry and the Dilemmas of Crime* (New York: Harper & Row, 1967); and John M. McDonald, *Psychiatry and the Criminal* (Springfield, Ill.: Charles C Thomas, 1969).

[5]Some examples are Jane and Glen Duncan, "Murder in the Family: A Study of Some Homicidal Adolescents," *American Journal of Psychiatry,* 127 (1971), 1498–1502; Steven Myers, "The Child Slayer," *Archives of General Psychiatry,* 17 (1967), 211–213; Emanuel Tanay, "Psychiatric Study of Homicide," *American Journal of Psychiatry,* 125 (1969), 1252–1258; and D. J. West, "A Note on Murders in Manhattan," *Medicine, Science and the Law,* 8 (1968), 249–255.

[6]Barbara Wootton, *Social Science and Social Pathology* (London: George Allen and Unwin, 1959), p. 207.

the varied nature of deviance and its relation to groups and the power structure are not considered. "When we relate crime to mental illness, we do not know whether the crime produced the mental illness, the mental illness the crime, or both were a product of a third factor."[7]

Unreliability of Diagnoses *Some writers, after extensive investigations, have concluded that psychiatric and psychoanalytic diagnoses are often unreliable and that psychiatrists cannot agree among themselves concerning what objective criteria are to be used in assessing degrees of mental well-being or mental aberration.*[8] To a great extent it is this very absence of objective criteria of either mental disorder or mental health that is responsible for the tendency of psychiatrists to equate "sickness" with, for example, delinquency and crime. As Mechanic has noted, the reliability of diagnoses in psychiatry is not high, since "psychiatrists disagree considerably among themselves on the meaning and applicability of the concept of mental illness."[9] Lacking such criteria, there is no way to distinguish between those whose criminal acts are excusable on the basis of mental disorder and those who, though committing criminal acts, are not mentally disordered.[10] Finding that they cannot distinguish "mentally healthy" criminals from "mentally unhealthy" ones, psychiatrists use criminal behavior itself as a criterion of mental disorder or of other abnormalities within the person. This dilemma, in essence, underlies the psychiatric explanation of deviant behavior and the psychiatric view concerning the treatment of deviants.[11] In fact, a leading psychiatrist, Thomas Szasz, and his followers have advocated since the early 1960s that the entire concept of mental disorder be abandoned, since they feel it is nonexistent and a value-laden, relativistic view of people's adjustment problems to living.[12]

Overemphasis on Childhood Experiences *Psychiatric theory has all too frequently assumed that adult behavior and personality are almost wholly determined by childhood experiences, most of them in the family, whereas evidence suggests overwhelmingly that behavior varies according to situations and social roles and that personality continues to develop throughout life.* Early family influences have probably been greatly overemphasized, sometimes to the virtual exclusion of the effect on personality of other groups such as the peer group, and of occupation, neighborhood, marriage, and other later social situations. Even in early life, the socialization of the child is

---

[7]C. Ray Jeffery, *Criminal Responsibility and Mental Disease* (Springfield, Ill.: Charles C Thomas, 1967), pp. 212–213.

[8]See Wootton, especially Chap. 7; Michael Hakeem, "A Critique of the Psychiatric Approach to Crime and Corrections," *Law and Contemporary Problems,* 22 (1958), 681–682; Michael Hakeem, "A Critique of the Psychiatric Approach to the Prevention of Juvenile Delinquency," *Social Problems,* 5 (1957–1958), 194–206; Arthur P. Miles, *American Social Work Theory* (New York: Harper & Row, 1954), pp. 122–130; Percival Bailey, "The Great Psychiatric Revolution," *American Journal of Psychiatry,* 113 (1956), 387–406; and Clinard.

[9]David Mechanic, *Mental Health and Social Policy* (Englewood Cliffs, N.J.: Prentice-Hall, 1969), p. 141. See Chapter 13, "Mental Disorder," for a further discussion of the unreliability of psychiatric diagnoses.

[10]See John Monahan, "Abolish the Insanity Defense? Not Yet." *Rutgers Law Review,* 26 (1973), 719–740.

[11]See Wootton; and Hakeem, "A Critique of the Psychiatric Approach to Crime and Corrections," for an elaboration of this problem.

[12]Thomas Szasz, *The Myth of Mental Illness* (New York: Harper & Row, 1961); and Szasz, "The Myth of Psychotherapy," *Psychotherapy and Psychosomatics,* 24 (1974), 212–221. For a critique of Szasz, see Lawrence S. Kubie, "The Myths of Thomas Szasz," *Bulletin of the Menninger Clinic,* 38 (1974), 497–502.

greatly influenced by the play group, by street play in urban areas, by preschool and kindergarten activities, and by neighbors and others such as relatives. The rigidity of character structure during the first year or two of life has been exaggerated, for life must be regarded as a continuous experience of social interaction which cannot be arbitrarily divided into infancy, childhood, and adult experience. Events occurring at 40 years of age, for example, may be explained by some occurrence at age 4. The theory of predetermination of adult behavior on the basis of heredity has largely disappeared; in its place is predeterminism based on early family interaction. For the most part, the sociological approach to deviant behavior, while certainly recognizing the importance of the family, does not agree with the psychiatric theory in its paramount emphasis on the family or on parental models as necessary determinants of either deviant or nondeviant behavior.

The previously mentioned survey of psychiatric writings on crime between 1966 and 1971 indicates a continued failure to appreciate broad social and cultural factors; in fact, only 3 of 39 articles did so. However, it would be unfair not to recognize that some psychiatrists have recently done so. In the area of crime, for example. Halleck has adopted the view that "even the most predisposed conformist will react in a criminal manner if his environment is sufficiently unfavorable,"[13] although along with this view he retains much of the traditional perspective of parental deprivation. Another psychiatrist, Diamond, has stated that "psychopathology alone . . . cannot account for the great bulk of criminal behavior. Criminal behavior is a much more complex phenomenon than most psychiatrists generally realize."[14] In a limited fashion some psychiatrists are giving recognition to broader cultural perspectives in the areas of drug use, alcoholism, mental disorder, and suicide. Part of this is the result of increased training of psychiatrists, who previously were exposed primarily to medical literature, in the social sciences. This area needs further expansion, as one psychiatrist stated as late as 1969. "Psychiatry as a branch of medicine is heavily dependent on the basic, the behavioral and social sciences. For this field which encompasses all of life, a broad education is necessary. Efforts to provide it are often woefully inadequate in our universities but also in our medical schools and psychiatric training centers."[15]

Scientific Status *Despite their claims, the explanations of psychiatrists concerning deviant behavior have not, for the most part, been scientifically verified.* The psychiatric approach has generally failed—indeed, it has often refused—to use experimental or more verifiable situations and more rigorous and controlled techniques to test hypotheses.[16] Psychiatrists often see crime, for example, as an individual's means of

---

[13]Halleck, *Psychiatry and the Dilemmas of Crime*, p. 85. Also see Seymour Halleck, "A Critique of Current Psychiatric Roles in the Legal Process," *Wisconsin Law Review*, (1966), 379–401.

[14]Bernard L. Diamond, "The Psychiatric View," in Seymour Halleck and Walter Bromberg, eds., *Psychiatric Aspects of Criminology* (Springfield, Ill.: Charles C Thomas, 1968), pp. 49–50.

[15]R. Grinker, Jr., "Emerging Concepts of Mental Illness and Models of Treatment: The Medical Model," *American Journal of Psychiatry*, 125 (1969), 865–869.

[16]See, for example, Lyle W. Shannon, "The Problem of Competence to Help," *Federal Probation*, 25 (1961), 32–39. Shannon suggests a number of positive criteria in evaluating a professional person's ability to deal effectively with deviant behavior: (1) the ability to predict human behavior; (2) the ability to control or modify human behavior; and (3) the existence of a body of scientific research that tends to support the explanation of the professional group in question and with which the therapy in question appears to be consistent.

trying to solve his personal problems. They do not explain why some people choose crime as a problem-solving technique while others do not.[17] As evidence, although the practice is less frequent today, almost complete reliance is often placed on interpretations by psychiatrists of a person's verbal recall of childhood experiences. Much of this type of activity has been criticized for using imagination and guesswork too freely. Another person going over the same material might find some other equally valid and significant explanation that does not employ the theory.

Most psychiatric studies have been concerned solely with deviant persons, and only a few studies have employed a control group of nondeviant persons. For research data, psychiatrists depend on a biased sample of those who have been arrested, institutionalized, or received psychiatric treatment, and much reliance is placed on other official records which often reflect the biases of persons who have prepared them.[18] This is understandable if one considers that psychiatrists specialize in treatment, but they frequently generalize without utilizing accepted scientific procedures, such as samples of sufficient size or representativeness. While they are increasingly using many larger samples in their studies, many psychiatrists continue to maintain that successes in therapy are proof of the validity of their theoretical systems. This is no more proof than the "cures" of patent medicine. Other factors, such as the subject's belief and acceptance of the interpretation, as well as his personal relations with the analyst, also enter into the so-called successful treatment.

Lack of Verified Theory for Practice   *Psychotherapy does not necessarily follow a theory, for often it is improvised to fit individual cases.* Furthermore, the results achieved by therapy may be due to other factors such as the intimate social relationship between practitioner and patient. Certainly some favorable therapeutic results are achieved by psychiatrists working with deviants, but more and more skepticism is being expressed about the effects of psychotherapeutic methods in the treatment of severe forms of deviant behavior. After reviewing the literature on alcoholism over an 11-year span, one writer stated that no conclusive opinion could be given as to the value of the psychotherapeutic method in the treatment of alcoholism.[19] Psychotherapy with drug addicts also does not appear to be very successful. Most addicts, due to the effects of addiction, have such an array of needs that a "doing" therapy is far more successful with them than a therapy which seeks to explore their basic personalities.[20] After having surveyed various studies of psychotherapy, Mechanic, an authority in the area of the treatment of mental disorders, has concluded as follows:

> We have few well-designed studies of psychotherapy; and we can criticize almost every investigation on one basis or another. But the over-all conclusion one draws from most of the investigations that attempted to have an adequate methodology is that psychotherapy is not very different in its effectiveness from many less costly procedures such as bed rest, simple interpersonal support. . . . Developments in the area of behavior therapy—

---

[17]Albert K. Cohen and James F. Short, Jr., "Crime and Juvenile Delinquency," in Robert K. Merton and Robert Nisbet, eds., *Contemporary Social Problems*, 4th ed. (New York: Harcourt Brace Jovanovich, 1976), pp. 70–71.

[18]Norman Denzin, *The Research Act* (Chicago: Aldine, 1970), p. 265.

[19]Morris E. Chafetz, "How Nations Drink: The Puzzle of Alcoholism," *Nation*, 199 (1965), 401–404. Also see F. Heyman, "Methadone Maintenance as Law and Order," *Society*, 9 (1972), 15–25.

[20]Heyman, p. 16.

treatment directed at specific symptoms and based on principles of learning theory—appear more promising. . . . Regardless of how one feels about traditional forms of psychotherapy, its effects are too limited and unimpressive and the expense of instituting it on a far-reaching basis is too great in terms of cost and personnel to justify it. Although older forms of psychotherapy will no doubt persist and new ones develop, at most psychotherapy will play only a limited role in the future organization of psychiatric rehabilitation.[21]

THE PSYCHOANALYTIC EXPLANATION OF DEVIANT BEHAVIOR

Psychoanalysis is closely related to psychiatry and its frame of reference, yet it has a particular system of explaining deviant behavior. This involves, as will be pointed out, what psychoanalysts call conflicts between the *id* and the *superego,* the masculinity-femininity conflict, infantile regression, and parent fixation.[22] Psychoanalytic work on deviance has greatly affected U.S. psychiatry in general as well as many social workers and other practitioners who deal with deviants. Psychoanalysis was founded by Sigmund Freud, a Viennese physician who died in 1939. As a result of Freud's work psychoanalysis has become an important part of the contemporary vocabulary and thinking of Western European society. Largely because of the emphasis on sex and symbolism, psychoanalytic works make particularly fascinating reading for both professional persons and laymen.

According to psychoanalytic writers, the chief explanation of behavior disorders must be sought in an analysis of the *unconscious mind,* which is said to consist of a world of inner feelings that are unlikely to be the obvious reasons for behavior or to be subject to recall at will. Antisocial conduct is a result of the dynamics of the unconscious rather than of the conscious activities of mental life. Much of the adult's behavior, whether deviant or nondeviant, owes its form and intensity to certain instinctive drives and to early reactions to parents and siblings.

Psychoanalysts generally rely on the use of lengthy free association and the analysis of dreams to infer unconscious experience and motivations. The analyst listens, often taking notes, while the patient, usually in a reclining position, rambles on, presumably verbalizing all the thoughts that come into his mind. Through this "free association" the patient is thought to be able to reveal words, phrases, and ideas ordinarily excluded from consciousness. The same principle holds in hypnosis, which is sometimes used, but which has many physical disadvantages over free association.

Child psychoanalysts often analyze a child's play activities, since the age of these patients and the general lack of verbalization skills of small children preclude the use of free association. Just as the free association of the adult presumably reveals significant

---

[21]Mechanic, *Mental Health and Social Policy,* © 1969, pp. 49–50. Reprinted by permission of Prentice-Hall, Inc., Englewood Cliffs, New Jersey.
[22]See, for example, Stuart S. Asch, "Some Superego Considerations in Crime and Punishment," *Journal of Psychiatry and Law,* 4 (1974), 159–181.

aspects of the unconscious, play activities of children are also thought to represent much deeper feelings. The nature of the child's play, particularly the symbolic meaning of the toys chosen and the manner of their use, are interpreted by the analyst as being consistent with psychoanalytic theory. One well-known child psychoanalyst gives an example of this kind of analysis:

> we see small girls drawing little stars or crosses, which signify feces of children, or older ones writing letters and numbers on a sheet of paper that stands for their mother's body or their own, and taking great care to leave no empty spaces. Or else they will pile up pieces of paper neatly in a box until it is quite full. Very frequently they will draw a house to represent their mother, and then put a tree in front of it for their father's penis and some flowers beside it for children.[23]

Dreams are supposed to have obvious as well as hidden meanings.[24] The part of the dream that one can recall is its obvious content, whereas the unconscious processes that give rise to the dreams are its hidden meanings. Since the latter are generally not acceptable to the dreamer, they must be transformed in some symbolic way to be made acceptable. The "censor," a mechanism of importance in this scheme, decides what may come to the dreamer's conscious mind and what may not. It also transforms, condenses, elaborates, and dramatizes the hidden content, through symbols, into the obvious content. These symbols often have sexual connotations. In dreams the father may be said to be symbolized as a king and/or various animals, the mother thought of as nature, and procreation by sowing or tilling.

Components of Personality

In the psychoanalyst's scheme, personality is thought of as composed of three parts: the primitive animal *id*, the *ego*, and the *superego*. Psychoanalysis assumes that the conscious self is built over a great reservoir of biological drives. Although biology, in the form of basic animal drives, plays an important part in psychoanalytic theory, these drives are present in everyone and do not necessarily represent individual biological differences.

1. The *id* is the buried reservoir of unconscious instinctual animal tendency or drive. From the Freudian standpoint these instincts are of two major types: the *libido*, including chiefly sexual drives, but not exclusively limited to them, and the love or life-trend instincts; and the sadistic or destructive instincts. These instincts operate in every activity.

2. The *ego* is elaborated from the large tract of instinctual tendencies as a result of the contact of the individual with the outer social world. Freud postulated here a dualistic conception of mind: the "id" or internal unconscious world of native or biological impulses and repressed ideas, and the "ego," the self, operating on the level of consciousness. These two may sometimes be compatible but more often are

---

[23]Melanie Klein, *The Psychoanalysis of Children*, rev. ed. (New York: Delacorte Press, 1975), p. 208.
[24]See, for example, Thomas M. French and Erika Fromm, *Dream Interpretation* (New York: Basic Books, 1964); and Calvin S. Hall and Robert L. Van de Castle, *The Content Analysis of Dreams* (New York: Appleton, 1966).

incompatible, unless adjusted through some psychological mechanism. There may be constant conflict between the "ego," the conscious part of the mind representing the civilized aspect of man, and the "id," the unconscious or "primitive" in man.

3. The *superego,* on the other hand, is partly conscious, partly unconscious; it is the conscious part which corresponds to the conscience. It is man's social self, derived from cultural definitions of conduct.

Deviance and Psychoanalysis

Some writers on psychoanalysis have made almost synonymous with criminal behavior the unresolved conflicts between the primitive id and its instinctive drives and the requirement of society. According to this view, crime arises out of inadequate social restrictions which society has placed on what psychoanalysts assume to be the original instinctive, unadjusted nature of man, which is savage, sensual, and destructive. Criminal behavior is thought of as an almost necessary outcome or expression of the personality, and hence does not always necessitate contacts with a "criminal" culture.

Psychoanalytic writers who deal with the problems of suicide have stressed the polarity principle of the life (love) and death (hate) instincts of the id. According to this view, there is a strong desire in the id for self-destruction. The superego, in turn, contains various social and moral restrictions on personal violence and self-destruction. The forces pulling toward self-destruction and self-preservation are in constant interaction, and when the former overcomes the latter, self-inflicted death ensues. Psychoanalysts often find hidden motives behind suicides, for example, self-mutilation or self-destruction. According to Menninger, the death wish, which is part of the id, may occur in alcoholics where chronic drunkenness is in a sense a slower method of self-annihilation than some of the other methods customarily employed.[25]

Every person, psychoanalytically, has both *masculine and feminine tendencies,* or, put another way, is naturally bisexual with homosexual and heterosexual components.[26] This results in a certain amount of conflict within the individual. Many psychoanalytic writers have emphasized the conflict, calling the masculine tendency aggressive and the feminine one passive. Murder is a sign of masculinity and may be a defense against "feminine" traits which the murderer abhors. Some psychoanalytic writers believe that alcoholism in the male represents the direct expression of his homosexual drives.

Psychoanalysts think of a normal personality as having *developed through a series of four stages.* The development of personality involves shifting interests and changes in the nature of sexual pleasure from the oral and the anal preoccupation of infant life to love of self, love of a parent of the opposite sex, and, finally, love of a person of the opposite sex other than one's parent. Some of these stages overlap and may go on simultaneously. Some persons do not progress through all of them;

---

[25]Karl Menninger, *Man Against Himself* (New York: Harcourt, Brace, 1938). Also see James Hillman, *Suicide and the Soul* (London: Hodder and Stoughton, 1964).
[26]See, for example, Edward M. Levine, "Male Transsexuals in the Homosexual Subculture," *American Journal of Psychiatry,* 133 (1976), 1318–1321.

consequently they have conflicts and develop personality difficulties. According to psychoanalysts, the newborn operates on a pain-pleasure principle, the environment consisting of desirable objects which merely serve to bring about bodily comfort and satisfaction, such as oral gratification through nursing and preoccupation with the activities of elimination. There is preoccupation with one's own body, but from the beginning this interest is increasingly blocked by cultural controls and restrictions; many psychoanalysts stress the fact that deviants are immature persons who have not developed into fully socialized adults, a situation termed "infantile regression." The activities of deviants unconsciously represent unresolved infantile desires. Others believe, for example, that the type of crime and the types of objects involved in the crime often indicate infantile regression. Some psychoanalysts have concluded that the etiology of schizophrenia is a retreat to a form of infantilism. The alcoholic has often been characterized by psychoanalysts as a passive, insecure, dependent, "oral" stage personality whose latent hostility has been obscured. Drug usage has been likened to infantile masturbation.[27] Homosexual behavior has been explained as a regression to the oral stage.[28]

In the psychoanalytic view the mother is definitely an object of a child's libido during its infancy: she is the first object to whom love impulses are directed, but she is also the first person to whom hate is directed since she is the first person who restricts pleasure. Based on this early attachment to the mother there arises an *Oedipus phase* in which the male child unconsciously becomes a rival of his father for his mother's sexual affections and therefore comes to hate his father. In the case of girls, the conflict with the mother over the father is termed the *Electra complex.*[29] Psychoanalytic writers have tried to show that many social phenomena can be understood only when viewed in the light of the Oedipus complex, which produces significant manifestations in almost every sphere of human activity. Sexual adjustment generally becomes heterosexual, with the love object outside the family; but with the deviant, this conflict is not solved. There are guilt feelings over the incestuous desires for the parent of the opposite sex and an unsatisfactory shift to other heterosexual persons. These guilt feelings are relieved by deviant behavior or by the punishment that arises from antisocial behavior. Criminals and neurotics have much in common, for example, for both feel that they need to be punished to relieve the guilt feelings arising from the Oedipal situation.[30] A posthumous psychoanalytic study of Lee Harvey Oswald, the assassin of President Kennedy, found that he had a manipulative, entrapping mother who generated an Oedipal complex.[31]

Similarly, the behavior difficulties associated with alcoholism lie in various

---

[27]Sandor Rado, "Fighting Narcotic Bondage and Other Forms of Narcotic Disorders," *Comprehensive Psychiatry,* 4 (1963), 160–167.

[28]See Irvin Bieber *et al., Homosexuality: A Psychoanalytic Study of Male Homosexuals* (New York: Vintage, 1965).

[29]Another conflict may result from overattachment to the mother, which turns to violent dislike and is called the *Orestes complex.* All these terms, of course, have their origin in the characters and plots of classic Greek plays.

[30]See Asch.

[31]David A. Rothstein, "Presidential Assassination Syndrome," *Archives of General Psychiatry,* 15 (1966), 260–266.

Oedipus or Electra conflicts.[32] Alcoholism is interpreted as an escape valve from these intolerable inner battles. Male homosexuality has been explained as a result of overattachment to the mother in an unresolved Oedipus complex which results in the individual's rejection of sexual relations with other women.[33] Psychoanalytic theories often explain prostitution as caused by the person's failure to reach sexual maturity. Because the prostitute suffers from, or has never outgrown, her Electra complex for her father, she is often incapable of receiving real sexual gratification. One psychoanalytic study sought to explain the high suicide rates of Sweden and Denmark and the lower rate of Norway in terms of differences in the reaction to childhood dependency on the mother, with the suicides in Sweden frequently representing a distinctive act aimed at both the person and the mother.[34]

Some Criticisms of Psychoanalytic Theory

Psychoanalysis has emphasized the meaningfulness of subjective experience, and as a theory it has contributed to the understanding of various psychological processes through which the mind avoids certain painful events. The emphasis on the unconscious, on symbolic expressions, and on mental conflict that has been developed from psychoanalytic writings has been noteworthy, even if overstressed in the explanation. There are, however, numerous criticisms with this approach.

Behavior is Social   *Contrary to psychoanalysis, evidence suggests that human behavior is a product of social experience and that it is not determined by an innate reservoir of animal impulses termed the id.* Depending upon social and cultural experiences, a person can be either cruel or gentle, aggressive or pacific, sadistic or loving. One can be either a savage Nazi Jew-baiter or a compassionate and tender human being like Albert Schweitzer or Mohandas Ghandhi. No detailed refutation is necessary, therefore, to disprove a psychoanalytic theory that some forms of criminality, for example, should be envisaged as outbursts of an id with "unsocialized original animal impulses." What constitutes criminal behavior and other forms of deviance is a matter of social determination, and impulses secure their social meaning only through the medium of social interaction. No savage individual is lurking under a veneer of socialization.

Conflicts as Sex-Based   *There is no evidence to support the theory that sex represents such an all-inclusive factor that it can explain most mental conflicts.* The psychoanalytic emphasis on sexual eroticism is a great overstatement of an important aspect of human behavior. Conflicts can arise in many other areas of human experience, for example, through economic competition, the achievement of status, and through religion.

---

[32]Eva Maria Blum, "Psychoanalytic Views on Alcoholism: A Review," *Quarterly Journal of Studies on Alcohol,* 27 (1966), 259–300.
[33]Aron Krich, ed., *The Homosexuals* (New York: Citadel Press, 1954).
[34]Herbert Hendin, *Suicide and Scandinavia* (New York: Doubleday, 1965).

Biological Emphasis *The entire psychoanalytic scheme is too bodily conscious rather than sufficiently socially conscious; the child's development is greatly influenced by social relationships that have little or no connection with bodily functions.* The evidence does not support the view that these rather presocial experiences involving oral and anal stimulation affect the entire course of human life. In a study of various societies, one writer considered the effects on personality of different methods of nursing, mothering, bowel training, and restraint of motion. He reached negative conclusions about their "specific invariant psychological effect upon children,"[35] concluding that the chief variables are the parental attitudes, which are derived from the culture. Sewell also concluded, from a study of 162 farm children, that different methods of infant breast feeding, weaning, and bowel training have practically no subsequent effect on personality.[36]

Universality of Conduct *Psychoanalytic theory has assumed that there are certain universal uniformities in human behavior which arise from the assumed uniformities in human biological drives, irrespective of cultural influences, historical eras, or variations in social structure.* An example of this erroneous approach is the view that the Oedipus complex is universal in all cultures. There is no universal cross-sex parental preference. It appears that Freud overrated the uniformity of family patterns and failed to perceive that sexual definitions are products of the child's social relationships.

Psychoanalysis as Antiscience *Psychoanalysis is not a scientific explanation.* First, most of psychoanalysis has not been verified, and for that reason it is possible to give a "symbolic" interpretation to almost everything.[37] The emphasis on the unconscious, as exemplified by the concentration on dream analysis, has never been scientifically established; it is a "ghost in a machine."[38] Second, a scientific theory must be stated in such a way that it is verifiable; in the case of psychoanalysis, "the theory is stated in language so vague and metaphysical that almost anything appears compatible with it."[39] As Nagel has written, "Can an adult who is recalling childhood experiences remember them as he actually experienced them or does he report them in terms of ideas which carry the burden of much later experience, including the experience of the psychoanalytic interview?"[40]

Lack of Agreement *Because of the lack of independent verification of the claims of psychoanalysts, psychoanalytic techniques are subject to widely differing interpretations, even from the same case situations.* Psychoanalysts, for example, often force their interpretations on their clients through the use of suggestion, or they simply assert the validity

---

[35]Harold Orlansky, "Infant Care and Personality," *Psychological Bulletin,* 46 (1949), 1–48.
[36]William H. Sewell, "Infant Training and the Personality of the Child," *American Journal of Sociology,* 58 (1952), 150–159.
[37]Andrew Salter, *The Case Against Psychoanalysis* (New York: Citadel Press, 1963), pp. 75–76.
[38]Ernest Nagel, "Methodological Issues in Psychoanalytic Theory," in Sidney Hook, ed., *Psychoanalysis, Scientific Method, and Philosophy* (New York: New York University Press, 1959), p. 47.
[39]Nagel, p. 41.
[40]Nagel, p. 52.

of their interpretations.[41] A client's acceptance of the interpretation can be taken, and usually is, as evidence of the validity of the interpretation in the first place.

Problems with Clinical Evidence *Finally, the only support of psychoanalytic claims is in the form of "clinical" evidence, which is not usually amenable to independent verification.* Clinical evidence is essentially information accumulated about specific cases in the form of clinical reports and case summaries or the oral and written evaluations of the therapist. Clinical evidence, however, is not adaptable to objective scrutiny; it tends to be highly subjective, depending upon the particular view of the specific therapist. Furthermore, clinicians often tend to interpret events in a manner consistent with their own preconceived theoretical views, thereby making the evidence fit the theory rather than serving as a check on the theory.

PERSONALITY TRAITS AND DEVIANT BEHAVIOR

Many efforts have been made, primarily by psychologists, but also by psychiatrists, to isolate by various tests those personality traits that would distinguish deviants from nondeviants, particularly delinquents, criminals, prostitutes, homosexuals, alcoholics, and drug addicts. It is assumed that the basic components of any personality are individual personality traits or generalized ways of acting. Many personality traits have been identified, such as aggressiveness or submissiveness; intense display of emotions or the lack of such a display when appropriate; suspiciousness or the lack of it; self-centered reactions as opposed to those directed toward the welfare of others; withdrawal from contacts with other persons as contrasted with a desire to be with others; and feelings that one is regarded with affection or is disliked. Although these traits have been enumerated as if they were distinct entities, in actuality most proponents assume that they shade between the two extremes. At one time, the term "temperament" was used to encompass all of these personality traits.

Many scientists used to believe that personality traits were hereditary and that some persons were "naturally" aggressive or "naturally" shy. This view is still held by many laymen today. Contemporary research has built up evidence, however, which reveals that such behavior patterns are primarily developed out of social experiences. Some psychological theory, like the psychiatric, attributes personality traits primarily to interaction in early childhood, particularly early experiences with the mother and father in the family. It is argued that, since the first experiences of the child with others are primarily within the family group, trait structures arising there form the basis for the entire structure of personality. Such traits are supposed to represent the patterning of attitudes in relation to others. As the young child adjusts to new situations, particularly in the family, he learns to adapt himself and to secure recognition for his needs by displaying anger, by withdrawing from contact with others, or by becoming aggressive.

---

[41]See, for example, Klein, p. 18.

Feelings of affection for others, antagonism toward others, or timidity grow out of these early experiences.

Dozens of tests, rating scales, and other psychological devices have been used to try to distinguish deviants from nondeviants. Traits are often ascertained and measured by a variety of pencil-and-paper type tests, such as the MMPI (Minnesota Multiphasic Personality Inventory) and the CPI (California Personality Inventory). The former is a lengthy questionnaire of 550 items which ask the subject to respond to statements as true or false applied to himself. Fourteen scales are usually scored, four as validity scales indicating the subject's accuracy and reliability and ten as clinical scales which are assumed to measure important phases and traits of personality. Projective tests are also used, such as the TAT (Thematic Apperception Test), which consists of a series of pictures about which the subject comments, and the Rorschach, which uses cards containing standardized inkblots, to which the subject responds by telling what they mean to him.

Delinquent and Criminal Behavior

Some psychologists have sought to type and to explain nearly all forms of delinquent and criminal behavior in terms of abnormalities in the psychological structure of the individual. They believe that inadequacies in personality traits interfere with the individual's adjustment to the demands of society. To establish this, a personality test is given to a group of delinquents or criminals, and their scores are then compared with test scores of a so-called control group of nondelinquents or noncriminals.[42] Studies have been made of emotional security, aggressiveness, conformity, conscientiousness, deception, self-assurance, social resistance, and suggestibility, and efforts have been made to distinguish moral judgments and ethical views. The assumptions of this approach to criminal behavior are that if one could ascertain the nature of trait structures that are related to criminal behavior, and if formation of these structures could either be prevented or treated successfully, much crime could be eliminated. To these psychologists delinquent or criminal behavior, even of a group nature, consists mainly of the actions of separate individuals.

There are, however, several major difficulties in distinguishing between the personality traits of offenders and those of nonoffenders. (1) The tests have not been able to distinguish the personality traits of criminal offenders from those of nonoffenders, as Glaser explains:

> There is considerable disagreement as to how useful personality measurement can be for assessing commitment to crime. Comparisons of personality test scores of criminals and

---

[42]For attempts to show the relation between personality traits and delinquency, see particularly Starke Hathaway and Elio D. Monachesi, *Analyzing and Predicting Juvenile Delinquency with the MMPI* (Minneapolis: University of Minnesota Press, 1953); Elio D. Monachesi, "Personality Characteristics and Socio-Economic Status of Delinquents and Non-Delinquents," *Journal of Criminal Law, Criminology and Police Science,* 40 (1950), 570–583; and Sheldon Glueck and Eleanor Glueck, *Unraveling Juvenile Delinquency* (Cambridge, Mass.: Harvard University Press, 1950). Also see Herbert Quay, "Personality and Delinquency," in Herbert Quay, ed., *Juvenile Delinquency Research and Theory* (Princeton, N.J.: Van Nostrand, 1965), pp. 139–170.

noncriminals have shown fairly marked and consistent differences only on scales that essentially ask questions about criminal values. . . . On other aspects of personality measured by verbal and projective tests, criminals are about as diverse as noncriminals, and for most purposes, differentiating them by their known criminal or noncriminal behavior appears to be more useful than assessing them on the basis of their paper and pencil test performances.[43]

(2) Samples of institutionalized offenders are customarily used, and they are undoubtedly not representative of offenders generally. (3) Test performances in an institutional setting may be unreliable. (4) It is also possible that stigmatization through arrests, court appearance, or imprisonment may so affect the personality traits of offenders that it is impossible to determine what they were like prior to these experiences. (5) Finally, very few studies of personality traits have distinguished among types of offenders.

Psychopathic Personality

One theory concerning the relation between personality traits and certain criminal behavior needs more detailed comment. The literature of many phases of deviant behavior contains references to a deviant personality type termed a *criminal psychopath* or a *psychopathic personality,* a habitual antisocial deviant.[44] Although there has been considerable dispute over the meaning of the term "psychopath," some of the characteristics of a so-called psychopath are said to be freedom from the signs or symptoms generally associated with psychoses or neuroses and demonstration of poor judgment and an inability to learn from experience, as is seen in "pathological lying," repeated crime, delinquencies, and other antisocial acts.[45] Psychopathic personalities "repeat apparently purposeless thefts, forgeries, bigamies, swindlings, distasteful or indecent acts in public, scores of times."[46]

Although many people believe that the concept of a psychopath is real and that such a personality type sufficiently explains numerous antisocial acts, it is subject to serious problems. For one thing, the term is used imprecisely and with a variety of meanings by those who are not clear as to the development processes of a psychopath; hence its usefulness can be seriously questioned. The lack of precision in

[43]Daniel Glaser, *Adult Crime and Social Policy* (Englewood Cliffs, N.J.: Prentice-Hall, 1972), p. 23. A review of all studies that had been made up to 1950 comparing personality characteristics of delinquents and nondelinquents and criminals and noncriminals concluded: "The doubtful validity of many of the obtained differences, as well as the lack of consistency in the combined results, makes it impossible to conclude from these data that criminality and personality elements are associated." Karl F. Schuessler and Donald R. Cressey, "Personality Characteristics of Criminals," *American Journal of Sociology,* 55 (1950), 476.
[44]Harrison Gough, "A Sociological Theory of Psychopathy," *American Journal of Sociology,* 53 (1948), 365. There are few more imprecise psychiatric terms, or with a longer history, than the term "psychopath." Originally, the terms "moral insanity" and "moral imbecility" were used. In the trial of Charles Guiteau in 1881 for the assassination of President Garfield, the issue of "moral insanity" was raised by the defense. Koch is credited with originating the term "psychopathic personality" in 1888 when he referred to a group of patients having no proper class of mental disorder, but who could not be considered entirely sane.
[45]Hervey Cleckley, *The Mask of Sanity* (St. Louis: C.V. Mosby, 1950).
[46]Cleckley, p. 415.

describing psychopathic traits has been shown by the wide differences in the diagnoses of "psychopathic" criminals in various institutions and by research on the traits.[47] Furthermore, the view that persons are psychopaths merely because they are repeaters or are persistent in their behavior is circular reasoning. Writing on the characteristic of persistent antisocial behavior as a criterion of a psychopath, Sutherland stated: "This identification of an habitual sexual offender as a sexual psychopath has no more justification than the identification of any other habitual offender as a psychopath, such as one who repeatedly steals, violates the antitrust law, or lies about his golf scores."[48]

Drug Addiction

A widely held belief is that differences in personality traits or the need to escape accounts for addiction to opiates. This view, while common among some psychiatrists and psychologists, is not generally supported by the research literature. In an exhaustive review of studies that have attempted to detect such personality mechanisms, Platt and Labate conclude:

> There is strong evidence for a position supporting the lack of importance of predisposing factors in three areas. First, current studies of the personality of the addict have failed to provide evidence for the existence of a single, unique, personality type associated with heroin addiction. Second, some of these studies suggest there may be subgroups of addicts, each using heroin for a different purpose. For example, one subgroup may use heroin to increase their levels of stimulation, while another may use it in order to narcotize themselves against such stimulation. Third, many studies, including the above, have consistently failed to demonstrate a specific type of psychopathy to be associated with heroin addiction.[49]

Addicts may exhibit personal problems, but it is not sound reasoning to assume that such personality traits existed before addiction, or led to the addiction.

Moreover, studies that attempt to find personality traits which differentiate addicts from nonaddicts do not answer the question of why individuals with the same personality traits as the addicts do not become addicted to drugs. Narcotic addiction will be explained later not in terms of the presence of predisposing personality trait

---

[47]Hakeem, "A Critique of the Psychiatric Approach to Crime and Corrections."

[48]Edwin H. Sutherland, "The Sexual Psychopath Laws," *Journal of Criminal Law, Criminology, and Police Science,* 40 (1950), p. 549.

[49]Jerome J. Platt and Christine Labate, *Heroin Addiction: Theory, Research and Treatment* (New York: Wiley, 1976), p. 316. The studies cited by these authors in support of this conclusion are J. I. Berzins, W. F. Ross, G. E. English, and J. V. Haley, "Subgroups among Opiate Addicts—Typological Investigation," *Journal of Abnormal Psychology,* 83 (1974), 65–73; J. J. Platt, "Addiction-Proneness and Personality in Heroin Addicts," *Journal of Abnormal Psychology,* 84 (1975), 303–306; J. I. Berzins, W. F. Ross, and J. J. Monroe, "A Multivariate Study of the Personality of Hospitalized Narcotic Addicts on the MMPI," *Journal of Clinical Psychology,* 27 (1971), 174–181; and A. C. Ogborne, "Two Types of Heroin Reactions," *British Journal of the Addictions,* 69 (1974), 237–242. One kind of statement not supported by this literature is the following: ". . . heroin addiction in some is symptomatic of an underlying chronic depression in a wounded personality, and in others of a failure of personality development." H. Dale Beckett, "Hypotheses Concerning the Etiology of Heroin Addiction," in Peter G. Bourne, ed., *Addiction* (New York: Academic Press, 1974), p. 37.

structures, but in terms of the availability of the drug, the process of drug usage, and the role of the drug subculture. "Which kinds of persons become addicted is a matter that is influenced by patterns of availability, by control policies, by social custom, and by many other factors."[50]

Alcoholism

To some people alcoholism is the result of personality maladjustment. According to this view, certain childhood experiences produce feelings of insecurity; these feelings, together with difficulties in interpersonal relations of adult life, produce tensions and anxieties reflected in certain personalities. Because the use of alcohol reduces anxiety a person may learn to depend upon it, and over a period of years dependence on alcohol becomes a way to escape difficulties with which the individual cannot deal.

Although this explanation is widely held, it has several limitations. First, efforts have been made to sketch an "alcoholic personality" that presumably applies to all alcoholics, yet surveys have concluded that scientific reports to date do not permit us to define such an alcoholic personality, or even to come to any substantial agreement as to just what it might be. Two reviews of all personality studies of alcoholics and nonalcoholics up to 1956, with the use of projective and nonprojective tests, found no reason to conclude that persons of one type are more likely to become alcoholics than persons of another type.[51] Second, such a theory is largely dependent for evidence on the personality traits of alcoholics and the differences between them and nonalcoholics. The personality traits of an alcoholic are usually measured after some 10 to 15 years of heavy drinking. During this period the individual has encountered many problems as a result of drinking—problems not only with family but with the police, the employer, and others—and has had many experiences foreign to the nonalcoholic. It cannot be assumed that the personality traits displayed by the alcoholic were there *before* the excessive drinking began. In fact, one study has pointed out that so-called alcoholic personalities undergo changes during drinking.[52]

Homosexual Behavior

Efforts have also been made to discover basic underlying personality traits of homosexuals, but they have not been successful. In an attempt to test this assumption a battery of attitude-scale projection personality tests were given to, and life histories secured from, 30 homosexuals who had not been in therapy or in an institution. Two experts who examined the results without knowing the subjects had difficulty in

---

[50]Alfred R. Lindesmith, *Addiction and Opiates* (Chicago: Aldine, 1968), p. 168.
[51]Edwin H. Sutherland, H. C. Schroeder, and C. L. Tordella, "Personality Traits and the Alcoholic: A Critique of Existing Studies," *Quarterly Journal of Studies on Alcohol,* 11 (1950), 547–561; and Leonard Symes, "Personality Characteristics and the Alcoholic: A Critique of Existing Studies," *Quarterly Journal of Studies on Alcohol,* 18 (1957), 288–302. Also see Craig MacAndrew and Robert F. Geertsna, "A Critique of Alcoholism Scales Derived from the MMPI," *Quarterly Journal of Studies on Alcohol,* 25 (1964), 68–76.
[52]Sheila B. Blume and Charles Sheppard, "The Changing Effects of Drinking on Changing Personalities of Alcoholics," *Quarterly Journal of Studies on Alcohol,* 28 (1967), 436–443.

distinguishing between the homosexuals and the heterosexuals on the basis of their records. Over half the homosexuals were rated as having a high degree of personal adjustment.[53]

Evaluation of Personality Trait Explanations

Although a number of criticisms of the personality trait explanation have been made or implied in the previous discussion, it might be well to summarize them here.

Behavior is Variable *Actually, human behavior consists primarily of social roles that are variable and socially determined and not static entities like so-called personality traits.* People learn to adapt and to play social roles (see pp. 38—39) according to given social situations, and in connection with these situations they display various normative behavior, deviant and nondeviant. Thus persons learn to play the nondeviant social roles of minister, doctor, or Boy Scout or the deviant roles of a youth gang member, drug addict, alcoholic, or prostitute. The theory also does not explain how specific behavior, such as techniques of stealing, are acquired.

Traits Before or After *It is almost impossible to isolate the effects of societal reaction and labeling on the behavior of deviants. One is never sure whether given personality traits were present before the deviant behavior developed or whether experiences encountered as a result of the deviation produced the traits.* Thus the fact that a criminal or a delinquent who has been convicted of an offense or has been confined in a correctional institution exhibits emotional insecurity is no proof that this person was insecure prior to committing the offense or prior to confinement in the institution. An alcoholic or a drug addict may have developed certain personality traits as a result of a long period of alcoholism or drug addiction, and consequent rejection and stigma, rather than having had the trait prior to the deviance.

Lack of Evidence *No evidence has been produced that so-called personality traits are associated with deviations from disapproved norms.* Comparisons with control groups have revealed that no series of traits can distinguish deviants from nondeviants in general. The studies do not show that all deviants have particular traits and that none of the nondeviants has them. Instead, practically all studies show an overlap in that a certain proportion of both deviants and nondeviants have a given trait. Some deviants, for example, are "emotionally insecure," but so also are some nondeviants. On the other hand, some deviants are "emotionally secure." It is difficult to interpret such mixed results without accounting for the fact that, though the proportions may vary, the same characteristics may be present in both deviant and nondeviant groups.

---

[53]Evelyn Hooker, "The Adjustment of the Male Overt Homosexual," in Hendrik Ruitenbeek, ed., *The Problem of Homosexuality in Modern Society* (New York: Dutton, 1963), p. 152. Also see Martin S. Weinberg and Colin J. Williams, *Male Homosexuals: Their Problems and Adaptations,* rev. ed., (Baltimore: Penguin Books, 1975), for a similar conclusion based on cross-national data.

Problems with Personality Tests *The internal construction and the arbitrary methods of weighting many personality tests have been questioned.*[54] It is difficult to judge the real validity of many tests purporting to measure personality traits. "Few personality scales lend themselves well to interpretations in terms of a single numerical score to be taken by itself and independent of scores in related test areas. The nature of the performance in some one area of the test usually affects and changes the significance of the score performance in another area."[55]

Early Family Experiences Again *Finally, like the psychiatric and psychoanalytic approaches, the personality trait explanation purports to show that the etiology of deviant behavior can be traced in the final analysis to family interaction, particularly the effect of early family experiences.*[56] The wider studies of socialization in later life and the use of role theory in the studies of adult life show that early life situations, particularly those in the family, often have less importance in the etiology of deviant behavior than the peer group, local community, school, marriage, and occupation.[57]

BEHAVIOR MODIFICATION OR BEHAVIOR THERAPY

The use of behavioral modification in the treatment of various forms of deviance in recent years has increasingly encountered both praise and criticism.[58] This approach has been applied in schools, clinical practice, mental hospitals, institutions for the mentally retarded, prisons, Army basic training units, vocational and industrial settings, and social planning.[59] Behavior modification programs involve a series of rewards and punishments designed to make the person socially acceptable and able to function adequately in a community. It is based on several psychological learning theories: It is behavioral in the sense that "cognitive" and attitudinal factors are not included, being deemed irrelevant in many respects. The main premise is that behavior is a function of its consequences, and the consequences are reinforcing (increasing the future probability of the behavior), punishing (decreasing the future probability), or neutral (no effect). There is a difference between a reward (something provided for the purpose of reinforcing behavior) and a reinforcement (something that actually has the effect of reinforcing the behavior).

---

[54]See, for example, George B. Vold, *Theroretical Criminology* (New York: Oxford University Press, 1958), pp. 126–138; and Don C. Gibbons, "Differential Treatment of Delinquents and Interpersonal Maturity Levels Theory: A Critique," *Social Service Review,* 44 (1970), 22—33.
[55]Vold, p. 127.
[56]Clinard, pp. 124–125.
[57]See Orville G. Brim, Jr., and Stanton Wheeler, *Socialization after Childhood* (New York: Wiley, 1966).
[58]See Robert L. Burgess and Don Bushell, eds., *Behavioral Sociology* (New York: Columbia University Press, 1969). The terms "operant conditioning" or "reinforcement" are sometimes used for behavior modification.
[59]See Eileen D. Gambrill, *Behavior Modification: Handbook of Assessment, Intervention, and Evaluation* (San Francisco: Jossey-Bass, 1977).

Behavior as a Consequence of Reinforcement

In this theory individual behavior is viewed as an outgrowth of past histories of reinforcement of behavior; people behave in particular situations because they have been rewarded or reinforced for similar behavior in similar situations in the past. In contrast, punishment for a specific behavior response tends to lead to the disappearance of that response from the individual's behavior. Both reinforcement and punishment can be positive or negative; positive refers to *adding* something to the environment or giving something (for example, *providing* approval, disapproval, praise, blame). Negative refers to *taking* something from the environment, such as withdrawing of status or privileges.[60]

Both deviance and conformity produce consequences that, in turn, affect future behavior. In terms of social control, the reaction of others in the form of sanctions is easily incorporated into a behavior modification framework. Positive sanctions for desirable or expected behavior are reinforcements, while negative sanctions for deviant behavior are punishments. Like sanctions, both reinforcements and punishments may be either social or nonsocial. Some examples are:

1. Reinforcement—social: praise, attention, approval, status, and membership.
2. Reinforcement—nonsocial: stealing money, food, or physical items such as TV sets.
3. Punishment—social: disapproval, criticism, ostracism, and exclusion.
4. Punishment—nonsocial: pain, fines, and incarceration.

This response orientation to the environment stands in contrast to other individualistic approaches, the traditional psychoanalytic, psychiatric, and clinical psychological perspectives, in which behavior is viewed as a function of antecedent stimuli. These differing views of causation have implications for methods of treatment and the control of deviant behavior. Whereas the traditional psychoanalytic school maintains that behavior change can come about only through a detailed search for, and treatment of, the underlying causes of the behavior, the behavior modification model rests on the supposition that the response behavior is the relevant area not only to study but to alter.

The roots of behavior modification may be found in the stimulus-response experiments of Pavlov, although they were limited primarily to reflexes, and to the behavior conditioning work of Watson. Skinner has provided the clearest basis for the operant conditioning model as it is utilized in the clinical treatment of deviant behavior today.[61] He claimed that an organism can be taught new functional responses on the basis of reinforcement techniques alone.[62] Each time a desirable behavior response occurs, such as a nonstuttering response in the case of a stutterer, the therapist or change agent rewards the subject through verbal conditioning or social recognition, or

---

[60]One of the most sophisticated statements of this approach can be found in Albert Bandura, *Principles of Behavior Modification* (New York: Holt, Rinehart and Winston, 1969).
[61]B. F. Skinner, *Science and Human Behavior* (New York: Macmillan, 1953).
[62]Skinner, *Science and Human Behavior.*

by giving other objects as rewards.[63] No rewards are given when the person stutters or displays similarly undesirable behavior. It is unnecessary to consider the effects of past performance and experiences in order to make use of this type of behavior modification. Gradualization is specifically built in: the person is taught, little by little, to replace deviant response patterns with new, nondeviant responses. In a manner similar to effective speech conditioning, "law-abiding" or other nondeviant behavior can be shaped, according to these principles. In institutions, juvenile delinquents or adolescents who have other unacceptable behavior problems but who follow programs considered to be beneficial for behavior modification receive rewards; those who violate rules are punished. In one Wisconsin program, for example, in the treatment of problem teenagers a system of "tokens" is used to encourage good behavior and discourage misbehavior. In this system various desirable behaviors are immediately rewarded by the giving of tokens, which can later be exchanged for such special privileges or rewards as movies, concerts, and passes for town. Patients receive tokens for being helpful to others, polite, cooperative, courteous at meal time, and being well groomed. Misbehaviors, such as being rude or destroying property, are "punished" by the removal of tokens.[64]

In this regard we see that operant conditioning is concerned not only with the environment in which the behavior takes place but also with "maintenance and extinction" of behavior.[65] It is not neutral behavior that is of interest to operant theorists but behavior that can and/or should be reinforced or punished. It is a process in which a stimulus is presented following a response for the purpose of increasing or decreasing the future occurrence of that response, whether the response is committing delinquent acts, drinking alcoholic beverages, performing good deeds, or any other that should be encouraged or discouraged.

Behavior Therapy

Through behavior therapy an attempt is made to modify the environmental consequences of the behavior. The difference between positive and negative reinforcement lies at the point at which an aversive stimulus, one the subject wishes to avoid, is terminated. Alcoholism was perhaps the first form of deviance for which therapies derived from the principles of behavior modification were used on a wide scale, largely because alcoholism has been thought to be the result of learning that alcohol use reduces tension and anxiety and thus reinforces its use.[66] Since alcoholism represents

---

[63]See R. M. Gilbert and J. R. Millenson, eds., *Reinforcement: Behavioral Analyses* (New York: Academic Press, 1972); and Jack T. Tapp, ed., *Reinforcement and Behavior* (New York: Academic Press, 1969).

[64]See "Mendota Behavior Program Detailed," *Wisconsin State Journal,* Madison, October 31, 1977, Section 3, p. 1.

[65]Weldon T. Johnson, "Exchange in Perspective: The Promises of George C. Homans," in Robert L. Hamblin and John H. Kunkel, eds., *Behavioral Theory in Sociology: Essays in Honor of George C. Homans* (New Brunswick, N.J.: Transaction Books, 1977), p. 64.

[66]See the discussion in Sam Hamburg, "Behavior Therapy in Alcoholism: A Critical Review of Broad-Spectrum Approaches," *Journal of Studies on Alcohol,* 36 (1975), 69–87. Actually, the evidence in support of this view of alcoholism is limited, although it has served as a central premise of behavioral therapy in alcoholism. See, for example, Howard Cappell and C. Peter Herman, "Alcohol and Tension Reduction: A Review," *Quarterly Journal of Studies on Alcohol,* 33 (1972), 33–64.

a pattern of drinking that has been reinforced by feeling "high" or "good," it is logical to believe that this process can be reversed and the problem thus resolved. This is accomplished by changing the stimulus value of alcohol, pairing it with the drug Antibuse that causes negative consequences: chemically produced nausea and vomiting each time a drink of alcohol is taken.

Sometime a punishment, such as a specific amount of electric shock, is applied after undesirable behavior occurs on the premise that the shock will lead to the elimination of the behavior. Under conditions of negative reinforcement, the shock would be applied until the subject develops a new, desirable response. An example of this process is the case of a young male under "treatment" for homosexuality. One writer has explained how this is accomplished.

> Electrodes are attached to his wrist, and a picture is projected on the screen. If it is female, nothing happens, but if it is a male, a mild electric shock would begin and would continue until he pressed a button to change the picture to that of a female. The electric shock would then be stopped, restoring calm and giving relief from the aversive stimulus.[67]

Similar techniques have been used with such behavior as smoking and the treatment of obesity.[68] Through the manipulation of small electric shocks and other aversive stimuli, the individual begins to associate the punishment with the behavior, and it is hoped that this association will prevent future acts. Covert sensitization conditioning, like aversive therapy, focuses to a great extent on punishing or extinguishing deviant responses. A practical example comes from work with alcoholics. Once relaxed and able to concentrate, the alcoholic is told to visualize himself entering a tavern, ordering a drink, having it put in front of him, picking it up and putting it to his lips, then having the feeling that his stomach is upset and he has to vomit. He is then asked to imagine the vomit as it comes up and covers himself and others around him. Finally, he visualizes himself embarrassed, humiliated, and sick, then leaving the tavern and feeling better.[69]

Evaluation of Behavior Modification

Behavior modification appears to have a number of clear advantages over the traditional psychoanalytic and psychiatric methods as a means of behavior change. The following advantages may be cited: (1) Behavior modification is short-term therapy. Psychoanalytic and psychiatric treatment may require years, depending upon the subjective progress of the patient-therapist relationship: since conditioning therapies are less time-consuming, more patients can be treated with lower cost. This is not to say, however, that "reconditioning" may not be necessary at a later time. (2) Behavior modification concentrates on the present and future, with little concern for uncovering the causes of the deviant behavior. The persistence or disappearance of

---

[67]Robert Henley Woody, *Psychobehavioral Counseling and Therapy: Integrating Behavioral and Insight Techniques* (New York: Appleton, 1971), p. 97.
[68]See J. P. Foreyt, *Behavioral Treatments of Obesity* (New York: Pergamon Press, 1977).
[69]Woody, p. 93. Also see the review in Ralph K. Schwitzgebel and David A. Kolb, *Changing Human Behavior: Principles of Planned Intervention* (New York: McGraw-Hill, 1974), pp. 51–53.

deviant response patterns will objectively determine the effectiveness of the therapy. (3) Behavior modification does not require persons to be their own change agents. Operant conditioning has proved to be successful with persons who are less amenable to direct, self-oriented behavior-change efforts. (4) Behavior modification in the form of reinforcement has been found to be compatible with the widely recognized sociological theory of differential association process in the causation of crime, which is termed, in behavior phraseology, the "differential association-reinforcement theory."[70] In a similar approach, it was found that positive and negative reinforcement, both physiological and social, generate opiate use and relapse.[71]

Although various degrees of success have been claimed in the application of behavior modification techniques in treating many forms of deviance, it is often difficult or even impossible to draw firm conclusions from the treatment data because of the great variations in the standards applied to follow-up investigations, the frequent lack of control groups, and other problems. Perhaps the most ingenious application that has emerged from the reinforcement operant model is one which reported the successful use of redeemable tokens as rewards for acceptable social behavior in the treatment of schizophrenics.[72] A combination of object rewards, social reinforcement, and relaxation was successfully used to modify stuttering in a schizophrenic boy.[73] In another report of the effectiveness of desensitization therapy on a group of 210 neurotic persons, it was stated that about 90 percent of them were apparently cured or had improved.[74] A study of alcoholics found behavior modification to be superior to nontreatment in a six-month follow-up study; 40 percent of the subjects treated were not drinking six months after treatment, whereas all persons in the nontreated group were still drinking.[75]

Yet, both the theory and the methods of behavior modification present a number of problems.

Contemporary Concerns

1. Behavior modification is an individualistic approach to behavior rather than one concerned with the role of broader social factors, such as the role of power and interest groups on definitions of deviance or the role that social control factors play in the deviance process.[76]

---

[70]Robert L. Burgess and Ronald L. Akers, "A Differential Association-Reinforcement Theory of Criminal Behavior," *Social Problems,* 14 (1966), 128–147. Formal learning theory puts a greater emphasis on reinforcement for *criminal patterns of behavior* than on *patterns of criminal association.* Also, in contrast to differential association, formal learning theory maintains that there are significant nonsocial reinforcements to much criminal behavior.

[71]Ronald L. Akers, Robert L. Burgess, and Weldon T. Johnson, "Opiate Use, Addiction, and Relapse," *Social Problems,* 15 (1968), 459–469.

[72]T. Ayllon and N. Azrin, *The Token Economy* (New York: Appleton, 1968). For a study that reached the opposite conclusion, see D. Richard Lewis, "The Failure of a Token Economy," *Federal Probation,* 38 (1974), 33–37.

[73]Woody, p. 67.

[74]Stanley Rachman, *The Effects of Psychotherapy* (New York: Pergamon Press, 1971), p. 134.

[75]Woody, p. 93.

[76]Recently some social learning theorists have posited a two-way causation process with both personal and environmental factors important in social behavior, but still with the emphasis on the individual. See, for example, Albert Bandura, *Social Learning Theory* (Englewood Cliffs, N.J.: Prentice-Hall, 1977).

2. Little is known about the long-term effects of behavior modification methods. Whether the deviant behavior is permanently eliminated or will return under a new set of circumstances is as yet unknown.

3. Behavior modification theorists have yet to establish with any certainty the conditions under which the techniques are likely to be effective and with whom. While therapists have claimed relatively high rates of success with some forms of deviance, for example, excessive eating, smoking, and alcoholism, it is not clear whether other forms of deviance, such as robbery and white-collar crime, are amenable to this type of therapy. As will be shown in a later chapter, the control of deviance is a complex issue, and it may not be addressed completely through techniques that focus only on the individual and neglect the larger social and political factors.

4. In a sense, behavior modification identifies individual deviance as behavior that is dysfunctional to society and, on this basis, should be eliminated. Deviance may, however, also serve a positive function in that it is said to contribute to social solidarity.

5. The underlying idea that the behavior of individuals can and should be manipulated raises some profound ethical questions. Sometimes the practice is even carried out without the person's permission. One therapist who has reflected on some of the problems involved has maintained that "the ultimate source of values is neither the patient's nor the therapist's wishes but the requirements of the society in which both live."[77] In essence, the ends of social conformity justify the means, and this may include license for violating the freedom of will of the individual. To this problem of ethics Skinner and others would reply that behavior is controlled anyway, but not as efficiently as it might be or for the most desirable behavior. The question is, then, not whether behavior ought to be controlled, but by whom and in what manner. Ultimately, the question may become how to control the behavior of the controllers.[78]

DEVIANCE AND THE MEDICAL MODEL

Today, the old sociological social pathology approach to deviance is represented by the medical model of psychiatrists and psychoanalysts who see the origin of deviance within the sphere of disease or psychological illness. The concept of mental illness and, therefore, deviations starting with a few behaviors has been extended by some to include "anything and everything in which they could detect any sign of malfunctioning, based on no matter what norm."[79] As one example, homosexuality is considered an illness because heterosexuality is the social norm.

A Central Assumption

Individualistic theories of deviance are based on an assumption of individual *qualitative differences.*[80] It is assumed that there are qualitative personality differences

---

[77]Leonard Krasner and Leonard Ullman, eds., *Research in Behavior Modification: New Developments and Implications* (New York: Holt, Rinehart and Winston, 1965), p. 363.
[78]See B. F. Skinner, *Beyond Freedom and Dignity* (New York: Bantam, 1971).
[79]This statement is from a criticism of this view by Szasz, *The Myth of Mental Illness,* p. 45.
[80]See Edwin M. Schur, *Radical Non-Intervention: Rethinking the Delinquency Problem* (Englewood Cliffs, N.J.: Prentice-Hall, 1973), pp. 29–78.

between deviant and nondeviant behavior. These differences may be conceived of in terms of personality structure, temperament, or dominant psychological needs of individuals. The question is, What types of persons commit deviant acts and how do they get that way? Because of the concern with this type of question, individualistic theories have been called "kinds-of-people" theories.[81] Since those persons who subscribe to individualistic theories are generally psychiatric and psychological clinicians whose orientation centers around the conception of individual "treatment," individualistic theories have come under attack as being examples of a "medical model" applied to the area of human behavior. The medical model views deviance as merely a symptom of some underlying individual "psychological sickness" which can be detected and treated only by professionals. Those who take this view regard most forms of deviance as a form of "mental illness" or psychological disorder. What is significant about a criminal act, for example, is not the behavior itself, as serious as it may be, but the fact that the criminal act is a symptom of the "real" problem which lies deep within the personality structure of the individual.

The Popularity of the Medical Model

The pervasiveness of the medical model in the treatment of deviance is evident in many official social control programs that deal with deviance, including psychiatric and counseling clinics and other individualistic approaches to deviance. Once the link has been made between deviance and "illness," whether it is real or inferred from behavioral indicators, the practical implications become clear: if deviance is an "illness," the appropriate action is medical in design. The treatment takes the form of some contact with a therapist. In the case of mental disorder, personality components have long been emphasized over the environmental or cultural.[82] The juvenile court, for example, is usually interested not in the act of delinquency but in the underlying problems of the individual delinquent that gave rise to the delinquent act. Those problems that are "diagnosed" by the court social work staff and the probation personnel are subsequently acted on by the court for "treatment" of the juvenile. Since each person's underlying problem is likely to be different, even though the same delinquent conduct may have resulted, the court emphasizes individualized treatment. Two girls arrested for the same crime may receive radically different court dispositions based on the court's perception of the underlying "problems" and "needs" of each individual.

The pervasive nature of the medical model can also be seen in the attitudes of the public and in the popular press. It is not hard to understand its popularity because it offers an explanation for those acts that seem to be "irrational" or unexplainable at first glance. How else, for example, can one account for the actions of a Lee Harvey Oswald or a Charles Manson? The medical model offers the explanation that these

---

[81]Albert K. Cohen, *Deviance and Control* (Englewood Cliffs, N.J.: Prentice-Hall, 1966), pp. 42–43.
[82]Nicholas Kittrie, *The Right To Be Different: Deviance and Enforced Therapy* (Baltimore: Johns Hopkins Press, 1971), pp. 409–410. Also see Heathcote W. Wales, "The Rise, the Fall, and the Resurrection of the Medical Model," *Georgetown Law Journal,* 63 (1974), 87–105.

persons are "sick." In this sense, deviance, as symptomatic of some other personal problem, is comparable to the use of the term "Mafia" by police officials to explain crimes so difficult that they cannot otherwise be explained or solved.[83] Similarly, the conception of mental illness can serve the same purpose for unusual or bizarre offenses: when all else fails, one can always claim that the deviant is "obviously" disturbed.

The medical model is effective in the treatment of physical illnesses where agreement on what constitutes health and what constitutes illness is more widely extended. A fever is indeed symptomatic of an infection somewhere in the body which the physician attempts to locate and to treat. In the area of social deviance, no such agreement about normative behavior exists. A number of more specific problems have become apparent with the medical model as it is applied to deviance.

Problems with the Medical Model

1. The fundamental problem with the medical model, like the social pathology view discussed in Chapter 3, is that personal qualities and characteristics do not inform us about the social nature of deviance, the interplay of social norms, sanctions and tolerance, and the meaning of deviance in society.[84] When the individual alone is considered one cannot know whose rules are being violated, the motivation of the social control agents, or the social circumstances under which some acts are singled out for control while others are not. Concluding that the drug addict is a "weak-willed" personality tells us nothing about the history of drug laws in this country, the social dynamics of drug enforcement, the interests of various groups in maintaining this activity as deviant, or the role of others in perpetuating deviant drug careers. A broader perspective is needed to address fully these latter concerns.

2. The medical model represents a contemporary elaboration of the social pathology view in more acceptable, seemingly value-free language. Since the causes of deviance are found within the individual, some form of individual therapy is indicated. If, for example, the causes of drinking are seen in some personality deficiency of the drinker in that the person "loses control" over alcohol consumption when confronted with stress, some form of individual counseling is appropriate. It is a short step from the identification of these personality deficiencies to making a moral judgment about them: the problem drinker is a "weak" personality or a "sick" person.

3. As applied to the study of deviance, the medical model is particularly prone

---

[83]See, for example, Dwight C. Smith, *The Mafia Mystique* (New York: Basic Books, 1975), particularly pp. 292–298.

[84]The discussion of the medical model should not be interpreted as meaning that there can be no individual factors which may produce, or help to produce, behavior that might be considered deviant. See Saleem A. Shah and Loren H. Roth, "Biological and Psychophysiological Factors in Criminality," in Daniel Glaser, ed., *Handbook of Criminology* (Chicago: Rand McNally, 1974), pp.101–173. This discussion points out that brain tumors and similar biological factors can on occasion produce behavioral manifestations of a deviant nature. Unfortunately, there seems to be no absolute symptomatology by which a judgment of organic disease can be made; that is, a brain tumor might produce certain behavior in some persons and quite different behavior in others.

to redundant or circular reasoning. Consider the following example. In 1966, Richard Speck entered an apartment in Chicago and brutally killed eight student nurses. In this nationally publicized and sensational case the immediate reaction of most persons was that Speck must be "crazy" because of the particularly shocking nature of the crime. The evidence offered in support of this claim was the behavior itself, since one *had* to be crazy to commit such an atrocious act. The medical model, therefore, has two uses for the term "illness." One is to take as evidence the deviant act of the illness, while the other is to use the concept of illness to explain the deviant act. In this case Speck's actions were taken as evidence of his illness, and that same illness was said to be the cause of the behavior. This circular reasoning is a common problem with the medical model. Often the deviance is taken as evidence of some underlying problem, and this presumed problem is then stated as the reason the behavior occurred. Obviously, what is required to break the tautology is to have evidence of the "problem" that is independent of the deviant act which is said to be simultaneously cause and effect of the problem.

SELECTED REFERENCES

Alexander, Franz G., and Sheldon T. Selesnick. *The History of Psychiatry.* New York: Harper & Row, 1966.

Asch, Stuart S. "Some Superego Considerations in Crime and Punishment," *Journal of Psychiatry and Law,* 4 (1974), 159–181.

Bandura, Albert. *Social Learning Theory.* Englewood Cliffs, N.J.: Prentice-Hall, 1977.

Burgess, Robert L., and Ronald L. Akers. "A Differential Association-Reinforcement Theory of Criminal Behavior," *Social Problems,* 14 (1966), 128–147.

Gambrill, Eileen D. *Behavior Modification: Handbook of Assessment, Intervention and Evaluation.* San Francisco: Jossey-Bass, 1977.

Hakeem, Michael. "A Critique of the Psychiatric Approach to Crime and Corrections," *Law and Contemporary Problems,* 22 (1958), 650–682.

Halleck, Seymour. *Psychiatry and the Dilemmas of Crime.* New York: Harper & Row, 1967.

Hook, Sidney, ed. *Psychoanalysis, Scientific Method and Philosophy.* New York: New York University Press, 1959.

Klein, Melanie. *The Psychoanalysis of Children,* rev. ed. New York: Delacorte Press, 1975.

MacDonald, John. *Psychiatry and the Criminal.* Springfield, Ill.: Charles C Thomas, 1969.

Mechanic, David. *Mental Health and Social Policy.* Englewood Cliffs, N.J.: Prentice-Hall, 1969.

Salter, Andrew. *The Case Against Psychoanalysis.* New York: Citadel Press, 1963.

Sewell, William H. "Infant Training and the Personality of the Child," *American Journal of Sociology,* 58 (1952), 150–159.

Shannon, Lyle. "The Problem of Competence To Help," *Federal Probation,* 25 (1961), 32–39.

Skinner, B. F. *Beyond Freedom and Dignity.* New York: Bantam Books, 1971.

Szasz, Thomas S. *The Myth of Mental Illness.* New York: Harper & Row, 1961.

CHAPTER 5

A crowded slum neighborhood in New York City. Urban living conditions frequently contribute to the extensive deviant behavior found in such areas.

Urbanization and Deviance

A LMOST everywhere, the spread of urbanization—in the United States, Europe, Latin America, Africa, and Asia—has been accompanied by a marked increase in various forms of deviant behavior. While city living has characterized some areas for centuries, urbanization has increased at such an accelerated rate over the past century that today it encompasses hundreds of millions of people throughout the entire world. Urban life has produced what some people have called the mass society. It has greatly increased social differentiation, the clash between norms and social roles, and the breakdown of interpersonal relations.[1]

The Growth of Cities

Cities first appeared in the Near East in about 3500 B.C., in Mesopotamia, in the region between the Tigris and Euphrates rivers.[2] A few centuries later they also appeared in the Nile Valley of Egypt and in the valley of the Indus River, in what is now Pakistan. Some cities, such as those in the Orient, were of considerable size. In general, however, only a small proportion of the people lived in them as compared with urban populations today, and few cities had over 100,000 persons. Athens, at its peak in the fifth century B.C., was estimated to have had between 120,000 and 180,000 persons; Rome had several hundred thousand; Florence in 1338, 90,000; and London in 1377, 30,000.[3]

Life in the large cities of several hundred years ago, both in Europe and in the Orient, was quite different from what it is in the same cities today. There were no forms of rapid transportation or mass communication, so that even though they were large, cities tended to be actually clusters of villages. Urban populations were much more permanent, and there was less migration into cities from rural areas; because of this people were able to know one another better than they do now.

In 1970, it was estimated that 69 percent of the people of the developed countries were living in cities of 20,000 or more, and 26 percent of those in the developing countries were in cities of this size or larger.[4] Forty-four percent of those in the developed countries were living in cities of 100,000 or more, while the figure for the developing countries was only 16 percent. Persons living in cities of a million or more made up 22 percent of the population in the developed countries and 8 percent in the developing ones. The proportion of the population living in cities of 100,000 or more in the developed counties increased 35 percent between 1950 and 1970; in the developing countries the increase was 83 percent.[5] During this same period the

---

[1]See Philip M. Hauser and Leo F. Schnore, *The Study of Urbanization* (New York: Wiley, 1965); and Noel P. Gist and Sylvia F. Fava, *Urban Society,* 6th ed. (New York: Crowell, 1964).

[2]Gideon Sjoberg, *The Preindustrial City: Past and Present* (New York: Free Press, 1960), pp. 25–51. Also see Kingsley Davis, "The Urbanization of the Human Population," in *Cities* (New York: Knopf, 1965), pp. 3–24.

[3]See Kingsley Davis, "The Origin and Growth of Urbanization in the World," *American Journal of Sociology,* 40 (1955), 429–437.

[4]Kingsley Davis, "The Role of Urbanization in the Development Process," *Conference Papers,* Rehovot Conference on Urbanization and Development in Developing Countries, August 16–24, 1971, Israel, p. 13.

[5]Davis, "The Role of Urbanization in the Development Process," p. 13.

proportion of the population in cities of a million or more inhabitants increased 47 percent in the developed countries and 136 percent in the developing ones.

In fact, by the year 2000, Kingsley Davis estimates that one fourth of the world's population will live in cities of over one million (in 1970, 12 percent lived in such cities); three cities will have more than 64 million people and one more than 100 million.[6] Some indication that these estimates may well be correct is that the largest, or "primate," cities of the less developed countries have been growing at a phenomenal rate. African cities like Abidjan, Dakar, Nairobi, Accra, and Kinshasa have doubled or even tripled in size during the past 10 years. For example, in 1940 Abidjan, capital of the Ivory Coast, had 20,000 inhabitants; in 1960, 250,000; in 1970, 500,000; by 1978 it was estimated to have nearly a million inhabitants. In Southeast Asia, greater Djakarta grew from 533,000 people in 1930 to over 5 million in 1970 and is continuing to increase rapidly.

Behind this phenomenal growth in urbanization, particularly in Western society, many forces have been operating, forces that can only be listed here: the breakdown of the feudal system and the loss of prescribed duties and obligations and an integrated way of village life; the growth of trade and commerce and later the Industrial Revolution, which produced a wide dispersion of the population, particularly to cities; the development of the factory system of production, and with it extensive occupational differentiation; the evolution of scientific thought, which brought a secular way of life by destroying many age-old beliefs and which also produced new forms of transportation as well as improvements in agriculture so that millions of people were freed from immediate dependence on the land to work and live in cities. Also essential for this growth of modern cities are more specific conditions: a level of agricultural production sufficiently high to provide a surplus that will allow people to concentrate in areas of nonagricultural production; enough power to provide large concentrations of persons with the means of industrial production and for the phenomenally expanded mass communication systems of the telephone, radio, and television. All of these forces have produced drastic changes in the interpersonal relations of those who moved to cities. As the large family has virtually disappeared, and with it many family functions and responsibilities, ties of family members to the land have been further weakened.

A countermigration to rural areas, however, started in the 1970s. In 1975, for the first time since 1920, rural areas were growing in population and urban areas declining.[7] Between 1970 and 1975, rural counties had a net gain of 1.8 million people compared with a new loss of 3 million during the 1960s. Urban counties had a net gain of 600,000 compared with a net gain of 6 million in the 1960s. Migrants went primarily to the rural counties of Florida, northern Michigan, the Ozarks, west of the Rockies, and northern New England. They included retired persons relocating to

---

[6]Kingsley Davis, *World Urbanization, 1950–1970,* Vol. II (Berkeley, Calif.: Institute of International Studies, 1972). Also see J. P. Pickard, "U.S. Metropolitan Growth and Expansion, 1970–2000," in S. M. Mazie, ed., *Population, Distribution and Policy,* Vol. V. (Washington, D.C.: U.S. Commission on Population Growth and the American Future, Government Printing Office, 1972).

[7]U.S. Census study reported in the *Wall Street Journal,* August 18, 1977.

warmer climates, blue- and white-collar workers leaving the cities for more pleasant living, and younger persons trying their hands at subsistence farming.

Cities in the United States

Following the Civil War, the United States changed from a society of rural communities to one of the most urbanized in the world. As Table 5.1 shows, in 1790 only 5.1 percent of the population lived in cities. By 1850 this figure had increased to 15.3, and in 1920 approximately half the people were urban. In 1950 the urban population of the United States was 64 percent of the total, and in 1970, 73.5 percent. In 1970 this amounted to 149,324,930 persons. In 16 states the percentage of urban population exceeds 75, the highest being California (90.9), followed by New Jersey (88.9), Rhode Island (87.1), New York (85.6), and Massachusetts (84.6).[8] The 1,563 cities of 100,000 persons and over contained more than one fourth (27.7 percent) of the total population of the United States in 1970. One in 10 Americans lives in a city of a million or more. A measure of urbanization, namely, "urbanized areas," which includes cities with a population of 50,000 or more and those persons residing in certain contiguous areas which are not part of the city, is now used. The 14 largest urbanized areas in the United States in 1960 are shown, in descending order, in Table 5.2. Some of these areas are larger than many European countries. The continuous urban conglomeration in the New York-northeastern New Jersey area is 16.2 million persons, in the Los Angeles-Long Beach area, 8.4 million, and in the Chicago-northwestern Indiana area, 6.7 million.

In 1970 slightly more than one half (58 percent) of the total U.S. population,

TABLE 5.1

Growth of the Urban Population in the United States, 1790–1970

Year	Percent Urban	Percent Rural
1790	5.1	94.9
1850	15.3	84.7
1900	39.7	60.3
1910	45.7	54.3
1920	51.2	48.8
1930	56.2	43.8
1940	56.5	43.5
1950	64.0	36.0
1960	69.9	30.1
1970	73.5	26.5

Source: United States Census of Population, 1970. Summary of Number of Inhabitants (Washington, D.C.: Bureau of the Census, 1971), pp. 3–6. The definition of "urban" changed in 1950, so that the comparable figure for that year was 59.6.

[8]Data from the Department of Commerce, Bureau of the Census, Supplementary Report, Population and Land Area of Urbanized Areas, 1970 and 1960 (Washington, D.C.: Bureau of the Census, 1970).

TABLE 5.2 The 14 Largest Urbanized Areas in the United States, 1960 and 1970

	Population in Millions	
Area	1960	1970
New York–northeastern New Jersey	14.1	16.2
Los Angeles–Long Beach area	6.5	8.4
Chicago–northwestern Indiana	6.0	6.7
Philadelphia-New Jersey area	3.6	4.0
Detroit	3.5	4.0
San Francisco–Oakland area	2.4	3.0
Boston	2.4	2.7
Washington–Md.–Va.	0.5	1.0
Pittsburgh	1.8	1.8
Cleveland	1.8	2.0
St. Louis, Mo.–Ill.	1.7	1.9
Baltimore	1.4	1.6
Minneapolis–St. Paul	1.4	1.7
Milwaukee	1.1	1.3

Source: United States Census of Population, 1970. Summary of Number of Inhabitants (Washington, D.C.: Bureau of the Census, 1971), pp. 1–50.

and about 73 percent of the urban population, were living in 248 urbanized areas. Of the 118.4 million persons living in urbanized areas, 63.9 million lived in the 308 central cities and 54.5 million in the fringe areas outside the cities. The 26 urbanized areas with more than one million inhabitants had a combined population of 71.9 million, or more than half of the total population of the 248 urbanized areas.

URBANIZATION AND DEVIANT BEHAVIOR

Since Greek and Roman times writers have contrasted the immorality of the city with the morality of rural areas. On the whole, modern cities, as compared with rural areas, do appear to have higher rates of crime, illegal drug usage, heavy drinking and alcoholism, homosexual behavior, and mental disorder. Official crime rates are generally much lower in rural areas, as studies of crime in the United States, France, Belgium, and many other European countries have shown.[9] Almost without exception the developing countries report that crime is rapidly increasing, and this increase is almost all due to the accelerated urbanization that has accompanied industrialization

---

[9]See Marshall B. Clinard, "The Relation of Urbanization and Urbanism to Criminal Behavior," in Ernest W. Burgess and Donald J. Bogue, eds., *Contributions to Urban Sociology* (Chicago: University of Chicago Press, 1965), pp. 541–558; Denis Szabo, *Crimes et Villes* (Louvain, France: Catholic University of Louvain, 1960); Denis Szabo, *Criminologie* (Montreal: University of Montreal Press, 1965); and Denis Szabo, "Urbanization et Criminalité," *Revue de Sociologie*, 1 (1963), 38–52.

and the migration to the cities of the rural youth.[10] In fact, most crime in less developed countries is concentrated in cities, particularly the larger ones, which account for a relatively small proportion of the total population of these countries.

> The lack of intimate ties, plus the protective cover of impersonality and anonymity, radically reduces both the internal and external control of criminal behavior. The city offers greater opportunities for theft and greater possibilities of collaboration with other offenders and with "fences" for the disposal of stolen goods. Urban areas generate the motivation, rationalization, skill, and low risk of detection of crime.[11]

While some criminal acts committed in rural areas are informally handled and are not officially reported, and while cities undoubtedly offer more opportunities to commit offenses, the differences between rural and urban crime rates are so great that differential reporting and opportunity account for only a small part of the increases.[12] Also, there is little evidence that the city attracts deviants from rural areas.[13]

Official burglary rates for urban areas in the United States are generally two and a half times greater than those for rural areas, larceny rates over three times greater, and those for robbery over twelve times greater (Table 5.3). The rates for crimes against the person are more equalized in urban and rural areas, but the rates for murder, forcible rape and aggravated assault are still higher in urban areas.

TABLE 5.3   Rates per 100,000 Population for Crimes Known to the Police in Rural and Urban Areas, United States, 1975

	Rate	
Offense	Urban	Rural
Murder and nonnegligent manslaughter	10.6	8.1
Forcible rape	31.3	12.0
Robbery	284.0	23.5
Aggravated assault	254.9	123.7
Burglary	1,747.9	785.9
Larceny-theft	3,195.6	941.6
Auto theft	586.2	102.4

Source: Uniform Crime Reports, 1975 (Washington, D.C.: Federal Bureau of Investigation, 1976), p. 49.

---

[10]Marshall B. Clinard and Daniel J. Abbott, *Crime in Developing Countries: A Comparative Perspective* (New York: Wiley, 1973). Also see Marshall B. Clinard, "The Problem of Crime and Its Control in Developing Countries." in David Biles, ed., *Crime in Papua New Guinea* (Canberra: Australian Institute of Criminology, 1976), pp. 47–71.

[11]Clinard and Abbott, *Crime in Developing Countries,* p. 255.

[12]See, for example, Marshall B. Clinard, "Rural Criminal Offenders," *American Journal of Sociology,* 50 (1944), 38–45; William P. Lentz, "Rural-Urban Differentials in Juvenile Delinquency," *Journal of Criminal Law, Criminology and Police Science,* 47 (1956), 311–339; and Marshall B. Clinard, "A Cross-Cultural Replication of the Relation of Urbanism to Criminal Behavior," *American Sociological Review,* 25 (1960), 253–257.

[13]See Theodore N. Ferdinand, "Demographic Shifts and Criminality: An Inquiry," *British Journal of Criminology,* 10 (1970), 169–175.

TABLE 5.4   **Rates per 100,000 for Crimes Known to the Police by City Size, United States, 1975**

Population	Offenses						
	Murder and Non.	Forc. Rape	Robbery	Agg. Ass.	Burg.	Larc.	Auto
Over 250,000	21.4	55.6	682.6	399.4	2,368.4	3,653.3	1,022.0
100,000 to 250,000	10.9	35.0	282.6	303.1	2,177.3	4,202.9	687.5
50,000 to 100,000	7.2	26.0	189.4	228.1	1,723.1	3,642.9	544.3
25,000 to 50,000	5.7	18.6	129.6	189.1	1,417.7	3,400.7	429.9
10,000 to 25,000	4.4	13.6	81.6	168.2	1,199.0	2,996.0	300.8
Under 10,000	3.9	11.5	49.4	166.7	1,037.5	2,633.6	209.9

Source: Uniform Crime Reports, 1975 (Washington, D.C.: Federal Bureau of Investigation, 1976), pp. 160—1.

Over 50 years ago, the French sociologist Emile Durkheim maintained that crime increases directly with the volume and density of the population. Studies of crime in France, Belgium, and other European countries have generally shown major differences in crime rates among cities of different sizes.[14] Comparisons in the United States of official crime rates by city size show some startling differences and, for most crimes, even a continuous progression in rates as the size of the city increases (see Table 5.4). In 1975, the rate per 100,000 population for burglaries reported to the police, probably the best comparable index of crime, rose steadily from 1,037.5 for cities under 10,000 persons to 2,368.4 for cities of over 250,000 population; robbery rates were 13 times as great for the largest cities.

The greater the size of a community, the greater the proportion of alcohol users it contains. This relationship is due to urban conditions rather than to the absence of rural ones (which encourage abstinence) and relates to the larger proportion of middle- to upper-status, white, and Protestant alcohol users in the more urban areas, as well as to a value system that is conducive to alcohol consumption.[15]

One should not assume from these generalities that there is always an automatic progression in official rates by city size. In fact, some very large cities may actually have rates more comparable to smaller cities because of a variety of circumstances (see p. 576). One example in Europe is the low crime rate of Zurich, a city of nearly half a million persons and a total metropolitan population of nearly 800,000.[16] The world's largest city, Tokyo, with 11.5 million population, is a classic example of a very large city with a low official crime rate.[17] One's chances of being murdered are 11 times

[14]Szabo, *Crimes et Villes;* Szabo, *Criminologie;* and Szabo, "Urbanization et Criminalité."

[15]Charles W. Peek and George D. Lowe, "Wirth, Whiskey, and WASP's: Some Consequences of Community Size for Alcohol Use," *The Sociological Quarterly,* 18 (1977), 209–222. Also see Claude S. Fischer, "The Effect of Urban Life on Traditional Values," *Social Forces,* 53 (1975), 420–432.

[16]Marshall B. Clinard, *Cities with Little Crime: The Case of Switzerland* (Cambridge: Cambridge University Press, 1978).

[17]*Tokyo: One City Where Crime Doesn't Pay!* A study of the reasons for Tokyo's low urban crime rate and what can be learned to help America's crime crisis (Philadelphia: The Citizens Crime Commission, 1975).

greater in New York City and 6 times greater in Philadelphia than in Tokyo. The chances of being mugged or robbed are 283 times greater in New York City and 82 times greater in Philadelphia. For assault the chances were found to be 7 and 3 times as great, respectively.

Many reasons may be cited for the situation in Tokyo. (1) The population of Japan is almost totally homogeneous, as compared with the United States or most other industrialized nations. (2) The household unit, even in the large cities, is a much more important element in Japanese society, and group controls are greater in that a person or family does not wish to lose face due to criminality. (3) Japanese life is highly disciplined. (4) Citizen participation in crime prevention and control is greater. (5) Handguns are virtually absent from Japanese life. (6) The criminal justice system is more efficient, and criminal sentences are in general short.

URBANISM AS A WAY OF LIFE

One must examine the effects of urbanization itself in order to explain differences in the incidence of deviant behavior in rural and urban areas, as well as the differences in rates by city size. The urbanization process itself brings about pronounced changes in the way of life.[18] This process connotes all kinds of changes; patterns of population distribution, work habits, housing, leisure pursuits, transactions with widening circles of people, and more opportunities for crime. It also means a more complex life, impersonality of relationships, subcultures, and less direct behavior controls. "It implies more opportunities for crime with less risk of detection and a disturbing juxtaposition of affluence and poverty."[19]

As a way of life, urbanism is often characterized by extensive conflicts of norms and values, rapid social change, increased mobility of the population, emphasis on material goods and individualism, a decline in intimate communications, and an increased release from informal social controls. It must be kept in mind, however, that these variables associated with the concept of urbanism may be found independent of city environments. In other words, "urbanism" is not synonymous with "city." Whereas "city" refers to an area distinguished principally by population size, density, and heterogeneity, "urbanism" refers to a complex of social relations. Although urbanism may more frequently arise within the city environments, this does not mean that it is limited to them. Rural areas in urban-industrial societies are also becoming "urbanized" as their way of life is experiencing such changes, but there are still pronounced differences between the two types. Some changes in rural society represent the spread of behavior patterns emanating from cities, but much of the change in rural areas has come about as the result of new relations among people who live in these areas.[20]

---

[18]J. John Palen, *The Urban World* (New York: McGraw Hill, 1975), pp. 112–113.
[19]*Social Defense Policies in Relation to Development Planning,* Working Paper, United Nations Congress on the Prevention of Crime and the Treatment of Offenders, Kyoto, Japan (New York: United Nations, 1970).
[20]See Richard Dewey, "The Rural-Urban Continuum: Real But Relatively Unimportant," *American Journal of Sociology,* 66 (1960), 60–66.

TABLE 5.5	**Schematic Version of Urbanism as a Way of Live**
Size An increase in the number of inhabitants of a settlement beyond a certain limit brings about changes in the relations of people and changes in the character of the community.	Greater the number of people interacting, greater the potential differentiation (mobility). Dependence upon a greater number of people, lesser dependence on particular persons. Association with more people, knowledge of a smaller proportion, and of these, less intimate knowledge. More secondary rather than primary contacts—increase in contacts which are face to face, yet impersonal, superficial, transitory, and segmental. More freedom from personal and emotional control of intimate groups. Association in a large number of of groups, no individual allegiance to a single group.
Density Reinforces the effect of size in diversifying men and their activities, and in increasing the structural complexity of the society.	Tendency to differentiation and specialization. Separation of residence from work place. Functional specialization of areas—segregation of functions. Segregation of people: city becomes a mosaic social world.
Heterogeneity Cities products of migration of peoples of diverse origin. Heterogeneity of origin matched by heterogeneity of occupants. Differentiation and specialization reinforces heterogeneity.	Without common background and common activities premium is placed on visual recognition: the uniform becomes symbolic of the role. No common set of norms and values, no common ethical system to sustain them; money tends to become measure of all things for which there are no common standards. Formal controls as opposed to informal controls. Necessity for adhering to predictable routines. Clock and the traffic signal symbolic of the basis of the social order. Economic basis: mass production of goods, possible only with the standardization of processes and product. Standardization of goods and facilities in terms of the average. Adjustment of educational, recreational, and cultural services to mass requirements. In politics, success of mass appeals—growth of mass movements.

Source: Schematic version by E. Shevky and W. Bell, *Social Area Analysis* (Stanford, Calif.: Stanford University Press, 1955), pp. 7–8, derived from Louis Wirth, "Urbanism as a Way of Life," *American Journal of Sociology.* 44 (1938), 1–24. Copyright 1938 by The University of Chicago Press.

Variations exist in the extent or degree to which areas can be characterized by urban qualities, some having less norm conflict, social change, mobility, individualism, and impersonality than others. Variations are also found within local areas of any given city. Certain cultural values in a society, moreover, may increase the effects of urbanization. If a culture emphasizes material possessions as a central value, as is true of the United States, the impersonality of urban life will tend to increase that emphasis. City living does not, of course, directly result in deviant behavior; it is just that many of the conditions associated with city life are, to a preponderant degree, conducive to deviation, such as crime and mental disorder.[21]

Norm Conflicts and Subcultures

The great diversity of interests and backgrounds of persons living in close contact with one another is a major characteristic of urbanism. Urban residents vary in age, race, ethnic background, and occupation, as well as in interests, attitudes, and values. Everywhere urban life is characterized by contrasts in wealth, abilities, and class structure. Large cities are really cities within cities, each area often with its own subculture, religious affiliation, or racial characteristic. Often groups have different customs as well as separate languages.[22] This heterogeneity of the population, the complex division of labor, the class structure, and, apparently, the simple physical dimension of population size, generally produce divergent group norms and values as well as conflicting social roles.[23]

Precisely because of the nature of urban life and the multiplicity of social groups in urban settings, urban experiences are not easily classified into types.[24] So differentiated and so conflicting have become the ends sought by different groups in these modern urban societies that individuals often do not know the conventional ways of behaving and suitable social rules in many areas of their lives. The simple fact that there are more people providing social expectations results in difficulties in fulfilling role obligations. Thus, urban residents tend not to agree about norms, show a tendency to ignore traditional norms, and often are not restrained by the social controls that have traditionally characterized rural areas. The behavioral result is often crime, high rates of mental disorder, drug addiction, alcoholism, suicide, and other forms of deviance.

Urban life also tends to foster increased individual freedom of normative choice.[25] Norm and role conflicts, or diversities of norms and behavioral standards,

[21]For a discussion of rural and urban ways of life and the manner in which they may lead toward or away from various forms of deviance, see John E. Conklin, *The Impact of Crime* (New York: Macmillan, 1975); and Eleanor Leacock, "Three Social Variables and Mental Illness," in Alexander H. Leighton, John A. Clausen, and Robert N. Wilson, eds., *Explorations in Social Psychiatry* (New York: Basic Books, 1957), pp. 308–338.

[22]For example, see Albert Hunter, *Symbolic Communities: The Persistence and Change of Chicago's Local Communities* (Chicago: University of Chicago Press, 1974).

[23]Bruce H. Mayhew and Roger L. Levinger, "Size and the Density of Interaction in Human Aggregates," *American Journal of Sociology,* 82 (1976), 86–110.

[24]Gerald D. Suttles, "Urban Ethnography: Situational and Normative Accounts," *Annual Review of Sociology,* 2 (1976), p.3.

[25]Arnold Rose, "The Problem of a Mass Society," in Arnold Rose, *Theory and Methods in the Social Sciences* (Minneapolis: University of Minnesota Press, 1954), p. 37.

create situations in which no single standard is likely to be upheld and in which deviation from it is not met with penalizing sanctions. Individuals who have been taught to accept the supremacy of a single rule may become skeptical of its validity when they discover, under urban conditions, that breaking the rule does not bring the social ostracism or the censure they had supposed.

The end result of urbanism is the creation and the strengthening of a variety of subcultures, and the norms of these subcultures are often conducive to deviance. The city does not always destroy social groups and subcultures; instead, it often tends to create them.[26] These subcultural groups become differentiated one from another by distinctive sets of beliefs and ways of living. Many of them are conventional, but others are considered to be deviant because of their lack of commitment to the dominant social order, their particular normative structure, and their unconventional types of behavior. Subcultures may be conventional; they may be considered only a bit "odd"—such as artists, missionaries of new religious sects, and certain types of intellectuals—or perhaps outright deviant—such as delinquent gangs, professional criminals, drug addicts and peddlers, and homosexuals. These groups can develop in the city due to the city's significant social diversity; the subcultures reflect this diversity. Rather than the destruction of social groups the urban process creates new ones; the city not only creates these groups but fosters and intensifies them. It is only within a large and complex population that certain of these subcultures can form and grow; the urban areas provide many groups the very opportunity to exist and to become stronger as persons are provided contacts with others of like interests, as well as with the opportunity for sustained interaction.

It is, then, the process by which these groups or subcultures are created and developed that indicates how deviance comes about, through processes of learning and support from others. The large city populations provide what is termed the "critical mass" of deviants as well as the opportunity to commit deviant acts. Fischer explains this well:

> Large population size provides a "critical mass" of criminals and customers for crime in the same way it provides a critical mass of customers for other services. The aggregation of population promotes "markets" of clients—people interested in purchasing drugs or the services of prostitutes, for example; and it provides a sufficient concentration of potential victims—for example, affluent persons and their property.[27]

Rapid Cultural Change

Rapid social and cultural change and disregard for the importance of stability through the generations also generally characterize urban life. Consequently, elements that are traditional, or "sacred," dwindle in importance. Sometimes the practical exigencies of urban life produce these changes; at other times, they seem to be outgrowths of the failure of informal controls to uphold and to maintain the older values and ideologies. Urban living has brought such great changes in the modern family, as has been

[26]Claude S. Fischer, *The Urban Experience* (New York: Harcourt Brace Jovanovich, 1976), pp. 35–38. Also see Claude S. Fischer, "Toward a Subcultural Theory of Urbanism," *American Journal of Sociology,* 80, (1975), 1319–1341.
[27]Fischer, *The Urban Experience,* p. 93.

pointed out, that it is often referred to as the "urban family." The reduced size of the modern family is both a characteristic and a result of urban life. Urban life has also led to the development of the concept of equality of the sexes both in marriage and outside it. The structuring of urban society into often fairly distinct peer groups has resulted in the magnification of age differences and the widening of the communication and status gaps between teenagers and adults, a situation that greatly increases the possibility of delinquency, crime, drug use, and different sex behavior.[28]

Mobility

It has been said that less than a century or more ago a person might live a lifetime without ever going far from home and without seeing more than a handful of strangers: today the picture is quite different. Modern transportation, particularly in urban areas, enables persons to move about rapidly and to have frequent contacts with many different people. People move again and again into strange localities. Packard refers to the United States as a "nation of strangers" where at least 40 million persons now lead "feebly rooted lives" as a result of this "deep upheaval" of life patterns.[29]

It appears that Americans move more often in their lifetimes than do persons in other countries. When allowances are made for variations in life expectancies, the average American moves about 14 times, the average Briton 8 times, and the average Japanese 5 times.[30] Between 1940 and 1960 more than 17.5 million people left the farms for the cities, or half of those living there in 1940. Approximately one in five persons moves each year; in 1962—1963, for example, some 35.4 million persons moved, and of this number about 28.7 million changed residence within the state and 6.7 million moved to another state. About 5 million crossed county lines, and approximately two in five moved across regional lines as well, many of them one or two thousand miles. Younger persons are more mobile than older persons; yet a large number of persons 65 and over also move. During 1970, 41.8 percent of those between 20 and 24 changed their places of residence, and nearly 9 percent of those 65 and over changed residence.

Urban societies generally tend to regard mobility favorably, but frequent moves may have unsatisfactory effects. They tend to weaken attachments to the local community, particularly among primary or face-to-face contacts, to make persons less interested in maintaining certain community standards, and to increase contact with secondary groups of diverse patterns, thus weakening bonds which help to provide the basis for social control among members of local groups. As persons become more mobile they come into contact with many different norms, and they begin to understand that other codes of behavior differ from their own. Mobility often means the loss of such personal relationships as kinship and neighborhood ties and fewer close

---

[28]Paul C. Friday and Jerald Hage, "Youth Crime in Post-Industrial Societies: An Integrated Perspective," *Criminology*, 14 (1976), 347–367.
[29]Vance Packard, *A Nation of Strangers* (New York: David McKay, 1972), p. 2.
[30]Larr H. Long, "On Measuring Geographic Mobility," *Journal of the American Statistical Association*, September 1970.

friendships. For child and adult alike, it may be necessary to acquire new friends and new norms, to change social roles, and to reconcile old norms and roles with new ones. As a result of these factors, social controls, and also legal controls, are weakened. Data on the effects of extensive mobility strongly point to a definite relationship between disrupted or anonymous life patterns and emotional stress. "The stress can in mild cases produce simply a generalized feeling of malaise, or it can in more stressful situations produce serious mental, physical, or personality disorders."[31] Studies have previously shown that migrants who move across state or national lines, for example, are more prone to mental disorders.[32]

As close relations with neighbors and relatives are severed, there is less control over the mobile person's behavior and a decline in the importance to him of having a "good reputation" in the eyes of these persons, thus contributing to criminal behavior. Too, the standards by which reputation is judged may become more diverse, depending less upon the specific ethical and moral qualities of the person than upon the "general impression" the person conveys. Children may have increasingly fewer contacts with grandparents and other relatives. Largely because of this mobility it is likely that a large proportion of young people today, living under urban conditions in America, cannot give the names of great grandparents on either side of the family. The identification of third cousins usually becomes impossible.

Materialism

External appearances and material possessions have become of primary importance in modern urban society, where people are more often known for their gadgets than for themselves. People increasingly come to judge others by how well they display their wealth, a display Veblen termed "conspicuous consumption." Under urban conditions, the types of clothes a person wears or the automobile he drives, the costliness of his home and its furnishings, the exclusiveness of the club or association to which he belongs, and the knowledge of his salary or the amount of his financial assets are the sole means others have of judging him or his success in life. Persons emphasize the importance of status symbols in urban society,[33] and it is on the basis of such readily "visible" criteria that status is assigned. Because of the status money and material goods provide, criminality, both in the lower and upper classes, becomes higher in urban areas.

Individualism

Urban persons tend to regard their own interests and self-expression as paramount in their social relations. The "I" feelings come to replace much of the feeling of

[31]Packard, p. 246.

[32]See Benjamin Malzberg, "Internal Migration and Mental Disease among the White Population of New York, 1960–61," *International Journal of Social Psychiatry* (1967), 184–191; Mildred Kantor, *Mobility and Mental Health* (Springfield, Ill.: Charles C Thomas, 1965); and Marc Fried, "Effects of Social Change in Mental Health," *American Journal of Orthopsychiatry,* 34 (1964), 3–28.

[33]See Erving Goffman, *The Presentation of Self in Everyday Life* (New York: Doubleday Anchor Books, 1959), especially Chap. 1.

cooperation characteristic of rural life. People increasingly feel that they must look after their own interests and increase their status through their own efforts. The urban person's strong belief in hedonism or personal happiness as the ultimate goal of life is increasingly seen. Competition has also been intensified as individualism has increased in urban society. The individual may feel that he is in ceaseless competition with the remainder of society, or at least with that part of the society in which he operates. The intensity with which a person strives for goals is, generally, in proportion to the values he attaches to them and the extent to which these goals can satisfy his socially induced needs. The extreme individualism and the competition of urban areas account, in part, for their higher rates of crime, alcoholism, suicide, and mental disorder.

Impersonality and Decline in Intimate Communication

Individuals may live or work where association with others is on a fairly personal basis, but in urbanized areas, particularly those where the population is dense and mobile, an extensive area of impersonality is often created for the residents. Associations among people outside their immediate contacts are scarcely more than acquaintances with people in their segmented social roles. Persons may even be regarded categorically much like physical objects, often objects to be "manipulated" without much feeling and primarily for personal satisfaction. Associations with others in urban settings tend to be brief and fragmentary; because of the impossibility of dealing with each association individually, they also tend to be stereotyped. In this connection Max Weber suggested some time ago that population density and the presence of large numbers of persons decrease the possibility of mutual acquaintanceships between individuals.[34] Because of the impossibility of developing a relationship with everyone one encounters in the city, urban residents use various categories for learning about and interacting with others. These categories, or stereotypes, are not necessarily derived from firsthand information but from secondary sources which tend to perpetuate the images. As Lofland puts it: "The cosmopolitan did not lose the capacity for knowing others personally. But he gained the capacity for knowing others categorically."[35]

Some people have suggested that the breakdown of intimate communication in an urban society lies at the center of many urban problems, as the individual finds he cannot easily communicate with his fellows and thus cannot orient his own values or put himself into harmony with the group.[36] Worst is probably the high-rise apartments of both low- and high-income families. While not invariably true, high-rise apartment dwellers tend to remain strangers, and the city's vast throngs, when they are not naturally subdivided into small-group affiliations, "tend to become coldly impersonal

---

[34]Max Weber, *The City,* Don Martindale, trans. (New York: Free Press, 1958).
[35]Lyn H. Lofland, *A World of Strangers: Order and Action in Urban Public Space* (New York: Basic Books, 1973), p. 177.
[36]Rose, "The Problem of a Mass Society."

and wary."[37] As people increasingly live in multiple-dwelling units made necessary by the imploding pressures of millions of rural and small-town people crowding into metropolitan areas, neighbors frequently live side by side in anonymity.[38]

The urban world of anonymity and the so-called blasé, sophisticated attitude of many big-city dwellers represent in part means people use to protect themselves from the intrusions of others. When they encounter difficulties in their interpersonal relations, they must often turn to professional counselors or psychiatrists. In many of the transitory relationships encountered the only things of interest are those directly pertaining to the situation; for example, whether a man will "stand" for a round of drinks or is a "good talker." This has helped to produce the loneliness of the urban world so well described by Auden:

> . . . This stupid world where
> Gadgets are gods and we go on talking
> Many about much, but remain alone
> Alive but alone, belonging—where?—
> Unattached as tumbleweed.[39]

Increase in Formal Social Controls

As urbanism increases and conformity to social norms becomes less affected by informal group controls, greater opportunities and inducements develop for behavior which deviates from that of others or the norms of others. As impersonality increases and intimate communication declines in the city, normative violations produce less and less informal censure of the kind seen in the rural areas. The conflicting normative experiences in an urban setting tend to weaken parental authority and other traditional controls over youth and also over all individuals. As a result, responsibility for controlling behavior in cities is shifting more and more to the police, the courts, and other agencies of govenment that tend to enforce the norms of certain power groups.

Urbanism as a Matter of Degree

The description of the characteristics of the urban way of life presented here should be considered only as an abstract type which can be compared with the characteristics of rural life. It is not meant to imply that the lives of all city persons are so characterized. One may have considerable personal relations, for example, with others in a city. Studies have shown that primary group life survives in urban areas in both developed and less developed countries. Gans, for example, found that close intimate relations exist in the Italian communities of a large city and that they are effective over considerable segments.[40]

---

[37]Packard, p. 3.
[38]Packard, p. 3.
[39]W. H. Auden, *The Age of Anxiety*, p. 44. Copyright © 1946 by Random House, Inc.
[40]Herbert Gans, *The Urban Villagers: Group and Class in the Life of Italian-Americans* (New York: Free Press, 1962). Also see William F. Whyte, *Street Corner Society* (Chicago: University of Chicago Press, 1943).

In other nonethnic situations, however, associations with relatives and friends in the city are often not in the local community, and they therefore differ considerably from such association in rural areas.[41] Even where people move within the city some retain active friendships in neighborhoods where they once lived.[42] According to Janowitz, sociologists have failed to take into consideration how impressive degrees and patterns of local community life do exist within metropolitan limits.[43] One study suggests that the role of mobility and impersonality in urban life should not be overstated in the factory and other work situations. "Even in the huge workplace where many thousands mass for the daily routine, the informal workgroup seems destined to go on performing its usual functions of controlling the workplace, initiating new members, deciding how far to go along with the boss, and making work a bit more like play."[44]

THE SLUM AND DEVIANCE

Almost universally people react to city slums in a negative manner, as if they represented something dark, evil, and strange. In fact, the very word "slum" is thought to be derived from "slumber," because slums were thought by most people to be "unknown, back streets or alleys, wrongly presumed to be sleeping and quiet."[45] Even today emotional attitudes toward the slum are reflected in popular definitions that emphasize the filth and squalor of the slum, the poor social conditions existing there, and the presence there of "vicious and dangerous persons." The slum popularly defined is a "street, alley, court, etc., situated in a crowded district or town or city and inhabited by people of a low class or by the very poor, or as a number of these streets or courts forming a thickly populated neighborhood or district of a squalid and wretched character."[46] Because of this general characterization of the slum, the word has sometimes been avoided in recent years, at least in the United States, and other terms have been substituted, such as "blighted," "deteriorated," "low-income," or "inner-core area" or "lower-class neighborhood." Hunter has pointed out, however, that "slum" is still a good word that carries real meaning.[47] A widely used term with

---

[41]See Gordon L. Bultena, "Rural-Urban Differences in Familial Interaction," *Rural Sociology,* 34 (1969), 5—15; and William H. Key, "Rural-Urban Social Participation," in Sylvia F. Fava, ed., *Urbanism in World Perspective* (New York: Crowell, 1968), pp. 305–312.

[42]Joel Smith, William H. Form, and Gregory P. Stone, "Local Intimacy in a Middle-Sized City," *American Journal of Sociology,* 60 (1954), 284. Also see Peter H. Rossi, *Why Families Move: A Study in the Social Psychology of Urban Residential Mobility* (New York: Free Press, 1956).

[43]Morris Janowitz, *The Community Press in an Urban Setting* (New York: Free Press, 1952), p. 19.

[44]Harold L. Wilensky and Charles N. Lebeaux, *Industrial Society and Social Welfare* (New York: Russell Sage Foundation, 1958), p. 124.

[45]Eric Partridge, *Origins: A Short Etymological Dictionary of Modern English* (London: Routledge & Kegan Paul, 1958).

[46]*The Oxford Universal Dictionary,* 1955 edition, p. 1921, notes that the word came into use in 1812. "Slumming" was a fashionable pursuit in 1884.

[47]David R. Hunter, *The Slums: Challenge and Response* (New York: Free Press, 1964), p. 6. The term has wide acceptance in other countries, particularly in developing countries.

strong emotional connotations is "ghetto," which originally referred to segregated urban Jewish areas and now refers to black slums.

Poor people are found on farms, in villages, and in small as well as very large cities. It is, therefore, incorrect to equate all poverty with the slum living found in most large cities. Poverty takes many forms, but in no place is the life of the poor made more complicated than by residence in slum communities. In fact, many of the conditions of slum living cannot by themselves be attributed to poverty. In rural areas the effects of poverty are often counterbalanced by many other features of traditional living. In areas of extensive urbanization and industrialization, where traditional and primary group ties are weakened, the stigma, the lack of power, and the low status of the poor in slum areas are much greater.

Ignoring the Slum Every urban society in the nineteenth century had its lower-class living in the slums, and in earlier times the low productivity of society and the great gap between the rich and the poor made this distinction seem natural and inevitable.[48] The upper classes did little to help, writing off the slum poor as the result of "God's will" and in general ignoring their starvation, illness, and despair. Occasionally persons of the wealthy class even found entertainment in their "slumming" expeditions, and occasionally philanthropically minded individuals visited the slums, feeling it to be their "Christian duty" to make some personal contribution. On the whole, however, the slum was taken for granted, assumed to be inevitable, or ignored by most people. A contemporary account reveals how little power slum dwellers had in civic affairs among the two million residents of the East End of London in 1882:

> Probably there is no such spectacle in the whole world as that of this immense, neglected, forgotten great city of East London. It is even neglected by its own citizens, who have never yet perceived their abandoned condition. They are Londoners, it is true, but they have no part or share in London; its wealth, its splendours, its honours, exist not for them. . . . No one is curious about the way of life in the east. . . . If anything happens in the east, people at the other end have to stop and think before they can remember where the place may be.[49]

As late as the 1890s many Americans in cities were really unaware of the serious conditions under which slum dwellers lived. Although several thousand people died each year in New York as a result of conditions in the slums, this fact was never emphasized in the newspapers: yet if the headlines proclaimed the drowning in a flood of a few hundred people or fewer, society became perturbed and millions of dollars were spent to prevent a recurrence of such a tragedy. Early studies of slum districts reflect a certain aloofness, with tenement dwellers being discussed as if they were a strange species of humanity with which the writers had little in common. Often in writings of the 1890s slum dwellers were described as being debased and undeserving

---

[48]Adapted from Marshall B. Clinard, *Slums and Community Development: Experiments in Self Help* (New York: Free Press, 1966).

[49]Quoted in Guy Thorne (Cyril Arthur Edward Ranger Gull), *The Great Acceptance* (New York: Hodder and Stoughton, 1913), pp. 1–2.

of sympathy, devoid of moral feelings and a sense of shame, and as living in "a commingled mass of venomous filth and seething sin, of lust and drunkenness, of pauperism and crime of every sort." A federal government report in 1894 described slum inhabitants as a "squalid and criminal population."[50]

Discovering the Slum   Since the turn of the century a more general conviction has gradually developed in many countries that the very presence of slums contradicts important values of society. Poverty might well be regarded as a personal matter, but the slums could not be as easily dismissed. Efforts to eliminate slums have largely been inspired more by emotional and esthetic revolt against their physical ugliness and their danger to the larger society than by full appreciation of the plight of the person living in the slums himself. In the United States, for example, the first real concern about the slum developed because of its effects upon the larger society, the slum areas being close to busy commercial districts and to better residential areas which were occasionally disturbed by rioting and brawling in the slums. Some people feared the slums as being sources of undesirable citizens, and others saw them as increasing threats to public health, particularly as the relation between slums and epidemics of typhoid, cholera, smallpox, and other diseases became recognized.

The tragedies of slum life were also "discovered" in part through the writings of Charles Dickens, who described the late nineteenth-century slums of London as "haunts of hunger and disease" and as "foul and frowsy dens." A number of American authors tried to imitate Dickens, but their approach was more lurid, using slums as backdrops for stories of crime and violence. Modern slum life has probably never been portrayed more brilliantly and more savagely than by such realistic novelists as James Farrell (the *Studs Lonigan* trilogy) in the 1930s, Willard Motley (*Knock on Any Door*) in the 1940s, and James Baldwin in the 1960s. In the 1950s the publication of a diary of a slum dweller in Brazil (*Child of the Dark*) had a wide impact.

The attitude of people today toward slums is vastly different than it was in past centuries or even past decades. In the past, there was acceptance of the inevitability of the correlation between slum conditions and social status; today there is increasing awareness among large segments of the population in many countries that slum conditions have to be changed, not only on humanitarian grounds but also to further the development of society as a whole. A belief is also emerging among a large proportion of U.S. slum dwellers that their situation is not inevitable and that it can be changed. This awareness of a "slum problem" is only recent in the developing countries, however, where even the physical conditions of life have not generally shocked the sentiments of those in positions of economic and political power.

Deviant Behavior in the Slum

One reason there is concern for eliminating slums is that a high incidence of deviant behavior—violence, property crime, prostitution, drunkenness, drug abuse, mental

---

[50]Quoted in Edith Elmer Wood, *The Housing of the Unskilled Wage Earner* (New York: Macmillan, 1919), p. 29.

disorder, suicide, illegitimacy—is associated with slum living. Yet, one should not overexaggerate the slum as a producer of deviance, for in middle- and upper-class suburbia there is also extensive white-collar crime, increasing youth crime, particularly vandalism, drug abuse, drunkenness and alcoholism, and various types of mental disorders. In general, however, overt crime is more pronounced in slum areas. A government survey of crime in the United States concluded that the offense occurs in, and the victims and offenders are more frequently from, slum areas, and this situation prevails in most countries in the world. "Study after study in city after city in all regions of the country have traced the variations in the rates for [serious] crimes. The results, with monotonous regularity, show that the *offense,* the *victims,* and the *offenders* are found most frequently in the poorest, and most deteriorated and socially disorganized, areas of cities."[51]

Crime and Delinquency   In nearly all countries, there is strong evidence that the slum neighborhood, rather than the individual or family, provides the milieu for juvenile delinquency and crime: it is here stolen goods are sold and attitudes of antagonism toward the police and outside authorities are developed. Gang delinquency in the form of theft or assault may be a natural means of adjusting not only to the social roles, behavior patterns, and norms of the groups but also to the slum neighborhood to which the gang delinquents belong. In developing countries the "criminalizing" effect of slums is potentially strongest on younger persons who migrate to areas with high crime rates, becoming at the same time emancipated from their village and home ties.[52]

It is estimated that in slums composing 20 percent of the population of a U.S. city there occur approximately 50 percent of all arrests, 45 percent of the reported major crimes, and 55 percent of the reported juvenile delinquency cases.[53] A number of studies made over a period of several years in Chicago, for example, have revealed that conventional crime, delinquency, mental disorder in general, and schizophrenia in particular, suicide, prostitution, vagrancy, dependency, illegitimacy, infant mortality, as well as high death and disease rates, are largely concentrated in the slum.[54] A study of Milwaukee showed that the slum, or inner core area of the city, which had 13.7 percent of the population, had 69 percent of the arrests for burglary, 21 percent of the aggravated assaults and 47 percent of other assaults, 60 percent of the murders, 72 percent of the arrests for commercial vice, 22 percent of the drunkenness, and 72 percent of the narcotics arrests.[55] Similar findings have been reported in such cities as

[51]*The Challenge of Crime in a Free Society,* President's Commission on Law Enforcement and Administration of Justice (Washington, D.C.: Govenment Printing Office, 1967), p. 35.

[52]Clinard and Abbott, *Crime in Developing Countries,* p. 140. Also see Marshall B. Clinard and Daniel J. Abbott, "Community Organization and Property Crime: A Comparative Study of Social Control in the Slums of an African City," in James F. Short, Jr., ed., *Delinquency, Crime and Society* (Chicago: University of Chicago Press, 1976), pp. 186–206.

[53]Hunter, p. 71.

[54]For a survey of these early studies, see Ernest R. Mowrer, *Disorganization, Personal and Social* (Philadelphia: Lippincott, 1942).

[55]*Milwaukee Study Committee on Social Problems in the Inner Core of the City,* Final report to Honorable Frank P. Zeidler, Mayor, City of Milwaukee (Milwaukee: Study Committee on Social Problems in the Inner Core of the City, 1960). Also see Charles T. O'Reilly, Willard E. Downing, and Steven I. Pflanczer, *The People of the Inner Core—North: A Study of Milwaukee's Negro Community* (New York: LePlay Research, 1965).

Cleveland, Jacksonville, Florida, and Indianapolis. A slum area in Cleveland, which contained only 2.5 percent of the city's population in its 333 acres, was responsible for 6.8 percent of its delinquency, 21 percent of its murders, and 26 percent of its houses of prostitution.[56] The rates for nearly all 29 types of crimes known to the police in Seattle, and arrests for these crimes, during the period 1949–1951, showed a decline as one moved out in six one-mile concentric zones from the center of the city. Slum areas were higher in 23 out of 29 crimes and were particularly high in robbery, prostitution, rape, gambling, and common drunkenness.[57] These problems and the trouble potential for those blacks living in a Washington, D.C., slum area called Winston Street have been described as follows:

> There is also Winston Street's own major trouble spot, the corner where the rougher streetcorner men hang out. Fights are rather common there, and the men occasionally show up with fresh knife wounds. True, most of the fights are within the group, and most of the people who have lived in the neighborhood for some time know the men well and are reasonably friendly with them; even so, they warn newcomers and visitors about this corner. Yet it is not so bad there, Winston Street people feel, as on the neighboring street where tough teenage boys hang out and are a menace to everybody who passes by.[58]
>
> Thus the people of the ghetto maintain a working knowledge of the potential for trouble in their environment. This knowledge undergoes constant revision, of course; and the concern with danger may also fluctuate, although it seems generally to be rather strong. At Winston Street people seem to be a little extra worried during the weeks before Christmas, when it is widely held that robberies and holdups increase in number— "people are desparate for money then, you know, to have something extra." (Besides, the victims may also carry more money, and it gets darker rather early.)[59]

Crimes involving violence, such as criminal homicide, assault, and forcible rape, are concentrated in the slums. Two detailed studies of criminal homicide in the United States, one in Houston and the other in Philadelphia, have shown a concentration of these offenses in lower-class slum areas.[60] Similarly, criminal homicides, assaults, and other crimes of violence in London have the highest incidence in slum areas, violence being used to settle domestic disputes and neighborhood quarrels.[61] Forcible rape is very largely committed by persons living in the slums; in fact, areas with high rates of

---

[56]R. B. Navin, W. B. Peattie, and F. R. Stewart, *An Analysis of a Slum Area in Cleveland* (Cleveland: Metropolitan Housing Authority, 1934).

[57]Calvin F. Schmid, "Urban Crime Areas: Part II," *American Sociological Review,* 25 (1960), 655–678.

[58]Reprinted from U. Hannerz: *Soulside*, New York; Columbia University Press, 1969, by permission of the publisher.

[59]Reprinted from U. Hannerz: *Soulside*, New York; Columbia University Press, 1969, by permission of the publisher. A survey of eight primarily low-income police districts for the year July 1, 1965, through June 30, 1966, in Chicago, Boston, and Washington, D.C., found that one in every five businesses and organizations had been burglarized, and in one Washington, D.C., district, one third had been. Albert J. Reiss, Jr., ed., *Studies in Crime and Law Enforcement in Major Metropolitan Areas* (Washington, D.C.: Government Printing Office, 1967), Vol. I, p. 80.

[60]Henry P. Lundsgaarde, *Murder in Space City: A Cultural Analysis of Houston Homicide Patterns* (New York: Oxford University Press, 1977); and Marvin E. Wolfgang, *Patterns in Criminal Homicide* (Philadelphia; University of Pennsylvania Press, 1958).

[61]F. H. McClintock, *Crimes of Violence* (London: Macmillan, 1963); and David J. Pittman and William Handy, "Patterns in Criminal Aggravated Assault," *Journal of Criminal Law, Criminology and Police Science,* 55 (1964), 462–470.

forcible rape have been found to correspond to areas having high rates of crimes against the person generally.[62] Violence may be used by younger persons in the slums to achieve sexual objectives. About conditions in East Harlem in New York City, one researcher has stated that many slum dwellers "live in a generalized state of fear—of being robbed, knifed, attacked, bullied, or having their children injured. The fear colors their whole lives; their ability to learn, to work, to stay sane and healthy, to venture out of their apartments or block, to live openly and freely, to be friends with their neighbors, to trust the world, outsiders, themselves. Fear is a crippler in the slum."[63] Teen-age boys in a Washington, D.C., slum have described how violence is commonplace:

> When I first started living around here it was really bad, but I have gotten used to it now. Been here 2 years. People getting shot and stuff. Lots of people getting hurt. People getting beat up. Gee, there's a lot of violence around here. You see it all the time.
>
> Sometime where I live at people be hitting each other, fighting next door. Then when they stop fighting then you can get some sleep.
>
> Drinking, cussing, stabbing people, having policemen running all around mostly every day in the summertime.[64]

Studies of Shaw, McKay, and Thrasher in Chicago several decades ago demonstrated the much higher rates of juvenile delinquency within slum districts.[65] Moreover, the Chicago slum areas had much higher rates in both 1900 and 1920, even though the ethnic composition of the area had almost entirely changed. Whether the slum areas were occupied successively by Swedes, Germans, Poles, or Italians, the rates were high, as they are today with a primarily black population. Similar findings have been reported in the United States for 8 other large metropolitan areas and 11 other cities, all widely separated geographically, including Boston, Philadelphia, Cleveland, Richmond, Birmingham, Omaha, and Seattle.[66] A study of Croydon a large English city near London, revealed the highest rates for delinquency were concentrated in areas populated by unskilled and semiskilled workers' families.[67]

Indications are that with the growth of urbanization, the cities of developing countries are beginning to face similar problems in their slums.[68] In developing countries, offenders involved in ordinary crime (not white-collar crime by persons in business and political corruption) come almost entirely from slum areas, and their offenses, whether theft or assault, are largely committed against other slum dwellers. This has been shown by studies in such varied cities as San Juan, Lima, Manila,

---

[62]Menachem Amir, *Patterns in Forcible Rape* (Chicago: University of Chicago Press, 1971); and Susan Brownmiller, *Against Our Will: Men, Women and Rape* (New York: Simon & Schuster, 1975), Chap. 6.
[63]Patricia Cayo Sexton, *Spanish Harlem: Anatomy of Poverty* (New York: Harper & Row, 1965), p. 116.
[64]*Task Force Report: Juvenile Delinquency and Youth Crime,* President's Commission on Law Enforcement and Administration of Justice (Washington, D.C.: Government Printing Office, 1967), p. 45.
[65]See Clifford Shaw, *Delinquency Areas* (Chicago: University of Chicago Press, 1929); and S. Kirson Weinberg, "Shaw-McKay Theories of Delinquency in Cross-Cultural Context," in Short, pp. 167–185.
[66]Clifford R. Shaw and Henry D. McKay, *Juvenile Delinquency and Urban Areas* (Chicago: University of Chicago Press, 1942).
[67]Terrence Morris, *The Criminal Area: A Study in Social Ecology* (London: Routledge & Kegan Paul, 1958).
[68]Clinard and Abbott, *Crime in Developing Countries.*

Bombay, Kuala Lumpur, and Kampala, Uganda. Studies of Kanpur and Lucknow in India, for example, showed that juvenile delinquency, juvenile vagrancy, and crime were primarily associated with slum areas.[69] Not all slum areas in a country have high crime rates, but the reasons for such variations have rarely been studied. One such study in Kampala, Uganda, showed that in two slum areas of quite similar physical conditions there were differences in crime rates. The area with the low crime rate was found to be more homogeneous in population and norms, and there was less mobility, a higher degree of intimate communication among the residents, more stability in family relationships, and greater participation in community organizations.[70]

Drug Use   Drug addiction, primarily to heroin, is heavily concentrated in the slums of large cities. In New York City, for example, 83 percent of adolescent drug users were found to live in slum areas populated by 15 percent of the city's census tracts.[71] Drug use for "kicks" is more common among teenagers and youth, partly because drugs are more readily available in these areas. There is also much talk about drugs. Within recent years drug use has been spreading into middle-class areas and into suburbia; when this problem existed almost entirely in the slum, middle-class people were much less concerned about drug use among adolescents. One study of a slum reported heroin peddling everywhere and its use by children as young as six. "As one Puerto Rican mother puts it: 'We don't care about marijuana here. If our kids just take marijuana, we consider ourselves lucky.'"[72]

Mental Disorder   A disproportionate amount of schizophrenic mental disorder appears to come from slum areas. In a Detroit study of two local communities the bulk of the schizophrenic cases (78.1 and 62.5 percent) had lived in slum areas before establishing residence there.[73] A survey of the prevalence of mental disorder in midtown New York revealed a higher rate among the lower class: in fact, 13 percent of the lower-class persons were classified as being psychotic as compared with only 3.6 percent of those from higher-status groups.[74] Schizophrenia was found to have a high incidence in a study of the slums and slum rehousing areas in San Juan, Puerto Rico, where it was, in part, related to the many role conflicts present in slum neighborhoods. The validity of these and the other studies depends, of course, upon the research procedures and the criteria used to determine "mental health," "mental disorder," "neu-

---

[69]Shankar S. Srivastava, *Juvenile Vagrancy: A Socio-Ecological Study of Juvenile Vagrants in the Cities of Kanpur and Lucknow* (New York: Asia Publishing House, 1963).
[70]Clinard and Abbott, *Crime in Developing Countries.*
[71]See, for example, Isidor Chein, Donald L. Gerard, Robert S. Lee, and Eva Rosenfeld, *The Road to H* (New York: Basic Books, 1964), p. 73. For a vivid description of the pervasiveness of drug use in a black slum, see Claude Brown, *Manchild in the Promised Land* (New York: Macmillan, 1965).
[72]Michael Dorman, *The Making of a Slum* (New York: Delacorte Press, 1972), p. 4.
[73]H. Warren Dunham, *Community and Schizophrenia: An Epidemiological Analysis* (Detroit: Wayne State University Press, 1965). His community explanation of this phenomenon is a cautious one, tying it to several other factors, including life chances. Also see Lloyd H. Rogler and August B. Hollingshead, *Trapped: Families and Schizophrenia* (New York: Wiley, 1965).
[74]Leo Srole, Thomas S. Langner, Stanley T. Michael, Marvin K. Opler, and Thomas A. C. Rennie, *Mental Health in the Metropolis: The Manhattan Midtown Study* (New York: McGraw-Hill, 1962); and Thomas S. Langner and Stanley T. Michael, *Life Stress and Mental Health* (New York: Free Press, 1963).

roses," and "psychoses" and adequately to take into account variations in societal reaction to mental disorders based on social class.

However great is the extent of certain forms of deviance in the slum, it is essential to reiterate that not all slum dwellers engage in them. In any slum area there exist, simultaneously, strong conventional value systems carried through certain individuals, schools, churches, and other sources.[75] The interaction of the conventional and unconventional value systems, such as delinquent and criminal values, may have a differential impact on those who live in these areas.[76] Moreover, it is also important to recognize the extensive nature of youth crime, drug usage, mental disorder, alcoholism, and suicide among middle- and upper-class groups. Among these groups are persons in business, lawyers, and physicians who commit white-collar crimes, most of which may be far more serious to the total society in the long run. Those who engage in such activities as price fixing, embezzlement, and bribery of public officials come from middle- or upper-class areas.[77] The discussion of deviance in slum areas, then, is not meant to convey the impression that all deviance is localized in the slums, even though, as stated above, the forms of deviance under discussion here are disproportionately slum-based.

THE SLUM AS A WAY OF LIFE

Slum areas are generally characterized as being overcrowded and congested, having bad and run-down housing, and being deficient in all amenities. Although slums do vary considerably from one type to another, as will be pointed out later, these general patterns of living conditions are almost universal; and although these general patterns of physical characteristics are almost without exception typical of slums, it would be a serious mistake to view slums only in such terms. The slum actually is far more than this; it is a *way of life*. Sociologically, it represents a subculture with its own set of norms and values, which is reflected in poor sanitation and health practices, often a lack of interest in formal education, certain deviance, and characteristic attributes of apathy and social isolation. In this sense "slums" may exist in areas of reasonably good physical facilities such as slum clearance projects. Slum residents have become isolated from the general power structure of the community and are looked upon as being inferior; in turn, they reflect, in their living and in their behavior, their own suspicions toward the world that they regard as the "outside."

Slums are of all types, shapes, and forms. New York has its Harlem and its Lower East Side, and Chicago has its Black Belt and its Uptown slum area of southern poor whites.[78] London has its well-known East End, and Bombay has its multistoried

---

[75]See, for example, Whyte.
[76]Solomon Kobrin, "The Conflict of Values in Delinquency Areas," *American Sociological Review,* 16 (1951), 653–661.
[77]See the collection of materials in Gilbert Geis and Robert F. Meier, eds., *White-Collar Crime: Offenses in Business, Politics and the Professions* (New York: Free Press, 1977).
[78]Todd Gitlin and Nanci Hollander, *Uptown: Poor Whites in Chicago* (New York: Harper & Row, 1970).

chawls. Southeast Asian families in Bangkok crowd together in "pile villages," wooden shacks raised on stilts along the waterfronts. Tin shacks, bamboo huts, or straw hovels crowd small lanes of Calcutta, Dacca, and Lagos, all of them steaming with high humidity and stinking from the open drains. The impoverished shanty-towns or squatter shacks of the slum dwellers cover the hillsides of Rio de Janeiro, Lima, Hong Kong, and other Asiatic, African, and South American cities. Few slums, however, are more crowded than those of Hong Kong and Singapore, where single rooms house from 10 to 40 families, each family with only "bed space" and no element of personal privacy. In Hong Kong hundreds of thousands of families live in waterfront sampan or "floating" slums.

The world's slums are populated by millions of persons, and because they constitute the chief sources of certain deviance in all places where they exist it is essential to understand the nature of the slum if one is to understand the reason for its relationship to deviant behavior. Slums differ in physical setting, degree of overcrowding, permanence of the inhabitants, degree of organization among the residents, and types of problems, such as deviant behavior, which they present.[79] They may, particularly in developing countries, lack even the most basic amenities and be constructed of nothing more than scraps, or they may be substandard tenement housing or even once the homes of middle-class wealthy residents. They also may be "slums of hope" where people may feel that they can still move out, or "slums of despair" where they feel that they cannot.[80]

PHYSICAL CHARACTERISTICS OF THE SLUM

Of all the characteristics of a slum, the physical conditions have been most often emphasized.

Housing Conditions

Slums have commonly been defined as those portions of a city where housing is crowded, neglected, deteriorated, and often obsolete. These inadequate housing conditions are in large part the result of poorly arranged structures, inadequate light and circulation, poor design, lack of sanitary facilities, overcrowding, and insufficient maintenance. Yet it must be recognized that the housing conditions of a slum area are often a product of neglect and sometimes willful destruction associated with the way of life found there. As a resident of a New York slum has said: "They come here and their kids write all over the walls, dump garbage and throw bricks. They fight all the time

---

[79]Slums and slum dwellers can also be classified in terms of social mobility and the reason for their involvement in the slum. See John R. Seely, "The Slum: Its Nature, Use and Users," *Journal of American Institute of Planners,* 25 (1959), 7–14; and Charles J. Stokes, "A Theory of Slums," *Land Economics,* 38 (1962), 187–197.

[80]Stokes, p. 197.

and ruin the cars parked on the block. I'm telling you, it ain't the landlord that tears up this building. The landlord don't live here."[81]

If slums in the United States are to be defined according to such standards as dilapidated housing, lack of adequate sanitary facilities, overcrowding, or location in an extremely undesirable area, it has been estimated that over five million families, or one sixth of the urban population, reside in slum environments.[82] In terms of physical conditions and housing standards, it is important to keep in mind, however, the comparative nature of the definition. A slum should be judged physically according to the general living standards of a country. Certainly slum housing in New York City or Chicago would be regarded as adequate, even good, in many parts of the world. The availability of running water, flush toilets, electricity, and cooking facilities, even though in limited supply, may make a slum not a slum in the physical sense in other parts of the world.

In spite of these differences there is a world-wide tendency to stress the physical aspects of the slum and to define it in these terms alone. In some cases there may be a partial relation between housing conditions and social deviance, but the explanation is more likely to be the slum way of life. Low economic status or discrimination forces people to live in low-rent areas where certain values prevail. This assumed relation of slum housing to deviant behavior has resulted in the erroneous belief that all that needs to be done is to provide new housing in slum areas.

> We hear that decent housing means less crime, less juvenile delinquency, lower costs for police and fire protection, and fewer welfare cases. From these assertions we get the impression that all the community has to do is remove the slums, and by this act it will wipe out social ills and their human and material costs.
>
> Several things are wrong with this picture. Certainly there is much evidence to substantiate the argument that the incidence of poverty, disease, vice, and crime is far greater in slum districts than in other parts of the metropolis. What the picture overlooks, however, is that the housing problems of slum occupants are generally inseparable from family and community disorganization, poverty, and disease. Human lives as well as houses are blighted in these areas. Merely moving occupants into better dwelling units will not cure other physical and social ills. Empirical evidence, in fact, is accumulating to show that improved housing does not have many of the social benefits initially attributed to it. . . . Yet the belief that delinquency, prostitution, alcoholism, crime, and other forms of social pathology magically inhere in the slums and will die with their demolition continues to persist.[83]

This view can be documented by studies in various parts of the world, including London, Caracas, Lima, Mexico City, Lagos, San Juan, and various mainland cities of the United States, which have shown that extensive deviant behavior, as well as poor health and sanitation practices, continue to exist with new housing. Even after the construction of new government housing projects in an English city, a study found that the rates of delinquency remained high.[84] It was concluded that an area's physical

---

[81]Woody Klein, *Let in the Sun* (New York: Macmillan, 1964), pp. 176–177.
[82]William G. Grigsby, "Housing and Slum Clearance: Elusive Goals," *The Annals,* 352 (1964), 107–118.
[83]John C. Bollens and Henry J. Schmandt, *The Metropolis: Its People, Politics and Economic Life* (New York: Harper & Row, 1965), pp. 255–256.
[84]Morris.

characteristics are of little relevance to crime and delinquency, except as an indirect determinant of the social status of the area. A survey of a large high-rise slum clearance project in St. Louis found that a significant proportion of the families had been involved in many problems since living there.

> For example, 41 percent of the households reported that something had been stolen from them since they moved into the project; 35 percent said someone in the family had been hurt by bottles or other objects dropped out of windows onto the walkways outside; 39 percent said some adult in the family had been "insulted" by teenagers cursing them outdoors; and 51 percent said their windows had been broken from outside. In addition, 16 percent of the women reported rapes or attempted rapes of a female in the family; 10 percent reported that someone in the family had been held up; and 20 percent reported cutting, shooting, or other kinds of physical assaults. These were all situations in which the family members affected were defined as victims, but in addition, other threatening situations involved family members as initiators or equal participants. One-fifth of the families reported adult quarrels and arguments with neighbors and one-fifth reported teenage fights involving family members.[85]

Another study of a large Midwestern high-rise development has been called the Vertical Ghetto, and the description lives up to the title. Teenagers in the project often identify with criminals and others who are adept at "beating the Man." "If an investigator approaches the right teenager, he can order almost any item (or buy back his own) that he wishes and expect to have it delivered. For example, if a prospective customer wants a special kind of hub cap for his car or a transistor radio or a tire, these teen-agers will get the items according to the customer's specifications at a small fraction of the actual cost. The purchaser, of course, in all probability, is receiving stolen, or 'hot,' goods. The teen-agers are well aware of puritanical hypocrisy. They do not hesitate to proclaim: 'Our best customers are the law-abiding citizens—nobody else has any money'."[86]

It is not difficult to explain why slum-clearance housing projects do not solve basic problems. The slum way of life continues to exist, the frictions and problems among the residents are not abated, and there is much greater social isolation and impersonality than previously existed in the former slum area. Slum-clearance projects bring together a group of strangers, and they destroy what community feelings and informal social controls previously did exist in these areas. Substitutes are usually formal controls by an external governmental housing agency set up to deal with the residents' problems through regulations, a situation which often results in negative counter reactions.

Overcrowding and Congestion

A slum may be overcrowded with buildings, or the buildings overcrowded with people, or both. High density is not the same as overcrowding: areas may have high

---

[85]Lee Rainwater, *Behind Ghetto Walls: Black Families in a Federal Slum* (Chicago: Aldine, 1970), p. 104.
[86]William Moore, Jr., *The Vertical Ghetto: Everyday Life in an Urban Project* (New York: Random House, 1969), p. 125.

densities, as in high-rise apartments, but not be overcrowded. Congestion may be so great that a judgment about the physical condition of the building must often be made in terms of the high density per block, acre, or the square mile. It has been pointed out, for example, that if the population density of New York City were as high as some of the worst blocks in Harlem, the entire population of the United States could fit into three of New York City's boroughs.[87] Whyte stressed the importance of overcrowding as a criterion for slum conditions when he described how he chose Boston's North End for a slum in his well-known sociological study of "street corner society." "It had more people per acre living in it than any other section of the city. If a slum meant overcrowding, this was certainly it."[88]

People who live under these crowded conditions obviously have little privacy, a factor that may be of great importance, especially in its effects upon interpersonal relations.[89] Frazier states that overcrowded housing probably explains why so many blacks congregate on the streets of black neighborhoods. "So far as the children are concerned, the house becomes a veritable prison for them."[90] The overcrowding and congestion of slum life mean that personal matters are difficult to keep to oneself in domestic life.

> Husbands and wives cannot keep their intimacies or arguments a private matter that others can at least pretend didn't happen. At times everyone may use the same towel, eat off the same plate, or indulge in a common obscenity. Fathers are seen in their underwear, mothers while in labor, sisters during their period, and boys when "beating their meat." Sometimes there are disclosures that could lead to serious consequences: abortions, incest, illegitimacy, adultery, and narcotics scars. More common, however, are those skeletons for which every family is supposed to have a closet: defecation, intercourse, parental arguments, and dressing.[91]

Poor Sanitation and Health

Slums are dirty places; they often are infested with rats, cockroaches, and other pests that complicate health and sanitation problems. It has been estimated that on the average the city slum areas, containing about 20 percent of the residential population, have 50 percent of all its diseases.[92] Areas in New York City that contain 27 percent of the total population are reported to account for 45 percent of the infant mortality deaths. In combating these problems a basic problem is the distribution of medical resources. One study concluded that the distribution of medical resources is unrelated to various population characteristics reflecting health needs. In fact, infant mortality rates in 109 of the largest metropolitan areas in the United States are in inverse

---

[87]Michael Harrington, *The Other America: Poverty in the United States* (Baltimore, Md.: Penguin Books, 1962), p. 70.
[88]Whyte, p. 283.
[89]For a discussion of the effects of slum overcrowding, see Alvin L. Schorr, "Housing and Its Effects," in Robert Guttman and David Popenoe, eds., *Neighborhood, City and Metropolis* (New York: Random House, 1970), pp. 709–729.
[90]E. Franklin Frazier, *The Negro in the United States,* rev. ed. (New York: Macmillan, 1957), p. 636.
[91]Gerald D. Suttles, *The Social Order of the Slum: Ethnicity and Territory in the Inner City* (Chicago: University of Chicago Press, 1968), p. 91.
[92]Hunter, p. 77.

proportion to such medical resources.[93] Thus, the slum population not only incurs higher probabilities of disease but these slum dwellers are also the least likely to receive medical help.

In the slum areas of developing countries the rates of disease, chronic illness, and infant mortality are exceptionally high. A migrant to the southern white Chicago slum area has said: "I was lookin right out the winder and this woman came right out of her house with a box of garbage. In place of puttin it in the garbage can somewhere, hell, she just dumped it right out in the damn street down there."[94] A person living in a New York tenement has commented: "If the people would cooperate there wouldn't be all the mess. Why can't these people bring garbage down instead of throwing it out of the windows? If they didn't feed the rats with garbage, there wouldn't be any rats. You take these people—they pee on the stairs. If you put these people somewhere else and tore these buildings down they'd do the same thing elsewhere."[95] A 16-year-old Washington, D.C., slum boy has described his area:

> Well, the neighborhood is pretty bad, you know. Trash around the street, stuff like that and the movies got trash all in the bathroom, dirt all over the floors. Places you go in for recreation they aren't clean like they should be, and some of the children that go to school wear clothes that aren't clean as they should be. Some of them, you know, don't take baths as often as they should. Well, my opinion is—it's not clean as it should be and if I had a chance, if my mother would move, I would rather move to a better neighborhood.[96]

SOCIAL BEHAVIOR OF THE SLUM

The social behavior of the slum can be analyzed in terms of its social organization, its social isolation, and its cultural patterns.

Social Organization

Detailed descriptive studies of slum communities often reveal a considerable degree of organization, with systematic and persisting features of social behavior.[97] Rather than being "disorganized," the slum often simply has its own organization, usually a type judged by the middle class to be unconventional. Miller states that lower-class culture is a cultural system in its own right, with its own integrity, set of practices, focal concerns, and ways of behaving, systematically related to one another rather than to

---

[93]Judith J. Friedman, "Structural Constraints on Community Action: The Case of Infant Mortality Rates," *Social Problems,* 21 (1974), 230–245.
[94]Gitlin and Hollander, p. 155.
[95]Klein, p. 176.
[96]*Neighbors of the President,* President's Commission on Juvenile and Youth Crime, 1963, as quoted in Robert W. Winslow, ed., *The Emergence of Deviant Minorities: Social Problems and Social Change* (San Ramon, Calif.: Consensus Publishers, 1972), p. 136.
[97]See, for example, Whyte, Gans; and Frederic M. Thrasher, *The Gang* (Chicago: University of Chicago Press, 1927).

corresponding features of middle-class culture.[98] Whyte has pointed out that in the American slum, behavior may be as highly organized, and social controls as effective, as in middle-class suburbia, except that the slum resident may not always conform to middle-class standards of proper conduct and respectability.[99] Formal governmental control may be ineffective and police and other government authorities may be held in disrespect, but this is replaced by some degree of informal control based on age, sex, occupation, or ethnic group. Sanitation and the health and child care beliefs and practices may also indicate a highly organized system, even though contrary to both scientific and middle-class beliefs.

Although some slums lack unity, this cannot be assumed to be a general phenomenon of the slum. Rather, each slum neighborhood must be examined in the light of its own type of subculture. In each case the particular subculture involved will be the dominant influence on the life patterns of the inhabitants, shaping their lives through the pressures of environmental and family backgrounds, cultural traditions, and major life concerns. Many years ago the rooming-house slum was described as a district of little social interaction among neighbors because people constantly were moving in and out without ever really becoming a part of the neighborhood.[100] The rooming-house slum differs greatly, however, from certain ethnic slums such as those of Italian-Americans in the United States, where many close common cultural ties are maintained. Studies of the more settled Italian slums in Boston found that the residents derived many satisfactions in their neighborhoods, and that while these areas were depressing places, they did provide an organized and familiar environment for those who lived there.[101] The strong friendship and family relationships made these people feel that their neighborhood was a real "home."

Upper- and middle-class areas in the city are, however, quite different from slum areas in their ecology, their social structure and, above all, their ability to participate and utilize effectively the resources of the larger city. Middle- and upper-class groups, particularly in the Western world, live in a neighborhood, but their actual participating area, where they shop, visit, and pursue recreational and cultural activities, is generally much larger. The world of slum people is much more fixed. It is centered in a smaller world which tends to create resentment and suspicion of the outside urban community.

Cultural Patterns

The slum has a culture of its own. The slum way of life is learned, and passes from generation to generation, in the process developing rationale, structure, and even defense mechanisms which provide means of continuation in spite of deprivations and

---

[98]Walter B. Miller, "Implications of Lower Class Culture," *Social Service Review,* 33 (1959), 219–236.
[99]William F. Whyte, "Social Organization in the Slums," *American Sociological Review,* 8 (1943), 34–39.
[100]Harvey W. Zorbaugh, *The Gold Coast and the Slum: A Sociological Study of Chicago's Near North Side* (Chicago: University of Chicago Press. 1929). p. 82.
[101]See Whyte, *Street Corner Society,* p. xv. Also see Walter Firey, *Land Use in Central Boston* (Cambridge, Mass.: Harvard University Press, 1947), p. 179; and Edward J. Ryan, "Personal Identity in an Urban Slum," in Leonard J. Duhl, ed., *The Urban Condition: People and Policy in the Metropolis* (New York: Basic Books, 1963), pp. 135–150.

difficulties. While all slum residents are influenced in some degree by this slum culture, all do not become a real part of it. For example, in parts of the world some members of the intellectual classes, including students and artists, choose to live in the slum yet they do not become slum dwellers in the full cultural sense. Others who have been forced to live in the slum at various times, such as the Jews and Japanese-Americans, have been able to a large extent resist the adoption of many slum cultural patterns.

Certain patterns or styles of life are typical of the slum culture. Life is usually gregarious and centered, for the most part, in the immediate area. Confusion and noise seldom abate; life has more spontaneity and behavior is more unrestrained than in the middle-class environment, whether in the home or on the street corner. Fried and Levin have cited some of the striking characteristics of social relations in the working-class slum community: "continuity of contact with the same people over long periods of time, spatial contiguity of residence, frequent interaction in a variety of circumstances, informality of contact in daily activities."[102] It is these factors that operate to create the context wherein "extremely close, mutually dependent relationships develop among clusters of people."[103]

In the slum culture toughness is often regarded as virtuous, and frequent resort to violence in the settlement of disputes is common. Also common is early initiation into sexual experiences, whether by marriage or otherwise, and for the most part middle-class standards of sex conduct are not widely followed. Above all, there is a greater tolerance of certain deviance, a higher rate of conventional crime, and an ambivalence toward quasi-criminal activities committed against the "outside world." In a settled Chicago slum of Italians, Puerto Ricans, Mexicans, and blacks the subculture consists of a wide range of personal information, shared understandings, ethnic customs, and mutual disclosures. In this slum much emphasis is put on gossip, innuendos, and slander to determine an individual's social character. Where the person might be negatively regarded as criminal or immoral in a middle-class area, the reputation of a person in the slums as being trustworthy might far outweigh such considerations. The content of the subculture has been described in terms of at least three concerns: (1) a concern about illegal activities and criminals with whom local residents are anxious to make friends; (2) a concern about each other's trustworthiness and loyalty, shown in a hesitation to reveal too much about oneself, lest one become vulnerable in some way; and (3) a concern over the exercise of brute force, which often becomes the basis on which leadership, social status, and continued association are assigned.[104]

The violence and force that are characteristic of the slum culture are not, however, accepted by slum residents, who recognize the dangers of the violence to them and to their communities. While the slum dweller might not respect a law that he feels makes differences between his rights and those of another, or a police force that applies laws in a differentiating manner, he "does recognize the law's duty to deal with lawbreakers, and he respects the policeman who does so with businesslike skill and

---

[102]Marc Fried and Joan Levin, "Some Social Functions of the Urban Slum," in Bernard J. Frieden and Robert Morris, eds., *Urban Planning and Social Policy* (New York: Basic Books, 1968), p. 72.
[103]Fried and Levin, p. 72.
[104]Suttles, *The Social Order of the Slum,* p. 232.

impartiality."[105] He knows that he lives in an area that is probably among the city's highest in crime rates, and he is anxious and even more desirous of police protection than those who live in safer regions of the same city.[106]

Throughout the slums, attitudes have led to the development of a generalized suspicion of the "outside world," which includes government and politicians, welfare groups, and the upper and middle classes generally. Slum people often fail adequately to utilize those very agencies, both public and private, which could be helpful to them, such as the health department, the educational facilities, or even the police. Police in ghetto areas are often perceived negatively, even though they provide one of the few means of protection in the most victimized areas of the city. Slum dwellers are generally dissatisfied with the quality of police services, the speed with which they are delivered, and the manner in which the services are administered.[107] When efforts are made to improve police services in the slums, however, another problem is encountered: increased manpower in slum areas, altered patrol priorities, and so on, all efforts to satisfy the complaints about poor and inadequate service, subsequently lead to complaints about police abuse.[108] Attempts to solve one problem here has only created or aggravated another. Slum residents' hostility thus includes an ever-widening group of institutions and of persons whose efforts have been primarily directed to help solve slum problems. Suttles has aptly described his research experience with the exclusiveness and suspicion of a Chicago slum he studied:

> When I first went into the Addams area, I entered several places where I was asked, "Whatta you want?" as if I were lost. At the time I thought them inhospitable or "prejudiced." What I did not know was that these places are almost never confronted by someone they have not known for years and that they are thoroughly tailored to the needs and personal peculiarities of a small network of friends within a single minority group. To them my presence was totally inexplicable. At worst, I could be a policeman, some sort of city inspector, or a troublemaker. At best, I might have got there by accident, not knowing any better.[109]

Those who live in slums adopt what Rainwater terms "coping," or strategies for survival—the expressive life-style, the violent strategy, the strategy of depressive adaptation, and, finally, the strategy of mobility.[110] In its benign-form expressive life-style, with its emphasis on having fun, dancing, and singing and an animated, colorful language, the impression is given of a happy, spontaneous existence which has an appeal and interest for the middle class who have been trained to be more serious and less animated. Yet Rainwater points out that it is the elaboration of this expressive life-style which plays a "central dynamic role in most forms of lower-class deviant behavior," being particularly relevant as a "motivating force for alcohol and drug involvement of all kinds."[111]

---

[105]*Task Force Report,* p. 43.
[106]*Task Force Report,* p. 43.
[107]Peter H. Rossi, Richard A. Berk, and Bettye K. Eidson, *The Roots of Urban Discontent: Public Policy, Municipal Institutions, and the Ghetto* (New York: Wiley, 1974), Chap. 6.
[108]Rossi, Berk, and Edison, especially p. 203.
[109]Suttles, *The Social Order of the Slum,* p. 47.
[110]Lee Rainwater, "Problems of Migrants to Cities," in Robert A. Dentler, *Major Social Problems,* 2d ed. (Chicago: Rand McNally, 1972), pp. 156–157.
[111]Rainwater, *Behind Ghetto Walls,* p. 379.

With the failure of this strategy, if the individual is unable to develop required skills or if the "audience is unappreciative," there is a tendency to adopt a violent strategy wherein force is adopted to gain what one wants. In general, this strategy is not popular among the lower classes, since on the whole persons of this class disapprove of the use of taking things by force. The strategy of depressive adaptation is characteristic of many who, having experienced repeated self-defeats, learn not to ask too much of life. "They come to hope simply that each day will bring nothing worse than the previous day, and that when there is trouble, they will be able to cope with it."[112] This is the strategy that is apparently adopted by more and more lower-class persons as they grow older. Finally, there is the strategy of mobility wherein lower-class persons strive to develop a "reasonable approximation of a stable working class way of life."[113]

Social Isolation

A slum represents an image in the eyes of the larger community which involves a negative societal reaction to slum dwellers. The nonslum dweller often associates the physical appearance and difficult living conditions of the slum with a belief in the "natural inferiority" of those who live there: because the slum is an inferior place, those who live there are also inferior. This reaction has important consequences for the social isolation of slum dwellers and their exclusion from power and participation in urban society. "The slums of virtually every American city harbor, in alarming amounts, not only physical deprivation and spiritual despair, but also doubt and downright cynicism about the relevance of the outside world's institutions and the sincerity of efforts to close the gap."[114] Those who live in the slum lack an effective means of communication with the outside world because of apathy, lack of experience in communicating with outsiders, or their own powerlessness to make their voices heard. "The common denominator of the slum is its submerged aspect and its detachment from the city as a whole. . . . The life of the slum is lived almost entirely without the conventional world."[115] The local politician often becomes the only "ambassador to the outside world," one who unfortunately frequently tries to manipulate it for his own benefit.[116] Regarding the isolation of a Washington, D.C., black slum area, Hannerz has offered this analysis:

> On the one hand there are the white people with whom the ghetto dweller has only impersonal relationships—the shopkeeper, the supervisor, the policeman, the social worker, the customer at the lunch counter downtown; on the other hand, there are the black people of the ghetto, the pool from which his partner in marriage, his intimate friends and enemies, his next door neighbor are all drawn. Ghetto dwellers do not only share a position with regard to the outside and experiences with it, they are also actual or potential participants in close personal relationships with one another.[117]

---

[112]Rainwater, *Behind Ghetto Walls,* p. 109.
[113]Rainwater, "Problems of Migrants to Cities," p. 157.
[114]*The Challenge of Crime in a Free Society,* p. 60.
[115]Zorbaugh, p. 152.
[116]Gans, p. 170.
[117]Reprinted from U. Hannerz: *Soulside,* New York: Columbia University Press, 1969, by permission of the publisher.

Slum people often feel relatively powerless to alter their life situations.[118] One writer has referred to this as the "feel" of a slum, the feel when an outsider is in a slum, the feel of things when one lives in the slum.

> The attitude of the slum dweller toward the slum itself, toward the city of which the slum is a part, toward his own chances of getting out, toward the people who control things, toward the "system"—this is the element which as much as anything else will determine whether or not it is possible to "do something" about slums. This is what makes slums a human problem rather than a problem of finance and real estate.[119]

With increasing social action and militancy among those who live in slum areas these characteristic attitudes of slum dwellers are changing rapidly. This is particularly the case with blacks, whose change in attitude and self-confidence is already being reflected in the emergence of self-help communities in slum areas and in their efforts to move out of them.

ELIMINATING THE SLUM

Slums have existed for centuries; they grow increasingly larger and new ones are spawned. In this sense they can be said to be self-perpetuating, either replenishing themselves from within or being augmented by new ones created through migration from without the city. In the past, in the United States at least, it has generally taken about three generations for a substantial proportion of families to move from the slums to middle-class areas. In developing countries this movement has hardly occurred at all, or if it has occurred it has taken many generations. Such a "natural" method of moving people out of these areas has generally worked, but it has been inefficient, slow, sometimes barbaric, and wasteful of human resources and talent. The problem is how to accomplish in one generation what has traditionally required several. Furthermore, since most large city slums contain not a few hundred people or even a few thousand, but hundreds of thousands, some way must be found to produce widespread change. The problem is more than moving people out of the slums: it is rather one of changing and even completely eradicating the slum. In spite of welfare and other services through the years, slums have generally continued to resist efforts to change them, and they have remained largely unaffected by the multitude of agencies and services offered, even in the developing countries. Thus far efforts have been directed toward ameliorating slum problems rather than eliminating the slum.

Changes in Society There must be, of course, basic changes in society if the problems of the slum are to be dealt with effectively. In both affluent and poor countries a more equitable distribution of wealth is urgently needed, along with the elimination of poverty; the realization of this objective in itself requires pronounced changes in the economic

---

[118]Warren C. Haggstrom, "The Power of the Poor," in Louis A Ferman, Joyce L. Kornbluh, and Alan Haber, eds., *Poverty in America* (Ann Arbor, Mich.: University of Michigan Press, 1965), pp. 315–334.
[119]Hunter, p. 18.

system and in social controls. Many individuals who are in positions of political and social power, however, are at present unwilling to promote these changes, whether because of economic costs, the elimination of a cheap supply of labor, the loss of political power, or an unwillingness on the part of middle- and upper-class persons to permit lower-class people, particularly those from minority groups, to live in or even near their own areas. It is conceivable that a reverse trend could take place, with middle- and upper-class persons relocating from suburbia in new housing in or adjacent to slum areas. This would bring them closer to the city's business and cultural facilities, a situation that would be advantageous to all groups. Multiclass housing construction has been tried in many parts of the world, particularly in Mexico City.

Dispersal of Slums   Slum people cannot successfully be integrated, however, if rigid class distributions by geographic areas are maintained in the cities and the lower-class groups are thus excluded from normal day-to-day contacts outside their restricted areas. In the United States class restriction is further complicated by racial discrimination.[120] While it is a mistake to assume that all slum residents are members of minority groups—millions of whites live in city slums—one need only look at population figures to see the heavy concentration of these groups in the cities.

The estimated central-city black population in the United States in 1970 was 13.6 million, and it could rise as high as 20.3 million by 1985, assuming the same nonwhite rate of migration as in the period 1960–1966.[121] By 1985 it has been estimated that the following cities will become 50 percent or more black in total population: Chicago, Philadelphia, St. Louis, Detroit, Cleveland, Oakland, Baltimore, New Orleans, Richmond, and Jacksonville. Already Washington, D.C., Newark, and Gary are over 50 percent black. While the suburban black population of the United States from 1960 to 1966 grew only at a rate of 33,000 a year, the white population of the suburbs went up to an average of 1,750,000 per year, partly as a result of the exodus of the white population from cities. In addition to blacks, about a million and a half other minority groups lived in the slums of large cities in 1966.

The voluntary movement of large numbers of black slum dwellers into suburban areas would involve radical changes in the present attitudes of both central-city blacks and suburban whites. While various recommended procedures, such as the busing of school children in order to break down racial antagonisms and improve the quality of education, might be effective over a period of time, they cannot solve many of the basic economic issues. One social scientist has approached the problem on a broad basis, and he proposes five effective arguments for dispersal of the black and other slum dwellers of the inner cities as opposed to a concentrated program of "enriching" and changing slum areas.[122]

First, factories, for various reasons, including taxes and space requirements, are being located in suburban areas, and there should be less rather than more divergence between where the jobs are and where the workers are. Second, U.S. Office of

---

[120]See Morton Grodzins, "The Metropolitan Area as a Racial Problem," in Guttman and Popenoe, pp. 479–501.

[121]These and other figures are from the *Report of the National Advisory Commission on Civil Disorders* (Washington, D.C.: Government Printing Office, 1968).

[122]The following discussion is derived from Anthony Downs, *Urban Problems and Prospects* (Chicago: Markham, 1970), pp. 60–62.

Education reports on equalities of educational achievement have tentatively concluded that the clustering of lower-income black students in segregated schools should be ended if their education is to be significantly improved.[123] If educational opportunities are to be provided for the most deprived groups to enable them to improve themselves they should be exposed to members of other social classes. Since there are insufficient numbers of the black middle-class children to provide this exposure, "this means some intermingling of children from the deprived groups with those from not-so-deprived white groups, at least in schools." In view of the difficulties of transporting large numbers of these students from the central city to suburban areas, the only sensible alternative is residential dispersal.

Third, in order to provide real freedom of choice in housing for blacks of all income levels and to develop adequate housing supplies for low- and middle-income families, many families in all income groups must move to the suburbs, which will necessitate programs of "positive incentives" and increased suburban housing construction. Fourth, dispersal of blacks and others away from the ghetto conditions of poverty, deprivation, and apathy is important in combating the increasingly high rates of crime and violence in the central city. Fifth, dispersal is needed to prevent the increasing concentration of blacks in the older, blighted core of the city while the suburban areas remain occupied mainly by whites, a situation that cannot lead to the development of "a truly integrated society in which race is not a factor."[124]

> Dispersal would involve specific policies and programs at least starting us toward reversal of the profoundly divisive trend now so evident in our metropolitan areas. It may seem extraordinarily difficult to begin such a reversal. But however difficult it may be now, it will be vastly more difficult in twenty years if the number of Negroes segregated in central cities is 8 million larger than it is today.[125]

Many Black Power advocates, on the other hand, see the need for greater black self-determination. They seek better housing, better schools, better jobs, and better personal security within all-black areas, with black social controls. To them, there is greater long-term hope in the "enrichment" of the areas where blacks now reside, and it is not compatible with their desires to live in white communities, even in suburbia, where they would be isolated from other blacks. Dispersal might still be in keeping with their views, since the number of persons moving out would probably not completely reduce the inner-city areas. Moreover, dispersal to suburbia probably could also furnish ample opportunity for blacks to live and work with other blacks.

CHANGING THE SLUM
WAY OF LIFE

As has been pointed out, most slum-clearance programs have not only failed to solve the problem of the slum way of life but often they have made it even worse. Likewise, charity, philanthropy, settlement houses, and welfare centers, along with the "uplift"

---

[123]See James Coleman et al., *Equality of Educational Opportunity* (Washington, D.C.: Office of Education, 1966); and U.S. Civil Rights Commission, *Racial Isolation in the Public Schools* (Washington, D.C.: Government Printing Office, 1967), both as reported by Downs, p. 61.
[124]Downs, p. 62.
[125]Downs, p. 62.

work of social workers, have neither prevented slums nor brought about much change. Many people believe that the slum can be changed simply by providing adequate wages, guaranteed minimum incomes, undiscriminatory employment policies, accessible and inexpensive credit plans, programs to train or to retrain youths and adults, more effective training for certain occupations and trade, increased social security and public assistance payments, and better teachers and improved programs for preschool as well as school-aged children.

Need for Self Help Others believe, however, that the slum problem requires more than these measures; the slum way of life must also be changed. To attack the problem in this way requires the concerted efforts of those who live there.[126] The dilemma of slum dwellers has been their own lack of power. Being lower in economic status, moving outside the sources of social and political power, and often apathetic or subject to political manipulation, they have become pawns of others in the larger urban world. Slum dwellers need to reach some measure of unity among themselves, as well as some degree of militancy, if they are to be recognized as part of the power structure and their legitimate demands for services and opportunities are to be met.[127] Community ties must be improved and new aspirations created. Since those who live in slums are generally apathetic, they need to recognize the necessity for change. In the process of developing a sense of respectability and of importance, the slum dweller may find the slum way of life incompatible with his new self-image.[128] Many advocates of Black Power, for example, point out the importance of black persons having control over their lives, institutions, and educational facilities in black neighborhoods, believing that this will be more advantageous to them in their efforts to escape from their subordination to a dominant white population. One writer views the development of a sense of self-respect among blacks as essential in the process of their assuming their proper role in society. Blacks can fulfill their proper role only by exerting "power over the decisions that directly affect [their] own members," because "a fully integrated society is not really possible until the Negro minority has developed its own internal strength."[129]

The importance of this change in identity has been particularly stressed in the Black Muslim movement and in other black groups in the United States.[130] Among the

---

[126]Clinard, *Slums and Community Development.* Urban community development projects are being carried out in slum areas in many parts of the world today, including the United States, where they are often called community action projects, Great Britain, Venezuela, Brazil, India, Pakistan, the Philippines, Indonesia, and Hong Kong. The People's Republic of China, as well as most of the other Socialist or Communist countries, such as Yugoslavia, have similar types of decentralized urban controls and responsibilities.

[127]See Saul Alinsky, *Reveille for Radicals* (Chicago: University of Chicago Press, 1946); and his *Citizen Participation and Community Organization in Planning and Urban Renewal* (Chicago: Industrial Area Foundation, 1962). Also see Charles E. Silberman, *Crisis in Black and White* (New York: Random House, 1964), pp. 321–328; and Kenneth Heller and John Monahan, *Psychology and Community Change* (Homewood, Ill.: Dorsey Press, 1977).

[128]See Haggstrom; and Marshall B. Clinard, "The Role of Motivation and Self-Image and Social Change in the Slum," in Vernon Allen, ed., *Psychological Factors in Poverty* (Chicago: Aldine, 1970).

[129]Downs.

[130]See C. Eric Lincoln, *The Black Muslims in America* (Boston: Beacon Press, 1961); and E. U. Essien-Udom, *Black Nationalism: A Search for an Identity in America* (Chicago: University of Chicago Press, 1962).

various occupants of slums in the United States, blacks alone have had little sense of identity or of ethnic or racial pride, and this has made it difficult for them to rise above the world of the slum in the same way that other ethnic groups have done. The cultural identity of blacks in the United States was erased by slavery, even to the extent of their losing knowledge of their exact African homeland, their past cultural heritage, and often even specific knowledge of their additional biological white ancestry where this had been added. The Black Muslims have tried to develop a new image of the black, working largely in some of the worst black slums. In their small mosques in neighborhood areas the Black Muslims stress pride in their African heritage and rejection of the appendages carried over from slavery. The new convert experiences a rebirth in self-image, in which he changes his name (the names of most blacks are those of their slave owners), his religion (Christianity was imposed by slavery), his idea of his African homeland, his moral and cultural values, and his very purpose in life. Among Black Muslims, pride in Africa means that new patterns of behavior must be practiced by the lower-class slum black if behavior and the new self-image are to be reconciled. A strict private and public morality is emphasized for the "new black"; crime, delinquency, drug addiction, and illegitimacy no longer fit this new self-image. Family roles are also redefined; a patriarchal system is substituted for a largely matriarchal one.

Indigenous Leaders   A new trend is emerging with respect to changing slum areas, namely, that efforts to bring about change should be carried out either through professional persons working with indigenous persons in the area or through giving the entire responsibility for change to nonprofessional or indigenous leaders. Such persons are viewed not merely as extensions of the professional worker but as having a distinct role themselves.

> Outside leaders have a definite but limited role. This approach to area reorganization places principal emphasis on the role of natural community leaders who are carriers of conventional conduct norms. Not only do such leaders serve as nondelinquent models for emulation by youngsters attracted to programs offered by projects of this type, but because these indigenous leaders have prestige in the local area, they easily attract adults, as well as children and youths, to project programs in the first instance. It is around natural community leaders, then, that legitimate social structures can be germinated and multiplied in delinquency-prone areas.[131]

Community Programs   Community action programs in slum areas are of various types. Some are loose organizations built around a single problem, others are more tightly organized on a local neighborhood basis and cover many problems. Some programs may involve a few hundred families while others may take in several thousand. Such organizations may deal with rent problems, sanitation and health problems, delinquency and crime, and drug use. In general, all such organizations serve as pressure groups on public authorities. There have also been efforts to delegate some decentralized political

---

[131]John M. Martin, "Three Approaches to Delinquency Prevention: A Critique," *Crime and Delinquency,* 7 (1961), 23. Also see Arthur Pearl and Frank Reissman, *New Careers for the Poor* (New York: Free Press, 1965).

authority to local school boards, and there have been proposals for local police boards, library boards, and local public health organizations. Increasing local government responsibility might well improve the work of law enforcement by changing the attitudes of slum dwellers toward the police, develop greater community interest in education and support for school programs, result in better cooperation on sanitation problems and public health problems, and afford local protection to such public facilities as schools and parks. Many U.S. small towns with as few as 2,500 persons administer and support their own schools, police and fire departments, libraries, parks, and other public facilities.

Probably the best-known effort to use people in local areas to control delinquency and other community problems is the Chicago Area Project, which began in about 1930 and continues to be very active today. Although primarily organized to counteract delinquency, it has indirectly stimulated many attempts to solve other slum problems. Initially the project was instituted to reduce the high delinquency in three areas of the slum; since then the work has been expanded to include seven other areas. The project has the same purpose as have other agencies—the control of delinquency—but its methods are different.

(1) It emphasizes the development of a program for the neighborhood as a whole. (2) It seeks to stress the autonomy of the local residents in helping to plan, support, and operate constructive programs which they may regard as their own. (3) It attaches special significance to the training and utilization of community leaders. (4) It confines the efforts of its professional staff, in large part, to consultation and planning with responsible neighborhood leaders who assume major roles in the actual development of the program. (5) It seeks to encourage the local residents to utilize to the maximum all churches, societies, clubs, and other existing institutions and agencies, and to coordinate these in a unified neighborhood program. (6) Its activities are regarded primarily as devices for enlisting the active participation of local residents in a constructive community enterprise, for creating and crystallizing neighborhood sentiment on behalf of the welfare of the children and the social and physical improvement of the community as a whole. (7) It places particular emphasis upon the importance of a continuous, objective evaluation of its effectiveness as a device for reducing delinquency, through constructive modification of the pattern of community life.[132]

Despite more effective programs of community action and participation in slum areas, the continued existence of slums cannot be dealt with effectively without dealing with the maldistribution of wealth and racial discrimination. In 1967, for example, the lowest fifth of the population in the United States made only 5.4 percent of the country's total income. On the other hand, the highest fifth of the population made 41.2 percent, and the top twentieth made 15.3 percent. In 1969, 1,211 persons had incomes of $1 million a year or more, which, figured at a minimum of $1 million each, totaled $1,211,000,000. Various palliatives, such as the many welfare benefits, the guaranteed minimum wage, and the more recent proposal for a guaranteed

---

[132]Clifford R. Shaw and Jesse A. Jacobs, "The Chicago Area Project: An Experimental Community Program for Prevention of Delinquency in Chicago" (mimeographed; Chicago: Institute for Juvenile Research, undated). Also see Solomon Kobrin, "The Chicago Area Project—A 25-Year Assessment," *The Annals,* 322 (1959), 19–29. Also see "The Chicago Area Project," in Harold Finestone, *Victims of Change: Juvenile Delinquents in American Society* (Westport, Conn.: Greenwood Press, 1976), pp. 116–151.

income, do not come to grips with the distribution of income.[133] Many people are presently expressing a certain cynicism regarding the possibilities of any durable solution to poverty as long as the current system of property and class relations prevails.[134]

SELECTED REFERENCES

Clark, Kenneth B., and Jeannette Hopkins. *A Relevant War against Poverty: A Study of Community Action Programs and Observable Social Change.* New York: Harper & Row, 1969.

Davis, Kingsley. *World Urbanization, 1950–1970,* Vol. II. Berkeley, Calif.: Institute of International Studies, 1972.

Clinard, Marshall B. *Slums and Community Development: Experiments in Self-Help.* New York: Free Press, 1966.

Clinard, Marshall B., and Daniel J. Abbott. *Crime in Developing Countries: A Comparative Perspective.* New York: Wiley, 1973.

Downs, Anthony. *Urban Problems and Prospects.* Chicago: Markham, 1970.

Fischer, Claude S. "The Effect of Urban Life on Traditional Values," *Social Forces,* 53 (1975), 420–432.

Fischer, Claude S. "Toward a Subcultural Theory of Urbanism," *American Journal of Sociology,* 80 (1975), 1319–1341.

Fischer, Claude S. *The Urban Experience.* New York: Harcourt Brace Jovanovich, 1976.

Fried, Marc, and Joan Levin. "Some Social Functions of the Urban Slum," in Bernard J. Frieden and Robert Morris, eds., *Urban Planning and Social Policy.* New York: Basic Books, 1968.

Hannerz, Ulf. *Soulside: Inquiries into Ghetto Culture and Community.* New York: Columbia University Press, 1969.

Hauser, Philip M., and Leo F. Schnore. *The Study of Urbanization.* New York: Wiley, 1965.

Hunter, David R. *The Slums: Challenge and Response.* New York: Free Press, 1965.

Jacobs, Jane. *The Death and Life of Great American Cities.* New York: Vintage, 1961.

Lofland, Lyn H. *A World of Strangers: Order and Action in Urban Public Space.* New York: Basic Books, 1973.

Moynihan, Daniel P. *The Politics of a Guaranteed Income: The Nixon Administration and the Family Assistance Plan.* New York: Random House, 1973.

Palen, J. John. *The Urban World.* New York: McGraw-Hill, 1975.

Rainwater, Lee. *Behind Ghetto Walls: Black Families in a Federal Slum.* Chicago: Aldine, 1970.

Rossi, Peter H., Richard A Berk, and Bettye K. Eidson. *The Roots of Urban Discontent: Public Policy, Municipal Institutions and the Ghetto.* New York: Wiley, 1974.

Suttles, Gerald D. *The Social Order of the Slum: Ethnicity and Territory in the Inner City.* Chicago: University of Chicago Press, 1968.

Suttles, Gerald D. "Urban Ethnography: Situational and Normative Accounts," *Annual Review of Sociology,* 2 (1976), 1–18.

---

[133]Daniel P. Moynihan, *The Politics of a Guaranteed Income: The Nixon Administration and the Family Assistance Plan* (New York: Random House, 1973).

[134]See, for example, David Matza and Henry Miller, "Poverty and the Proletariat," in Robert K. Merton and Robert Nisbet, eds., *Contemporary Social Problems,* 4th ed. (New York: Harcourt Brace Jovanovich, 1976), pp. 639–673. See particularly Maurice Zeitlin, ed., *American Society, Inc.: Studies of the Social Structure and Political Economy of the United States,* 2d ed. (Chicago: Rand McNally College Publishing Co., 1977).

PART TWO

DEVIANT BEHAVIOR

CHAPTER 6

An exhibit of weapons confiscated from a teen-age gang by Chicago police when they inter-rupted a threatened gang battle. (*Chicago Daily News* photograph. Reprinted with permission of Field Enterprises, Inc.)

Criminal Behavior

ONLY within the past hundred years or so have efforts been made to study scientifically the factors that underlie criminal behavior.[1] Although there had previously been much interest and considerable speculation about the nature of crime, little attention had been focused on the criminal. Near the end of the eighteenth century, several writers, notably Cesare Beccaria in Italy, suggested that a crime was simply a rationally planned act wherein the pleasure derived from the criminal act exceeded the possible pain that might result from any punishment imposed.[2] This conception of crime was based on the principles of hedonistic philosophy, which assumed the behavior of all persons to be entirely a matter of individual responsibility and all behavior to be motivated by the anticipation and expectation of pleasure. In 1807, Gall published his first volume on the relationship between certain areas of the brain and criminal behavior.[3] The origin of scientific criminology is usually traced, however, to the work of Cesare Lombroso, an Italian army doctor, who was originally influenced by his work with mental hospital patients whose various physical measurements he took. His work was also greatly influenced by Darwin's theories of evolution, which claimed that contemporary humans had antecedents in various forms of more primitive humans.[4] He had become convinced that some criminals were born with certain common physical features, and he developed a system of classifying them into those who were "born" criminals and those who were insane or "criminaloid." About his physical measurements of "born" criminals he wrote:

> Thus were explained anatomically the enormous jaws, high cheekbones, prominent superciliary arches, solitary lines in the palms, extreme size of the orbits, handle-shaped or sessile ears found in criminals, savages, and apes, insensibility to pain, extremely acute sight, tattooing, excessive idleness, love of orgies, and the irresistible craving for evil for its own sake, the desire not only to extinguish life in the victim, but to mutilate the corpse, tear its flesh, and drink its blood.[5]

Criminaloids were persons who had not been born with physical stigmata, that is, with physical characteristics that were more common at an earlier evolutionary period, but who had innate tendencies toward committing crimes. Lombroso's theory was later shown to be incorrect, but his work did a great deal to arouse an interest in the actual scientific study of individual criminals and in criminal behavior generally. Most of the interest stimulated by his studies was directed at efforts to disprove his biological view of crime and subsequently to shift the approach instead to learning and the social factors in the explanation of criminal behavior.

---

[1] For a survey of the scientific approach to criminal behavior and an examination of our present knowledge, see Gwynn Nettler, *Explaining Crime*, 2d ed. (New York: McGraw-Hill, 1978); Edwin H. Sutherland and Donald R. Cressey, *Criminology*, 10th ed. (Philadelphia: Lippincott, 1978); Sue Titus Reid, *Crime and Criminology* (Hinsdale, Ill.: Dryden Press, 1976); and Gresham M. Sykes, *Criminology* (New York: Harcourt Brace Jovanovich, 1978).

[2] Cesare Beccaria, *An Essay on Crimes and Punishment* (New York: Stephen Gould, 1809).

[3] See Leonard Savitz, Stanley H. Turner, and Toby Dickman, "The Origin of Scientific Criminology: Franz Joseph Gall as the First Criminologist," in Robert F. Meier, ed., *Theory in Criminology: Contemporary Views* (Beverly Hills, Calif.: Sage Publications, 1977), pp. 41–56.

[4] Cesare Lombroso, *L'uomo delinquente* (Turin: Bocca, 1896–1897). Also see Gina Lombroso Ferrero, *Lombroso's Criminal Man* (New York: Putnam, 1911); and Cesare Lombroso, *Crime, Its Causes and Remedies*, H. P. Horton, trans. (Boston: Little, Brown, 1912).

[5] Ferrero, p. xv.

NATURE OF A CRIME

The nature of a crime or a criminal act may be examined in two ways, as a violation of the criminal law or as a violation of any law punished by the state, depending upon how one approaches illegal behavior. *Sociologically a crime is any act that is considered to be socially injurious and that is punished by the state, regardless of the type of punishment.* From a strictly legal standpoint, an act is a crime only when the statutes so specify; these statutes, and their subsequent interpretations by the courts, constitute the criminal law. The criminal law may be defined as a body of specialized rules of a politically organized society that contains provisions for punishment to be administered in the name of the political state when a violation has been substantiated through the judicial process.

Many criminal laws develop from social conflict. Conflicts are inevitable in any society—conflicts between states, between groups, and between cultural units; they are the normal consequences of social life. Group cohesion is assured by some form of coercion and constraint through the criminal law as exercised by certain persons and groups who have the power to determine the conduct of others. To illustrate with two examples of embezzlement and vagrancy, historical analyses of these particular laws indicate that the statutes evolved through a conflict process whereby the new law was seen as a device to protect the development of industrial interests in English society at the time by forcing people into the cities to work.[6] These interests were of such importance that those persons and groups powerful enough to introduce and have enacted certain legislation used the criminal law-making process to their advantage: the advantage in the embezzlement law related to the crown's concern for the safety of funds in foreign trade and commerce, while the vagrancy law related to securing labor for manufacturing and industrial purposes. In his presentation of the origin of criminal law, Quinney claims that crime actually constitutes behavior which conflicts with the interests of those segments of society that have the power to shape criminal policy.[7] Although this definition applies to much crime of the type regulating political behavior and personal morality, as well as the avoidance of the criminal law by certain powerful groups, the definition is too broad to include all crimes. Crimes such as burglary, larceny, robbery, and auto theft are generally regarded as crimes by all social strata in society; they would remain crimes no matter who has power in the social structure.[8] If

---

[6]Jerome Hall, *Theft, Law and Society,* 2d ed. (Indianapolis: Bobbs Merrill, 1952), Chaps. 1 and 2; William J. Chambliss, "A Sociological Analysis of the Law of Vagrancy," *Social Problems,* 11 (1964), 67–77; and William J. Chambliss, "The State, the Law and the Definition of Behavior as Criminal or Delinquent," in Daniel Glaser, ed., *Handbook of Criminology* (Chicago: Rand McNally, 1974), pp. 7–43.

[7]Richard Quinney, *The Social Reality of Crime* (Boston: Little, Brown, 1970), pp. 16–18. Also see Richard Quinney, *Criminology: Analysis and Critique of Crime in American Society* (Boston: Little, Brown, 1975). For a discussion of the relation among conflict, power, and crime, also see Austin T. Turk, *Criminality and Legal Order* (Chicago: Rand McNally, 1969); William J. Chambliss and Robert B. Seidman, *Law, Order and Power* (Reading, Mass.: Addison-Wesley, 1971); and Barry Krisberg, *Crime and Privilege: Toward a New Criminology* (Englewood Cliffs, N.J.: Prentice-Hall, 1975).

[8]Sections of the lower class may, under certain circumstances, approve the use of assault to settle disputes (see Chap. 7). Moreover, assault and criminal homicide arising from assault in certain cases where provoked by the victim may not be condemned as much by the middle and upper classes. For a more general statement, see Ernest van den Haag, *Punishing Criminals: Concerning a Very Old and Painful Question* (New York: Basic Books, 1975).

those in the lower class were in power, however, they might well lower the length of sentences for these crimes to make them more comparable to those for white-collar crimes. It is true, as Quinney claims, that those segments of society with the power to shape the enforcement and administration of the criminal law through agents such as the police and the courts do influence what criminal laws are actually enforced.[9]

As the criminal law has developed through legislative and court action almost every kind of norm has been punished by the state at some time under it. For centuries, however, before any legislation was enacted certain acts were crimes under the common law, and most of what are now termed conventional crimes like burglary and robbery were covered under common law. At some time or other under criminal law a variety of behavior has been covered, including engaging in recreational activities on the Sabbath, practicing witchcraft, cigarette smoking, failing to show proper respect to a noble, wearing a one-piece bathing suit, listening to illegal radio programs, selling alcoholic beverages, and many others. As the written criminal codes came into being to cover great varieties of behavior, sanctions against such acts were included, since many of them had their origins in institutional norms and values. Lawyers refer to the violations of these laws, which have their origins and partial support in the mores, as *mala in se,* because they are considered bad in themselves. Certain other types of behavior which constitute a considerable portion of the criminal law have no such bases in the mores or in common law, and lawyers refer to them as *mala prohibita,* or as bad simply because they have been prohibited by law. Most of these latter offenses have grown out of more recent technological and cultural changes in society. Many are associated with the automobile, building codes, the manufacture and selling of impure foods and drugs, acts in restraint of trade, fraudulent or negligent acts of bank officials resulting in insolvency of banks, sales of fraudulent securities, and improper conduct in labor relations.

White-Collar Violations

With this background, one can see how lawbreaking has often been divided into two categories: the conventional crimes such as larceny, burglary, and robbery, usually punished under the criminal law; and those other violations of law that have come to be known as *white-collar crimes,* or perhaps more appropriately, occupational crimes. The latter are seldom punished under the criminal law.[10] They include violations of the law by persons in small and large businesses, employees, politicians, government employees, labor union leaders, doctors, and lawyers in connection with their occupations.[11] The definition of a crime solely in terms of the criminal law seems to be too

---

[9]Quinney, *The Social Reality of Crime,* pp. 18–20. See also Herman Schwendinger and Julia Schwendinger, "Social Class and the Definition of Crime," *Crime and Social Justice,* 7 (1977), 4–13; and John F. Galliher and James L. McCartney, *Criminology: Power, Crime and Criminal Law* (Homewood, Ill.: Dorsey Press, 1977).

[10]See Chap. 7.

[11]See Robert F. Meier and Gilbert Geis, "The White-Collar Offender," in Hans Toch, ed., *The Psychology of Crime and Criminal Justice* (New York: Holt, Rinehart and Winston, 1978). See also Carl B. Klockars, "White Collar Crime," in Edward Sagarin and Fred Montanino, eds., *Deviants: Voluntary Actors in a Hostile World* (Morristown, N.J.: General Learning Press, 1977), pp. 220–258.

restrictive, however, for an adequate explanation of criminal behavior. Many students of the problem believe that a crime should be defined not only in terms of the criminal law but in broader terms as *any act punishable by the state, regardless of whether the penalty is a criminal one or is administrative or civil in nature.* They believe that the strict legal definition of a crime solely under the criminal law is too limited and biased. They point out, moreover, that in many cases the regulation of white-collar and occupational offenses provides for the criminal law along with alternative sanctions such as civil and administrative actions. The fact that considerations of power mean that the alternatives are primarily employed does not mean that the criminal sanction is not also provided.

Crimes such as burglary, committed primarily by lower-class persons, are governed by criminal sanctions alone. The state, however, has many ways of compelling individuals, business concerns, and labor unions to obey the law under administrative law. It may withdraw a doctor's, lawyer's or druggist's right to practice, and it may suspend a tavern or restaurant owner from doing business for a few days, a year, or even permanently. If an individual or a company makes a product illegally, such as alcohol, or if a concern manufactures foods in violation of pure food laws, the products may be seized and destroyed by the government without compensation. If a business concern or a union defies the law, the government may institute under civil law an injunction to "cease and desist" from further violations; if further violations occur, contempt of court proceedings may be instituted. Many other examples of government penalties could be cited to indicate that the criminal law is not the only sanction used by political institutions to secure compliance with conduct norms.

Many people believe that violations leading to penalties of this type are not really crimes and that the "crime" and "criminal" should be arbitrarily restricted to the more overt acts of ordinary criminals which are punished by the criminal law. These acts fit the more common stereotype of crime; they are acts that persons who have such stereotypes would not commit themselves, and these acts are perceived by the public as being more serious violations of the law.[12] This arbitrary distinction is made not on the basis of illegal behavior but according to how the judicial process—namely, the criminal law—reacts to it. The difficulty in limiting the definition of a crime to the criminal law becomes evident when one compares the punishment of a fine, a jail sentence, or probation given an apprehended burglar or bank robber with the different kind of punishment often given a person in legitimate occupations. Unless a more inclusive concept of what constitutes "crime" is used, it is impossible to deal analytically with the different illegal activities that are punished by law according to occupation and social class. A conviction in the criminal court is not an adequate criterion, since a large proportion of those who commit crimes are not convicted in the criminal courts.[13] Sutherland stated that this criterion should be supplemented, and as this is done the criteria of the crimes of one class should be kept consistent in general terms with those of other crimes.

---

[12]Peter H. Rossi, Emily Waite, Christine E. Bose, and Richard E. Berk, "The Seriousness of Crimes: Normative Structure and Individual Differences," *American Sociological Review,* 39 (1974), 224–237.
[13]Edwin H. Sutherland, "White Collar Criminality," *American Sociological Review,* 5 (1940), p. 5.

Adolescent Violations

A person below the age of 18[14] who commits a crime is generally regarded as a "delinquent" rather than a criminal, but one must not assume that *juvenile delinquency* is comparable to adult criminality in all respects except age; nor should one assume that adolescents who are apprehended for delinquency and sent to state training schools are always "junior criminals." Actually, some behavior that falls in the category of "delinquency" does not fall into the definition of a crime, since many of these acts would not come before the criminal courts if they had been committed by adults. The offenses are, rather, "delinquencies" that can be committed only by adolescents; they include being unmanageable at home, truancy, and running away from home. These offenses are commonly termed *status offenses,* which means that they are offenses which are crimes only because of the age status of adolescent persons in our society. Regardless of the offense, delinquent youths technically are not "prosecuted" in a court as are adults. The state is expected to act in the child's or youth's best interest to prevent further difficulties, the penalties are not specific, and the judge is permitted great latitude and discretion in judgment.[15] Because of the broader definition and conception of delinquency, the judges' powers of case disposition range from dismissal to institutional commitment for every offense coming before them, whether the case involves truancy or, as in nearly all states, even homicide.

The extremely varied nature of the acts covered under juvenile delinquency makes it difficult to study all of this behavior analytically. Actually, there is little reason to make a distinction in such acts merely on the basis of age, since a large proportion of serious crime, such as burglary, auto theft, and even robbery, is committed by persons under 18. Perhaps the most appropriate solution to this problem is to consider as *crimes* only those delinquent acts which would be considered crimes were they to be committed by adults, as shall be done in the following discussion.[16] Partly because of the extent and the seriousness of actual juvenile crime there has been a movement, beginning in the 1970s, to reduce the case load from the jurisdictions of juvenile courts and to "decriminalize" status offenses. All persons committing such acts would either be diverted from the juvenile court system entirely and handled in special counseling programs or would be ignored.[17]

SOURCES OF CRIMINAL ATTITUDES

Thus far the discussion of crime has attempted to clarify the nature of delinquent and criminal acts. It has been shown that behavior becomes criminal because it is socially harmful and is subject to punishment by the state. Attention will now be focused on

---

[14]Most states provide for concurrent jurisdiction at age 16 or 17, allowing the prosecution in certain serious crimes, such as homicide, to proceed against the offender either as a juvenile or an adult.
[15]See, for example, Malcolm Klein, ed., *The Juvenile Justice System* (Beverly Hills, Calif.: Sage Publications, 1976).
[16]Marshall B. Clinard and Richard Quinney, *Criminal Behavior Systems: A Typology,* rev. ed. (New York: Holt, Rinehart and Winston, 1973); and William B. Saunders, *Juvenile Delinquency* (New York: Holt, Rinehart and Winston, 1976), pp. 3–11.
[17]See Edwin M. Schur, *Radical Non-Intervention: Re-Thinking the Delinquency Problem* (Englewood Cliffs, N.J.: Prentice-Hall, 1973); and Robert M. Carter and Malcolm W. Klein, eds., *Back on the Street: The Diversion of Juvenile Offenders* (Englewood Cliffs, N.J.: Prentice-Hall, 1976).

the sources of various conflicting norms which either are in opposition to laws forbidding certain behavior or fail to support them.

Criminals develop attitudes and definitions of situations through group association in the same fashion as do noncriminals. Most, but not all, crime is learned as anything else is learned and is a product of *differential association* with criminal norms.[18] There is differential association with various conflicting norms supporting and opposing criminal behavior; some norms tend to push the individual away from criminal behavior whereas others pull the person toward it. An important part of an offender's role is the extent to which a lawbreaker acquires the techniques, rationalizations, and philosophy of a criminal career.[19]

Much crime is learned in interaction with other persons; intimate and personal associations undoubtedly have the greatest influence in the acquisition of criminal norms. Most of these associations are likely to be of a group nature, such as through certain companions, gangs, occupations, or neighborhoods. Their effect depends on the frequency, duration, priority, and intensity of exposure to noncriminal and criminal norms. The *frequency* and *duration,* or length of time of the associations, have much to do with the development of criminal behavior. Exposure to criminal norms in associations in early life *(priority)* has greater effect on determining whether or not criminal behavior will take place. The *intensity* of the association is related to the prestige of persons with criminal norms with whom an individual associates and to the individual's reactions to such persons.

Group experience involves not only the family but also peer groups, school, neighborhood, clubs, church, occupation, marriage—in fact, all life in its interaction with the culture and the subculture. Both criminality and noncriminality are "natural" in the sense that they are the outgrowths of processes of social definitions. In the discussion that follows, the relation between criminal behavior, the mass media, the family, occupation, neighborhood, companions, and gangs will be discussed.

The Mass Media

The great interest of juveniles and young adults in crime stories on television and in motion pictures has caused some people to overestimate the importance of these

---

[18]The theory of differential association was originally developed by Edwin H. Sutherland nearly 45 years ago and has become the leading framework for explaining the development of criminal behavior, although some people currently point out that, as originally stated, it was too broad and difficult to test. For a full statement of the theory, see Sutherland and Cressey, Chap. 4. The details of the theory have been criticized and modified slightly but remain essentially the same, namely, a learning theory of criminality. It is in basic agreement with general theories of socialization, set theory, and elements of behavior modification or operant conditioning. See Robert L. Burgess and Ronald L. Akers, "A Differential Association-Reinforcement Theory of Criminal Behavior," *Social Problems,* 14 (1966), 128–147; Melvin L. DeFleur and Richard Quinney, "A Reformulation of Sutherland's Differential Association Theory and a Strategy for Empirical Verification," *Journal of Research in Crime and Delinquency,* 3 (1966), 1–22; and Donald R. Cressey, "The Language of Set Theory and Differential Association," *Journal of Research in Crime and Delinquency,* 3 (1966), 22–27. Some modifications have included the addition of self-concept, reference groups, and differential identification of the offender. For a general discussion of the theory and for much evidence to support it, see Sutherland and Cressey. Also see Harwin L. Voss, "Differential Association and Reported Delinquent Behavior: A Replication," *Social Problems,* 12 (1964), 78–85; C. R. Jeffery, "Criminal Behavior and Learning Theory," *Journal of Criminal Law, Criminology and Police Science,* 56 (1965), 294–300; Reed Adams, "Differential Association and Learning Principles Revisited," *Social Problems,* 20 (1973), 458–470; and Robert E. Clark, *Reference Group Theory and Delinquency* (New York: Behavioral Publications, 1972).

[19]Frank E. Hartung, *Crime, Law and Society* (Detroit: Wayne State University Press, 1965), pp. 62–88.

media; others tend to discount them in their explanations of delinquency and crime. Without question television and motion pictures often present a version of our culture that emphasizes wealth, materialism, and conflicting conduct, both criminal and sexual, which furnishes juveniles with models conducive to delinquency.[20] A broad survey of television use conducted by a scientific research team some years ago found that from the age of 3 to 16 the average child was devoting about a sixth of waking hours to watching television, and that more than half the children studied watched "adult" programs such as crime and Western themes as well as shows featuring emotional problems.[21] The investigators analyzed 100 hours of programs in the so-called children's hours, from 4 to 9 P.M. During these 100 hours they counted 12 murders, 16 major gun fights, 21 persons shot, and 21 other violent incidents involving stranglings, robberies, a horse grinding a man under his hoofs, a woman killed by falling from a train, a tidal wave, an earthquake, and even one guillotining. Many researchers in such fields as education, psychology, and concerned groups associated with television are currently engaged in studying the effects of exposure to television in all aspects of youth development. The public tends, however, to take the easiest course in dealing with social problems such as crime, often attributing it to the mass media rather than to the broader social and neighborhood conditions within the society. In relation to crime specifically, a more realistic appraisal of both television and motion picture programs indicates that on the whole their direct influence on juveniles and youth serves only to aggravate whatever deviant attitudes and subcultural roles already exist. It is conceivable, moreover, that even if all the media were to disappear from a society such as the United States, there would probably still be almost as much delinquency and crime as there now is. Certainly extensive delinquency and crime existed before the present mass media were considered to be of any consequence. Children both learn and are influenced by the various media of mass communication, but all of what they receive passes through another set of influences, such as the family, the school, and the church, before it becomes a vital guide to actions. A study has concluded that "what television does to children is less significant than what children do with television; and what children do with television . . . depend(s) on their homes, their schools, their peer group relations, and many other factors quite outside the mass media.[22]

With respect to the question of whether or not television does promote aggressive acts by viewers, three different views have been proposed: first, that television teaches aggressiveness; second, that it reduces aggressiveness by serving as an outlet; and third, that it has no demonstrable effect on viewers. Some researchers have found a more direct role for the television media in the learning and modeling of aggressive

---

[20]Primarily for this reason, for some time children in Sweden under the age of 14 have not been permitted to see most motion pictures, which are primarily American, and certain crime films are censored for adults. In the United States little can be done to prevent adolescents from seeing adult television programs, but certain restrictions do apply to motion pictures.

[21]Wilbur Schramm, Jack Lyle, and Edwin B. Parker, *Television in the Lives of Our Children* (Stanford, Calif.: Stanford University Press, 1961). Also see Joseph Klapper, *The Effects of Mass Communication* (New York: Free Press, 1960). The research reported here was conducted by a team at Stanford University Institute for Communication Research, and findings were based on responses from 6,000 children, 2,000 parents, and 300 teachers.

[22]Wilbur L. Schramm, ed., *Mass Communications* (Urbana: University of Illinois Press, 1960), p. 466.

behavior.[23] In another study a negative conclusion was reached in a project involving almost 400 boys, part of whom viewed aggressive programs and the other part serving as a control group that watched nonaggressive programs.[24] The conclusion in this study was that exposure to aggressive television programs over a six-week period produced no increment in aggressive behavior; the only measure on which the controls decreased relative to the aggressive television viewing group was "fantasy aggression." "About all one can state regarding this latter finding is that boys who witness mostly nonaggressive content in television make up fewer stories in which fighting takes place than boys who watch a great deal of fighting on television."[25] It was generally felt, in fact, that viewing aggressive programs reduces rather than stimulates the actual acting out of aggressive tendencies in certain types of boys. Another writer stated that there is no clear general influence from watching television, and when there is, it is due to the interaction between the influence of the mass media and other factors. Newspapers and television provide examples to be emulated by murderers, kidnappers, and hijackers, but an overwhelming majority of readers and viewers do not carry out these acts. This suggests the importance of other factors for those who do, "such as previously reinforced illegal behaviors as well as the opportunity available in the current situation, and the possession of appropriate skills as well as the influence of serious psychological disturbance."[26] An extensive review of existing evidence concerning the impact of television on subsequent violent conduct has shown that viewing violence has not been demonstrated to have significant effects on aggressive behavior.[27]

While it is difficult to demonstrate a direct relation between the mass media and criminal acts, there is no question but that the mass media, in their desire to make money, do present an image of a crime-ridden, violent society and that they also give the impression that the typical criminal comes from the lower- and blue-collar classes rather than from the white-collar groups and corporations. This image, of course, is accurate only for those crimes that contain the most dramatic appeal (for purposes of television, particularly, this element is crucial); evidently, acts of price fixing, as an example, are not as exciting to the public as acts of armed robbery or homicide.

The Family

The family, as an institution, has been undergoing great social changes, particularly in urban areas, which have resulted in the decline of its importance in general social life. As traditional functions of the family have declined, the socialization of young children

---

[23]Robert M. Liebert, John M. Neale, and Emily S. Davidson, *The Early Window: Effects of Television on Children and Youth* (New York: Pergamon, 1973); and Albert Bandura, *Aggression: A Social Learning Analysis* (Englewood Cliffs, N.J.: Prentice-Hall, 1973).

[24]Seymour Feshbach and Robert D. Singer, *Television and Aggression* (San Francisco: Jossey-Bass, 1971). The authors went on to say that there should be some qualification in regard to the groups to which this finding applies, since the effect is pronounced in children with certain personality and social characteristics and either weak or absent in others.

[25]Feshbach and Singer, p. 140.

[26]M. Philip Feldman, *Criminal Behavior: A Psychological Analysis* (New York: Wiley, 1977), p. 86.

[27]Robert M. Kaplan and Robert D. Singer, "Television Violence and Viewer Aggression: A Reexamination of the Evidence," *Journal of Social Issues*, 32 (1976), 35–70.

has increasingly been taken on by other groups, such as the school and the street gang. As kinship ties have become weaker and as the mother is increasingly employed outside the home, the urban child may spend less time with immediate family members. Among large sections of the urban population today the family no longer plays the dominant, idealized role that certainly remains in the minds of those who think of it as the primary factor in encouraging or preventing delinquency and crime. Furthermore, the modern family tends to reflect the norms of the social class and the neighborhood of which it is a part, the occupation of the father, and the neighborhood locale. It is difficult to speak of a family as such without referring to its place in the social structure.

Some people believe that unsatisfactory family influences constitute the chief source of criminal behavior. A number of possible family influences might be related to illegal behavior, including the one-parent (or broken home) situation and the family itself as a source of criminal patterns and attitudes. The evidence indicates that although there may be some direct tutelage in criminal acts by father, mother, or siblings, this is of minor importance and that it is relatively rare. In one study that compared the criminal behavior patterns of fathers and sons over time, no evidence was found of any direct family connection to crime, although for certain offenses, notably drunkenness and minor larceny, there was some evidence that attitudes about crime were transmitted from one generation to another.[28] In general, however, the sons of offenders were not found to be more criminal than their fathers.

Persistent efforts have been made to link youth crime to broken homes, on the assumption that such a break in family ties, due to separation, desertion, divorce, or death, may well lead the young person to commit delinquent acts. Some studies do show that between 30 and 60 percent of delinquents come from broken homes, but these figures must be judged in terms of the fact that a large percentage of children in the United States are reared in homes broken by divorce, separation, desertion, or death, or in situations where the father's employment takes him away from the family for long periods of time. They also must be considered in terms of sex, age, race, and the social conditions in the local community. It is not the broken family as such that is important, but rather the local community conditions surrounding the family. More-over, the effect of a broken home may be quite different, depending upon the identification with one parent or the other. Both earlier and more recent studies reveal that the proportion of broken homes, however, is greater among blacks than among whites and among females than among males.[29] The higher percentage of young females has been explained as being due to the fact that they are more often arrested for sexual offenses which represent an attempt to obtain affectional relationships outside the home. This view, however, makes the dubious assumption that females

---

[28]Joan McCord, "Father and Son Criminality: A Comparative Study of Two Generations of Native Americans," in Meier, pp. 83–92.

[29]For the earlier studies of the relation between delinquents from broken homes and race, see Thomas P. Monahan, "Family, Status and the Delinquent Child: A Reappraisal and Some New Findings," *Social Forces,* 35 (1957), 250–258. For the comparisons between males and females, see Jackson Toby, "The Differential Impact of Family Disorganization," *American Sociological Review,* 22 (1957), 505–512.

have more "craving" for love than do males.[30] These figures have little meaning unless they are compared with control groups.

The effort to link delinquency with broken homes is unlikely to yield much in the way of either new information or insight into the etiology of delinquency. The relationship between broken homes and delinquency is seriously confounded by a selection process in the juvenile justice system which is difficult to control in any examination of this relationship. The evidence is strong that juveniles from broken homes are more likely to be arrested, convicted, and sentenced to a juvenile institution.[31] A study of juvenile court cases in Florida, for example, indicated that delinquents had come disproportionately from disrupted families, with lower-class and serious offenders most often coming from incomplete families: but again this may reflect in part differential processing of the cases.[32]

Any family encounters some difficulties in trying to keep a young person away from criminal influences in a neighborhood. Parental discipline is, of course, not the only factor in the dynamics of family interaction; other important factors are family discipline, value agreement, mutual recreation, parental interaction, and rejection by parents. In one study it was reported that these factors have a greater impact for young females than for young males.[33]

Occupation

Persons are inducted into illegal practices within their occupations as well as in their specific businesses. Techniques of violations in business, for example, are picked up from conversations with other people in business and from descriptions of violations appearing in trade publications and in the general press. Many violations indicate such ingenuity that they undoubtedly represent the assistance of lawyers hired for this very purpose. Advertising specialists learn how to prepare misleading advertising; in turn, these persons train others in their acquired skills. Illegal practices are diffused among corporations. Illegal practices in restraint of trade and misrepresentation in advertising are common; frequently they are adopted by others as they develop. Large concerns often diffuse illegal practices among other subsidiaries.[34]

> When one corporation in an industry uses an illegal method, the other corporations in that industry adopt the same illegal method in order that the first may not have a

---

[30]For more recent studies of the relation between delinquent youth offenders from broken homes and sex, see Dorie Klein, "The Etiology of Female Crime: A Review of the Literature," *Issues in Criminology,* 7 (1973), 3–30. See also Anthony R. Harris, "Sex and Theories of Deviance: Toward a Functional Theory of Deviant Typescripts," *American Sociological Review,* 42 (1977), 3–16.
[31]Schur, p. 121.
[32]Roland J. Chilton and Gerald E. Markle, "Family Disruption, Delinquent Conduct and the Effect of Subclassification," *American Sociological Review,* 37 (1972), 93–99.
[33]See F. Ivan Nye, *Family Relationships and Delinquent Behavior* (New York: Wiley, 1958).
[34]Donald R. Cressey, "Restraint of Trade, Recidivism, and Delinquent Neighborhoods," in James F. Short, Jr., ed., *Delinquency, Crime and Society* (Chicago: University of Chicago Press, 1976), pp. 209–238; and George A. Hay and Daniel Kelly, "An Empirical Survey of Price Fixing Conspiracies," *Journal of Law and Economics,* 17 (1974), 13–38.

competitive advantage over them. The corporations in an industry or a branch of an industry belong to trade associations in which policies are discussed and adopted. These associations through conferences, publications, and other means act as centers for diffusing techniques of law violations and of a common ideology regarding violations of law. Consequently, the corporations which belong to a trade association tend to act in a uniform manner and to have approximate equality in the number of decisions against them.[35]

Certain types of corporations also appear to have low rates of violations, presumably because there is more emphasis on maintaining the good reputation of the business. Moreover, corporations moving into a new industry tend to have patterns of illegal behavior that resemble those in that industry.[36]

Service repairmen learn the rackets associated with the repair of television sets, radios, appliances,[37] and automobiles.[38] Training of this type is seen in the following case of a college graduate:

> When I graduated from college I had plenty of ideals of honesty, fair play, and cooperation which I had acquired at home, in school, and from literature. My first job after graduation was selling typewriters. During the first day, I learned that these machines were not sold at a uniform price but that a person who haggled and waited could get a machine at about half the list price. I felt that this was unfair to the customer who paid the list price. The other salesmen laughed at me and could not understand my silly attitude. They told me to forget the things I had learned in school, and that you couldn't earn a pile of money by being strictly honest. When I replied that money wasn't everything they mocked at me: "Oh, no? Well, it helps." I had ideals and I resigned. . . .
>
> Then I got an opportunity in the used-car business. I learned that this business had more tricks for fleecing customers than either of those I had tried previously. Cars with cracked cylinders, with half the teeth missing from the fly wheel, with everything wrong, were sold as "guaranteed." When the customer returned and demanded his guarantee, he had to sue to get it and very few went to that trouble and expense: the boss said you could depend on human nature. If hot cars could be taken in and sold safely, the boss did not hesitate. When I learned these things I did not quit as I had previously. I sometimes felt disgusted and wanted to quit, but I argued that I did not have much chance to find a legitimate firm. I knew that the game was rotten but it had to be played—the law of the jungle and that sort of thing. I knew that I was dishonest and to that extent felt that I was more honest than my fellows. The thing that struck me as strange was that all these people were proud of their ability to fleece customers. They boasted of their crookedness and were admired by their friends and enemies in proportion to their ability to get away with a crooked deal: it was called shrewdness. Another thing was that these people were unanimous in their denunciation of gangsters, robbers, burglars, and petty thieves. They never regarded themselves as in the same class and were bitterly indignant if accused of dishonesty; it was just good business.
>
> Once in a while, as the years have passed, I have thought of myself as I was in

---

[35]Marshall B. Clinard, *The Black Market* (New York: Holt, Rinehart and Winston, 1952), p. 301.

[36]Hay and Kelly.

[37]Diane Vaughan and Carlo Giovanna, "The Appliance Repairman: A Study of Victim Responsiveness and Fraud," *Journal of Research in Crime and Delinquency,* 13 (1975), 153–161.

[38]According to a 1977 Federal Trade report, approximately 14 billion out of 40 billion automobile repairs made annually in the United States are unnecessary.

college—idealistic, honest, and thoughtful of others—and have been momentarily ashamed of myself. Before long such memories became less and less frequent and it became difficult to distinguish me from my fellows. If you had accused me of dishonesty I would have denied the charge, but with slightly less vehemence than my fellow business-men, for after all I had learned a different code of behavior.[39]

Neighborhoods

The neighborhood or local community is primarily one of personal relationships, where people live and where their local institutions are situated. It is an area of more personal participation in which the activities of child and adult tend to be organized around agencies, such as local stores, the school, the church, playgrounds, and sometimes even a motion picture theater. It is a world of meaningful experiences to the individual. At the same time, neighborhoods often reflect different normative standards which may lead to criminal behavior.

Neighborhoods differ as to social class, in the variety of the composition of racial, ethnic, and religious groups, and in the stability of the population. Even more important, there may be pronounced differences in the presence of norms supporting obedience to law and those supporting criminal activities in the local community. Some local areas are organized primarily around noncriminal norms, while in others deviant norms and criminal standards predominate.[40] In either instance, no local community has norms exclusively of one type or another; rather, conflicting standards are present in varying proportions. Persons who live in middle- and upper-class suburbia may express approval of violations of laws affecting their own businesses or professions while condemning other law violations. Persons in high-crime-rate areas may have opportunities for many close associations with people who engage in or even encourage them to engage in crime. A study of slum areas in three cities concluded that

> nearly every youngster on the slum block, whether in New York, Washington, or Chicago (with few but conspicuous exceptions), does develop some kind of a "larceny sense." In all probability, while still quite young, he will learn to steal and he will learn what the risks are—including when, where, and how not to go too far. Just as experimentation with sex approaches universality, so with theft.[41]

Some persons are critical of the emphasis on neighborhood factors in delin-quency and crime, pointing out that at most generally only about one half to two thirds of youthful offenders have been arrested, and that only one fourth of the boys, even in the worst crime areas, have appeared before the juvenile court. One writer has attempted to answer this argument by noting that official delinquency, as measured by

---

[39]Personal document from *White Collar Crime* by Edwin H. Sutherland. Foreword by Donald R. Cressey. Copyright 1949 by Holt, Rinehart and Winston, Inc. Foreword © 1961 by Donald Cressey. Reprinted by permission of Holt, Rinehart and Winston.
[40]See Irving Spergel, "Male Adult Criminality, Deviant Values and Differential Opportunities in Two Lower Class Negro Neighborhoods," *Social Problems,* 10 (1963), 237–250; and Richard A. Cloward and Lloyd E. Ohlin, *Delinquency and Opportunity: A Theory of Delinquent Gangs* (New York: Free Press, 1960).
[41]Bernard Rosenberg and Harry Silverstein, *The Varieties of Delinquent Experience* (Waltham, Mass.: Blaisdell Publishing, 1969), p. 97.

arrests or juvenile court statistics, represents only a small proportion of actual offenders.[42]

Companions and Delinquent Gangs

Attitudes favorable to crime are primarily acquired through companions and by participation in small, intimate groups, such as gangs, in much the same manner as law-abiding norms are transmitted. The view that most conventional crime and delinquency arise from the adoption of deviant norms, particularly through the tutelage of others, has been supported by studies of juvenile and youth crime, adult theft, burglary and robbery, and organized crime.[43]

A national survey of crime in the United States estimated that between 60 and 90 percent of all delinquent acts are committed with companions. The typical delinquent operates in the company of peers, and this fact alone "makes youth groups of central concern in consideration of delinquency prevention."[44] Most young offenders are often arrested in company of others, and it can safely be assumed that those who had no companions at the time of arrest had had at least one at the beginning of their delinquencies. In considering the role of companions in crime most persons have in mind only juvenile gangs or the more organized criminal syndicates. Yet many associations of youths with criminal norms are not with organized groups, but instead with one or two companions. Petty larceny and vandalism are commonly committed by two or three "best friends."[45] This study concluded that the probability of an individual boy's committing a specific kind of delinquency was dependent upon such an act being committed by his two best friends, although this relation varied with the type of delinquency. The most serious offenses are committed in groups, and they are the ones that largely get into the official arrest records.[46]

Such differential association with criminals or delinquents by means of contacts with one or two persons appears to be the type most characteristic of rural and village areas, and these companions have been found to be more often chance acquaint-

---

[42]Solomon Kobrin, "The Conflict of Values in Delinquency Areas," *American Sociological Review,* 16 (1951), 653–661.

[43]See, for example, Clifford R. Shaw and Henry D. McKay, *Juvenile Delinquency and Urban Areas,* 2d ed. (Chicago: University of Chicago Press, 1970); Andrew Walker, "Sociology and Professional Crime," in Abraham S. Blumberg, ed., *Current Perspectives on Criminal Behavior* (New York: Knopf, 1974), pp. 87–113; and James A. Inciardi, "Vocational Crime," in Glaser, *Handbook of Criminology,* pp. 299–401. Also see Maynard L. Erickson and Gary F. Jensen, " 'Delinquency Is Still Group Behavior!': Toward Revitalizing the Group Premise in the Sociology of Deviance," *Journal of Criminal Law and Criminology,* 68 (1977), 262–273.

[44]*The Challenge of Crime in a Free Society,* President's Commission on Law Enforcement and the Administration of Justice (Washington, D.C.: Government Printing Office, 1967), p. 66. Also see Maynard L. Erickson, "Group Violations and Official Delinquency: The Group Hazard Hypothesis," *Criminology,* 11 (1973), 127–160. Also see Eric W. Linden and James Hackler, "Affective Ties and Delinquency," *Pacific Sociological Review,* 27 (1973), p. 42.

[45]Albert J. Reiss, Jr., and A. Lewis Rhodes, "An Empirical Test of Differential Association Theory," *Journal of Research in Crime and Delinquency,* 1 (1964), 5–18.

[46]Maynard L. Erickson, "The Group Context of Delinquent Behavior," *Social Problems,* 19 (1971), 114–129.

ances.[47] In urban areas larger group patterns of crime in the form of youth gangs are the more typical method of association. This apparent difference in the pattern of associates is due to the greater effectiveness of informal social control in farm and village areas, although these patterns are changing somewhat as urbanization increasingly affects the rural areas.

Gang delinquency is a world-wide phenomenon today, and it is not confined to the United States. Primarily it is a phenomenon of urbanization with the structuring of groups on the basis of age. Gangs are reported to be extensive in places far apart, for example, England, France, Sweden, Belgium, South Africa, Israel, Australia, the Federal Republic of Germany, Japan, the Soviet Union, and the developing countries of Asia, Africa, and Latin America.[48] In France and Belgium they are known as *blousons noirs,* in England as "teddy boys," in Sweden as *raggare,* in Poland and Russia as "hooligans," and in South Africa as *tsotsios.* An intensive research project on the *blousons noirs* in Belgium in the 1960s pointed out that in spite of the wide geographic distribution of these young gangs throughout the world, there is an astonishing similarity in their fundamental characteristics.[49] Many studies have shown the high incidence of gang membership among youthful offenders. Approximately two thirds, for example, of a sample of Swedish criminal offenders had belonged to a group of youth who stole.[50]

Gangs engage in all types of criminal activities from theft and burglary to armed robbery. In fact, most juveniles who do engage in robberies operate in gangs, particularly those who engage in strong-arm robberies. In one government study of crimes of violence in 17 cities, youth groups and gangs were found to be involved in a significant percentage of all robberies. An analysis of major crimes cleared by arrest showed that 9.5 percent of youth groups or gangs were involved in armed robbery and 6.8 percent in unarmed robbery. In the case of groups or gangs in which the majority of offenders were juveniles, the percentage involved in armed robbery was 14.1 and in unarmed robbery 18.6.[51]

Certain large U.S. cities are experiencing significant increases in violent youth gangs. Not only do official statistics show increases in these gang activities, but

---

[47]Marshall B. Clinard, "Rural Criminal Offenders," *American Journal of Sociology,* 50 (1944), 38 – 45. Also see John E. Conklin, *The Impact of Crime* (New York: Macmillan, 1975), Chap. 6.

[48]Fyvel has examined gang delinquency in a number of countries. See T. R. Fyvel, *Troublemakers: Rebellious Youth in an Affluent Society* (New York: Schocken Books, 1962). Specific treatments of gang activity in other countries can be found in Edmund W. Vaz, "Juvenile Delinquency in Paris," *Social Problems,* 10 (1962), 23 – 31; Peter Willmott, *Adolescent Boys of East London* (London: Routledge & Kegan Paul, 1966); and Valery Chalidze, *Criminal Russia: Essays on Crime in the Soviet Union* (New York: Random House, 1977), Chap. 5, "Hooliganism." For a discussion of the role of companions and gangs in youth crime in developing countries, see Marshall B. Clinard and Daniel J. Abbott, *Crime in Developing Countries* (New York: Wiley, 1973), Chap. 7.

[49]A. Racine, C. Somerhausen, C. Debuyst, G. De Bock, and L. DeBray, *Les Blousons Noirs* (Paris: Editions Cujas, 1966), pp. 1 – 19 and 131 – 132.

[50]Marshall B. Clinard, "A Cross Cultural Replication of the Relation of the Process of Urbanism to Criminal Behavior," *American Sociological Review,* 25 (1960), 253 – 257; and Marshall B. Clinard, "The Relation of Urbanization and Urbanism to Criminal Behavior," in Ernest W. Burgess and Donald J. Bogue, eds., *Contributions to Urban Sociology* (Chicago: University of Chicago Press, 1964).

[51]Donald J. Mulvihill and Melvin Tumin, *Crimes of Violence,* National Commission on the Causes and Prevention of Violence, Staff Report Series (Washington, D.C.: Government Printing Office, 1970), Vol. 12, p. 610.

informal estimates and mass media accounts suggest increases in the number of criminal gangs and their involvement in more violent action against individuals and other groups than in the past. They are involved in gang-related killings, assaultive encounters with other gangs, and assaults and intimidation of students and teachers in schools; they collect protection money from gang-controlled territories, inflict major damage to school buildings, and extort money from local business concerns. The high rates of violent gang activity in the United States in the 1930s, in the 1950s, and again in the 1970s have led one observer to speak of the "cyclical" nature of youth gangs.[52] Once gang violence reaches a certain level of intensity, it produces a set of severe control responses on the part of the police, social service agencies, and citizens' groups, resulting in decreasing numbers, visibility, and organization of gangs. In a 1975 survey of six cities (New York, Los Angeles, Chicago, Philadelphia, Detroit, and San Francisco), Miller found that there had been a "new wave" of gang violence, particularly in New York, Los Angeles, and Detroit, and that the nature of gang activity changes over time. Unlike in earlier epochs, most modern gang members whose criminal activities are violent are predominantly black or Hispanic slum residents rather than others. Miller reports that while the classic "rumble" still occurs, "forays by small bands, armed and often motorized, appear to have become the dominant form of inter-gang violence."[53]

Neighborhood Values   Criminal and delinquent gangs tend to reflect *neighborhood values* such as those of the slum, and it is largely this factor that determines whether or not they will engage in criminal activities. In certain areas gang members may engage in noncriminal activities, while in other areas they may bring the delinquent norms of the area into intimate contact with the individual. This gang delinquency in the form of stealing and vandalism may be regarded as a natural adjustment to the social roles, behavior patterns, and norms of the group as well as to those of the neighborhood of which the group is a part. Many youth gangs in large urban areas have long histories; some have been in existence for many years, so that the members may have older brothers or even fathers who were once members. Some big-city gangs appear to be large, often having several hundred or thousands of members in a loose federation of small gangs such as the well-known Vice Lords in Chicago.[54] In the six large cities studied by Miller estimates ranged from 760 to 2,700 gangs with 28,500 to 81,500 members and an average membership between 30 and 40.[55] Some individuals belong to gangs because of the personal protection they afford or the opportunity for large-scale racketeering or "shakedowns" of business establishments. Many youth maintain a loose and tenuous relation to the large and even the smaller gangs, some dropping in and others dropping out; some participate in some gang activities while others do not.[56]

---

[52]Walter B. Miller, "American Youth Gangs: Past and Present," in Blumberg, pp. 210–239.
[53]Walter B. Miller, *Violence by Youth Gangs and Youth Groups as a Crime Problem in Major American Cities* (Washington, D.C.: National Institute for Juvenile Justice and Delinquency Prevention, 1975), p. 76.
[54]R. Lincoln Keiser, *The Vice Lords: Warriors of the Street,* fieldwork edition (New York: Holt, Rinehart and Winston, 1979).
[55]Miller, *Violence by Youth Gangs and Youth Groups as a Crime Problem in Major American Cities,* p. 75.
[56]James F. Short, Jr., and Fred L. Strodtbeck, *Group Process and Gang Delinquency* (Chicago: University of Chicago Press, 1965), p. 283.

Criminal Techniques Gangs that have directed their activities toward crime and delinquency for some time furnish excellent *training in criminal techniques*. They teach new members how to empty slot machines, shoplift, obtain "junk" illegally, open freight cars, snatch purses, "roll" drunks, secure skeleton keys to steal autos or enter houses, purchase guns, steal automobiles, engineer holdups, sell stolen goods to "fences," and, finally, bribe a policeman or otherwise "fix" a case. New members may progress from truancy and stealing petty objects and "junk" to more serious activities like burglaries, automobile thefts, and even armed robbery.[57]

Mutual Excitation The effectiveness of delinquent gangs in disseminating knowledge of crime lies in the fact that through *mutual excitation* the gang makes illegal acts attractive to the individual. Members enjoy the thrill of common intimate participation in interests involving conflict.

> When we were shoplifting we always made a game of it. For example, we might gamble on who could steal the most caps in a day or who could steal in the presence of a detective and then get away. We were always daring each other that way and thinking up new schemes. This was the best part of the game. I would go into a store to steal a cap, by trying on one and when the clerk was not watching walk out of the store, leaving the old cap. With the new cap on my head I would go into another store, do the same thing as in the other store, getting a new hat and leave the one and when the clerk was not watching walk out of the store, leaving one hat at night. It was fun I wanted, not the hat. I kept this up for months and then began to sell the things to a man on the west side. It was at this time that I began to steal for gain.[58]

Justifying Delinquency *Rationalizations or techniques of neutralization* for delinquent behavior are extremely important to justify deviant behavior in the face of adult disapproval and legal sanctions, and they are largely derived from gang associations.[59] These include "denial of responsibility" by blaming parents, and so on; "denial of injury" by claiming, for example, that the act was a prank or that the stolen car was "borrowed"; "denial of the victim" by arguing that the delinquent act was justified under the circumstances; "condemnation of the condemners" by pointing to cruel police methods; and, finally, the "appeal to higher loyalties" by claiming that association in gangs is more important than loyalty to the larger society. These rationalizations, together with the associations gang members have had with an inconsistent legal system and its agents, come increasingly to mean that gangs break their ties with the legal and "drift into delinquency."[60]

Some youth gangs disappear after a while, but others continue for many years. Although there is no hard and fast line of demarcation between a gang of younger

---

[57]See Gerald D. Robin, "Gang Member Delinquency in Philadelphia," in Malcolm W. Klein, ed., *Juvenile Gangs in Context: Theory, Research and Action* (Englewood Cliffs, N.J.: Prentice-Hall, 1967), pp. 15–24.
[58]Chicago Area Project, *Juvenile Delinquency*, a monograph prepared by the Institute for Juvenile Research and the Chicago Area Project, rev. ed. (Chicago, 1953), p. 5.
[59]For a brief survey of many of these theories, see Daniel Glaser, "Social Disorganization and Delinquent Subcultures," in Herbert C. Quay, ed., *Juvenile Delinquency: Research and Theory* (Princeton, N.J.: Van Nostrand, 1965), pp. 27–62.
[60]David Matza, *Delinquency and Drift* (New York: Wiley, 1964).

offenders and one of older offenders, the latter tend to become involved in more career stealing. The membership of criminal gangs of older adults appears to be drawn chiefly from those juveniles who have had a record of incarceration in correctional institutions. Criminal gangs often become associated with organized criminal rackets. They develop connections as part of criminal syndicates, work with political machines, and specialize in types of rackets. Youth gangs constitute the main entry, as will be pointed out later, into conventional criminal careers and organized crime.

Status in Gangs   The position or *social status* of gang members is measured by entirely different means from those used by conventional youth groups. A gang member achieves high status by displaying courage and skill in the commission of a crime, by having a long record of delinquencies, and, better still, by having been incarcerated in a correctional institution. He learns to acquire social status in his group by the skill he has developed in these illegal activities. In a gang robbery, for example, one of the most important roles is that of "wheel man," the person who must obtain a get-away car, plan the escape route, and drive away from the robbery scene.[61] This is often considered to be the most important part of a robbery since quick escape is vital. The wheel man also may function as a lookout and, on occasion, participate directly in a robbery. As a result of their participation in gang behavior, the members develop fairly uniform attitudes toward their opposition to authority, their contempt for traitors, the recognition and prestige gained through delinquency, hero worship, the stigma of petty theft, and the gang's control over its members.[62] In street gangs devoted primarily to fighting and violence, a member's social position depends upon frequent exhibitions of "heart" and his skill in using violence.[63] Fighting gangs are almost constantly involved in negotiating with each other, and many agreements and contracts are worked out to demonstrate their respective strengths. In one city, the bulk of the assaultive incidents among street gang members involved contests wherein the defense or preservation of honor was the central issue.[64] The individual gang member who uses drugs can lay claim to "rep" only if he can display an ability to obtain the drugs and to increase the experience of the "kick."

In fact, the behavior of the delinquent gang can largely be explained by status processes within the group rather than by forces outside the society such as anomie[65] (see pp. 67–73). Gang behavior is largely a product of *status strivings within the gang*

---

[61]John E. Conklin, *Robbery and the Criminal Justice System* (Philadelphia: Lippincott, 1972), p. 99.

[62]Chicago Area Project, p. 5. See also LaMar T. Empey, "Delinquency Theory and Recent Research," *Journal of Research in Crime and Delinquency,* 4 (1967), 28–42.

[63]One recent study has discussed the context in which gang violence occurs in a Mexican-American community. Most acts are directly tied to situations in which one party impugns the honor of an adversary. See Ruth Horowitz and Gary Schwartz, "Honor, Normative Ambiguity and Gang Violence," *American Sociological Review,* 39 (1974), 238–251.

[64]Lewis Yablonsky, *The Violent Gang* (New York: Macmillan, 1962).

[65]Short and Strodtbeck. Unfortunately, Short and Strodtbeck largely neglect the norms of the local community in which the delinquent gang behavior tends to take place. They also fail to see the gang as an aspect of the conflict of youth culture with the larger urban adult social world. This broader perspective has been adopted in Travis Hirschi, *Causes of Delinquency* (Berkeley: University of California Press, 1969). Here delinquency is viewed as the result of a weakening or breaking of the social bonds that relate the

rather than an attempt to achieve status denied by the larger society. Thus gang behavior is a rational balancing of immediate loss of status and esteem within the group and the risk of punishment by the criminal law. Gang delinquency is not as much a failure to attain certain adult goals in society as it is a failure to achieve status within the context of the adult, middle-class-dominated institutions such as the school, the church, and the economic and political institutions. The formation of a gang subculture involves the establishment of new groups with new rules by which members may compete successfully to obtain status by stealing and by violence. Money acquired by gang members is usually spent not for economic necessities but for status rewards within the group, such as expensive shoes or other items of clothing, and for "kicks," alcoholic beverages, and drugs.

Leadership in Gangs   Nowhere are the status values of the gang better seen than in the *gang leader* who comes to exemplify them. His control over the gang depends upon his demonstration of those qualities. It is he who helps to invoke the codes of the gang and to punish and ridicule those who do not live up to the standards of conduct the gang demands. One leader of a city youth gang has written:

> The boys I ran around with were just like me, steal anything they get their hands on. One boy would make plans for stealing money, and we would give him jiggers and help him out if he needed help, and the other boys would do the same. We would meet every Saturday night in the pool room and set down in the pool room and plan our schemes out for the following week. The leader of each group was supposed to be tough. He would take most of the money and split the rest of it with the rest of the boys. I was leader, and never did cheat the other fellows out of a dime, and they had me for their leader until I was sent to Eldora Training School. The gang then got them a different leader, and they continued to take part where I left off. Then in Eldora they came and seen me and told me I could be their leader when I was released, but I said I wasn't going to be another leader, and they called me names such as coward. Well, I couldn't very well take those names, so I was their leader again when I was released, but I wished I wouldn't of for it got me only in trouble again, while the other boys was released on probation. It didn't offer me nothing but bad luck.[66]

---

individual to the larger social order. Other explanations of gang behavior, such as that of Miller, claim that it is a product of lower-class culture which has a number of local concerns (values) like toughness, excitement, fate, and autonomy leading to crime. The focal concerns of the lower class, however, are a tautology; they are derived from the observation of gang behavior which they seek to explain. Moreover, the lower-class theory neglects the fact that middle-class values and agents also impinge on slum boys through the law and the schools. The focal concerns are probably experienced most in large city slums and less elsewhere; such a theory fails to explain middle-class delinquency. See Walter B. Miller, "Lower Class Culture as a Generating Milieu of Gang Delinquency," *Journal of Social Issues,* 14 (1958), 5–19. Cloward and Ohlin's theory of delinquency and opportunity is discussed in Chapter 3: see Cloward and Ohlin. Albert K. Cohen's theory of the origin of delinquent norms and subcultures as an outgrowth of shared hostility to middle-class values has received little support. See Albert K. Cohen, *Delinquent Boys: The Culture of the Gang* (New York: Free Press, 1955). For criticisms of a number of theories, see David Bordua, "A Critique of Sociological Interpretations of Gang Delinquency," *The Annals,* 338 (1961), 120–136. For a discussion of middle-class gangs, see Edmund W. Vaz, ed., *Middle Class Juvenile Delinquency* (New York: Harper & Row, 1967).
[66]From a personal document collected by Marshall B. Clinard.

CLASSIFICATION AND TYPOLOGY OF CRIMINAL OFFENDERS

The term "criminal" does not refer to a homogeneous group; in fact, it has little meaning except as it refers to lawbreakers. Instead, there are various classifications of criminal offenders, depending on whether the offenders are distinguished by types of crime committed, by characteristics such as sex and age, or in terms of behavior systems. Classification by offense is useful in studying the legal definitions of offenses; classification by sex and age is necessary in enumerations for statistical purposes.[67] From a scientific point of view, however, offenders are best grouped according to their behavior patterns and the processes through which the criminal behavior is developed. An adequate explanation of criminal behavior should show how it applies to all criminal behavior and how it should be modified to explain various types.[68]

Classification by Crime

Criminal offenders are often classified from a legal point of view by the *type of crime committed,* such as murder, arson, and burglary. Such a classification enables us, presumably, to group offenders neatly according to what they did and to show something of the tolerance limits of crimes as reflected in the different penalties of the criminal law. This method of grouping may be quite misleading, inasmuch as persons of extremely diverse types may commit the same type of crime; moreover, the seriousness of a criminal act is not always correlated with criminal behavior patterns in offenders. Distinctions based on misdemeanants and felons are also unsatisfactory. Finally, a large amount of serious crime committed by persons in business, politicians, government officials, doctors, and lawyers, as well as corporations, does not find its way into conventional discussions of crime and criminal statistics. Generally, much of this behavior is not detected and prosecuted, and if it is, it is by a variety of governmental agencies whose operations are outside the criminal law and thus seldom reported in the news media.

The major legal division of crimes is into officially reported *personal* and *property* crimes. Personal crimes, or crimes against persons, such as murder, manslaughter, and assault, actually constitute a small percentage of all reported crimes; in 1975, for example, crimes of this type accounted for 9 percent of all officially reported crimes. The 20,510 murders committed actually constituted slightly less than one half of 1 percent of all crimes. During 1975, 91 percent of the total 11,256,600 reported offenses were property crimes. Over 3 million cases of burglary were reported and almost 6 million cases of serious larceny (See Table 6.1). Most crimes reported to the police reflect acts committed by lower-class persons, a large percentage of whom are youth; they do not include occupational and corporate crimes.

---

[67]For a survey of classification schemes, see Daniel Glaser, "The Classification of Offenses and Offenders," in Glaser, *Handbook of Criminology,* pp. 45–83.
[68]Clinard and Quinney.

TABLE 6.1 **Estimated Number of Crimes Reported to the Police and Rate per 100,000 Population in the United States, 1975**

Crimes	*Estimated Crime*	
	Number	Rate per 100,000 Population
Total	11,256,600	5,281.7
Violent	1,026,280	481.5
Property	10,230,300	4,800.2
Murder	20,510	9.6
Forcible rape	56,090	26.3
Robbery	464,970	218.2
Aggravated assault	484,710	227.4
Burglary	3,252,100	1,525.9
Larceny-theft	5,977,700	2,804.8
Auto theft	1,000,500	469.4

Source: Uniform Crime Reports, 1975 (Washington, D.C.: Federal Bureau of Investigation, 1976), p. 11.

Classification by Sex

Criminal offenders may also be classified according to *sex.* This distinction used to have perhaps greater significance when nearly all offenses committed by women were prostitution and drunkenness as opposed to the property and violent crimes of men. Women are now engaging in almost as wide a variety of offenses as men, but not as frequently, except for shoplifting, a common offense for women. As measured by arrests, the proportion of crime among women appears to be increasing rapidly. In 1960 female arrests in the United States accounted for 10.9 percent; in 1975 the percentage was 16.7. In this same period female arrests rose 101.7 percent, while male arrests rose only 22.8. More spectacular was the increase in arrests in the under-18 age group: for females the increase was 253.9 percent, for males 125.3 percent. This increase, of course, must be examined in terms of the much lower rate at which women started. Furthermore, due to the differential treatment of women in the criminal justice process and the lower likelihood of arrests of women, the arrest statistics are even less reliable as a measure of crime than the male arrest figures.[69] On the other hand, women are less likely to be subjects of police suspicion in certain types of crime such as burglary or auto theft. Women are also not as likely to be arrested for the same offenses if their behavior is within the traditional women's role.[70]

[69]See Joseph G. Weis, "Liberation and Crime: The Invention of the New Female Criminal," *Crime and Social Justice,* 6 (1976), 17–27.
[70]See Meda Chesney-Lind, "Judicial Enforcement of the Female Sex Role: The Family Court and the Female Delinquent," *Issues in Criminology,* 8 (1973), 51–69, and her "Judicial Paternalism and the Female Status Offender: Training Women To Know Their Place," *Crime and Delinquency,* 23 (1977), 121–130. Also see Lois De Fleur, "Biasing Influences on Drug Arrest Records: Implications for Deviance Research," *American Sociological Review,* 40 (1975), 88–103.

Although it is increasingly difficult to distinguish clearly among offenses in terms of the sex of the offender, the apparently lower general ratio of crimes committed by women can be explained in a number of ways. (1) Women often participate in crimes committed by men but they are not as easily detected as are men. (2) Because women can engage in prostitution they need not turn to burglary or larceny. Certainly women now participate sufficiently in the general society, however, to be able to steal a car or to burglarize a home. (3) The differential access to, or pressures toward, criminally oriented subcultures and crimes means that women do not as frequently belong to gangs and are more isolated from criminal norms.[71] (4) It has also been suggested that differential sex role expectations mean that women more often develop a conception of themselves in terms of future parental responsibilities, making their participation in serious crimes less likely.[72] These differences have been built into both socialization patterns and the application of social control measures. (5) Differences in opportunities to commit particular offenses and in sex differences have been incorporated into the crime categories themselves.

As the women's movement progresses and women are placed in more positions of opportunity to commit crimes, a much larger amount of female crime can be expected. Simon has stated that "increased participation in the labor force provides women with more opportunities for committing certain types of crimes. As those opportunities increase, women's participation in larceny, fraud, embezzlement, and other financial and white-collar crimes should increase."[73] In those situations where they have the opportunity, as in shopping, they do commit a high proportion of crimes; while most shoplifting offenses are simple, some of these offenders are extremely professional in the skill.[74] It may be maintained, however, that the women's movement may result in both increases and decreases in crime because of the greater economic opportunities and the decreased importance of prostitution. Looking at the total situation, one researcher has concluded that the degree of urbanization and the percentage of women in the labor force are more linked to the increases in women's crime than other variables.[75]

Classification by Age

Age is another distinction often used to classify offenders; supposedly younger and older offenders denote different degrees of criminal development. Serious crimes most frequently are committed by persons under 25 (see Table 6.2). In the United States in 1975 the highest arrest rate for larceny, burglary, and motor vehicle theft was in the age group between 15 and 17. The next highest group was that between 18 and 20; after 20 the rates dropped off directly in proportion to age increases. This general picture of a large percentage of conventional crimes being committed by those under

---

[71]Dale Hoffman-Bustamente, "The Nature of Female Criminality," *Issues in Criminology,* 8 (1973), 117.
[72]Hoffman-Bustamente, p. 117.
[73]Rita James Simon, *Women and Crime* (Lexington, Mass.: Heath, 1975), p. 19.
[74]See, for example, Freda Adler, *Sisters in Crime* (New York: McGraw-Hill, 1975); and Simon.
[75]Michael L. Radelet, "The Effect of Female Social Position on the Sex Ratio of Arrests," unpublished paper, Department of Psychiatry, University of Wisconsin, Madison, 1977.

TABLE 6.2

Percentage of All Arrests in the United States by Selected Age Groups, 1975

Offense	Under 15	15—17	18—20	21—24
Murder and nonnegligent manslaughter	1.1	8.4	15.6	19.7
Forcible rape	3.9	13.6	19.5	21.0
Robbery	9.6	24.6	23.4	19.3
Aggravated assault	5.2	12.3	14.7	17.3
Burglary	18.1	32.5	20.0	12.6
Larceny-theft	20.1	25.0	17.7	12.7
Auto theft	14.4	40.2	18.5	11.5

Source: Derived from *Uniform Crime Reports,* 1975 (Washington, D.C.: Federal Bureau of Investigation, 1976), pp. 188–189.

18 holds true for nearly all the developed countries.[76] In the developing countries the age of offenders is still young, but it is often about two years older.[77]

Although all types of crimes are committed by persons of any age, the probability is far greater that a young person will be arrested for the most serious crimes. In the general population only about 30 percent are under the age of 18, yet in 1975 approximately one in every two burglars arrested was under this age (see Table 6.3). Over two thirds (73.1 percent) of all those arrested for auto theft were under 21 and over one half (57.7 percent) of all those arrested for robbery. Three fourths of those arrested for larceny were under 25, as well as over four fifths (84.6 percent) of those arrested for automobile thefts and over three fourths of the arrested burglars. If one combines larceny, burglary, and motor vehicle theft, one half of those arrested were under 18, and two thirds were under 25. Nearly half of all persons arrested for forcible

TABLE 6.3

Arrests in the United States by Cumulative Younger Age Groups, 1975

Offense	Percent under 18	Percent under 21	Percent under 25
Murder and nonnegligent manslaughter	9.5	25.2	44.9
Forcible rape	17.6	37.0	50.6
Robbery	34.3	57.7	77.0
Aggravated assault	17.6	32.2	49.6
Burglary	52.6	72.6	85.2
Larceny-theft	45.1	62.8	75.4
Auto theft	54.5	73.1	84.6

Source: Uniform Crime Reports, 1975 (Washington, D.C.: Federal Bureau of Investigation, 1976), p. 190.

---

[76]See, for example, D. J. West, *The Young Offender* (London: Duckworth and Penguin Books, 1967), for the situation in England.
[77]Clinard and Abbott.

rape were under 25. A different picture is revealed in arrests for other offenses, particularly those involving drunkenness, driving while intoxicated, gambling violations, homicide, aggravated assault, and white-collar and professional crime, all of which are largely committed by older persons.

In all probability the age at which ordinary crimes are actually committed is even lower than the figures suggest. In the first place, many offenders in the age group 14–16 are not included because the figures cited above are computed from fingerprint cards submitted voluntarily by local police departments; moreover, juvenile offenders are often not fingerprinted, or their fingerprints may not be reported to the FBI. In the second place, arrests tabulated in a given year *do not indicate the age of first arrest.* If it were possible to know when offenses *first* started, a greater frequency might be found below 18 and even below 15 years of age.

Classification of offenders by age has little merit because the "hardness" of an offender has little relation to age. An offender is "hardened" if the individual has definite antisocial attitudes toward laws, property, and the police, professional knowledge of the techniques used to commit crimes and avoid prosecution, and a framework of rationalizations to support this conduct. These attitudes may be well developed in a person of 17 and yet be absent in a "criminal" of 40. For example, 76.6 percent of all arrests for robbery are of persons under 25, and this offense is almost always preceded by other crimes, usually involving the use of a gun, and indicating definite criminal attitudes.

Criminal Behavior Systems

A more useful way of distinguishing between criminal offenders is a typology based on *behavior systems.* This involves four aspects: the criminal career of the offender, the group support of criminal behavior, the correspondence between criminal and legitimate behavior patterns, and the societal reaction to the behavior.[78] A typology in these terms will be used in Chapter 7 to describe and analyze a number of types of crimes: violent personal, occasional property, political, occupational, corporate, conventional, organized, and professional. Before discussing these types, however, the nature of a criminal behavior system should be explained in more detail.[79]

Criminal Career of the Offender The criminal career of the offender is determined by the extent to which criminality has become a part of an offender's life organization and the person has moved from primary to secondary deviation. It includes playing a criminal role, conception of self as criminal, progression in crime, and the extent to which criminal behavior has identified with and become a part of the offender's life organization.

Although individuals may commit crimes that are legally similar, this behavior actually has a different significance for each. In some individuals the delinquent and criminal activity may represent only a minor and relatively unimportant part of their

---

[78]Clinard and Quinney.
[79]For a recent discussion and critique of typologies, see Don C. Gibbons, "Offender Typologies—Two Decades Later," *British Journal of Criminology,* 15 (1975), 140–156; and Don C. Gibbons, *Society, Crime and Criminal Careers,* 3d ed. (Englewood Cliffs, N.J.: Prentice-Hall, 1977), pp. 239–263.

social roles and life organization, while crime may pervade the lives of others. The extent of incorporation of criminal attitudes reflects the relative degree of development of criminal social roles and identification with a criminal way of life. Thus, offenders may play roles varying all the way from that of an occasional offender to less sophisticated roles such as those of "tough guy," "young punk," "smart operator," "big shot," "strong-arm man," and the "big boss." Greater participation in criminal activities means that crime has become integrated into the person's life organization and that criminal habits and attitudes have been well established.

Closely associated with an identification with delinquency or crime is the self-identity and social role a criminal offender develops. While conception of self as a criminal is highly developed among conventional, organized, and professional offenders, most personal, occupational, corporate, and political offenders do not conceive of themselves as such. Societal reaction in the form of law-enforcement agencies is related to the acquisition of one's self-conception as a delinquent or a criminal; for this reason the first arrest or incarceration is often of prime importance in an offender's criminal career. Once an offender has developed the self-concept of a delinquent, prostitute, confidence man, or robber it is often hard to change it. Some sociological studies have suggested differences in self-conception as the reason that certain youth residing in a delinquency area do not become delinquents.[80] One group of researchers stated that the conception of self and others is "the differential response component that helps to explain why some succumb and others do not, why some gravitate toward socially unacceptable patterns of behavior and others veer away from them."[81] Others have criticized this finding, however, on the grounds that the self-concept measures were not adequate and that some delinquents reject the appraisal of others.[82]

The history of a criminal career type shows a progressive acquisition of criminal techniques and knowledge. This progression varies with different types of crimes. Career burglars and robbers, for example, show a progression as youths from petty thefts to more serious larcenies to crimes such as ordinary burglaries and auto thefts and then on to highly skilled burglaries or armed robberies. Criminality may proceed from trivial to more serious crimes, from being a sport to being a business, and from occasional crime to more frequent crime. Along with the progression in crime, offenders develop a philosophy of life that justifies their criminal actions. White-collar and professional crime, as well as much political crime, however, do not progress in these terms.

The individual may gain considerable satisfactions from the acceptance of group

---

[80]See Leon Fannin and Marshall B. Clinard, "Differences in the Conception of Self as Male among Lower and Middle Class Delinquents," *Social Problems,* 13 (1965), 205–214. For a discussion of differences between working-class and middle-class delinquency, see Don C. Gibbons, *Delinquent Behavior.* Also see Walter C. Reckless, Simon Dinitz, and Ellen Murray, "Self Concept as an Insulator against Delinquency," *American Sociological Review,* 21 (1956), 744–746; and Walter C. Reckless, Simon Dinitz, and Barbara Kay, "Self-Component in Potential Delinquency and Non-Delinquency," *American Sociological Review,* 22 (1957), 566–570.

[81]Reckless, Dinitz, and Kay, p. 570.

[82]For a critical survey of research on the self concept as a variable in delinquency, see Sandra S. Tangri and Michael Schwartz, "Delinquency Research and the Self-Concept Variable," *Journal of Criminal Law, Criminology and Police Science,* 58 (1967), 182–191. Also see James D. Orcutt, "Self-Concept and Insulation against Delinquency: Some Critical Notes," *The Sociological Quarterly,* 11 (1970), 381–391.

norms and will orient his life around them. Thus if a young man identifies himself with the activities of a group of "young punks," this relationship may become as satisfying as if he identified his activities with a group of Boy Scouts. Yet mere membership in a group or contact with criminal norms does not tell us what the behavior means to the individual. Much conventional, as well as organized and professional criminality, is the result of a person's identification with others to whom the criminal behavior seems acceptable.[83] Occasional, occupational, corporate, and political offenders usually do not identify with crime.

Group Support of Criminal Behavior   The offender's behavior is shaped by the extent to which criminally defined norms and activities become a part of the individual's career. This career includes the social roles played, the conception of self, the progression in criminal activity, and the identification with crime. Offenders vary in the degree to which criminally defined behavior has become a part of their life organization. Although most crime is learned from association from others, there are variations in the extent to which the behavior of a criminal offender is supported by norms of the group or groups to which he belongs. Some of these may be companions, gangs, occupations, or local communities. This includes the differential association of the offender with both criminal and noncriminal norms and the integration of the offender into deviant social groups.

Correspondence between Criminal Behavior and Legitimate Behavior   Criminal acts vary in the extent to which the criminal behavior is consistent with legitimate patterns of behavior in the society. This includes the extent to which criminal behavior corresponds to valued goals and means which are regarded as legitimate by the dominant or power segments of the society. Businessmen who commit white-collar offenses, for example, develop many rationalizations that they are contributing to the goals of society in making wealth and producing goods. The values of the political offender, such as the conscientious objector to war who seeks to "improve" society by his actions, are different in nature but similar to those of the total society. On the other hand, the correspondence between the goals of most conventional criminals and the norms of legitimate society is slight.

Societal Reaction   Finally, various groups in a society who have the power to shape policy regard types of crime in different ways, reacting more strongly to one than to another. The reactions may take the form of law enforcement through criminal prosecution, conviction, and sentencing, or through civil or administrative action by governmental agencies. Some crimes are reacted to with severe sentences, others with slight sentences if any at all. Societal reactions are affected by the visibility of the offense and the degree to which the criminal behavior corresponds to the interests of the power structure of the society. Different patterns of detection, arrest, prosecution, conviction, sentencing, and punishment exist for each type of criminal behavior. Occupational crime and organized crime are reacted to differently with different degrees of punish-

---

[83]Daniel Glaser, "Criminality Theories and Behavioral Images," *American Journal of Sociology,* 61 (1956), 433–445.

ment. Likewise, offenders of certain types are not as likely to encounter enforcement measures. Labeling by arrest, conviction, or imprisonment has important effects on the self-conception of the criminal offender. In the following chapter we will discuss a number of types of criminal behavior systems in more detail, using largely the analytical system.

SELECTED REFERENCES

Carter, Robert M., and Malcolm W. Klein, eds. *Back on the Streets: The Diversion of Juvenile Offenders.* Englewood Cliffs, N.J.: Prentice-Hall, 1976.

Chambliss, William J. "The State, the Law, and the Definition of Behavior as Criminal or Delinquent," in Daniel Glaser, ed., *Handbook of Criminology.* Chicago: Rand McNally, 1974.

Chambliss, William J., and Robert B. Seidman. *Law, Order and Power.* Reading, Mass.: Addison-Wesley, 1971.

Clinard, Marshall B., and Daniel J. Abbott. *Crime in Developing Countries.* New York: Wiley, 1973.

Clinard, Marshall B., and Richard Quinney. *Criminal Behavior Systems: A Typology,* rev. ed. New York: Holt, Rinehart and Winston, 1973.

Empey, LaMar T. "Delinquency Theory and Recent Research," *Journal of Research in Crime and Delinquency,* 4 (1967), 28–42.

Glaser, Daniel. "The Classification of Offenses and Offenders," in Daniel Glaser, ed., *Handbook of Criminology.* Chicago: Rand McNally, 1974.

Glaser, Daniel, ed. *Crime in the City.* New York: Harper & Row, 1970.

Kaplan, Robert M., and Robert D. Singer. "Television Violence and Viewer Aggression: A Reexamination of the Evidence," *Journal of Social Issues,* 32 (1976), 35–70.

Klein, Dorie. "The Etiology of Female Crime: A Review of the Literature," *Issues in Criminology,* 7 (1973), 3–30.

Matza, David. *Delinquency and Drift.* New York: Wiley, 1964.

McCord, Joan. "Father and Son Criminality: A Comparative Study of Two Generations of Native Americans," in Robert F. Meier, ed., *Theory in Criminology: Contemporary Views.* Beverly Hills, Calif.: Sage Publications, 1977.

Miller, Walter B. *Violence by Youth Gangs and Youth Groups as a Crime Problem in Major American Cities.* Washington, D.C.: National Institute for Juvenile Justice and Delinquency Prevention, 1975.

Morris, Terence. *The Criminal Area: A Study in Social Ecology.* London: Routledge & Kegan Paul, 1958.

Sellin, Thorsten. *Culture Conflict and Crime.* New York: Social Science Research Council, Bulletin 41, 1938.

Shaw, Clifford R., and Henry D. McKay. *Juvenile Delinquency and Urban Areas,* 2d ed. Chicago: University of Chicago Press, 1969; originally published in 1942.

Short, James F., Jr., and Fred L. Strodtbeck. *Group Process and Gang Delinquency.* Chicago: University of Chicago Press, 1965.

Simon, Rita James. *Women and Crime.* Lexington, Mass.: Heath, 1975.

Sutherland, Edwin H., and Donald R. Cressey. *Criminology,* 10th ed. Philadelphia: Lippincott, 1978.

Wolfgang, Marvin E., Robert M. Figlio, and Thorsten Sellin. *Delinquency in a Birth Cohort.* Chicago: University of Chicago Press, 1972.

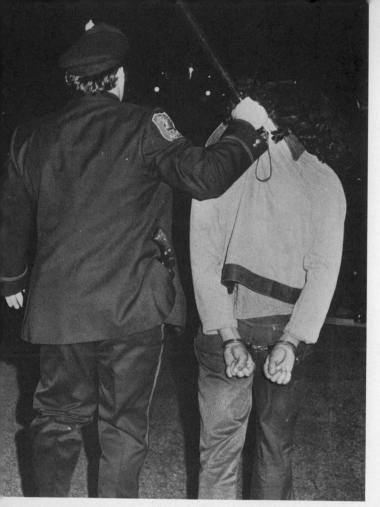

CHAPTER 7

Criminal offenders are of many types. Here a police officer is arresting a conventional type of offender. Most other types, such as the occupational and the corporate, are not subject to this type of arrest. (Wide World Photos)

Types of Criminal Behavior

CRIMINAL offenders can be classified according to the degree to which they are *career criminals.* A criminal career can be distinguished from a noncriminal career by the extent to which the person has developed criminal norms that lead to criminal acts and by how the person views the criminal behavior. As distinguished from a noncriminal career, a criminal career involves a life organization of roles built around criminal activities, such as: (1) identification with crime; (2) conception of self as a criminal; (3) extensive association with criminal activities and with other criminals; and finally, (4) a progression in crime that involves the acquisition of more complex techniques and more frequent offenses.

Offenders can be divided into the following types along a continuum from noncareer to career and embodying the nature of the group support, the relation to noncriminal values, and the societal reaction. Most personal offenders are of the noncareer type, or primary criminal deviants, whereas property offenders are more likely to be of the career, or secondary, type. At one end of the continuum are violent personal criminal offenders and occasional property offenders; at the other are organized and professional offenders. In between are political offenders, occupational and corporate violators, and conventional criminal offenders (see Figure 7.1).[1] In other chapters, an analysis will be presented of public order types of behavior that are often criminal—illegal drug usage, drunkenness, prostitution, and homosexuality.

VIOLENT PERSONAL CRIMES

Collective violence has been common in the past and in contemporary society, in the form of wars, civil riots, and violent demonstrations. This violence involves thousands of individual acts of assault, murder, arson, vandalism, and theft. War is a good example of collective violence. During World War I, 17 million soldiers were killed or missing in battle, and there were 20 million civilian deaths; in World War II, 10 million soldiers were killed or missing in battle, and 43 million civilians were killed.[2] The Nazi control of Europe resulted in the brutal extermination of 6,500,000 Jews. The total number of deaths, both military and civilian, in the Indochina war of the 1960s and early 1970s will probably never be accurately known, but it was in the hundreds of thousands. In the My Lai massacre alone there were 346 deaths. Use of violence by the government, often unnecessary, by means of the police and army against political dissenters and civilian protestors has frequently resulted in deaths and injuries. Unwarranted acts of collective violence by the police against individuals suspected of political crime and even beatings or other torture by authorities of a government are

---

[1]See also Marshall B. Clinard and Richard Quinney, *Criminal Behavior Systems: A Typology,* rev. ed. (New York: Holt, Rinehart and Winston, 1973), pp. 18–20; and James A. Inciardi, *Reflections on Crime* (New York: Holt, Rinehart and Winston, 1978), Chap. 5.

[2]One study of 110 nations has shown that even the postwar homicide rates generally increased substantially after a war in both victorious and defeated nations. Homicidal rate increases occurred with particular consistency among nations with large numbers of combat deaths. See Dane Archer and Rosemary Gartner, "Violent Acts and Violent Times: A Comparative Approach to Postwar Homicide Rates," *American Sociological Review,* 41 (1976), 937–963.

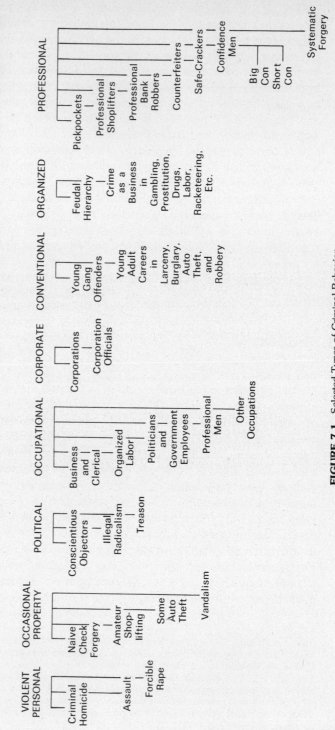

FIGURE 7.1 Selected Types of Criminal Behavior.

by no means uncommon; indeed, such tactics are often even sanctioned by the highest civil authorities.[3] Wolfgang states that labor and race riots, lynching mobs, fights among delinquent gangs, and attacks by organized criminal syndicates "are all forms of collective violence that have punctuated the history of social change.[4]

These forms of violence are all collective; on the whole their origin and nature are quite different from individual acts of violence such as criminal homicide, assault, and forcible rape, which are designated as *violent personal offenses*. All involve the accomplishment of an objective through violence, whether it is an argument, a personal dispute, or sexual intercourse. Offenders who commit these personal types of offenses generally do not have criminal careers in such offenses. In fact, most murderers and assaulters do not conceive of themselves as being "criminals," because there is seldom identification with crime, and criminal behavior as such is not a meaningful part of their lives. Forcible rapists, on the other hand, are likely to have a record of other offenses.

Subculture of Violence

Most acts of violence grow out of an interaction situation in which the act comes to be defined as requiring violence and in which the victim plays a part in precipitating it, whether it results in criminal homicide, assault, or forcible rape. General cultural and subcultural patterns seem to determine the frequency of crimes of violence, and the extent of acceptance of the use of violence varies from country to country, region to region, and state to state. It also varies by neighborhood within a city and by social class, occupation, race, sex, and age. These variations have been explained as *subcultures of violence,* or the normative systems of a group or groups. According to Wolfgang and Ferracuti, specific populations, for example, social classes or ethnic groups, have different attitudes toward the use of violence.[5] The favorable attitudes toward violence are organized into a set of norms that are culturally transmitted. Such subcultural groups exhibit norms having to do with the importance of human life in the scale of values, the kinds of reactions to certain types of social stimuli in the evaluation of these stimuli, and the general socialization process. It should be emphasized again that the proponents of a "subculture" of violence base the existence of the theory on differences in *rates* of violence among various groups. This does not, of course, mean that *all* persons in any group share the values supposedly reflected in a subculture of violence or, conversely, in a subculture of nonviolence; nor does it mean that a person uses violence under all situations and under all conditions.

This theory has been challenged in a few studies, however, which claim it is difficult to test. One study concluded that there was little empirical evidence by social class for the subcultural theory based on the degree of self-esteem, violence in the

---

[3]Paul Takagi, "A Garrison State in a Democratic Society," *Crime and Social Justice,* 1 (1974), 27–33.
[4]Marvin E. Wolfgang, "A Preface to Violence," *The Annals,* 364 (1966), 2. Also see James F. Short, Jr., and Marvin E. Wolfgang, eds., *Collective Violence* (Chicago: Aldine, 1972); and Lewis A. Coser, "Some Social Functions of Violence," *The Annals,* 364 (1966), 8–18.
[5]Marvin E. Wolfgang and Franco Ferracuti, *The Subculture of Violence: Towards an Integrated Theory in Criminology* (London: Tavistock, Social Science Paperbacks, 1967). Also see Hugh Davis Graham, ed., *Violence: The Crisis of American Confidence* (Baltimore: Johns Hopkins Press, 1971).

form of fighting, and the conferral of esteem by others for using violence, thereby casting doubt on whether violence is socially rewarded in lower-class groups.[6] Another study which analyzed the differences in values among persons with differing degrees of involvement with violence found no significant differences in the value orientations of persons who reported "no," a "moderate," or a "high" degree of participation in violence at different times in their lives.[7] These studies, however, deal with attitudes toward and the *use of violence* rather than *serious violence* leading to homicide, aggravated assault, and forcible rape. Obviously, physical violence is used to some extent by all groups, and this is not the issue. Moreover, they offer no alternative theory for the great variations in the rates of use of serious violence by certain types of groups, something that the subculture of violence does offer.

Criminal Homicide and Assault

The type of criminal homicide discussed here consists of both murder and nonnegligent manslaughter, but does not include justifiable homicide or accidental death. Another type of criminal homicide not included is negligent manslaughter, in which a death is attributable to the negligence of some person other than the victim. Technically "murder" is determined by the police and the court through a legal process. In aggravated assault there is an attempt to use physical force to settle an argument or a dispute.[8] Nearly all criminal homicide represents some form of aggravated assault, the chief difference being that the victim died.

Most criminal homicide, like assault, is an outgrowth of personal disputes and altercations, some immediate and some long-standing in nature. Relatively few of these offenses are associated with the commission of other crimes such as robbery. The acceptance of the use of violence to settle disputes is related to general cultural patterns. The acceptance of murder as a method of solving interpersonal conflicts varies a great deal in time, from country to country, from region to region, and by local areas, race, social class, and age.

Variations by Country The use of personal violence to settle disputes, even though it results in assault and murder, appears to have been common in nearly all of Europe a few centuries ago, even among the upper classes. Whereas at present most European countries, particularly most Scandinavian countries, the United Kingdom, and Ireland have low rates, the Latin American and African countries generally have high rates.[9]

---

[6]Howard S. Erlanger, "The Empirical Status of the Subculture of Violence Thesis," *Social Problems,* 22 (1974), 280–292. For a discussion of some of the methodological and statistical problems in testing the subculture of violence hypothesis, see Howard S. Erlanger and Halliman H. Winsborough, "The Subculture of Violence Thesis: An Example of a Simultaneous Equation Model in Sociology," *Sociological Methods and Research,* 5 (1976), 231–246.

[7]Sandra J. Ball-Rokeach, "Values and Violence: A Test of the Subculture of Violence Thesis," *American Sociological Review,* 38 (1973), 736–749.

[8]Physical assault on children by their parents is permitted if it does not result in serious injury; all too frequently it does. See Naomi Feigelson Chase, *A Child Is Being Beaten: Violence against Children, an American Tragedy* (New York: McGraw-Hill, 1975).

[9]Marshall B. Clinard and Daniel J. Abbott, *Crime in Developing Countries: A Comparative Perspective* (New York: Wiley, 1973).

The higher homicide rates of Latin American countries are related to the attitude of masculinity or "machismo," involving particularly the customary recourse to the use of violence when one is personally insulted or when one's honor is challenged. The rates of violence in Turkey and Finland are higher than those in other European countries, and the rate in Ceylon is particularly high for Asia.[10] The United States ranks about in the middle.

Regional Variations   In the United States homicide rates in the southern states are considerably higher than those in other regions, although the rates in the West are rapidly increasing.[11] The differences are due largely to the fact that cultural definitions demand personal violence in certain situations and that weapons are more frequently carried in some areas than in others. While the high rates of violence in the South appear to be products of a subculture in which violence has long been used to settle disputes and in which the carrying of hand guns has been common, this subculture is not easy to explain.[12] Some people maintain, for example, that the high rate is due to the extremely high rates of violence among blacks, who constitute a large part of the population. Actually, there is no correlation between these two factors; in fact, sometimes states rank lower in violent crimes as the proportion of the black population increases. Another explanation is that the South has a higher percentage of lower-class persons, a group prone to violence. Further study, however, actually shows that southern cities with high homicide rates have a higher percentage of whites in higher-status positions.

Homicide rates also show variation within many other countries. For example, the rates are higher in Sardinia than in any other part of Italy; here the use of violence, particularly of vendetta (homicides), is regulated by a set of norms or a "code" that supersedes and superimposes Italian criminal law. An intensive study compared Sardinia's violent offenders with the nonviolent offenders and, in turn, with violent offenders from other parts of Italy.[13] Psychological tests yielded few attitudes of difference; no data contradicted the hypothesis of a subculture of violence, of the existence of violent, socially learned and reinforced responses of Sardinian offenders.

Local Areas   The fact that rates are highest in the large city slums is one indication of the importance of the subcultural factors.[14] Slum areas have long been characterized by violence, not so much because of the physical characteristics of slum poverty but because of the slum way of life in which the use of force may be approved to settle disputes. Two studies of homicide in Houston, Texas, for example, found these crimes

---

[10]See Franco Ferracuti and Graeme Newman, "Assaultive Offenses," in Daniel Glaser, ed., *Handbook of Criminology* (Chicago: Rand McNally, 1974), pp. 194–195.

[11]William G. Doerner, "A Regional Analysis of Homicide Rates in the United States," *Criminology*, 13 (1975), 90–101, and Robert S. Munford, Ross S. Kazer, Roger A. Feldman, and Robert B. Stivers, "Homicide Trends in Atlanta," *Criminology*, 14 (1976), 213–232.

[12]Sheldon Hackney, "Southern Violence," in Hugh Davis Graham and Ted Robert Gurr, *Violence in America*. Staff Report to the National Commission on the Causes and Prevention of Violence (Washington, D. C.: Government Printing Office, 1969), Vol. 2, pp. 387–404.

[13]Franco Ferracuti, Renato Lazzari, and Marvin E. Wolfgang, eds., *Violence in Sardinia* (Rome: Mario Bulzoni, 1970).

[14]*To Establish Justice, To Insure Domestic Tranquility,* Final Report of the National Commission on the Causes and Prevention of Violence (Washington, D.C.: Government Printing Office, 1969), p. 23.

to be concentrated in a relatively small area of largely lower-class residents.[15] One found that over 87 percent of the homicides occurred in four areas not far apart in certain slum areas near the city center. Two thirds of the homicides studied in Cleveland occurred in 12 percent of the city, primarily in black slum areas.[16] Studies of criminal homicides and other crimes of violence in London showed them also to be concentrated in slum areas. This was the case not only in domestic strife and neighborhood quarrels but even in fights in public houses, cafes, and streets where persons involved were working-class people from the same neighborhood.[17]

Race   Due largely to slum living racial disparity is greatest in arrest rates for crimes of violence. In 1975 when blacks made up 12 percent of the total U.S. population they accounted for one half (54 percent) of all criminal homicide arrests.[18] In the Philadelphia homicide study the rate among blacks was four times that of whites, indicating the role of the subculture of the slum and the isolating effects of segregation from the general norms of society.[19] A Cleveland study showed that while three fourths of the offenders in homicide cases were black, only 11 percent of the population were black.[20] In a Houston study blacks made up only one fourth of the population but accounted for two thirds of the offenders.[21] In a Chicago study the criminal homicide rate for nonwhites was approximately 10 times that of whites; in fact, the rate for nonwhite females was approximately twice that of white males.[22]

The relation of group factors to crimes of violence can be seen in the fact that in nearly all crimes of violence in the United States both offender and victim are of the same race. This is true of homicide, aggravated assault, and rape. Crimes of violence are *intraracial* rather than interracial. This results from the tendency for social relations to be still largely with members of one's own race. Only 6 percent of Houston homicide cases were interracial in nature.[23] The finding of a large-scale study based on *arrests* in 17 large U.S. cities supports the intraracial nature of violence. "Racial fears underlie much of the public concern over violence, so one of our most striking and relevant general conclusions is that serious 'assaultive' violence—criminal homicide,

---

[15]Henry Allen Bullock, "Urban Homicide in Theory and Fact," *Journal of Criminal Law, Criminology and Police Science,* 45 (1955), 565–575. Also see Henry P. Lundsgaarde, *Murder in Space City: A Cultural Analysis of Houston Homicide Patterns* (New York: Oxford University Press, 1977), pp. 47–50 and 105–106.

[16]Robert C. Bensing and Oliver Schroeder, Jr., *Homicide in an Urban Community* (Springfield, Ill.: Charles C Thomas, 1960).

[17]F. H. McClintock, *Crimes of Violence* (London: Macmillan, 1963), pp. 44-45. Also see S. Venugopal Rao, *Murder: A Pilot Study of Urban Patterns with Particular Reference to the City of Delhi* (New Delhi: Government of India, 1968).

[18]Federal Bureau of Investigation, *Uniform Crime Reports—1975* (Washington, D.C.: Government Printing Office, 1976), p. 192.

[19]Marvin E. Wolfgang, *Patterns in Criminal Homicide* (Philadelphia: University of Pennsylvania Press, 1958).

[20]Bensing and Schroeder, p. 22.

[21]Alex D. Pokorny, "A Comparison of Homicides in Two Cities," *Journal of Criminal Law, Criminology and Police Science,* 56 (1965), 479–487.

[22]Harwin L. Voss and John R. Hepburn, "Patterns in Criminal Homicide in Chicago," *Journal of Criminal Law, Criminology and Police Science,* 59 (1968), 501. Also see John R. Hepburn and Harwin L. Voss, "Patterns of Criminal Homicide in Chicago and Philadelphia," *Criminology,* 8 (1970), 21–45.

[23]Lundsgaarde, p. 118.

aggravated assault and forcible rape—is predominantly *intraracial* in nature."[24] The majority of these crimes involved blacks assaulting blacks; most of the rest involved whites victimizing other whites. Where race was known, one fourth of the homicides and assaults were between whites and two thirds between blacks; only 6 percent involved blacks killing whites and 4 percent whites killing blacks.[25]

Social Class   Crimes of violence are found almost entirely in the lower class. Nine out of 10 criminal homicides in Philadelphia involved persons in lower-class occupations; laborers, for example, committed far more criminal homicides than clerks.[26] In a London study of crimes of violence, primarily homicides and assaults, the majority of the offenders were found to be unskilled or casual workers.[27] The higher-class clerical workers accounted for no more than 5 percent of the total. In Delhi, India, nearly four fifths of all murderers were from the poor classes, as were two thirds of all the victims.[28] Of those involved in a sample group of assaulters in St. Louis, four fifths of the offenders, as well as a like percentage of the victims, were from the working class.[29] Rarely do criminal homicides occur among middle- and upper-class groups, even in the southern part of the United States or in Latin American countries where rates are generally high.

Age   Personal violence in urban areas is generally higher among the younger age groups; homicide arrest rates in the United States are much higher among males aged 18 to 24.[30] For aggravated assault the 15–24 age group has the highest rate. It should be remembered, however, that many cases of homicide and assault also occur among older age groups.

Interaction between Offender and Victim   Most murders and aggravated assaults represent a response, growing out of social interaction between one or more parties, in which a situation becomes defined as requiring the use of violence. Generally before such an act takes place, all parties concerned must come to believe that the situation cannot be resolved without the use of violence. The violence may result from a single argument or dispute, while in other cases it may result from a long series of disputes between husband and wife, lovers, neighbors, or fellow-employees. Increasingly verbalization declines and resort is made to violence. Typical cases of homicide and assault have

---

[24]*Crimes of Violence,* Staff Report to the National Commission on the Causes and Prevention of Violence, prepared by Donald J. Mulvihill and Melvin M. Tumin, with Lynn A. Curtis (Washington, D.C.: Government Printing Office, 1969), Vol. 11, p. 208. This study had been the most comprehensive study of violence in the United States until the Dangerous Offender Project directed by John P. Conrad and Simon Dinitz. A series of nine volumes with several authors and dealing with various aspects of the project will be published by Lexington Books. The first volume was John P. Conrad and Simon Dinitz, *In Fear of Each Other: Studies of Dangerousness in America* (Lexington. Mass.: Lexington Books, 1977).
[25]*Crimes of Violence,* p. 209.
[26]Wolfgang, *Patterns in Criminal Homicide.*
[27]McClintock, *Crimes of Violence,* pp. 131–132.
[28]Rao, pp. 19–21.
[29]David J. Pittman and William Handy, "Patterns in Criminal Aggravated Assault," *Journal of Criminal Law, Criminology and Police Science,* 55 (1964), 462–470.
[30]*To Establish Justice, To Insure Domestic Tranquility.* p. 22.

two characteristics in addition to the mutual recognition that violence is appropriate. First, the events are usually nonscheduled in time and place, "developing" rather than being planned beforehand. Second, the violence is escalated by a "character contest, a gamey confrontation in which the offender and victim attempt to save or establish face at the expense of each other by standing strong and steady in the face of adversity."[31]

It is thus apparent that homicides and assaults are often "precipitated" by the victims themselves. In one study more than one in four criminal homicides was precipitated by the victim in that the victim was the first to show or to use a deadly weapon, or to strike a blow in an altercation.[32] In another study it was found to be one case out of every three.[33] Victim-precipitated homicides were found to be significantly associated with blacks, victim-offender relationships involving male victims of female offenders and mate slayings.[34]

Many cases of violence develop from what might be regarded as trivial disputes. What is considered "trivial" by a person is related to his judgment derived from age, social class, and other background factors. Such homicides may involve the nonpayment of a small debt, a petty jealousy, or a small neighborhood quarrel, but these matters may be extremely important to the person involved. The role of these subcultural situations among the lower class in precipitating violence is that

> the significance of a jostle, a slightly derogatory remark, or the appearance of an object in the hands of an adversary are stimuli differentially perceived and interpreted by Negroes and whites, males and females. Social expectations of response in particular types of social interaction result in differential "definitions of the situation." A male is usually expected to defend the name and honor of his mother, the virtue of womanhood (even though his female companion for the evening may be an entirely new acquaintance and/or a prostitute), and to accept no derogation about his race (even from a member of his own race), his age, or his masculinity. Quick resort to physical combat as a measure of daring, courage, or defense of status appears to be a cultural expectation, especially for lower socio-economic class males of both races.[35]

Relationship of Offender and Victim　Assaultive crime, whether or not it leads to homicide, is intergroup behavior. Studies indicate that *close relationships* usually exist between offenders and victims of homicide or assault.[36] They usually involve relatives, close friends, or acquaintances, and they usually occur inside buildings rather than on the streets. Males kill males, women kill women, and persons over 25 kill others of the same age group.[37] In other words, people kill and assault those persons with whom

---

[31]David F. Luckenbill and William B. Sanders, "Criminal Violence," in Edward Sagarin and Fred Montanino, eds., *Deviants: Voluntary Actors in a Hostile World* (Morristown, N.J.: General Learning Press, 1977), p. 113.

[32]Wolfgang, *Patterns in Criminal Homicide,* p. 252; and Lundsgaarde, pp. 53–54.

[33]Voss and Hepburn, p. 506.

[34]Voss and Hepburn, p. 506.

[35]Wolfgang, *Patterns in Criminal Homicide,* pp. 188–189.

[36]*To Establish Justice, To Insure Domestic Tranquility,* pp. 25–26. Also see Federal Bureau of Investigation, *Uniform Crime Reports—1975;* and Lundsgaarde, p. 181, where an analysis of 232 homicide cases showed that 86 percent occurred with the use of firearms.

[37]Ferracuti and Newman, pp. 184–185. For this reason, these authors term criminal homicide the most intimate of violent crimes (p. 185).

they are likely to have the most contact. It is not surprising that domestic violence should also be a situation where homicide can result. One study attempted to address the question of why some abused wives have continued to stay with their husbands even though they have been beaten.[38] Three major factors were brought out: (1) the less severe and less frequent the violence, the more a wife remains with her husband; (2) the more a wife was struck as a child by her parents, the more likely she is to remain with her abusive husband; and (3) the fewer resources and the less power a wife has, the more likely she is to stay with her violent husband. Previous experiences in violence appear to condition the wife not to view it as unusual and may also have raised her threshold of tolerance for violence. In one study in which drug-using homicide victims and nondrug-using victims were examined, both groups were found likely to be killed within the confines of domestic or love relationships.[39] "Over half of the non-users were killed in such situations and a third of the drug-using women were. Traditional domestic, especially marital, contexts, then, still prove the most lethal for women."[40]

Urban residents greatly fear physical assaults by strangers on the street, yet according to a survey of various studies by a Presidential Commission, personal violence is actually less likely to be perpetrated by a stranger. This survey found that about 70 percent of all willful killings, nearly two thirds of all aggravated assaults, and high percentages of forcible rape are committed by family members and others previously known to their victims.[41] Similarly, a large government survey of 17 major U.S. cities found that only one in seven homicides and one in twenty assaults involved strangers.[42] Studies in England, Denmark, Italy, and India, all having different cultures, also revealed the significance of personal contacts in criminal homicide.[43]

Forcible Rape

Forcible rape, or unlawful sexual intercourse with a woman against her will, is distinguished from statutory rape or sexual intercourse, with or without consent, with a female under a specified age, generally 16 or 18 in the United States and 15 abroad. Many women regard forcible rape as a "political act," because it is an exercise of power by one group (males) over another (females). One commentator has said that "rape is to women as lynching was to blacks: the ultimate physical threat."[44] Rape represents an act of overt social control, an act that insures the continued oppression of women and a perpetuation of a male-dominated society. While recognizing the violent nature of forcible rape, the expectation of sexual gratification for the offender

---

[38]Richard J. Gelles, "Abused Wives: Why Do They Stay?" *Journal of Marriage and the Family,* 38 (1976), 659–668.

[39]Margaret A. Zahn, "The Female Homicide Victim," *Criminology,* 13 (1975), 400–415.

[40]Zahn, p. 413.

[41]*The Challenge of Crime in a Free Society,* President's Commission on Law Enforcement and Administration of Justice (Washington, D.C.: Government Printing Office, 1967), p. 18.

[42]*Crimes of Violence,* Vol. 11, p. 219.

[43]Ferracuti and Newman, pp. 185–187.

[44]Susan Brownmiller, *Against Our Will: Men, Women and Rape* (New York: Simon & Schuster, 1975), p. 254. Also see Marcia J. Walker and Stanley L. Brodsky, eds., *Sexual Assault: The Victim and the Rapist* (Lexington, Mass.: D. C. Heath and Co., 1976).

would seem to be another dimension, however, that is not present in ordinary assault and beating of women.

Degree of Violence   There is claimed to be a further political context to rape. Women historically have not enjoyed equal protection under the law in a number of areas, such as employment and marital property rights.[45] The law has adopted what has been termed a "paternalistic" approach to women: females typically have been seen as in need of protection and shelter from some of the harsher realities faced by men. In this sense it might appear that they have been protected as well in the rape laws: the law has treated females as if they were property of men, and a crime of rape has been treated as though it were a crime against the husband or father of the victim, not against the woman. "It is telling that a man cannot legally rape his wife, and that it is extremely difficult to win a conviction of rape against a man who rapes a prostitute—she does not belong to another man."[46]

Although forcible rape traditionally has been seen as a sexual crime motivated by the offender's desire for sexual relations, actually it cannot be described adequately without reference to the use of violence. Conceptualizing forcible rape as a deliberate act of violence has done much to reorient thinking about rape and to challenge various myths that have arisen about this offense. Perhaps the most long-standing myth is that rape is impossible if the victim resists sufficiently. Rape is like other predatory crimes, however, in the sense that the victim has no choice: "physical force is *always* present or implied."[47] It does not matter if the force is overt, such as using a weapon during the rape, or threatened—the use of force limits the choice of the victim, who is not physically as strong as the aggressor.[48]

Most instances of forcible rape parallel other forms of interpersonal violence such as homicide, assault, and wife-beating in terms of the characteristics of both offenders and victims. This indicates that a large proportion of rape comes out of a subculture of violence. Certain cultural values that are learned in interaction with others appear to be more conducive to forcible rape. One important component of the learning of sexual roles is expectations about the role of the other sex. Groups who contribute disproportionately to rape statistics as offenders also seem to be those whose conceptions of females as objects of sexual gratification are most strong. The male role, at the same time, is one that requires physical aggression on occasion, especially when one's masculinity is impugned or threatened. The assertion of masculinity, whether through the use of competitive sports, displays of physical prowess, or forcible rape, may constitute an important aspect of the everyday lives of some males in urban slum and other lower-class areas. Lower-class individuals often have difficulties in constructing their identities in terms that most middle- and upper-class persons understand—materialism, success, and social mobility. Males may thus be forced to

---

[45]See Karen DeCrow, *Sexist Justice* (New York: Random House, 1974).

[46]Dorie Klein and June Kress, "Any Woman's Blues: A Critical Overview of Women, Crime and the Criminal Justice System," *Crime and Social Justice*, 5 (1976), 39.

[47]Julia R. Schwendinger and Herman Schwendinger, "Rape Myths: In Legal, Theoretical and Everyday Practice," *Crime and Social Justice*, 1 (1974), 20. Also see J. L. Barkas, *Victims* (New York: Scribner's, 1978). This book deals with how the crimes of murder, assault, and forcible rape affect the victims.

[48]The laws in some states have been rewritten in such a way that the use of violence in rape is emphasized.

seek an identity in other realms of everyday living and in emphasizing the differences between themselves and females. Physical strength and force are devices very suitable to this purpose: they are readily available to males, they represent a biological difference between them and females, and they convey a sense of power when used.

Reporting of Rapes Various surveys have indicated that many cases of forcible rape are not reported to the police. This is readily understandable for several reasons. (1) Rape is an emotionally upsetting and deeply humiliating experience for the victim, who often reports it to the authorities with the greatest reluctance. (2) There is still a strong stigma, even within their own families, attached to victims of rape, although this situation is now changing. (3) Because of various myths associated with rape, victims are often seen somehow to have consented, either by not having resisted sufficiently or by having "led on" the assailant to the point where passion controlled the situation. (4) When rapes have been reported, some officials in the criminal justice system have tended not to believe the victim and to treat her as if she had been a party to the crime. (5) The victim is usually given a comprehensive physical examination to verify the rape, and she is often questioned in detail about the circumstances of the rape. (6) Of a more serious nature is the victim's treatment in the courtroom, usually under questioning by the attorney for the defense, who examines her, in a public hearing, in relation to her previous sexual history, the provocative circumstances relating to the rape, and whether or not she resisted the attack with "sufficient determination." Some states require that the judge make a statement to the jury before the case is handed over to the jury as a final protection for the defendant. Such a statement says in effect that rape is an easy charge to allege but difficult to prove.[49]

Because of the vast underreporting of forcible rape in the United States, official estimates have little meaning. Furthermore, most of the available information about forcible rapists is obtained from a selected population, those reported and those arrested. One study in 17 large U.S. cities indicated that 90 percent of the forcible rapes were intraracial; in one third of them both parties were white, in two thirds both were black, in 10 percent whites had raped blacks, and in less than 1 percent blacks had raped whites.[50] Amir, in a Philadelphia rape study that used official police statistics, found that the demographic pattern for rapists paralleled that for other violent offenders.[51] It was generally committed by a young, unmarried male, aged 15 to 25, from an inner-city area. Forty percent of the offenders were between 15 and 19 years of age; if the age bracket 15 to 24 were to be used, it would cover two thirds of the offenders. Ninety percent of the offenders belonged to the lower occupational status groups and came from slum areas with generally high rates of crimes of violence. Amir found the proportion of black offenders to be four times that of the white population, as was the proportion of black victims. There was also a high percentage (43 percent) of multiple rapes in which the victim was raped by more than

---

[49]For a useful collection of papers on this subject and other legal issues, see Duncan Chappell, Robley Geis, and Gilbert Geis, eds., *Forcible Rape: The Crime, the Victim and the Offender* (New York: Columbia University Press, 1977).

[50]*Crimes of Violence,* Vol. 11, p. 209.

[51]Menachem Amir, *Patterns of Forcible Rape* (Chicago: University of Chicago Press, 1971).

one male.[52] This probably suggests a possible bias in the type of arrested offender because those most frequently arrested were young adults.

The nature of any previous relationship between rapist and victim is difficult to ascertain completely from the research studies. In one study it was reported that about half of the victims had known the assailants before the rape.[53] A review of the literature by two other writers concluded, however, that forcible rape is more commonly perpetrated by strangers.[54] This confusion may be due to the fact that the offender and the victim might possibly have known each other, but the acquaintance was quite casual in nature.[55] After they have met in this manner at a party, a bar, or at some other function, for example, some interaction might ensue followed by force or the threat of force to assure that sexual relations take place. The victim's resistance may even be interpreted as a cue for continuing the rape; after the rape, the offender may attempt to "cool out" the victim, trying to convince her that it was a "love" act in which he had been carried away by passion or as a result of alcohol, or that there had been a misunderstanding wherein the offender thought the victim wanted forceful lovemaking.[56]

Some Legal Issues   In forcible rape, the element of lack of consent or victim precipitation is legally crucial. It has been claimed that this represents male bias in the formulation and administration of the law.[57] Some state codes have been revised to emphasize the use of force or assault in such cases regardless of the victim's possible attitude. Most judgments regarding victim precipitation in any case come from the police activity reports that often do not accurately or objectively state the events as they actually occurred. For example, Amir's study reported that one in five forcible rapes in his Philadelphia study were "victim precipitated," in the sense that the victim actually, or so it was interpreted by the offender, had agreed to sexual relations, but then had either retracted her consent before the act or did not resist strongly enough when the suggestion was made by the offender or the offenders.[58] This figure might be high, again because police arrest records and their views of the offense were used in the study. A quite contradictory result was found in another study in which comparisons were made of the degrees of victim precipitation in four crimes against the person: murder, aggravated assault, robbery, and forcible rape.[59] The findings pointed to the conclusion that some sort of provocation on the part of the victim was common with

---

[52]Amir, p. 200.

[53]Amir, p. 200.

[54]Ferracuti and Newman, p. 185.

[55]John H. Gagnon, "Sexual Conduct and Crime," in Glaser, p. 262.

[56]Kurt Weis and Sandra Borges, "Victimology and Rape: The Case of the Legitimate Victim," *Issues in Criminology,* 8 (1973), 71–115.

[57]Amir, pp. 259–264.

[58]This, of course, is not to say that forcible rape is to be condoned in those situations in which the victim somehow "invited" sexual intercourse and then refused. For a discussion of male bias in the formulation and administration of rape laws, see Camille E. LeGrand, "Rape and Rape Laws: Sexism in Society and Law," *California Law Review,* 61 (1973), 919–941.

[59]Lynn A. Curtis, "Victim Precipitation and Violent Crime," *Social Problems,* 21 (1974), 594–605. Also see Lynn A. Curtis, *Criminal Violence: National Patterns and Behavior* (Lexington, Mass.: Lexington Books, 1974).

murder and aggravated assault, less frequent but still noteworthy with robbery, and of the least relevance with rape.

Because of the serious nature of these issues, as well as the need for greater sensitivity to rape victims, action with respect to rape has been evidenced at the local level, largely through private groups. Most large cities as well as a number of smaller ones now have rape crisis centers which offer a range of services, educating the public about rape, holding self-defense classes for women, providing transportation and official escorts after dark, serving as a referral agency to coordinate rape services, and giving direct counseling and support to rape victims. These centers, which are usually associated with other centers or agencies that provide a wide range of services from birth control information to family difficulties, have also been quite active in lobbying for legal changes both in the content of the law and in the procedures that govern rape trials.

Societal Reaction to Crimes of Personal Violence

As expressed in the law, societal reaction is extremely severe against murder, manslaughter, and forcible rape. At the same time these forms of interpersonal violence are not punished with the same degree of intensity or severity. One study found that murders which occurred between intimates (husband and wife, close friends, and so on) were punished with a much lower penalty than were homicides occurring between strangers.[60] Sociologically murderers are the least "criminal" of all offenders; persons who commit murder in a personal dispute do not conceive of themselves as criminals. Rarely are they recidivists, their criminal careers consisting of a single offense. Most murderers are not eligible for probation, and therefore they spend much time in prison, the minimum time served not uncommonly being 10 to 15 years. The death penalty has been restored in a large number of states for selected types of murder such as multiple murders, murder associated with kidnapping and robbery, and the killing of a police officer or prison guard. These murders are not typical and constitute only a small proportion of all murders committed.

OCCASIONAL PROPERTY OFFENDERS

Many offenders have criminal records consisting of little more than an occasional or infrequent property offense, such as illegal auto "joy riding," simple (naive) check forgery, misuse of credit cards, shoplifting, employee theft, and vandalism. Such crimes are incidental to the way of life of occasional property offenders, and in no way do such offenders make a living from crime nor do they play a criminal role. This type

---

[60]Lundsgaarde.

of criminal behavior is usually of a fortuitous nature, the offense is often committed alone, and there are seldom prior criminal contacts. With the exception of the act of vandalism, the offender has little group support for the behavior, such as sustained contact with a criminal culture or with a slum area. Occasional crimes need little group support because they are fairly easy to commit in the sense that few skills are needed. The present wide-scale mass display of merchandise in stores, with inadequate supervision, presents limitless opportunities for shoplifting and makes training in sophisticated techniques unnecessary. To "borrow" a car illegally often involves little more than driving it away.

Occasional offenders do not conceive of themselves as criminals. Most of them are able to rationalize their offenses in such a way as to explain it to themselves as a noncriminal act, such as that a large store can afford shoplifting or that there had been no intention to steal the auto, only to borrow it. The offenses show little sophistication in crime techniques: there is little knowledge about crime, and generally there is no need for it because the offenses are simple. There is also no vocabulary of criminal argot. The occasional offender makes no effort to progress to types of crime requiring greater knowledge and skills.[61]

Auto theft in the form of "joy riding" is not a career type of offense. It usually is done only by youth, and the offenses are usually sporadic.[62] The theft of an auto under these conditions is like "borrowing" the car: it is usually driven around for a while and then abandoned. It involves no techniques commonly associated with the conventional career types in which "stripping" is learned, as well as the selection of special kinds of cars, and "fences" are found for the sale of the car or its parts. This occasional auto offender, the "joy rider," does not necessarily progress in techniques and skills, and this type of illegal behavior is usually terminated with adulthood. Obviously, not all auto theft involves "joy riding" or youth. Offenders may steal an automobile not for the short-term transportation of joy riding but for long-term transportation, for use or sale, or in the commission of another crime.[63] Age and degree of sophistication in stealing enter into these types of auto theft.

It has been estimated that at least three fourths of all *check forgeries* are committed by persons who have no previous pattern of such behavior. Analyzing a small samples of cases, Lemert concluded that such persons generally do not come from a delinquency area, have no previous criminal record, and have had no previous contact with delinquents and criminals. Novice check forgers generally come from the higher socioeconomic groups, and they do not conceive of themselves as criminals. Lemert suggests that this offense is a product of certain difficult social situations in which persons find themselves, a certain degree of social isolation, and a process of "closure" or "constriction of behavior alternatives subjectively held as available to the forger."[64] Check usage is declining, increasingly being replaced with *credit cards* for all

---

[61]See William W. Wattenberg and James Balistieri, "Automobile Theft: A 'Favored-Group' Delinquency," *American Journal of Sociology,* 57 (1952), 575–579.

[62]Wattenberg and Balistieri.

[63]Charles H. McCaghy, Peggy C. Giordano, and Trudy Knicely Henson, "Auto Theft: Offender and Offense Characteristics," *Criminology,* 15 (1977), 367–385.

[64]Edwin M. Lemert, "An Isolation Closure Theory of Naive Check Forgery," in Edwin M. Lemert, *Human Deviance, Social Problems, and Social Control,* 2d ed. (Englewood Cliffs, N.J.: Prentice-Hall, 1972), p. 139.

types of purchases and services. These cards are unsupported by sufficient bank funds as checks are required to be, and when they are stolen they are used fraudulently to obtain not only items but also such things as airline tickets, meals in restaurants, and so on.

Shoplifting and employee theft are closely related. While sometimes both large and small expensive items are shoplifted, most theft of this kind involves relatively small and less expensive items. Shoplifting is associated with current methods of large-scale merchandising through supermarkets, discount stores, and merchandise marts. Enormous quantities of goods are displayed with little supervision, although stores are increasingly using such security measures as closed-circuit television and metal detectors attached to garments which will set off alarms if not properly removed by clerks. A government report has explained some of the factors underlying the growth of shoplifting.

> In retail establishments, managers choose to tolerate a high percentage of shoplifting rather than pay for additional clerks. Discount stores, for example, experience an inventory loss rate almost double that of the conventional department store. Studies indicate that there is in general more public tolerance for theft of property and goods from large organizations than from small ones, from big corporations or utilities than from small neighborhood establishments. Restraints on conduct that were effective in a more personal rural society do not seem as effective in an impersonal society of large organizations.[65]

It is impossible to estimate with any degree of accuracy the total amount lost annually by merchants due to these illegal activities. One study estimated that the probable proportions for total shrinkages are due one third to clerical errors, a third from employee and supplier thefts, and the remaining third to customer shoplifting.[66] Even a 2 percent shrinkage represents an enormous financial loss which could be as high as $5 billion a year.[67]

Shoplifters may be found among all groups of persons, including college students who often claim they do it because of the low risk of apprehension.[68] Generally, however, shoplifters appear to be either youth or "respectable" employed persons and even housewives, largely of the middle class.[69] The latter can generally afford the things they steal. Among adult shoplifters, women appear to constitute by far the largest proportion, but when one considers that traditionally women do most of the shopping, this difference may not be particularly great if one bases the rate on the proportion of women and men in a store at a given time. Just how small the risk of apprehension actually is was demonstrated in a study in which researchers, with permission of the management but without the knowledge of the employees, deliber-

---

[65]See *The Challenge of Crime in a Free Society,* President's Commission on Law Enforcement and Administration of Justice (Washington, D.C.: Government Printing Office, 1967).

[66]R.L. Adair, "Shrinkage Control Is Everyone's Job," *Financial Executive,* April 1973, pp. 36–46.

[67]Joseph F. Hair, Jr., Ronald F. Bush, and Paul Bush, "Employee Theft: Views from Two Sides," *Business Horizons,* December 1976, pp. 25–29.

[68]See Robert E. Kraut, "Deterrent and Definitional Influences on Shoplifting," *Social Problems,* 23 (1976), 358–369.

[69]Mary Owen Cameron, *The Booster and the Snitch: Department Store Shoplifting* (New York: Free Press, 1964), p. 110.

ately "lifted" items from department and grocery stores.[70] Less than 10 percent of all shoplifting activities were detected; most customers were unwilling to report even the most flagrant cases they observed.

Shoplifters generally do not conceive of themselves as criminals nor of their activities as "crimes." They do, however, regard themselves as "pilferers," and they rationalize these offenses on the basis that the items taken are generally of modest price and that the large stores can well absorb the losses. Few of these offenders have criminal records. Employee theft is rationalized in a similar manner. For example, in a study of theft of items for their own use by workers in an electronics plant, it was discovered that the workers were highly selective about the property they stole from the plant, based primarily on their conception of who "really" owned the property and their certainty of that ownership.[71] They also avoided labeling their acts as "theft." Pilfering was rationalized in terms of such verbalization as "the company expects it" or "the company doesn't mind."[72]

Vandalism includes many acts of willful destruction of property. It is practically impossible to estimate either the extent or the cost of vandalism in the United States today. Schools are prime targets of vandalism, and one estimate of a Senate committee in 1975 reported costs of around $500 million for school vandalism alone.[73] Windows are broken, and both moveable and stationary equipment of all kinds are destroyed or stolen. Libraries are also vandalized extensively, pages from books ripped out, or entire books ruined. Besides the main target of schools, all types of public property seem to attract youth who deface and destroy park and playground equipment, road signs and markers, as well as trees, shrubs, and fountains intended to beautify an area. Even necessities such as public toilets and telephones are rendered useless, often repeatedly. Autoists constantly report the slashing of tires, broken car windows, and body damages. Golf clubs report that benches, markers, flags, and even expensive putting greens and trees are defaced or broken. Railroads complain about, and demand protection from, destruction of freight car seals, the throwing of objects at passenger car windows, and the tampering with of switches and rails, which, like the removal of road signs, can pose threats to safety. Vacant houses offer particular attractions for vandals, who seem often to delight in creating as much disorder as possible by breaking whatever they can find, emptying the contents of catsup and mustard bottles and all kinds of drinks over furniture and rugs, rendering completely unusable as much equipment as they can find. Damages to theater, train, and bus seats are almost everyday occurrences costing millions of dollars in repair and replacement costs.

Vandalism is generally a worldwide phenomenon, and the vandals' targets are much the same regardless of the country. It has been reported that in the Soviet Union

---

[70]Erhard Blankenburg, "The Selectivity of Legal Sanctions: An Empirical Investigation of Shoplifting," *Law and Society Review,* 11 (1976), 110–130.
[71]Donald N. M. Horning, "Blue-Collar Theft: Conceptions of Property, Attitudes toward Pilfering, and Work Group Norms in a Modern Industrial Plant," in Erwin O. Smigel and H. Laurence Ross, eds., *Crimes against Bureaucracy* (New York: Van Nostrand Reinhold, 1970), pp. 46–64.
[72]See Gerald Robin, "White-Collar Crime and Employee Theft," *Crime and Delinquency,* 20 (1974), 251–262.
[73]Birch Bayh, "Our Nation's Schools: A Report Card—'A' in School Violence and Vandalism" (Washington, D.C.: Government Printing Office, 1975).

common acts of vandalism are "breaking street lamps and windows, throwing stones at passing trains, putting public telephones out of order, and desecrating tombstones. Smashed-up monuments are a common sight in Russian cemeteries."[74] In West Germany and in Sweden damage and destruction of road signs, street lights, bus and streetcar seats, and telephone booths are common.

Vandalism has been classified in terms of meanings, motives, and patterns into acquisitive, tactical, vindictive, play, and malicious.[75] Acts of vandalism are committed largely by youth without a criminal orientation toward themselves or what they do: their acts are regarded primarily as "pranks" or "raising hell."[76] The fact that often nothing is stolen during acts of vandalism tends to reinforce the vandals' conception of themselves as merely "hell raisers," not delinquents. Property destruction appears to provide fun and excitement for adolescents and to serve as a protest against ill-defined roles and ambiguous status in the social structure. One study of self-reported vandalism found that the major motivation was anger toward parents and school officials.[77]

Groups commit acts of vandalism, but the acts do not derive from any subculture. In fact, acts of vandalism seldom utilize or even require prior sophisticated knowledge. They grow out of *collective interaction;* few are deliberately planned in advance.[78] It is spontaneous behavior, the outgrowth of social situations in which group interaction takes place. Each interactive response by a participant builds upon the actions of another participant, and the group act of vandalism results.[79] Participation in the acts gives status and group interaction to each person, and through direct involvement the individual avoids becoming a marginal member of the group.

Societal Reaction to Occasional Offenders

In most cases societal reaction toward occasional offenders is not severe unless the theft or damage done in the acts is particularly large. Occasional offenders seldom have prior records. Generally they are dismissed or acquitted by the courts or placed on probation. It has been found that the formal arrest of shoplifters, naive check forgers, and vandals helps to redefine the act in their eyes as a "crime." Adult pilferers or shoplifters do not, for example, think of themselves, prior to their arrest, as thieves and can conceive of no group support for themselves in that role, but their arrest forces them to reject the role and to conceive of themselves as law violators.[80]

---

[74]Valery Chalidze, *Criminal Russia: Essays on Crime in the Soviet Union* (New York: Random House, 1977), pp. 82–83.

[75]Colin Ward, ed., *Vandalism* (London: The Architectural Press, 1973).

[76]Andrew L. Wade, "Social Processes in the Act of Juvenile Vandalism," in Marshall B. Clinard and Richard Quinney, *Criminal Behavior Systems: A Typology* (New York: Holt, Rinehart and Winston, 1967), pp. 94–109. Also see Don C. Gibbons, *Changing the Lawbreaker* (Englewood Cliffs, N.J.: Prentice-Hall, 1965), pp. 74–94; John M. Martin, *Juvenile Vandalism* (Springfield, Ill.: Charles C. Thomas, 1961); and William Bates and Thomas McJunkins, "Vandalism and Status Differences," *Pacific Sociological Review,* 5 (1962), 89–92.

[77]Pam Richards, "Patterns of Middle-Class Vandalism: A Case Study of Suburban Adolescence," unpublished doctoral dissertation, Northwestern University, Evanston, Illinois, 1976.

[78]Wade, pp. 94–109.

[79]Wade, pp. 99–108.

[80]Cameron, p. 165.

POLITICAL CRIMINAL OFFENDERS

Political crime exists wherever the state invokes its laws to punish those who present a threat to the government and where, for alleged reasons of state, governments themselves violate the law. All societies, regardless of the political and economic system, designate certain acts as crimes against the state. No government is ambivalent about its existence; all enact legislation against acts that are considered by the group in power as endangering the state or not to the advantage of the state. Democratic states attempt to protect themselves from those who would overthrow democracy; communist states and military dictatorships try to protect themselves from those who would overthrow their political systems.

Crimes against the government involve attempts to protest, to express beliefs about or alter in some way the existing social structure. Included in political crime is a wide range of acts—treason, sedition, sabotage, assassination, hijacking, violation of military draft laws, civil rights violations, violations resulting from the advocacy and support of "radical" ideas (either left or right) and actions, and failure to conform to certain laws because of religious beliefs. *Crimes by government* and its agents include violations of citizens' rights and their civil liberties, such as the violations of constitutional guarantees and civil rights legislation by various government officials; criminal acts committed in the course of enforcing the laws of the state, as exemplified by assault and murder of citizens by the police and among prison officials; and violations condoned by governments such as conspiracy to obstruct justice, perjury, acceptance or solicitation of bribes, and other forms of political corruption.

Against Government

Political crimes against government are distinguished from other criminal behavior in that they are directed largely at improving the world or the existing political system. Offenders who commit crimes as a protest against the existing political or economic order are considered political criminals.[81] Such individuals frequently express in their self-conceptions the morality and the rationality of their political beliefs. To understand the political offender one must have a conception of a person quite different from the ordinary stereotype of the "criminal."[82] This offender cannot be viewed as a product of impersonal forces such as the slum. Political offenders are different from conventional offenders, for example, because they are seeking to challenge the existing system. Thus political offenders represent a paradox, since they carry on their illegal activities in the pursuit of their particular ideals. They do not scheme to extract large sums of money from unsuspecting victims, and basically they are not motivated to kill persons, although they claim that such crimes may be unavoidable in pursuit of their ideals.[83] For the most part, they are idealists who are devoted to a cause, even though the cause is controversial, which they consider more important than patriotism or even

---

[81]W. William Minor, "Political Crime, Political Justice and Political Prisoners," *Criminology*, 12 (1975), 385–398.
[82]See Clinard and Quinney, rev. ed., 1973, pp. 163–164.
[83]Mabel A. Elliott, *Crime in Modern Society* (New York: Harper & Row, 1952), p. 180.

personal safety. During the Vietnam war of the 1960s most were opposed to the war generally and to the draft, and they often participated in violent demonstrations in which they were beaten and injured. One imprisoned conscientious resister vividly expressed his moral convictions:

> I believe in brotherhood and loving people. I suppose that on an individual basis it's a natural thing for a man to protect himself as a matter of self-defense, but it becomes a different thing, even for self-defense when it's institutionalized. I think that military institutions have disunited and separated men, and that is contrary to a basic belief of mine. I don't think any war is ever justified. While I do believe that I'm against war in general, this one particularly just doesn't have anything to do with anything I believe in. I think all war is an expression of the sickness of mankind, part of that sickness which he should try to overcome. I just don't look at it as being a natural thing—like some people do. I just don't understand people who can think of war as a part of the way of life. I feel this is not me, and I can't participate in something like a war which seems crazy merely because some agency says I should. Basically, I'm just not a violent person.[84]

Characteristics like age, sex, ethnicity, and social class do not differentiate political offenders as a whole from the general population. Despite this, they do share some characteristics. Usually they do not conceive of themselves as criminals, and they do not identify with the conventional idea that what they do is a "crime." When the government defines them as political outlaws, saboteurs, and so on, however, they may perceive of themselves as criminals against the state, as political revolutionaries. Their goals are usually ideological rather than personal, the violation of the law being only incidental to other objectives. The political offender is committed to some form of political and social order, although it is usually not the existing one. Schafer has termed the political offender a "convictional" criminal "because he is convinced of the truth and justification of his own beliefs, and this conviction in him is strong enough to cause him to give up egoistic aspirations as well as peaceful efforts to attain his altruistic goals, thus leading him to illegitimate ways to bring about something he believes is good for the social group. He is not like the prosaic violators of law; he has a passion for the impossible that he believes is possible."[85] There are also "pseudoconvictional" criminals who use the cover of political crime to achieve criminal or other objectives, as in the case of some robberies, kidnappings, and hijackings.

Generally, political criminal behavior is of a group nature in that these persons identify and associate with others who share similar values. They receive support from particular politically organized groups and often from other segments of society who are not as committed to overt social action. In the more militant groups support may range from advice to technical knowledge about committing various illegal acts. These groups serve the same functions that countercultures do for other deviants: they lessen the stigma from the outside society by offering group solidarity and the means to interact with persons of similar ideas, and they facilitate other contacts in a social network committed to the common cause of committing acts against government.

---

[84]Willard Gaylin, *In the Service of Their Country: War Resisters in Prison* (New York: Grosset & Dunlap, 1970), p. 278.
[85]Stephen Schafer, *Introduction to Criminology* (Reston, Va.: Reston Publishing Co., 1976), p. 138. Also see Stephen Schafer, *The Political Criminal: The Problem of Morality and Crime* (New York: Free Press, 1974).

By Government

Violations of the law by governments have been extensive in many countries over a long period of time. Through the eighteenth century it was a common practice in Great Britain and France, for example, to sell public office to the highest bidder. In fact, Montesquieu felt that in this way one could secure better appointees than by means of appointment by the throne. President Lincoln suspended such civil rights as *habeas corpus* on a large scale; and civil rights were violated on a grand scale by the actions in the 1920s against alien radicals by a U.S. Attorney General, and in the 1960s by the U.S. government against Vietnam war protesters. Under the Harding administration in the 1920s, the Veterans Administration, the Department of the Navy, and the Department of the Interior were involved in major corruption; the Secretary of the Navy resigned, and the Secretary of the Interior was imprisoned. Corruption during the presidencies of Eisenhower and Johnson affected their closest advisers, both of whom were forced to resign. The culmination of this type of crime occurred in the 1970s in the vast violations of the law by President Nixon and his associates, which resulted in the imprisonment of 25 high ranking officials, including the attorney general and two top presidential aides.[86] The President himself was spared from the strong possibility of punitive action only by a presidential pardon. The violations of law by these men included obstruction of justice, conspiracy to obstruct justice, perjury, burglarizing the offices of citizens, the sale of ambassadorships, accepting illegal contributions or bribes from corporations, bribing persons to prevent testimony, illegal tactics or "dirty tricks" in conducting campaigns, the destruction of evidence, and misuse, for their own purposes, of the FBI, the CIA, and the Internal Revenue Service. Another member of the Nixon Administration, Vice President Agnew, who had been the governor of Maryland, was forced to resign in 1973 after pleading no contest to a variety of bribery and corruption charges. In the United States violations of law have been extensive by governors, senators, congressmen, judges, prosecutors, and police officials. Police officers may be involved in misconduct and brutality, as well as corruption, illegal use of force, harassment, illegal entry, and seizures. In other countries wholesale illegal arrests, beatings, torture, and even murder have been carried out by governments against groups and individuals who oppose them. In the 1970s there has been extensive use of imprisonment, torture, and murder by governments of some countries, such as Uganda, South Africa, Chile, and Argentina.

A classification of crimes committed by government in the United States has been made by Lieberman:

1. *Crimes against the Individual*
   a. Dismissal from jobs or prosecution, to coerce or force the individual to desist from lawful activity or in retaliation for revealing government corruption;
   b. Prosecution of individuals under laws not enforced against other violators;
   c. Manufacturing or suppressing evidence to secure convictions;

---

[86]See, for example, Leon Jaworski, *The Right and the Power: The Prosecution of Watergate* (New York: Pocket Books, 1977). Also see Jack D. Douglas, "Watergate: Harbinger of the American Prince," *Theory and Society,* 1 (1974), 89–97; and Arthur J. Vidich, "Political Legitimacy in Bureaucratic Society: An Analysis of Watergate," *Social Research,* 42 (1975), 778–811.

      d. Devotion of resources and time to investigate and prosecute individuals for "crime" that is not the real object of social disapproval;

      e. Denial of procedures guaranteed under law;

      f. Unlawful sentencing or other unlawful deprivation of liberty.[87]

2. *Crimes Affecting Groups,* such as radicals, war resisters, suspects, minority group members, prisoners, the poor, aliens.

3. *Crimes Affecting Everyone,* such as illegal expenditures of public funds, illegal campaign practices.

Societal Reaction to Political Offenders

The degree of societal reaction to political offenses against government depends in part on the extent to which policies and actions of government are accepted. Public officials usually do not recognize the moral character of the political offender; rather, they react severely toward him because he threatens the existing political structure and his loyalty to the state is in question. Official reaction is, therefore, often severe. Radicals are often harassed, deported, jailed, and even killed. If convicted of an offense, their sentences may be long, and in some cases they may receive death sentences.

Offenses committed by government are seldom reacted to strongly unless the situation becomes particularly flagrant, as in the Watergate scandal, or where there is a change in government and government officials and politicians of the previous regime are investigated and punished. Individual acts of politicians and government officials are more frequently punished, but not with the severity accorded conventional criminal offenders.

OCCUPATIONAL OFFENDERS

Some persons commit crimes in connection with their occupations. This includes employees who commit crimes against their employers.[88] These offenses occur in all legitimate occupations, such as repair services of all types (automobile, television, and other appliances), small and large businesses, political offices, government, the medical, legal and pharmaceutical professions, and many others. There are few occupations, in fact, in which there are not some law violations. The offenses of murder and robbery, which could be committed by persons of any occupation, are not included, nor are illegitimate occupations such as prostitution or professional or organized crime.

---

[87]Jethro K. Lieberman, *How the Government Breaks the Law* (Baltimore, Md.: Penguin Books, 1972), pp. 28–29. Lieberman also includes the private crimes of government officials, offenses included here under occupational crime. Also see Jack D. Douglas and John M. Johnson, eds., *Official Deviance: Readings in Malfeasance, Misfeasance, and Other Forms of Corruption* (Philadelphia: Lippincott, 1977).

[88]Clinard and Quinney, pp. 187–204. Also see Richard Quinney, "The Study of White Collar Crime: Toward a Reorientation in Theory and Research," in Gilbert Geis and Robert F. Meier, eds., *White-Collar Crime: Offenses in Business, Politics and the Professions* (New York: Free Press, 1977), pp. 283–295.

For those occupations of particularly high social and economic status, the term *white-collar crime* is used as a subdivision of occupational crime.[89]

Crime is extensive among persons in *business,* and it includes income tax violations, illegal financial manipulations such as embezzlement and various types of frauds, misrepresentation in advertising, expense account misuse, and bribery of public officials. In the investment business, fraudulent securities are sold, asset statements are misrepresented, and customer assets may be used illegally by brokers.[90] A New York City commission named to investigate allegations of graft and corruption in the Police Department uncovered information about illegal practices in the construction industry.[91] The commission found that bribes paid to the police by contractors and subcontractors were the rule rather than the exception, constituting a major source of graft. These payments were not confined to uniformed police officers, and larger payoffs were given to building inspectors and permit-granting personnel. These payoffs are not hard to understand: To erect a building in New York City a builder must obtain a minimum of 40 to 50 different permits and licenses from various city departments. The total permits needed may increase to 120 or more for very large projects. Contractors do not bother to obtain all of the permits, only the major ones, and they do so by making payments to appropriate city officials.

A quite recent and incredibly involved type of criminal behavior has developed in the occupational area of computer technology, and usually it involves offenses connected with business.[92] The total losses resulting from computer crimes are high, generally greater than those for other types of white-collar crimes. These losses usually include thefts of large sums of money illegally siphoned off in various ways by persons technically trained in the use of computer programming. As computers increasingly play a dominant role in almost every aspect of the lives of individuals and in all types of businesses, large numbers of persons, perhaps as many as two million, are directly involved in programming and operating the many steps related to the collection, storage, and use of tremendous amounts of computer data. The very skill that persons who are trained in complex computer technology have enables them to commit crimes that bring them great financial rewards and that are almost impossible to detect. It has been estimated, in fact, that approximately 90 percent of these crimes go undetected, largely because a person who programs a crime can at the same time program the elimination of it, leaving no "audit trail" in the process. Most persons who commit crimes of this nature do so for the very reasons that others, particularly embezzlers, in positions of financial trust commit them—having a nonsharable problem and the "know-how."

---

[89]Edwin H. Sutherland, "White Collar Criminality," *American Sociological Review,* 5 (1940), 1–12. Also see Edwin H. Sutherland, *White Collar Crime* (New York: Dryden Press, 1949).
[90]Hurd Baruch, *Wall Street: Security Risk* (Washington, D.C.: Acropolis Books, 1971). Also see Michael Gartner, ed., *Crime and Business* (Princeton, N.J.: Dow Books, 1971).
[91]The Knapp Commission, "Official Corruption and the Construction Industry," in Douglas and Johnson, pp. 225–232.
[92]For good analyses of computer crimes and abuses, see Donn B. Parker, *Crime by Computer* (New York: Scribner, Sons, 1976); and Thomas Whiteside, "Annals of Crime (Computers—1)," *The New Yorker,* August 22, 1977; and Thomas Whiteside, "Annals of Crime (Computers—2)," *The New Yorker,* August 29, 1977. Also see August Bequai, *Computer Crime* (Lexington, MA: Lexington Books, 1978)

In addition to fraudulent activities in the computer industry, *repairmen* who service automobiles, television sets, radios, and other appliances make many unnecessary repairs.[93] One study has shown how auto dealers often sell new cars for small profits with the expectation that they will be able to recoup by higher margins on used cars and by overcharging for repairs.[94] Auto mechanics may also fail to replace parts, yet charge the customer for them, or simply paint old parts to make them appear new. They also may calculate time spent according to a false prearranged "time-repair formula" rather than the actual time worked.

Politicians and government employees commit offenses for personal gain, including personal misappropriation of public funds or the illegal acquisition of these funds through padded payrolls, through the illegal placement of relatives on government payrolls, or through monetary "kickbacks" from appointees.[95] Their illegal activities are usually more subtle. Politicians and government employees may gain financially by furnishing some favor to business firms. Favors for which politicians may be rewarded by certain persons in business include illegal commissions on public contracts, issuance of illegal licenses or certificates of building or fire inspections, and tax exemptions or lower tax valuations. Criminal syndicates may share the proceeds of gambling or other profits with public officials who give protection from arrest. Political corruption exists not only at the local and state levels, but reaches into Congress and even the Executive Office of the President itself, where bribery, perjury, and influence peddling are by no means uncommon. In the period 1968–1972 alone, five congressmen or their aides went to prison for such offenses.[96]

Labor union officials may engage in such criminal activities as misappropriation or misapplication of union funds, defiance of the government by failure to enforce laws affecting their labor unions, collusion with employers to the disadvantage of their own union members, and the use of fraudulent means to maintain control over unions.

Certain activities in the *medical profession* are not only unethical but illegal. They include giving illegal prescriptions for narcotics, performing illegal abortions, making fraudulent reports such as in Medicare payments and giving false testimony in accident cases, and fee splitting. Fee splitting, in which a doctor splits the fee charged with the referring physician, is against the law in many states because of the danger that such referrals will be based on the size of the fee rather than on the proficiency of the practitioner. This practice actually involves the very life of the patient if the physician refers him to an inferior surgeon for the prime purpose of obtaining a portion of the surgical fee. No less crucial are cases of *pharmacists* who violate federal and state regulations pertaining to the content of prescriptions and the control of narcotics.

---

[93]For a study of victim-responsiveness and fraud in relation to one specific case of an appliance repairman, see Diane Vaughan and Giovanna Carlo, "The Appliance Repairman: A Study of Victim-Responsiveness and Fraud, *Journal of Research in Crime and Delinquency,* 12 (1975), 153–161.

[94]William N. Leonard and Marvin G. Weber, "Automakers and Dealers: A Study of Criminogenic Market Forces," in Geis and Meier, pp. 133–148.

[95]See Douglas and Johnson.

[96]Mark J. Green, James M. Fallows, David R. Zwick, *Who Runs Congress?* (New York: Grossman, 1972), p. 144. Also see Herbert E. Alexander, ed., *Campaign Money: Reform and Reality in the States* (New York: Free Press, 1977).

In one study it was concluded that deviance is tolerated and even condoned by the "norm group" because of the nature and the press of modern pharmaceutical practices.[97]

Lawyers engage in such illegalities as misappropriating funds in receivership, securing perjured testimony from witnesses, and various forms of "ambulance chasing," usually to collect fraudulent damage claims arising from accidents. In ambulance chasing, a lawyer seeks out persons who have been injured, trying to have them sign a contingent-fee contract entitling the lawyer to a fixed percentage of any settlement or award paid to the client.[98] When such cases are discovered, the offender is more apt to be disbarred than prosecuted criminally.

Self-Conception of Occupational Offenders

Any consideration of conventional or ordinary crimes gives an erroneous impression of the extent and effects of crime on society as well as of the nature of "criminals."[99] The major difference between occupational crime and many other forms lies in the offender's conception of himself. Since the offenses take place in connection with a legitimate occupation and the offender generally regards himself as a respectable citizen, he does not see himself as a criminal. He may play a variety of other roles, such as that of a respected citizen; hence the degree of recognition of the conflict between this role and that of being a "criminal offender" is great. Because he is likely to regard himself as a respectable citizen, at most he thinks of himself as a lawbreaker and not as a criminal. In this sense he has the attitude of some offenders convicted of such crimes as statutory rape, nonsupport, or drunken driving. The higher social status attached to the legitimate occupation of such an offender makes it difficult for the general public, while not condoning their activities, to conceive of them as being associated with real criminal behavior, which is largely stereotyped as the more overt offenses. This attitude, in turn, is reflected in the conception that white-collar offenders have of themselves as noncriminals.

The maintenance of a "noncriminal" self-concept is an essential element in occupational crime. In cases of embezzlement, for example, Cressey found the offenders to be trusted persons who stole funds under three conditions:[100] (1) a nonsharable financial problem, a problem about which the person will tell no one; (2) knowledge of how to violate the law and the violator's awareness that the financial problem could be secretly resolved by violating a position of trust; and (3) suitable rationalizations for the embezzlement of money to resolve the individual's self-conception as a trusted person. Potential trust violators define the situation through rationalizations in terms that enable them to look upon the criminality as essentially

[97]Albert I. Wertheimer and Henri R. Manasse, Jr., "Pharmacist Practice Deviance," *Social Science and Medicine,* 10 (1976), 232. Also see Richard Quinney, "Occupational Structure and Criminal Behavior: Prescription Violations by Retail Pharmacists," in Geis and Meier, pp. 189–196.
[98]Jerome E. Carlin, *Lawyer's Ethics: A Survey of the New York City Bar* (New York: Russell Sage, 1966).
[99]See Marshall B. Clinard, "White Collar Crime," *International Encyclopedia of the Social Sciences* (New York: Crowell-Collier and Macmillan, 1968).
[100]Donald R. Cressey, *Other People's Money* (Belmont, Calif.: Wadsworth, 1971), p. 30.

noncriminal in nature; for example, they justify their stealing as merely "borrowing," as part of the "general irresponsibility" for which they are not completely accountable, or as due to unusual circumstances that are different in their case.[101]

Occupational offenders are able to rationalize their lawbreaking behavior as "noncriminal," "necessary," "others are doing it," and "it is the only way to carry on one's occupation." In many cases the justification is in terms of attitudes toward the law itself. If the law is considered "unfair" for good business and profits, then one can reconcile the self-image. Such views are as much a rationale for violating as a rationalization subsequent to the violation. Moreover, the occupational offender's life organization is not built around a criminal role: the person plays a variety of roles, the most prominent often being that of a "respectable citizen."

Differential Association

Persons may learn to violate the law with impunity in any occupation. A beginner learns techniques for violating the law, along with the rationalizations to justify them. The diffusion of the varied illegal practices are transmitted to new persons entering the occupation from those already in it and from one business establishment, political machine, or other occupational group to another. Violations are increasingly seen as "normal" in the business situation. As in other forms of deviance, occupational offenders are part of a larger social group from which they derive social and other support and even encouragement. In some occupations it is the nonviolator who is considered by the group as deviant, not the occupational offender. What distinguishes occupational offenders and their subculture from other deviants and their subcultures is the amount of power and social standing held by the occupational offenders by virtue of their other social roles.[102] Moreover, with other occupational offenders the subculture has a more generalized function. In addition to those functions, the subcultures generally perform as in other forms of deviance. The occupational group's subculture provides support for legal activities as well as the illegal ones; it does so because the subculture blurs the distinction between legal and illegal practices.

Some occupational offenses are related to the occupational structure. In the medical profession, for example, physicians quite commonly refer patients to one another, and this general pattern is conducive to illegal fee splitting. In the case of pharmacists, one study of retail pharmacists suggested that occupational violations often arise from the two divergent occupational role expectations in the profession, the professional training role of strict ethical conduct and the business or profit role.[103]

---

[101]Some suggestions for the prevention of embezzlement based on this research are given in Cressey, *Other People's Money,* pp. 153–156.

[102]Vilhelm Aubert, "White-Collar Crime and Social Structure," in Geis and Meier, p. 172.

[103]See Quinney, "Occupational Structure and Criminal Behavior." The finding of the effects of role divergencies was not verified in another study of pharmacy violations, and this was thought to be largely due to the fact that both the violators and the nonviolators questioned about their views of advertising, the professional training of pharmacists, and the provision of professional services were closely matched on such relevant variables as pharmacy being a business, a profession, or a combination of both. In other words, violations were found equally in the professional and the business groups. See Wertheimer and Manasse.

A number of factors tend to isolate persons in business from unfavorable definitions of illegal activity.[104] First, the mass media decry conventional crime, while often treating white-collar crime, unless it is sensational, much more leniently. Second, persons in business are often shielded from severe criticism by government officials, many of whom either were formerly in business, have accepted contributions from business sources, or associate socially with business people in clubs and other organizations. Finally, business people associate chiefly with each other, both professionally and socially, so that the implications of white-collar crime are not objectively scrutinized.

Although many cases of occupational crime can be satisfactorily explained by a theory of differential association, such a general theory as an explanation for *all* cases has several limitations. This is particularly true if there had been continuous and intimate association with unethical and illegal differential norms and at the same time some isolation from other norms. Some individuals do *not* engage in these practices, even though they are familiar with the techniques and the rationalizations of violations, and frequently associate with persons who are similarly familiar with these practices. It is doubtful if any individual could be in a given line of business for any length of time without acquiring a rather complete knowledge of the illegalities associated with it. In part, persons tend to accept or to reject opportunities for white-collar crime according to their orientations toward their roles and their attitudes toward general social values. Some of these factors are the relative importance attached to status symbols of money as compared with law obedience and the relative importance attached to personal, family, or business reputations.[105]

Societal Reaction

Seldom are occupational offenders apprehended, partly because of limited government agency enforcement staffs. Where they are, legal actions such as the use of administrative sanctions of license withdrawal or criminal penalties such as fines are not often used. Either nothing is done or social control is left to the professional organization, as in the case of the bar associations or medical societies. These organizations, however, seldom use internal sanctions themselves. Even when legal actions are taken against various occupational offenders, there is no assurance that violators will be stigmatized, particularly if they are white-collar offenders. One study reported that malpractice suits against physicians actually had the effect of *increasing* their business in spite of the bad publicity and any official sanctions from the medical boards. It seemed that other physicians felt sorry for them and increased referrals to them because they thought they would not otherwise get patients.[106] A study of pharmacy deviance found that the illegal behavior of the violator pharmacists resulted

---

[104]Sutherland, *White Collar Crime,* pp. 247–253. Also see Gilbert Geis, "Avocational Crime," in Glaser, pp. 273–277.

[105]Marshall B. Clinard, *The Black Market* (New York: Holt, Rinehart and Winston, 1952). Also see Robert A. Lane, "Why Businessmen Violate the Law," *Journal of Criminal Law, Criminology and Police Science,* 44 (1953), 161–163.

[106]Richard D. Schwartz and Jerome H. Skolnick, "Two Studies of Legal Stigma," in Howard S. Becker, ed., *The Other Side: Perspectives on Deviance* (New York: Free Press, 1964), p. 111.

in no known rejection of those pharmacists by others among the group studied. The conclusion was, in fact, that it would be "presumptuous" to classify these persons as outsiders based on the study's findings.[107]

CORPORATE CRIMINAL BEHAVIOR

Large corporations are huge conglomerates with assets and sales often totaling in the billions of dollars and with enormous economic and political power. The total sales of many of them exceed the gross national product of most nations.[108] Some control broad aspects of the U.S. economy; for example, 95 percent of all prepared soups are controlled by Campbell Soup Company, and 85 percent of all breakfast foods are produced by four food-manufacturing corporations. With the growth of these large corporations in the United States during the past 50 years or so, laws have been passed to regulate various illegal acts committed by them, such as restraint of trade (price fixing and monopoly control); fraudulent sales; illegal financial manipulation; misrepresentation in advertising; issuance of fraudulent securities; income tax violations; misuse of patents, trademarks, and copyrights; manufacture of unsafe foods and drugs; illegal rebates; unfair labor practices; and environmental pollution.[109] The enforcement of regulations designed to control these practices rests largely with administrative agencies like the Federal Trade Commission, the Food and Drug Administration, the Securities and Exchange Commission, the Environmental Protection Agency, the Consumer Products Safety Commission, and some of the more specific law-enforcement agencies like the Anti-Trust Division of the Department of Justice. Although only corporation officers can be sent to prison, corporate liability is increasingly common under criminal law, and corporations are being punished by heavy fines under this law. Generally, however, corporate violations are dealt with by more administrative and civil enforcement actions, such as consent orders and agreements not to repeat the violation, seizure or recall of the commodity, and court injunctions to refrain from further violations.

With their extensive control over the economy, large corporations can market foods that are grossly overpriced and that often are not essential to good nutrition, emphasizing seldom-needed vitamins or taste instead of basic protein content.[110] Even basically nutritious foods such as prepared meats and peanut butter are often so processed and filled with fats and adulterants that their total nutritional values are reduced.[111] Of all food products, the most highly advertised, and often the most

---

[107]Wertheimer and Manasse, p. 232.

[108]See Ralph Nader and Mark J. Green, eds., *Corporate Power in America* (New York: Grossman, 1973).

[109]See, for example, Sutherland, *White Collar Crime;* Geis and Meier; Robert L. Heilbroner, *In the Name of Profit* (New York: Doubleday, 1972); and John E. Conklin, *"Illegal But Not Criminal": Business Crime in America* (Englewood Cliffs, N.J.: Prentice-Hall, 1977). Also see Mark J. Green, ed., *The Monopoly Makers* (New York: Grossman, 1973).

[110]See Beatrice Trum Hunter, *Consumer Beware* (New York: Simon & Schuster, 1971). Also see James S. Turner, *The Chemical Feast* (New York: Grossman, 1970); and Warren Magnuson and Jean Carper, *The Dark Side of the Market Place* (Englewood Cliffs, N.J.: Prentice-Hall, 1972).

[111]Hunter, pp. 301–306.

overpriced, are breakfast cereals, which are often not really nutritious but are attractively packaged in a manner often designed to be deceptive as to weight. A survey conducted in 1963 by the National Bureau of Standards found more than 80 percent of all prepackaged foods to be under the specified weight.[112] It is almost impossible for the conscientious consumer to penetrate the facade of modern packaging, some of which must be turned over and over and practically examined with a magnifying glass to find in the small print the net weight.[113] Even then the amounts are often in unfamiliar weights and measurements confusing to consumers, even with the introduction of "unit" pricing.

Fake and deceptive corporate advertising, which approaches real fraud, is common in newspapers, magazines, billboards, and television and has been subjected to much investigation.[114] This includes "puffing," obvious falsities, social-psychological misrepresentations, literally misdescriptive names of products, and false mock-ups.[115] Among the many "puffery" examples current today in advertising are:[116]

> Blatz is Milwaukee's finest beer
> King of beers (Budweiser)
> We try harder (Avis)
> Ford gives you better ideas
> GM—always a step ahead
> Come to where the flavor is (Marlboro)
> Breakfast of Champions (Wheaties)
> You expect more from Standard, and you get it
> You can be sure if it's Westinghouse

It is extremely difficult to distinguish "puffing" from illegal deception. An example of countless misleading mockups in television advertising is the display of a specific window cleaner being used on two windows. In the "after" picture far better results for the advertised cleaner are obtained simply by having no glass in the window frame. A case in the 1970s involving a full-page national advertisement for the Campbell Soup Company showed the great lengths to which "puffing" goes.

> Campbell's problem was that showing the solid ingredients is vital, but when the soup stands still the solids settle to the bottom of the bowl and the resulting photograph shows nothing but the broth. The solution adopted was to place marbles in the bottom of the bowl before pouring in the soup. This would cause the solid ingredients to poke above the surface where they would appear attractively in the photograph. So far so good—it was a legitimate mock-up because it would show the product only as it really was. What happened, however, was that the mock-up got out of hand. The executive in charge of marbles put so many of them into the bowl that the photographed soup displayed a far greater proportion of solid ingredients than Campbell's vegetable soup actually has. The

[112]"Quote without Comment," *Consumer Reports,* May 1963, p. 206.
[113]Hunter, p. 23.
[114]See Kearl W. Kintner, *A Primer on the Law of Deceptive Practices* (New York: Macmillan, 1971).
[115]See Ivan L. Preston, *The Great American Blow-Up: Puffery in Advertising and Selling* (Madison: University of Wisconsin Press, 1975).
[116]Preston, derived from pp. 18–19.

result was a 1970 FTC-imposed agreement in which the company consented to avoid such practices in the future.[117]

Subject to particularly scathing criticism have been the manufacturers of unsafe automobiles and tires, which contribute to the 55,000 annual deaths on highways and the over 4.5 million injuries.[118] In addition, consumers have often suffered financial losses and experienced great frustrations by automobiles advertised and sold primarily for enormous corporate profits but with many defects. In the pharmaceutical industry corporations have been subjected to attack for marketing drugs and other chemical products that are often worthless, overadvertised, overpriced, and even dangerous to health.[119] The Food and Drug Administration has charged that many manufacturers of prescription drugs violate federal laws prohibiting false and misleading advertising. It has also been stated that about a fourth of the total spent to manufacture drugs goes for advertising and promotional purposes. Among the violations noted in this industry are the submission of false research claims about the safety or usefulness of the drug, claims for usefulness beyond that approved in the final printed label of the product, and advertisements that make either obsolete or false claims.[120]

The extensive nature of law violations by corporations has been widely revealed by many governmental investigative committees, both state and federal. These investigations have covered banking operations, the oil industry, stock exchanges, public utilities, foodstuffs, drugs, real estate, insurance, railways, and munitions. A significant case of corporate crime involved a complicated and far-reaching conspiracy in price fixing and price rigging, both violations of the federal antitrust laws, by many leading electrical equipment concerns in the United States. Twenty-nine companies, including General Electric and Westinghouse, and 45 executives of the companies involved, were convicted in the 1960s of illegalities in the sale of heavy electrical equipment that totaled $1,750,000,000 a year.[121] Because of these violations both government and private purchasers had been deceived about the open competitive nature of bids, paying sums far in excess of a regular bid and thus in the end costing the taxpayers in the case of purchases made by government agencies. Consequently, the convictions were later followed by civil suits totaling millions of dollars filed by federal, state, and local agencies in an attempt to recover damages from the companies involved. Since then other cases of large-scale price fixing have been prosecuted successfully by the government, although this represents only a small portion of the price-fixing activity believed to take place.[122] In 1967, for example, major pharmaceutical manufacturers such as American Cyanamid, Charles Pfizer, and Bristol-Myers were found guilty of

---

[117]Preston, pp. 241–242.
[118]Ralph Nader, Lowell Dodge, and Ralf Hotchkiss, *What To Do with Your Bad Car: An Action Manual for Lemon Owners* (New York: Grossman, 1971).
[119]Heilbroner, pp. 106–127; and Turner. Also see Milton Silverman and Philip R. Lee, *Pills, Profits and Politics* (Berkeley: University of California Press, 1974).
[120]See Turner. Also see Silverman and Lee.
[121]See John Herling, *The Great Price Conspiracy: The Story of the Anti-Trust Violations in the Electrical Industry* (Washington, D.C.: Robert B. Luce, Inc. 1962).
[122]Stuart L. Hills, *Crime, Power, and Morality* (Scranton, Pa.: Chandler Publishing Company, 1971), pp. 166–167.

participation in a long-term price-fixing scheme and of trying to monopolize a $100-million market that involved the sale of antibiotic "wonder drugs."[123] In 1969 three major plumbing manufacturers (Borg-Warner, American Standard, and Kohler), who were among 15 corporations with total annual sales of over $1 billion—comprising about 98 percent of total enameled cast-iron plumbing sold in this country—were convicted by a federal court jury of raising and fixing plumbing-fixture prices over a four-year period. Convicted of similar charges were high-ranking officials in each of the three corporations.

More sophisticated violations are occurring in corporations through the use of computers (see p. 214), as in the Equity Funding case, the largest-known single-company fraud.[124] This crime, which was discovered in 1973, involved an estimated $2 billion in losses, and the victims were the company's insurance customers. It involved illegal activities in securities and insurance frauds, which made the Equity Funding Corporation of America appear to be one of the most successful, largest, and fastest-growing financial institutions in the world. The scheme was carried out by company management itself, principally by inflating reported company earnings, primarily by use of the computer and false bookkeeping. One fraudulent operation, for example, involved 64,000 fictitious insurance policies out of 97,000 claimed to have been issued. This operation was for the purpose of securing funds to cover fraudulent activities elsewhere, and its creation and concealment were possible only with the use of the computer. A computer specialist, at company direction, programmed the computer to create fictitious insurance policies with a value of $430 million and a total yearly premium of $5.5 million.

Nature of Violations

In his study of the illegal behavior of large corporations Sutherland found many types of violations of law to be industry-wide in that practically all firms in the industry violate the law.[125] He concluded that (1) the criminality of corporations is persistent; (2) there is generally little loss, if any, of status by an offender among business associates;[126] (3) in those areas immediately affecting white-collar offenders contempt for the government as a whole is quite general, as well as contempt for the law and those who administer it; and (4) most corporate crimes are organized in the sense that the violation is a corporation affair or may extend to several corporations or subsidiaries.

---

[123]Hills.

[124]For details of this well-known case, see Whiteside; Parker, Chapter 13, "Equity Funding—A Computer Fraud?"; and Conklin, pp. 46–47. Also see William E. Blundell, "Equity Funding: "I Did It for the Jollies," in John M. Johnson and Jack D. Douglas, *Crime At The Top: Deviance in Business and the Professions* (Philadelphia: Lippincott, 1978), pp. 153–186. [Reprinted from *Swindled* (New York: Dow Jones Books, 1976).]

[125]Sutherland, *White-Collar Crime*, p. 218.

[126]Sutherland, *White-Collar Crime*, pp. 217–220. Sutherland's conclusions have direct implications for the control of this behavior. See Christopher D. Stone, *Where the Law Ends: The Social Control of Corporate Behavior* (New York: Harper & Row, 1975). Also see Donald R. Cressey, "Restraint of Trade, Recidivism and Delinquent Neighborhoods," in James F. Short, Jr., ed., *Delinquency, Crime and Society* (Chicago: University of Chicago Press, 1976), pp. 209–238.

There is considerable support for corporate crime among similar, even competing, individuals and businesses; in fact, lawbreaking can become a normative pattern within certain corporations. The corporate executives learn the necessary values, motives, rationalizations, and techniques favorable to particular types of crime, and persons in these positions are not only often shielded from criticism of their illegal activities but may even find support for them in the mass media.

Differential Association

In his study of violation of labor relations and trade practice laws among shoe manufacturers Lane concluded that the manufacturers who associate with men whose attitudes favor violation are more likely to break the law.[127] The importance of group factors was also indicated in the electrical equipment conspiracy by the fact that actual plans and procedures were jointly drawn up by the corporations. Some of the plans were as ingenious as those found in organized or professional crime: secret meetings in hotel rooms had been arranged by company representatives, and participants were cautioned to conceal their bids in expense-account reports. At these meetings pricing schedules were arranged and plans made for each to submit the lowest bid for each of the various contracts. One of the most involved conspiracies, also the best organized and of the longest duration, occurred in the switch-gear division, which handles the sales of electric circuit breakers and the like.[128] Conspirators had developed a special language (argot) of their own and special operating procedures: attendance lists at the secret meetings were "Christmas card lists" and meetings were "choir practices." The companies involved in this particular conspiracy were General Electric, Westinghouse, Allis-Chalmers, Federal Pacific, and ITE, all of them being given code numbers which were used in the book price listings and in communications between executives.

Self-Conception

Corporation officials do not conceive of themselves as actually being criminals. They rationalize their behavior in terms of the unfairness of the law and the need to make a profit. Geis has analyzed the rational nature of most of their illegal actions in his study of the electrical conspiracy cases. A combination of factors must be present prior to participation in violations: first, the offenders had to perceive that financial gains would accrue from the violations, either personal or professional; second, they had to be able to rationalize their acts in terms of the image they had of themselves as upstanding, law-abiding, respected individuals; and third, a clearly indicated relationship that is often overlooked in explaining criminal behavior had to exist between "extrinsic conditions and illegal acts."

> When the market behaved in a manner the executives thought satisfactory or when enforcement agencies seemed particularly threatening, the conspiracy desisted. When

---

[127]See Lane.
[128]Herling, pp. 106–114.

market conditions deteriorated, while corporate pressures for achieving attractive profit-and-loss statements remained constant, and enforcement activity abated, the price-fixing agreements flourished.[129]

Societal Reaction and the Control of Corporate Crime

Public opinion polls have shown that large segments of the public have grave doubts about the honesty and the integrity of major U.S. corporations. Yet the corporations are so large, the violations so complex, and so diffused among great numbers of persons, as in the case of consumer violations and such fraud cases as the Equity Funding, that it is difficult to generate the same degree of public reaction to the crimes committed as for conventional or occupational offenses and offenders. Still, consumer and other groups have increasingly been advocating strong action against them.

Government regulatory agencies have been effective in controlling some corporate violations, but often enforcement of the laws is negligible, and probably a large proportion of law violations by corporations go undetected due to certain protective attitudes of most regulatory agencies toward the industries they regulate, the influence of large corporations, and the limited size of the enforcement staffs.[130] The influence of the corporate power structure makes it difficult for Congress to enact really strong enforcement measures or to appropriate sufficient funds for enforcement.[131] When violations are discovered seldom is strong legal action taken against influential corporations. Usually an injunction is issued or a fine levied, which in most cases can easily be absorbed by the corporation. Even before these measures are taken corporations are frequently given advance warning or notice of their violations, and they may be asked simply to modify their advertising claims or to withdraw their products from the market. Their response is often the issuance of "new" versions of the same product. Increasingly, however, consumers are demanding more adequate regulations to protect the public.

As a result of consumer pressures, court decisions making corporation officers personally liable, heavier monetary penalties, and other factors, stronger actions in cases of corporate violations in the future seem certain. With these developments redefinitions of criminal responsibility will significantly facilitate more vigorous legal action and increases in criminal convictions. In 1975, for example, the Supreme Court held the president and executive officer of a large national food chain personally liable criminally, by virtue of his responsibility and power, for the unsanitary storage

---

[129]Gilbert Geis, "The Heavy Electrical Equipment Antitrust Cases of 1961," in Geis and Meier, pp. 130–131. See also Robert F. Meier and Gilbert Geis, "The White-Collar Offender," in Hans Toch, ed., *The Psychology of Crime and Criminal Justice* (New York: Holt, Rinehart and Winston, 1978).
[130]See Turner; Robert Fellmeth, *The Interstate Commerce Omission* (New York: Grossman, 1970); Mark J. Green with Beverly C. Moore, Jr., and Bruce Wasserstein, *The Closed Enterprise System* (New York: Grossman, 1972); and Sutherland, *White Collar Crime,* pp. 232–233.
[131]Green, Fallows, and Zwick.

conditions found in one of the company's warehouses.[132] Others are of the opinion that stronger sanctions and enforcement alone cannot control corporate crime. Nader advocates the licensing of corporations to bring them under stricter controls in much the same way that public utilities are licensed.[133] On the other hand, Stone takes the view that corporate structure must be reorganized to insure more closely supervised activities and the ascertainment of responsibility, including the appointment of public members to the boards of trustees to insure greater compliance with the law.[134]

CONVENTIONAL CRIMINAL CAREERS

Conventional criminal offenders represent the stereotyped idea of a "criminal" to most persons. They move progressively from youth gang offenses, primarily theft, to adult criminal behavior of a more serious type, chiefly burglary or robbery. Their careers involve early group experience with delinquent behavior patterns as gang members. They adapt to a number of social roles and achieve high status through their gang activities. They continuously acquire techniques and develop rationalizations to explain their crimes as they move from petty to more serious offenses. During this progression, they have many experiences with official agencies, including the police, courts, juvenile authorities and institutions, reformatories, and, finally, prison. Institutional experiences add to their status and sophistication and help mold the conceptions they have of themselves as criminals. The degree of career development and sophistication among conventional criminals, however, is much lower than among professional criminals. Their careers in crime usually terminate somewhere between the early twenties and the late twenties or early thirties.

The career patterns of conventional offenders can be illustrated in a comparison study of persons convicted of armed robbery with a group of other property offenders.[135] As juvenile delinquents, the former frequently carried and used weapons of violence, and their arrest histories showed an average of 18 arrests. The armed robbers showed early patterns of stealing from their parents, school, and on the streets, truancy with either expulsion or suspension from school, street fighting, association with older delinquents, and membership in juvenile delinquent gangs. In comparison with the persons in the other criminal categories, greater involvement was evidenced in the destruction of property and in more frequent fights and delinquent activities, including more muggings and purse snatching. In addition, they had more often been leaders of youth gangs, basing their claims to leadership on their superior

---

[132]Tony McAdams and Robert C. Miljus, "Growing Criminal Liability of Executives," *Harvard Business Review*, 55 (1977), 36–39.
[133]Ralph Nader, Mark J. Green, and Joel Seligman, *Taming the Corporation* (New York: Norton, 1972); and Nader and Green.
[134]Stone.
[135]Julian B. Roebuck and Mervyn L. Cadwallader, "The Negro Armed Robber as a Criminal Type: The Construction and Application of a Typology," *Pacific Sociological Review*, 4 (1961), 21–26.

skill and strength. "Criminal progression appeared to occur at a more rapid rate with an early trend toward crimes of violence—from petty thefts and playground fights, to the rolling of drunks and homosexuals, and on to holdups with such weapons as pistols and knives."[136]

As conventional criminal offenders associate increasingly with youth of similar backgrounds, they become more involved in a subculture that is either neutral to or in opposition to the law, and their acts are frequently part of the way of life and the norms of a local slum community (see p. 145). They have learned early to commit illegal acts, and they have found group support for them, all of which enables them to progress readily to adult criminal behavior of a more substantial and sophisticated type.[137] As they identify more and more with crime, their conceptions of themselves as criminals become more concrete. Offenders who pursue criminal activities sporadically tend to vacillate in the conceptions they have of themselves, but for those who commit offenses regularly and are continuously isolated from law-abiding segments of society, a criminal self-conception is almost inescapable. They are also more and more severely dealt with before the law, further cementing their regard of themselves as criminals. A history of long criminal records may provide a vicious circle, because the offender, once stigmatized, finds it even more difficult to enter law-abiding society. In this sense, the person is forced into a life of crime, yet skills and organization, characteristic of the more organized and professional criminals, are lacking, making the individual even more likely to be arrested and imprisoned. Largely for these reasons, the conventional criminal offenders constitute a large proportion of the prison population, generally more than one half.

A large number of youth gang delinquents discontinue criminal behavior as they grow older, as has been indicated, and it has been suggested that this results from the lessening of deviant and criminal associations as family and other adult responsibilities are assumed. These changes are probably more important in breaking criminal patterns than are most of the current attempts at rehabilitation in correctional institutions. The movement from gang delinquent to adult criminal is not uniform, and it is affected by other noncriminal opportunities available to a person and by his conception of the future.

Societal Reaction to Conventional Offenders

The severe punishments given persons who have committed burglaries and robberies indicate the strong societal reaction to conventional offenders. These penalties in part represent society's desire to protect property and to punish harshly whenever violence

---

[136]Roebuck and Cadwallader, p. 24. Also see Julian B. Roebuck, *Criminal Typology: The Legalistic, Physical-Constitutional-Hereditary, Psychological-Psychiatric and Sociological Approaches* (Springfield, Ill.: Charles C Thomas, 1967), pp. 106–117.
[137]See Harold S. Frum, "Adult Criminal Offense Trends Following Juvenile Delinquency," *Journal of Criminal Law, Criminology and Police Science,* 49 (1958), 29–49; Gerald D. Robins, "Gang Member Delinquency in Philadelphia," in Malcolm W. Klein, ed., *Juvenile Gangs in Context: Theory, Research and Action* (Englewood Cliffs, N.J.: Prentice-Hall, 1967), p. 24; and D. H. Stott and D. M. Wilson, "The Adult Criminal as Juvenile: A Follow-Up Study of Glasgow Juvenile Delinquents into Adulthood," *British Journal of Criminology,* 17 (1977), 47–57.

is used to obtain it. They also represent a difference in orientation toward this type of lower-class crime as compared with occupational and corporate crime. Because these offenders usually have extensive records as juveniles and young adults, prosecuting attorneys are likely to have a stereotyped view of them and are usually successful in securing from them a guilty plea to a lesser but still severe charge. The official processing of conventional criminal offenders results in a lengthy series of arrests and convictions. The types of offenses they commit, often with but little skill, may lead to a considerable risk of apprehension and a high risk of conviction and incarceration in prisons. In this regard, they differ from professional criminals. Many spend much time in correctional institutions, and since society generally holds against a person the fact of imprisonment rather than what the person did, these offenders are among the most stigmatized.

ORGANIZED CRIME
AND CRIMINALS

Like professional offenders, members of organized criminal syndicates earn their living through their criminal activities. The very nature of these activities is fundamental in organized crime: supplying illegal goods and services—prostitution, massage parlors, pornographic establishments and films, usurious financial loans, illegal gambling, illegal narcotics, and stolen goods to voluntary customers—and the subsequent use of funds obtained in these activities to conduct operations in legitimate businesses.[138] It is the aspect of these operations related to legitimate businesses, together with the public demands for the services provided, that make organized crime and the organized criminal an incredibly complex and difficult problem. In addition, organized crime engages in racketeering to extort money and help maintain control over certain business services and labor unions.

Although perhaps the most basic characteristic of organized crime today is its feudal system, a number of general characteristics are important in its structure and operation.

1. Hierarchical structure involving a system of specifically defined relationships with mutual understandings, obligations, and privileges.
2. Unlimited political or geographic boundaries—intracity or intercity; intrastate or interstate.
3. Dependence upon:
   a. the possible use of force and violence to maintain internal control and restrain competition;
   b. securing and maintaining permanent immunity from interference from law enforcement and other agencies of government.
4. Criminal operations directed at large financial gains and specializing in one or more combinations of enterprises that fall into the areas of social deviation where public opinion is divided.

---

[138]See Francis A. J. Ianni and Elizabeth Reuss Ianni, *The Crime Society: Organized Crime and Corruption in America* (New York: New American Library, 1976), pp. 1–2.

5. Establishment of monopolistic control or establishment of spheres of influence between or among different criminal organizations.

The feudal basis of organized crime appears to rest on the "family," as associated generally with the terms "Mafia" or "Cosa Nostra." Actually the claims for the existence of such groups and these organizations are sharply debated by some. The generally accepted view is derived from information of the U.S. Department of Justice and contained in a report of a Presidential Commission and in the writing of Donald Cressey, who did the research for the Commission.[139] According to these findings, there is a national organization of approximately 24 "families" of Cosa Nostra operating in large cities and directed by a governing council whose task it is to divide operational territories in the United States and to settle jurisdictional disputes among the families. According to the government report, these "families" are exclusively Italian, they frequently communicate with each other, and the smooth functioning of their operations is assured by a national board of overseers.[140] These organized criminal groups operate throughout the country. Most cities have only one such group, which may contain as many as 700 persons, but New York City is reported to have five. The wealthiest and most influential groups are centered in New York, New Jersey, Illinois, Florida, Louisiana, Nevada, Michigan, and Rhode Island, and illegal activities in many other states are controlled by the large organizations. Some writers have claimed, however, that in spite of the government report the existence of the Cosa Nostra, some of its supposed operations, and even the name have not been sufficiently documented.[141] One writer has stated that the belief in a Mafia in the United States is the result of a combination of ulterior motives and sensational reporting.[142] It is claimed that such a "mystique" about organized crime has conditioned the measures of crime control that are often used against this form of criminality.

Organization

Presuming that these crime syndicates, or "families," do exist, one sees that the very nature of the "family" is crucial to its power. Leaders of particular syndicates appear to have the allegiance of several underlords who, in turn, have coteries of henchmen varying from lieutenants to what might be called "soldiers" (see Figure 7.2). Their strict code of behavior not to inform on members and other aspects of a code of honor are characterized by "(1) intense loyalty to the organization and its governing elite, (2) honesty in relationships with members, (3) secrecy regarding the organization's structure and activities, and (4) honorable behavior which sets members off as morally superior to those outsiders who would govern them."[143] This type of crime depends

---

[139]See *The Challenge of Crime in a Free Society;* and Donald R. Cressey, *Theft of the Nation* (New York: Harper & Row, 1969).

[140]*The Challenge of Crime in a Free Society,* p. 192.

[141]Norval Morris and Gordon Hawkins, *The Honest Politician's Guide to Crime Control* (Chicago: University of Chicago Press, 1970), pp. 203–225. See also Joseph L. Albini, *The American Mafia: Genesis of a Legend* (New York: Appleton, 1971).

[142]Dwight C. Smith, Jr., *The Mafia Mystique* (New York: Basic Books, 1975).

[143]Cressey, *Theft of the Nation,* p. 171. (Author's italics omitted.)

An Organized Crime Family

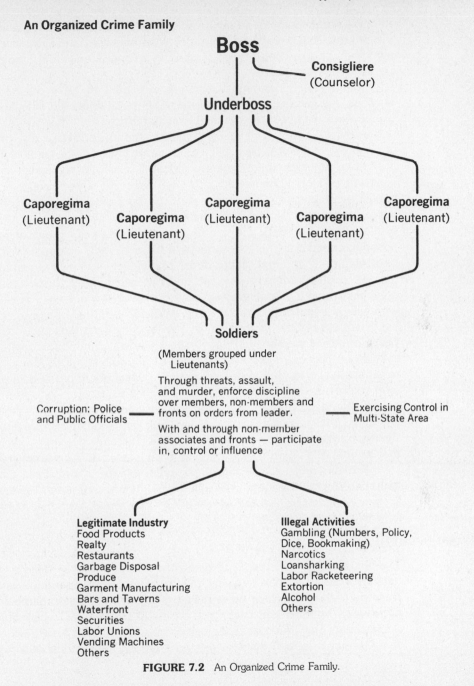

FIGURE 7.2 An Organized Crime Family.

From *The Challenge of Crime in a Free Society*, Report of the President's Commission on Law Enforcement and Administration of Justice (Washington, D.C.: Government Printing Office, 1967), p. 194.

upon the potential use or threat of force and violence, plus intimidation and bribery to ensure large economic gains, to control illegal activities, and to survive in competition with other groups. The so-called gangster in an organized criminal group performs any acts of violence required.

In addition to its feudal hierarchy designed to carry out particular criminal activities, syndicates are also organized to keep members out of legal entanglements. Connections with political machines or with branches of the legal system, such as the police or the courts, insure almost permanent immunity from arrest, or if there should be an arrest, make possible a "fix," or an arrangement in the criminal justice system to have the charges dropped. Organized criminal syndicates maintain their close associations with political machines either through direct payoffs or through delivery of votes, honest or fraudulent. The payoffs are used by politicians, police commissioners, or police captains or lieutenants either as personal assets or as contributions to the political machine. Both the contributions and the aid in delivering votes, which possibly require only the endorsement of the party by the criminal syndicate leader in local communities, bring either direct or indirect immunity. Immunity also comes through the appointment of councilmen, police officers, prosecutors, judges, and other government officials who will cooperate with the leaders of organized crime and who will pass along the word that the syndicate is to be left alone.

The large-scale organization of a crime syndicate makes generalizations about backgrounds of members difficult.[144] Most syndicate members came originally, however, from the slum and have had a record of youth crime.[145] Many of their histories resemble the conventional criminal career in which there has been a progression in a long series of delinquencies and crime, as well as association with a tough gang of young offenders. Instead of ending their criminal careers while young, they have continued their activities in association with some organized criminal syndicate. A significant factor in this continuance is their habituation to crime, which means that they may attach themselves to criminal groups as conditions seem suitable.

For the most part, seven areas predominate in organized crime: (1) illegal gambling; (2) racketeering; (3) illegal drugs; (4) usury or loan sharking; (5) illicit sex; (6) sale of stolen or hijacked goods; and (7) control of legitimate business.

Illegal Gambling

The lucrative returns from illegal gambling enterprises make them most attractive to organized crime. In most large cities illegal bookmakers associated with crime syndicates specialize in bets on horse racing, professional boxing, baseball, hockey, and professional football and basketball. Formerly betting was concentrated on professional events only, but college football and basketball have also drawn their attention. The "numbers racket" involves placing a bet on the possible occurrence of certain

---

[144]For a general discussion of criminal organization, see Albert K. Cohen, "The Concept of Criminal Organization," *British Journal of Criminology,* 17 (1977), 97–111.

[145]Francis A. J. Ianni, *Black Mafia: Ethnic Succession in Organized Crime* (New York: Simon & Schuster, 1975). Also see Robert T. Anderson, "From Mafia to Cosa Nostra," *American Journal of Sociology,* 81 (1965), 302–310.

numbers, such as the last three digits of the daily U.S. Treasury balance.[146] A complicated organization is required to distribute forms and to collect and pay off bets. For efficient operations, the gambling syndicates employ writers or runners, pick-up men or collectors of bets, cashiers, clerks, checkers, and operators. Tickets with winning numbers are redeemed by cashiers on the spot; if holders are not present, the money is delivered by runners. Numbers runners are usually small-time criminals who are part of the larger syndicate. Their income is based on a percentage of the take, and since they are engaged in illegal activities, their income is not reported and is therefore tax-free. Generally, they receive between 15 and 25 percent of all bets they take in, from a third to a half of the losses of a new customer, and a 10 percent tip from the customer who wins.[147]

Racketeering

A big source of illegal income for organized crime is from racketeering, the systematic extortion of money from persons or organizations to force some service on them, to extort money, or to maintain control. Most racketeering is concentrated in organizations engaged in the distribution of services and commodities, including, for example, the wholesaling of perishable foods and the laundry and cleaning businesses. Concerns are forced to pay tribute to "protect" themselves from violence, such as damaging clothes in a cleaning and dyeing establishment, or to maintain price fixing. Tribute may also be demanded to avoid a wildcat strike. Racketeering has been used to maintain control of union members or to defeat another union that is competing for members. Although racketeering activities have affected many industries, they have been particularly prevalent in the motion-picture industry, the building trades, liquor stores, laundry and cleaning establishments, and the waterfront, trucking, and loading businesses.[148]

Illegal Drugs

A major role of organized crime is in importing and distributing illegal drugs (see Chapter 9).

Usury

Usury, or loan sharking, is an important function of organized crime, and large profits are made. Money is made available at rates far above the legal limits, which are usually a maximum of 12 percent, to persons who are desperately in need of cash but who have neither the collateral nor the financial reputation to secure it through legitimate sources.

---

[146]See Ivan Light, "Numbers Gambling among Blacks: A Financial Institution," *American Sociological Review,* 42 (1977), 892–904.
[147]Thomas Plate, *Crime Pays!* (New York: Ballantine Books, 1975), p. 75.
[148]See Robert Kennedy, *The Enemy Within* (New York: Harper & Row, 1960); and Gus Tyler, ed., *Organized Crime in America* (Ann Arbor: University of Michigan Press, 1962). Also see John Landesco, "Racketeering," in Ianni and Ianni, pp. 173–185.

Illicit Sex

Organized crime still plays a large role in shakedowns in prostitution, in the ownership of topless and bottomless bars, and in the distribution of pornographic literature and films (see p. 411).

Sale of Stolen or Hijacked Goods

Organized criminals have engaged in the sale, often in interstate commerce and sometimes the actual theft, of valuable goods. Some of these goods are stolen from airports and similar loading or storage facilities. More recently, they have engaged in the sale of stolen credit cards.

Legitimate Business

In addition to the control of illegal activities, organized crime has infiltrated legitimate businesses. This has been accomplished through illegal means or the investment of large sums of money from the profits of illegal activities.[149] Legitimate businesses are sometimes used as fronts, but more recently organized crime has used legitimate businesses as major sources of revenue. They have a vested monopoly in some legitimate enterprises, like cigarette vending machines and jukeboxes. Crime syndicates own a wide variety of enterprises such as real estate, retail firms, restaurants and bars, hotels, automobile agencies, trucking concerns, food companies, linen and tavern supply outlets, garbage-collection routes, and other service concerns.

In addition to their legitimate income, legitimate businesses can be used illegally by criminal syndicates in several ways. One such scheme is the planned bankruptcy. After a business has been acquired the new owner runs up large debts, either through purchasing merchandise or borrowing money directly from banks, and he then files for bankruptcy. If successful, all debts are cancelled, and the new owner has a profit from his dealings before he went to court.[150]

Societal Reaction and Social Control of Organized Crime

Although societal reaction is strong against organized crime as such, there have been few effective measures to control it.[151] Many reasons may be cited for this failure: (1) The very nature of organized crime creates a major problem. As it is largely an

---

[149]In a case study of one "family" which had both legitimate and illegitimate holdings, Ianni found, however, that the profits from the illegitimate business never crossed over into the legitimate business, and vice versa: there was a clear distinction between the source of revenue and the purpose to which it would be put. This is contrary to other evidence and, moreover, in this instance it is impossible to generalize this finding from a single case study to other syndicates. See Francis A. J. Ianni, *A Family Business: Kinship and Social Control in Organized Crime* (New York: Russell Sage, 1972).

[150]Plate, pp. 137–138.

[151]See, for example, Denny F. Pace and Jimmie C. Styles, *Organized Crime: Concepts and Control* (Englewood Cliffs, N.J.: Prentice-Hall, 1975).

"illegitimate" business, it usually consists of different types of individual crimes rather than the "organized" element being a crime in itself.

> It is not against the criminal law for an individual or group of individuals rationally to plan, establish, develop, and administer an organization designed for the perpetration of crime. Neither is it against the law for a person to participate in such an organization. What is against the law is bet taking, usury, smuggling and selling narcotics and untaxed liquor, extortion, murder, and conspiracy to commit these and other specific crimes.[152]

(2) The public demands many of the services provided, such as gambling and usury. (3) Many difficulties are encountered in obtaining proof of criminal activities, particularly because of the intimidation of witnesses. (4) The corruption of public officials prevents possible prosecution. (5) Greatly lacking are effective resources to deal with the possible nation-wide operations of some crime syndicates. (6) Local, state, and federal organized crime agencies are poorly coordinated. (7) Even the sanctions that are available are ineffectively used, sentences seldom being commensurate with the financial rewards obtained from the illegal activities. (8) Finally, the image of the organized criminal as a great success and even a "hero" to certain slum dwellers makes it difficult to deal with this problem by soliciting community support.[153] The President's Commission has concluded:

> The public demands action only sporadically, as intermittent, sensational disclosures reveal intolerable violence and corruption caused by organized crime. Without sustained public pressure, political office seekers and office holders have little incentive to address themselves to combatting organized crime. A drive against organized crime usually uncovers political corruption; this means that a crusading mayor or district attorney makes many political enemies. The vicious cycle perpetuates itself. Politicians will not act unless the public so demands; but much of the urban public wants the services provided by organized crime and does not wish to disrupt the system that provides those services. And much of the public does not see or understand the effects of organized crime in society.[154]

Organized crime has become an integral part of U.S. society in two ways. First, it has had its roots in newly arrived immigrant groups such as the Irish and the Italians who viewed this activity as a means of social mobility.[155] On discovering that they had been relegated to the lowest rung on the social ladder in their new country, such persons turned to criminal activities, using some of the skills and the organizational principles of similar organizations in their home lands. It is not surprising, therefore, that there is ethnic succession in the criminal syndicate membership. In New York City, for example, there is evidence that organized crime is increasingly becoming an area for blacks and Puerto Ricans, with the present predominantly Italian members slowly moving into more legitimate enterprises.[156]

Second, just as organized crime seems to have originated in the most American of processes, social mobility or "getting ahead," so too has it paid its way into U.S. life

---

[152]Cressey, *Theft of the Nation,* p. 299. Also see Frederic D. Homer, *Guns and Garlic: Myths and Realities of Organized Crime* (West Lafayette, Ind.: Purdue University Press, 1974), pp. 139–168.
[153]Elizabeth Ruess Ianni, "A Community Self-Study of Organized Crime," in Ianni and Ianni, pp. 367–373.
[154]*The Challenge of Crime in a Free Society,* p. 200.
[155]Daniel Bell, "Crime as an American Way of Life: A Queer Ladder of Social Mobility," in *The End of Idology,* rev. ed. (New York: Free Press, 1962), pp. 127–150.
[156]Ianni, *Black Mafia.*

by offering services and goods that are valued by many segments of the population: gambling, illicit sex, loans difficult to obtain, illegal drugs, and, before the repeal of Prohibition, illegal alcohol. Organized crime could not exist without the demands for goods and services commonly available in this country, although many satisfy their desires through legal outlets, for example, going to Las Vegas to gamble and using legal drugs. In addition to servicing demands from customers, organized crime often attempts to stimulate and to create demand for goods and services. Either directly or indirectly it encourages usage of these services and loans money at high interest rates, possibly driving some of its customers to other crimes such as embezzlement or theft to repay the loans. In short, "organized crime is built not only on the premise of supplying existing public demands, but also on the idea of expanding such demands."[157]

Most people believe that the best solution to illegal gambling through organized crime is to legalize it as is done in Nevada. Most countries have state lotteries, sweepstakes, or other forms of betting that bring in much revenue for the state after the winners have been paid.[158] Several states in the United States have similar lotteries. In 1976 the state of Delaware began a state sports lottery with betting on professional football games. It is questionable, however, if commercialized gambling could be legalized throughout the country with the same results as in many European countries.[159] It is argued that it would be too large an enterprise for the government and that any legalized gambling in the United States as a whole might well become infiltrated by the same criminal elements now in control of illegal gambling, as has happened to a considerable extent in Nevada. There is no assurance that legalization of gambling would eliminate the profits in organized crime; the members might well shift to some other field as they turned to gambling after the repeal of the Prohibition laws and as they are now doing in loan sharking, illegal drugs, and illicit sex.

THE PROFESSIONAL OFFENDER

Of all offenders the "professionals" have the most highly developed criminal careers, social status, and skills. They probably have never been numerous, and there is indication that their numbers have declined to such an extent during this century that Cressey has referred to them as "old-fashioned criminals."[160] Various preventive

---

[157]John E. Conklin, *The Crime Establishment: Organized Crime and American Society* (Englewood Cliffs, N.J.: Prentice-Hall, 1973), p. 5. Also see Matthew G. Yeager, "The Gangster as White-Collar Criminal," *Issues in Criminology*, 8 (1973), 49–73; and George B. Vold, *Theoretical Criminology* (New York: Oxford University Press, 1958), p. 240.

[158]Sweden, for example, legalized betting on sports pools in 1934, the betting supervised by a corporation consisting of members of several sports organizations. Some of the revenue is used for these organizations and for expenses, but the largest share goes to the government.

[159]See Cressey, *Theft of the Nation*, pp. 292–297. For an opposite view see Gilbert Geis, *Not the Law's Business? An Examination of Homosexuality, Abortion, Prostitution, Narcotics and Gambling in the United States* (Washington, D.C.: National Institute of Mental Health, Center for Studies of Crime and Delinquency, 1972), pp. 222–250.

[160]Donald R. Cressey, *Criminal Organization* (New York: Harper & Row, 1972), p. 45.

devices have made professional forgery, for example, more difficult, and there is a possibility that it, as well as other types of professional crime, is declining.

Professional offenders are characterized by the following: (1) *skill*—a complex of techniques for committing crimes; (2) *status*—their positions in the world of crime are high; (3) *consensus*—professional criminals share common values, beliefs, and attitudes; (4) *differential association*—primarily associations with other professional criminals rather than law-abiding persons and other types of criminals; and (5) *organization*—activities are pursued in terms of knowledge and through an information and assistance system. Related to these characteristics are several others associated with group support that underlies professional crime.[161]

Skill

Professional criminals as a group engage in a variety of highly specialized crimes. The individual develops a great deal of skill in a particular type of offense, including pickpocketing; shoplifting; confidence games; sneak-thieving from stores, banks, and offices; stealing from jewelry stores by substituting inferior jewelry for valuable pieces; stealing from hotel rooms; and a variety of miscellaneous offenses such as passing forged checks, counterfeiting, and extorting money from others engaged in illegal activities. The specialized skills exhibited by the professional check forger are quite different from those of the amateur or naive forger.[162] There are also professional robbers, bank robbers, safecrackers, and burglars.

Professional pickpockets, or "class cannons," as they call themselves, ply their trade at airports, race tracks, amusement parks, and areas frequented by tourists.[163] Working in a "mob" of three or four, each with a specific role to play, they select a "mark" on the basis of their guesses, as well as the mark's dress and demeanor as to whether or not the person has money. The actual snatch is quick, sometimes with a jostle or bump, the cannon quickly passes the loot to another member of the mob, and they immediately leave the area. Although the amount varies, it has been estimated from their own reports that class cannons have average incomes of about $23,000 a year.[164] A hard-working mob will "hit" 10 to 15 marks a day with an average take of $10 to $25. When detected by the mark, probably not more than one in a hundred, pickpockets can often talk their way out by offering the victim's money back to him, often with a bonus.

The *professional shoplifter* sells the stolen merchandise rather than using it as does the amateur. Professional shoplifters usually work in small "troupes," touring the country, staying long enough in a given place to "clout" (shoplift) and dispose of

[161]Edwin H. Sutherland, *The Professional Thief* (Chicago: University of Chicago Press, 1937).

[162]Edwin M. Lemert, "The Behavior of the Systematic Check Forger," *Social Problems,* 6 (1958), 141–149; and James A. Inciardi, "Vocational Crime," in Glaser, pp. 314–318.

[163]David W. Maurer, *Whiz Mob: A Correlation of the Technical Argot of Pickpockets with Their Behavior Pattern* (New Haven, Conn.: College and University Press, 1964).

[164]See James A. Inciardi, "In Search of the Class Cannon: A Field Study of Professional Pickpockets," in Robert S. Weppner, ed., *Street Ethnography: Selected Studies of Crime and Deviance in a Natural Setting* (Beverly Hills, Calif.: Sage Publications, 1977) pp. 55–77; and James A. Inciardi, "The Pickpocket and His Victim," *Victimology,* 1 (1976), 446–453.

stolen merchandise. They are skilled in techniques, using devices such as "bad bags" (old printed paper bags from a store), large "booster" overcoats, and "booster boxes," boxes observably ready for mailing.[165] They know the risk of being apprehended is small, even if they are detected.

Confidence games are divided into the "short con" and the "big con." In the former, money is secured illegally from an individual directly and in a brief time, through the sale, for example, of false jewelry.[166] The big con usually requires a longer period of time and involves a larger sum of money, which is secured, for example, through the operation of a "money-making machine" or the sale of fraudulent securities.[167] A great asset for the con man is the fact that his victim is often also out to violate the law, either in accepting the illegal proposition of the confidence man or in engaging in illegal activity to raise money for the confidence game. A special type of con man is the professional "hustler," who makes his living betting against his opponents—often with a backer—in various types of pool or billiard games and in so doing engaging in various deceitful practices, such as hiding his own high degree of skill in the games. His conning involves an "extraordinary manipulation of other people's impressions of reality and especially of one's self, creating 'false impressions.'"[168]

Status

The high status of professional criminals is reflected by the attitudes of other criminals and by the special treatment usually accorded them by the police, court officials, and others. Offenders of lower-status groups tend to look up to the professional, whereas professional thieves are contemptuous of amateurs and have many epithets for them, such as "snatch-and-grab thief" and "boot-and-shoe thief." Highly skilled criminal activities, however, do not alone make a professional. Of greater importance is the individual's social role, which is the result of extensive contacts with others in the profession. Professional thieves have in common "acquaintances, congeniality, sympathy, understandings, agreements, rules, codes of behavior, and language." In terms of social role Sutherland has said that "a person who is received in the group and recognized as a professional thief is a professional thief."[169]

Differential Association

As in other professions, professional criminals are trained in their occupation. A newcomer learns from other professionals; frequently the techniques used have long

---

[165]Cameron, pp. 42–50.

[166]Julian B. Roebuck and Ronald C. Johnson, "The 'Short Con' Man," Crime and Delinquency, 10 (1964), 235–248.

[167]See, for example, the biography of the most famous U.S. confidence man, Joseph R. Weil, "Yellow Kid" Weil (as told to W. T. Brannon) (New York: A. S. Barnes, 1948).

[168]Ned Polsky, "The Hustlers," Social Problems, 12 (1964), 14; and Andrew Walker, "Sociology and Professional Crime," in Abraham S. Blumberg, ed., Current Perspectives on Criminal Behavior: Original Essays on Criminology (New York: Knopf, 1974), pp. 87–113. Also see David M. Hayano, "The Professional Poker Player: Career Identification and the Problem of Respectability," Social Problems, 24 (1977), 556—565.

[169]Sutherland, The Professional Thief, p. 207.

histories.[170] Frequently they are recruited from persons in their twenties who have shown a potential for professional criminality or who have some specialized skill; for example, professional counterfeiters may recruit someone who works as an engraver. Pickpockets may be recruited from hotel clerks who show unusual skill with their hands, and confidence men chosen from persons who show exceptional intelligence, presence, and "gift of gab." At first he is given jobs of minor capacity and is helped to improve his skills. If he does this assignment well, he is promoted to more important ones. During this apprenticeship, he is taught the morality and code of his profession. He acquires the important characteristic of a "larceny sense," a term that refers to a criminal ability to exploit situations through his skills. He learns how to dispose of stolen goods and which contacts are most valuable to him for this purpose.[171] He also learns how to "fix" cases if apprehended, and he builds up associations with other professional criminals. If successful, he is admitted to full status with other professional offenders and acquires a reputation in his field, among both other criminals and public officials.

Probably the best example of differential association in professional crime is the special argot by which members communicate with one another in a separate set of symbols, much as special terms are used in any profession. This language is not employed to hide anything, for its use in public would attract attention among laymen. It is handed down from generation to generation; hence many terms used by professional criminals, like some terms used by doctors, can be traced back several hundred years.[172] They give unity to the group and serve as a specialized language for specialized activities, as in any group, and other terms are adapted to their needs.[173] The following are examples of typical words and expressions used by professional thieves.

> *Boost:* the racket of shoplifting.
> *Cannon:* the pickpocket racket, or a member of a mob engaged in picking pockets.
> *Hang paper:* to write fraudulent checks.
> *Heel:* sneak thief from stores and offices.
> *Hook:* member of a pickpocket mob who takes the wallet from the pocket of the victim.
> *Hotel prowling:* stealing from hotel rooms.
> *Penny-weighting:* substituting fake for real jewelry.
> *Poke:* pocketbook.
> *Score:* Successful theft, referring to the value of the stolen property.

For purposes of recruitment and the identification of appropriate places to victimize, the professional criminal subculture performs an important role for the professional criminal. Because of his extensive mobility, each is known personally by a large number of other professional thieves. Information regarding methods and situations becomes known and shared by all professionals, as is illustrated by phrases

---

[170]James A. Inciardi, *Careers in Crime* (Chicago: Rand McNally, 1975), pp. 5–13.
[171]We know relatively little about the professional fence, although his role is an important one. See Duncan Chappell and Marilyn Walsh, "Receiving Stolen Property: The Need for Systematic Inquiry into the Fencing Process," *Criminology,* 11 (1974), 484–497. An excellent case study of a professional fence can be found in Carl B. Klockars, *The Professional Fence* (New York: Free Press, 1974).
[172]Inciardi, "Vocational Crime," pp. 328–331.
[173]See David W. Maurer, *The Big Con* (New York: Pocket Books, 1949), pp. 282–283. Also see Sutherland, *The Professional Thief,* pp. 235–243; and Maurer, pp. 200–216.

such as "Toledo is a good town," "The lunch hour is the best time to work that spot," and "See Skid if you should get a tumble in Chicago." A professional thief may warn another, or he may take up a collection to help a thief who is in jail or to assist his family.

Organization

Professional criminals are generally loosely organized, although this depends somewhat on the nature of the crime to be committed. Pickpocket mobs tend to work together for long periods of time, but there is turnover in personnel. Some of them, such as "heavy criminals" (professional burglars or robbers), form groups for specific purposes and disband when the need for collaboration no longer exists.[174] In the case of a professional armed robbery, for example, where organization does exist, it is a more permanent organization.[175] They must keep in touch with one another, if by reputation alone, however, so that they may be recruited for another robbery job in the future. It is important, for example, that the organizer of an armed robbery knows which "wheel man" to drive the get-away car is available at the time so he can be contacted about the job.

Societal Reaction to Professional Crime and Its Social Control

Generally, the public is not as aware of professional crime as it is of organized crime. Occasionally a well-publicized case or a popular motion picture, such as *The Sting* in the early 1970s, brings this type of crime to the public's attention. In fact, because of their highly developed skill, professional criminals are usually accorded special treatment by the police, the court, and other official persons. Sometimes they are able to buy protection and can generally arrange a "fix" to avoid punishment. They are often able to avoid conviction because of these informal processes; moreover, the fact of their not having a previous record does not fit the usual public stereotype of a highly developed offender. "Even perfect technique fails occasionally, but the advantage the professional shoplifter has (as with most professional thieves) over other shoplifters is to use his influence and 'know-how' in resolving a lengthy jail or prison sentence. An attorney will have been carefully selected for his 'right' connections."[176]

SUMMARY

The discussion of various types of criminal behavior systems and the differences between them can be summarized briefly as follows:[177]

---

[174]Don C. Gibbons, *Crime, Society and Criminal Careers,* 3d ed. (Englewood Cliffs, N.J.: Prentice-Hall, 1977), pp. 279–282.
[175]Werner J. Einstadter, "The Social Organization of Armed Robbery," *Social Problems,* 17 (1969), 67–68. For the organization in safe-cracking, see Bill Chambliss, *Box Man: A Professional Thief's Journey* (New York: Harper & Row, 1972). (The story of Harry King, as told to and edited by Bill Chambliss.)
[176]Cameron, pp. 47–48.
[177]The following is adapted from Clinard and Quinney, pp. 16–21.

Violent Personal Criminal Behavior The offenders do not conceive of themselves as criminals. They are often persons with no previous records, but they commit personal offenses because of certain particular circumstances. The offenses are not directly supported by any group, but there may be subcultural definitions favorable to the general use of violence. These offenses produce strong societal reaction.

Occasional Property Criminal Behavior These offenders do not usually conceive of themselves as criminals, and they are able to rationalize their criminal behavior. They usually uphold the general goals of society and find little support for their behavior in subcultural norms. These behaviors violate the value placed on private property. There is leniency in legal processing, and societal reaction is not severe when the offender has no previous record.

Political Criminal Behavior Governments create laws to protect their own existences. Specific criminal laws, such as conspiracy laws, as well as traditional laws, are made to control and punish those who threaten the state. Political offenders, acting out of conscience, do not usually conceive of themselves as criminals. Governmental crimes are related to the efforts of a government to maintain power and legitimacy.

Occupational Criminal Behavior These offenders violate the law in the course of their occupational activities. They do not consider themselves criminals and are able to rationalize their conduct. Some occupations, or groups within occupations, tolerate or even support the offenses. Because they are committed by "respectable" persons, societal reaction has traditionally been mild. Official penalties have been lenient, often restricted to the sanctions administered by the professional associations. Public reaction is becoming less tolerant.

Corporate Criminal Behavior Criminal laws and administrative regulations have been established to regulate the restraint of trade, false advertising, the manufacture of unsafe foods and drugs, pollution, and many other areas. The criminal behaviors are often an integral part of corporate business operations. Violations are rationalized as being basic to business enterprise. Corporate crime involves a great amount of organizations among the participants. Strong legal actions have not usually been taken against corporations and their officials. Public reactions and legal actions are increasing.

Conventional Criminal Behavior Offenders begin their careers early in life, often in gang associations; they vacillate between the values of the larger society and those of a criminal subculture. Some continue primary association with other offenders, while others pursue different careers. Their behavior is consistent with the goal of economic success, but inconsistent with the sanctity of private property. There are usually many arrests and convictions and often severe penalties.

Organized Criminal Behavior These offenders pursue crime as a livelihood. In the lower echelons they conceive of themselves as criminals, associate primarily with other criminals, and are isolated from the larger society. In the top levels they associate with persons of legitimate society and often reside in the better residential neighborhoods. Illegal services desired by legitimate society are provided by organized crime. The public tolerates organized crime, partly because of the services it provides and partly because of the complex problems in dealing with its operation. Conviction is usually for minor offenses.

Professional Criminal Behavior Professional crimes are distinguished by the nature of the criminal behavior rather than by specific criminal laws. Professional criminals pursue crime as a livelihood and way of life. They conceive of themselves as criminals, associate with other professionals, and have high status among other criminals. The extent of organization among professional offenders varies with the kind of offense. Many cases of professional criminal behavior are "fixed" in the course of legal processing.

SELECTED REFERENCES

Bequai, August. *White-Collar Crime: A 20th Century Crisis.* Boston: D. C. Heath and Co., 1978.

Blankenburg, Erhard. "The Selectivity of Legal Sanctions: An Empirical Investigation of Shoplifting," *Law and Society Review,* 11 (1976), 110–130.

Cameron, Mary Owen. *The Booster and the Snitch: Department Store Shoplifing.* New York: Free Press, 1964.

Chappell, Duncan, Robley Geis, and Gilbert Geis, eds. *Forcible Rape: The Crime, the Victim and the Offender.* New York: Columbia University Press, 1977.

Clinard, Marshall B., and Richard Quinney. *Criminal Behavior Systems: A Typology,* rev. ed. New York: Holt, Rinehart and Winston, 1973.

Conklin, John E. *Robbery and the Criminal Justice System.* Philadelphia: Lippincott, 1972.

Conklin, John E. *"Illegal But Not Criminal": Business Crime in America.* Englewood Cliffs, N.J.: Prentice-Hall, Inc., 1977.

Cressey, Donald R. *Theft of the Nation: The Structure and Operations of Organized Crime in America.* New York: Harper & Row, 1969.

Cressey, Donald R. "Restraint of Trade, Recidivism, and Delinquent Neighborhoods," in James F. Short, Jr., ed., *Delinquency, Crime and Society.* Chicago: University of Chicago Press, 1976, pp. 209–238.

Erlanger, Howard S. "The Empirical Status of the Subculture of Violence Thesis," *Social Problems,* 22 (1974), 280–292.

Erman, M. David, and Richard J. Lundman. *Corporate and Governmental Deviance: Problems of Organizational Behavior in Contemporary Society.* New York: Oxford Press, 1978.

Ferracuti, Franco, and Graeme Newman. "Assaultive Offenses," in Daniel Glaser, ed. *Handbook of Criminology.* Chicago: Rand McNally, 1974, pp. 175–207.

Geis, Gilbert, and Robert F. Meier, eds. *White-Collar Crime: Offenses in Business, Politics and the Professions.* New York: Free Press, 1977.

Goff, Colin H., and Charles E. Reasons. *Corporate Crime in Canada: A Critical Analysis of Anti-Combines Legislation.* Scarborough, Ont.: Prentice-Hall of Canada, Ltd., 1978.

Hills, Stuart L. *Crime, Power, and Morality.* Scranton, Pa.: Chandler, 1971.

Ianni, Francis A. J., and Elizabeth Ruess Ianni, eds. *The Crime Society: Organized Crime and Corruption in America.* New York: New American Library, 1976.

Inciardi, James A. *Careers in Crime.* Chicago: Rand McNally, 1975.

Inciardi, James A. "In Search of the Class Cannon: A Field Study of Professional Pickpockets," in Robert S. Weppner, ed., *Street Ethnography: Selected Studies of Crime and Deviance in a Natural Setting.* Beverly Hills, Calif.: Sage Publications, 1977, pp. 55–77.

Johnson, John M., and Jack D. Douglas. *Crime at the Top: Deviance in Business and the Professions* (Philadelphia: Lippincott, 1978).

McCaghy, Charles H., Peggy C. Giordano, and Trudy Knicely Henson. "Auto Theft: Offender and Offense Characteristics," *Criminology,* 15 (1977), 367–385.

Schafer, Stephen. *The Political Criminal: The Problem of Morality and Crime.* New York: Free Press, 1974.

Stone, Christopher D. *Where the Law Ends: The Social Control of Corporate Behavior.* New York: Harper & Row, 1975.

Stott, D. H., and D. M. Wilson. "The Adult Criminal as Juvenile: A Follow-Up Study of Glasgow Juvenile Delinquents into Adulthood," *British Journal of Criminology,* 17 (1977), 47–57.

Sutherland, Edwin H. *The Professional Thief.* Chicago: University of Chicago Press, 1937.

Wolfgang, Marvin E. *Patterns in Criminal Homicide.* Philadelphia: University of Pennsylvania Press, 1958.

Wolfgang, Marvin E., and Franco Ferracuti. *The Subculture of Violence: Toward an Integrated Theory in Criminology.* London: Tavistock Social Science Paperbacks, 1967.

CHAPTER 8

Social Control of Criminality
The Criminal Justice System

THE social control of delinquent and criminal behavior represents the most highly structured, formal system used by society to attempt to control one type of deviance. The well-developed system of controlling crime and delinquency, commonly referred to as the *criminal justice system,* explicitly enunciates society's great disapproval of "crime," unlike many other forms of deviance. The laws, enacted by legislatures and modified by court decisions, define delinquent and criminal behavior; they also specify the sanctions imposed for violations. Because these laws and decisions are written, one does not face the same degree of ambiguity in defining or in studying this type of deviance as one does, for example, with mental disorder. Systems for caring for mentally ill persons have been developed by society; as yet, however, no definitive systems of behavior are accepted as constituting deviance of this type (see Chapter 13).

The very nature of the highly formalized criminal justice system makes it more readily amenable to empirical studies of these social controls than is possible with other structures of social control.[1] In view of its institutional nature, moreover, processes of social control can be studied from different perspectives. They include the organizational, that is, the structure and function of official agencies such as the police; the social-psychological, for example, the process of individual police officer decision-making or the use of police discretion; and the sociological, such as the impact of police activities on crime rates in terms of the crimes the police may discover and those they may prevent. It is also possible to examine the generally widespread dissatisfaction with the criminal justice system, both as a whole and with respect to many aspects of it, the training of police, the exercise of police discretion, the use of police violence, the limitations of full enforcement of the law, the sentencing disparities in the courts, the role of punishment in society, and the function of prisons in controlling criminality. This chapter deals with these important issues.

THE CRIMINAL LAW

Two centuries ago the writings of an Italian nobleman and essayist, Cesare Beccaria, set a pattern that has affected the punishment of criminal offenders under the law in every country in the world. His philosophy was simply that an act such as a crime that produced "pleasure" must be counteracted by a "pain" such as imprisonment. All laws that prescribe sentences such as one year for petty theft, five years for auto theft, ten years for burglary, and twenty for robbery can be traced to Beccaria. A similar philosophy was expressed by certain hedonistic psychologists, of whom Jeremy Bentham of England was one of the best known.[2] The legal view of Beccaria coincided with the ideas of the new Age of Enlightenment, with its humanitarian ideals as opposed to the barbarous penal practices of that day. At a time when the same crime was punished differently by various judges or even by the same judge, with little or no

---

[1]See Graeme Newman, *Comparative Deviance: Perception and Law in Six Cultures* (New York: Elsevier, 1976), Chap. 2, pp. 9–27.

[2]Jeremy Bentham, *An Introduction to the Principles of Morals and Legislation* (New York: Hafner, 1948; originally published in 1780).

punishment for a nobleman and great severity for a serf, Beccaria's famous work, *Essay on Crimes and Punishment* (1764), suggested uniform penalties for a given crime, penalties scaled according to the severity of the crime. He recommended the abolition of torture and other inhumane physical punishments then in common use, including capital punishment. He pointed out that punishments that were secret, cruel, and final, such as the death penalty, were not necessarily preventive, and that if the nature of the punishment were known in advance a person could calculate the pain-pleasure ratio prior to committing the act.

Beccaria's writing had great influence in his day. He was invited, for example, to help revise the criminal codes of Prussia on the invitation of Frederick the Great and of Russia on the invitation of Catherine the Great. These revised codes then became the basis for the Code Napoleon. The conception of punishment advanced in all of these writings still underlies the criminal law of nearly all countries today, with a specific number of years of imprisonment, for example, for each type of crime.

The Changing Concept of the Law

The establishment of uniform penalties did indeed provide a more humanitarian approach to the severe punishments of a century or so ago, but the underlying concept was found lacking some time later. In fact, the entire concept of law, its purpose and its scope, has been changing radically in recent years. It is no longer considered to be a static, rigid code of norms and punishments, but rather an on-going action. Law is quantitative in that it involves actions associated with law. "A complaint to a legal official, for example, is more than no complaint, whether it is a call to the police, a visit to a regulatory agency, or a lawsuit. . . . So is the recognition of a complaint, whether this is simply an official record, an investigation, or a preliminary hearing of some kind. In criminal matters, an arrest is more law than no arrest, and so is a search or an interrogation."[3]

Law also changes, as do the uses of law. Sociologists are interested in the nature of the changes and the conditions that bring them about. In this century there has been an increasing reliance on law to regulate the activities and thus the lives of people. As the law has proliferated to incorporate many more behaviors, many changes in penalties for certain crimes have also occurred.[4] These increases will invariably result in more social control and in further changes in the control methods. In other words, as more behavior is considered to be criminal, the more acts will become the interest of the police, the courts, and the prison system.

The process by which norms are moved from the social to the legal level is termed the process of *legalization*. Not all social norms are laws or legal norms; in fact, only certain norms are translated into legal norms. The question becomes, then, why the violation of certain norms is chosen to be incorporated into the criminal code and the violation of others is not. Turk has identified four social forces involved in the

---

[3]Donald Black, *The Behavior of Law* (New York: Academic Press, 1976), p. 3.
[4]See, for example, Herbert L. Packer, *The Limits of the Criminal Sanction* (Stanford, Calif.: Stanford University Press, 1968).

legalization or creation of legal norms: moral indignation, a high value on order, response to threat, and political tactics.[5]

1. ***Moral Indignation***   Legal norms may be created by the actions of relatively small groups of persons who have become morally outraged at some actions they regard as reprehensible. A number of studies have interpreted the creation of various legal norms and structures as arising from moral indignation. Persons who act in this manner are termed "moral entrepreneurs," people who are sufficiently outraged that they will take positive action to insure passage of a law or support others who take such action.[6]

2. ***A High Value on Order***   Persons wish to control the contingencies of life and to make society as orderly as possible. Sometimes this is possible only through legislation, as in regulating traffic flow. It would be chaotic were there no traffic signals, rules of the road, or speed laws; the law insures this uniformity.

3. ***Response to Threat***   This source may come either from the individual or from the group level; it involves the use of law as a tool of social engineering to back up other, informal, social controls in the face of some threat, either real or imagined. Certain acts may be regarded as more damaging than others to the social order, and this may necessitate the implementation of legal procedures. Drug abuse may be seen as being both morally incorrect and socially and physically harmful both to the user and to others; in this case, then, it would appear certain that it would be outlawed.

4. ***Political Tactics***   A final source of legalization may be termed political in that here the law is used for the benefit of some groups to the exclusion of others. This source is perhaps best identified with the conflict perspective to be discussed shortly (also see Chapter 3); here the law is viewed as a tool to be manipulated by powerful groups for their own benefits in situations where their needs best fit into the legal structure.

Legalization or origin of law can also be viewed through two quite broad, and different, perspectives, the *functionalist* and the *conflict* approaches.[7] The functionalist perspective is best illustrated in Durkheim's traditional view of crime and law.[8] (1) The

---

[5]Austin T. Turk, *Legal Sanctioning and Social Control* (Rockville, Md.: National Institute of Mental Health, 1972). Also see Andrew Hopkins, "On the Sociology of the Criminal Law," *Social Problems,* 22 (1975), 608–619.

[6]See, for example, Howard S. Becker, *Outsiders: Studies in the Sociology of Deviance,* enlarged ed. (New York: Free Press, 1973); and Anthony Platt, *The Child Savers,* 2d ed. (Chicago: University of Chicago Press, 1976). For contrary evidence, see Martin Looney, "Social Control in Cuba," in Ian Taylor and Laurie Taylor, eds., *Politics and Deviance* (Baltimore: Penguin Books, 1973), pp. 42–60; and Edwin M. Lemert, "Beyond Mead: The Societal Reaction to Deviance." *Social Problems.* 21 (1974). 457–468.

[7]The account given here draws heavily from William J. Chambliss, "Functional and Conflict Theories of Crime: The Heritage of Emile Durkheim and Karl Marx," in William J. Chambliss and Milton Mankoff, eds., *Whose Law? Whose Order? A Conflict Approach to Criminology* (New York: Wiley, 1976), pp. 1–28. See also John Horton, "Order and Conflict Theories of Social Problems as Competing Ideologies," *American Journal of Sociology,* 71 (1966), 701–713.

[8]Emile Durkheim, *Division of Labor in Society* (New York: Free Press, 1938). A slightly divergent discussion of legal systems and social conditions that draws on Durkheim, and others, can be found in Roberto Mangabeira Unger, *Law in Modern Society: Toward a Criticism of Social Theory* (New York: Free Press, 1976).

law represents a value consensus of society; laws are the natural evolution of agreed-upon norms and values of the social group as is found in the collective conscience of the group. (2) The law represents, moreover, the norms and values considered essential to the continuing social order; it is in the public's interest to protect these values through the law. (3) The state, as represented in the legal system, is value-neutral and impartial, and in pluralistic societies, it merely arbitrates conflict between competing groups and interests.

The conflict view (see Chapter 3) states, on the contrary, that law represents only certain powerful segments of the community, not the community as a whole. Marx was a strong advocate of this view. (1) Crime becomes centered in the lower classes because the laws made by the rulers of society define as criminal many actions of the lower class. (2) The ruling class not only controls the law-defining machinery of the state but it also maintains its control over the law-enforcement, or the criminal justice, system. (3) The disproportionate penalties for burglary versus the penalties for many forms of white-collar and corporate crime reflect the ability of the upper classes to institute less severe penalties for any criminal actions they might commit and also to enforce the penalties more severely against the lower class through the official social control system. (4) When one's interests are made part of the criminal law, they are legitimized and come to have greater authority. In this way the ruling class not only makes the law but is also able to control its enforcement.

The long sentences given to the members of the lower class, who commit most of the violent personal and conventional property crimes, reflect the power of certain segments of society to shape the image of crime and the severity of penalties. To the mass media, largely, these are the "crimes" and these are the "criminals." Occupational and corporate offenders are rarely prosecuted criminally and even less frequently imprisoned. The losses to the public of *one* crime of illegal price fixing and price rigging in violation of the U.S. antitrust laws committed by 29 leading electrical companies in 1961 involved hundreds of millions of dollars, a loss far greater than the money taken in *all* burglaries in the country during that year. Yet for this crime seven executives at the policy-making level were sentenced to only 30 days in jail; 24 others received suspended sentences.[9] Despite violations of the price and rationing regulations by businessmen during World War II, only a few were criminally prosecuted, and where there were prosecutions, penalties were slight and few went to prison.[10]

A large proportion of white-collar and occupational offenses are dealt with by administrative sanctions that sometimes involve only a promise to change the practices. The differential implementation of the law toward corporations has been attributed to the status of business persons and to their influence on the legislature and the courts and to the relatively unorganized resentment of the public against these largely invisible and nonviolent crimes.[11]

---

[9]Gilbert Geis, "The Heavy Electrical Equipment Antitrust Cases of 1961," in Gilbert Geis and Robert F. Meier, eds., *White-Collar Crime: Offenses in Business, Politics and the Professions* (New York: Free Press, 1977), pp. 117–132.

[10]Marshall B. Clinard, *The Black Market: A Study of White Collar Crime* (New York: Holt, Rinehart and Winston, 1952).

[11]Edwin H. Sutherland, *White Collar Crime* (New York: Dryden Press, 1949), pp. 46–51. Also see M. David Ermann and Richard J. Lundman, eds., *Corporate and Governmental Deviance: Problems of Organizational Behavior in Contemporary Society* (New York: Oxford University Press, 1978).

The functionalist and the conflict views, then, represent disagreement concerning the origin and nature of the criminal law and the purpose to which the law is to be put. The most widespread difference concerns whether the law should be viewed as "law in action" in response to conflict and if it is beneficial to the whole society, or only to those segments that control the legal apparatus.[12] It is clear, however, that not all persons have equality before the law; some are more privileged than others and are better able to use the law to their own advantage.

Deterrence and the Law

Beccaria's conceptual framework of crime and punishment, the "pleasure" of the rewards of crime versus the "pain" of punishment, forms the basis of what is now known as the "deterrence doctrine."[13] The law should formulate "fair" punishments; that is, punishments that are proportionate to the seriousness of the offense, and known to all beforehand. The penalties should also outweigh the benefits of the crime, or the gain to be derived from the criminal act.

Most persons subscribe in principle to the idea of deterrence, if only because it is reinforced in their everyday living. Children, for example, do not often deliberately disobey their parents in front of them because this increases the chances they will be punished for their actions. The great majority of individuals pay income taxes not out of a deeply felt conviction but because of the financial and other penalties that would be incurred if they failed to pay them. Many persons adhere to the speed limit because they fear getting a ticket for speeding.

Some persons liken the deterrence doctrine to most economic situations: "If the price of gasoline rises from $.40 to $.70 a gallon, and all other factors remain more or less the same, we expect people to buy less gasoline. This is the law of supply and demand."[14] Similarly, if penalties, or costs, are increased for certain acts, it is assumed that the probabilities are decreased that they will be committed. This is the core of the deterrence doctrine. This does not mean that no one will buy gasoline or commit crimes; it means rather that there will be a change in the rate in that particular behavior due to the increased costs involved. The traveling salesperson will be willing to pay the extra money; so too will the professional thief be willing to risk the penalty for thievery (the individual knew, after all, that thievery was risky but still decided to pursue that line of work).

Punishment can be examined from two points of view. First, it deters others from committing offenses (termed *general deterrence*); and second, it deters the person from repeating the offense once he has been punished (termed *specific deterrence*). In Beccaria's classic discussion of the deterrence doctrine, he specified that legal threats would serve as deterrents according to the operation of three variables: (1) the severity

---

[12]One recent example of this dispute can be found in Austin T. Turk, "Law as a Weapon in Social Conflict," *Social Problems,* 23 (1976), 276–291.

[13]The term "deterrence doctrine" is from Jack P. Gibbs, *Crime, Punishment and Deterrence* (New York: Elsevier, 1975). Also see Johannes Andenaes, "General Prevention: Illusion or Reality?" *Journal of Criminal Law, Criminology and Police Science,* 43 (1952), 176–198; and Charles R. Tittle, "Crime Rates and Legal Sanctions," *Social Problems,* 16 (1969), 409–423.

[14]Lawrence M. Friedman, *Law and Society: An Introduction* (Englewood Cliffs, N.J.: Prentice-Hall, 1977), p. 119.

of the punishment; (2) the certainty that it would be applied; and (3) the celerity, or speed, with which it would be applied. To maximize the deterrent effect, then, the punishment should be severe, certain, and swiftly administered. Research generally supports the view that certainty of punishment is more important than severity for achieving deterrence (the celerity of punishment, while highly thought of, has not been the object of empirical test). Legal threats appear to depend on certain characteristics of the potential offender, such as the individual's value system and prior socialization experiences, aspects of the to-be-committed crime, the nature of the situation, and the presence of other social controls regulating the behavior in question.[15]

Differential Effect   Punishment may work best with those individuals who are "future oriented" and who are thus worried about the effect of punishment on their future plans and their social status rather than being concerned largely with the present and having little or no concern about their status. For this reason gang boys may be deterred by punishment less strongly than the white-collar professional person. A study of delinquency among all boys born in 1945 in Philadelphia and living there from the tenth to the eighteenth year of their lives showed that of 9,945 boys, 3,475 had at least one police contact.[16] Among the important conclusions was that repeated punishment may be ineffectual and that it may actually lead to more serious crimes for certain of the boys. Punishment also depends on the individual's perception of the chances of being apprehended. It probably has more effect on those who take a more pessimistic rather than an optimistic view about such chances. Finally, the degree to which early socialization to general law obedience takes place is related to deterrence; the "square" may try to obey all laws.

Striking differences are found in the effect of legal threats leading to deterrence when one examines types of criminal behavior. Crimes such as violent personal and collective violence, where there is an emotional element and considerable interaction with the victim, appear to be less deterred by punishment than are other types. Other social controls may be more effective than legal threats. Offenses committed by broad segments of the population and not *mala in se,* such as traffic offenses, are not as deterred by punishment.[17] Where there is a strong motivational element, such as professional shoplifting or mugging by a drug addict to secure funds to support the drug habit, or in the case of political crime, the possibility of deterrence is lessened. Since most ordinary property crimes are committed by youth, status within the peer group may be more important than the legal threats regulating these crimes. On the

---

[15]Summaries of the research literature can be found in Franklin E. Zimring and Gordon Hawkins, *Deterrence: The Legal Threat in Crime Control* (Chicago: University of Chicago Press, 1973); Charles R. Tittle and Charles H. Logan, "Deviance and Sanctions: Evidence and Remaining Questions," *Law and Society Review,* 7 (1973), 371–392; William J. Chambliss, "Types of Deviance and the Effectiveness of Legal Sanctions," *Wisconsin Law Review,* (1967), 25–35; Johannes Andenaes, *Punishment and Deterrence* (Ann Arbor: University of Michigan Press, 1974); and Andenaes, "General Prevention Revisited: Research and Policy Implications," *Journal of Criminal Law and Criminology,* 66 (1975), 338–365.

[16]Marvin E. Wolfgang, Robert M. Figlio, and Thorsten Sellin, *Delinquency in a Birth Cohort* (Chicago: University of Chicago Press, 1972).

[17]See Wolf Middendorff, *The Effectiveness of Punishment* (South Hackensack, N.J.: Fred B. Rothman, 1968).

other hand, professional and organized offenders may be more affected by severe penalties, provided that they are actually apprehended and, if apprehended, not "fixed." All of this suggests that deterrence is not merely an all-or-none process but depends on features of the offender, the offense, and the situation.

For these reasons, research has uncovered differences in the extent of deterrence with respect to marijuana use and theft, as two separate offenses.[18] Moreover, younger persons seem less deterred from crimes than older, more established professional persons.[19] Justifying the criminal law in terms of its deterrent effectiveness, however, does not mean that all offenders must be deterred, only some (unspecified) number of them. To many persons, even if a small percentage of crimes is deterred, this is sufficient to employ the criminal law as a deterrent.

If the threat of punishment is to be an effective deterrent, it must be communicated to the audiences affected by the mass media and other means. They must know that the behavior is prohibited, that the chances of apprehension are great (perhaps, even if they are not), and that the penalties they will receive for violation of the law outweigh possible gains from the crime. The evidence available at present indicates that much of the public and even the affected audiences (potential offenders) are poorly informed about such matters. Surveys in California and Nebraska, for example, have shown that people do not know much about minimum and maximum penalties, and that, in general, most people do not know that the penalty for a crime has been increased.[20] Rather than knowing the specific penalty for a crime, however, it may be more important that persons know only that they will be punished, either in the form of public ridicule or imprisonment.

The prison sentences imposed in the United States are longer than those of any other country in the world. One view is that penalties for crimes should be increased if current penalties are not working; if doubling penalties does not work, then tripling them should do even better. In Illinois, for example, there are sentences of 199 years; a judge in Texas in 1972 gave a young offender a 2,500-year sentence. The evidence does not support the effectiveness of long sentences, though, of course, the particular person so sentenced will be prevented from committing any more crimes while in prison. A few years ago, after an especially brutal rape case involving an old woman and a child, Pennsylvania increased the penalty for forcible rape without injury from 15 to 20 years and added a new category of life imprisonment for those convicted of rape involving bodily injury. A study showed no effect on the rape rate, either in frequency or intensity.[21] It is possible, however, that increases in the certainty that the

---

[18]Gordon P. Waldo and Theodore G. Chircos, "Perceived Penal Sanction and Self-Reported Criminality: A Neglected Approach to Deterrence Research," *Social Problems* 19 (1972), 522–540.

[19]See Harold G. Grasmick and Herman Milligan, Jr., "Deterrence Theory Applied to Socioeconomic/Demographic Correlates of Crime," *Social Science Quarterly,* 57 (1976), 608–617; Wayne E. Hensley, "Probability, Personality, Age and Risk Taking," *Journal of Psychology,* 95 (1977), 139–145; and Gilbert Geis, "Deterring Corporate Crime," in Ralph Nader and Mark J. Green, eds., *Corporate Power in America* (New York: Grossman, 1973), pp. 182–197.

[20]See *Public Knowledge of Criminal Penalties: A Research Report* (Sacramento: State of California Assembly Research Office, 1968); and a poll conducted for the Center for Studies in Criminal Justice at the University of Chicago, reported in Franklin E. Zimring, *Perspectives on Deterrence* (Washington, D.C.: National Institute of Mental Health, 1971), p. 57.

[21]Barry Schwartz, "The Effect in Philadelphia of Pennsylvania's Increased Penalties for Rape and Attempted Rape," *Journal of Criminal Law, Criminology and Police Science,* 59 (1968), 509–516.

older penalty would be applied would have yielded more deterrence than simply increasing the penalty and leaving the level of certainty unchanged.

Informal Context   The context of deterrent threats is perhaps the most misunderstood component of the deterrence doctrine.[22] Legal threats of punishment do not exist in isolation; they represent only one mechanism of social control that regulates behavior. A multiplicity of controls affect the behavior of most persons at any given time. Probably most persons do not refrain from committing crimes because they have been deterred by the criminal law, but because of informal controls and other reasons. Most persons refrain from homicide not because they fear being apprehended and imprisoned, or even put to death, but because of the strong moral and personal inhibitions about killing another human being. A teenager may refrain from committing a burglary not because of fear of subsequent involvement with the police, but because his family would think less of him, whether or not he was apprehended. Those persons who do not use marijuana or other drugs may not refrain because of legal threats but because of moral reasons, unknown health hazards, or the lack of knowledge of where to get it or how to use it.

It is in this context, then, that the impact of legal threats of punishment must be evaluated. Unfortunately, this context of a number of other social controls makes research on the subject even more difficult. How does one know, when an act of conformity is observed, whether this act was because the person was deterred or because of the other controls regulating the behavior? Given this context for legal threats, however, it may well be that whatever changes are made in the level of legal threat (for example, increasing the certainty of punishment for crimes through more vigorous police action and better detection techniques) will not substantially affect crime rates. The informal sanctions regulating behavior may be essentially more important than are legal threats, and increasing the legal threats does not add appreciably to the control already present.

Capital Punishment   The death penalty is one of the most obvious, controversial, and emotional issues in the use of deterrence because it is the most severe form of punishment. In 1972, the U.S. Supreme Court stopped all executions on the grounds that the death penalty was not uniformly administered, its use was a matter of choice, even prejudice, and very few persons were being executed (some years only one person was executed and at other times none in the entire country). Largely because the majority of the public believes that capital punishment does indeed deter, and has shown great concern about violent crime, over 30 states since 1972 have rewritten their criminal laws to make more specific the use of capital punishment, as well as to restrict it to certain offenses. The laws excluded most murders, since they involve the killing of a relative or acquaintance in anger. In general, the laws were rewritten to include such specific offenses as multiple killings; killing in connection with a robbery, rape, kidnapping, or holding a hostage; murder for hire; killing a police officer or prison guard; and treason. The Supreme Court in 1976 affirmed the validity of most such

---

[22]Robert F. Meier and Weldon T. Johnson, "Deterrence as Social Control: Legal and Extralegal Factors in the Production of Conformity," *American Sociological Review,* 42 (1977), 292–304.

laws, and the first execution in the United States in 10 years was carried out in Utah in 1977. At the beginning of 1977, over 400 persons were awaiting execution.

Supporters of capital punishment maintain that it is a deterrent to others and that it protects society; moreover, it removes the possibility of the offender's repeating the act, constitutes retribution for society and the victim's family, and serves to protect police officers and prison guards. However, the arguments against the death penalty are many, and the issue of deterrence is only one of the arguments.[23] Its abolition in a number of states resulted in no consistent reaction; sometimes there was an increase in the number of murders, sometimes not. No significant differences were found between states with and without it. The evidence indicates, moreover, that juries are less willing to convict a person when the penalty is death. If an injustice has been done, it can never be remedied; and where the taking of human life is contrary to most religious and social beliefs, executions have a debasing effect on society. The death penalty is more likely to affect the poor and minority group members, and it is cruel and inhuman punishment, particularly in the long waiting period before execution takes place. It is not in line with the contemporary view that emphasizes the possibility of change in offenders.

As of 1978, more than 10 states still did not have the death penalty, and four states, including New York, had it on a very restricted basis, usually only for murder of a police officer or by a person serving a life sentence. Four states abolished the death penalty long ago and have not restored it as of 1978: Michigan (1847), Wisconsin (1853), Maine (1887), and Minnesota (1911). As of 1978, all western European countries, with the exception of France and Spain, and Canada had abolished the death penalty. France has seldom used it in recent years, and it appears likely that as Spain becomes increasingly democratized, it will eventually abolish it.

The question actually faced here, however, is not whether the death penalty does deter, but whether it deters *more* than does life imprisonment, the most commonly used penalty. Most persons, in other words, wish to know whether or not capital punishment creates more deterrence than the penalty that would be used if there were no such penalty available. Not surprisingly, varied and confusing answers have been given. In 1975 Isaac Erhlich published an article purporting to show that each execution in the United States between 1933 and 1967 had deterred about eight potential murderers.[24] Other research, however, has seriously questioned the claim that the death penalty is more of a deterrent than life imprisonment.[25]

Deterrence and White-Collar Crime   An important issue is how effectively the law deters white-collar and corporate criminality. Occupational and corporate offenders are rarely criminally prosecuted and even more rarely imprisoned. A large proportion of these

---

[23]See the summary of evidence in Edwin H. Sutherland and Donald R. Cressey, *Criminology,* 10th ed. (Philadelphia: Lippincott, 1978); and Sue Titus Reid, *Crime and Criminology* (Hinsdale, Ill,: Dryden Press, 1976), pp. 473–492. Also see Isaac Ehrlich, "Capital Punishment and Deterrence: Some Further Thoughts and Additional Evidence," *Journal of Political Economy,* 85 (1977), 741–788.

[24]Isaac Ehrlich, "The Deterrent Effect of Capital Punishment: A Question of Life and Death," *American Economic Review,* 65 (1975), 394–417.

[25]William J. Bowers and Glenn L. Pierce, "The Illusion of Deterrence in Ehrlich's Research on Capital Punishment," *Yale Law Journal,* 85 (1975), 187–208.

offenders are handled through administrative and civil sanctions. The differential implementation of the law toward corporations has been attributed to the status of persons in business and to their influence on the legislature and the courts, the trend away from punishment in many newer types of *mala prohibita* crimes, and to the relatively unorganized resentment of the public against largely invisible and nonviolent crimes.[26] Detecting and proving crimes of this type present complex problems, far more complex than those involving most ordinary crimes. It is necessary that government prosecuting agencies expend tremendous resources and time in their investigation and prosecution of some white-collar offenders.[27] Moreover, since corporations cannot be sent to prison, the most severe punishment is a fine and the prosecution of certain management officials. A task force report by the President's crime commission of the 1960s pointed out that "Careful scrutiny of a huge mass of data for weeks or months may be necessary to produce the required evidence of criminality. A complicated security fraud investigation, for example, may involve several years of investigation by a team of law enforcement personnel."[28]

It is ironic that the penalties for white-collar crime are the least severe, while they are given to the very persons who might be the most affected by them or who might "benefit" the most from them. In other words, if these offenders are potentially the most deterred, an increase in punishments and the intensity of enforcement might result in the greatest benefit to society.[29] The very complexities of many of the laws, however, effectively result in the maintenance of the status quo. Not only should the structure of the laws be simplified, but the law-enforcement apparatus will have to be improved if such benefits are to be seen.

THE POLICE

Police play a major role in the implementation of the law. In the United States, there are over 40,000 different governmental agencies with law-enforcement powers and approximately 600,000 public law-enforcement officers of various types, exclusive of government security guards and private police.[30] The cost of police law-enforcement services exceeds $2.5 billion a year. The establishment of organized, uniformed, and armed police as a response to problems of social control in modern societies has in turn created many problems: the maintenance of citizen civil rights, the development

---

[26]Sutherland; and Colin H. Goff and Charles E. Reasons, *Corporate Crime in Canada: A Critical Analysis of Anti-Combines Legislation* (Scarsborough, Ontario: Prentice-Hall, 1978). Also see John M. Johnson and Jack D. Douglas, eds., *Crime at the Top: Deviance in Business and the Professions* (Philadelphia: Lippincott, 1978).

[27]Some of the problems in combating white-collar crime are discussed in Stuart L. Hills, *Crime, Power and Morality: The Criminal Law Process in the United States* (Scranton, Pa.: Chandler, 1971), pp. 181–202. Also see Laura Shill Schrager and James F. Short, Jr., "Toward a Sociology of Organizational Crime," *Social Problems,* 25 (1978), 407–419

[28]*Task Force Report: Crime and its Impact—An Assessment,* President's Commission on Law Enforcement and Administration of Justice (Washington, D.C.: Government Printing Office, 1967), p. 106

[29]Geis, "Deterring Corporate Crime."

[30]See Michael J. Hindelang, Michael R. Gotfredson, Christofer S. Dunn, and Nicolette Parisi, *Sourcebook of Criminal Justice Statistics—1976* (Washington, D.C.: Department of Justice, 1977).

of efficient and impartial enforcement of the laws, the political neutralization of the police, and the organization and discipline of the police as servants of the public will.[31] In a sense the police serve as mediators between the community and the legal system; they are responsible for enforcing all criminal laws irrespective of whether citizens wish to be policed or not. Reiss has termed the police "the major emergency arm of the community in times of personal and public crisis."[32]

It has been estimated that the actual time spent dealing with crime itself constitutes less than 10–20 percent of the average police force time.[33] If one takes into account only the approximately six million arrests for the more serious conventional crimes, it roughly comes to about twelve arrests per year per policeman; if one takes into account arrests for all offenses except ordinary traffic violations, it probably is about 20–22. The rate for policemen assigned to specialized squads is, of course, much higher. Police actually have many duties of a noncriminal nature, and they have increased during the past 50 years as they have assumed more and more regulatory functions. One study showed that even on police radio calls no more than a third of the calls involved criminal matters that might result in an arrest, and only about 5 percent actually did.[34] They are expected to perform such varied functions as find lost children, missing persons, and straying pets; check on homes when families are out of the city; help disabled persons; give first aid; handle mentally ill persons; act as escorts at funerals and many other functions; help to settle family quarrels; and, of course, one of their largest duties, direct traffic. So many of their duties resemble those of social workers that some have even suggested that persons with this training might be hired as policemen.

Role Conflicts

Despite these manifold functions, the police have a role given to no other group: they have the authority to use coercive force if necessary to make an arrest, to keep the peace, and to maintain order. Bittner points out that it is this potential use of force that gives homogeneity to the diverse policing procedures and their more humanitarian activities.[35] Because of this ever-present authorized capacity to use force, the line of demarcation between "lawful" and "unlawful" use of force is slim. If a person, for example, will not go with an officer, the policeman has the legal right to use such means as will subdue the person.

The police in a democracy like the United States face a particularly difficult role

[31]David Bordua, "Police," *International Encyclopedia of the Social Sciences* (New York: Macmillan, 1968), Vol. 12, pp. 175–181. See also Peter K. Manning, "The Police: Mandate, Strategies and Appearances," in Jack D. Douglas, ed., *Crime and Justice in American Society* (Indianapolis: Bobbs Merrill, 1971), pp. 149–195.

[32]Albert J. Reiss, Jr., *The Police and the Public* (New Haven, Conn.: Yale University Press, 1971), p. 1.

[33]Some of the literature reporting "time studies" of the police is reported in Clarence Schrag, *Crime and Justice: American Style* (Rockville, Md.: National Institute of Mental Health, 1971), pp. 146–147.

[34]*Task Force Report: Science and Technology,* President's Commission on Law Enforcement and Administration of Justice (Washington, D.C.: Government Printing Office, 1967), p. 93.

[35]Egon Bittner, *The Functions of the Police in Modern Society* (Rockville, Md.: National Institute of Mental Health, 1970), p. 44. Another list of crime-solving tasks which often require the use of, or the potential for, force is found in Herman Goldstein, *Policing a Free Society* (Cambridge, Mass.: Ballinger, 1977), p. 61.

conflict: on the one hand, they must maintain law and order, often using force, and on the other, they must do so under the rules of law. In a democracy, the ideological conflict between the norms that govern the maintenance of order and the basic principle of accountability to the rule of law justify the many and varied demands on the police officer. "He may be expected to be rule enforcer, father, friend, social servant, moralist, streetfighter, marksman, and officer of the law."[36] More specifically, police officers often claim that in order to achieve law and order they must often use a degree of force not deemed proper by the courts, make illegal searches, use informers to arrest drug pushers and to recover stolen property, use illegal methods of entrapment to apprehend prostitutes, and also use illegal methods to obtain confessions. Skolnick has well summarized these contradictions:

> As functionaries charged with maintaining order, they are part of the bureaucracy. The ideology of democratic bureaucracy emphasizes initiative rather than disciplined adherence to rules and regulations. By contrast, the rule of law emphasizes the rights of individual citizens and constraints upon the initiative of legal officials. This tension between the operational consequences of ideas of order, efficiency, and initiative, on the one hand, and legality, on the other, constitutes the principal problem of police as a democratic legal organization.[37]

Discretion

Because of the very nature of their duties, great discretionary powers of law enforcement have been delegated to the police. In one sense, this discretion constitutes "justice without trial."[38] This discretionary power is evident whether a police officer is acting in conflict situations or in suppressing crime. His task is "to maintain order under circumstances such that the participants and the observer are likely to disagree as to what constitutes a reasonable and fair settlement and he is likely to be aware of hostility, alert to the possibility of violence, and uncertain that the authority symbolized by his badge and uniform will be sufficient for him to take control of the situation."[39]

In his role of suppressing crime, he is expected to use discretion to judge the likely future behavior of persons based on appearances and attitudes and to deal with persons he considers to be "suspicious" in terms of laws that "either say nothing about his authority to question and search short of making an arrest or give him ambiguous or controversial powers."[40]

A study of police discretion has shown that arrests are not often made for trivial offenses (for example, drunkenness) or for conduct considered to reflect the standards of a community (for example, marital fighting). Arrests are not made if the victim does

---

[36]Jerome H. Skolnick, *Justice without Trial: Law Enforcement in a Democratic Society,* 2d ed. (New York: Wiley, 1975), p. 17.
[37]Skolnick, p. 6.
[38]Skolnick, p. 6.
[39]James Q. Wilson, *Varieties of Police Behavior: The Management of Law and Order in Eight Communities* (New York: Atheneum, 1968), p. 278.
[40]Wilson, p. 278.

not or will not request prosecution, if the arrest would be inappropriate or ineffective (for example, homosexual behavior), if it would cause loss of public support for the police (for example, social gambling), or if it would cause harm either to the offender (an upper-class person) or to the victim (exhibitionism or statutory rape) that would outweigh the risk from inaction.[41] Moreover, there are also offenses that might be more serious for which the police will take no action if, in their immediate judgment, the circumstances do not permit or demand an arrest.[42]

Police discretion may lead to selective enforcement and thus be prone to abuse. Presumably decisions on whether or not to arrest are made on strictly legal grounds: a crime has been committed and the police have "probable cause" to make an arrest. A number of factors, however, govern or affect the decision: particular police depart-ment policies that govern the actions of line officers regarding specified offenses (for example, "crack-down" situations where officers are told to pay more serious atten-tion to drunk driving over holiday periods); the demeanor of the suspect; and the suspect's race and sex.[43] Abuses of police discretionary powers are directed, for the most part, at members of minority groups such as blacks, Chicanos, and Indians and also at the poor, slum dwellers, "hippies," addicts, radical activists, and prostitutes. These abuses involve particularly the making of arrests, violation of due process of law by false arrest or by unlawful search and seizure, systematic police harrassment, the framing of suspects, and brutality in making arrests ("summary punishments").[44] Such practices tend to undermine the legitimacy of the police in the eyes of those affected, since they sense the surveillance under which they are being kept.

This use of discretion is an inevitable element of policing. Various proposals have been made, however, to limit or to control its abuse. The most feasible proposal at present appears to be the use of administrative rules within police departments which would serve as guidelines for the officer in making arrest decisions.[45] This means formally recognizing that discretion does exist, which police officials have been reluctant to do because it implies that they are selectively enforcing the law and without legislative approval, and deciding in what manner it can best be handled. Other proposals have suggested the adoption by the police of a discretionary rule-making process; under this proposal, the rules would be developed by the police under a court mandate.[46] Whatever method ultimately is adopted, the problems connected with police discretion are likely to remain.

---

[41]Wayne R. LaFave, *Arrest: The Decision To Take a Suspect into Custody* (Boston: Little, Brown, 1965).

[42]See Kenneth Culp Davis, *Police Discretion* (Minneapolis, Minn.: West Publishing Company, 1975). Also see Goldstein, pp. 93–130.

[43]Many of the studies have been done with juveniles. See Davis; Nathan Goldman, *The Differential Selection of Juvenile Offenders for Court Appearance* (Hackensack, N.J.: National Council on Crime and Delinquency, 1963); Irving Piliavin and Scott Briar, "Police Encounters with Juveniles," *American Journal of Sociology,* 70 (1964), 206–214; Theodore N. Ferdinand and Elmer G. Luchterhand, "Inner-City Youth, the Police, the Juvenile Court and Justice," *Social Problems,* 17 (1970), 510–527; and Donald J. Black and Albert J. Reiss, Jr., "Police Control of Juveniles," *American Sociological Review,* 35 (1970), 63–77.

[44]See Paul Chevigny, *Police Power: Police Abuses in New York City* (New York: Random House, 1969).

[45]See Theodore K. Moran, "Judicial-Administrative Control of Police Discretion," *Journal of Police Science and Administration,* 4 (1976), 412–418.

[46]Kenneth Culp Davis, "An Approach to Legal Control of the Police," *Texas Law Review,* 52 (1974), 709.

The Use of Force

Traditionally, the police have used different methods in dealing with citizens from the "respectable" classes, including more polite manners. In dealing with members of the lower classes, white or black, their methods may be different, the most likely victim of excessive force being a lower-class man of either race.[47] The most common practice in dealing with such persons is abusive and profane language, as well as commands to go home or move on, stopping and questioning persons and searching them and their cars, threats of the use of force if their commands are not obeyed, prodding with a nightstick or even coming forward with a pistol, and the use of physical force or violence itself.[48]

Police use of force generates as much controversy as any aspect of policing. The police are the only agency authorized to use "necessary" force in the pursuit of their duties, and for good reason: offenders are often reluctant to submit passively to police authority on their own volition. Force must often be employed if they are going to carry out some of their function, but in many instances they overstep their authority and use force unnecessarily or indiscriminately. Police-citizen interactions, called encounters, may take place over many matters—inquiries about identification, explanation of a citizen's presence in a particular locale, interviewing witnesses of a crime, or responding to a citizen's call for help. During the course of an encounter a special set of norms arises to structure the interaction; these norms place both the police and the citizen into particular roles. Specifically, the citizen must show proper respect to the police because the police represent the "law."[49] When a citizen fails to show this deference, the implicit normative structure of the citizen-police encounter is violated, and the probability of an arrest and/or the use of force increases. In other words, citizens who are disrespectful or who otherwise show a contempt for the police are more likely to be arrested or to become victims of police violence.[50]

An overt display of disrespect cannot go unchallenged, because the authority of the police is at stake. This helps to explain the higher rates of police violence among certain groups of victims, such as minority group members and lower-class persons regardless of race. These groups are more reluctant to display proper deference to the police, particularly those members of minority groups who have had a long history of interaction with the police which has often been interpreted as harassment. Youths are particularly prone to violate the deference norm.[51]

The Police and Society

While the police are presumably politically neutral, they have always responded to considerations of political and social power. Organized police forces originally devel-

---

[47]Albert J. Reiss, Jr., "Police Brutality—Answers to Key Questions," in Michael Lipsky, ed., *Law and Order Police Encounters* (Chicago: Aldine, 1970), p. 77. Also see Reiss, *The Police and the Public*.

[48]Reiss, "Police Brutality," p. 59.

[49]See Richard E. Sykes and John P. Clark, "A Theory of Deference Exchange in Police-Citizen Encounters," *American Journal of Sociology*, 81 (1975), 584–600.

[50]Reiss, "Police Brutality," pp. 59–77. See also Hans Toch, *Police, Prisons, and the Problem of Violence* (Rockville, Md.: National Institute of Mental Health, 1977), pp. 12–33.

[51]See Piliavin and Briar. Also see Theodore L. Becker and Vernon G. Murray, eds., *Government Lawlessness in America* (New York: Oxford University Press, 1971), pp. 1–93.

oped, in fact, out of political conditions that enabled certain classes in society to create specialized forces to protect their property and their lives.[52] Since the law, by definition, is the result of a political process that is dominated by the most powerful interests in any society, the police are servants of the same interests. Police activities against persons on strike, on the supposition that private property must be protected from violence and damage, are only one example of the political nature of the police. In several large cities, for example, Philadelphia and Minneapolis, the political power of the police and the support they have been able to enlist have resulted in the election of police personnel to the office of mayor.[53]

The police depend upon the public for the effective performance of their crime control duties, but there is ambivalence about how effective they should be. Skolnick observes that while no reasonable person wants a "flaccid, inefficient, or untrained" police force, at the same time there is increasing reliance upon the police for social stability, and this "constitutes a pretty good indication of the weakness of bonds of social community." As a society we want both to "improve the police while minimizing their significance as a social institution."[54] The police do deal with the practical problems of order and social control in everyday events, solving crimes, pursuing offenders, regulating traffic, and so on, but they also control by their mere "presence." Their most significant product has been termed "symbolic: their distinctive uniforms, their displays of police presence in public crowd situations, at important crimes (what is called 'showing the flag' by the English police); their almost random encounters with the everyday world of the citizen, all ritualize and create in everyday life the appearance of a consensual, constraining moral order."[55]

While the police depend upon a certain degree of favorable public attitudes toward them, they can be made more accountable to the public in various ways. Much has already been accomplished by the courts. (1) The Supreme Court, for example, has handed down decisions guaranteeing legal representation to a suspect, and it has also outlawed forced confessions. (2) It has handed down decisions regulating interrogation and the admissibility of evidence, though these decisions are not always practiced by all police forces.[56] (3) Where minority groups have been successful in capturing political power at the local level, they have been able often to secure changes in police practices toward minorities and have opened police hiring practices to include minorities. Further changes have been made through (4) citizen review boards as well as the appointment of an "ombudsman" to hear citizen complaints. (5) Appointments of more civilians, such as lawyers, to high police posts are frequently

---

[52]See Sidney Harring, "The Development of the Police Institution in the United States," *Crime and Social Justice,* 5 (1976), 54–59. Also see Sidney Harring and Lorraine McMullin, "The Buffalo Police, 1872–1900: Labor Unrest, Political Power and the Creation of the Police Institution," *Crime and Social Justice,* 4(1975), 5–14; and Center for Research on Criminal Justice, *The Iron Fist and the Velvet Glove,* 2d ed. (Berkeley, Calif.: Center for Research on Criminal Justice, 1977).
[53]See Goldstein, p. 139.
[54]Skolnick, p. 273.
[55]Peter K. Manning, "Dramatic Aspects of Policing: Selected Propositions," *Sociology and Social Research,* 59 (1974), 26. See also Peter K. Manning, *Police Work: The Social Organization of Policing* (Cambridge, Mass.: MIT Press, 1977).
[56]See William J. Chambliss and Robert B. Seidman, *Law, Order and Power* (Reading, Mass.: Addison-Wesley, 1971), pp. 368–395.

made in some countries in Europe.[57] (6) As a guarantee against unwarranted police practices, it has been suggested that the police issue each citizen a receipt for any police-work contact, as is now done in part of New York City and in New Orleans.[58]

JAILS

Many persons begin their paths toward prison while they are incarcerated in lockups and jails, either awaiting hearing or a trial or serving a misdemeanor sentence. Many of these places are physically degrading, poorly managed, and devoid of any meaningful activity for their inmates. In 1972, the population at one time of 3,921 jails in the United States was 141,588 persons.[59] The estimated number of persons entering jails over a single year is far greater: in California alone the estimated number of jail bookings in 1967 was over a million, and total commitments in one year to the Illinois jails were about 169,000.[60] Few of these facilities provide comprehensive medical services, educational opportunities, or recreational outlets. In addition to these inadequacies, many inmates have not been convicted of a crime; they have been put in jail awaiting a judicial determination of their cases. One observer has remarked that our prisons "are used to incarcerate men convicted of serious crimes and our jails (while housing some convicted men) primarily hold people who are awaiting trial, who have been convicted of nothing; yet, our jails are far worse than our prisons."[61]

While prison populations are relatively homogeneous, made up mostly of lower-class persons with little education and few occupational skills, jail populations are usually more heterogeneous because of the more diverse functions of the jail in most communities. Often jails provide social welfare services by accommodating homeless drunks and vagrants, furnishing involuntary temporary lodging for transients, and providing a holding facility for other types of persons with behavior problems which may or may not be appropriate for continued confinement.[62] Jails may detain material witnesses for trial or mentally ill persons for whom alternative arrangements could not be made immediately. Juveniles may also be detained temporarily, as well as alcoholics and drug addicts, although there is a trend in the United States to use other facilities for these persons. Jails serve such a wide variety of persons and problems that it is difficult to devise a coherent program that would reasonably take into account this diversity.

Conditions in Jails

In a survey of the 3,319 U.S. jails at the county level or located in municipalities of 25,000 or more population, 86 percent were found to provide no facilities for exercise

---

[57]George E. Berkeley, *The Democratic Policeman* (Boston: Beacon Press, 1969).
[58]Reiss, *The Police and the Public,* pp. 203–207.
[59]Hindelang, Gottfredson, Dunn, and Parisi, pp. 230 and 237.
[60]Hans W. Mattick and Ronald P. Sweet, *Illinois Jails: Challenge and Opportunity for the 1970s* (Chicago: Center for Studies in Criminal Justice, the Law School, University of Chicago, 1969).
[61]Ronald Goldfarb, *Jails: The Ultimate Ghetto* (New York: Doubleday, 1976), p. 5.
[62]See Edith Flynn, "Jails and Criminal Justice," in Lloyd E. Ohlin, ed., *Prisoners in America* (Englewood Cliffs, N.J.: Prentice-Hall, 1973), pp. 55–57.

or recreation, 90 percent no educational facilities, only 50 percent medical facilities, and one in four no visiting facility.[63] Of the 100,000 cells in these jails, one in four had been in use longer than 50 years, and more than 5,000 cells are over 100 years old. Extracts from a 1969 Illinois jail survey, probably the best study that has been made, give some idea of the overall jail conditions to be found in most parts of the United States.[64]

> Jails are built to hold secure the most dangerous prisoner they are thought likely to hold, so archaic ideas about human nature are frozen into fortress-like plants or dungeons that last forever. The dilapidated physical condition of Illinois jails damns more jail administrators and damages more inmates than any other single fact about local conditions. [page D]

> Less than 10 percent of Illinois jails have the physical capacity to separate the four main classes of prisoners: males, females, adults and juveniles. If we add three more main classes of prisoners: unsentenced and sentenced, felons and misdemeanants, and first offenders and recidivists, all classes of which would be separated in a rational penal system, we see how limited Illinois jails are. Adding a violent drunk, a mentally disturbed person and an aggressive homosexual would make rational jail administration impossible for all but three jails in Illinois. [page D]

> In Illinois, 82 percent of all jails have an average of 45 square feet or less per bed, including the space occupied by the bed; 35 percent have 25 square feet or less. These are the dehumanizing conditions that nurture kangaroo courts, barn boss systems and occasional "mad dog" prisoners. An evaluation of sanitary facilities, i.e., toilets, wash basins and showers, on the basis of number and accessibility, indicates that 20 percent of the jails have inadequate toilets for adult males, 30 percent have inadequate wash basins and more than 80 percent have inadequate showers. If these facilities had also been evaluated on the basis of mechanical functionality, the ratings would have been much worse. [page D]

> More than half the jails do not require inmates to strip for security searches, hygienic purposes or medical examinations. Only four Illinois jails extend routine medical attention to all inmates, while 77 jails conduct no medical examinations during receiving procedures. [page E]

> The supervision of inmates varies enormously depending upon available man power, hour of day or night, and cell-locking policies. Considering the average cell sizes, entirely too much reliance is placed on simply locking prisoners in. If "active supervision" is defined as: direct observation of inmates by a member of the jail staff at least once every half hour, only 15 percent of all inmates receive such supervision during daytime hours. Nighttime supervision is much less frequent. [page E]

> Despite the demoralizing idleness of inmates, only five of 160 jails have any recreational facilities or programs that afford physical exercise. In 95 percent of all jails prisoners must depend on the availability of cards, board games, radio, T.V. or reading matter, the latter

---

[63]Mattick and Sweet. See also National Advisory Commission on Criminal Justice Standards and Goals, "Local Adult Institutions," and Law Enforcement Assistance Administration, "The Nation's Jails," both in Robert M. Carter, Daniel Glaser, and Leslie T. Wilkins, eds., *Correctional Institutions,* 2d ed. (Philadelphia: Lippincott, 1977), pp. 67–90 and 91–101.
[64]The following excerpts appear on the lettered pages as indicated, from Mattick and Sweet. Reprinted by permission of the publisher.

largely magazines or comic books. Only 25 percent of county jails permit all inmates access to radio and only three percent to T.V. From the standpoint of physical health and mental stimulation the jails of Illinois offer idleness and debilitation, immaturity and emptiness. [page J]

The overwhelming majority of the 3561 persons who work in Illinois jails are workers whose principal duties are outside the jails but happen to include the handling or servicing of prisoners or some aspect of jail administration. About 60 percent of these are law enforcement officers rather than correctional personnel. The law enforcement psychology of a policeman is to put offenders *into* jail; the rehabilitative psychology of a correctional worker should be to prepare an inmate to get *out* of jail as a law-abiding citizen. This psychological contradiction is worth pondering. Of the nearly 3000 custodial and supervisory personnel who have the primary responsibility for jails and inmates, few are trained for jail work. [page L]

In the 30 largest jails, only five claim civil service or merit systems of employment for all or some employees. Political patronage and personal friendship are the main sources of employment in these jails. [page M]

Such conditions could be changed by (1) making improvements in the physical conditions and in the programs of the jails.[65] (2) At the most, there should be direct state control and administration of all jails, and at the least, the state should set and properly enforce minimum jail standards. (3) Jail personnel should be trained correctional officers rather than simply law-enforcement officers. (4) Most of those under jail sentences could be on outside programs of work and education during the day, as is done in some states, particularly California and Wisconsin, the latter a state that under Huber laws has followed this procedure for over 60 years.[66] (5) Persons who are awaiting trial could be separated, for example, from convicted offenders. (6) Bail and release on personal recognizance could be more widely used. In fact, efforts are now being made in some places to eliminate the requirement for bail, which falls heavily on poor persons and results in their being disproportionately confined in jails. (7) Fines could be paid in installments instead of a term in jail ordered because of inability to pay a fine. (8) Financial restitution to the victim in place of a jail or prison sentence and in connection with probation might be more widely employed than it is. (9) Courts could dispose of cases more rapidly to avoid lengthy jail incarcerations. (10) Those who are acquitted should be indemnified for financial losses suffered as a result of detention, a procedure that has existed for a long time in European countries. (11) Finally, the decriminalization of many offenses, such as public drunkenness (since as much as half the jail population often consists of persons jailed for this offense), the possession of marijuana for personal use, prostitution, and many other public order offenses would greatly reduce the jail population (see pp. 326, 372, and 406–408).

PRISONS

Although many people think that prisons are the only way to treat serious law violators, prisons as they are known today are a relatively recent invention, being not even two centuries old. Serious offenders—thieves, burglars, and robbers—except for

---

[65]Law Enforcement Assistance Administration.
[66]See Alvin Rudoff and T. C. Esselstyn, "Evaluating Work Furlough: A Follow-up," *Federal Probation,* 37 (1973), 48–53.

those sent to the galleys, were formerly not imprisoned. Either they were executed or they were punished by being subjected to physical torture, branded, maimed, sent to the pillory, or transported to a penal colony, usually in another hemisphere.[67] Penal servitude in the galleys was widely used from about 1500 until early in the eighteenth century.

Near the end of the eighteenth century, the Quakers of Pennsylvania were responsible for a number of correctional reforms, including the establishment of the first prison in the United States, and probably in the world. Forerunners of these prisons were jails where criminals were kept awaiting other punishment, usually execution; special places of confinement for nobles and others who were not generally subjected to the harsh penalties for peasants; and work houses that had been first set up in England in 1556 for debtors, prostitutes, and other minor offenders. The Quakers had become appalled at the brutal methods used to punish ordinary criminals, particularly the death penalty, which was meted out for hundreds of crimes. Because of their efforts, the Pennsylvania legislature reduced the punishments for a number of offenses and began to institute imprisonment for many others. The Walnut Street Jail in Philadelphia, built in 1790, was used for these offenders, who served their sentences in solitary confinement.[68] Imprisonment has now become the chief means of dealing with convicted offenders. In the United States there are about 590 state and 40 federal correctional facilities; as of December 31, 1976, these institutions contained 283,145 prisoners.[69] The prison population at this time showed an increase of 12 percent over that of 1975 and represented an all-time high for inmates ever incarcerated in correctional institutions in this country. The inmate population has been rising since 1972, although some states have experienced a decline.[70]

Objectives of Imprisonment

Originally, the Quakers believed that meditation and religious training would bring about individual reformation, which was the real objective of imprisoning law violators, but today public attitudes are extremely confused and contradictory about the purpose of incarceration. Prisons seem to exist for widely divergent purposes— retribution, deterrence, incapacitation, and rehabilitation.[71] The most important func-

---

[67]Sellin claims that originally these types of punishments had been used for slaves who had disobeyed their masters and that they were then later extended to free men who broke the law. See Thorsten Sellin, *Slavery and the Penal System* (New York: Elsevier, 1976), especially pp. 70–71.

[68]For an account of early U.S. prisons, originally published in 1833, see Gustave de Beaumont and Alexis de Tocqueville, *On the Penitentiary System in the United States and Its Application in France* (Carbondale, Ill.: Southern Illinois University Press, 1964). For a discussion of the political and economic context of the development of the Walnut Street Jail, see Paul Takagi, "The Walnut Street Jail: A Penal Reform To Centralize the Powers of the State," *Federal Probation,* 39 (1975), 18–25.

[69]*Prisoners in State and Federal Institutions on December 31, 1976,* Advanced Report from the Department of Justice (Washington, D.C.: National Prisoner Statistics, 1977). Also see Vernon Fox, *Introduction to Corrections,* 2d ed. (Englewood Cliffs, N.J.: Prentice-Hall, 1977).

[70]*Prisoners in State and Federal Institutions on December 31, 1975* (Washington, D.C.: National Prisoner Statistics, 1977), p. 1. Those states that reported a decrease in population are Maine, Minnesota, South Dakota, and Mississippi, while some others reported about the same population as the year before. See *Prisoners in State and Federal Institutions on December 31, 1976.*

[71]This list does not exhaust the possibilities. Hawkins mentions others, including containment, control, punishment, restraint, and reintegration. See Gordon Hawkins, *The Prison: Policy and Practice* (Chicago: University of Chicago Press, 1976), p. 30.

tion of prisons, some persons believe, is to extract *retribution* for a crime—"an eye for an eye and a tooth for a tooth"—a principle based partly on the assumption that individuals are responsible for their actions and that punishment should be proportionate to the injury to society. Persons who hold this view regard the prison as the mechanism by which society is able to extract vengeance and "make right" the wrong done. Criminals are punished because they "deserve" to be punished, and the prison is the principle punishment mechanism. Criminals are persons who, at the very least, should not be rewarded when apprehended; because committing a crime is "wrong" and not valued, criminals should be punished for their acts.[72]

To other persons, the very existence of prisons *deters* some potential offenders from committing crimes they would otherwise commit. As our earlier discussion indicates, such a view distinguishes between general and specific deterrence, the former referring to the threat of prison directed toward the population as a whole, the latter referring to those who have experienced prison and refrain from crime because they do not wish to experience it again.

Still other persons regard prisons as methods of *incapacitation,* or getting offenders out of the way by confinement. An incapacitated offender cannot commit other crimes, at least during confinement. No accurate information is presently available on the extent to which prisons serve this function of incapacitation, although many people believe it is an important function.[73] Estimates of the reduction of crime as a result of incapacitation have ranged from 80 percent to under 10 percent. One recent study that examined the effect of imprisonment on a group of violent offenders found that a five-year mandatory sentence would have prevented no more than 4 percent of the violent crimes in the jurisdiction from which the offenders had come.[74] Maximizing the effect of prison incapacitation is, however, limited; most of the crimes in this country, both property and violent crimes, are committed by youth, and there has traditionally been a great reluctance on the part of the public, as well as the functionaries of the criminal justice system, to impose lengthy sentences on young persons, who constitute a very large proportion of offenders.

Persons who regard prisons as *rehabilitative* believe that they should be places where offenders are classified into various types and a program devised for their institutional treatment, after they have undergone thorough social and psychological studies carried out by specialists such as psychiatrists, psychologists, and sociologists, among others. A primary conflict has existed between the other objectives of imprisonment and "rehabilitation." We may know to some extent how to extract vengeance, to manipulate prison conditions to maximize whatever deterrence emanates from them, and to incapacitate individuals with a high degree of security: we know very little about how to "rehabilitate" in the sense of changing various norms, values,

---

[72]For a sophisticated account of retribution, see Graeme Newman, *The Punishment Response* (Philadelphia: Lippincott, 1978).

[73]See James Q. Wilson, *Thinking About Crime* (New York: Basic Books, 1975); and Ernest van den Haag, *Punishing Criminals: Concerning a Very Old and Painful Question* (New York: Basic Books, 1975).

[74]Stephen Van Dine, Simon Dinitz, and John Conrad, "The Incapacitation of the Dangerous Offender: A Statistical Experiment," *Journal of Research in Crime and Delinquency,* 39 (1977), 22–34. Also see Stephen Van Dine, John Conrad, and Simon Dinitz, *The Incapacitation of the Dangerous Offender: A Retrospective and Prospective Look* (Lexington, Mass.: Lexington Books, 1978).

attitudes, and group identification patterns, primarily because of the impact of the prison subcultures. While it is difficult, many persons do reconcile the prison both as a place for punishment and a place for rehabilitation. "In my view," writes one noted observer, "penal purposes are properly retributive and deterrent. To add reformative purposes to that mix—as a purpose of the sanction as distinct from a collateral aspiration—produces neither clemency nor justice. To add incapacitative purposes is likewise unjust."[75]

Disagreement is likely to persist on the proper objectives of the prison, though in recent years there has been much reflection on what the prison *is* able to do rather than on what one would *like* it to be able to do. Such assessments have tended to stress the punishment-like objectives of imprisonment and to de-emphasize the rehabilitative aspects. The trend seems to be one of recognizing what the prison is geared toward (punishment) and attempting to carry out that purpose in a just and equitable manner. Following this viewpoint, some of the suggested reforms would do away with indeterminant sentencing alternatives (one to ten, one to life) for judges which were available under a system in which offenders convicted of the same crime might serve different lengths of time. This discretion would be replaced with fixed sentences such as 10 years for robbery, according to legislative action. Another proposal is to do away with parole so that each person serves the same time minus good behavior time in prison. This, it is claimed, would insure more equitable and fair punishment and would eliminate the problems of the abuse of judicial discretion.[76]

Characteristics of Prison Life

The United States, and this is the case in most other countries, has a great variety of state and federal prisons, with differences in size, type, and programs.[77] Some prisons are maximum security institutions, others medium and minimum security; some are small, others have populations of thousands; some have well-developed training and educational programs, others have little more than a custodial environment. It is thus obviously difficult to generalize about prisons except in terms of the "average" prison, which, of course, does not exist. Prisons provide little or no freedom comparable to the civilian life to which nearly all prisoners return; the environment is a restricted and isolated one.[78] Few opportunities are given prisoners to make decisions. They cannot generally go where they wish, eat what and when they please, enjoy as many radio and television programs as they desire, or even take a shower at any time, let alone when they may need one. Although there is some work choice, it is limited; where an inmate is fortunate enough to have full-time employment, the pay is rarely more than 25 cents a day. Most prison inmates are marched everywhere; at night they are confined to their cells; and at all times at maximum security institutions guards with

---

[75]Norval Morris, *The Future of Imprisonment* (Chicago: University of Chicago Press, 1974), p. 58.
[76]See Andrew von Hirsch, *Doing Justice: The Choice of Punishments* (New York: Hill and Wang, 1976).
[77]For a discussion of the variety of prison systems, see Robert M. Carter, Richard A. McGee, and E. Kim Nelson, *Corrections in America* (Philadelphia: Lippincott, 1975), especially pp. 96–125.
[78]For what prison is like to those incarcerated, see interviews with prisoners on various aspects of prison life in Leonard J. Berry, *Prison* (New York: Grossman, 1972).

lethal weapons are stationed in gun towers. Furthermore, prisons are psychologically insecure places in which to live; they are, in fact, dangerous because violence is the inmate's constant companion. This violence is less likely to come from prison staff than from other inmates. In spite of recent increases in violent incidents, few inmates assault staff. "Individual custodial attacks on inmates are also—despite prison folklore—few. Overt violence in prison is mostly confined to inmate attacks on fellow inmates or upon themselves."[79] Whereas fist fights between inmates were formerly regarded as effective means for the inmates to "let off steam," the use of lethal weapons such as knives and other weapons by inmates has changed this; what might have resulted in a beating in the past is now likely to result in death from stabbing.[80]

Prison violence appears to be due largely to attitudes and values brought by inmates into the prison and to certain features of prison life. It has been found to be related to the proportion of inmates incarcerated for violent offenses, those detained for more than one year, and, to a lesser extent, the age of the perpetrator.[81] A number of sources in the social structure of the prison can be cited for prison violence. The inmate social system, for example, stresses a distinction between "we" and "they" due to inmate distrust of prison staff and to the wishes of inmates to handle their own problems. Central values in prisons, moreover, have long been superior strength and courage, qualities that serve as criteria for "maleness" and status within the walls.[82]

What particularly widens the social distance between prison officials and inmates are the endless prison rules which have been built up in the history of a prison. Some of these rules are probably necessary, but they often result from the incarceration of thousands of men under maximum security in larger prisons. There are many rules, however, which completely govern the inmate's behavior, prescribing such things as obedience, care of the cell, personal hygiene, talking, visiting, eating, going to chapel, and respect for officers. Most rules are so petty that they could not be generally enforced in a free society, in an industrial plant, or even in a military establishment. Guards may display unwarranted authority over inmates because of the vague nature of many rules and the wide latitude with which they may be interpreted. Infractions of rules are usually arbitrarily punished, with few rights for the prisoners in questioning witnesses, and they largely result in the withdrawal of certain privileges, additional prison time, and solitary confinement.

The artificiality and social isolation of prison life and the multiplicity of rules are great hindrances to any program that attempts to change criminal attitudes. As long as prisons in general do not allow more social contacts with the outside world it is unlikely that institutional treatment can achieve much in the way of attitude changes or satisfactory emotional adjustment. To change attitudes there must be opportunities to assimilate those of the conventional culture. Prison confinement allows only rare outside social contacts; visits from the outside are infrequent and rigidly supervised, the general practice being only once a month; letters are limited in number and censored; and even choices of reading materials, radio programs, and movies are

[79]Toch, p. 53.

[80]Robert Sommer, *The End of Imprisonment* (New York: Oxford University Press, 1976), p. 55.

[81]Desmond Ellis, Harold G. Grasmick, and Bernard Gilman, "Violence in a Prison: A Sociological Analysis," *American Journal of Sociology,* 80 (1974), 16–43.

[82]Albert K. Cohen, "Prison Violence: A Sociological Perspective," in Albert K. Cohen, George F. Cole, and Robert G. Bailey, eds., *Prison Violence* (Lexington, Mass.: Lexington Books, 1976), pp. 3–22.

often restricted. The one-sex nature of prison communities results in great mental suffering and excessive discussion of sex, and the impossibility of heterosexual intercourse encourages homosexual practices among many inmates. The difficulties connected with the sex problem in prison communities make it one of the most serious and demoralizing features of prison life.[83]

The Prison Social System

Every prison has its "prison subculture" involving a complex social system of inmates and officers. In the social structure of the prison, some inmates have higher status than others, some play certain social roles but not others, and some values are espoused but not others.[84] Thus all inmates do not participate equally in this prison subculture. Some inmates seek status primarily among those who make a career out of crime; others by participation in the formal prison system where they are considered "good prisoners."[85] The norms of the prison subculture generally exert a greater influence over the prisoners' actual behavior than the system of formally prescribed rules, and violations of these norms by inmates evoke sanctions ranging from ostracism to physical violence. Some of the *informal* rules are described in the following general maxims:

a. Don't interfere with the interests of inmates. Concretely, this means that inmates "never rat on a con," or betray each other. It also includes these directives: "Don't be nosey," "Don't put a guy on the spot," and "Keep off a man's back." There are no justifications for failing to comply with these rules.

b. Keep out of quarrels or feuds with fellow inmates. This is expressed in the directives, "Play it cool," "Do your own time."

c. Don't exploit other inmates. Concretely, this means, "Don't break your word," "Don't steal from the cons," "Don't welsh on debts," and "*Be right.*"

d. Don't weaken; withstand frustration or threat without complaint. This is expressed in such directives as, "Don't cop out" (cry guilty), "Don't suck around," "*Be tough,*" and "*Be a Man.*"

e. Don't give respect or prestige to the custodians or to the world for which they stand. Concretely, this is expressed by "Don't be a sucker," and "Be sharp."[86]

In addition to these informal rules of behavior, inmates share a prison argot that expresses their code or value systems. By means of this argot they communicate to one another stereotypes of prison officials and of the prison world. Guards are known as "hacks" or "screws" and are to be treated with distrust and suspicion. Inmates who

---

[83]See John H. Gagnon and William Simon, "The Social Meaning of Prison Homosexuality," in Carter, Glaser and Wilkins, pp. 227–237.

[84]See Donald Clemmer, *The Prison Community,* rev. ed. (New York: Holt, Rinehart and Winston, 1958); and Donald R. Cressey, "Adult Felons in Prison," in Lloyd E. Ohlin, ed., *Prisoners in America* (Englewood Cliffs, N.J.: Prentice-Hall, 1973), pp. 133–138.

[85]See Cressey, "Adult Felons in Prison"; Charles W. Thomas, "Toward a More Inclusive Model of the Inmate Contraculture," *Criminology,* 8 (1970), 251–262; and Charles W. Thomas and Samuel C. Foster, "Prisonization in the Inmate Contraculture," *Social Problems,* 20 (1972), 229–239.

[86]Gresham M. Sykes and Sheldon L. Messinger, "The Inmate Social System," in *Theoretical Studies in the Social Organization of the Prison* (New York: Social Science Research Council, 1960), pp. 6–8. See also Erving Goffman, "On the Characteristics of Total Institutions: The Inmate World," in Donald R. Cressey, ed., *The Prison: Studies in Institutional Organization and Change* (New York: Holt, Rinehart and Winston, 1961), pp. 15–67.

conform to the values of the prison officials (by accepting the ideal of hard work and of submission to authority) are labeled "suckers." In addition, there is great preoccupation with "rats" who "squeal" on another inmate to gain favors.[87] The "yard" serves as a place to talk about prison life, about crime, and about the vagaries of society. The inmate who tries to be part of the inmate subculture and at the same time tries to benefit from the professional and administrative staff generally finds himself playing contradictory social roles. The control of the inmate subculture, as one writer has described it, is in the hands of "politicians" and "right guys."[88]

Depending upon the type of institution, this informal prison system assigns appropriate roles and statuses to prisoners.[89] In general, a new prisoner is questioned by other prisoners as to his attitudes toward the prison system, and his performance as an inmate is later evaluated. The inmate social system also sets up expectations of mutual care and protection. This system of reciprocal relations, however, is not supported by those prisoners who wish to go along with official prison policies. The system is strong, but not invincible.

While there is no consensus, there are two explanations of the origin of the inmate subculture, which have been termed the "deprivation" model and the "importation" model.[90] According to the first model, on entering prison inmates are faced with a number of major social and psychological problems, including "deprivation or frustration in the areas of social acceptance, material possessions, heterosexual relations, personal autonomy, and personal security."[91] Cohesion in the inmate system is crucial, since "the greater the degree to which the society of captives moves in the direction of inmate solidarity . . . the greater is the likelihood that the pains of imprisonment will be rendered less severe for the inmate population as a whole."[92] The prison subculture has developed, then, as a response to the problems faced by all prison inmates. Given the nature and seriousness of the problems encountered, individualistic solutions are unlikely to succeed in alleviating these deprivations; rather, a system of inmate roles is created, each role having a corresponding status and function, to face the problems on a collective level. The elimination of heterosexual contacts gives rise to homosexual roles; the deprivation of material goods and services gives rise to inmate roles centered around the acquisition of these goods, either through theft or bartering with guards.

The "importation" model has been offered as an alternative explanation for the inmate subculture.[93] This approach views inmates as doing more than responding to

---

[87] See Gresham M. Sykes, *The Society of Captives* (Princeton, N.J.: Princeton University Press, 1958).
[88] Hans Reimer, "Socialization in the Prison Community," *Proceedings,* American Prison Association, New York, 1937, pp. 152–153.
[89] Peter G. Garabedian, "Social Roles and the Process of Socialization in the Prison Community," *Social Problems,* 11 (1963), 139–152.
[90] An excellent summary of these perspectives can be found in Charles W. Thomas and David M. Petersen, *Prison Organization and Inmate Subcultures* (Indianapolis: Bobbs Merrill, 1977).
[91] Sykes, p. 106.
[92] Sykes, p. 107.
[93] See John Irwin, *The Felon* (Englewood Cliffs, N.J.: Prentice-Hall, 1970); Charles Wellford, "Factors Associated with Adoption of the Inmate Code: A Study of Normative Socialization," *Journal of Criminal Law, Criminology and Police Science,* 58 (1967), 197–203; and Charles W. Thomas and Samuel C. Foster, "The Importation Model Perspective on Inmate Social Roles: An Empirical Test," *Sociological Quarterly,* 14 (1973), 226–234.

immediate, prison-specific, problems. Certain cultural elements are "imported" into the prison from the outside, from their lives prior to their becoming inmates. Prisoners bring with them a collection of values, norms, and attitudes which are important in determining the content of the inmate subculture. These factors include preprison experiences in the form of learning criminal attitudes, association with other criminals, and participation in a criminal or delinquent subculture. While the "importation" model may explain some facets of life in certain prisons, basically the "deprivation" model can be viewed as the chief explanation for a prison subculture.

Social Organization of Women's Prisons

Most of the research on prisons and their inmate systems has been carried out in men's prisons. A disproportionate number of inmates in women's prisons are sentenced for homicide, check forgery, shoplifting, and violations of narcotics laws; it is not as likely that female inmates have committed, and consequently are serving sentences for, robbery, burglary, or auto theft. Some women are less likely to be convicted, and they are more often given probation; there is usually a greater proportion of those from minority groups, and, as in men's prisons, few come from the middle and upper classes.

While there are many similarities to men's prisons, differences do exist in women's prisons.[94] Most states have different types of men's prisons, but there is generally only one prison for women. The entire federal system in the United States has only two women's prisons, for example, and as a result all types of federal offenders are confined there. The cottage system, typical of women's prisons, takes the place of cells, and while this gives the impression of being a more open institution, there is often greater security and constant checks. Programs in women's institutions emphasize the domestic arts such as housekeeping and secretarial work, on the assumption that most crime has grown out of the fact that the female offender has not sufficiently played the woman's role. Beginning in the 1970s, a number of "co-ed" prisons have been established. In most cases this has involved the transfer of a limited number of men to women's prisons, where they participate jointly in most activities but are kept sexually segregated. In Denmark, however, a co-ed prison arrangement has been established with adjoining cells and promiscuous sexual relations.

A woman's prison can be thought of as a microsociety made up of three main groups in addition to the prison staff.[95] The first group, the "squares," consists of those women who are largely from the "square" conventional society and who are experiencing their first prison term. These women have been committed, for the most part, for situational homicides or middle-class embezzlement; they regard themselves as respectable persons and prison as a place to which only criminals go. The second

---

[94]See David A. Ward and Gene G. Kassebaum, *Women's Prison* (Chicago: Aldine, 1965); Rose Giallombardo, *Society of Women: A Study of a Woman's Prison* (New York: Wiley, 1966); and Esther Heffernan, *Making It in Prison: The Square, the Cool and the Life* (New York: Wiley-Interscience, 1972). Also see Kathryn W. Burkhart, *Women in Prison* (New York: Doubleday, 1973), for a useful source of descriptive material on women's prisons.
[95]Heffernan.

group is made up of the "professionals," who have pride and who look upon their difficulties in, for example, professional shoplifting as an occupational hazard. They adopt a "cool" system which supports a maximum advantage of prison amenities without endangering their chances for parole or release. Habitual women criminals are the third group; they have been in and out of prisons from an early age. Prison life for them, with its "familial" and status aspects, furnishes a substitute for the rejected or rejecting larger society. In addition to these three groups, there is an emergent political prisoner group, in both men and women's prisons, which views such institutions as part of the oppressive nature of the larger society and which must be destroyed or reformed.

Women's prisons have inmate status systems comparable to those of men's prisons, and there is similar emphasis on the norms of the informal prison structure, "doing time," or "minding your own business." Interaction of the inmates with the prison staff or guards, work supervisors, professionals, and administrators is complex, as it is in men's prisons, but because of the smaller size, the personnel are almost constantly present. Women inmates appear to build more effective friendship and "family" relationships than do men, finding substitutes for various family roles.[96] Conjugal role-playing is common, overt homosexuality is relatively frequent. When violence occurs, it is usually in connection with conflicts in sexual roles.

Evaluations of Imprisonment

Contradictory elements are evident in the use of prisons as a means of dealing with crime in modern society. As a means of incapacitating persons for periods of time, and as places of punishment, prisons are successful. They are, however, extremely costly to the public whose tax dollars support them. They are also costly to the prisoner. It is in prison that many inmates become embittered human beings, filled with hatred for society. Inmates are exposed to a degrading environment, violence from other inmates, and homosexuality which characterizes all one-sex communities. Under these conditions it is difficult to "rehabilitate" an inmate; because of the very experience of having been imprisoned, society sets such individuals apart, eyeing them as former "dangerous convicts." Ex-convicts frequently find it difficult to face this stigma, which is reinforced through discriminatory employment practices based on a prison record. Because of these problems some ex-inmates undoubtedly return to criminal activities in spite of their best intentions to go "straight."

Persons incarcerated in prisons are not the only criminals in society, nor are they necessarily the worst. Only a small percentage of all crimes committed, for example, about 20 percent of the burglary cases, results in an arrest; a still smaller percentage is prosecuted, convicted, and imprisoned. Many who do go to prison are often persons who could not afford a good lawyer, who lacked sufficient influence on the prosecutor or judge, or who were members of a minority group, such as blacks, Native Americans, or Chicanos. Most imprisoned persons come from lower-class backgrounds;

---

[96]Heffernan, pp. 87–104.

persons from these classes commit the most crimes for which one is imprisoned, such as robbery, larceny, and auto theft. There are extensive violations of the law among the middle and upper classes, but few of these persons are sent to prison, reflecting the attitude of society that these persons are less dangerous.

It is difficult to assess the degree to which prisons achieve either general or specific deterrence. Using the proportion of prison admissions to crimes committed and the mean length of time served in prison as indicators of the certainty and severity of punishment, respectively, one study reported that punishment factors did have a negative relationship to the general crime rate.[97] With respect to specific deterrence, the evidence is even less conclusive, although when Glaser interviewed some 1,200 prisoners he reported that "the aspect of prison most often mentioned by inmates as of the greatest assistance in helping them 'go straight' was the unpleasantness of the confinement experience."[98]

Prisons may have a far less general deterrent effect, however, than has commonly been thought. The probability of incarceration for the commission of a crime is statistically low, perhaps as few as 2 percent of those arrested ending up in prison. The high-risk factor of being sent to prison is largely a myth reinforced by the media. The public thinks that this probability is high, however, and this fiction may be more important in the general deterrence process than any other factor.[99]

Measuring the outcome of prison confinement presents difficult conceptual and methodological problems. If, for example, a person released from prison does not commit another crime (that is, is not a recidivist), it may be that the person would not have committed another crime again under any circumstances, whether or not the individual had been sent to prison. In this case, the prison had no effect one way or the other. It might also be that the person is an example of specific deterrence; he did not commit another crime because he did not wish to experience prison and its deprivations again. Still a further reason might be that the person did not find the prison uncomfortable enough in terms of punishment, but was rehabilitated by a prison treatment program. The question is, of course, how can one tell which of these reasons is correct? Unfortunately, at the present time, it is practically impossible to know what processes actually occurred.

Similar problems are evident in assessing the "rehabilitative" function of prisons. There is no conclusive evidence that any method or mode of rehabilitation or treatment currently in use in prisons, either for juveniles or adults, is effective in producing changes in persons exposed to it that make them significantly different from those who have not been so exposed.[100] This is due chiefly to the fact that the inmate

---

[97]Charles H. Logan, "General Deterrent Effects of Imprisonment," *Social Forces,* 51 (1972), 64–73.

[98]Daniel Glaser, *The Effectiveness of a Prison and Parole System* (Indianapolis: Bobbs Merrill, 1964), p. 481.

[99]See Robert F. Meier, "The Deterrence Doctrine and Public Policy: A Response to Utilitarians," in James A. Cramer, ed., *Preventing Crime* (Beverly Hills, Calif.: Sage Publications, 1978), pp. 233–247.

[100]Gene Kassebaum, David A. Ward, and Daniel Wilner, *Prison Treatment and Parole Survival: An Empirical Assessment* (New York: Wiley, 1971); Paul Lerman, *Community Treatment and Social Control* (Chicago: University of Chicago Press, 1975); and Douglas Lipton, Robert Martinson, and Judith Wilks, *The Effectiveness of Correctional Treatment: A Survey of Treatment Evaluation Studies* (New York: Holt, Rinehart and Winston, 1975).

social system is largely antitreatment in orientation, its value system minimizing prison efforts to change prisoners. The stronger the inmate subculture and the more pervasive the norms that emphasize "doing your own time," and avoiding contacts with the prison staff that are meaningful in terms of rehabilitation, the less likely are treatment programs to be effective. In addition, the typical prison population consists largely of persons who have previously been failures in the criminal justice system and who have had longer contacts with criminal norms. The most comprehensive studies of the effectiveness of imprisonment were made of a representative sample of released inmates from U.S. federal prisons in 1960, one of the most highly regarded prison systems in the world.[101] Glaser found that one in three men (35 percent) could be classified as a "failure" in that he had been returned to prison for a new offense as a parole violator or was given a nonprison sentence for a felony-type offense. He suggested that where there had been reformation, it could not all be attributed necessarily to prisons but to changes in the prisoner's life situation, for example marriage, new friendship patterns, and employment outlook, factors that are often products of aging and other, nonprison, circumstances. Prisons cannot, however, be reasonably subjected to charges that they have completely failed in their crime control function.[102] They may not have much of an impact on the crime rate, but it is by no means clear that prisons always make matters worse in individual cases.[103]

Prisons are indeed undesirable places. They are meant to be just that; it would be an odd prison that could be considered an attractive environment. Traditionally the emphasis on making prisons unpleasant was deliberate: the offender had violated the law, and the appropriate response to the act was a punishment. In a system based on the idea that prisoners deserve punishment, the regime was constructed around the loss of individuality, freedom, and other deprivations, "an eminently reasonable response."[104] Even those institutions that have paid the greatest lip service to rehabilitation, with a wide variety of "treatment programs," remain places of punishment first, treatment second. The social structure of the prison permits no other arrangement.

Changing Prisons

The preceding discussion points to some of the changes which are needed if the prison is to be made both more humane and more effective within the limits that these goals are compatible and reasonable. Over the years a number of proposed changes have been adopted in various places, including work-release programs in which inmates work in paid employment or attend educational institutions during the day, diversified types of institutions, reductions in prison size to make the inmate populations more manageable and amenable to treatment, the employment of more minority group members on prison staffs, the upgrading of vocational and educational programs to

---

[101]Glaser, *The Effectiveness of a Prison and Parole System.* Also see Leslie T. Wilkins, *Evaluation of Penal Measures* (New York: Random House, 1969).

[102]See Charles R. Tittle, "Prisons and Rehabilitation: The Inevitability of Disfavor," *Social Problems,* 21 (1974), 385–395.

[103]A similar conclusion is reached by Gibbons with regard to juvenile institutions. See Don C. Gibbons, *Delinquent Behavior,* 2d ed. (Englewood Cliffs, N.J.: Prentice-Hall, 1976).

[104]David F. Greenberg, "Problems in Community Corrections," *Issues in Criminology,* 10 (1975), 29–30.

better prepare the inmates for release, and the maintenance of closer ties with the family and home community. Brief, periodic home furloughs would help in this aspect, as well as in the reduction of homosexual behavior in prison. Conjugal visits should be provided, where possible, for many prisoners and certainly for those ineligible for furloughs. Sweden and practically all Latin American countries allow conjugal visits; in the United States, Mississippi has long had it, and California has adopted it for certain prisoners.[105] In addition to these privileges, prisoners might also be allowed to make outside telephone calls, be permitted more freedom in style of personal dress, and in some cases given higher pay for prison work. One of the most famous European prisons, the Utrecht prison in the Netherlands for habitual older offenders, uses many techniques to bring the individual inmate into wider participation with the society. Prisoners, for example, are invited to have a Sunday and holiday dinner with the same family, and excellent results have been reported.

The work- and educational-release programs mentioned above offer great possibilities. This new type of approach, which has been adopted by many states and the federal prison system, combines an institutional program with a plan for the inmates to work for private concerns or go to high school, vocational school, or college during the day.[106] Sometimes inmates in these programs are transferred to halfway houses in a community, a plan to be discussed later. In prisons and jails the inmates associate only with other criminals, but in work-release programs they have opportunities to associate with noncriminals. These programs generally provide for payment of regular wages from which are deducted the costs of food and clothing, travel, contributions to the support of the person's dependents, and payment of obligations. Inmates in these programs work in a variety of occupations, primarily blue-collar jobs. Work release has multiple benefits, such as providing funds to support dependents, pay legitimate debts, and accumulate a release "nest egg." A large proportion of those on this type of program remain on the same job after they have completed their sentences. The main problem with such work- and educational-release programs is that offenders still associate only with inmates during evenings and on weekends. This means that the prison subcultural setting is still partially retained and the results so far have not been as encouraging as had originally been hoped.

The use of prison unions, begun in Sweden in the early 1970s, has been directed toward involving inmates in the prison decision-making process.[107] The Prisoner's Labor Union in Ohio, for example, has formulated a set of goals for its organization; objectives include obtaining the minimum wage for prison labor, obtaining Workmen's Compensation benefits, correcting dangerous working conditions, combating abuse within the prison, and establishing affiliation with outside unions. Generally, prison officials have not been receptive to the idea of organization by prisoners, for whatever purpose. The idea is also abhorrent to many segments of the public. A major problem with prisoners' unions is, first, that the inmate is one who, by virtue of having committed a crime and having been sent to prison as punishment,

---

[105]For an account of conjugal visits in Mexico, Latin America, and parts of the United States, see Norman S. Hayner, "Attitudes Toward Conjugal Visits for Prisoners," *Federal Probation,* 36 (1972), 43–50.
[106]*Graduated Release* (Rockville, Md.: National Institute of Mental Health, 1971).
[107]C. Ronald Huff, "Unionization behind the Walls," *Criminology,* 12 (1974), 175–194.

may not "qualify" for the benefits of those mechanisms such as unions which operate outside the walls. The prisoner-custodial staff relationship is not at all like that between employee and employer. Second, there is serious question as to whether the denial of the right to form a union is a denial of the civil rights of a prisoner because the primary need in a prison is to maintain order.[108]

ALTERNATIVES TO IMPRISONMENT

Increasingly, alternatives to imprisonment are being found; among them are "decarceration," probation, fines, restitution to the victim, community-based correctional facilities, diversion from the criminal justice system, and community service. These alternatives are available at the sentencing phase of the criminal process, and they provide the sentencing judge with a number of options better fitting the need for social control in relation to the serious or dangerous nature of the deviant act.

Decarceration

A major reform has been directed at the idea of "decarceration." This issue is regarded as the most radical innovation. In the extreme decarceration means the closing of prisons and the use of various alternatives for offenders. The trend toward decarceration has extended not only to prisons but to other social control institutions, including mental hospitals.[109] The rationale behind decarceration in these institutions is essentially a combination of humanitarianism and pragmatic results. It is increasingly seen as being more humane to deal with deviants in the community rather than to isolate them from society. Others have argued that it is the rising costs of institutional care, without accompanying documentable evidence of the success of correctional institutions, which has spearheaded the movement toward decarceration. Perhaps the best-known example of decarceration with respect to criminality was the Massachusetts experience. In 1969, this state began a series of reforms which ultimately led to the closing of its juvenile institutions in 1972, except for a small one near Boston. By 1975, 40 percent of the 1,912 youths being served by the Department of Youth Services were on traditional parole, and 56 percent were receiving other nonresidential services. Of all youth not on parole, 19 percent were in foster homes, 23 percent were in group-care situations, and 10 percent in secure-care settings.[110] A preliminary evaluation of this radical change in the method of handling offenders found no rise in

---

[108]See Barry M. Fox, "Criminal Law: The First Amendment Rights of Prisoners," *Journal of Criminal Law, Criminology and Police Science,* 63 (1972), 163–185. Also see *Jones v. North Carolina Prisoners' Labor Union, Inc.* (No. 75-1874), decided June 23, 1977.

[109]See Andrew T. Scull, *Decarceration: Community Treatment and the Deviant—A Radical View* (Englewood Cliffs, N.J.: Prentice-Hall, 1977).

[110]Lloyd E. Ohlin, Alden D. Miller, and Robert B. Coates, *Juvenile Correctional Reform in Massachusetts: A Preliminary Report of the Center for Criminal Justice of the Harvard Law School* (Washington, D.C.: Government Printing Office, 1976).

recidivism rates as a result of this change.[111] The Massachusetts experience seems to suggest that it is possible to have large numbers of youth in more open settings without increasing the danger to the community from recidivating youth.

Another example of decarceration is the probation-subsidy program instituted in California in the 1970s. It involved a subsidy program to reward counties with financial incentives for *not* committing youths to the California Youth Authority.[112] The financial savings to the state was probably the motivation to reduce commitments, but the official rationale was usually phrased in terms of providing better probation services to local communities. Based on the number of reduced commitments compared to some previous base-year rate, each county received a sum of money to be used to expand its probation services. The state thus saved the money it would otherwise have spent on costs for inmates by having less inmates, the counties received money for not committing youth to institutions and could better afford more and improved probation services, and offenders were more likely to receive some community sentencing alternative. The California probation-subsidy program, however, has not worked out the way its founders had intended. Rather than saving money, the program actually cost the state far more than anticipated. While each county was to receive $4,000 for each person *not* committed to a state facility (based on the cost to the state of keeping each person), the cost to the state actually increased to $6,000 or so while the program was operating. So, while there were indeed fewer commitments, those who were committed stayed longer, increasing the cost to the state beyond the $4,000 figure. The state ended up spending more money per inmate, largely as a result of inflation and the increased sentences, as well as paying money to the counties.

Community-Based Correctional Facilities

As prisons have come more and more under attack on the basis of their ineffectiveness, high cost, and removal from the inmates' communities, community-based correctional facilities have been increasingly established, as, for example, in the state of Massachusetts.[113] Under these programs inmates are sent to local facilities, known by such terms as halfway houses, residential treatment centers, probation hostels, and group foster homes. Generally they are small, and they are located in residential areas, as close as possible to where the offender lives and works or goes to school. Some inmates have been transferred from conventional correctional facilities; others have been committed directly to the new facility by the court; still others are operated by the state, some by local community workers. These centers usually have a resident social worker, and broad community services are provided. In these programs it is expected that the offender will have far greater contacts with persons with conventional norms

---

[111]Lloyd E. Ohlin, Robert B. Coates, and Alden D. Miller, "Radical Correctional Reform: A Case Study of the Massachusetts Youth Correctional System," *Harvard Educational Review,* 44 (1974), 74–111.
[112]Lerman, especially Chap. 8.
[113]National Advisory Commission on Criminal Justice Standards and Goals, "Corrections and the Community," in Carter, Glaser and Wilkins, pp. 394–411.

and that the local community will take responsibility for its own problems. Presumably individuals would not be stigmatized, as would be true if they were placed in regular prisons, and this would facilitate their readjustment upon release.

The correctional day care center is one example of a community-based correctional program. Offenders go daily to such a center for counseling and discussions with other offenders and staff members, while continuing to live at home, have a job, or go to school. These centers represent an alternative for probation failures or for offenders in need of more intensive care than probation allows and who would not benefit from incarceration. One well-known center has been the Provo (Utah) Experiment in which youth offenders continued to live at home but were required to meet each day in the late afternoon for a program of counseling and other activities.[114] The personnel was largely volunteer, group-counseling sessions were conducted, and public school teachers assisted in remedial reading and other educational programs.

The advantages claimed for community-based correctional facilities are many. (1) The local community is expected to become involved in these programs, thus giving the offender far greater contacts with noncriminal norms. (2) The individual would not be as stigmatized, presumably, as would be the case in a conventional institution. (3) Individuals who enter these centers on transfers from an institution would have an opportunity to become adjusted to a free society under some supervision and would also have an opportunity to acquire some savings prior to release. (4) The cost for the community-based center is much less than prisons. While some may claim that this type of program does not constitute punishment, persons suffer "punishment" under any circumstances when they are under the control of the law and their freedom is restricted, and they are subject to a certain amount of stigmatizing. Many of these programs, however, have not been as successful as might be anticipated, primarily because individuals with experience in crime are still associating with each other, if not during the entire day, at least during part of the day and at night.

Probation

It is generally agreed to be wiser, from the standpoint of efficiency, to concentrate on a wide and effective use of probation rather than to attempt to change offenders' attitudes within the artificial confines of jails or prisons. Probation is a judicial status which grants a convicted offender the privilege of remaining in the community, under court supervision and with certain restrictions, rather than being incarcerated, and to receive such counseling and assistance as might be required.[115] Effective probation can help to modify the group, neighborhood, or occupational factors involved in criminality. If it is to be effective, probation must be well supervised and administered by trained staffs. Programs are now being instituted, with encouraging results, in which non- or paraprofessionals are used to relieve the probation officers' workload. The rapid expansion in the use of nonprofessionals as agents of direct service has probably

---

[114]See LaMar T. Empey and Maynard L. Erickson, *The Provo Experiment: Impact and Death of an Innovation* (Lexington, Mass.: Lexington Books, 1972).

[115]See Howard Abadinsky, *Probation and Parole: Theory and Practice* (Englewood Cliffs, N.J.: Prentice-Hall, 1977).

been one of the most significant developments in the field of corrections in recent years. It has also been said to be the most realistic alternative for alleviating the manpower shortage in the field.[116]

Differences in total resources and in the quality of trained personnel have led states to use probation to a varied extent. Some states, such as Wisconsin and Rhode Island, use probation for more than 90 percent of convicted offenders; other states make far less use of these services. Probation services are centered around two main functions: (1) an investigative function, which provides the sentencing judge with social background information about the offender; and (2) a supervisory function, which constitutes the actual contact between probation officer and client once an offender has been granted probation. The investigative function terminates with the submission of a presentence report to the judge, a document that details all pertinent aspects of the offender's life situation, with particular attention to the circumstances under which the offender committed the crime, and makes a sentencing recommendation to the judge. The supervisory function takes the form of regular contact between probation officer and probationer where counseling, employment advice, and other interpersonal services are rendered.

There is little evidence that probation provides much treatment, as commonly defined. Probation officers generally have high caseloads and are burdened by many bureaucratic requirements which preclude intensive individualistic work with probationers.[117] In spite of this, the results of studies measuring the effectiveness of probation are generally good—with estimates of recidivism usually being lower than 20 percent in some jurisdictions. In light of our earlier remarks, however, this encouraging result cannot necessarily be attributed to probation procedures; the success of probation as a correctional alternative lies often in the selection of persons for probation. The officers who make the recommendations about the offenders to the judge are unlikely to recommend probation for those who are not good risks. Moreover, judges are unlikely to grant probation to offenders whom they think will reinvolve themselves in trouble with the law. As a result, probation caseloads are overrepresented with offenders who are good risks, persons who are likely to succeed on probation (and perhaps persons who would not commit another crime even if they were not on probation). Whatever the reason for the success rates for probation, this alternative to imprisonment seems to be a reasonable one for many types of offenders. Undoubtedly its use will continue and will probably expand as prisons come under increasing attack.[118] In fact, there is good reason for not even putting some offenders on probation, but instead suspending their sentences. This avoids stigmatizing the offender and saves a great deal of expense. In Switzerland, for example, there is no adult probation; instead, approximately two thirds of all prison sentences are generally suspended, and this figure is increasing.[119] The primary purpose is to prevent

[116]See Charles R. Horejsi, "Training for the Direct-Service Volunteer in Probation," *Federal Probation,* 37 (1973), 38–41.

[117]Lewis Diana, "Is Casework in Probation Necessary?" *Focus,* 34 (1955), 1–8.

[118]See John A. Wallace, "Probation Administration," in Daniel Glaser, ed., *Handbook of Criminology* (Chicago: Rand McNally, 1974), pp. 949–969.

[119]Marshall B. Clinard, *Cities with Little Crime: The Case of Switzerland* (Cambridge: Cambridge University Press, 1978).

offenders from slipping into recidivism. Only a small percentage of suspension orders are revoked; the proportion in 1972 was only 13 percent.

Fines

The imposition of fines has long been used as a punishment and it preceded imprisonment; it might well be used again more frequently as an alternative to jail and imprisonment. Many justifications exist for this implementation of the punitive reaction: (1) the fine is the most economical penalty as it costs the state practically nothing when it is not associated with imprisonment for default; (2) it is easily divisible and can be readily adjusted to fit the individual circumstances; (3) since it does not carry the public stigma associated with imprisonment, it does not interfere with the reformation of the offender; (4) it affects money, one of the most universal interests, and thus is the most generally efficacious measure; and (5) it also provides some income for the state, county, or city. Some poor persons, however, cannot pay fines and thus some method of installment payment must be used. It has been suggested that fines be levied perhaps in terms of a person's income per day rather than a certain set sum; certainly one of the most difficult aspects for a justice system is that a fine for a wealthy person can easily be paid and thus does not have the same effect.

Fines are more commonly used with misdemeanors, either alone or combined with probation or incarceration, but they may also be imposed in felony cases depending upon the statutory law. It is not at all unusual for fines to be imposed for various white-collar offenses such as embezzlement, income tax evasion, and corporate fraud.[120] Judges have generally been reluctant to impose fines on other types of felony offenders, both because the statutes do not permit the imposition of fines and because judges view imprisonment as punishment enough for a felony violation.

Restitution to the Victim

Increased interest has also been shown in requiring the offender to make restitution to the victim in lieu of, or in addition to, imprisonment or a fine.[121] In 1977, restitution programs were reported as being successful in California, Illinois, Ohio, Colorado, Oklahoma, Georgia, and Florida. In cases of vandalism and shoplifting, restitution offers a more realistic and perhaps a more inconvenient punishment than an impersonal fine, which goes not to the victim but the state. Vandals, for example, could be forced to repair the damage they have caused in homes, schools, parks, or business establishments.

The offender might be required to restore to the victim twice the value of goods stolen or burglarized; in the case of assault, manslaughter, or even murder, the offender would be required to pay to the victim or close relative a compensatory sum

---

[120]Donald J. Newman, *Introduction to Criminal Justice*, 2d ed. (Philadelphia: Lippincott, 1978), p. 281.
[121]See, for example, Gilbert Geis and Herbert Edelhertz, *Public Compensation to Victims of Crime* (New York: Holt, Rinehart and Winston, 1974); Gilbert Geis, "Compensating Victims of Crime," *Tennessee Bar Journal,* 11 (1975), 24–27; and Gilbert Geis, "Restitution by Criminal Offenders: A Summary and Overview," in Joe Hudson, ed., *Restitution in Criminal Justice* (St. Paul: Minnesota Department of Corrections, 1976), pp. 246–261.

of money. Juvenile offenders might be required to work around the yard, paint the house, or perform other duties for the victim. The wider use of such a penalty would directly benefit the victim of a theft, burglary, assault, or vandalism in a manner not possible if a fine is paid to the state where the only personal satisfaction can be retribution. Furthermore, the bringing together of the victim and the offender helps to overcome the impersonality of much crime, particularly in a large city where offenders usually have never seen the victim before, as in the case of a burglary. Partly for this reason, one proposal has suggested that victims be part of the plea-bargaining process so that their interests are represented in any deal made in regard to the punishment between the offender and the state.[122]

Community Service

The Criminal Justice Act of 1972 of England and Wales, which is directed at the reduction of the use of imprisonment, includes community service of from 40 to 240 hours, usually on weekends, in lieu of imprisonment. Two examples of the community-service alternative used in 1973 may be cited. A 40-year-old man with 18 previous convictions and sentences who was convicted of theft was ordered to perform 100 hours of community service: he was assigned to decorating work, and his first job was to decorate the house of a single-parent family. Another man, aged 18 with six previous convictions, convicted of assault, was ordered to perform 200 hours of service, helping with the cooking at a hospital for discharged mental patients.[123]

Community service appears to be a useful substitute for imprisonment. This approach might help to change the attitudes of the offender, who is punished through loss of free time, and of the community, where a citizen has been injured by theft or assault and where there have been police and court costs. Work could be done in hospitals, nursing homes, parks, and so on. Community service is particularly useful in the case of juveniles, in cases of vandalism, for example, where the offender cannot pay a fine. Perhaps even better would be some combination of community service, restitution to the victim, and probation.

Diversion from the Criminal Justice System

This history of correctional innovations appears to be one of an idea gaining acceptance with juveniles in the juvenile justice system, then, once established, progressing to the adult system. Probation, for example, was not widely used in this country until it had been used with juveniles for some time. Largely because of a lack of knowledge of the low average age of "criminal offenders," the public seems to be less threatened by juvenile crime and is thus more open to change and innovation at that level than at the adult level. One recent innovation that began with juveniles, and is now being expanded to adults, is the use of diversion programs. Diversion programs are organized around the removal of the offender from the tradition of court appearances and

---

[122]Morris, pp. 55–57.
[123]*The Observer* (London), April 1, 1973.

a criminal record. Instead, the person is placed directly in a situation where he can receive individual and family counseling, as well as vocational and educational services. If no additional arrest occurs, records of the original charge are destroyed. The purposes of diversion are to eliminate the stigma that the offender might otherwise receive from being processed through the traditional justice system, to provide better services than incarceration offers, and to allow the justice system to concentrate on more serious offenders.[124]

One concern with diversion programs involves the manner in which clients participate in the programs. Ideally, diversion programs should be completely voluntary. "But often youths are not just diverted from the juvenile court, they are diverted into a treatment program."[125] The choice between going to court and participating in a diversion program is not difficult for most persons; most would prefer to face the dialogue of a counselor than the demands of a judge. True diversion would make the choice completely free and noncoercive. Diversion programs are expanding from those pioneering programs with juvenile offenders (actually, minor juvenile offenders) to areas of adult criminality, such as public drunkenness, motor vehicle offenses, and failure to pay child support.[126]

SELECTED REFERENCES

Bittner, Egon. *The Functions of the Police in Modern Society.* Rockville, Md.: National Institute of Mental Health, 1970.

Black, Donald. *The Behavior of Law.* New York: Academic Press, 1976.

Carter, Robert M., Daniel Glaser, and Leslie T. Wilkins, eds. *Correctional Institutions,* 2d ed. Philadelphia: Lippincott, 1977.

Cohen, Albert K. "Prison Violence: A Sociological Perspective," in Albert K. Cohen, George F. Cole, and Robert G. Bailey, eds., *Prison Violence.* Lexington, Mass.: Lexington Books, 1976.

Cressey, Donald R., ed. *The Prison: Studies in Institutional Organization and Change.* New York: Holt, Rinehart and Winston, 1961.

Gibbons, Don C. *Changing the Lawbreaker: The Treatment of Delinquents and Criminals.* Englewood Cliffs, N.J.: Prentice-Hall, 1965.

Gibbs, Jack P. *Crime, Punishment and Deterrence.* New York: Elsevier, 1975.

Goldfarb, Ronald. *Jails: The Ultimate Ghetto.* New York: Doubleday, 1976.

Goldstein, Herman. *Policing a Free Society.* Cambridge, Mass.: Ballinger, 1977.

LaFave, Wayne R. *Arrest: The Decision To Take a Suspect into Custody.* Boston: Little, Brown, 1965.

---

[124]For a collection of statements on the goals and procedures of diversion, see Robert M. Carter and Malcolm W. Klein, eds., *Back on the Street: The Diversion of Juvenile Offenders* (Englewood Cliffs, N.J.: Prentice-Hall, 1976).

[125]Paul Nejelski, "Diversion: Unleashing the Hound or Heaven?" in Margaret K. Rosenheim, ed., *Pursuing Justice for the Child* (Chicago: University of Chicago Press, 1976), p. 97.

[126]See Malcolm Klein, Kathie S. Teilmann, Joseph A. Styles, Suzanne Bugas Lincoln, and Susan Labin-Rosenweig, "The Explosion of Police Diversion Programs: Evaluating the Structural Dimensions of a Social Fad," in Malcolm W. Klein, ed., *The Juvenile Justice System* (Beverly Hills, Calif.: Sage Publications, 1976), pp. 101–119; and Robert P. Rhodes, *The Insoluble Problems of Crime* (New York: Wiley, 1977), pp. 39–40.

Lerman, Paul. *Community Treatment and Social Control.* Chicago: University of Chicago Press, 1975.

Lipton, Douglas, Robert Martinson, and Judith Wilks. *The Effectiveness of Correctional Treatment: A Survey of Treatment Evaluation Studies.* New York: Holt, Rinehart and Winston, 1975.

Meier, Robert F., and Weldon T. Johnson. "Deterrence as Social Control: Legal and Extralegal Factors in the Production of Conformity," *American Sociological Review,* 42 (1977), 292–304.

Morris, Norval. *The Future of Imprisonment.* Chicago: University of Chicago Press, 1974.

Newman, Donald J. *Conviction: The Determination of Guilt or Innocence.* Boston: Little, Brown, 1966.

Newman, Donald J. *Introduction to Criminal Justice*, 2d ed. Philadelphia: Lippincott, 1978.

Newman, Graeme. *The Punishment Response.* Philadelphia: Lippincott, 1978.

Reiss, Albert J., Jr. *The Police and the Public.* New Haven, Conn.: Yale University Press, 1971.

Sellin, Thorsten. *Slavery and the Penal System.* New York: Elsevier, 1975.

Skolnick, Jerome H. *Justice without Trial: Law Enforcement in a Democratic Society*, 2d ed. New York: Wiley, 1975.

Sykes, Richard E., and John P. Clark. "A Theory of Deference Exchange in Police-Citizen Encounters," *American Journal of Sociology,* 81 (1975), 584–600.

Thomas, Charles W., and David M. Petersen. *Prison Organization and Inmate Subcultures.* Indianapolis: Bobbs Merrill, 1977.

Wallace, John A. "Probation Administration," in Daniel Glaser, ed., *Handbook of Criminology.* Chicago: Rand McNally, 1974.

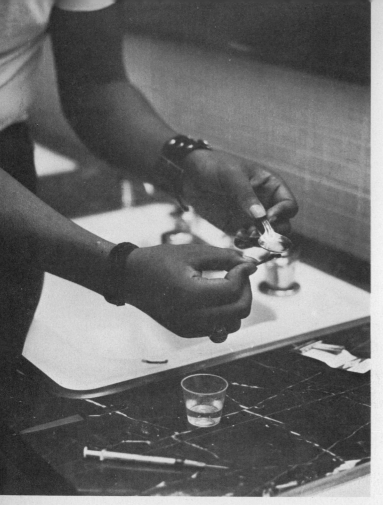

CHAPTER 9

Heroin is being "cooked" with water prior to being injected into the vein with the syringe in the foreground. (Photo courtesy NIDA Nilo Olin)

Drug Use and Addiction

D RUGS have been used for centuries and for various reasons. They are used in medicine to treat disease, to ease pain, or to control the appetite in dieting; they are used for sedation, for social relaxation, and for relief from tensions, boredom, and anxiety; they are used for pleasure, to satisfy curiosity, and to open the mind to new feelings of sensitivity; they are used to create a bond of fellowship, to increase sexual performance, and to give more meaning to life. In the case of heroin, they are often used simply to relieve the harsh pains of being on the drug. For whatever reason drugs are used, it is important to understand the nature of drugs, their use and abuse, as well as the social meanings they have for those who use them.

DEVIANCE AND DRUGS

Drug use, and the societal reaction to it, has varied extensively in time and in place; drug usage has not always been regarded as deviant behavior. In fact, in terms of a relative view of deviance (see Chapter 1), there is little reason to doubt that much marijuana and opiate use is not regarded as being deviant.[1] In India, for example, a country in which there is a strong, religiously associated aversion to alcohol in the higher castes, such forms of marijuana as bhang are not only tolerated but actually prescribed by social custom and religious usage. It is often expected that bhang, a liquid form of marijuana mixed with milk or fruit juices, be served at weddings, and if certain priests who use marijuana and opium become addicted to opium it is not considered particularly reprehensible or unusual. Lindesmith and Gagnon also point out that opium was considered the main therapeutic agent known to medicine for nearly 2,000 years, and its use has been recommended at one time or other for almost all human ailments. "During these centuries there were unquestionably millions of persons who became addicts simply by following the advice of physicians or by acting in accord with widespread popular beliefs concerning the therapeutic power of opium and its derivatives."[2]

Opium, which is easily obtained from a poppy, was and is, in its various forms, the most widely used drug, not only in Europe and the United States, but particularly in the Orient.[3] Its early use in medical treatment tended to spread it. Two important drugs were derived from opium: morphine, a potent drug, in 1804; and heroin, about three times as powerful as morphine, in 1898. These drugs, as well as opium, which could be smoked or drunk, became widely used in the nineteenth century in the United States, particularly by women, who took them in patent medicines for "female

---

[1]See Alfred R. Lindesmith and John H. Gagnon, "Anomie and Drug Addiction," in Marshall B. Clinard, ed., *Anomie and Deviant Behavior: A Discussion and Critique* (New York: Free Press, 1964), pp. 162–163.
[2]Lindesmith and Gagnon, p. 163. Also see Alfred R. Lindesmith, *Addiction and Opiates* (Chicago: Aldine, 1968); John C. Ball, "Two Patterns of Narcotic Drug Addiction in the United States," *Journal of Criminal Law, Criminology and Police Science,* 56 (1965), 204; and Roger Smith, "Status Politics and the Image of the Addict," *Issues in Criminology,* (1966), 157–176.
[3]Hong Kong today is estimated to have a high number of addicts. See Hong Kong Legislative Council, *The Problem of Narcotic Drugs in Hong Kong* (Hong Kong: S. Young, Government Printer, 1962); and Albert G. Hess, *Chasing the Dragon* (New York: Free Press, 1965).

disorders." At that time many of these drugs could be easily and legally purchased. In fact, heroin was first made by pharmaceutical chemists to be sold over the drugstore counter as a cough remedy.

Changes in Social Attitudes

The attitude of the public toward drug users in the United States during the nineteenth century was different from what it is today. While drug use was not approved, there was considerable tolerance of it, drug addiction was regarded as a personal problem, and addicts were generally pitied. Not until later did drug users come to be regarded as deviant characters, and most people associated addiction with criminal behavior. This change in public attitude was due in part to the prevalence of opium smoking among certain criminal elements at the time.

The Harrison Act, passed in 1914, strictly regulated the sale and use of opiates and cocaine in the United States. This legislation, and subsequent statutes, made the selling and using of these drugs, as well as marijuana, illegal without a doctor's prescription.[4] One consequence of this legislation was to make drug addicts criminals and drugs to be regarded as mysterious and evil. The result was that public attitudes against drug use were reinforced, and it became difficult for persons to secure or use drugs without associating with other users. For this reason some people have claimed that the laws, particularly those dealing with marijuana, have served not so much to control this drug as to create victims of law enforcement.[5]

In 1977 President Carter recommended to Congress that the possession of small amounts (one ounce or less) of marijuana be decriminalized, removing for this offense the penalty of up to one year in prison and a fine as high as $5,000; instead, he urged that civil penalties be used. The President's request drew a dividing line between personal use and trafficking in marijuana, which would remain a serious criminal offense. Most state laws provide similar punishment for possession and sale of drugs. In 1978, several cities and 10 states had decriminalized the possession of marijuana: Oregon, Alaska, Maine, Colorado, California, Ohio, South Dakota, Minnesota, New York, and North Carolina; several states, however, have retained the possible use of civil penalties.[6]

By 1977, moves to decriminalize possession of small amounts of marijuana were also gaining momentum in several other states. In Nevada, a bill to legalize and tax marijuana, as cigarettes are taxed, has been introduced into the legislature, and in New Mexico, a bill has been introduced to legalize possession of marijuana in a private residence and to decriminalize possession for use in public. Under this measure

---

[4]A comprehensive discussion of the origins of narcotics legislation is contained in David F. Musto, *The American Disease: The Origins of Narcotic Control* (New Haven, Conn.: Yale University Press, 1973); and Musto, "Early History of Heroin in the United States," in Peter G. Bourne, ed., *Addiction* (New York: Academic Press, 1974), pp. 175–185.

[5]See, for example, Erich Goode, "Notes on the Enforcement of Moral Crimes," in Harvey A. Farberman and Erich Goode, eds., *Social Reality* (Englewood Cliffs, N.J.: Prentice-Hall, 1973), pp. 254–264.

[6]An excellent discussion of the history of social and legal changes in policy surrounding the use and control of marijuana can be found in Richard J. Bonnie and Charles H. Whitebread, II, *The Marihuana Conviction: A History of Marihuana Prohibition in the United States* (Charlottesville: University of Virginia Press, 1974).

possession of up to three ounces would be lawful in a private residence and possession of up to one ounce in public would be subject to a maximum fine of $50; the offense would be handled like a traffic citation, with the criminal penalties remaining for possession of larger amounts. It has been claimed that the number of arrested marijuana possession offenders dropped by almost 50 percent in California in 1976 as a result of decriminalization (it is now a civil offense), with a savings to the state of at least $25 million, according to the Justice Department.

The administration of these laws has resulted in increased numbers of arrests for the violation of drug laws. By 1975, a large number of persons were arrested; in fact, the number was exceeded only by arrests for drunkenness and larceny. In 1975, 601,400 persons were arrested for violation of drug laws, as compared with 182,909 in 1969 and 400,606 in 1971. Most of those arrested were young and male.[7] Not all addicts are eventually processed as criminals, however, for the federal Narcotic Addiction Rehabilitation Act (NARA) of 1966, as well as similar laws in California and New York, provide for the civil law commitment of certain narcotic addicts who desire this in place of prosecution—which would give them a criminal record. In California in 1972, 2,125 persons were given civil commitments. These persons are then treated in hospitals and through community services. Not all addicts are eligible; under the federal civil commitment program the following are ineligible:

1. Individuals who are charged with or convicted of "crimes of violence," such as voluntary manslaughter, rape, mayhem, kidnapping, robbery, burglary or housebreaking at night, assault with a dangerous weapon, or assault with intent to commit an offense punishable by imprisonment for more than one year.

2. Individuals charged with unlawfully importing, selling, or conspiring to import or sell, a narcotic drug.

3. Individuals who have been convicted of a felony on two or more occasions, or who have been civilly committed on three or more occasions.

4. Individuals with pending prior charges of felonies which have not been finally determined or who are on probation or whose sentences following conviction have not been fully served.[8]

Neither the punitive nor the nonpunitive efforts to control drug abuse appear to have been successful. In fact, in 1973 the Drug Enforcement Administration was created to help coordinate the federal government's programs to correct these failures. This agency consolidated the former Bureau of Narcotics and Dangerous Drugs, the Office of National Narcotics Intelligence, and the Office for Drug Abuse Law Enforcement into one major one with the overall responsibility of enforcing the federal narcotics and dangerous drugs laws. This major reorganization was necessitated by the failure of previous attempts to stem the narcotics problem, a failure due in part to lack of coordination and the overlapping of the various federal agencies with jurisdictional authority relating to narcotics.[9] The Drug Enforcement Administration is also responsi-

---

[7]Federal Bureau of Investigation, *Uniform Crime Reports—1975* (Washington, D.C.: Government Printing Office, 1976), pp. 179, 183, 189.
[8]"The Narcotic Addict Rehabilitation Act of 1966," Public Health Service Publication No. 1782, revised May 1969, Department of Health, Education and Welfare, Washington, D.C., p. 3.
[9]Robert D. Pursley, *Introduction to Criminal Justice* (Encino, Calif.: Glencoe Press, 1977), p. 157.

ble for regulating and inspecting nearly 5,000 drug manufacturing and distribution firms to prevent possible diversion of legally manufactured drugs to illicit sources.

The Example of Marijuana

The story of how marijuana became illegal is instructive of the role of certain interest groups in making the criminal law. At the turn of the century in the United States extracts derived from marijuana were almost as commonly used for medicinal purposes as aspirin is today. "Not only was cannabis [marijuana] a proprietary medication which could be purchased without a prescription in any drug store but it was also prescribed by physicians for the treatment of a broad variety of medical conditions, from migraines and excessive menstrual bleeding to ulcers, epilepsy, and even tooth decay."[10] Part of the enthusiastic reception given marijuana use medicinally was due to the scientific knowledge available about the drug at this time. In fact, it was generally conceded among "the American scientific community in the 1930s that marihuana users did not evidence the tolerance and withdrawal symptoms characteristic of physical addiction."[11] As late as 1930, only 16 states had passed laws barring marijuana use. In 1937 Congress passed the Marijuana Tax Act, designed to stamp out its use by criminal law proceedings, which in turn influenced the other states to pass such criminal legislation. Becker maintains that there was little public concern, but the passage of the criminal legislation was the result of the almost singlehanded efforts of the Federal Bureau of Narcotics, as the "moral entrepreneur," which made the public aware of the problem on the basis of rather limited data and cases. Becker states that while it is hard to know the motives of the officials of the Bureau, "we need assume no more than that they perceived an area of wrongdoing that properly belonged in their jurisdiction and moved to put it there."[12] Their efforts in pressing for marijuana legislation took two forms: cooperating in the development of state legislation affecting marijuana use and providing data for distributing accounts of the problem.

This previously widely accepted explanation of the original federal marijuana legislation, however, has been challenged. In a 1977 study, two researchers reported that contrary to the results of most studies of the Marihuana Tax Act, the evidence was insufficient to conclude that there was a major effort by the Federal Bureau of Narcotics to generate a public marijuana crisis to create pressure for the legislation. A review of newspapers, as well as the Congressional Record, did not indicate a nationwide marijuana crisis. Furthermore, this legislation, they found, is not the important legislative change implied by these other studies; it is merely a symbolic gesture involving a Bureau promise of no increased funding required by the law's passage.[13] On the basis of this reexamination, the Becker claim that the federal

---

[10]Solomon H. Snyder, *Uses of Marijuana* (New York: Oxford University Press, 1971), p. 3.
[11]Bonnie and Whitebread, p. 189.
[12]Howard S. Becker, *Outsiders: Studies in the Sociology of Deviance,* enlarged ed. (New York: Free Press, 1973), pp. 138–139. Also see Donald T. Dickson, "Bureaucracy and Morality: An Organizational Perspective on a Moral Crusade," *Social Problems,* 16 (1968), 143–156; and his "Marijuana and the Law: Organizational Factors in the Legislative Process," *Journal of Drug Issues,* 3 (1973), 115–122.
[13]John F. Galliher and Allyn Walker, "The Puzzle of the Social Origins of the Marihuana Tax Act of 1937," *Social Problems,* 24 (1977), 366–376.

legislation against marijuana was only a product of a government agency can be rejected as an overstatement.

The influence of the federal legislation has been great. In 1978 many states still punished by criminal law procedures the simple *possessor* of marijuana on the *first* offense, and many states had severe penalties for this offense in comparison with their penalties for conventional crimes such as larceny and burglary. Within the last few years, however, many states have seriously been reevaluating their statutes relating to the possession and use of marijuana.

A Presidential Commission in 1972 reported that marijuana use, as a behavior, "has created fear, anger, confusion and uncertainty among a large segment of the contemporary American public." The Commission felt that three interrelated factors have fostered the definition of marijuana as a national problem. First, the illegal behavior was highly visible to all segments of the society. Second, such drug use was perceived as a threat to personal health and morality and that of the society. Third, it has grown out of broader issues affecting changes in the status of the youth and wider social conflicts and issues. According to the Commission:

> More than anything else, the visibility of marihuana use by a segment of our population previously unfamiliar with the drug is what stirred public anxiety and thrust marihuana into the problem area. . . . For decades, its use was mainly confined to the underprivileged socioeconomic groups in our cities and to certain insulated social groups, such as jazz musicians and artists. As long as use remained confined to these groups and had a negligible impact on the dominant social order, the vast majority of Americans remained unconcerned. From the other side, the insulated marihuana user was in no position to demand careful public or legislative scrutiny. However, all this changed markedly in the mid-1960's. For various reasons, marihuana use became a common form of recreation for many middle and upper class college youth. The trend spread across the country, into the colleges and high schools and into the affluent suburbs as well. Use by American servicemen in Vietnam was frequent. In recent years, use of the drug has spanned every social class and geographic region. . . . Such mass deviance was a problem and the scope of the problem was augmented by frequent publicity. The topic of the usage of marihuana by the young received considerable attention from newspapermen and television reporters.
>
> . . . The symbolic aspects of marihuana are the most intangible of the items to which the Commission must address itself, and yet they may be at the heart of the marihuana problem. Use of marihuana was, and still is, age-specific. It was youth-related at a time in American history when the adult society was alarmed by the implications of the youth "movement": defiance of the established order, the adoption of new life styles, the emergence of "street people," campus unrest, drug use, communal living, protest politics, and political radicalism. In an age characterized by the so-called generation gap, marihuana symbolizes the cultural divide. For youth, marihuana became a convenient symbol of dissaffection with traditional society, an allure which supplemented its recreational attraction. Smoking marihuana may have appealed to large numbers of youth who opposed certain policies or trends, but who maintained faith in the American system as a whole. In a time when symbolic speech is often preferred to the literal form, marihuana was a convenient instrument of mini-protest. It was also an agent of group solidarity, as the widely publicized rock concerts so well illustrate.[14]

---

[14]*Marihuana: A Signal of Misunderstanding,* First Report of the National Commission on Marihuana and Drug Abuse (Washington, D.C.: Government Printing Office, 1972), pp. 6–9.

In summary, the Commission report indicated that marijuana itself is not as much the object of all the legislation against it, but rather more fundamentally it is the style of life that goes with marijuana smoking. Kaplan has pointed out that this style of life emphasizes, "immediate experience, present rather than delayed gratification, noncompetitiveness, and lessened interest in the acquisition of wealth."[15]

On the other hand, a large proportion of the U.S. public reacts highly negatively to "hard-drug" users. To a large extent the public's attitudes toward drug addicts, that is, those addicted to hard drugs, represent a stereotype of what has been termed the "dope fiend" myth. This stereotype has been fortified by the work-oriented Protestant ethic of U.S. society, which reinforces the idea that all drug peddlers and addicts are unproductive. The existence of the extensive drug laws serves to confirm these views about the deviant nature of drugs.

Most Western European countries have a drug problem, and some of them have taken a different approach to the problem. In contrast to the severe penalties under the laws in the United States, many of them regard drugs and marijuana use more as a medical than a criminal problem. The use of the hard drugs—heroin, cocaine, and morphine—is considered a medical problem in which medical authorities are permitted to prescribe the drugs a person requires. While there are laws on the statute books in England, for example, prison terms for marijuana use are virtually never imposed for first or second offenses, and they are almost routinely treated as misdemeanors meriting only token fines. Consequently, the addict or marijuana user is not regarded by the British public as being "criminal." A man does not have to steal drugs to secure some source of supply for himself, and a woman does not have to turn to prostitution. They are, therefore, generally regarded as noncriminals. Because of an increase in drug addiction, however, measures have been adopted within the past few years to create a degree of centralization in issuing prescriptions to drug users through hospital doctors. Previously any physician could prescribe drugs.[16]

LEGAL DRUG USAGE

Drugs are physical substances other than those required for the normal maintenance of health, such as food, which affect the structure or the function of the body.[17] The use of illegal drugs such as heroin and marijuana, while disapproved, have their widely used counterparts in such legally approved drugs as alcohol, cigarettes, tranquilizers for relaxation, barbiturates for sleeping and relaxing, and other minor pain-killing drugs such as aspirin. Coffee and tea are also drug stimulants which can have

---

[15]Robert Kaplan, *Drug Abuse: Perspectives on Drugs* (Dubuque, Ia: William C. Brown, 1970), p. 4. See also John H. McGrath and Frank R. Scarpitti, *Youth and Drugs: Perspectives on a Social Problem* (Glenview, Ill.: Scott, Foresman, 1970); and Clayton A. Hartjen, *Possible Trouble: An Analysis of Social Problems* (New York: Holt, Rinehart and Winston, 1977), p. 256.

[16]See Edwin M. Schur, *Narcotic Addiction in Britain and America: The Impact of Public Policy* (Bloomington: Indiana University Press, 1962); and Andrew Scull, "Social Control and the Amplification of Deviance," in Robert A. Scott and Jack D. Douglas, eds., *Theoretical Perspectives on Deviance* (New York: Basic Books, 1972), pp. 282–316.

[17]Harold Kalant and Oriana Josseau Kalant, *Drugs, Society and Personal Choice* (Don Mills, Ontario: PaperJacks, General Publishing Company, 1971), p. 14.

considerable effect when consumed regularly in large quantities. Much scientific literature has clearly established that caffeine is a stimulant whose actions fairly closely resemble those of the amphetamines. While most persons use it in such moderation that no ill effects are suffered, an occasional person drinks so much coffee that he develops symptoms of sleeplessness, nervousness, elevated blood pressure, and hyperirritability that can be produced by equivalent doses of amphetamine. "This same type of reasoning can be used with respect to the nicotine contained in tobacco, and it is very easy to show that alcohol must also be considered a drug because of its many similarities to the barbiturates and other groups of central nervous system depressants."[18]

Some idea of the wide-scale use of the more accepted and legal drugs is indicated by the fact that over a million pounds of *barbiturate* derivatives, for example, are manufactured each year in the United States, the equivalent of 24 half-grain doses for each person in the country, enough to kill each twice.[19] In 1957 it was estimated that 7 percent of the adult population was regularly using tranquilizers, sedatives, and drug stimulants; in 1967 one out of every four persons, or 27 percent, was doing so.[20] In 1970, 202 million legal prescriptions for psychoactive drugs—stimulants, sedatives, tranquilizers, and depressants—were filled in pharmacies in the United States for persons who saw their physicians first. A New York state survey of 1968–1969 showed the wide prevalence and incidence of the use of various ordinary drugs. Of the total population aged 14 and older, 19.6 percent had used barbiturates, and 2.8 percent of the population (377,000) regularly were using the drugs at least six times a month. Relaxants and minor tranquilizers had been used by 19.8 percent of the population, and 3.8 percent, or 525,000 persons, were using them regularly. Pep pills had been used by 6.3 percent of the population, and 0.8 percent (110,000) were using them regularly. Prescription diet pills had been used by 11.5 percent, with 1.6 percent (225,000) using them regularly.[21]

The use of *amphetamines,* which include all types of stimulant drug products and pep and diet pills, now reaches extensive proportions. It was estimated in 1972 that 100,000 pounds of these products were being produced annually in the United States by well-known manufacturers—an amount equivalent to 50 5-milligram doses for each person in the nation. It was also estimated that as much as half of these products finds its way into the illicit market.[22] As a result, it has been said that there are probably more high-dosage intravenous amphetamine users in large metropolitan areas than heroin users.[23] Initially, the amphetamines work in a manner just the

---

[18]Kalant and Kalant, p. 14.

[19]John C. Pollard, "Some Comments on Nonnarcotic Drug Abuse," paper presented at the Nonnarcotic Drug Institute, Southern Illinois University, Edwardsville, Ill., June 1967.

[20]Hugh Parry, "Tranquilizer Users," *Wayfarers Magazine,* February 1969. Also see Hugh Parry, M. B. Balter, G. D. Mellinger, I. H. Cisin, and D. I. Manheimer, "National Patterns of Psychotherapeutic Drug Use," *Archives of General Psychiatry,* 28 (1973), 769–783.

[21]Carl D. Chambers, *Differential Drug Use within the New York State Labor Force* (New York: Narcotic Addiction Control Commission, 1971).

[22]See James A. Inciardi and Carl D. Chambers, "The Epidemiology of Amphetamine Use in the General Population," *Canadian Journal of Criminology and Corrections,* 14 (1972), 2.

[23]See John C. Kramer, Vitezslav S. Fishman, and Don C. Littlefield, "Amphetamine Abuse Patterns and Effects of High Doses Taken Intravenously," *Journal of the American Medical Association,* 201 (1967), 305–309.

opposite to the barbiturates, stimulating rather than relaxing the central nervous system. Similar to the body's adrenalin in function, they are often taken by long-distance drivers, night-shift workers, fatigued housewives, students preparing for exams, and many others for general stimulation, pleasure, or fun. They were first synthesized early in this century, came into the spectrum of medical use during the 1930s, and were commonly sought during World War II by soldiers to counteract fatigue. They are sometimes combined with barbiturates to achieve a desired medical effect, the combination being useful as a weight-reducing agent. This combination with barbiturates can lead to addiction, but, unlike barbiturates, the amphetamines are not themselves physically addictive. The body can build up a tolerance to them, but users experience no physical withdrawal symptoms. Psychologically, however, the amphetamines can be habituating: known as "pep" pills, they hide fatigue and create a feeling of euphoria, exhilaration, and unusual perceptiveness. Under the influence of these drugs a state of mind can turn to a feeling of confidence and energy, but as the effect wears off a mild letdown occurs. Excessive use may lead to insomnia, and later exhaustion and deep depression. Overdoses of pep pills cause loss of judgment, and the user may imagine himself able and sometimes actually attempt to perform impossible feats.

Use of Legal Drugs

A Senate subcommittee on juvenile delinquency reported in 1972 that as many as one million Americans, mostly between the ages of 30 and 50, are "hooked" on barbiturates. Virtually all of the barbiturates are being abused. The subcommittee said that "the problem reaches into every area of American life, affecting such diverse groups as school children, college students, industrial workers, middle-class party goers, residents of our ghettos and barrios, and middle-aged adults who started using barbiturates under a physician's supervision."[24] Moreover, virtually all of the barbiturates and amphetamines that are abused originate from legitimate drug companies. These drugs are then "diverted" into the illicit market via hijackings and theft, spurious orders from nonexistent firms, forged prescriptions, and numerous but small-scale diversions from family medicine chests and legitimate prescriptions.[25] A national survey conducted for the National Commission on Marihuana and Drug Abuse[26] confirms many of these estimates. The survey reported that 6 percent of U.S. youth (ages 12 through 17) and 13 percent of adults had had some experience with stimulants; and 4 percent of youth and 5 percent of adults had used stimulant drugs obtained by prescription at least once for nonmedical reasons. Stimulant use was greater among better-educated adults who resided in metropolitan areas and in the West. Trend data of college student involve-

---

[24]United Press International news release, reported in *The Wisconsin State Journal,* Madison, December 5, 1972.

[25]David E. Smith and Donald R. Wesson, "Legitimate and Illegitimate Distribution of Amphetamines and Barbiturates," in David E. Smith and Donald R. Wesson, eds., *Uppers and Downers* (Englewood Cliffs, N.J.: Prentice-Hall, 1973), p. 109.

[26]*Drug Use in America: Problem in Perspective,* Second Report of the National Commission on Marihuana and Drug Abuse (Washington, D.C.: Government Printing Office, 1973). See also J. Fred E. Shick, David E. Smith, and Donald R. Wesson, "An Analysis of Amphetamine Toxicity and Patterns of Use," in Smith and Wesson, *Uppers and Downers,* pp. 23–61.

ment with these drugs indicated that student stimulant use had increased 41 percent between 1970 and 1972.

A recent ambitious study attempted to estimate the incidence of drug taking of all types by interviewing 2,510 males aged 20 through 30.[27] Twenty-seven percent of the sample had used stimulants, and 12 percent admitted continuing their use at the time of the interview (1974–1975). Twenty percent had used sedatives, and 44 percent admitted having tried heroin or cocaine at any time prior to the interview. If one includes the drugs of alcohol and tobacco, 70 percent of the sample had used tobacco in the form of cigarettes, and 97 percent of them had consumed alcohol; 92 percent indicated that they had continued the use of alcohol.

The use of depressant and stimulant drugs may be related to cultural characteristics of a particular society. Amphetamines, for example, have been widely used by adults in countries such as Japan, Sweden, and the United States where there is a strong emphasis on productivity and personal achievement.[28] Most likely, the persons who use amphetamines in these nations feel that their activities are further aided by the use of stimulants. Recent revelations in the mass media concerning the use of amphetamines by professional athletes and entertainers also suggest that this is the case.

Sources of Legal Drugs

One study has charged the pharmaceutical companies with encouraging the increased use of drugs by subjecting physicians and the general public to intensive advertising campaigns.[29] Some 60 drug companies spend over $750 million annually to reach and convince 180,000 physicians to use their products. This increase in the widespread and legal use of drugs has been largely the result of the urging of physicians to prescribe drugs to relieve simple problems of everyday existence. A recent work has this to say about such practices:

> While the pharmaceutical industry has been expanding its market of both prescription and nonprescription drugs, it has in doing so created an increased need . . . In the context of current usage, drugs are medical agents whose function is the solution of medical problems. Only to the extent that interpersonal and other problems can be construed as medical psychiatric problems can they be considered appropriate targets for drug treatment. As more and more facets of ordinary human conduct, interactions, and conflicts are considered to be medical problems, physicians and, subsequently, patients become convinced that intervention through the medium of psychoactive drugs is desirable or required.
>
> The pharmaceutical industry is redefining and relabeling as medical problems

---

[27]John A. O'Donnell, Harwin L. Voss, Richard R. Clayton, Gerald T. Slatin, and Robin G. W. Room, *Young Men and Drugs—A Nationwide Survey* (Rockville, Md.: National Institute on Drug Abuse, 1976).
[28]Everett H. Ellinwood, "The Epidemiology of Stimulant Abuse," in Eric Josephson and Eleanor E. Carroll, eds., *Drug Use: Epidemiological and Sociological Approaches* (New York: Wiley, 1974), pp. 303–329. Also see John A. Clausen, "Drug Use," in Robert K. Merton and Robert Nisbet, eds., *Contemporary Social Problems*, 4th ed. (New York: Harcourt Brace Jovanovich, 1976), p. 153.
[29]Henry L. Lennard, Leon J. Epstein, Arnold Bernstein, and Donald C. Ransom, *Mystification and Drug Misuse: Hazards in Using Psychoactive Drugs* (San Francisco: Jossey-Bass, 1971). Also see Milton Silverman and Philip R. Lee, *Pills, Profits and Politics* (Berkeley: University of California Press, 1974).

calling for drug intervention a wide range of human behaviors which, in the past, have been viewed as falling within the bounds of the normal trials and tribulations of human existence. Much evidence for this position is to be found in the advertisements of drug companies in medical journals, in direct mailings to physicians, and in advertising directed to the general public.[30]

Physicians are constantly bombarded by a barrage of "drug literature"—by direct mail or in medical journal advertisements—that has been likened to the best marketing techniques of Madison Avenue.[31] The use of photographs of attractive women (frequently wearing little clothing, in the case of dermatology-related drugs), sensational situations, and slogans permeate the advertisements, on the basis of which physicians choose one drug over another.

After conducting hearings on the drug industry in 1972 Senator Gaylord Nelson said that the United States has "become a nation of irrational pill poppers," with the public as well as the drug companies to blame. Drug companies, according to Senator Nelson, "deserve to be exposed and censured and the law needs to be tightened to control their advertising." Americans seem to want to take a pill for every ache and pain, for nervous tension, for anxiety, and for the ordinary stresses and strains of daily living, he said. As a result, "we have become massively addicted to taking drugs whether we need them or not. We have created a drug culture and many of the youth of America are simply doing what they learned from their parents."[32]

The wide-scale syndrome of pill taking is encouraged by advertising. In 1972 the Director of the Bureau of Narcotics and Dangerous Drugs said that

> from sunrise to closing benediction in the late evening, the American public is bombarded on radio and television by catchy little jingles, cute sketches, and somber warnings, offering drugs and medicines to cure most little symptoms of real or imagined illness—or to provide escape from reality. The average medicine cabinet gives testimony to the success of this mass media campaign. The rows of bottles and vials of pills and tablets are a sad commentary on a society that once was noted for its ability to endure hardship in seeking its destiny.[33]

Federal Communications Commissioner Nicholas Johnson called television "the principal pusher to a junkie nation" and urged a grass-roots campaign for legislation to regulate television drug advertising. Johnson said: "We've got a drug problem in America: it's called television."[34] This cultural setting of "taking something" for everything has meaningful implications for drug use among the young in contemporary Western society. For them, drug taking is a method of facilitating human

---

[30]Lennard *et al.*, pp. 18–19.

[31]Donald R. Wesson, David E. Smith, and George R. Gray, "The Politics of Barbiturate and Amphetamine Abuse," in Smith and Wesson, *Uppers and Downers*, p. 99. See also Robert Seidenberg, "Advertising and Drug Acculturation," in Robert H. Coombs, Lincoln J. Fry, and Patricia G. Lewis, eds., *Socialization in Drug Use* (Cambridge, Mass.: Schenkman, 1976), pp. 19–25.

[32]As reported in an Associated Press news release in *The Wisconsin State Journal,* Madison, December 5, 1972.

[33]As reported in a United Press International news release in *The Wisconsin State Journal,* Madison, October 5, 1972.

[34]As reported in a United Press International news release in *The Wisconsin State Journal,* Madison, November 15, 1972.

interaction and of providing new or missing experiences, much in the way that adults use alcohol and various prescription or nonprescription pills. Young people take drugs "in the pursuit of novelty and drama; to generate feelings of closeness, warmth, and awe in man and nature; and even to generate an experience of the uncanny, the horrible, the magical, and the loathesome."[35]

This situation is not confined to the United States. Heavy sales of drugs that modify mood and behavior through legitimate channels are reported in Canada, indicating that Canadians are leaning heavily on these drugs. In addition, illicit manufacture, importation, and sales seriously contribute to drug consumption.[36] In Great Britain about 6 percent of all prescriptions under the National Health Service are for barbiturates, with an estimated 75,000–125,000 persons being dependent on them and 400,000–600,000 being regular users without being dependent on them.[37] Amphetamines represent about 2.5 percent of all National Health prescriptions, with about 50,000–100,000 persons regularly taking them by prescription.

TYPES OF DRUGS INVOLVED IN ILLEGAL USE

From the standpoint of physiological effect, drugs fall roughly into two categories, the depressants and the stimulants. As their names imply, depressants decrease mental and physical activity in varying degrees, depending upon the dosage, whereas the stimulants excite and sustain activity and diminish symptoms of fatigue (see Table 9.1). The most important depressant drugs are morphine, heroin, methadone, and marijuana. *Opiates,* heroin and morphine, which, together with semisynthetics and synthetics, such as methadone and ineperidine, with qualities similar to real opiates, account for the greatest proportion of *drug addiction* in the United States. A study of 1,013 first admissions in 1971 to the then federal NIMH Clinical Research Center in Lexington, Kentucky, showed that heroin was the drug most often preferred.[38] Other specific drugs, including sedative hypnotic relaxants, stimulant-type drugs, and hallucinogens, are listed in Table 9.2.

The opiates *heroin* and *morphine,* white powdered substances derived from opium, are most frequently taken by injection, either subcutaneously or directly into the vein. Almost immediately after the injection of either drug the person becomes flushed and experiences a mild itching and tingling sensation. Gradually he becomes drowsy and relaxed and enters a state of reverie. Soon this state of euphoria is reached only with larger injections of the drug. Thus the addict builds up his *tolerance* for the drug as well as his dependence upon it. As this tolerance builds up, the addict becomes comparatively immune to the toxic manifestations of the drug. With mor-

---

[35]Lennard *et al.,* p. 45.
[36]G. H. Ettinger, "The Problem of Overprescription," *Addictions,* 15 (1968), 10.
[37]Jock Young, *The Drugtakers: The Social Meaning of Drug Use* (London: Paladin, 1971), p. 25.
[38]Private communication from Dr. Robert S. Weppner, National Institute of Mental Health Clinical Research Center, Lexington, Kentucky, 1972.

TABLE 9.1 Some Substances Used for Nonprescribed Drugging Effects

Substance	Slang Name	Active Ingredient	Source	Pharmacologic Classification	Medical Use
Morphine	White stuff, M.	Morphine sulphate	Natural (from opium)	Central nervous system depressant	Pain relief
Heroin	H., horse, scat, junk, smack, scag, stuff, Harry	Diacetylmorphine	Semi-synthetic (from morphine)	CNS depressant	None, legally
Codeine	Schoolboy	Methylmorphine	Natural (from opium), semi-synthetic (from morphine)	CNS depressant	Ease pain & coughing
Paregoric		Tincture of camphorated opium	Natural (from opium) and synthetic	CNS depressant	Sedation, counteract diarrhea
Meperidine		Meperidine hydrochloride	Synthetic (morphine-like)	CNS depressant	Pain relief
Methadone	Dolly	Methadone hydrochloride	Synthetic (morphine-like)	CNS depressant	Pain relief
Cocaine	Corrine, coke, flake, snow, gold dust, star dust, Bernice	Methylester of benzoylecgonine	Natural (from coca leaves)	Stimulant, local or topical anesthetic	Local or topical anesthesia
Marijuana	Pot, grass, tea	Tetrahydro-cannabinols	Cannabis sativa	CNS toxin	Experimental research only
Hashish	Hash	Tetrahydro-cannabinols	Cannabis sativa	CNS toxin	Experimental research only
Barbiturates	Barbs, red devils, yellow jackets, phennies, peanuts, blue heavens, candy	Phenobarbital, pentobarbital, secobarbital, amobarbital	Synthetic	CNS depressant	Sedation, relieve high blood pressure, epilepsy
Amphetamines	Bennies, dexies, hearts, pep pills, speed, lid proppers, wake-ups	Amphetamine, dextroamphetamine, methamphetamine (desoxyephedrine)	Synthetic	CNS stimulant	Control appetite, narcolepsy; some childhood behavioral disorders
LSD	Acid, big D, sugar, trips, cubes	D-lysergic acid diethylamide	Semi-synthetic (from ergot alkaloids)	Hallucinogen	Experimental research only
DOM	STP, "serenity, tranquility, peace"	4-methyl-2, 5-dimethoxy alpha methyl phenethylamine	Synthetic	Hallucinogen	None
THC		Tetrahydrocannabinol	Synthetic	Hallucinogen	None
DMT	Businessman's special	Dimethyltryptamine	Synthetic	Hallucinogen	None

Substance	How Taken	Usual Form of Product	Effects Sought	Long-term Possible Effects	Physical Dependence Potential	Psychological Dependence Potential	Organic Damage Potential
Morphine	Swallowed or injected	Powder (white), tablet, liquid	Euphoria; prevent withdrawal discomfort	Addiction, constipation, loss of appetite	Yes	Yes	Yes, indirectly
Heroin	Injected or sniffed	Powder (white gray, brown)	Euphoria; prevent withdrawal discomfort	Addiction, constipation, loss of appetite	Yes	Yes	Yes, indirectly
Codeine	Swallowed	Tablets, liquid (in cough syrup)	Euphoria; prevent withdrawal discomfort	Addiction, constipation, loss of appetite	Yes	Yes	Yes, indirectly
Paregoric	Swallowed or injected	Liquid	Euphoria; prevent withdrawal discomfort	Addiction, constipation, loss of appetite	Yes	Yes	Yes, indirectly
Meperidine	Swallowed or injected	Tablets, liquid	Euphoria; prevent withdrawal discomfort	Addiction, constipation, loss of appetite	Yes	Yes	Yes, indirectly
Methadone	Swallowed or injected	Tablets, liquid	Prevent withdrawal discomfort	Addiction, constipation, loss of appetite	Yes	Yes	Yes, indirectly
Cocaine	Sniffed, injected or swallowed	Powder (white), liquid	Excitation	Depression, convulsions	No	Yes	Probable
Marijuana	Smoked or swallowed	Plant particles (dark green or brown)	Euphoria, relaxation, increased perception	Usually none; bronchitis, conjunctivitis possible	No	Possible	Not determined
Hashish	Smoked or swallowed	Solid, brown to black, resin	Relaxation, euphoria, increased perception	Usually none; conjunctivitis, psychosis possible	No	Possible	Not determined
Barbiturates	Swallowed or injected	Tablets or capsules	Anxiety reduction, euphoria	Severe withdrawal symptoms; possible convulsions, toxic psychosis	Yes	Yes	Yes
Amphetamines	Swallowed or injected	Tablets, capsules, liquid, powder (white)	Alertness, activeness	Loss of appetite, delusions, hallucinations, toxic psychosis	Possible	Yes	Probable
LSD	Swallowed	Tablets, capsules, liquid	Insight, distortion of senses; exhilaration	May intensify existing psychosis, panic reactions	No	Possible	Not determined
DOM	Swallowed	Tablets, capsules, liquid	Stronger than LSD effects	?	No	Possible	Not determined
THC	Smoked or swallowed	In marijuana or liquid	Stronger than marijuana effects	?	No	Possible	Not determined
DMT	Injected	Liquid	Shorter term than LSD effects	?	No	Possible	Not determined

TABLE 9.1 Some Substances Used for Nonprescribed Drugging Effects (*cont.*)

Substance	Slang Name	Active Ingredient	Source	Pharmacologic Classification	Medical Use
PCP	Hog, peace pill, angel dust	Phencyclidine	Synthetic	Hallucinogen	Veterinary anesthetic
Mescaline	Mesc	3, 4, 5-trimeth-oxyphenethyl-amine	Natural (from peyote cac-tus)	Hallucinogen	None
Psilocybin		3 (2-dimethylamino) ethylindol-4-oldihydro-gen phosphate	Natural (from psilocybe: fungus on a type of mushroom)	Hallucinogen	None
Coffee, Tea, Colas	Java, coke	Caffeine	Natural	CNS stimulant	Mild stimulant
Alcohol	Booze, juice, sauce	Ethanol ethyl alcohol	Natural (from fruits, grains)	CNS depressant	Solvent, anti-septic, seda-tive
Tobacco	Fag, coffin nail	*Nicotinia tabacum*	Natural	CNS toxin (nicotine)	Emetic (nico-tine)
Glue		Aromatic hydrocarbons	Synthetic	CNS depressant	None

Source: "Teaching about Drugs, A Curriculum Guide, K-12," Kent Ohio, American School Health Association. By permission of the American School Health Association and the Pharmaceutical Manufacturers Association, © July 1978.

phine, for example, the tolerance may be as high as 78 grains in 16 hours, a dosage strong enough to kill 12 or more unaddicted persons. The safe therapeutic dosage of morphine given in hospitals is usually considered to be about one grain in the same period of time.

The heroin or morphine addict becomes dependent upon his injections over a varying length of time, usually quite short, the addiction increasing slowly in intensity thereafter. Authorities are generally agreed that this dependence is favored more by the regularity of administration than by the amount of the drug or the method of administration. The addict becomes as dependent on drugs as he is on food, and if he is receiving his usual daily supply he is not readily recognized as an addict. Even intimate friends and family may not know of the addiction. If the individual does not receive this daily supply, however, clearly characteristic symptoms, referred to as *withdrawal distress* or the abstinence syndrome, will appear within approximately 10–12 hours. He may become nervous and restless, he may develop acute stomach cramps, and his eyes may water and his nose run. Later, he stops eating; he may vomit frequently, develop diarrhea, lose weight, and suffer muscular pains in the back and legs. During this period the "shakes" may develop, and if the addict cannot get relief by obtaining drugs he is in for considerable mental and physical distress. Consequently, an addict will go to almost any lengths to obtain a supply of drugs to relieve the suffering of withdrawal distress. Once the drugs are obtained, he appears normal again within about 30 minutes.

Substance	How Taken	Usual Form of Product	Effects Sought	Long-term Possible Effects	Physical Dependence Potential	Psychological Dependence Potential	Organic Damage Potential
PCP	Smoked or swallowed	Tablets, powder in smoking mixtures	Harsher than LSD	?	No	Possible	Not determined
Mescaline	Swallowed	Tablets, capsules	Same as LSD	?	No	Possible	Not determined
Psilocybin	Swallowed	Tablets, capsules	Same as LSD	?	No	Possible	Not determined
Coffee, Tea, Colas	Swallowed	Liquid	Alertness	May aggravate organic actions	No	Yes	No
Alcohol	Swallowed or applied topically	Liquid	Sense alteration, anxiety reduction	Toxic psychosis, addiction; neurologic damage	Yes	Yes	Yes
Tobacco	Smoked, sniffed, chewed	Snuff, pipe-cut particles, cigarettes	Relaxation	Loss of appetite, habituation	Possible	Yes	Possible
Glue	Inhaled	Plastic cement	Intoxication	Impaired perception, coordination, judgment	No	Yes	Yes

This physiological and psychological dependence on opiate drugs, with the stage always set for the withdrawal syndrome, makes this drug addict a particularly serious problem, both for himself and for society. As tolerance for the drug is developed and more and more must be taken to relieve the physiological and psychological symptoms of withdrawal distress, the habit is well established. It is difficult to break the habit.

Methadone (dolophine) is a synthetic narcotic analgesic which was originally developed in Germany during World War II. It is a potent, long-lasting narcotic which comes in pill, injectable liquid, or oral liquid form. For some years it has been used to treat heroin addicts who are put on a methadone-maintenance program with one dose which may last up to a day, as contrasted to the three minimum daily dosages taken by most addicts. The idea behind the methadone-maintenance program is that the addict is brought up to a relatively large dosage, which theoretically establishes enough cross tolerance that euphoria with other drugs, particularly the less potent heroin, is impossible. Methadone now appears, however, to be physically and psychologically addicting, does not always block the euphoric effects of other opiates, and has increasingly presented problems as it has become used in place of other drugs.[39]

Cocaine, the best-known stimulant drug, is most commonly inhaled or "snorted" through the nose. Cocaine is considered a recreational drug and one that

[39]Robert S. Weppner, Richard C. Stephens, and Harold T. Conrad, "Methadone: Some Aspects of Its Legal and Illegal Use," *American Journal of Psychiatry,* 129 (1972), 451–455. Also see Dan Waldorf and Douglas W. Daily, "Debunking Popular Myths about Addicts and Addiction," in Robert H. Coombs, ed., *Junkies and Straights: The Camarillo Experience* (Lexington, Mass.: Lexington Books, 1975), pp. 45–46.

TABLE 9.2 Drug Preferred by First Admissions to NIMH Clinical Research Center, Lexington, Kentucky, 1971

(By Race and Sex)

Drug	White				Black			
	Male		Female		Male		Female	
	No.	Percent	No.	Percent	No.	Percent	No.	Percent
Narcotic Analgesics								
Heroin	158	54.3	34	37.3	359	67.7	61	60.4
Dilaudid	22	7.6	9	9.9	0	0.0	2	1.9
Morphine	14	4.8	3	3.3	1	0.2	1	0.9
Numorphan	8	2.7	7	7.7	1	0.2	2	1.9
Cough syrups	3	1.0	1	1.1	14	2.6	3	2.9
Opium	2	0.7	1	1.1	2	0.3	0	0.0
Other narcotic analgesics	23	7.9	7	7.7	6	1.1	5	5.0
Sedative Hypnotic Relaxants								
Tuinal	2	0.7	1	1.1	0	0.0	2	1.9
Seconal	1	0.3	2	2.2	0	0.0	1	1.0
Valium	1	0.3	0	0.0	0	0.0	0	0.0
Other sedative hypnotic relaxants	2	0.7	2	2.2	0	0.0	0	0.0
Stimulant-Type Drugs								
Cocaine or derivatives	12	4.1	4	4.4	95	17.9	12	11.9
Methedrine	10	3.4	6	6.4	1	0.2	0	0.0
Other stimulant-type drugs	2	0.7	5	5.5	1	0.2	1	0.9
Hallucinogens								
Marijuana	20	6.9	7	7.7	42	7.9	5	4.9
LSD	6	2.1	2	2.2	5	0.9	2	2.0
Peyote	1	0.3	0	0.0	0	0.0	0	0.0
Psilocybin	1	0.3	0	0.0	0	0.0	0	0.0
Other hallucinogens	0	0.0	0	0.0	0	0.0	1	1.0
Alcohol	3	1.0	0	0.0	3	0.6	3	2.9
Total	291	99.9[a]	91	99.9[a]	530	99.9[a]	101	99.9[a]

[a]Does not total to 100 percent because of rounding errors.
Source: Dr. Robert S. Weppner, NIMH Clinical Research Center, Lexington, Kentucky, private communication, 1972.

facilitates social interaction. It produces a euphoria, a sense of intense stimulation and a sense of psychic and physical well-being accompanied by reduced fatigue. Illicit cocaine is sold as a white crystalline powder frequently diluted to about half its volume by other ingredients, particularly sugar. Cocaine is extremely expensive; its current (1977) street price ranges from $60–$100 a gram (about 1/30th of an ounce).[40] The combination of the high price and the exotic properties attributed to it has contributed

[40]Robert C. Petersen, "Cocaine: An Overview," in Robert C. Petersen and Richard C. Stillman, eds., *Cocaine: 1977* (Washington, D.C.: National Institute of Drug Abuse Research, Monograph 13, Government Printing Office, 1977), p. 5.

to cocaine's street reputation as *the* status drug. American use patterns are character-ized by infrequent use of small quantities of cocaine.[41] In one study 85 regular users of cocaine were observed. Although the subjects' self-reported experiences were quite positive, negative effects were also indicated, such as restlessness, anxiety, hyperirrita-bility, and, for some (5 percent), paranoia.[42] Cocaine is not physiologically addictive, but it has a potential psychological dependence.

Barbiturates are sedatives and hypnotics that exert a powerful calming action on the central nervous system, and thus are of great value to those who suffer from nervous tension, high blood pressure, and epilepsy, as well as from a number of other physical and psychological conditions. These synthetic drugs, derived from barbital and produced in solution, tablet, or capsule form, are legal when prescribed by a licensed physician. There are three general classifications: long-acting, slow-starting drugs like phenobarbital; intermediates such as amobarbital sodium and butabarbital sodium; and short-acting, fast-starters, pentobarbital sodium and secobarbital sodium. When properly prescribed and taken as directed, barbiturates have no lasting adverse effect. The patient's system will absorb the drug, make it harmless by liver or kidney action, depending upon the drug ingested, and eventually pass whatever residue may be left. If carelessly used, however, barbiturates often lead to psychological depen-dency and physiological addiction. In their direct action on the body, they are potentially more dangerous than opiates, and an overdose may well lead to death because the drug can depress the brain's respiratory control to the point where breathing ceases. Under the influence of barbiturates addicts are confused and lose their sense of timing, thus they are prey to overdosages. Superficial signs of excessive barbiturate use are quite similar to the classic stages of alcohol intoxication: relaxation and increased sociability, then gloominess and irritability, then staggering, incoher-ence, and a lapse into deep sleep. Overdosage turns sleep into a coma, and if there is not prompt medical attention death may result.

The *hallucinogens* include marijuana and hashish and the "consciousness expanders," such as mescaline and peyote, produced from certain mushrooms, morning glory seeds, and other plants. They also include LSD, a chemical synthetic mainly from lysergic acid. It is not clear exactly in what physiological manner the hallucinogens work; while it is obvious they have a chemical effect upon the brain, the process is unclear. These drugs are not thought to be addicting or physically habituat-ing, but the sensations they produce, startling and sometimes pleasurable, may lead to repeated usage. The effects of such natural hallucinogens as peyote are not as great as those of LSD if not taken in prolonged overdoses, but LSD is a different matter. A tiny amount (1/300,000 of an ounce) of it causes delusions or hallucinations, some pleasant while others are terrifying. It tends to heighten sensory perceptions, often to the point where they are wildly distorted, even to the extent of depersonalizing the individual's ego identity, and frequently even the body images of the user. It is claimed, therefore, by some users that this has the effect of "opening up the mind,"

---

[41]Donald R. Wesson and David E. Smith, "Cocaine: Its Use for Central Nervous System Stimulation Including Recreational and Medical Uses," in Petersen and Stillman, pp. 137–152.
[42]Eduardo Siguel, "Characteristics of Clients Admitted to Treatment for Cocaine Abuse," in Petersen and Stillman, pp. 201–210.

even to the extent of awakening latent talents. If large doses are taken (over 700 mcg), confusion and delirium frequently ensue. During LSD use material that has been repressed may be unmasked, and some individuals may not be able to handle it. Although the experience usually lasts from 4 to 12 hours, it may continue for days.

Marijuana (marihuana)—bhang, hashish in stronger cake form, cannabis, or popularly "grass" or "pot"—is derived from the leaves and tender stems of the hemp plant, often known as Indian hemp, and it is usually inhaled by smoking specially prepared cigarettes called "reefers" or "joints." The general technical term for this drug is *cannabis,* an annual herb native to Asia. The hemp fiber is used for various forms of cordage and other products. The female flowering tops of the plant are the source of marijuana and hashish.

The usual effect produced by smoking these products is euphoria, a state of "dreaminess," an intensification of feelings, loquacity, inappropriate laughter, and a distorted sense of time and space, all with few unpleasant after-effects. In spite of some controversy about the effects of using marijuana, it is not usually considered by investigators in this country as a real form of drug addiction in a physical sense, although it may, to some extent, be psychologically addicting. Claims have been made that marijuana use affects performance, for example, in auto driving, that it causes psychotic episodes, that it has long-range negative effects, that it causes bodily and brain damage, and that it causes a long-term loss of ambition. The research up to 1972, on which these claims have been based, has been critically examined by such authorities as Erich Goode, and he has concluded that none of them has any real validity.[43] Many of these studies are contradictory and based on unrepresentative samples, and the data do not support the conclusions.

The National Commission on Marijuana and Drug Abuse concluded in 1972 that "From what is now known about the effects of marihuana, its use at the present level does not constitute a major threat to public health."[44] The commission found little or no evidence that marijuana can cause addiction or brain damage or lead to crime or violence or necessarily to the use of more powerful drugs such as heroin. It did find that its use while driving could be a threat to public safety. The commission gathered information on its use, conducted extensive hearings, sponsored more than 50 research projects, and studied the effects on long-term users in countries where it has been widely used for many years—Jamaica, Greece, India, and Afghanistan. A 1976 study by the Department of Health, Education and Welfare also failed to show any definitely negative physiological or psychological effects of marijuana use. The report stated, however, that present marijuana users smoke relatively low-potency material and largely only occasionally. While this does not produce demonstrable negative effects or health hazards other than while driving a motor vehicle while intoxicated with marijuana, it is possible that this might change with more frequent use or if stronger material were used.[45] Another scientific study of the literature on marijuana use has concluded that "marihuana is a relatively safe intoxicant that is not

---

[43]Erich Goode, *Drugs in American Society* (New York: Knopf, 1972), pp. 63–96.
[44]*Marihuana: A Signal of Misunderstanding,* p. 90.
[45]*Marihuana and Health,* Report to the Congress from the Secretary, Department of Health, Education and Welfare (Washington, D.C.: Government Printing Office, 1976), p. v.

addicting, does not in and of itself lead to the use of harder drugs, is not criminogenic, and does not lead to sexual excess, and the evidence that it may lead to personality deterioration and psychosis is quite unconvincing."[46] An examination of the British situation and the report of the Canadian Commission of Inquiry into the Nonmedical Use of Drugs reached similar conclusions.[47] And as President Carter concluded in recommending the decriminalization of marijuana in 1977, "Penalties against possession of a drug should not be more damaging than the use of the drug itself."

EXTENT OF MARIJUANA USE

The United Nations Commission on Narcotic Drugs estimated in 1956 that over 200 million persons in the world regularly used marijuana, and in all probability this figure is far greater today. In 1972 the National Commission on Marijuana and Drug Abuse in the United States reported that from surveys they had done an estimated 24 million persons had tried marijuana. Of this number 8,300,000 generally used it less than once a week, and there were 500,000 heavy users, those who used it more than once a day. The Commission found that the use of marijuana had tripled in the two and a half years before the report. A 1976 government report confirms the view that marijuana usage is steadily increasing. It was estimated that 36 million Americans had at one time or another used marijuana, and nearly 15 million persons were considered current users, that is, had used it within the preceding month. Twice as many men as women over 18 had used marijuana (29 percent versus 14 percent) (see Table 9.3). Marijuana use is still largely associated with the younger age groups. In fact, the relationship between usage and age is striking: past age 25 experimentation with marijuana and its continued use become less common; over age 35 marijuana

TABLE 9.3

Marijuana Use among Adults, 1971–1976

	Percent Ever Used				*Percent Current Use***			
	1971	1972	1975	1976	1971	1972	1975	1976
All adults	15	16	19	21	5	8	7	8
Age								
18–25	39	48	53	53	17	28	25	25
26–34	19	20	29	36	5	9	8	11
35+	7	3	4	6	—*	—*	—*	1
Sex								
Male	21	22	24	29	7	11	9	11
Female	10	10	14	14	3	5	5	5

*Less than 0.5%.
**Used during last month.

[46]Lester Grinspoon, *Marihuana Reconsidered* (Cambridge, Mass.: Harvard University Press, 1971), p. 323.
[47]Michael Schofield, *The Strange Case of Pot,* Canadian Commission of Inquiry into the Nonmedical Use of Drugs (LeDain Report) (Ottawa: Queen's Printer for Canada, 1970).

TABLE 9.4

Marihuana Use among Youth, 1971–1976

	Percent Ever Used				Percent Current Use*			
	1971	1972	1975	1976	1971	1972	1975	1976
All youth	14	14	23	22	6	7	12	12
Age								
12–13	6	4	6	6	2	1	2	3
14–15	10	10	22	21	7	6	12	13
16–17	27	29	39	40	10	16	20	21
Sex								
Male	14	15	24	26	7	9	12	14
Female	14	13	21	19	5	6	11	11

*Used during last month.
Source: Marihuana and Health. Sixth Annual Report to the U.S. Congress from the Secretary of Health, Education and Welfare (Rockville, Md.: National Institute on Drug Abuse, 1976), p. 5.

experience, and particularly continued use, are rare. As the marijuana-using population ages this may well change. One fourth of those between 18 and 25 years of age were classified as "current users." Among males aged 20–24 approximately 1 in 10 reported use on a daily basis. If the analysis is restricted to those in this age group who report ever having used it, nearly one in five (17 percent) did so daily. There was a steady progression by age from 6 percent of those aged 12–13 "ever used" to 40 percent aged 16–17 (see Table 9.4). The increase in the percentage of current users was even more dramatic. Just over 8 percent of the nation's 1976 high school graduates reported virtually daily marijuana use; this was 40 percent greater than the number frequently using alcohol. In Toronto, Canada, it was found that marijuana use was increasing so rapidly among students in the upper grades that a replica of a 1968 study conducted in 1970 concluded that at the current rate of increase it would take only four years until more students used marijuana than alcohol and less than six years until all high school students were using it.[48]

EXTENT OF OPIATE ADDICTION

While it is not possible to know exactly how many heroin addicts there are today in the United States, it is clear that addiction is a serious and growing problem. Because the taking of drugs for nonmedical purposes is illegal, in all probability some addicts are neither officially reported as such nor arrested. Most heroin users carefully protect their suppliers so that great skill is required to detect both users and suppliers. It is even difficult to estimate the extent of addiction in the United States. At present there is disagreement concerning the best methodology by which such estimates are to be derived and the appropriate instrumentation for measurement. Differences are even

[48]R. G. Smart and Dianne Fejer, "Recent Trends in Illicit Drug Use among Adolescents" (Toronto: Mental Health Division, National Health and Welfare, 1971).

found in the definition of addiction. As a result, the widely differing estimates should be treated with caution.[49] Arrest statistics, for example, are likely to reflect certain groups whose vulnerability to arrest is greater.[50]

The estimated number of drug addicts in the United States has generally continued to climb. In 1951, the Federal Bureau of Narcotics estimated there were between 50,000 and 60,000 addicts.[51] In the early 1970s, the estimates varied between 400,000 and 600,000. One estimate put the number of active heroin users in the United States in 1975 at 660,000.[52] In 1977, the Interim Report of the House Select Committee on Narcotics Abuse and Control estimated about 800,000 heroin addicts, of whom only about a third were under any type of treatment. One expert has pointed out that more young people are using heroin today than ever before in U.S. history. The rate of heroin usage, and addiction, has jumped enormously from 1967 to the present, certainly as much as two times and possibly as much as five times.[53] A national survey in 1969–1970 of a random sample of 7,948 students attending four-year colleges with at least 1,000 enrollment, however, showed that only 0.6 percent of them had ever used heroin.[54]

The United States leads all Western countries in the magnitude of the narcotics problem. Even Japan has a relatively minor addiction problem for a highly urbanized country with half the population of the United States. According to government reports, there were only about 6,000 narcotic addicts in the late 1960s, a large proportion of whom became addicted not through the illicit use of narcotics but under medical treatment.[55] Several European countries, notably Great Britain and Sweden, have recently reported increases in drug addiction, but the situation in Europe is, as yet, nothing like that in the United States.

Since 1962, there have been reports of much increase in the use of heroin by college and high school students. Goode points out, however, that while the numbers as well as the percentage of young heroin users have dramatically increased recently, it is as fallacious to exaggerate the extent of heroin use as it is to minimize it: "It is a rare college campus where one student in ten has even tried heroin; on most campuses, the figure is closer to one in a hundred."[56]

Some indication of the widespread use of heroin in lower-income areas in New York is the fact that a 1971 government study of two such areas showed 70 to 233 persons per 10,000 were addicted to heroin.[57] Of the residents questioned, 43 percent

---

[49]For an excellent discussion of these problems, see Joan Dunne Rittenhouse, ed., *The Epidemiology of Heroin and Other Narcotics* (Menlo Park, Calif.: Stanford Research Institute, National Institute on Drug Abuse, 1976).

[50]Bruce Bullington, John G. Munns, Gilbert Geis, and James Raner, "Concerning Heroin Use and Official Records," *American Journal of Public Health*, 59 (1969), 1887–1893.

[51]John Gerrity, "Truth about the 'Drug Menace,'" *Harper's Magazine*, 204 (1952), 27–31.

[52]Leon Gibson Hunt and Carl D. Chambers, *The Heroin Epidemics: A Study of Heroin Use in the United States, 1965–1975* (New York: Spectrum Publications, 1976), p. 73.

[53]Goode, *Drugs in American Society*, p. 159.

[54]Eugene Groves, in a report for the National Institute of Mental Health, cited in the *Drinking and Drugs Practice Surveyor*, No. 4 (1971).

[55]Ministry of Health and Welfare, *A Brief Account of Narcotics Abuse and Counter Measures in Japan*, Tokyo, 1970.

[56]Goode, *Drugs in American Society*, p. 160.

[57]Reported in an United Press International news release in *The Wisconsin State Journal* (Madison), July 24, 1972.

knew someone who used heroin, 13 percent had been offered heroin at least once, and 24 percent had friends who used it. A study of the residential distribution of heroin users in San Antonio, Texas, found that use of the drug varied inversely by socioeconomic status and that it was associated with minority status.[58] The high addiction rate among blacks is largely a product of the fact that the concentration of the traffic in black areas makes the drug particularly readily available there, and as time passed the number of blacks experimenting with such drugs as heroin and marijuana has apparently increased steadily.[59] A more recent study confirmed a similar concentration of high rates of heroin addiction among areas of low socioeconomic groups with a high percentage of minority group members.[60]

The predominant pattern is the drug user from urban areas. In the past there was considerable drug addiction among whites in the rural South, but the numbers are now decreasing. A study of southern opiate addicts has shown that factors leading to addiction are quite different from those in large metropolitan areas in the United States and, therefore, quite different from the general pattern of addiction.[61] The largest group became addicted because of medical treatment with drugs, an individual pattern more common 25–50 years ago. Second in importance was the use of drugs in treating alcohol excesses, and the last was pleasure seeking through associations with others. The median age of over 30 was much older.

There is recent evidence that the pattern of heroin use is changing from that found as little as 10 years ago, with increased rates of new use occurring in new populations and geographic areas.[62] These areas are smaller cities, particularly cities of 500,000 population and less. This latest trend in heroin use is contrasted with an almost exclusively urban pattern that prevailed up until the early 1970s. Hunt and Chambers have sketched a rough chronology of intravenous heroin use in the United States as follows:

1. 1930s—use begins to develop
2. Post-1945—first widespread use in larger cities
3. 1950–Early 1960s—most cities probably experience low and constant incidence of new heroin use
4. 1960s—new use begins to grow rapidly, rising to local peaks in the late 1960s and then falling rapidly
5. Early 1970s—analyses begin to appear forecasting the end of "the epidemic" based on consistent peak-incidence years, 1968–1969
6. Mid-1970s—analysts begin to revise their forecasts based on city-specific data that show a distinct sequence of peak years by city size and spread over a much longer period (1968–1974, or later). These new data indicate that by 1971 all metropolitan areas of a million or more have already experienced peak use.[63]

---

[58]John Redlinger and Jerry B. Michael, "Ecological Variations in Heroin Abuse," *Sociological Quarterly,* 11 (1970), 219–229.
[59]Lindesmith and Gagnon, p. 172.
[60]Redlinger and Michael, pp. 219–227.
[61]John A. O'Donnell, *Narcotic Addicts in Kentucky* (Washington, D.C.: National Institute of Mental Health, Government Printing Office, 1969); and Ball, p. 211.
[62]Hunt and Chambers.
[63]Hunt and Chambers, p. 53.

These authors go on to state that "assuming current analyses of incidence peaks and geographic diffusion are substantially correct, future estimates of heroin addiction should be based upon (1) a continuing endemic incidence from our larger cities, plus (2) 85,000–280,000 new cases generated from population concentrations of 500,-000 or less."[64] In other words, while the heroin epidemic of the 1960s in cities over 500,000 may have leveled off, the rates of new cases of addiction in smaller cities are increasing. This may signal more increases in addiction due to increased supplies of heroin and a new user population.[65] Based on a 1975 National Institute of Drug Abuse study of 24 metropolitan areas, New York had an estimated 69,000 heroin addicts in 1975; Los Angeles was second with 60,000; Chicago third with 47,700; Detroit fourth with 33,200; San Francisco fifth with 28,600; and Philadelphia sixth with 23,800.[66] On a per capita basis, however, the 10 cities with the most heroin addicts per 100,000 population were:

1. San Francisco 915
2. Los Angeles 864
3. Phoenix 796
4. Detroit 792
5. San Diego 788
6. Chicago 677
7. San Antonio 657
8. New York 608
9. Seattle 607
10. Miami 530

The Changing Nature of Opiate Addiction

The nature of opiate addiction is changing. Today, addiction to opiates is heavily concentrated among young urban males from large cities, particularly among blacks and Puerto Ricans. Such a pattern is much different from the one the nineteenth century users of opiates presented. There was no similar concentration noted; about two thirds of the users, according to early surveys, were women, and addiction in the medical profession was noted. Most observers felt it was less prevalent in the lower than in the middle and upper classes. The average age of addicts at that time was found to be between about 40 and 50, and some investigators believed that addiction was a problem of middle age, since most addicts took up the habit after the age of 30.[67] Some idea of the changes occurring between 1937 and 1962 was revealed by a comparison of addict patients at Lexington and Fort Worth hospitals during these periods.[68] The male patients were younger by some eight years. The use of heroin

---

[64]Hunt and Chambers, p. 53.
[65]Jerome J. Platt and Christina Labate, *Heroin Addiction: Theory, Research and Treatment* (New York: Wiley, 1976), p. 330.
[66]National Institute of Drug Abuse.
[67]Lindesmith and Gagnon, pp. 164–165.
[68]Ball.

prior to admission had increased, whereas the use of morphine had decreased. The proportion of patients who came from northern metropolitan centers had increased notably. Nevertheless, high rates of hospitalization have continued from many of the southern states. "Thus, the major change has been the increasing preponderance of heroin addicts from minority groups of our largest cities."[69] A St. Louis study in 1967 of a sample of the general black population, for example, found that 1 out of 10 city-born black men had been addicted to heroin.[70]

AGE AT FIRST OPIATE USE AND LENGTH OF ADDICTION

Narcotics are first used at quite an early age. Of 1,013 first admissions in 1971 to the NIMH Clinical Research Center in Lexington, Kentucky, approximately two thirds of both white male and black male addicts began to use drugs between 15 and 19 years of age (see Table 9.5). In fact, 13.5 and 8.8 percent, respectively, began before fifteen. Approximately one half of both the white women addicts and the black first used narcotics between 15 and 19 years of age. These figures are roughly the same as those obtained in a national analysis of age of first narcotic use.[71]

All studies indicate a high rate of relapse among opiate addicts: a period of six months to five years, varying from 70 to 90 percent. While this is, in part, a product of the strong societal reaction on the part of many against the use of drugs, which may, in

TABLE 9.5		**Age at First Narcotics Use for First Admissions to NIMH Clinical Research Center, Lexington, Kentucky, 1971 (By Race and Sex)**						

Age	White				Black			
	Male		Female		Male		Female	
	No.	Percent	No.	Percent	No.	Percent	No.	Percent
Less than 15	39	13.5	12	13.3	47	8.8	8	8.0
15–19	189	65.4	47	52.2	346	65.2	52	52.0
20–24	44	15.1	20	22.2	107	20.1	28	28.0
25–29	10	3.7	4	4.4	20	3.7	7	7.0
30–34	2	0.7	4	4.4	6	1.1	4	4.0
35–39	2	0.7	2	2.2	5	0.9	1	1.0
40–44	3	1.0	1	1.1	0	0.0	0	0.0
Total	289	99.8[a]	90	99.8[a]	531	99.8[a]	100	100.0

[a]Does not total to 100 percent because of rounding errors.
Source: Dr. Robert S. Weppner, NIMH Clinical Research Center, Lexington, Kentucky, private communication, 1972.

---

[69]Ball, p. 211.
[70]Lee N. Robins and George E. Murphey, "Drug Use in a Normal Population of Young Negro Men," *American Journal of Public Health,* 57 (1967), 1580–1596.
[71]Hunt and Chambers, p. 79.

turn, lead to a deviant career,[72] relapse cannot be entirely explained by labeling. Stephens' study of 236 male narcotic addicts found that the extent of prior labeling by formal agencies was not related to relapse but that informal labeling by the family and addict friends was related to it.[73]

Some two thirds of the drug addicts eventually appear to leave addiction or to become inactive.[74] A study made of those who were inactive in 1960 but had been active in 1955 involved 5,333 men and 1,681 women. Their ages ranged from 18 to 76, with the average age 35.1.[75] Addicts in this study included only regular users of opium derivatives, such as heroin, and of synthetic opiates, such as meperidine (Demerol). The average length of addiction was 8.6 years, although some had been addicted for over 50 years. Inactivity increased cumulatively by age, with three fourths of the dropouts occurring by the age of 36.2. Inactivity takes place largely in the thirties, with 79 percent becoming inactive between 25 and 44. Statistical tests showed that this was not a statistical artifact, for the proportion of addicts becoming inactive in each group was not dependent on the proportion of addicts in that age group in the total active addict population. The reasons for leaving addiction are not clear; a number of hypotheses are that it is a function of the life cycle of juvenile addiction, the number of years of addiction itself, or that addicts leave the more youthful drug subculture as they grow older. Contrary to labeling theory, it appears that sustained societal reaction from formal agencies and from informal sources (that is friends, family, and neighbors) introduces a process that may result in eventual abstention from drug use. This is due to the fact that official labeling of the addict occurs long after addiction has taken place in most cases, and over time the addict's appetite for drugs often outstrips the resources to provide them. "The effect of society's reaction at this point is to place an unbearable amount of pressure on the addict to abstain for good, and sooner or later most do."[76] Just as becoming addicted is a social process, so too is becoming an ex-addict.

RELATION OF OCCUPATION TO OPIATE USE

Although there is wide divergence in the occupations of narcotic addicts, certain occupations are known to offer more hazards. The New York state survey, for example, showed the rate of regular use of heroin per 10,000 population to be highest

---

[72]Earl Rubington, "Drug Addiction as a Deviant Career," *International Journal of the Addictions,* 2 (1960), 3–20.

[73]Richard C. Stephens, "Relapse among Narcotic Addicts: An Empirical Test of Labeling Theory," unpublished Ph.D. dissertation, University of Wisconsin, Madison, 1971. See also Jay R. Williams, *The Effects of Labeling the "Drug-Abuser": An Inquiry* (Rockville, Md.: National Institute on Drug Abuse, 1976).

[74]Study of the Federal Bureau of Narcotics, cited in Charles Winick, "Maturing Out of Narcotic Addiction," *Bulletin on Narcotics,* 14 (1962), 6.

[75]Winick, "Maturing Out of Narcotic Addiction."

[76]William E. McAuliffe, "Beyond Secondary Deviance: Negative Labeling and Its Effects on the Heroin Addict" in Walter R. Gove, ed., *The Labeling of Deviance: Evaluating a Perspective* (New York: Sage/Halsted, 1975), p. 236.

among sales workers and among clerical and other low-level white-collar workers.[77] The medical profession has an excessive share of addicts.[78] Goode estimated in 1974 that there were three to four thousand physician narcotic addicts in the United States, or about one in every 85 to 115 physicians (based on a total of about 350,000 physicians).[79] Other countries have reported a substantial incidence of addiction among physicians. In England physicians are reported as being the occupational group most heavily represented among addicts, accounting for 17 percent of the addicts there. One report, summarizing United Nations data on the subject, stated that 1 physician in every 550 in England and 1 in every 95 in Germany were addicts.[80] Doctors can obtain drugs easily and rather inexpensively. Moreover, physicians have knowledge of what drugs can do for someone who is tense or tired, which is an important factor in their becoming addicted. Many of these physicians do not come to the attention of authorities because they can often maintain their addiction without detection.

In a study of 98 physicians who either were or had been opiate addicts, pronounced differences were found between them and the typical addict who buys drugs from a "pusher."

> The most obvious difference is that the age at which the physicians began to use drugs is just about the age that the typical addict stops using drugs, whether by "maturing out" or for other reasons. The "street" addict typically begins drug use in adolescence, while the physician begins when he is an established community and professional figure. The "street" addict takes heroin, while the typical physician addict took meperidine. The physician can get a pure quality of his drug, although it is not as strong as heroin. The "street" addict gets a diluted drug. He often starts with marijuana, although none of the physicians ever smoked marijuana.
>
> The physician is usually discovered by the indirect evidence of a check of prescription records, while the "street" addict is usually arrested because he has narcotics in his possession or has been observed making an illegal purchase. The physician is usually not arrested, while the typical "street" addict is arrested. Money to obtain drugs was not a problem for the physicians, as it usually is for the typical addict, who must steal in order to obtain money to buy drugs illegally. The physicians could use their professional access to narcotics to obtain drugs without much money. Even if they paid, the legal prices of narcotic drugs are very low.
>
> Most non-physician addicts associate with other addicts. In contrast, the physicians interviewed almost never associated with other physician addicts, or did not do so knowingly. They did not have any occasion for doing so, either for the purpose of getting drugs or for passing time, or for emotional support. They were solitary about their addiction. The "street" addict usually talks in a special jargon and often has a kind of wry insight into drug use, which stems from his extended discussions with his peers. The physicians did not talk in jargon and manifested very little insight into their drug use.[81]

---

[77]Chambers, p. 224.

[78]Charles Winick, "Physician Narcotic Addicts," *Social Problems,* 9 (1961), 174–186. Also see Florence Heyman, "Methadone Maintenance as Law and Order," *Trans-Action (Society),* 9 (1972), 25.

[79]Erich Goode, "The Criminology of Drugs and Drug Use," in Abraham S. Blumberg, ed., *Current Perspectives on Criminal Behavior: Original Essays on Criminology* (New York: Knopf, 1974), p. 169.

[80]Lawrence Kolb, "The Drug Addiction Muddle," *Police,* 1 (1957), 57–62. Also see Goode, "The Criminology of Drugs and Drug Use," p. 169.

[81]Winick, "Physician Narcotic Addicts," pp. 178–179. Copyright © 1961 by the Society for the Study of Social Problems. Reprinted by permission of the publisher.

Performers in the entertainment world, such as jazz musicians, sometimes become marijuana users, largely because such drug use appears to be much less disapproved by their associates. The use of drugs was studied among 357 jazz band musicians in New York City, 73 percent of whom were white.[82] Heroin was used by a large proportion: 53 percent at least once, 24 percent occasionally, and one in six, or 16 percent, regularly. A number of group factors are related to the musician's drug use. One was the extent of use by the band itself. About half (53 percent) felt that the use of drugs was related to upward or downward mobility. For example, a young musician may take a drug to accelerate progress to the top. Drugs may be used to help tide a musician over periods of unemployment. About one in five, especially those over 30, felt that drug use was related to "one nighters" because this type of traveling is tiring for musicians. As one heroin user described it:

> I was traveling on the road in 1952. We had terrible travel arrangements and traveled by special bus. We were so tired and beat that we didn't even have time to brush our teeth when we arrived in a town. We'd get up on the bandstand looking awful. The audience would say, 'Why don't they smile? They look like they can't smile.' I found I could pep myself up more quickly with heroin than with liquor. If you drank feeling that tired, you'd fall on your face.[83]

THE PROCESS OF USING MARIJUANA

One becomes a marijuana user, either on a regular or irregular basis, through a learning process, bolstered by subcultural support for its continued use. When one uses marijuana for pleasure, one must first learn to conceive of the drug as something that can produce pleasurable sensations.[84] The user must learn three things: (1) to smoke the drug in a way that will produce certain effects; (2) to recognize these effects and to connect the drug with them; and (3) finally, to enjoy the sensations. These three steps occurred in all the marijuana users whom Becker studied. He claims that first users do not ordinarily "get high" because they do not know the proper technique of drawing the cigarette or pipe and holding the smoke. Even after learning the technique, they do not form a conception of smoking as being related to pleasure. Even though there are pleasurable sensations, the new marijuana users may not feel that the pleasures are enough, or they may not be sufficiently aware of their specific nature to become regular users. They learn to feel the sensations of "being high" as defined by others. With greater use, and guidance from others, they learn to appreciate more of the sensations of the drug.

Finally, one more step is necessary to continue the use of marijuana. The person must learn to enjoy the sensations experienced with the use of the drug. Feeling dizzy, being thirsty, misjudging distances, or a tingling scalp may not of themselves be pleasurable experiences. The user must learn to define them in this way. Association

---

[82]Charles Winick, "The Use of Drugs by Jazz Musicians," *Social Problems,* 7 (1959–1960), 240–254.
[83]Winick, "The Use of Drugs by Jazz Musicians," p. 246.
[84]Becker, pp. 235–242.

with other marijuana users helps to define sensations that were frightening into those that are pleasurable and to be looked forward to. An experienced marijuana user has described how newcomers are helped to define the use of the drug as giving pleasurable sensations:

> Well, they get pretty high sometimes. The average person isn't ready for that, and it is a little frightening to them sometimes. I mean, they've been high on lush (alcohol), and they get higher that way than they've ever been before, and they don't know what's happening to them. Because they think they're going to keep going up, up, up until they lose their minds or begin doing weird things or something. You have to like reassure them, explain to them that they're not really flipping or anything, that they're gonna be all right. You have to just talk them out of being afraid. Keep talking to them, reassuring, telling them it's all right. And come on with your own story, you know: "The same thing happened to me. You'll get to like that after awhile." Keep coming on like that; pretty soon you talk them out of being scared. And besides they see you doing it and nothing horrible is happening to you, so that gives them more confidence.[85]

The use of marijuana is a group activity, lending itself to friendships and participation in a group setting. It is smoked in intimate groups, which, in turn, has a relation to its impact on the individual. This group nature, according to Erich Goode, is reflected in the group setting where one's social relations are with intimates, friends of intimates, or potential intimates rather than with strangers; the long-term continuing social relations within the group; a certain degree of value consensus within the group; a convergence of values as a result of progressive group involvement; the maintenance of the circle's cohesive nature through the joint activity which reaffirms its social bonds by acting them out; and the definition of the group themselves, as well as others, partly on the basis of whether they have or have not participated in the activity.[86] Group contacts are needed in order to get a supply, to learn the special technique of smoking to gain maximum effect, and to furnish psychological support for engaging in an illegal activity. Marijuana is nearly always smoked in a group. "There is no cannabis equivalent to the secret drinker, who hides a bottle in his or her room and develops a dependence on alcohol unknown to his friends or family."[87] One could hardly call an experimenter, that is, one who has tried it a few times a true member of a group; on the other hand, a person will become more involved the more he smokes marijuana, his bonds with other smokers becoming stronger and his bonds with nonsmokers weaker. Goode provides a more extensive description and analysis of this social context of marijuana use.

> Group processes operate at the very inception of the individual's marijuana using experience. Being "turned on" for the first time is a group experience. Only three percent of my respondents were alone when they had their first marijuana experience. And four percent were in the company of at least one other individual, each of whom was also experiencing marijuana for the first time. All of the remainder—93 percent—had their first marijuana experience in the company of at least one individual who had already smoked marijuana. It is clear, then, that the neophyte marijuana smoker, at the point of

---

[85]Becker, p. 240. Copyright © 1973 by The Macmillan Publishing Co., Inc. Reprinted by permission of the publisher.
[86]Erich Goode, "Multiple Drug Use among Marijuana Smokers," *Social Problems,* 17 (1969), 54.
[87]Schofield, p. 131.

his first exposure to the drug, is subject to group definitions of the desirability of the experience, as well as the nature of its reality. Marijuana use, even at its very inception, *is simultaneously participation in a specific social group*. This generalization holds equally as strong for the *continued* use of marijuana. Marijuana is characteristically smoked in groups, not in isolation. In the sample, only five percent claimed to smoke at least half of the time alone, and almost half—45 percent—said that they *never* smoked alone. Marijuana cannot be understood apart from the web of social relations in which it is implicated.

Moreover, the *nature* of the group character of marijuana use also significantly determines its impact. Marijuana is not merely smoked in groups, but it is also smoked in *intimate* groups. The others with whom one is smoking are overwhelmingly *significant* others. One rarely smokes with strangers, with individuals whom one does not care for, or is indifferent to, or whom one does not expect to like in the future. Even at large parties where marijuana is smoked, small cliques will form, oases of compatibles, wherein all will share the same activity. Smoking marijuana is symbolic in ways that more accepted behavior is not; it resembles communal eating in civilizations for whom eating well is a rare or intermittent festivity. Brotherhood is an element in the marijuana ritual, as is the notion of sharing something treasured and esteemed. Emphasis is placed on passing a given "joint" around to all present, thus completing a circle; this procedure is generally preferred to that of each participant lighting up his own "joint" and smoking it by himself, without any group continuity. And of course, the clandestine nature of the activity, the fact that it is legally "underground," lends an air of excitement and collective intrigue to marijuana smoking which would be absent in a context of licitness, as with drinking. All of these factors make marijuana use a highly significant (to the participants) and emotionally charged activity.[88]

Marijuana and Heroin

Many people believe that heroin addiction is facilitated by marijuana use; in fact, a national survey in 1970 found that the majority of the persons questioned felt that marijuana smoking causes people to want to use stronger drugs like heroin. So far, however, this relation has not been substantiated. The National Commission on Marijuana and Drug Abuse concluded, in 1972, that the overwhelming majority of marijuana users do not progress to other drugs, either remaining with marijuana or changing to alcohol. "Marihuana use per se does not dictate whether other drugs will be used; nor does it determine the rate of progression, if and when it occurs, or which drugs will be used. The user's social group seems to be the strongest influence on whether other drugs will be used; and, if so, which drugs will be used."[89] A government report to Congress in 1971 stated that "it is generally conceded that marijuana does not necessarily lead directly to the use of other drugs. On a worldwide basis, there is little evidence of a progression from the use of marijuana to that of opiates or hallucinogens."[90] Actually, a large variety of drugs might be immediate precursors to heroin addiction.[91] Goode has concluded that while heroin addiction may imply a

---

[88]Goode, "Multiple Drug Use among Marijuana Smokers," pp. 54–56. Copyright © 1969 by the Society for the Study of Social Problems. Reprinted by permission of the publisher.
[89]*Marihuana: A Signal of Misunderstanding*, pp. 88–89.
[90]*Marihuana and Health*, p. 8.
[91]See Robert S. Weppner and Michael H. Agar, "Immediate Precursors to Heroin Addiction," *Journal of Health and Social Behavior*, 12 (1971), 10–18.

one-time use of marijuana, marijuana "need not imply eventual use of heroin among all groups."[92] This is confirmed by the fact that there probably are at least 15 to 20 times more regular users of marijuana than of heroin.

Marijuana Subcultures

While the initiate must first learn how to use marijuana, its use is maintained through the subculture. The marijuana subculture contains a number of conduct norms, at least within white racial groups, which prescribe marijuana use and other behavior as appropriate in certain situations. A number of these conduct norms have been identified. The participant in this subculture is expected to (1) interact with marijuana users; (2) use marijuana or hashish if offered; (3) use them with some regularity (once a month or more); and (4) buy from or sell marijuana to friends if one possesses a quantity.[93] The major difference between white and black drug subcultures lies in the other drugs that regular marijuana users might be expected to use. Marijuana-using blacks are more likely to be expected to use cocaine and heroin; whites to use hallucinogens, amphetamines, barbiturates, and methedrine.[94] It is not, therefore, the use of marijuana per se that may lead the user to experiment with other drugs, possibly of a dangerous nature, but the drug subculture that leads its participants to them. It is also the subculture that inhibits nondrug activities, depending on the degree of involvement of the individual.

A major difference between the marijuana and heroin subcultures relates to the fact that marijuana use is overwhelmingly recreational in nature, while heroin is not easily perceived in these terms. The use of marijuana, like social drinking, serves a symbolic function for users, identifying members of the subculture and serving as a lubricant in social settings. Whereas heroin is used alone or with another person in order to share resources (money, "works," and the like), marijuana is almost never used alone; it is a group activity from the time of initiation through continued use. Goode notes that "when one person offers another a smoke of a marijuana cigarette, there is communication taking place between the two, as the person who offers consciously thinks of sharing and participating in a common activity."[95] The importance of one's associations and the sociability of using marijuana has been noted in a recent English study. The general conclusion reached was that

> being a drugtaker was more important to many of those observed and interviewed than were the effects of the drugs they used. First, drugtaking experiences had usually been fostered by contact with, and encouragement by, friends who were held in high regard. Such contact with drugtakers and the apparent peer support for drug use in effect provided a "neutralization" of any fears or doubts concerning drug use, and it resocialized individuals to regard drugtaking as harmless, pleasant, or desirable. It seemed that, in

---

[92]Erich Goode, ed., *Marijuana* (New York: Atherton, 1969), p. 62.
[93]Bruce D. Johnson, *Marihuana Users and Drug Subcultures* (New York: Wiley, 1973), p. 194. Also see John Langer, "Drug Entrepreneurs and Dealing Culture," *Social Problems*, 24 (1977), 377–387.
[94]Johnson, p. 196.
[95]Erich Goode, *The Marijuana Smokers* (New York: Basic Books, 1970), pp. 23–24. See also Erich Goode, *The Drug Phenomenon: Social Aspects of Drug Taking* (Indianapolis: Bobbs Merrill, 1973), especially pp. 37–40.

general, individuals had become drugtakers in order to affirm values they believed to be important.[96]

THE PROCESS OF OPIATE ADDICTION

Opiate addiction is learned just as other behavior is learned—primarily from association with others who are addicts. Some indication of this is the fact that although drug addiction used to be common among Chinese in the United States, by the 1960s this group of addicts had almost ceased to exist.[97] The usual pattern is that of association for other reasons rather than one person seeking another simply because the other person is an addict. Opium addiction is taken over by an individual in much the same way as other cultural patterns are transmitted. Addicts must first learn how to use drugs. They must be aware of the drug, know how to administer it, and be able to recognize its effects. Beyond this, there must be some motive for trying the drug—to relieve pain, please someone, achieve acceptance in a group, produce euphoria, or achieve some other goal. This goal need have little to do with the narcotic's specific effects. "Moreover, the motivation or goal of initial drug use must be sharply distinguished from the motivation to maintain a drug habit. The latter is a product of learning which seems to depend on the interaction between drug effects, especially in the first experience of withdrawal, and the self-conception of the drug user."[98]

Addiction and Recognition of Withdrawal Distress

Lindesmith, one of the leading sociologists in the area of opiate addiction, has explained addiction to opiates on the basis of the addict's association of the drug with the distress accompanying sudden cessation of its use. Using opiates is one thing; becoming addicted to them is another. Users who fail to realize the connection between the distress and the opiate escape addiction, whereas those that link the distress and the opiate, and thereafter use it to alleviate the distress symptoms, invariably become addicted.[99] Addiction is distinguished by "an intense, conscious desire for the drug and by a tendency to relapse, evidently caused by the persistence of attitudes established in early addiction. Other correlated aspects are the dependence upon the drug as a twenty-four hour necessity, the impulse to increase the dosage far beyond bodily need and the definition of one's self as an addict."[100]

Many persons may use heroin over a long period of time and not become addicted to it, while others become addicted in a brief time. An addicted individual

---

[96]Martin A. Plant, *Drugtakers in an English Town* (London: Tavistock, 1975), p. 253.

[97]John C. Ball and M. P. Lau, "The Chinese Narcotic Addict in the United States," *Social Forces,* 45 (1966), 68–72.

[98]John A. Clausen, "Social and Psychological Factors in Narcotics Addiction," *Law and Contemporary Problems,* 22 (1957), 39.

[99]Lindesmith, *Addiction and Opiates.*

[100]Lindesmith, *Addiction and Opiates,* p. 64.

who does not receive a daily supply begins to experience withdrawal distress, or the abstinence syndrome, within 10–12 hours. The physiological or biological effects of drugs are insufficient to produce addiction, although they are indispensable preconditions.

> The effect which the biological events associated with using drugs has on human behavior is seen as one that is mediated by the manner in which such events are perceived or conceptualized by the person who experiences them. Persons who interpret withdrawal distress as evidence of the onset of an unknown disease act accordingly, and, if they are not enlightened, do not become addicted. Persons who interpret the symptoms of opiate withdrawal as evidence of a need for the drug also act accordingly and, from using the drug after they have understood, become addicted.[101]

Then as the addict applies the attitudes of his society to addiction toward his own behavior and experiences he faces the problem of becoming adjusted to the implications of being an addict in this hostile society. As he tries to rationalize his behavior he is inevitably drawn to those who are also addicted.

Lindesmith claims that it is impossible to become addicted without recognizing the withdrawal distress which may come several hours after a "shot" and in some cases may be difficult to detect. Doctors may successfully prevent addiction by keeping patients unaware of the effects of the drug upon them. Patients who have experienced withdrawal distress without understanding the connection between it and the drug have escaped addiction: some crucial cases have been cited of persons receiving drugs without becoming addicted but who, when they later took drugs and began to associate the taking of drugs with the fear of withdrawal symptoms, became addicted. This interpretation is supported by the fact that an addict seldom experiences the uplift or buoyancy attributed to the drugs unless he has been "taught" to expect it. Even the argot of addicts themselves in the word "hooked" indicates the process of addiction. The following case shows how a person begins to realize that he is addicted.

> Mr. G. was severely lacerated and internally injured in an accident. He spent thirteen weeks in a hospital, in the course of which he received opiates frequently both by mouth and hypodermically. He was unconscious part of the time and suffered considerable pain during convalescence despite the intake of opiates. He did not know what he was getting and noticed no effects except that his pain was relieved by the shots. He was discharged from the hospital but in several hours he began to feel restless and uncomfortable, without recognizing his condition. That night he became nauseated and vomited blood. Fearing that he was going to die, he summoned his family doctor. The physician did not realize what was the matter and administered a mild sedative. During the next day Mr. G.'s condition became steadily worse, and by the second night he was in such misery that, as he said, he began to wish that he would die. He again summoned his family doctor. This time the doctor began to suspect that Mr. G. was suffering from opiate withdrawal and prepared an injection of morphine. Mr. G. remembers nothing after the injection except that the doctor sat down by his bed and asked him how he felt. He replied that he noticed no effect, but the doctor said, "You will in a few minutes." Soon

---

[101]Lindesmith, *Addiction and Opiates*, pp. 95–96. Animals and infants appear to become addicted without conscious motivation. Lindesmith implies that none of the lower animals respond to opiates in the same way that human addicts do.

the patient fell asleep and continued in perfect comfort for many hours. When he awoke, he was informed of the true nature of the relieving dose by his wife and by the physician's comment: "Now we're going to have a hell of a time getting you off." The patient remained free of the drug for a few days and then purchased a syringe and began to use it himself.[102]

Lindesmith has summarized the evidence in support of his view that opiate addiction is a social-psychological process associated with recognition of withdrawal symptoms; drug addiction is continued for fear of the pain or discomfort associated with withdrawal:

> (1) the fact that some addicts deny ever experiencing euphoria from the drug; (2) that persons may and do become addicts without ever taking the drug voluntarily; (3) that addicts can be deceived about whether they are under the influence of the drug or not; (4) that euphoria is associated primarily with the initial use of the drugs and virtually disappears in addiction; (5) that the addict maintains that his shots cause him to feel "normal," and (6) that marihuana and cocaine, which do not create tolerance and physical dependence, are regarded as nonhabit-forming and that the habit-forming propensity of various substances seems to be roughly proportional to the severity of withdrawal symptoms and not to the euphoria they produce. One may say that the undoubted euphoria which opiates often initially produce is the bait on the hook rather than the hook itself.[103]

In becoming an opiate addict the individual changes his conception of himself and of the behavior he must play as a "drug addict." These new conceptions have both social-psychological and sociological implications. The more he associates with others who are "hooked" and finds that he cannot free himself from dependence on drugs, the more he comes to play the new role of the addict.

> It is evident that the drug addict assumes the group's viewpoint with respect to his experience of withdrawal distress by virtue of the fact that, prior to addiction, he has been a non-addict and a participating member of society. In view of the very use of language symbols, in terms of which the processes of re-evaluation which constitute addiction proceed, the addict necessarily shares the traditional heritage which includes knowledge of, and attitudes toward, the drug habit. Prior to addiction addicts acquire the attitudes of non-addicts, and when they become addicted they must adjust themselves to these attitudes.[104]

Criticism of the Theory

Lindesmith's theory of addiction, particularly his view that the primary motivating factor in continued use of opiates is the relief of withdrawal symptoms rather than the euphoria produced by the opiates, has been challenged by two investigators. One problem with Lindesmith's theory is his apparent claim that once dependence is established, euphoria does not take place, thereby removing euphoria as a causal

---

[102]Lindesmith, *Addiction and Opiates,* p. 77.
[103]Alfred R. Lindesmith, "Basic Problems in the Social Psychology of Addiction and a Theory," in John A. O'Donnell and John C. Ball, eds., *Narcotic Addiction* (New York: Harper & Row, 1966), pp. 102–103.
[104]Lindesmith, *Addiction and Opiates,* p. 194.

factor in addiction. In a study of long-term addicts, McAuliffe and Gordon found that these addicts do indeed experience euphoria, although not to the extent that newer addicts do.[105] This is due to the economic restraints put on the longer-term addicts because the drug cost prevents them from obtaining as much as they would like in order to increase the euphoria. Such addicts, however, do appear to orient their behavior around the achievement of euphoria as produced by heroin.

To these criticisms Lindesmith has replied that, first, he never claimed that drug addicts used withdrawal symptoms as a motivation for continued addiction. An addict's craving for drugs is produced or caused not by a motive but by the repetition of a particular experience. Second, the criticism of his treatment of the relation of euphoria to addiction, says Lindesmith, reduces itself to two points:

> I did not emphasize it sufficiently, and I did not attribute causal significance to it. Apropos of the first point, I did in fact assign a significant function to euphoria when I said it might be thought of as the bait on the hook—the bait that lures the user into a trap. McAuliffe and Gordon seem to view addiction not as a trap but, rather, as a conscious and more or less rational pursuit of pleasure. As I see it, they are so preoccupied with the bait that, like fish about to be hauled in by the fisherman and like the beginning user of drugs, they do not see the hook. Thus they give little attention to the many painful and unpleasant effects of addiction other than financial costs and risks of arrest. With respect to the second point, I have already indicated that causal significance cannot be attached to experiences that follow from addiction instead of preceding it. . . . The craving that characterizes the addict arises in conjunction with the use of the drug after physical dependence is established and recognized. It is characteristically at this point that the compulsive, irrational, ecstatic themes seem for the first time to enter into the addict's behavior and his reports on his experience and attitudes: he begins to show signs of falling in love with his drug.[106]

Platt and Labate have pointed out another difficulty with Lindesmith's theory, stating that while it "suggests that cognitive elements are important in the addiction process, [Lindesmith does not] specify the nature of the individual cognitive process in operational terms."[107] In other words, while Lindesmith claims that the addict must "learn" to be an addict, he does not define this learning in terms sufficiently clear to be tested.

Initial Use

Most drug addicts are knowingly initiated into drug usage, usually by a friend, acquaintance, or marital partner. Rarely does the use of drugs during illness lead to addiction. As for the large numbers who take them because of curiosity, there has usually been some association with persons already addicted. There is a desire to "try something once," especially if it happens to be something frowned upon by society in general, as is drug addiction. Some adolescents and others take drugs for the "kick,"

---

[105]William E. McAuliffe and Robert A. Gordon, "A Test of Lindesmith's Theory of Addiction: Frequency of Euphoria among Long-Term Addicts," *American Journal of Sociology,* 79 (1974), 795–840.
[106]"A Reply to McAuliffe and Gordon's 'A Test of Lindesmith's Theory of Addiction,'" *American Journal of Sociology,* 81 (1975), 149–150.
[107]Platt and Labate, p. 317.

as something tabooed by "squares," and to heighten and intensify the present
moment of experience and differentiate it from the routine of daily life.[108] The chain-
reaction process of addiction has often been called a "sordid and tragic pyramid
game" in which the average addict introduces several friends into the habit, often as a
means of solving his own supply problem. Persons are often initiated at parties where
the first "shots" are "on the house" in order to initiate the beginner.[109] Persons
commonly become aware of the possibility of using drugs when they learn that a
friend is using them: "if the novice is a girl, this person is likely to be a boyfriend; if a
boy, a roommate or relatively long-time intimate. That a person standing such a
relationship to a novice takes drugs at all is a strong argument for the novice to take
them as it dispels prior ideas that only 'dope fiends' and 'derelicts' of one kind or
another would ever consider doing so."[110] Rationalizations for using drugs are also
learned from others: using drugs becomes "natural." While some may continue to use
drugs in a limited pattern, "recreational users," others move on to a more systematic
pattern, the "heads," including street-level pushing or selling of drugs, with increased
techniques and rationalizations about drug use.

The group nature of heroin addiction can clearly be seen from both the
subcultural nature of the phenomenon, to be discussed presently, and the social
nature of the initial use. The learning process of initial use, and the subcultural support
of continued use, both suggest a social learning interpretation of heroin addiction. In a
study of 417 heroin addicts in five different treatment facilities in New York, Waldorf
found that the initial heroin use is *not* a solitary activity. "Persons are initiated in a
group situation among friends and acquaintances. Only 17 (4 percent) of our sample
of 417 males reported that they were alone the first time they used heroin; by far the
majority (96 percent) reported that they used heroin the first time with one or more
persons."[111] The other persons were almost always friends, usually of the same sex;
white persons in the sample tended to use the drug in larger groups than did the blacks
and the Puerto Ricans. More often than not, moreover, the persons who initiated the
men and boys of this study into heroin use had used it previously themselves, but most
were not addicted. Initiates may be more wary of addicts as "teachers" than nonaddicts, since addicts represent, and quite visibly, the potential danger of using heroin.

The process of drug addiction results in both stigma and rejection as a product of
societal reaction, and this, in turn, affects the individual's self-image. The more the
addict associates with other drug addicts and the drug subculture, and the more he
finds he cannot free himself from drug dependency, the more he adopts the self-
conception of being an addict and plays the social role of an addict. The final step in
the process, of course, is the self-identification as "addict" or "junkie." "Even the drug

---

[108]Harold Finestone, "Cats, Kicks and Color," *Social Problems,* 5 (1957), 3–13.

[109]Isidor Chein, Donald L. Gerard, Robert S. Lee, and Eva Rosenfeld, *The Road to H* (New York: Basic
Books, 1964), Chap. 6; and John P. Fort, Jr., "Heroin Addiction among Young Men," *Psychiatry,* 17
(1954), 251–259.

[110]James T. Carey, *The College Drug Scene* (Englewood Cliffs, N.J.: Prentice-Hall, 1968), p. 52.

[111]Dan Waldorf, *Careers in Dope* (Englewood Cliffs, N.J.: Prentice-Hall, 1973), p. 31. A recent case study
illustrates this process, with the addict's uncle initially serving as "tutor" and supplier. See Richard P. Rettig,
Manual J. Torres, and Gerald R. Garrett, *Manny: A Criminal-Addict's Story* (Boston: Houghton Mifflin,
1977), especially pp. 33–34.

user in respectable society, who may have few or no addicted associates, secretly labels himself as a 'drug addict' or 'dope fiend.' "[112]

Types of Addicts

The career type of addict is the "street addict," as Stephens terms him. Street addicts belong to a drug subculture largely made up of urban slum-dwelling male members of minority groups who adhere to a deviant drug-related set of values.[113] They favor the use of heroin and cocaine, use the intravenous method, have frequent withdrawals from drug use, and engage in many "hustles" to support the habit. Their lives revolve around three main events: (1) the "hustle" (obtaining money illegally to purchase drugs); (2) "copping" (buying heroin); and (3) "getting-off" (injecting heroin).[114] Conventional activities occupy little time in the life of the "junkies." Many forms of "hustles" in which they are constantly engaged may be cited: they include prostitution for female addicts, simple theft such as shoplifting and burglary, or more cunning schemes involving variants of con games. All "hustles" contain similar elements and all are illegal activities.[115]

One study of the life-style of the heroin user has refined the notion of the "street addict" by specifying five types of heroin addict roles: (1) "expressive students" who try drugs, including heroin, in attempts to explore the cultural and social world; (2) "social world alternators" who use heroin in connection with exploiting diverse social opportunities in the pursuit of hedonism; (3) "low riders" who use heroin symbolically to express cohesiveness in motorcycle groups; (4) "barrio addicts" who use heroin as a ritual of sociability; and (5) "ghetto hustlers" who use drugs as an aspect of the adventure of "living by one's wits."[116] This last type of addict is the closest to the street addict described by Stephens and Levine, though the other types of users may slide into a street-addict role at a later time. Maintaining the street-addict role requires involvement in the addict subculture in order to receive social support from other, similarly placed individuals and to guarantee a source of heroin supply.

The Subculture of Drug Addiction

Much of drug addiction involves an elaborate subculture. Not only do persons learn how to use drugs and appreciate them but they also learn a series of positive beliefs about the benefits of drugs, beliefs that others help to reinforce constantly.[117] The new

---

[112]Lindesmith, *Addiction and Opiates,* p. 63. Also see Harld Alksne, Louis Lieberman, and Leon Brill, "A Conceptual Model of the Life Cycle of Addiction," *International Journal of the Addictions,* 2 (1967), 221–240; and Dan Waldorf, "Life Without Heroin: Some Social Adjustments during Long-Term Periods of Voluntary Abstention," *Social Problems,* 18 (1970), 228–243.

[113]See Richard S. Stephens and Stephen Levine, "The Street Addict Role: Implications for Treatment," *Psychiatry,* 34 (1971), 351–357.

[114]Michael Agar, *Ripping and Running: A Formal Ethnography of Urban Heroin Addicts* (New York: Seminar Press, 1973), p. 21.

[115]Agar, pp. 46–47.

[116]Virginia Lewis and Daniel Glaser, "Lifestyles among Heroin Users," *Federal Probation,* 38 (1974), 21–28.

[117]See Carey for a discussion of the subculture on a college campus.

addict also learns about the sources of supply and how he must remain part of the group in order to assure this supply. Even the spread of the intravenous technique of administering opiate drugs with a needle from 1935 to 1965 is an example of the individual's involvement in the drug subculture.[118]

Drugs must be imported illegally into the country and then distributed through suppliers and peddlers. There are "pushers" who help to indoctrinate new persons into addiction. Those who use the drugs are, to a large extent, also part of this subculture, since drug addicts must generally associate with "pushers," usually other addicts, in order to secure their supply. Drug addiction involves an elaborate subculture supported by group norms which one writer has called a "survival system."[119] This involves the justification or ideology for drug usage and the "reproductive" system, namely, that addicted persons must continually recruit new members in order to sell them drugs to support their habit. There is also defensive communication with its own argot for drugs, supplies, and drug users, which must be learned by the initiates, and the "neighborhood warning systems" by which addicts are protected by others. The support of the habit requires a complex distribution network of the illegal drugs. Such information as the coming of the police, or the kind of heroin for sale and where, is said to pass rapidly and accurately, with greater safety than provided by the telephone, and information is sifted out according to a reliability consensus of different persons.

To understand why illegal trade in narcotics flourishes and why it is so difficult to wipe out, one must realize the potential large profit in the handling of illegal drugs. The price for a shot of heroin varies considerably and is often what the traffic will bear. It costs from $25 to $100 a day or more to support a heroin habit. While the police often have little difficulty in apprehending the common addict who is searching restlessly for his next shot, it is much more difficult to track down the supplier or successive line of suppliers to the source. Many addicts would rather sweat out the "shakes" than disclose the name of their supplier, and often there is a high degree of organization among those who manage to get supplies of drugs illegally into the country.

The extremely high profits involved in the sale of illegal drugs can be seen from the return which is likely on one kilogram (approximately 35 ounces) of heroin. This amount of 86 percent pure heroin in Europe costs about $10,000, and it might cost as much as $10,000 more to smuggle it into the United States. The wholesaler's profit is about $18,000, the dealer makes $32,000, and the pusher who peddles the drugs $70,000. The cost, to the addict, of one kilogram of relatively pure heroin after it has been diluted with as much as 90 percent milk sugar amounts, then, to $225,000. The profit on the original cost of the heroin is $215,000.[120] Where profits of this size exist it is inevitable that well-organized techniques will be developed to protect them. It is also inevitable that such an enterprise should become a fertile field for organized crime.

Youth addiction is group in nature. In their attempts to acquire status among

---

[118]John A. O'Donnell and Judith P. Jones, "Diffusion of the Intravenous Technique among Narcotic Addicts in the United States," *Journal of Health and Social Behavior,* 9 (1968), 120–230.

[119]Seymour Fiddle, "The Addict Culture and Movement into and out of Hospitals," in U.S. Senate, Committee on the Judiciary, Subcommittee to Investigate Juvenile Delinquency, *Hearings,* Part 13, New York City, September 20–21, 1962 (Washington, D.C.: Government Printing Office, 1963), p. 3156.

[120]Arthur D. Little, Inc., "Drug Abuse and Law Enforcement," a report to the President's Commission on Law Enforcement, Administration of Justice, January 18, 1967.

their peers, adolescents in certain areas often appear to be willing to explore socially unacceptable areas of behavior. Drug use among youths, consisting primarily of heroin and marijuana, flourishes in the slum areas of large cities in the United States. In New York, for example, almost 90 percent of the cases are concentrated in only 13 percent of the census tracts.[121] In fact, in some of the tracts as many as 10 percent of the young men aged 16–20 were known, during a three-year period, to be involved with drugs. In such areas the desire to enjoy life by having new experiences and taking chances means that there is a readiness to try the drug, because, they are told, it will give them an immediate "kick" or a "high" feeling. A study of male Puerto Rican addicts showed that they smoked marijuana and associated with neighborhood boys who were known addicts before starting to use heroin themselves. "The neighborhood addicts who provided the drugs and technical knowledge to the neophyte were invariably described by him as 'friends.'"[122] Great determination is required to escape the pull or, rather, push of delinquent subcultures which are associated with the use of drugs. Great pressure is also exerted to fall in with the aggressive "cats," and an adolescent finds the taunting accusations of "chicken" and "square" hard to ignore. Speaking of young addicts in a Chicago low-income area Finestone states:

> An orientation to life which gives zestful sanction to many forms of unconventional activity appears to have spread the welcome mat for narcotics use. Much of the behavior reported by these young addicts clearly indicates that they had actively sought out narcotics—and not only heroin, but every other substance of which they had heard which yielded a "kick" such as marijuana, cocaine, benzedrine, and the barbiturates. The activity centering around these narcotics had many of the characteristics of a fad—that is, the restless searching, the uncertainty and excitement and exclusive preoccupation with a novel experience, the pressures to "go along," and the final capitulation on the part of many, despite the existence of strong initial doubts and inhibitions.[123]

A study of Chicago juvenile gangs found that extensive drug use is not a generally supported gang activity, although it tended to be more common among black than white gangs.[124] Most juvenile gangs that use drugs often try to set the limits of drug usage by their members. In a study of 18 gangs it was found that 65 percent of the members were opposed to the use of heroin, or felt ambivalent about it, but very few gang members had strong feelings about the use of marijuana.[125] Any leader who became a drug addict was demoted. Delinquent gangs are more tolerant of occasional use, but resist immoderate usage on the ground that it interferes with their stealing or that it will get the gang into trouble. Some writers have referred to a type of delinquent gang that, in its inability to achieve the conventional goals of society, becomes preoccupied with the use of drugs rather than stealing except to get money for drugs.[126]

---

[121]See Chein et al., Chap. 2.

[122]John C. Ball, "The Onset of Heroin Addiction in a Juvenile Population: Implications for Theories of Deviancy" (Lexington, Ky.: Addiction Research Center, National Institute of Mental Health, 1966), p. 8.

[123]Harold Finestone, "Narcotics and Criminality," Law and Contemporary Problems, 22 (1957), 73–74.

[124]James F. Short, Jr., and Fred L. Strodtbeck, Group Process and Gang Delinquency (Chicago: University of Chicago Press, 1965), pp. 1, 63–64, and 82.

[125]Chein and Rosenfeld.

[126]Richard A. Cloward and Lloyd E. Ohlin, Delinquency and Opportunity: A Theory of Delinquent Gangs (New York: Free Press, 1960).

There is a widespread assumption that young addicts are introduced to the drug habit by drug peddlers. One study has shown that the first shot of heroin came through some adult in only 10 percent of the cases.[127] Nearly all were introduced to the drug in the company of a boy their own age or in a group of boys. The first trial use of drugs was free to most. Only 10 percent had to pay for the first "shot" or "snort." The first dose was often taken in the home of one of the boys, although a large number tried it on the street, in a cellar, or even on a roof top. Frequently, it was taken before a party as a bracer to give poise and courage. Clausen reports: "There is general agreement that the great majority of these [marijuana and heroin] users were not tricked into addiction by drug peddlers."[128]

Suppliers and most addicts live in a world that often has its own meeting places, values, and argot. Possibly nothing more clearly demonstrates the fact that addiction has cultural components than the argot which is used. It includes special terms for the drugs, for those who supply the drugs, and for addiction itself. It also includes special descriptive terms for those who use the drugs.

Selected Glossary of Terms Used by Addicts[129]

Burn (n, v.t.): less heroin than an amount of money should purchase.
Cooker (n.): small receptacle in which to dissolve heroin.
Dynamite (adj.): high-quality heroin.
Fix (n, v.t.): inject heroin intravenously.
Flash (n.): physical sensation of heroin entering system.
Goofballs (n.): barbiturates.
Heart (n.): courage.
House Connection (n.): dealer who operates in a private home.
Hype (n.): heroin addict.
The Life (n.): life of a heroin addict.
Panic (n.): shortage of heroin in the market.
Ropes (n.): veins.
Smack (n.): heroin.
Strung Out (adj.): physically addicted to heroin.
Tracks (n.): scars along a vein resulting from frequent injection.
Works (n.): paraphernalia for injecting heroin.

In summary, through the addict's subculture, he is able to connect with dealers, employ a number of "hustles," and protect himself from outside interference, particularly from the police. The addict subculture thus plays a number of important functions for the addict, not the least of which is the opportunity to meet others like himself and benefit from mutual association. "This obviously enhances his morale and gives him some defense against the antagonistic larger society."[130] This observation should not surprise us; we encountered similar descriptions in our discussion of slums and the reactions of slum residents to outsiders. Moreover, most of us gravitate toward persons like ourselves—persons of similar ages and with like interests, tastes, and activities—because we find them easy to communicate with and feel a shared sense of experi-

---

[127]Chein and Rosenfeld, p. 58.
[128]Clausen, p. 40.
[129]Derived from Agar, pp. 157–165. Also see Smith and Wesson, *Uppers and Downers,* pp. 142–151.
[130]Waldorf, *Careers in Dope,* p. 31.

ence. Heroin addicts find similar comfort with other addicts. Since most of the street addict's life centers around the identification of heroin supplies, the purchase of heroin, and the injecting of heroin, it is of little surprise that the subculture facilitates these activities. The addict is, through his associations, placed in the drug market, meeting and getting to know dealers and places where he can "shoot up." The drug subculture also has its negative features, however, since it isolates the addict from conventional society; the only persons the addict is likely to know are other addicts, and they tend to reinforce the addiction process rather than providing positive social support to remain off drugs. Like other subcultures of a deviant nature, the drug subculture does not prepare its members to reenter the conventional world, and, in fact, inhibits that reentry. Moreover, the nature of addiction and the role of the drug subculture mean that the effect of severe legal deterrent measures is limited.

CRIME AND DRUG ADDICTION

The use of narcotics is so expensive that an addict must often engage in various illegal activities to maintain his supply. As noted earlier, once an individual becomes addicted to a narcotic drug like heroin, his dependence upon a continuous supply usually becomes the most important single feature of his daily life. As tolerance to the drug is increased, and the addict requires larger and larger doses, the daily expenditure is generally more than he can earn legitimately; moreover, since the addict's life is centered around obtaining drugs and getting high, the addict has little time for those occupations that would support the habit, were he qualified. For these reasons, the addict employs the "hustle" to obtain money for drugs. By their nature, "hustles" are illegal.

Some indication of the cost of a heroin habit can be gleaned from the following: Between 1948 and 1953, heroin was available at 30 to 40 percent purity for $2 to $2.50 a packet (about 10 milligrams). In the 1960s, a 2 percent mixture cost $5.[131] Dupont and Greene have reported that the cost of a milligram of street heroin was about $1.50 in early 1972; a year later it had increased to $5.80.[132] This kind of financial burden on addicts, as most need 10–30 milligrams of pure heroin a day, forces these persons to engage in the forms of "hustling" that best suit their habit needs. Estimates of the amount of criminality by addicts are notoriously unreliable, in view of the difficulties in obtaining precise figures on which crimes were committed by addicts and which by nonaddicts. Several estimates have been made, however. Scher estimates that each addict in the United States, in order to maintain his habit, steals

---

[131]Charles Winick, "Epidemiology of Narcotics Use," in David M. Wilner and Gene G. Kassebaum, eds., *Narcotics* (New York: McGraw-Hill, 1965), pp. 3–18.

[132]Robert L. DuPont and M. H. Greene, "The Dynamics of a Heroin Addiction Epidemic," *Science,* 181 (1973), 716–722. This figure is probably high. It is difficult to estimate the actual cost of heroin because costs vary from one part of the country to another, and they also change with the supply. Newmeyer found a San Francisco sample, in 1975, was paying from 13.5¢ to $1.56, or an average of 83.5¢ per milligram of pure heroin. See John Newmeyer, "Indications of Drug Abuse—Buys," *Epidemiology of Drug Abuse: Current Issues* (Washington, D.C.: U.S. Government Printing Office, March 1977), pp. 130–134.

between $50,000 to $150,000 in merchandise, equipment, or funds each year from business and industry.[133] On the basis of 63,000 addicts, each of whom requires between $50 to $100 or more per day to support his habit, a total of $3.5 million in cash or $35 million in merchandise is stolen each day in the United States, according to Scher. This represents a substantial increase from Winick's estimate in the early 1960s that heroin addiction was costing over $250 million annually for all addicts.[134]

Much crime, consequently, is committed by addicts because they are addicts. In a New York State study 38 addicts reported committing 6,766 offenses during a period of four years.[135] For every 120 crimes there was only one arrest. The offenses were nearly all against property (97 percent), with burglary the largest of them (35 percent). In the past crimes committed by addicts largely involved stealing, burglary, and prostitution, but there is evidence that addicts in large urban areas are increasingly turning to robbery and mugging to support their habits.

For most contemporary narcotic addicts, criminal involvement is a part of their life-style after becoming addicted to narcotics but not necessarily prior to some drug experimentation.[136] The vast majority of narcotic addicts support their addictions by committing crimes, but this is not the result of any property of the drug; merely the cost of the drug. That most addicts should be involved in criminality after addiction suggests that (1) drugs are expensive and (2) the heroin subculture facilitates criminal behavior by providing opportunities for crime and stressing the need for continued heroin use. Not all narcotic addicts resort to crime, however. One study reported that 36 percent of heroin users at a treatment clinic in San Francisco obtained their drugs legally (through an occupation, spouse, welfare, or some other legal means).[137] The remaining 64 percent indicated that they engaged in various "hustles" to obtain funds for their drugs.

MAKING SENSE OF DRUG ADDICTION

One problem that any theory of addiction faces is the nature and meaning of the term "addiction" itself. "The term 'drug addiction' has been variously defined. Some definitions stress uncontrollable psychological craving on the part of the user, and others stress physiological dependency on a particular drug."[138] Thus, even the basic definition of addiction is not commonly agreed upon by those experts who study this

[133]J. M. Scher, "The Impact of the Drug Abuser on the Work Organization," in J. A. Scher, ed., *Drug Abuse in Industry* (Springfield, Ill.: Charles C Thomas, 1973), pp. 5–16. This estimate may be somewhat high because it assumes that the addict is using drugs most of the year.

[134]Winick, "Epidemiology of Narcotic Use."

[135]James A. Inciardi and Carl D. Chambers, "Criminal Involvement of Narcotic Addicts," *Journal of Drug Issues*, 2 (1972), 57–64.

[136]Carl D. Chambers, "Narcotic Addiction and Crime: An Empirical Review," in James A. Inciardi and Carl D. Chambers, eds, *Drugs and the Criminal Justice System* (Beverly Hills, Calif.: Sage Publications, 1974), p. 140.

[137]J. Newmeyer, "The Junkie Thief," unpublished paper, Haight-Ashbury Free Medical Clinic, San Francisco, as cited in Leroy C. Gould, "Crime and the Addict: Beyond Common Sense," in Inciardi and Chambers, *Drugs and the Criminal Justice System*, p. 61.

[138]Clausen, pp. 146–147.

problem. Even if one decides to construct a definition around such terms as "habitua-tion," "craving," "detrimental drug effects," and "psychological dependency," one sees that even these terms cannot be defined in operational terms that would produce complete agreement.[139]

One term, "tolerance," would appear to be agreed upon by many, and be a necessary condition of addiction, however defined. Theories of addiction that stress tolerance (and, to an extent, dependence) are plentiful, and some observers claim that tolerance, more than any other single element in the addiction process, determines and dominates the behavior of the addict and the nature and course of the addic-tion.[140] Unfortunately, theories that rely entirely on the concepts of tolerance and dependence fail to take into account the important roles of interpersonal learning and subcultural support, which appear to be more predictive of the course of the addiction than the physiological properties of heroin, even with long-term addicts. Moreover, even the terms "tolerance" and "dependence," while they seem to have clear empirical referents, are ambiguous when applied to addiction. "Despite intensive and exhaustive experimental work over the past century, and more especially over the past ten years, the phenomena of tolerance to and dependence on the narcotic analgesics are puzzling and intriguing. They have puzzled and intrigued pharmacologists for many years; the mechanisms responsible for their initiation, maintenance, and loss still remain obscure."[141] It would seem that we cannot rely solely on physiological properties of opiates on which to base a theory of addiction. It is to these social considerations that we now turn.

Throughout this discussion the social, rather than the physiological or psycho-pathological, nature of drug taking and addiction has been stressed since addiction, essentially, is a social process that can be viewed independently from the physical properties of drugs and their impact on the human organism. One particular social theory that has attempted to deal with lower-class drug usage, and addiction in particular, is Merton's theory of anomie (see Chapter 3). According to this theory, the addict is one who has pursued high (and unrealistic) cultural goals, but who has turned to illegitimate means to achieve them when the legitimate means have become blocked. This "retreat" from the social scene results in the use of drugs.[142] A more recent version of this theory, which has been updated to account for the increasing numbers of addicts in the middle and upper classes, suggests that this new type of addict, rather than being deficient in the intellectual and educational skills required to reach his goal, may be deficient in the personal skills needed for success or may be frustrated by economic realities.

> With increased expectations of ready access to culturally defined goals, such as a job and status—developed on the basis of his high attainment relative to comparable nonad-dicts—the failure to reach these goals has a detrimental effect upon his self-esteem and

---

[139]See Reginald G. Smart, "Addiction, Dependence, Abuse or Use: Which Are We Studying with Epide-miology?" in Josephson and Carroll, pp. 23–42.

[140]Peter G. Bourne, "Issues in Addiction," in Bourne, *Addiction,* p. 16.

[141]J. Cochlin, "Factors Influencing Tolerance to and Dependence on Narcotic Analgesics," in S. Fisher and A. M. Freedman, eds., *Opiate Addiction: Origins and Treatment* (Washington, D.C.: Winston, 1974), p. 23. For a review of various theories of tolerance and dependence, see Platt and Labate, pp. 70–78.

[142]Robert K. Merton, *Social Theory and Social Structure,* enlarged edition (New York: Free Press, 1968).

he turns to heroin use to escape from the unpleasant subjective consequences and affect that result.[143]

Alternatively, Lindesmith's theory of addiction emphasizes the addict's learning, first, how to use the drug from others, and, second, that continued use of the drug will relieve the withdrawal distress which results from discontinued use.[144] We have commented previously on Lindesmith's difficulty in identifying and operationalizing the personal cognitive elements in this process, and the fact that some people maintain, at least for long-term addicts, that continued use of addicting drugs also seems oriented around the achievement of euphoria, rather than only the elimination of withdrawal distress. But Lindesmith's account of the addiction process as essentially a learning process would seem to make better sense of the information that has been presented.

Addiction begins with others taking the role of "teachers" with those to be initiated into the use of drugs; persons have to learn about the drug, how to use it, and the reactions it will produce. This information comes most reliably from those who have experienced the drug at some earlier time and whose judgment is trusted by the initiate. The addiction process is best made sense of in social learning terms. The maintenance of addiction is, similarly, best accounted for not with the physical properties of the drug (though the relief of withdrawal distress and the achievement of euphoria are important motivating forces), but with the drug-supporting role of the addict subculture. If learning initial drug use from others begins the process, the subculture perpetuates it.

This interpretation is consistent with the recent evidence on the changing nature of heroin addiction. Trends in the incidence of heroin use show that the rates of addiction in larger cities has probably leveled off and that for smaller cities are increasing. This trend, which may point to a new kind of heroin epidemic, also suggests a learning interpretation. Hunt and Chambers present three types of evidence showing that heroin usage spreads among closely associated individuals in small groups. "(1) users typically describe their initiators as friends or peers; (2) the statistics on the initiator-successor relationship are consistent with the structure of association groups; and (3) the empirical behavior of the spreading process . . . matches simple diffusion in reported peer populations."[145] In short, the use of heroin parallels the diffusion of other trends in society throughout different populations and regions; this diffusion process is essentially a learning process.

The learning of drug use is most strikingly seen in the process of juvenile initiation into drugs, whether marijuana or heroin. While popular opinion holds that youthful drug use is predominantly experimental, with the adolescent being curious about the presumed effects of drugs, a desire for adventure or excitement, or a form of vengeance on society, the induction into juvenile drug use is a complex social process embodying such curiosity initially perhaps, but also the availability of tutors and the opportunity to take drugs. Rather than drug use being an escape from reality, one

---

[143]Platt and Labate, p. 320.
[144]Lindesmith, *Addiction and Opiates.*
[145]Hunt and Chambers, p. 25. These authors put the matter more bluntly: "The most basic conclusion is that heroin use is naturally contagious" (p. 25).

study reported that "our evidence shows overwhelmingly the great majority of youngsters become users as a means of embracing reality."[146] This reality is a social one, with drug use being an integral part of the activities of the group. For youth, drug subcultures do not arise from use, but use comes about through participation in the subculture. For certain users, notably upper-class males, the process and seduction of the drug subculture is such that drug use can develop from anticipatory socialization rather than direct contact with members of the subculture. That is, college-oriented high school students, perceiving marijuana use as a part of the collegiate style of life, will be more likely to use marijuana than will high school students not expecting to go to college.[147]

DRUG ADDICTION AND SOCIAL CONTROL

All studies of the results of treatment indicate that narcotic addiction, particularly the use of heroin, is one of the most difficult forms of deviant behavior to treat because of a high percentage of relapse. A follow-up study of male addicts found, for example, that if relapse were defined as any reuse of narcotics, the observed relapse rate of 87 percent is equivalent to the 80–90 percent relapse rates reported in most other studies.[148] Although no relation was found between length of addiction and relapse, age was found to be related to relapse. Specifically, it was found that patients under 30 years of age used narcotics regularly or became readdicted at a much higher rate than those over 30. Similarly, the rates of total abstinence or occasional use of narcotics were higher for those over 30. Another study found a readdiction rate of more than 90 percent within five years of discharge from the treatment program.[149]

Rehabilitation of the addict will always be difficult as long as the "larger society treats rehabilitation as the passage between two moral worlds."[150] The strong moral interpretation of drug addiction in the larger society encourages relapse among ex-addicts who were motivated to change their behavior. Inevitably, despite rehabilitation agents, the individual often "finds that the only people who, in his terms, 'accept' him for what he is are the old addict friends."[151]

The high recidivism rate of the opiate addict can be attributed to sociopsychological rather than merely physiological reasons. Since the majority of addicts have had to turn to stealing and prostitution, and in these activities fulfill the criminal image held by others, rejection of the drug culture is difficult.[152] Moreover, recidivism in drug usage is

---

[146]Herbert Blumer, with Alan Sutter, Roger Smith, and Samir Ahmed, "Recruitment into Drug Use,"in Coombs, Fry, and Lewis, p. 172.
[147]Armand L. Mauss, "Anticipatory Socialization toward College as a Factor in Adolescent Marijuana Use," *Social Problems,* 16 (1969), 357–364.
[148]Richard Stephens and Emily Cottrell, "A Follow-Up Study of 200 Narcotic Addicts Committed for Treatment under the Narcotic Addict Rehabilitation Act (NARA)," *British Journal of Addiction,* 67 (1972), 45–53.
[149]G. H. Hunt and M. E. Odoroff, "Follow-up Study of Narcotic Drug Addicts after Hospitalization," *Public Health Reports,* 77 (1962), 41–54.
[150]Troy Duster, *The Legislation of Morality* (New York: Free Press, 1970), p. 211.
[151]Duster, p. 211.
[152]Lindesmith, *Addiction and Opiates,* Chapter 6, "Cure and Relapse."

a product of long experience with drugs, the conception of oneself as an addict, association with other addicts, and the recognition of the effects of drugs. Because the person is frequently isolated from the conventional world, an addict who stops taking drugs is forced to associate with those who are still addicted. At times, even the boredom of being a nonaddict is a significant factor in relapse. The individual may still believe in the efficacy of the drug, may still interpret the vicissitudes of life somewhat in terms of opiates, and does not exhibit feelings of disgust or moral indignation toward drug use in the same way he might have done before addiction. "These changes are produced by the influence of withdrawal distress, as has been demonstrated, but once formed, they are independent of the withdrawal symptoms."[153]

The Use of Criminal Penalties

The use of the criminal law to suppress completely such narcotic drug usage as heroin has not been successful in the United States. It is believed that suppression has actually increased the difficulties of controlling the illegal drug traffic because it has made necessary the development of an elaborate organization for illicit supply which seeks to extend itself by inducing nonaddicts to become users of narcotics. Because of their attempts to obtain enough money to buy illicitly—or to steal—high-priced drugs that could be obtained legally for a fraction of the cost charged by peddlers, crimes are committed by persons who would not otherwise commit them. Drug users become "criminals" under these laws and drugs something mysterious and evil: the very stigma of having an arrest record makes the rehabilitation of drug addicts more difficult. The effects of such drug-related crimes and imprisonment are to make a career for many out of what was originally addiction to the drug. A study of heroin addicts from Puerto Rico revealed that more than three fourths of them remained more or less continuously addicted over the average 16-year period since the onset of drug use, despite the fact that many had had many felony arrests, many related directly to narcotics.[154] While it could not be concluded that heroin caused their criminality, it was evident that it figured heavily in their illicit activities. A particularly frequent violation was the selling of narcotics. "Overall, this study of long-term correlates of addiction presents a dismal picture of the life patterns of these human beings. For the most part, they have remained continuing problems to their society and to themselves."[155]

In the process of enforcing the criminal law the civil rights of drug users are commonly violated. Various methods are used to entrap drug sellers, particularly the use of other drug users and prostitutes as informants, various "inside" and "outside" buying situations, and the use of marked money.[156] By being informants individuals

---

[153]Lindesmith, *Addiction and Opiates,* p. 139.

[154]Lois R. DeFleur, John C. Ball, and Richard W. Snarr, "The Long-Term Social Correlates of Opiate Addiction," *Social Problems,* 17 (1969), 233.

[155]DeFleur, Ball, and Snarr, p. 233.

[156]For a discussion of the informant in the narcotics enforcement pattern, see Jerome H. Skolnick, *Justice without Trial: Law Enforcement in a Democratic Society,* 2d ed. (New York: Wiley, 1975), pp. 139–163. Also see Peter K. Manning, "Rules in Organizational Context: Narcotics Law Enforcement in Two Settings," *The Sociological Quarterly,* 18 (1977), 44–61.

protect their own supplies and avoid arrest. Because of these forced associations and conflicts, both inside and outside the law, it is not surprising that a deeply ingrained "drug subculture" has developed in this country. Thus while it is not, and never has been, a criminal offense just to *be* an addict (possession is the criminal offense), the addict lives in almost perpetual violation of one or several criminal laws, which gives him a special status not shared by other criminal offenders. "Together with the fact that he must have continuous contact with other people in order to obtain drugs, it also gives him a special exposure to police action and arrest, and, in areas where the addiction rate is high, a special place in police statistics and crime rate computations."[157]

Consequently, many authorities and such commissions as the Joint Committee on Narcotic Drugs (of the American Bar Association and the American Medical Association) have long recommended that drug addiction be regarded primarily as a medical problem, as it is in Great Britain and in many Western European countries.[158] They have recommended a complete review of laws in order to abolish prison terms for addicts, to allow qualified doctors to dispense narcotics, and to establish experimental outpatient clinics rather than to rely upon hospitalization for addict care. It is suggested that the power to control addiction now being exercised by legislators, lawyers, judges, prosecutors, and the police be transferred to the medical profession. Doctors would be given great freedom in dispensing drugs to addicts. There are indications that such an approach is slowly coming in the United States, as is demonstrated by methadone-maintenance programs.

The advantages of a shift from the use of the criminal law to suppress drug use have been summarized by Lindesmith:

1. Prevention of the spread of addiction and a resultant progressive reduction in the number of addicts.
2. Curing current addicts of their habits insofar as this can be achieved by present techniques or by new ones which may be devised.
3. Elimination of the exploitation of addicts for mercenary gain by smugglers or by anyone else.
4. Reduction to a minimum of the crime committed by drug users as a consequence of their habits.
5. Reducing to a minimum the availability of dangerous addicting drugs to all nonaddicts except when needed for medical purposes.
6. Fair and just treatment of addicts in accordance with established legal and ethical precepts, taking into account the special peculiarities of their behavior and at the same time preserving their individual dignity and self-respect.
7. Antinarcotic laws should be written so that addicts do not have to violate them solely because they are addicts.
8. Drug users are admittedly handicapped by their habits but they should nevertheless be encouraged to engage in productive labor even when they are using drugs.

---

[157] *The Challenge of Crime in a Free Society,* President's Commission on Law Enforcement and Administration of Justice (Washington, D.C.: Government Printing Office, 1967), p. 221.
[158] *Drug Addiction: Crime or Disease?* Interim and Final Reports of the Joint Committee of the American Bar Association and the American Medical Association on Narcotic Drugs (Bloomington: Indiana University Press, 1960).

9. Cures should not be imposed upon narcotics victims by force but should be voluntary.
10. Police officers should be prevented from exploiting drug addicts as stool pigeons solely because they are addicts.
11. Heroin and morphine addicts should be handled according to the same principles and moral precepts applied to barbiturate and alcohol addicts because these three forms of addiction are basically similar.[159]

Treatment

A person who is on drugs does not always fail to function effectively in society. Substantial numbers of addicts can be responsible and productive members of the community. For this reason, clinical programs in New York City and elsewhere have been directed at keeping thousands of addicts on *methadone maintenance* while efforts are made to bring about their rehabilitation. In this way, they can be kept free in society and can work and even go to school. The addict usually comes daily to a clinic for a dosage of methadone (a substitute for heroin to prevent withdrawal distress), usually given in a glass of juice. In this way an illegal addiction is replaced by a legal one. In other cases, methadone is distributed by doctors directly to the drug patient.

The results of the methadone-maintenance program have generally been reported as encouraging, but serious questions have been raised about this type of program. There has also been evidence of abuses in the use of methadone itself.[160] Many individuals are becoming addicted to the use of methadone, and it is increasingly being recognized that not all patients will be able to relinquish the prop of methadone support, with some in need of methadone indefinitely.[161] Thus when the term "success" is applied to methadone-maintenance programs it may mean that while the user is not on heroin or some other addicting drug he is nevertheless being given an addicting drug. One measure of the effectiveness of such a program is the extent of dropouts from the programs: one study found that one fifth of the dropouts of the largest methadone-maintenance program in New York City were on methadone at other programs, 43 percent were drug free, one fourth were using heroin again, and 14 percent were in institutions.[162]

There is some evidence that methadone-maintenance programs do reduce somewhat the amount of "addict crime" by providing a legal source of drugs. This particular benefit of the programs, however, seems limited to those who voluntarily participate and remain in the program for a period of time.[163] A recent study has also found that dropouts of methadone-maintenance programs did not have as low a crime

[159]Alfred R. Lindesmith, *The Addict and the Law* (Bloomington: Indiana University Press, 1965), pp. 269–270.
[160]See, for example, Robert S. Weppner, Richard C. Stephens, and Harold T. Conrad, "Methadone: Some Aspects of Its Legal and Illegal Use," *American Journal of Psychiatry,* 129 (1972), 451–455.
[161]See Leon Brill and Carl D. Chambers, "A Multimodality Approach to Methadone Maintenance Treatment of Narcotic Addicts," *Social Work,* 16 (1971), 39–51.
[162]James Boudouris, "A Follow-up Study of Dropouts from a Methadone Maintenance Program," *The International Journal of the Addictions,* 11 (1976), 807–818.
[163]Robert G. Newman, Sylvia Bashkow, and Margot Cates, "Arrest Histories before and after Admission to a Methadone Maintenance Treatment Program," *Contemporary Drug Problems,* 2 (1973), 417–430.

rate as those who remained in the program, but that they had reduced their criminality from their preprogram levels.[164] These results suggest that, like other forms of drug treatment, voluntary participation, an indicator of motivation and cooperation in the rehabilitative process, is extremely important if such programs are to help addicts.

Partly because of problems associated with methadone-maintenance programs some researchers in this country have recommended legal heroin-maintenance programs. It is hoped that such programs might reach the vast population of addicts who now remain outside the reach of the methadone programs and other efforts.[165] Such a program would not differ greatly from the treatment of opiate addiction in the United Kingdom and several other Western European countries where addiction is considered to be a medical problem, to be treated largely by outpatient care by physicians (in Great Britain with those attached to hospitals), with drugs being prescribed at low cost. Distribution of the drugs is supervised by public health authorities; a register of known addicts is maintained, and addicts must utilize only one doctor and one prescription pharmacy. Physicians are supposed to prescribe a minimum dosage and to make programmed attempts to cure the addict: British officials, as well as the public, therefore, do not regard the addict as a "criminal." British addicts appear to be relatively noncriminal, and the addict does not have to steal or become a prostitute or peddle heroin in order to obtain heroin. Recently, however, serious questions have been raised about the European results of heroin maintenance, because rates of addiction have risen rapidly, although they are still low in comparison to the United States. In 1971, for example, Great Britain passed the Misuse of Drugs Act which further restricts the rights of physicians to prescribe certain dangerous drugs, puts the penalty for trafficking to a maximum of 14 years, and permits unlimited fines.

Where *hospitals* or sanatoria are used, the optimum treatment period is a few months. Newly admitted drug addicts are first given thorough medical examinations and treatment, which includes building up their general physical condition along with removal of drugs. Drug dosages are gradually reduced to minimize the severity of withdrawal symptoms. Currently the most frequently used drug is methadone because it gives much milder abstinence symptoms than either heroin or morphine. The next step, removal of the patient's psychological dependence on drugs, is much more difficult. It usually involves counseling, recreational and occupational therapy, and vocational training. The addict usually receives follow-up supervision, since most relapses among addicts occur within the first two years after hospital release.[166] Addicts are being less and less confined for lengthy periods in hospitals, private sanatoria, or other in-patient facilities. Many are often treated for a while in some in-patient facility, however, and then released to after-care supervision where they can be monitored while living at home. There are also many therapeutic community facilities which provide in-patient facilities to some extent. To avoid stigma, California uses a method

[164]Jacob Schut, Robert A. Steer, and Frank I. Gonzalez, "Types of Arrests Recorded for Methadone Maintenance Patients before, during and after Treatment," *British Journal of Addictions,* 70 (1975), 80–93.

[165]See James M. Markham, "What's All This Talk of Heroin Maintenance?" *The New York Times Magazine,* July 2, 1972.

[166]See Jerome Levine and Jac. J. Monroe, "Discharge of Narcotic Drug Addicts against Medical Advice," *Public Health Reports,* 79 (1964), 13–18.

of "civil commitment" to hospitals rather than utilizing the criminal law. Under either alternative, however, forced treatment is involved.

Addict Self-Help Programs

Other treatment methods employed in the United States have been carried out largely by self-help groups of addicts themselves, such as more widespread groups like Narcotics Anonymous and Synanon and various local groups. Narcotics Anonymous was established in 1948 by a former drug addict and is similar to Alcoholics Anonymous in both its activities and its structure. It uses an informal organization in combating drug addiction, recognizes the difficulties faced by former addicts in keeping off drugs, and involves the belief that addicts would be more likely to stay off drugs if they could join some sort of group comprised of ex-addicts who could understand and help each other in dealing with their difficulties. Branches exist in most large cities in the United States and Canada. Similar to the pattern of Alcoholics Anonymous, new members are assigned to an older member who can be called upon for help when the initiate is having difficulties. The process in Narcotics Anonymous is similar to that of A. A., in that norms and attitudes favoring the use of drugs are replaced by norms and attitudes opposed to their use. In addition, N. A. members adhere to a set of prescribed steps similar in content to those of A. A. The first step, for example, requires that members admit that they are addicts. "We admit that we were powerless over drugs—that our lives had become unmanageable."[167] In general, Narcotics Anonymous has not been as successful as A. A. in terms of affecting permanent change. Some people believe that the comparative ineffectiveness of N. A. is due to the absence of public and community support, while others suggest that the public attitude toward addiction in the United States is responsible for the tremendous handicaps an addict faces in being reaccepted by society. There is no doubt that the public attitude toward drug addiction is much more negative than it is toward alcoholism.

A group method that deals with drug addicts is the organization of drug addicts—men and women—called Synanon (which got its name from an addict who was trying to say "seminar"), founded in 1958 by a member of Alcoholics Anonymous.[168] There are Synanon establishments in many parts of the country. Typically, Synanon establishment drug addicts live voluntarily together in a number of buildings for the purpose of freeing themselves and each other from drug addiction. Some have been criminals and prostitutes before addiction, but most of them have had to engage in criminal activities and prostitution to support their addiction. They manage their own offices and carry out the physical operations of the establishment. Membership in a Synanon group can be divided into three groups, which represent stages in progress toward rehabilitation. In the first stage they live and work in the residential center; in the second they have jobs outside but still live in the house; in stage three persons graduate to living and working on the outside.

An important part of the program is that each evening members meet in small

---

[167]John M. Murtagh and Sara Harris, *Who Live in Shadow* (New York: McGraw-Hill, 1959), p. 178.
[168]Lewis Yablonsky, *The Tunnel Back: Synanon* (New York: Macmillan, 1965).

groups, or "synanons," of 6 to 10 members, and membership is rotated so that one does not regularly interact in the small group with the same persons. The trend of the discussions is up to the members; no professional persons are present. The purpose of these group sessions is to "trigger feelings" and to precipitate "a catharsis." Because members of Synanon live together, their behavior is under constant scrutiny by the others and affords material for every session. In the discussions there is an "attack therapy," or "haircut," in which members insist on the truth and cross-examination; hostile attack and ridicule are expected. "An important goal of the 'haircut' method is to change the criminal–tough guy pose."[169]

It has been claimed that the program unknowingly applies the differential association theory or explanation of criminal behavior to the treatment of drug addicts because it brings them into contact with an antidrug subculture in which they learn to play nonaddict roles. The main aspects of the program are:

1. A willingness expressed by the individual, who gives up his own desires and ambitions, in order to become completely assimilated with a group dedicated to "hating" drug addiction.
2. The discovery by the addict that he belongs to a group that is "antidrug," "anticrime," and "antialcohol," as he hears over and over again each day that his stay at Synanon depends upon his staying completely free from drugs, crime, and alcohol—the group's basic purpose.
3. The maximization of a family-type cohesion wherein the members are deliberately thrown into continuous mutual activity, all designed to make each former drug addict fully realize that he is in this respect like each other member of the family-type group.
4. Explicit programs for giving to each member certain status symbols in exchange for their staying off drugs and even developing antidrug attitudes. The entire experience is organized into a hierarchy of graded competence unrelated to the usual prison or hospital status roles of "inmate" and "patient."
5. Specific emphasis on complete disassociation from the former drug and criminal culture and the substitution of legitimate, noncriminal cultural patterns.[170]

While no direct evidence is seen that "haircuts, synanons, and both formal and spontaneous denunciations of street talk and the code of the streets have important rehabilitative effects on the actors . . . it seems rather apparent, however, that an individual's own behavior must be dramatically influenced when he acts in the role of a moral policeman and 'takes apart' another member."

In one study of 372 Synanon enrollees a number of years ago 29 percent were found to be "off" drugs. Of more significance, however, of the 215 persons who had remained there for at least one month, approximately one half were still off drugs, while of the 143 who had stayed for at least three months, two thirds were still nonusers, and of the 87 who had remained at least seven months in the program, 86 percent were nonusers. These statistics appear to be relevant in that they indicated that once an addict has actually become a member of the antidrug community, as

---

[169]Yablonsky, p. 241.
[170]From Rita Volkman and Donald R. Cressey, "Differential Association and the Rehabilitation of Drug Addicts," *American Journal of Sociology,* 69 (1963), 129–142.

indicated by three to six months of participation in it, the less likely it is that he will leave and revert to drug usage.[171] It might be expected that those who do complete the preliminary period of time and harrassment would be more highly motivated, however, to become freed of their drug habit and that their eventual success, if it does occur, might just as well be due to this motivation rather than to any special qualities of the program itself.

Prevention of Drug Use

Two strategies underlie the attempts to prevent drug use: the employment of threatlike tactics to "scare" potential users into not using drugs, and the use of special education programs that alert potential users to the dangers and consequences of drugs. The former strategy is difficult to evaluate, primarily because the use of scare tactics has not been formally incorporated into programs of drug education. Drug education programs, on the other hand, are formalized, structured attempts to provide objective information to potential drug users so that they themselves might evaluate and, it is to be hoped, reject drug use.

Drug educational programs are generally confined to persons who do not have extensive drug experience or backgrounds. It has been reported that the more a person has been exposed to drugs in the past, the more the person is likely to find "drug education" among peers in the community rather than through a drug education program.[172] For this reason some studies report that these programs have both retarding and enhancing effects: in other words, for some persons the drug education program will inhibit drug usage while for others it may stimulate further use. These educational programs must cautiously select the contents of their programs as well as the population to which they are to be directed, and they must carefully assess the prior experiences of this "target" group.[173] Until it is possible to isolate the conditions under which such programs do inhibit drug use, they will probably continue to be inhibiting factors in some cases, perpetuating factors in others, and having no effect in still others.

As is true with most problems of deviant behavior, the prevention of drug use is not an easy task. The taking and widespread use of drugs is well ingrained in our society, and the line separating legal from illegal drug use is extremely fine in many social situations. The prevention of drug use, particularly in respect to heroin and other addicting substances, will probably remain more a matter of informal social control than of formal social control. The extremely questionable use of law as an important tool for drug control has long been voiced by persons who work and do research in this area, and increasingly alternative approaches for handling this problem are being advocated.

---

[171]Volkman and Cressey, p. 232.
[172]See Richard H. Blum, with Eva Blum and Emily Garfield, *Drug Education: Results and Recommendations* (Lexington, Mass.: Lexington Books, 1976).
[173]Richard Dembo and Michael Miran, "Evaluation of Drug Prevention Programs by Youths in a Middle-Class Community," *The International Journal of the Addictions,* 11 (1976), 881–903.

SELECTED REFERENCES

Agar, Michael. *Ripping and Running: A Formal Ethnography of Urban Heroin Addicts.* New York: Seminar Press, 1973.

Bonnie, Richard J., and Charles H. Whitebread II. *The Marihuana Conviction: A History of Marihuana Prohibition in the United States.* Charlottesville: University of Virginia Press, 1974.

Chambers, Carl D., and Leon Brill. *Methadone: Experiences and Issues.* New York: Behavioral Publications, 1972.

Coombs, Robert J., Lincoln J. Fry, and Patricia G. Lewis, eds. *Socialization in Drug Use.* Cambridge, Mass.: Schenkman, 1976.

DuPont, Robert L., and M. H. Greene. "The Dynamics of a Heroin Addiction Epidemic," *Science,* 181 (1973), 716–722.

Galliher, John H., and Allyn Walker. "The Puzzle of the Social Origins of the Marihuana Tax Act of 1937," *Social Problems,* 24 (1977), 366–376.

Goode, Erich. *Drugs in American Society.* New York: Knopf, 1972.

Johnson, Bruce C. *Marihuana Users and Drug Subcultures.* New York: Wiley, 1973.

Josephson, Eric, and Eleanor E. Carroll, eds. *Drug Use: Epidemiological and Sociological Approaches.* New York: Wiley, 1974.

Hunt, Leon Gibson, and Carl D. Chambers. *The Heroin Epidemics: A Study of Heroin Use in the United States, 1965–1975.* New York: Spectrum, 1976.

Lennard, Henry L., Leon J. Epstein, Arnold Bernstein, and Donald C. Ransom. *Mystification and Drug Misuse: Hazards in Using Psychoactive Drugs.* San Francisco: Jossey-Bass, 1971.

Lindesmith, Alfred R. *Addiction and Opiates.* Chicago: Aldine, 1968.

McAuliffe, William E., and Robert A. Gordon. "A Test of Lindesmith's Theory of Addiction: Frequency of Euphoria among Long-Term Addicts," *American Journal of Sociology,* 79 (1974), 795–840.

Musto, David R. *The American Disease: The Origins of Narcotics Control.* New Haven, Conn.: Yale University Press, 1973.

O'Donnell, John A., and John C. Ball, eds. *Narcotic Addiction.* New York: Harper & Row, 1966.

O'Donnell, John A., Harwin L. Voss, Richard R. Clayton, Gerald T. Slatin, and Robin G. W. Room. *Young Men and Drugs—A Nationwide Survey.* Rockville, Md.: National Institute of Drug Abuse, 1976.

Petersen, Robert C., and Richard C. Stillman, eds. *Cocaine: 1977.* Washington, D.C.: National Institute of Drug Abuse Research Monograph 13; Government Printing Office, 1977.

Platt, Jerome L., and Christine Labate. *Heroin Addiction: Theory, Research and Treatment.* New York: Wiley, 1976.

Silverman, Milton, and Philip R. Lee. *Pills, Profits and Politics.* Berkeley: University of California Press, 1974.

Winick, Charles. "Physician Narcotic Addicts," *Social Problems,* 9 (1961), 174–186.

Young, Jock. *The Drugtakers: The Social Meaning of Drug Use.* London: Paladin, 1971.

An alcoholic sleeping off a binge. Alcoholism is far more prevalent, and the social and economic costs to society far greater, than the use of hard drugs such as heroin and cocaine. (© Mimi Cotter)

CHAPTER 10

Drunkenness and Alcoholism

ALCOHOL is by far the most widely used mood-altering drug in America today.[1] Although increased concern has been expressed about the use of "drugs" by large segments of the public, and through the mass media, alcohol is often not regarded as a drug. Excessive drinking and alcoholism actually present far greater problems numerically than the use of other drugs, and the total effects upon individual behavior and decreased physical and psychological functioning as a result of alcohol use are more serious. It can lead to both physical and psychological dependency, to impaired social relationships, and to poor work performance.[2] Alcohol is not physiologically habit-forming in the sense that certain other drugs are, and one does not become a chronic drinker as a result of the first, twentieth, or even the one hundredth drink. Furthermore, it has never been demonstrated that the craving for alcoholic beverages is inherited.

PHYSIOLOGICAL AND PSYCHOLOGICAL ASPECTS OF ALCOHOL

Alcohol is a chemical substance derived through a process of fermentation or by distillation. Although the process of distillation of alcoholic beverages from barley, corn, wheat, and other grains is of fairly recent origin, nearly all societies have made some form of fermented beverages, such as wine, beer, and similar products for thousands of years.[3] Following the intake of alcoholic beverages, a certain amount of alcohol is absorbed into the small intestine. It is carried in the blood to the liver and then disseminated in diluted form to every part of the body. Because there can never be more than 1 percent of alcohol in the bloodstream, it cannot directly cause organic brain damage, neither "corroding," "dissolving," nor in any way directly harming the brain cells. In fact, all substances classed as colatile anesthetics, such as ether, can produce precisely the same reactions upon the brain.

The effect of alcohol is determined by the rate of its absorption into the body; this depends upon the kind of beverage consumed, the proportion of alcohol contained, the speed with which it is drunk, and the amount and type of food in the stomach, as well as on certain individual physiological differences. In moderate quantities, alcohol has relatively little effect on a person, but large quantities disturb the activity in the organs controlled by the brain and cause the phenomenon known as "drunkenness." The effect on behavior of different kinds and quantities of alcoholic beverages on the human system of a healthy 150-pound person who has not eaten a large quantity of food is shown in Table 10.1.

Alcohol produces a number of psychological effects on emotional and overt

---

[1]Harrison M. Trice and Paul M. Roman, *Spirits and Demons at Work: Alcohol and Other Drugs on the Job* (Ithaca, N.Y.: Industrial and Labor Relations Paperback, 1972), p. 1.
[2]Peter Wuthrich, "Social Problems of Alcoholics," *Journal of Studies on Alcohol,* 38 (1977), 881–890.
[3]Charles H. Patrick, *Alcohol, Culture and Society* (Durham, N.C.: Duke University Press, 1952), pp. 12–39.

TABLE 10.1 The Effect of Alcoholic Beverages

Amount of Beverage Consumed	Concentration of Alcohol Attained in Blood	Effect	Time Required for All Alcohol To Leave the Body
1 highball (1½ oz. whisky) or 1 cocktail (1½ oz. whisky) or 3½ oz. fortified wine or 5″ oz. ordinary wine or 2 bottles beer (24 oz.)	0.03%	No noticeable effects on behavior	2 hrs.
2 highballs or 2 cocktails or 7 oz. fortified wine or 11 oz. ordinary wine or 4 bottles beer	0.06%	Feeling of warmth—mental relaxation—slight decrease of fine skills—less concern with minor irritations and restraints	4 hrs.
3 Highballs or 3 cocktails or 10″ oz. fortified wine or 16½ oz. (1 pt.) ordinary wine or 6 bottles beer	0.06%	Increasing effects with variation among individuals and in the same individuals at different times Buoyancy—exaggerated emotion and behavior—talkative, noisy, or morose	6 hrs.
4 highballs or 4 cocktails or 14 oz. fortified wine or 22 oz. ordinary wine or 8 bottles (3 qts.) beer	0.12%	Impairment of fine coordination—clumsiness—slight to moderate unsteadiness in standing or walking	8 hrs.
5 highballs or 5 cocktails or (½ pt. whisky)	0.15%	Intoxication—unmistakable abnormality of gross bodily functions and mental faculties	10 hrs.

For those weighing considerably more or less than 150 pounds the amounts of beverage indicated above will be correspondingly greater or less. The effects indicated at each stage will diminish as the concentration of alcohol in the blood diminishes.
Source: Reprinted from "Intoxication and Alcoholism: Physiological Factors," by Leon A. Greenberg in Volume No. 315 of *The Annals of The American Academy of Political and Social Science*

behavior.[4] In moderate amounts, alcohol can lessen tensions and worry and in general may ease the fatigue associated with anxiety. The belief that alcohol is primarily consumed, however, for its tension-reducing effects has been questioned in a survey of the entire literature where findings were contradictory.[5] The use of alcohol presents an illusion of being a stimulant because it reduces or alters the cortical control over action. Alcohol has a negative effect on task performance, although this is dependent on the experience of the person, the complexity of the work, and the amount of alcohol consumed. The inexperienced drinker tends to overreact to the sensations of alcohol, and he may be merely fulfilling what he perceives to be the socially expected behavior in response to drinking. Such a reaction is commonly seen in groups of teenagers who can behave as if intoxicated under the influence of small quantities of alcohol.[6]

Alcohol plays an important role for persons on skid row in large cities. Drunkenness is often prolonged and steady, with a constant saturation of alcohol, and there is general agreement that alcohol produces euphoria and a warm glow of optimism. Feelings of loneliness are dulled, as are feelings of social inadequacies.[7] Three skid row alcoholics have described their feelings:

> Alcohol is marvelous at removing obstacles for a while. Everyone gets to the point where he is just fed up and scared and worried. He doesn't know where to turn. Alcohol takes care of that. The important becomes unimportant. Your problems aren't anywhere near what you thought.

> When I'm sober, Skid Row is a transient place—there is nothing there. When I'm drunk, I don't pay any attention to the smut and dirt. I am enjoying talking to my own kind. The scenery is in the background, I just ignore it.

> When you sober up there is a futile feeling. You begin to see yourself as you really are. You know you made an ass of yourself. You wonder what others thought of you.

Considerable evidence supports the view that much of so-called *drunken behavior* or drunken comportment is the product of socialization and not the result of the alcohol itself that automatically releases controls. An anthropological survey of the way different cultural groups react to drunkenness shows that among some the normal inhibitions on behavior remain in effect. In many societies alcohol is often consumed in very large quantities without producing appreciable changes in behavior except for a progressive impairment in the exercise of one's sensorimotor capabilities, such as coordination.[8] For example, among the Onitsha of Nigeria, the ability to appear sober

---

[4]For a review of the literature on psychological effects, see Julian B. Roebuck and Raymond B. Kessler, *The Etiology of Alcoholism: Constitutional, Psychological, and Sociological Approaches* (Springfield, Ill.: Charles C Thomas, 1972), pp. 61–138.

[5]Howard Cappell and C. Peter Herman, "Alcohol and Tension-Reduction," *Quarterly Journal of Studies on Alcohol,* 33 (1972), 33–64.

[6]Robert Straus, "Alcoholism and Problem Drinking," in Robert K. Merton and Robert Nisbet, eds., *Contemporary Social Problems,* 4th ed. (New York: Harcourt Brace Jovanovich, 1976), p. 204.

[7]Jacqueline P. Wiseman, *Stations of the Lost: The Treatment of Skid Row Alcoholics* (Englewood Cliffs, N.J.: Prentice-Hall, 1970). Excerpts from p. 15.

[8]Craig MacAndrew and Robert B. Edgerton, *Drunken Comportment: A Social Explanation* (Chicago: Aldine, 1969), p. 36.

in spite of heavy drinking is respected, while exhibited drunken behavior brings shame.[9] On the other hand, in some societies, people generally may display considerable physical aggression toward others when drunk. The drinker in some societies becomes "euphoric" or happy but neither sexually "loose" nor aggressive. Certain normal constraints on the relation between the sexes may fall but without accompanying changes in sexual aggressiveness. In still others, the opposite may occur, aggression becoming "both rampant and unbridled, but without any changes whatsoever occurring in one's sexual comportment."[10]

The continuous use of alcohol, such as in cases of alcoholism which will be discussed later, results in a greatly diminished appetite. If this drinking is not curbed disease may follow, not primarily from the alcohol consumed but rather because nutritional deficiencies result from prolonged drinking. These deficiencies may produce an organic condition called polyneuritis, or, less technically, beriberi, caused by a lack of vitamin B_1, or pellagra, caused by a deficiency of niacin. The fact that these deficiencies are present has caused some researchers to believe that alcoholism can be prevented or controlled by proper nutrition, although such an approach fails properly to take into account the sociological aspects of drinking. The disease most commonly associated with alcoholism is cirrhosis of the liver. Although this disease occurs proportionately more often among heavy drinkers than among nondrinkers, it is not caused directly by alcohol but instead is due to some nutritional deficiency.

PREVALENCE OF DRINKING IN THE UNITED STATES

In the United States the drinking of alcohol, in order of amount consumed and cost, consists chiefly of beer, followed by distilled spirits and wine fermented from grapes. Over the past century there has been a downward trend in the drinking of distilled spirits and an increase in the consumption of beer. In the year 1850, almost 90 percent of the absolute alcohol consumed, that is, the alcohol content of a beverage, in the United States was in the form of distilled spirits, and nearly 7 percent was beer. From the period 1860–1870 to 1960, the consumption of distilled spirits declined well over a third, while the consumption of beer almost doubled.[11] In 1960, only 38 percent was in the form of spirits, 51 percent beer. Since World War II, the consumption of beer has risen less than 11 percent, while the consumption of distilled spirits has risen by 50 percent.[12] In a single year over $10 billion is spent on alcoholic beverages of all types. In 1974, $8 billion was collected in excise taxes on alcohol and tobacco products.[13]

---

[9]Ifekandu Umunna, "The Drinking Culture of a Nigerian Community: Onitsha," *Quarterly Journal of Studies on Alcohol,* 28 (1967), 529–537.

[10]MacAndrew and Edgerton, p. 172.

[11]Mark Keller and Vera Efron, *Selected Statistical Tables on Alcoholic Beverages, 1950–1960, and on Alcoholism, 1930–1960* (New Brunswick, N.J.: Quarterly Journal of Studies on Alcohol, 1961), p.3.

[12]See *Alcohol and Health: New Knowledge,* Second Special Report to the U.S. Congress from the Secretary of Health, Education and Welfare (Washington, D.C.: Government Printing Office, 1974).

[13]As of 1978, the federal excise tax rate on distilled spirits was $10.50 per proof gallon.

Alcoholic beverages have been produced in the United States since 1640 and have been subject to taxes since 1791. One of the major effects of Prohibition repeal was the concentration of alcohol manufacture into the hands of four main distillers—Distillers Corporation (Seagrams, Ltd.), Schenley Distillers Corporation, National Distillers Products Corporation, and Walker.[14] In addition to the manufacturers, the liquor industry includes distributors, retailers, and, of course, drinkers.

Between 1970 and 1976, the annual average per capita consumption of absolute or 100 percent alcohol (100 proof is actually 50 percent alcohol), for those over 14, was 1.5 gallons.[15] If this figure seems high, one should realize that in 1830 it was estimated that each individual American consumed an average of 9.5 gallons per year. The 1976 per capita consumption of distilled spirits was 2.0 gallons, wine 1.8 gallons, and beer 21.8. This does not mean that persons drank all of them, since some persons, for example, are exclusively beer drinkers. Moreover, since these figures are averages, and since some persons drink no alcoholic beverages at all, much larger amounts of alcohol are consumed by average drinkers. If this average consumption is compared with that of other countries, the U.S. per capita consumption of alcohol is less than that of France and Italy, two heavy wine-drinking countries which head the list. France also consumes, in addition, large quantities of stronger spirits, such as brandy or cognac. It appears that the Soviet Union also has an extremely high per capita consumption rate, perhaps the highest in the world, although its figures are not normally released.[16]

Since 1940 there have been marked increases in the percentage of adult drinkers in the United States, the largest being in the percentage of women drinkers.[17] A Gallup poll report in 1976 indicated that about 71 percent of those over 18 used alcoholic beverages, up sharply from the 55 percent in 1955. One must add to the total of adult drinkers the substantial number of teenagers below 18 who drink, as numerous studies have shown that their use of alcohol is rapidly increasing. By 1976 the number of women who reported that they drank had increased to 66 percent, up from 45 percent in 1958, which is a much greater rate of increase than among men. All of these drinkers are not regular drinkers, however, and when the infrequent drinkers and the abstainers are added, the adult population is rather evenly divided between the 47 percent who do not drink or who drink less than once a month and the 53 percent who drink once a month or more.

More recently, it appears that each new generation tends to have a larger proportion of persons who drink, and most of them remain drinkers throughout life.

---

[14]See the discussion of the liquor industry in Norman K. Denzin, "Notes on the Criminogenic Hypothesis: A Case Study of the American Liquor Industry," *American Sociological Review,* 42 (1977), 905–920.

[15]Carl Cannon, "Spirits of '77—Americans Drink Less," *Los Angeles Times,* April 21, 1977, p. 1.

[16]Vladimir G. Treml, "Production and Consumption of Alcoholic Beverages in the USSR," *Journal of Studies on Alcohol,* 36 (1975), 285–320. Also see Walter D. Connor, *Deviance in Soviet Society: Crime, Delinquency and Alcoholism* (New York: Columbia University Press, 1972).

[17]Don Cahalan, Ira H. Cisin, and Helen M. Crossley, *American Drinking Practices: A National Survey of Drinking Behavior and Attitudes* (New Brunswick, N.J.: Rutgers Center of Alcohol Studies, 1969). See also Don Cahalan and Ira H. Cisin, "Drinking Behavior and Drinking Problems in the United States," in Benjamin Kassin and Henri Begleiter, eds., *Social Aspects of Alcoholism* (New York: Plenum Press, 1976), pp. 77–115; and Mark Keller, "Problems of Epidemiology in Alcohol Studies," *Journal of Studies on Alcohol,* 36 (1975), 1442–1451.

Some drinkers, although a small proportion, do give up drinking, and, of course, many who abstain from alcohol remain abstainers throughout life. About half of the abstainers in the urban areas in the United States appear to abstain for moral reasons, while the other half give such reasons as dislike of the taste and lack of interest.[18] As the proportions of adults and young persons who drink increase, a stronger "drinking culture" is developed. At present, the extreme of the "drinking culture" is probably found in France, where only 4 percent of the population are abstainers.[19] There are also few nondrinkers in Italy, and a Polish survey on a representative sample of the population aged 20 or over found only about 8 percent of the men and 25 percent of the women were nondrinkers.[20]

Statements about the proportion of drinkers in the general population are often misleading, however, because they give no indication of the frequency and amount of drinking.[21] A study of drinking behavior conducted during 1964–1965, using a large sample of U.S. adults, found that 32 percent of the population were classified as "abstainers" because they said that they drink less than once a year if at all. The group of drinkers was divided into the heaviest drinking (heavy drinkers)—12 percent of the population, based on quantity, frequency, and variability of intake (those who drank several times a week with usually three or more drinks per occasion, or nearly every day with five or more drinks at least once in a while); and the "infrequent" to "moderate" drinkers—56 percent of the population.[22]

Variations in Drinking Behavior

Great variation is seen in drinking frequency by age, education, income, size of community, marital status, and religion. In a national U.S. sample approximately 79 percent of those between 21 and 39 drink, 70 percent between 40 and 59, and 56 percent aged 60 and older.[23] Generally, those adults with a higher education drink more than those with less education; the percentage with seventh-grade or less education was 46, high school, 79, and college, 89. Drinking also increases directly with income. The proportion of drinking generally increases also with the size of the community—60 percent of those living in areas under 2,500 but 76 percent in cities over 500,000. With reference to religion, the proportion of those who drink is highest

---

[18]Genevieve Knupfer and Robin Room, "Abstainees in a Metropolitan Community," *Quarterly Journal of Studies on Alcohol,* 31 (1970), 108–131.

[19]See David J. Pittman, "International Overview: Social and Cultural Factors in Drinking Patterns, Pathological and Nonpathological," in David J. Pittman, ed., *Alcoholism* (New York: Harper & Row, 1967), pp. 12–13.

[20]Andrzej Swiecicki, "Survey on Alcohol Consumption in Poland," *Archives of Criminology,* 2 (1964), 385–391.

[21]Cahalan, Cisin, and Crossley.

[22]Harold A. Mulford, "Drinking and Deviant Behavior, USA," *Quarterly Journal of Studies on Alcohol,* 25 (1964), 634–650; and Allan Beigel and Stuart Chertner, "Toward A Social Model: An Assessment of Social Factors Which Influence Problem Drinking and Its Treatment," in Benjamin Kassin and Henri Begleiter, eds., *Treatment and Rehabilitation of the Chronic Alcoholic* (New York: Plenum Press, 1977), pp. 197–233.

[23]Mulford. For a more general discussion, see Keller, "Problems of Epidemiology in Alcohol Studies."

among Jews, Catholics, and Lutherans and the least among other large Protestant denominations. A survey of high school drinking in 1959 concluded that a large proportion of youth aged 14 to 18 has had some experience with drinking, frequently with parental consent, but that the drinking practices of young people can be understood only in terms of their social class, economic status, religious affiliation, and the drinking customs of their parents.[24] Currently, alcohol consumption in this age group appears to have had a marked increase.

PUBLIC DRUNKENNESS

A Harris public opinion poll in the early 1970s showed that the American people were two to one against arresting persons for public drunkenness if they cause no trouble. Despite this, an estimated two million arrests for public drunkenness are made in the United States each year. This represents about one fourth of all arrests for other than traffic offenses. At least half the populations of most jails consists of persons arrested for drunkenness. The typical public drunkenness statute contains two elements: (1) the intoxication takes place in a "public place"; and (2) "loud and boisterous" or "disorderly" conduct is involved. Several common features characterize the statutes: they do not relate to immediate acts of violence; since no "victims" are involved, enforcement is initiated by the police; and by implication, they are primarily directed against lower-class and skid row persons. The laws provide usually maximum jail sentences ranging from five days to six months, although 30 days is more customary. Some states punish habitual drunkenness as a felony with a two-year prison sentence. Drunkenness under certain specified conditions, such as while driving a motor vehicle, is severely punished in the United States and most countries.[25]

Arrests for drunkenness among those under 21 years of age are disproportionately smaller compared to older age groups; arrests for violations of laws prohibiting the purchase of alcohol by minors are disproportionately higher.[26] A St. Louis study showed that although persons 10 through 21 made up 15 percent of the population, this age group accounted for only 2 percent of arrests for public intoxication and 3 percent of the drunken driving arrests, but 23 percent of law violations relating to the purchase of liquor.[27]

Laws against public drunkenness originated in church attitudes, particularly Protestant, toward personal morality and more specifically, moral ideas about the individual's lack of control and the inability if intoxicated to carry out the will of God

---

[24]Raymond G. McCarthy, "High School Drinking Studies," in Raymond G. McCarthy, ed., *Drinking and Intoxication* (New York: The Free Press, 1959), p. 205.

[25]For a general discussion of the use of legal regulations, see Robert E. Popham, Wolfgang Schmidt, and Jan de Lint, "The Effects of Legal Restraint on Drinking," in Kassin and Begleiter, *Social Aspects of Alcoholism,* pp. 579–625.

[26]Federal Bureau of Investigation, *Uniform Crime Reports—1975* (Washington, D.C.: Government Printing Office, 1976).

[27]Muriel W. Sterne, David J. Pittman, and Thomas Coe, "Teen-Agers, Drinking, and the Law: A Study of Arrest Trends for Alcohol-Related Offenses," *Crime and Delinquency,* 11 (1965), 81.

effectively in work and family relationships. Under English common law intoxication itself was not a crime: it was tolerated whether in a public place or not unless it resulted in some form of breach of the peace or disorderly conduct. In England it was not until 1606 that intoxication in public first became a criminal offense, and it still remains so in most U.S. jurisdictions. The value conflicts over the use of alcohol actually represent a struggle between the Calvinistic tradition that it is the community's responsibility to supervise the individual's drinking and to take criminal action against drunkenness and an individualistic tradition that regards drinking as a matter of free choice.

Arrests for public drunkenness are not evenly distributed across the social spectrum; in most jurisdictions upper- and middle-class men who violate the law are either not detected, ignored, or simply given transportation to their homes by the police.[28] The arrests occur primarily among the lower classes. A study in the District of Columbia showed that of approximately 27,000 persons arrested for public intoxication in 1965, 56 percent had been arrested 5 or more times, 29 percent 20 or more times, and 12 percent 50 or more times.[29] A large proportion of those frequently arrested were from skid row areas. In fact, a Seattle study of "urban nomads" who lived on skid row showed that jail confinement for drunkenness (they termed it "the bucket") was a common experience: one fourth had been jailed 26 to 50 times, a fourth 50 to 100 times, 12 percent between 100 and 200 times, and 7 percent more than 200 times.[30]

Members of minority groups are also more frequently arrested and incarcerated for drunkenness. In one study chronic drunk police cases were found to constitute 18 percent blacks, although blacks represented only 2 percent of the population.[31] Similarly, Indians are more frequently arrested than whites, particularly in areas near reservations.[32] On the other hand, women are less likely to be arrested in proportion to their population representation. In Great Britain in 1974, for example, 3,412 females were arrested for simple drunkenness, and 46,551 males, a ratio of almost 14 to 1.[33] In a Boston study of female arrests, it was found that few women were arrested for drunken driving and that the arrests which were made were usually in connection with an accident.[34]

Regardless of the reason for the arrest, drunk persons are usually put into a large, specially prepared cell called a "tank," which may contain as many as 50 to 100 persons, with inadequate ventilation and sanitary facilities and smelling of vomit and urine. In addition, the drunken behavior of some inmates may be hazardous to

---

[28]James P. Spradley, *You Owe Yourself a Drunk: An Ethnography of Urban Nomads* (Boston: Little, Brown, 1970), p. 80.

[29]Raymond T. Nimmer, *Two Million Unnecessary Arrests: Removing a Social Service Concern from the Criminal Justice System* (Chicago: American Bar Association, 1971).

[30]*Task Force Report: Drunkenness,* President's Commission on Law Enforcement and Administration of Justice (Washington, D.C.: Government Printing Office, 1967), p. 73.

[31]David J. Pittman and C. Wayne Gordon, *The Revolving Door* (New York: Free Press, 1958).

[32]Sidney Harring, "The Effect of Language Retention on the Indian Arrest Rate," unpublished master's thesis, University of Wisconsin, Madison, 1970.

[33]Carol Smart, *Women, Crime, and Criminology: A Feminist Critique* (London: Routledge & Kegan Paul, 1976), p. 14.

[34]Milton Argeriow and Donna Paulino, "Women Arrested for Drunken Driving in Boston: Social Characteristics and Circumstances of Arrest," *Journal of Studies on Alcohol,* 37 (1976), 648–658.

persons who have been arrested for their own safekeeping and protection.[35] The morning following his arrest, the drunk is generally brought before the judge, who is often seeing many similar cases and thus processing them rather hurriedly. Often there are few due process of law safeguards, persons arrested and held for prosecution almost never have legal representation, and they are almost always found guilty.[36] Since many of these alcoholics have been arrested from 100 to 200 times annually, they serve in their lifetimes up to 10 or 20 years.

DRINKING AS A SOCIAL AND GROUP PHENOMENON

Alcoholic beverages of one type or another have been widely used for centuries by most ancient and modern peoples. The people of Western Europe and the American colonists were no exception. In fact, ale and beer were part of the daily diet in New England and the middle and southern colonies of the eastern seaboard; it was believed that these beverages were necessary to maintain health.[37] Yet from the earliest days drunkenness was frowned upon, and persons who drank excessively were punished. In the late eighteenth century rum, whose alcohol content far exceeds that of beer or ale, was an important part of the colonists' economic and social life, and numerous distilleries were in operation.

Thus, patterns of drinking have come down to us through a long past, and the knowledge, ideas, norms, and values involved in the use of alcoholic beverages have passed from generation to generation, thus maintaining the continuity of an alcohol subculture. Drinking patterns today vary in terms of beverages used, the circumstances under which the drinking takes place, the time, the amount, and the individual's own attitude and that of others toward his drinking. All drinking patterns are learned, as are all behavior patterns. One writer on alcohol has stated that there are no really universal patterns of drinking for John, the average American citizen: "In any event, John will not drink like a Zulu or an Austrian or a Japanese; in fact, he will not drink like a New Yorker or a Californian or a ditch digger or a Yale man or a Kentucky mountaineer, unless he is or has been in socially significant contact with such a group."[38]

Drinking plays a significant role in everyday interpersonal affairs. Alcohol is used by many people to celebrate national holidays, such as Christmas and New Year's, and to rejoice in victories, whether those of war, the football field, or the ballot box. The bride and groom are often toasted, and the father may celebrate the birth of a child with a drink "all around." Promotions, anniversaries, and important special

---

[35] *Task Force Report: Drunkenness,* p. 2.
[36] Raymond G. McCarthy, "Alcoholism: Attitudes and Attacks," *The Annals,* 315 (1958), 13.
[37] *Task Force Report: Drunkenness,* p. 2.
[38] Seldon D. Bacon, "Sociology and the Problems of Alcohol," *Memoirs of the Section of Studies on Alcohol* (New Brunswick, N.J.: Quarterly Journal of Studies on Alcohol, 1946), pp. 17–18. Also see MacAndrew and Edgerton.

events of achievement by the family and close friends often call for a drink. Businessmen may negotiate contracts over a few glasses, and meeting an old friend is often the occasion for a drink. In many homes guests are welcomed with a drink or cocktails before dinner to help get the guests acquainted. The cocktail party itself is built around the serving of alcoholic beverages and social objectives of the party often seem secondary.[39] Even some religious ceremonies and, on occasion, the bereavement of death, as in the Irish wake, are accompanied by alcoholic beverages. On a more inclusive level, it has been said that the "notion that in alcohol is magic" is imbedded in the culture pattern, a magic that frees the human spirit and "permits it to soar into the heavens unhampered by the ills of the flesh."[40]

Despite the widespread use of alcohol in connection with many social functions, the value systems implicit in U.S. drinking patterns differ from those in Europe where traditionally drinking has been one phase of a deeply rooted, stable, and a generally integrated social and recreational pattern. Rather than alcohol drinking being a "vice" or a social problem it has remained just one element in a traditional recreational practice. In other words, where drinking in the European tradition has been one aspect of a group's coming together, U.S. drinking has often been the opposite; gathering together has all too frequently provided the occasion for drinking.[41] In the United States, furthermore, and elsewhere as well, drinking among teenagers represents peer-group identification, within the context of an age-graded social system, as well as a status transformation into adult roles.[42] For at least some teenagers, drinking is related to the passage from youth into adult roles in our society. Group drinking patterns are also found among college students whose "bull sessions" commonly involve beer or other drinking. In European universities there were, and still are, "drinking fraternities" for which members have qualified by their ability to consume a large quantity of wine, beer, ale, or other liquor.

Public Drinking Houses

A large proportion of drinking is done in a group context in public drinking houses, which are found in most of the world today under a variety of names: American taverns and bars, British pubs, French bistros, German beer halls, Italian wine houses, and African or Japanese bars. Public drinking houses are more than places where alcoholic beverages are sold for consumption on the premises. They have several important characteristics: (1) they involve group drinking; (2) this drinking is commercial in the sense that anyone can buy a drink as contrasted to bars of private clubs; (3) they serve alcohol and can thus be distinguished from the coffee houses of the Middle East or the teahouses of the Orient; (4) their bartenders or "tavernkeepers" serve as functionaries of the institution, and around them, in part, the drinking gravitates; (5)

---

[39]David Riesman, Robert J. Potter, and Jeanne Watson, "The Vanishing Host," *Human Organization,* 19 (1960), 17–28.
[40]Ernest R. Mowrer, *Disorganization: Personal and Social* (Philadelphia: Lippincott, 1942), p. 264.
[41]See Herbert A. Bloch, "Alcohol and American Recreational Life," *American Scholar,* 18 (1949), 56–57.
[42]See Christofer Sower, "Teen-Age Drinking as Group Behavior," *Quarterly Journal of Studies on Alcohol,* 20 (1959), 656.

many customs are connected with them, including the physical surroundings, types of drinks, and the hours of sale.[43] In the United States alone there are over 200,000 bars and taverns, and they are widely patronized.

The important social nature of tavern or bar drinking can be seen in the historical development of public drinking establishments as far back as Babylon, Greece, and Rome.[44] Taverns played a significant role in England and in Colonial America. In part because it was believed that drinking not done in public was likely to be excessive, whereas the sale of liquor in a tavern could be regulated, the Puritan authorities in Massachusetts in 1656 even enacted a law making towns liable to a fine for not maintaining an "ordinary" (tavern).[45] The scientific validity of this view is shown in a Canadian study that tested the relation of tavern frequenting, the amount of alcohol consumed, and drunkenness, concluding that convictions for drunkenness and tavern rates in Ontario "showed a quite markedly negative relationship when plotted through time."[46] The rate of arrest for drunkenness in relation to the number of pubs (taverns) per 100,000 in various counties in England and Wales also failed to show a positive relationship.[47]

In Colonial America taverns served as coach stations or wayside stops and as places for lodging strangers. They were used as schools, courthouses, public meeting houses, post offices, job markets, and as places for celebrations of weddings and national holidays. One writer has asserted that in Colonial America the people found that "the tavern was their club, their board of trade, their 'exchanges,' and indeed, to most of the colonists it served as their newspaper."[48] As the Industrial Revolution brought thousands of migrants, particularly single men, to the cities to work in the factories, a new type of public drinking house, the "saloon," replaced the wayside tavern. The saloon became common in urban areas and was characterized by strictly male patronage, drinking at an elaborate bar with "free meals," and a special "family entrance." Most of them performed an important function of helping to relieve the poverty, loneliness, and monotony of city life, although some were centers of drunkenness, gambling, and prostitution.

The modern tavern made its appearance after the repeal of Prohibition. It differed from the saloon in that women were generally permitted, the surroundings were more attractive, and patrons more frequently drank at tables rather than at a bar. At least five different varieties of public drinking places emerged, the types being largely associated with certain areas of a city: the skid row bar, the downtown cocktail lounge and bar, the dine and dance establishment, the night club, and the neighborhood tavern. The patrons of skid row taverns are drifters, transients, and alcoholics; drunkenness, prostitution, gambling, and violations of other state laws and ordinances

[43]See Marshall B. Clinard, "The Public Drinking House and Society," in David J. Pittman and Charles R. Snyder, eds., *Alcohol, Culture and Drinking Patterns* (New York: Wiley, 1962), pp. 270–292; and E. E. LeMasters, *Blue-Collar Aristocrats: Life-Styles at a Working-Class Tavern* (Madison: University of Wisconsin Press, 1975).
[44]W. C. Firebaugh, *Inns of Greece and Rome* (Chicago: Fm. M. Morris, 1928).
[45]Eugene Field, *The Colonial Tavern* (Providence, R.I.: Preston and Rounds, 1897), pp. 11–12.
[46]Robert E. Popham, "The Urban Tavern: Some Preliminary Remarks," *Addictions*, 9 (1962), 22.
[47]Popham, p. 22.
[48]Field, pp. 232–233.

are not uncommon. Patrons of cocktail lounges are largely a higher-status group of regular customers, and in large cities often a major function is the facilitation of casual sexual encounters between middle- and upper-class men and young, unattached women.[49] The neighborhood tavern is the most numerous type, constituting probably three fourths of all taverns. It is patronized by people in the neighborhood and serves as a meeting place as well as providing general relaxation.

Tavern drinking is not, of course, the only evidence of the social and group aspects of the consumption of alcoholic beverages. Middle- and upper-class drinking, although generally not oriented around a public drinking house, is similarly social in nature and centers around various group events, the cocktail party, and the bar in the country club or dining establishment. In this setting, alcohol is used as a social lubricant, stimulating conversation as well as serving as a sign of friendship and a good time. Cocktail parties are usually private functions, although some business firms and corporations use them as a business device to entertain customers or for the traditional Christmas party for employees.

TYPES OF DRINKERS

Drinkers can be classified in terms of the deviation from norms of drinking behavior within a culture and dependence on alcohol in the life organization of the individual. This includes the amount of alcohol consumed,[50] the purpose and meaning of drinking as an aspect of role-playing, the degree to which such drinking handicaps the individual in his interpersonal relations, and his ability to refrain from taking a drink. More specifically, the classification of types of drinkers involves the analysis of behavioral phenomena in connection with (1) the amount of consumption of beverage alcohol (2) in an excessive manner indicating preoccupation with alcohol which (3) interferes with the drinker's interpersonal relationships.[51] One study has devised a scale to measure preoccupation with drinking so that the differences between types of responses to the use of alcohol may be measured, with Group I representing the most highly preoccupied with alcohol and Group IV the least preoccupied (see Table 10.2).

The three main types of drinkers are social or controlled drinkers, heavy drinkers, and alcoholics. A *social or controlled drinker* drinks for reasons of sociability,

---

[49]See Sheri Cavan, *Liquor License: An Ethnography of Bar Behavior* (Chicago: Aldine, 1966); and Julian Roebuck and S. Lee Spray, "The Cocktail Lounge: A Study of Heterosexual Relations in a Public Organization," *American Journal of Sociology,* 72 (1967), 388–395.

[50]The amount of alcohol considered socially permissible is itself culturally determined, as well as the resources available to drinkers. In this connection one study concluded that alcoholic consumption relies heavily upon three conditions: (1) one's resources for drinking; (2) activities that may compete for these resources; and (3) the economic cost of drinking in one's particular social status. See Thomas Storm and Ronald Cutler, "Alcohol Consumption and Personal Resources: A General Hypothesis and Some Implications," *Journal of Studies on Alcohol,* 36 (1975), 917–924.

[51]Harold A. Mulford and Donald E. Miller, "Drinking in Iowa, IV: Preoccupation with Alcohol and Definitions of Alcohol, Heavy Drinking and Trouble Due to Drinking," *Quarterly Journal of Studies on Alcohol,* 21 (1960), 279–291. See also the replication of this study: Harold A. Mulford and Donald E. Miller, "Preoccupation with Alcohol and Definitions of Alcohol: A Replication of Two Cumulative Scales," *Quarterly Journal of Studies on Alcohol,* 24 (1963), 682–696.

TABLE 10.2   The Iowa Scale of Preoccupation with Alcohol

Item	Content of Statement	Method of Scoring
I	I stay intoxicated for several days at a time.	Agree on any two.
	I worry about not being able to get a drink when I need one.	
	I sneak drinks when no one is looking.	
II	Once I start drinking it is difficult for me to stop before I become completely intoxicated.	Agree on any two.
	I get intoxicated on work days.	
	I take a drink the first thing when I get up in the morning.	
III	I awaken next day not being able to remember some of the things I had done while I was drinking.	Agree on any two.
	I take a few quick ones before going to a party to make sure I have enough.	
	I neglect my regular meals when I am drinking.	
IV	I don't nurse my drinks; I toss them down pretty fast.	Agree on any two.
	I drink for the effect of alcohol with little attention to type of beverage or brand name.	
	Liquor has less effect on me than it used to.	

Source: Adapted from Harold Mulford and Donald E. Miller, "Drinking in Iowa. IV. Preoccupation with Alcohol and Definitions of Alcohol, Heavy Drinking and Trouble Due to Drinking." Reprinted by permission from *Quarterly Journal of Studies on Alcohol,* Vol. 21, pp. 279–291, 1960. Copyright by Journal of Studies on Alcohol, Inc., New Brunswick, NJ 08903. The scale is cumulative in that with few exceptions respondents beginning with the bottom item agree to each item up to a point and then reject the remaining items.

conviviality, and conventionality. He may or may not like the taste and the effects produced by alcohol. Above all else, he is able to desist from using intoxicating beverages when he so chooses; he drinks in a take-it-or-leave-it manner. Social drinkers may be either occasional or regular drinkers. The former drink sporadically and may have only a few drinks a year, whereas the regular social drinker may drink three or more times a week.

The *heavy drinker* uses alcohol more frequently; in addition and occasionally, he may consume such quantities that he becomes intoxicated.[52] Some studies have

[52]Trice and Roman have termed this category "deviant drinking" in that it "both exceeds the bounds of community definition and impairs role performance." See Trice and Roman, *Spirits and Demons at Work,* p. 16. The use of this term is somewhat misleading since the separate category of "alcohol addiction" is also included as "deviant drinking."

defined a heavy drinker as one who takes three or more drinks of liquor at a "sitting" more than once a week. He sometimes, but not always, has weekend binges or, at a party, may drink too heavily or take a few more than anyone else. Whatever else may be said about excessive drinkers, they, in common with social drinkers but with greater difficulty, may be able to curtail or even completely to cease drinking on their own volition. Depending upon circumstances, they may continue drinking in this manner for the rest of their lives; they may later reduce the frequency and quantity of their alcohol consumption, or they may become alcoholics. Approximately 1 in 10 of all drinkers in a national survey reported themselves to be either heavy drinkers or as "having trouble due to drinking," or both.[53] Another survey of problem drinking among U.S. males aged 21 to 59 concluded that almost three fourths (72 percent) of those interviewed in their homes had at some time experienced a problem associated with heavy drinking. Typical problems reported were frequent quarrels with wives over drinking, the cost of alcoholic beverages, and belligerence when intoxicated. Drinking problems with the most serious consequences were reported most frequently by men from the lowest social class and least frequently by men from the upper-middle class or those in high social positions.[54] The distinction between "social" and "heavy" drinkers may be related to the judgments of one's peers and drinking companions. Blue-collar workers, for example, seem to base such judgments on an individual's work record and performance; if the drinker can perform satisfactorily at work, he is not considered a heavy drinker, no matter how much he consumes.[55]

Although problem drinkers are heavy drinkers, not all heavy drinkers are problem drinkers. Some idea of the characteristics of those who get into "trouble" because of alcohol use and who are likely to constitute a high proportion of alcoholics has been shown in a nation-wide survey. Heavy drinkers have been found to be most often white males and black females; men aged 40 to 49; males and females of lower status groups; males who had completed high school but not college; single, divorced, or separated males and females; residents of large cities; and Protestants of no established denominations, Catholics, and those without a religious denomination.[56]

Largely on the basis of his findings in a national study that those who encounter "trouble" due to drinking were primarily Baptists or members of small or unspecified denominations, Mulford reported that the drinker in a group where drinkers are less prevalent is more likely to encounter trouble because of his drinking. This suggests the hypothesis that whether an individual's drinking leads to trouble depends as much or more upon the reactions of others as it does upon his own actions.[57]

Alcoholics are persons whose frequent and repeated drinking of alcoholic beverages is in excess of the dietary and social usages of the community and is of such an extent that it interferes with health or social or economic functioning. The alcoholic

---

[53]Mulford.
[54]Don Cahalan and Robin Room, *Problem Drinking among American Men* (New Brunswick, N.J.: Rutgers Center of Alcohol Studies, 1974). Also see Don Cahalan and Robin Room, "Problem Drinking among American Men Aged 21–59," *American Journal of Public Health*, 62 (1972), 1473–1482.
[55]LeMasters, p. 161. For females, such judgments were made on the basis of the neglect of children rather than absence from work.
[56]Cahalan, Cisin, and Crossley.
[57]Mulford, p. 646.

is unable to control consistently, or to stop at will, either the start of drinking or its termination once started.[58] *Chronic alcoholics,* the most severe form of alcoholism, characteristically have a "compulsion" to drink continually. Of particular importance are such other characteristics as solitary drinking, morning drinking, and general physical deterioration. A study has indicated that the presence of one or more of the following major criteria indicates alcoholism.[59]

1. Withdrawal symptoms—gross tremor, hallucination, seizure, or delirium tremens when deprived of alcohol.
2. Tolerance—high blood levels of alcohol without gross evidence of intoxication; daily consumption of a fifth of a gallon of whiskey, or an equivalent intake of beer or wine, by an individual weighing 180 pounds.
3. Continued drinking in the face of strong penalties—medical warnings, loss of job, disruption of marriage, arrest for drunkenness or drunken driving.
4. Major illness—fatty degeneration, alcoholic hepatitis, cirrhosis, pancreatitis, and a number of other syndromes and ailments associated with alcohol.

Alcoholism is a serious problem for the individual; although a sense of euphoria may permeate the individual while he is drinking, it is followed by great complications in personal living. Alcoholics have ugly hangovers in which they may collapse physically and become filled with remorse and self-disgust leading to terrifying doubts when their plans for control of the drinking seem no longer to work. Nausea becomes a frequent morning-after experience, blackouts increase, and the time of their onset grows steadily earlier. They gulp drinks, particularly to make certain of having enough "under the belt" before going out even to events where they know they will be able to drink, simply to avoid the risk of not getting enough. Signs of drinking appear at inconvenient and even wrong times when others are sober, and the attitudes of persons who react strongly against their alcoholic behavior only cause further drinking.

As drinking continues, social and physical deterioration continues, even to the extent that a loss of time sense occurs. Extremely ingenious methods are developed to safeguard the alcoholic's supply; it is almost impossible to describe the alcoholic's terror at being without a drink, so the person resorts to hiding his liquor under pillows, under porches, and in any place where they may go undetected. A "sip" is needed for everything, feelings of unsteadiness, headaches, or the "shakes." The day may be started with 8 ounces of gin or whiskey, and each day the alcoholic may consume quantities of alcohol far in excess of the customary amounts of his drinking group. One study showed that alcoholics had usually developed their patterns of drinking over a period of 10 to 20 years of drinking, having become intoxicated for the first time at a mean age of 18.3 years and by the age of 29.5 had already experienced "blackouts"

---

[58]See Mark Keller, "Alcoholism: Nature and Extent of the Problem," *The Annals,* 315 (1958), 1–11, and his "Definition of Alcoholism," *Quarterly Journal of Studies on Alcohol,* 21 (1960), 125–134. Some authorities feel that such broad definitions make it difficult for scientists to replicate research. Consequently, an operational definition of alcoholism in terms of community standards and societal reaction has been used involving frequent arrests for drunkenness, contact with social agencies, clinics, mental hospitals, or Alcoholics Anonymous. See William and Joan McCord, *Origins of Alcoholism* (Stanford, Calif: Stanford University Press, 1961), pp. 10–11.

[59]National Council of Alcoholism standards issued in 1972, as reported in the *Wisconsin State Journal,* Madison, August 3, 1972.

TABLE 10.3   Symptoms and Mean Onset Ages (Years) of 13 Selected Symptoms in a Wisconsin Study Group of 252 Alcoholics, 1955

Symptoms	Mean Age
First drink for self	17.6
First intoxication	18.3
First blackout	29.5
First frequent blackouts	33.6
First morning drinking	35.6
First daytime bouts	35.7
First "benders"	36.0
First loss of control	36.0
First drinking alone	36.1
First convulsions	37.6
First protecting of supply	37.8
First drunk on less liquor	38.4
First tremors	38.6

Source: Derived from Harrison M. Trice and J. Richard Wahl, "A Rank Order Analysis of the Symptoms of Alcoholism." Reprinted by permission from *Quarterly Journal of Studies on Alcohol,* Vol. 19, pp. 636—648, 1958. Copyright by Journal of Studies on Alcohol, Inc., New Brunswick, N. J. 08903.

during intoxication.[60] By 35.6 years they were drinking in the morning, at 36.1 they began drinking alone on a regular basis, by 37.8 they were first protecting their supply of alcohol, and by 38.6 years, they were having their first tremors (see Table 10.3). On the average, alcoholics reach their lowest point, and conceive of themselves as having reached this lowest point, in their late thirties or early forties. During this period of one or two decades of drinking, they have tried to change their environments, and have begun losing working time, jobs, friends, and family. They also have irrational fears, resentments, and "remorse," which is particularly characteristic. The characteristics of alcoholics—their drinking behavior, smoking habits, life-style, and emotional state—are even seen in the causes of their deaths, due not only to cirrhosis of the liver but frequently to falls, fires, and poisoning.[61]

EXTENT OF ALCOHOLISM

To determine the estimated number of alcoholics in the United States, the figure for chronic alcoholics is usually multiplied by four. Estimates of the number of alcoholics with complications—chronic alcoholics—are generally derived by multiplying the

[60]Harrison M. Trice and J. Richard Wahl, "A Rank Order Analysis of the Symptoms of Alcoholism," *Quarterly Journal of Studies on Alcohol,* 19 (1958), 636–648. Also see E. M. Jellinek, "Phases in the Drinking History of Alcoholics," *Memoirs of the Section of Studies on Alcohol* (New Brunswick, N.J.: Quarterly Journal of Studies on Alcohol, 1946).
[61]See Wolfgang Schmidt and Jan de Lint, "Causes of Death of Alcoholics," *Quarterly Journal of Studies on Alcohol,* 33 (1972), 171 185.

reported number of deaths from cirrhosis of the liver by a certain ratio, usually three in the United States. In 1973, an estimate was made of 5.5 million alcoholics, 500,000 of whom were women, based on a certain percentage of deaths from cirrhosis of the liver.[62] This would amount to about one alcoholic in five or six persons who generally drink some alcoholic beverage. Although there are other methods of estimating the prevalence of alcoholism, such as the consumption level of alcohol or projection of deaths from alcoholism, a study made in Ontario found that all of them resulted in similar estimates of alcoholism.[63] An effort has been made to determine the extent of alcoholism by interviewing a sample of the general population about their preoccupation with alcohol (see Table 10.2). This method, however, presents many problems due to the necessity for using large samples.

Countries with the highest rates of alcoholism are nearly all European nations. France has the highest known rate, followed by Chile, Portugal, and the United States. Somewhat lower, but still high rates, are found in Australia, Sweden, Switzerland, the Union of South Africa, and Yugoslavia.[64] Alcoholism and drunkenness appear to be increasing in the Soviet Union, and the government uses extensive measures to deal with these problems. The sale of strong alcoholic drinks is permitted only between 11 A.M. and 8 P.M., and chronic drunks are subjected to compulsory treatment methods.[65]

Male alcoholics outnumber females. Drinking among women has increased greatly during the past few decades, and their rate of alcoholism has thus tended to increase, although the rate increase has not been great.[66] Typically, drinking is more common among the male population, and men consume more alcohol more frequently than do women. Since exposure to alcohol is related to alcoholism, one would thus expect a lower rate among women. The symptomatology and drinking habits of men and women are quite different.[67] Several reasons appear to account for the differences between the rates of alcoholism among men and women. (1) Proportionately fewer women than men drink. (2) Greater social stigma is attached to excessive drinking by women than by men. (3) Housewives do not face the same occupational drinking hazards that men face. (4) Women up to now have generally not been as directly involved in the competitive economic struggle, and in spite of rapid changes in the family situation, women still have the major responsibility for the care and upbringing of the children and are not as "free" to drink regularly as the men, particularly in the lower classes. (5) A woman's self-image is not as seriously threatened; because her role is more restricted, failure in this role is less likely to be known to outsiders. A man can fail both in his family role and in his occupational role, and thus

---

[62]Earl Rubington, *Alcohol Problems and Social Control* (Columbus, O.: Charles E. Merrill, 1973), pp. 50–51.

[63]Wolfgang Schmidt and Jan de Lint, "Estimating the Prevalence of Alcoholism from Alcohol Consumption and Mortality Data," *Quarterly Journal of Studies on Alcohol,* 31 (1970), 957–964.

[64]See Mark Keller and Vera Efron, "The Prevalence of Alcoholism," *Quarterly Journal of Studies on Alcohol,* 16 (1955), 634.

[65]See Treml; and Connor.

[66]Edith S. Lisansky, "The Woman Alcoholic," *The Annals,* 315 (1958), 73–82.

[67]Kenneth W. Wanberg and John L. Horn, "Alcoholism Patterns of Men and Women," *Quarterly Journal of Studies on Alcohol,* 31 (1970), 40–61.

there is a greater possibility that his self-image will be publicly deflated.[68] It is generally agreed, however, that as women continue to enter business and professional fields they will increasingly be subject to the same situations that lead to excessive drinking among men.

Costs of Alcoholism

Industry loses large sums of money due to excessive alcohol consumption, in the form of absenteeism, inefficiency on the job, and accidents. It has been estimated that between 3 and 4 percent of an average work force will be deviant drinkers at one time.[69] According to Trice and Roman, the work-based costs of problem drinking are (1) those that stem directly from an employee's work behavior, (2) the deviant drinker's effect on other employees; and (3) the costs of trying to do something about the problem drinker once the tolerance limits are reached.[70]

The annual economic cost of alcohol-related problems has been roughly estimated at 25 billion dollars.[71] This figure is termed "conservative" and includes the costs of lost production of goods and services attributed to male problem drinkers; expenditures for alcohol-related health and medical problems; alcohol's contribution to the costs of automobile accidents and insurance rates; alcohol-related costs of maintaining the criminal justice system of police, courts, and prisons; costs of programs of treatment, education, and research on alcohol problems; and alcohol-related costs of social welfare programs. More than 8 billion dollars was estimated as the annual cost of alcohol-related health and medical problems. This comprised 12 percent of all adult health expenditures and 20 percent of the total adult costs for hospitalization. Of all patients in U.S. Veterans Hospitals in 1971, 17 percent were alcoholics. In one general hospital, problem drinkers had an average stay of 11.2 days compared with 7.7 days for other patients, their average utilization of intensive care facilities was 5.3 days compared with 3 days, and their average hospital charges were $1,506 compared with $964.[72]

Although the costs are high for industry, the price of alcoholism to the individual is also great. In addition to the actual costs of the beverages, alcoholics face loss of wages, medical care costs, court costs and fines, the loss of home or business furnishings and equipment, and many other expenses. They also have higher rates of accidental death than do nonalcoholics. A study of accidental deaths among 1,343 San Francisco Bay area alcoholics showed that they were 7 times more likely to become victims of fatal accidents than were other area residents of the same age and sex. They were 4.5 times more likely to die in a motor vehicle accident, 16 times more likely to die of an accidental fall, and 30 times more likely to die of accidental poisoning. Women alcoholics had an accidental death rate 16 times and men alcoholics 6 times more than expected. These high death rates are the result not only of the

[68]McCord and McCord, *Origins of Alcoholism*, p. 163.
[69]Trice and Roman, *Spirits and Demons at Work.*
[70]Trice and Roman, *Spirits and Demons at Work*, p. 2.
[71]*Alcohol and Health: New Knowledge*, pp. 49–57.
[72]Robert Straus, "Alcohol and Society," *Psychiatric Annals*, 3 (1973), 72.

alcohol consumption but of the life-styles of alcoholics, the state of their health, their personalities, and the differential care received when they are ill or injured.[73] Alcoholics have also been found to have significantly worse driving records than nonalcoholics.[74] Suicide rates among alcoholics are far in excess of the 4 percent figure for the general population. This has been explained as being due primarily to societal reaction, since the rates are greater for males and whites than for women and blacks.[75]

Alcoholism and the Medical Model

The medical profession has adopted a medical model within which alcoholism is likened to any other disease, to be treated by medical measures. There is much disagreement, however, about treating alcoholism or problem drinking as a disease, and whether or not a physician can or should treat the problem.[76] One observer has noted that if alcoholism is a disease, "is it a disease of some organ system of the body, or is it what some would call a mental illness? Is it a problem for internal medicine or psychiatry? As is well known, this issue is far from resolved."[77] Another states that "viewing alcoholism as a disease is of no value in either describing what alcoholism is or what causes it. Although it is generally agreed that the 'disease' involves a loss of control—in the sense that a person cannot refrain either from starting to drink or from continuing to drink once started—it is also recognized that no physiological factor has been isolated that accounts for this."[78] The adequacy of the medical model of alcoholism depends ultimately on the meaning of "disease." If alcoholism is a disease, it is unlike any other presently known to medicine, having not only physical organic characteristics but also psychological and sociological components. At present, moreover, it is not possible to know if alcohol is a symptom of the disease or if it is the disease itself.

The popularity of the medical model of alcoholism will probably continue, in view of the public's inclination to adopt medical perspectives on alcoholism, as well as drug addiction, which reduces the extent to which alcoholics are considered to be responsible for their actions. The medical approach to problem drinking does have the advantage of giving it a more humane setting, for example, treatment in a medical facility rather than confinement in a jail. If this model is adopted, however, and the problem drinker is regarded as a "sick" person, it is then logical to conceive of him as

---

[73]Berthold Brenner, "Alcoholism and Fatal Accidents," *Quarterly Journal of Studies on Alcohol,* 28 (September 1967), 517–528.

[74]Wolfgang S. Schmidt and Reginald G. Smart, "Alcoholics, Drinking and Traffic Accidents," *Quarterly Journal of Studies on Alcohol,* 20 (1959), 631–644.

[75]William A. Rushing, "Suicide and the Interaction of Alcoholism (Liver Cirrhosis) with the Social Situation," *Quarterly Journal of Studies on Alcohol,* 30 (1969), 93–103.

[76]See, for example, J. Hershon, "Alcoholism and the Concept of Disease," *British Journal of Addictions,* 69 (1974), 123–132. Also see Benjamin Kassin, "Theory and Practice in the Treatment of Alcoholism," in Kassin and Begleiter, *Treatment and Rehabilitation of the Chronic Alcoholic,* p. 33.

[77]Gerald Goldstein and Charles Neuringer, *Empirical Studies of Alcohol* (Cambridge, Mass.: Ballinger, 1976), p. 2.

[78]Charles H. McCaghy, *Deviant Behavior: Crime, Conflict and Interest Groups* (New York: Macmillan, 1976), p. 271. Also see Walter B. Clark, "Loss of Control: Heavy Drinking and Drinking Problems in a Longitudinal Study," *Journal of Studies on Alcohol,* 37 (1976), 1256–1290.

irresponsible for his behavior, yet deviant.[79] The person is then not responsible for his actions because of his condition (which, of course, was the result of his actions), not because of choice, a perspective that may be appropriate for conditions such as physical handicaps or mental retardation (see Chapter 15), but questionable in terms of the realities of problem drinking and alcoholism.[80]

Societal Reaction

Excessive drinking does not itself make the alcoholic. If it is continued for a long enough time, however, the alcoholic may increasingly become involved in *difficulties that arise from the drinking* itself, and it is the degree of reaction to these difficulties that lead to alcoholism. The alcoholic may lose his job, his friends, and his spouse because of this drinking; he may even be arrested and jailed. Drinking may become a way of getting away from problems caused by the drinking. The alcoholic becomes involved in a circular process; as he drinks excessively he faces additional problems that can be solved only with more drinking. At this stage a true alcoholic condition has been established. The Protestant ethic seems to play a role in this because drunkenness is looked upon as indicating a lack of moral strength, will power, and dedication to goals of personal discipline and work. Societal reaction to drunkenness may be expressed through husband or wife, employer, work associates, parents, in-laws, neighbors, or church members. In some countries, including the United States, the image of the alcoholic is a negative one; at the same time the person is considered to be "sick." A similar negative image of the alcoholic was found among New Zealanders, where a representative sample of urban dwellers found a third of them felt alcoholism to be due to moral weakness. A third of the sample interviewed said they would not like to live next door to an alcoholic, and 73 percent said they would not like working with an alcoholic.[81]

Trice and Roman point out the complexity of the self-reaction of the heavy drinker or alcoholic to being labeled as such.[82] This labeling generally results in the exclusion of alcoholics from various social gatherings, which in itself further complicates the problem because they increasingly associate with others in heavy-drinking groups whose members have undergone similar ostracism. Extreme deviance is tolerated in these groups, and normalization, in a sense, is complete because deviant drinking and intoxication are the norms.[83] The deviant may then think more and more of himself as a deviant, which further encourages his continued excessive drinking. This isolating experience has been observed among both middle- and lower-class persons. As they become heavier and heavier drinkers some gravitate to taverns of a lower-class nature: the middle-class or white-collar worker begins to frequent working-

---

[79]See James D. Orcutt, "Ideological Variations in the Structure of Deviant Types: A Multivariate Comparison of Alcoholism and Heroin Addiction," *Social Forces,* 55 (1976), 419–437.

[80]Fred Montanino, "Alcohol: Use and Abuse," in Edward Sagarin and Fred Montanino, eds., *Deviants: Voluntary Actors in a Hostile World* (Morristown, N.J.: General Learning Press, 1977), pp. 326–367.

[81]Peter J. Blizard, "The Public Image and Social Rejection of the Alcoholic in New Zealand," *Quarterly Journal of Studies on Alcohol,* 30 (1969), 686–700.

[82]Trice and Roman, *Spirits and Demons at Work,* pp. 32–37.

[83]Trice and Roman, *Spirits and Demons at Work,* p. 34.

class taverns so that his colleagues will not observe his increasing drinking difficulties. Similarly, the working-class drinker goes through a process of downward mobility, patronizing skid row bars and taverns.[84]

In some cases, however, the social sanctioning by others may be sufficient to curtail the extensive drinking. In other situations, the person may discount his own labeling, reacting to the labelers by labeling them as "prudes." Where the label is applied by a psychiatrist, a local alcoholic agency, or a mental hospital it may have a much stronger stigmatizing effect even though, at the same time, the individual's being labeled "ill" or "sick" may remove the moral stigma and serve further to facilitate drinking. For this reason a person may seek such "middle men" as the family physician, a clergyman, a social worker, or a teacher whose appraisal does not carry the same official sanction.

GROUP AND SUBCULTURAL FACTORS IN EXCESSIVE DRINKING AND ALCOHOLISM

Group associations and cultural factors play important parts in determining who becomes an excessive drinker and who does not. Different drinking customs are evident in each modern society and also in the subcultural groups of the society. Subgroups differ in the way in which alcohol is used, in the extent of drinking, and in attitudes toward drunkenness. The correlation of diverse cultural drinking patterns with alcoholism can help us to test a number of hypotheses. Some people believe that frequent drinking will lead to alcoholism; yet those groups with relatively high frequencies of drinking, such as U.S. Jews, particularly the Orthodox, and Italian-Americans, have low rates of alcoholism.[85] Still others say that frequency of drunkenness leads to alcoholism, yet the Aleuts, the Andean Indians, and those of the northwest coast of North America, among whom drunkenness is common, appear to have little alcoholism.[86] The Camba Indians of Bolivia drink a particularly potent drink at fiestas, where mass drunkenness takes place, but they do not drink on other occasions, and they have little alcoholism.[87] All drinking is communal, and drinking and drunkenness

---

[84]LeMasters, pp. 156–157.

[85]See Charles R. Snyder, *Alcohol and the Jews* (New York: Free Press, 1958); Giorgio Lolli, Emilio Serianni, Grace M. Golder, and Pierpaolo Luzzatto-Fegis, *Alcohol in Italian Culture* (New York: Free Press, 1958); and Beigel and Ghertner. Snyder's classic study has been recently reprinted. See Charles R. Snyder, *Alcohol and the Jews* (Carbondale, Ill.: Southern Illinois University Press, 1978).

[86]Chandler Washburne, *Primitive Drinking: A Study of the Uses and Functions of Alcohol in Preliterate Societies* (New Haven, Conn.: College and University Press, 1961); Gerald D. Berreman, "Drinking Patterns of the Aleuts," *Quarterly Journal of Studies on Alcohol,* 17 (1956), 503–514; William Mangin, "Drinking among Andean Indians," *Quarterly Journal of Studies on Alcohol,* 18 (1957), 55–66; and Edwin M. Lemert, *Alcohol and the Northwest Coast Indians,* University of California Publications on Culture and Society, Vol. 2, No. 6 (Berkeley: University of California Press, 1954).

[87]Dwight B. Heath, "Drinking Patterns of the Bolivian Camba," in Pittman and Snyder, pp. 22–36.

become means of acceptance rather than of rejection of the person. Among Polynesians stigma is also rare for heavy drinking, and no guilt develops over drunkenness even though it threatens other Polynesian values of friendship patterns.[88] Even with this ambivalence there is little alcoholism.

The role of the *integration of drinking behavior patterns* has been used to explain low rates of alcoholism.[89] If conformity to drinking standards is supported by the entire culture or subculture, and the values and sanctions are well established, consistent, and known and agreed to by all, rates will be low. If the individual drinker does not know what is expected, or if the expected situation varies, he is in a position of ambivalence. Alcoholism is associated with culture where there is conflict over its use, where children are not introduced to it early, where drinking is done outside of meals, and where it is drunk for personal reasons and not as a part of the ritual and ceremony or part of family living. Among the West African Kofyar, for example, beer has a ritual, ceremonial, and convivial use; drinking is always regulated within a social setting, and there is no solitary drinking.[90]

In some modern societies such as the United States, Ireland, France, and Sweden, marked ambivalence is seen regarding alcohol use with resulting conflicting and coexisting values and high rates of alcoholism.[91] In other societies with low rates of alcoholism like Italy, Spain, and Japan, and among Jewish groups, attitudes about alcohol are permissive and positive. The differences between permissiveness and ambivalence about alcohol seem to be definitely related to excessive drinking and alcoholism. More specifically, the role of group and subcultural factors in producing excessive drinking and alcoholism can be shown in relation to the societal reaction to alcoholism, companions and excessive drinking, skid row drinking, occupation and excessive drinking, religious differences in excessive drinking, sex differences, and ethnic differences in drinking. In summary, these group and ethnic differences indicate the importance of the social learning and cultural values as dominant forces in problem drinking. What a person does with alcohol, and what he or she thinks about it, are functions of group membership and the feelings of identification with these groups. Drinking also takes place in social situations in which the drinker believes his own behavior is approved by the group.[92] Although the amount of alcohol consumed is a factor in problem drinking and alcoholism, social and cultural factors appear to be all-important. In those groups where there is agreement about drinking customs and

[88]Edwin M. Lemert, "Forms and Pathology of Drinking in Three Polynesian Societies," *American Anthropologist,* 66 (1964), 361–374.

[89]Albert D. Ullman, "Sociocultural Backgrounds of Alcoholism," *The Annals,* 315 (1958), 48–55. Also see Margaret K. Bacon, "Alcohol Use in Tribal Societies," in Kassin and Begleiter, *Social Aspects of Alcoholism,* pp. 1–36. In testing this hypothesis of the integration of drinking patterns and low rates of alcoholism, one study found little support for it unless one were to take into account the amount of alcohol consumed. See Paul C. Whitehead and Cheryl Harvey, "Explaining Alcoholism: An Empirical Test and Reformulation," *Journal of Health and Social Behavior,* 15 (1974), 57–65.

[90]Robert Netting, "Beer as a Locus of Value among the West African Kofyar," *American Anthropologist,* 66 (1964), 375–384.

[91]See Robin Room, "Ambivalence as a Sociological Explanation: The Case of Cultural Explanations of Alcohol Problems," *American Sociological Review,* 41 (1976), 1047–1065.

[92]See Robert B. Bell, *Social Deviance: A Substantive Analysis,* rev. ed. (Homewood, Ill.: Dorsey Press, 1976), p. 169.

values, and where there are social supports for moderate drinking and negative sanctions for excessive drinking, low rates of alcoholism will be found.[93] Where these factors do not operate in this manner, one should expect higher rates.

Moreover, the importance of a given set of drinking and nondrinking norms is influenced by the relative importance of a group to an individual.[94] The evidence seems to indicate that many problem drinkers are "processed" into their drinking patterns, being encouraged to use alcohol as a means of adjusting to personal difficulties by these informal drinking groups.[95]

Companions and Excessive Drinking

Drinking generally takes place in small groups, and within these groups special drinking norms tend to develop.[96] In fact, the person who drinks alone in the presence of others may be regarded somewhat as a deviant.[97] While conformity between drinking habits and drinking norms is the rule in small groups, identification with a group is a variable on the basis of which it is possible to explain an individual's drinking norms and behavior.[98]

A close relationship exists between the development of alcoholism and the types of companions one has. Drinking norms appear to conform closely to those of age contemporaries, particularly of friends or the marital partner.[99] Fellow employees may also influence drinking norms. Among adolescents, the behavior of one's friends has an extremely important influence in determining whether or not a young person will begin to drink, as well as influencing other behavior and attitudes toward alcohol.[100]

---

[93]E. Blackner, "Sociocultural Factors in Alcoholism," *International Psychiatry Clinics,* 3 (1968), 51–80; and Ullman.

[94]Donald E. Larsen and Baha Abu-Haban, "Norm Qualities and Deviant Drinking Behavior," *Social Problems,* 15 (1968), 441–450.

[95]Harrison M. Trice, "The Problem Drinker in Industry," *ILR Research* (Ithaca, N.Y.: New York State School of Industrial and Labor Relations, 1956), II, p. 11.

[96]Several studies have shown the group nature of drinking. In a Finnish study it was found that more than two thirds of the drinking occasions among men, for example, in rural areas involved groups of two to four persons. A study in Poland found that excessive drinking was primarily a group phenomenon, with men drinking approximately four times more in the company of friends than in the family circle. See P. Kuusi, *Alcohol Sales Experiment in Rural Finland* (Helsinki: Finnish Foundation for Alcohol Studies, 1957); and Andrzej Swiecicki, *Alcohol: Zagadnienia Polityki Spolczne* (Alcohol: Problems of Social Police) (Warsaw, Poland, 1968).

[97]Robert Sommer, "The Isolated Drinker in the Edmonton Beer Hall," *Quarterly Journal of Studies on Alcohol,* 26 (1965), 95–110.

[98]Eric Allardt, "Drinking Norms and Drinking Habits," in *Drinking and Drinkers* (Helsinki: Finnish Foundation for Alcohol Studies, 1957).

[99]John L. Haer, 'Drinking Patterns and the Influence of Friends and Family," *Quarterly Journal of Studies on Alcohol,* 16 (1955), 178–185.

[100]C. Norman Alexander, Jr., and Ernest Q. Campbell, "Peer Influences on Adolescent Drinking," *Quarterly Journal of Studies on Alcohol,* 28 (1967), 444–453. The use of certain drugs may be condoned in some peer groups to a greater extent than other drugs: alcohol and nicotine are permitted in most groups more than other drugs. See Harrison M. Trice and Janice M. Beyer, "A Sociological Property of Drugs: Acceptance of Users of Alcohol and Other Drugs among University Students," *Journal of Studies on Alcohol,* 38 (1977), 58–74.

Skid Row Drinking

Group drinking plays a major part in the lives of "homeless" men on skid row. Although alcohol is a major preoccupation with them, they are not all problem drinkers. One study has estimated that only one in three are problem drinkers, a third drink only moderately, and the others drink little or not at all.[101] The evidence also shows that only a minority of the skid row residents have been driven there by excessive drinking.[102] The drinking in these areas appears to be due to the social and cultural dynamics of the area rather than the result of a drinking problem acquired prior to coming to the area.

Nevertheless, among the "urban nomads" of skid row the drinking of alcoholic beverages to become intoxicated is institutionalized. To them drinking is a symbol of social solidarity and friendship, and group drinking and collective drunkenness are completely acceptable in their culture.[103] The most important primary group among them is the "bottle gang," and no one who wishes to join is turned down.[104] The big problem for these bottle gangs is where to drink, since public drinking is largely forbidden except in taverns, night clubs, and restaurants, all of which are usually too costly for them. On the other hand, if they find other outside places they might be arrested: three fourths of one arrested Seattle sample had been drinking in public.[105] The major function of these drinking groups is to provide the social and psychological context for the drinking among its members who mutually support each other both in obtaining the alcohol and sharing it.[106] So great are these group influences on skid row that if an individual is to deal effectively with his alcoholism he must leave.

Even the extensive argot of skid row "drunks" indicates the learned group and cultural aspects of alcoholism in that it functions among drinking acquaintances as a language to deal with all aspects of drinking episodes, including activities, objects, people involved in them, and states of mind and body. Some examples from a study of 500 terms from drunk argot are:

> *ammunition:* alcohol in some form.
> *cook the pot:* to scheme about ways of obtaining money.
> *hammer:* solicit money for drinks.
> *lush:* a drink, a lover of whisky, whisky itself.
> *needle:* fortify any drink with additional alcohol.

---

[101]See Howard M. Bahr, *Skid Row: An Introduction to Disaffiliation* (New York: Oxford University Press, 1973), p. 103. Also see David Levinson, "Skid Row in Transition," *Urban Anthropology,* 3 (1974), 79–93; and McCaghy, p. 269.

[102]See Harvey A. Siegel, David M. Petersen, and Carl D. Chambers, "The Emerging Skid Row: Ethnographic and Social Notes on a Changing Scene," *Journal of Drug Issues,* 5 (1975), 160–166.

[103]Spradley, p. 117. Also see Joan K. Jackson and Ralph Connor, "The Skid Row Alcoholic," *Quarterly Journal of Studies on Alcohol,* 14 (1953), 475; and Donald J. Bogue, *Skid Row in American Cities* (Chicago: University of Chicago Press, 1963), pp. 272–304.

[104]Rubington, *Alcohol Problems and Social Control,* pp. 91–102.

[105]Spradley, p. 121.

[106]Pittman and Gordon, p. 71. Also see W. Jack Peterson and Milton A. Maxwell, "The Skid Row 'Wino,'" *Social Problems,* 5 (1958), 316; and George David Kuedeking and Howard M. Bahr, "A Smallest Space Analysis of Skid Row Men's Behavior," *Pacific Sociological Review,* 19 (1976), 275–290.

> *rum-dumb:* drunken stupor.
> *shakes:* tremors in alcohol withdrawal.
> *Sneaky Pete:* inexpensive fortified wine.
> *sparrow:* inferior liquor.
> *stumble bum:* alcoholic.
> *stew bum:* any drunk in poor condition, dirty, poorly clothed, unshaven.[107]

Occupation and Excessive Drinking

There is a slight tendency for the percentage of drinkers to increase with *occupational status,* although this is not the case with problem drinkers. Mulford found the highest percentage of drinkers in the top occupational categories, such as lawyers and doctors, but the percentage of problem drinkers in these same categories was the lowest of any occupational group.[108] In contrast, "the second highest percentage of drinkers (college professors, scientists, and engineers) had the highest percentage of problem drinkers (24 percent)."[109]

The social patterns in some occupational categories call for more immoderate drinking than in others. Certain business occupations are often associated with frequent and heavy drinking. Organizations themselves often informally stimulate the idea that drinking is an important part of performing the job. "Thus, work histories of sales managers, purchasing agents, and representatives of labor unions who have become alcoholics strongly suggest that their organizations tacitly approve and expect them to use alcohol to accomplish their purposes effectively."[110] The informal power struggles which characterize the upper echelons of many companies and corporations in the business world appear to be a more important factor in the development of alcoholism among this group than any individualistic, psychiatric explanation in terms of the "medical model." In one study of 552 business executives, members of Alcoholics Anonymous in New York, it was found that as these persons participated more actively in the status struggle of the business world they drank more.[111] Their college drinking patterns appear to have had no relation. The alcoholism symptoms were concentrated in the mid-thirties to the early fifties and showed that the beginning of real symptoms of alcoholism coincided with their career development. On-the-job-absenteeism, that is, going to work out of a strong responsibility when in poor work condition, appears frequently as they ascend the bureaucratic ladder. A partner in a Wall Street brokerage firm put it this way: "I was drinking with a lot of my friends. I don't recall it as anything unusual. What stands out in my mind was hopes to get with a 'going' outfit, one with a future for me."

---

[107]Earl Rubington, "The Language of 'Drunks,'" *Quarterly Journal of Studies on Alcohol,* 32 (1971), 721–740. Also see Howard M. Bahr and Theodore Caplow, *Old Men Drunk and Sober* (New York: New York University Press, 1973).

[108]Mulford.

[109]Beigel and Ghertner, p. 208.

[110]Harrison M. Trice, *Alcoholism in America* (New York: McGraw-Hill, 1966), p. 79.

[111]Harrison M. Trice and James A. Belasco, "The Aging Collegian: Drinking Pathologies among Executive and Professional Alumni," in George Maddox, ed., *The Domesticated Drug: Drinking among Collegians* (New Haven, Conn.: College and University Press, 1970), pp. 218–234.

Entertaining prospective customers for cocktails and dinner is often regarded as a traditional way of doing business and is provided for in expense accounts. Daily luncheons are often preceded by martinis, followed later by the leisurely drinking of highballs. In addition, important negotiations are often conducted over a drink in a bar. The executives who commute generally leave the office early enough to have two or three "for the road" before boarding the train. When they arrive home they usually find that their wives have cocktails ready, or that they have been invited out for cocktails at the home of some acquaintance.

Merchant seamen provide an excellent illustration of occupational heavy drinkers. Various studies among Swedish seamen, for example, have shown that chronic alcoholism is common.[112] Life at sea for many becomes monotonous, frustrating, and socially isolating. Since social outlets aboard ship are limited, seamen look forward to having a good time when the ship docks at the various ports of call. "Having a good time" in port involves many things, and almost invariably it includes excessive drinking. It is not surprising, then, that a high percentage of seamen appear eventually to become alcoholics. In the tradition of their occupation, some form "bottle gangs," and they tend to lose their individuality in these groups. Often the men know little about each other, sometimes nothing more than nicknames: yet, in reference to norms such as excessive drinking and sexual promiscuity, they may act as one. Sailors often, for example, share their pay in order to continue drinking.

A large percentage of alcoholics have had experiences in an all-male society where drinking is a symbol of manliness and group integration, and these experiences appear to have affected their heavy drinking patterns. In groups such as the army, navy, merchant marine, and isolated work camps of all kinds, the monotonous and protective, yet controlled, routines are broken by the free hours that offer drinking opportunities. Drinking often becomes for them a preoccupation, and through their talks filled with drinking tales an imagery and love of drinking are built up that help to reduce the routine of the job, the sexual deprivation, and the loneliness of the all-male society.[113]

Religious Differences in Excessive Drinking

Marked differences in drinking patterns are found among religious groups. A California study showed that almost universally the Irish Catholics were high in heavy drinking, the Jews low. For example, 36 percent of the Irish Catholics drank daily, but only 26 percent of the white Protestants and 18 percent of the Jews. Similar differences existed in the amount of drinking. Few Jews were abstainers, but in general

---

[112]Anonymous, "Alcoholism—An Occupational Disease of Seamen," *Quarterly Journal of Studies on Alcohol,* 8 (1947), 498–505. Also see Anders Otterland, "Alcohol and the Merchant Seafarer," Twenty-sixth International Congress on Alcohol and Alcoholism, Stockholm, August, 1–5, 1960, *Abstracts,* pp. 206–207. On the other hand, drinking appears not to constitute a major problem among domestic servants. Due to the close supervision exercised in this occupation, a developing alcoholic is usually noticed quickly and dismissed. See Robert Straus and Miriam Winterbottom, "Drinking Patterns of an Occupational Group: Domestic Services," *Quarterly Journal of Studies on Alcohol,* 10 (1949), 441–460.
[113]Pittman and Gordon, p. 67.

they were less likely to approve of drunkenness than either the Irish or the Protestants.[114] Studies have also indicated that in spite of the fact that drinking is quite pervasive among the Jewish people, their rates for alcoholism fall far below what one might expect.[115] Only 4 percent of Jewish students in one study experienced social complications due to their drinking, as contrasted with Episcopalians, 39 percent; Methodists, 50 percent; and nonaffiliates, 57 percent.[116] In a limited study, Methodists, who belong to America's largest religious denomination, were found largely to disapprove of the use of alcohol, and this fact predisposed those who drank to show greater alcohol problems than did Jews, conditioned as they had been about the negative consequences of drinking since childhood.[117] Fewer of the Methodists had drunk alcohol before the age of 11, and far more had had their first drink away from home or in an auto. From these findings it was concluded that the teaching of abstinence, associating drinking with intemperance, tends inadvertently to encourage intemperance among those students of abstinence backgrounds who disregard the injunction on drinking. On the other hand, more frequent religious participation, even among those students who do drink, tends to diminish resulting social complications.[118]

The appropriate and inappropriate uses of alcohol appear to be far less clear among a larger proportion of U.S. Anglo-Saxon Protestants than among Jews; even when agreement about drinking behavior is apparent, it is not usually deeply rooted in the culture, and seldom is it free of conflicting attitudes.[119] Certain generalizations may be made, however, even though there are differences between denominations. Among Protestants of northern European descent who drink, drinking is usually not associated with other activities, having the specific purpose to escape or to have a good time. There is a general sense of uneasiness about the enjoyment of drinking. There appears to be no agreement among this group about how to act in response to drunkenness, and while people seem to feel somewhat uncomfortable and even guilty about getting drunk, "the absence of clear guidelines is striking."[120]

On the other hand, Orthodox Jews have been found to have less drunkenness and less alcoholism than Protestants or more secular Jews and generally to use alcohol differently.[121] Wine drinking is almost universal among Orthodox Jews, as nearly all occasions—births, deaths, confirmations, religious holidays—require it by both prescription and tradition. The Orthodox Jew thus becomes used to alcohol in modera-

---

[114]Genevieve Knupfer and Robin Room, "Drinking Patterns and Attitudes of Irish, Jewish and White Protestant American Men," *Quarterly Journal of Studies on Alcohol,* 28 (1967), 676–699.

[115]Snyder, *Alcohol and the Jews;* Robert F. Bales, "Cultural Differences in Rates of Alcoholism," *Quarterly Journal of Studies on Alcohol,* 6 (1946), 480–500; and Beigel and Ghertner, p. 206.

[116]Jerome H. Skolnick, "Religious Affiliation and Drinking Behavior," *Quarterly Journal of Studies on Alcohol,* 19 (1958), 452–470.

[117]Skolnick. The study allowed for differences in social class, age, region, and religious activity among denominations.

[118]Skolnick, p. 470.

[119]See Thomas F. A. Plaut, *Alcohol Problems: A Report to the Nation by the Cooperative on the Study of Alcoholism* (New York: Oxford University Press, 1967), pp. 126–127.

[120]Plaut, p. 127.

[121]Snyder, *Alcohol and the Jews,* Chap. 6.

tion; he starts using it in childhood, later drinks with great frequency but largely in ritualistic contexts. Early socialization in alcohol use and ceremonial drinking is not as common among non-Orthodox Jews, who therefore use alcohol in less moderation. Patterns of Orthodox drinking and their ritualistic associations are further supported by a normative structure of ideas of drunkenness as a Gentile vice. The strength of the taboo among Orthodox Jews can be seen from an old folk saying: "Drunk he is, drink he must, because he is a Gentile." Snyder's comparative study pointed out that Jews bring powerful moral sentiments and anxieties counter to intoxication through their deeply ingrained ideas that sobriety is a Jewish virtue while drunkenness is a vice of Gentiles.[122] Great implications are associated with this finding: "where drinking is an integral part of the socialization process, where it is interrelated with the central moral symbolism and is repeatedly practiced in the rites of the group, the phenomenon of alcoholism is conspicuous by its absence. Norms of sobriety can be effectively sustained under these circumstances even though the drinking is extensive."[123]

Sex Differences in Drinking

Differences are found in the drinking patterns of men and women; they are particularly marked among adult excessive drinkers. One study that compared married and unmarried men and women alcoholics found that men were younger when they took their first drink and that they were more likely to engage in more social drinking than women.[124] These variations reflect the differing expectations for men and women in our society. Among the women, a strong relation was seen between heavy drinking and marital instability, but it is not clear if marriages failed because of heavy drinking or if heavy drinking precipitated the marital problems. Female alcoholics appear to have backgrounds unlike those of male alcoholics; for example, they have a higher incidence of alcoholism in their families. Women alcoholics generally appear to have more family disruption histories than do women as a whole.[125] Just as male alcoholics often have had difficulties in their jobs, the women alcoholics have experienced more difficulties in their marriages. This situation may well change. A 1976 study found that adolescent sex differences in the use of alcohol are disappearing, due to increasingly similar status positions, responsibilities, and activities for males and females, and this may have an effect in equalizing the future sex rates of alcoholism.[126]

---

[122]Snyder, *Alcohol and the Jews,* p. 182.

[123]Snyder, *Alcohol and the Jews,* p. 202. Also see Charles R. Snyder, "Inebriety, Alcoholism, and Anomie," in Marshall B. Clinard, ed., *Anomie and Deviant Behavior* (New York: Free Press, 1964), pp. 189–213; and Charles R. Snyder, "Culture and Jewish Sobriety: The Ingroup-Outgroup Factor," in Pittman and Snyder, pp. 188–215.

[124]Evelyn Bromet and Rudolf Moos, "Sex and Marital Status in Relation to the Characteristics of Alcoholics," *Journal of Studies on Alcohol,* 37 (1976), 1302–1312.

[125]Linda S. Beckman, "Women Alcoholics: A Review of Social and Psychological Studies," *Journal of Studies on Alcohol,* 36 (1975), 797–824.

[126]Henry Wechsler and Mary McFadden, "Sex Differences in Adolescent Alcohol and Drug Use; A Disappearing Phenomenon," *Journal of Studies on Alcohol,* 37 (1976), 1291–1301.

Ethnic Differences in Excessive Drinking

Pronounced differences are seen in the extent of excessive drinking patterns of various ethnic groups. These differences are, in turn, related to differences in the extent of drunkenness and alcoholism among the groups.

The Irish   Excessive drinking has long been associated with the Irish, and many of these patterns have carried over to the Irish-Americans. Studies have indicated that their rates of alcoholism probably exceed those of any other single ethnic group.[127] Their drinking habits cannot be attributed to a biological basis; Irish men drink because their culture permits general drinking, particularly strong beer and ale and whiskey. Their drinking is not confined to ceremonial purposes. A study of Irish drinking behavior suggests that the cultural factors are the most important determinants of excessive alcohol consumption. Typically, Irish society has been characterized by a pattern of high socioeconomic aspirations, late marriage, and much emphasis on the virtues of abstaining from sex until marriage. As a result of the cultural limitations on marriage and the consequent sex segregation, "bachelor groups" characterize the Irish social structure. Married men are also a part of this bachelor group, and they are often leaders in socializing younger men into their drinking practices. "A boy became a man upon initiation into the bachelor group, that is, when first offered a drink in the company of older men in the local public house. Farm and marriage might be a source of male identity for a few, but hard drinking was a more democratic means of achieving manhood."[128] Drinking is a source of prestige and esteem among men who live in a male segregated world. But the hard drinker in Irish society was, and still is, seldom a persistent drunkard, because chronic drunkenness has not been culturally sanctioned. Even today the rate of alcoholism in Ireland is comparatively low. Drinking patterns in England, Scotland, and Ireland point to the conclusion that "Irish drinking" has not been unique to Ireland.[129] Nevertheless, the "heavy drinker" stereotype followed Irish immigrants to the United States where it was translated not into heavy drinking but into drunkenness and alcoholism. They brought with them the tradition of public house drinking, the obligation to "stand" for a drink for others, who then had to reciprocate, and a suspicion of those teetotalers who were not one of the hard-drinking "boys."[130]

The Italians   A reverse situation exists among Italians in Italy who have always had a tradition of using wine with meals. Despite their extensive use of alcohol, the Italians have a very low incidence of alcoholism; in fact, the U.S. rate is eight times as great. Although the rate of alcoholism is also low among Italian-Americans, it appears to be higher than in Italy, even though the total consumption of alcoholic beverages is higher among the

---

[127]William and Joan McCord, with Jon Gudeman, "Some Current Theories of Alcoholism: A Longitudinal Evaluation," *Quarterly Journal of Studies on Alcohol,* 20 (1959), 746.
[128]Richard Stivers, *A Hair of the Dog: Irish Drinking and American Stereotype* (University Park, Pa.: Pennsylvania State University Press, 1976), p. 165.
[129]Stivers, Chap. 2.
[130]Bales, "Cultural Differences in Rates of Alcoholism."

Italians in Italy. A research project on the use of alcohol among Italians and among first-, second-, and third-generation Italian-Americans found that generally it was regarded as healthful to drink wine with meals.[131] Such an attitude appears, in part, to prevent alcoholic excesses and addictions. Most Italians first drink wine early in life, both men and women drink wine, and there is little opposition to the drinking of wine by young persons. An interesting fact is that single persons appear to drink less wine; it thus appears that wine, used as it is in conjunction with food events, loses much of its appeal for unattached individuals in the Italian culture where alcoholic beverages are seldom used for "escape" purposes.[132]

These drinking patterns were, in general, found to be only partially present among Italian-Americans, and their absence leads to excessive drinking and alcoholism. For example, 70 percent of Italian men, and 94 percent of the women, did all of their drinking at mealtimes, in comparison with only 7 percent of the first-generation Italian-American men and 16 percent of the women, and 4 percent of the men and 11 percent of the women in the second generation. All of these drinking patterns, particularly the consumption of wine with meals, have tended to "inoculate" the Italians and the Italian-Americans from alcoholism, but as they have declined in importance alcoholism has increased.

The French Persons in both Italy and France drink about the same large quantities of alcohol each day (900 to 1,000 cubic centimeters), but the rates of alcoholism are much greater in France, which is thought to have the highest rate of alcoholism in the world.[133] This difference can be explained by a number of factors: (1) Nearly all the alcoholic intake in Italy is wine, consumed at mealtime, while in France a substantial amount of the alcohol intake is in the form of distilled spirits and aperitifs between and after meals. In fact, in France, alcoholism rates are much lower in the southern part of the country where wine is largely consumed and where it is used in connection with meals. (2) Exposure to alcohol in childhood is viewed quite differently in the two countries: the French have rigid parental attitudes either favoring or opposing drinking among children.[134] Most Italians accept the drinking of wine in childhood as a "natural" part of a child's development. (3) The Italians have a much lower "safe limit" for amounts of alcohol consumption than the French, and they tend to view drunkenness as a personal and family disgrace. (4) The French view drinking, particularly of copious quantities, as associated with virility, while the Italians do not.[135]

Chinese-Americans In the United States Chinese-Americans often do not drink, but when they do, they usually drink in moderation and consequently have a low alcoholism rate.

[131]Lolli *et al.*
[132]Lolli *et al.*, p. 79.
[133]Roland Sadoun, Giorgio Lolli, and Milton Silverman, *Drinking in French Culture* (New Brunswick, N.J.: Rutgers Center of Alcohol Studies, 1965). Also see Lawrence Wylie, *Village in the Vaucluse* (New York: Harper & Row, 1964).
[134]Barbara Gallatin Anderson, "How French Children Learn To Drink," *Transaction (Society),* 5 (1968), 22.
[135]The alcoholism rate is high in Switzerland, and a study of Swiss alcoholics found their drinking patterns more similar to those of the French than to the Italians'. See Pierre Devrient and Giorgio Lolli, "Choice of Alcoholic Beverages among 240 Alcoholics in Switzerland," *Quarterly Journal of Studies on Alcohol,* 23 (1962), 459–467.

The social control exercised by the Cantonese Chinese subculture is such that alcohol is largely consumed as a part of social functions, public drunkenness is disapproved, and children are educated to observe these patterns.[136] One study pointed out, however, that gambling serves as a functional equivalent to alcoholism among the Chinese; as they become increasingly integrated into the general norms of U.S. society and as gambling declines, their rates of alcoholism may be expected to increase.[137]

American Indians   Excessive drinking is a serious problem among American Indians (Native Americans), and arrests for drunkenness generally seem greatly to exceed those for most other groups in the United States. The rate of arrests for alcohol-related crimes among Indians is 12 times greater than the national average.[138] Although some of this difference is real, a considerable part, undoubtedly, is due to discrimination in making arrests. The pattern of excessive drinking is not racially determined, for there is no evidence that the Indian is inherently more susceptible to intoxication or to alcoholism. It is caused by a combination of historical, social, and cultural factors.[139] Drinking was heavy on the American western frontier during the nineteenth century. Pioneer farmers, trappers, and cowboys drank more heavily than those persons they left behind because of group norms and the breakdown of social controls over intoxication on the frontier. It was with these heavy-drinking persons that Indians came into contact in the nineteenth century. Moreover, many traders and trappers used various devices to get Indians interested in the excessive use of alcohol.[140] Too, most Indians were unfamiliar with the use of alcohol before the coming of whites. When the excessive use of alcohol later became common among Indians, federal laws were enacted, beginning with a rather general law in 1802 and a final, more specific one in 1893 and again in 1938, which made it an offense, punishable by imprisonment and heavy fine, to serve any intoxicants to an Indian. These laws were not repealed until 1953. Among the Navaho, as among most Indian tribes, when alcohol was illegal it was usually purchased secretly, at exorbitant prices and consumed by small groups until it was finished.[141] It is difficult to generalize about Indian drinking, however; one study of Oneida Indian youth, for example, found equal numbers of abstainers and light, moderate, and heavy drinkers among this group as among a control group of white youth.[142]

American Blacks   Despite the fact that most studies suggest that alcoholism, as well as problem-drinking rates, are generally higher for American blacks than for whites, relatively few

---

[136]Milton L. Barnett, "Alcoholism in the Cantonese of New York City: An Anthropological Study," in Oskar Deithelm, ed., *Etiology of Chronic Alcoholism* (Springfield, Ill.: Charles C Thomas, 1955), pp. 179–227.

[137]George Chu, "Drinking Patterns and Attitudes of Rooming-House Chinese in San Francisco," *Quarterly Journal of Studies on Alcohol,* Supplement 6, 1972, pp. 58–68.

[138]Omer Stewart, "Questions Regarding American Indian Criminality," *Human Organization,* 23 (1964), 61–66.

[139]Edward P. Dozier, "Problem Drinking among American Indians: The Role of Socio-Cultural Deprivation," *Quarterly Journal of Studies on Alcohol,* 27 (1966), 72–87.

[140]Allan M. Winkler, "Drinking on the American Frontier," *Quarterly Journal of Studies on Alcohol,* 29 (1968), 413–445.

[141]Dwight B. Heath, "Prohibition and Post-Repeal Drinking Patterns among the Navaho," *Quarterly Journal of Studies on Alcohol,* 25 (1964), 119–135.

[142]Donald E. Weast, "Patterns of Drinking among Indian Youth: The Significance of Anomie and Differential Association," *The Wisconsin Sociologist,* 9 (1972), 12–28. There are indications that tribal backgrounds, familial structure, and degree of acculturation are also important variables inhibiting generalizations about Indian drinking. See Beigel and Ghertner, p. 213.

studies have been made of drinking patterns and alcoholism among the black population.[143] There seems to be no question that black women have a higher rate of alcoholism, at least on the basis of those hospitalized, than white women. When controlled for education, hospitalization rates are three to six times greater, depending upon the level.[144] That this difference is a real one is indicated by the fact that similar differences are found when inpatient and outpatient cases are considered.[145] Other studies have shown that the rates of arrest, conviction, or incarceration for public intoxication tend to be higher for blacks than for whites.[146] Some of these rate differences are due to discrimination against blacks in the criminal justice system.

There is no racial factor in drinking behavior among blacks; the determining factor in the use of alcoholic beverages is cultural.[147] The pronounced differences among lower-, middle-, and upper-class blacks in relation to alcohol-drinking behavior make it extremely difficult to generalize about blacks as a group. Middle- and upper-class blacks generally are either abstainers or more moderate in their drinking behavior, tend to regard lower-class heavy drinking and drunkenness, and the fighting sometimes associated with it, as reflecting negatively on blacks as a group. The most pronounced variations by socioeconomic status occur in the choice of public versus private places for drinking, the "elaboration of the drinking ritual and attention to the symbolic values of alcoholic beverages, and permissible behavior accompanying drinking—especially in regard to aggression."[148] Drinking appears to be extensive in black slum areas of large urban communities, both in the North and in the South. A study of drinking in a South Carolina mill town whose population was one fourth black found that intoxication generally was sanctioned negatively and that alcohol was pervasive in terms of the numbers of men and lower-status women who used it and in relation to its association with recreation, "touchy" behavior, and nonmarital sexual behavior. "Alcohol use is one of the axes along which social status is measured in a community whose access to individual recognition and achievement in the larger society is severely limited."[149]

ALCOHOL-RELATED CRIME AND DRUNKEN DRIVING

Drunkenness is undoubtedly of some significance in some violent personal crimes such as murder, aggravated assault, and forcible rape, but claims that it plays a major

---

[143]For surveys of the literature in this area, see Muriel W. Sterne, "Drinking Patterns and Alcoholism among American Negroes," in Pittman, pp. 71–74; and Beigel and Ghertner, p. 212. Also see R. Strayer, "A Study of the Negro Alcoholic," *Quarterly Journal of Studies on Alcohol,* 22 (1961), 111–123.

[144]See, for example, B. Z. Locke and H. J. Duvall, "Alcoholism among Admissions to Psychiatric Facilities," *Quarterly Journal of Studies on Alcohol,* 26 (1965), 521–534; and B. Z. Locke, M. Kramer, and B. Passamanick, "Alcoholic Psychoses among First Admissions to Public Mental Health Hospitals in Ohio," *Quarterly Journal of Studies on Alcohol,* 21 (1960), 457–474.

[145]Margaret B. Bailey, Paul W. Haberman, and Harold Alksne, "The Epidemiology of Alcoholism in an Urban Residential Area," *Quarterly Journal of Studies on Alcohol,* 26 (1965), 19–40.

[146]Sterne, pp. 74–77.

[147]John R. Larkin, *Alcohol and the Negro: Explosive Issues* (Zebulon, N.C.: Record Publishing, 1965), p. 245.

[148]Sterne, p. 98.

[149]Sterne, p. 89.

part in such crimes are greatly exaggerated.[150] In Wolfgang's criminal homicide study in Philadelphia, it was concluded that there is a significant association between violent homicide and the presence of alcohol in the offender of either sex. He found that 60 percent of all criminally violent homicide offenders had been drinking before the crime, while the remainder had not been; among those who had killed nonviolently half had been drinking prior to the crime while the other half had not been drinking.[151] Offenses of violence against the person in Finland, where they are common, are often committed in a state of intoxication. Yet it is estimated that 43 percent of those who drink in Finland continue drinking to a state of drunkenness once they begin to drink, indicating that only a small proportion of those who are intoxicated engage in acts of violence.[152]

The exaggerated claims about the relation of alcohol to violence may be questioned on a number of grounds. (1) First, the commission of a crime, whether violent or nonviolent, after "drinking," as in the Philadelphia study, does not mean a great deal unless it can be shown that the person had drunk enough to have become intoxicated. (2) In most crimes of violence, and in crimes generally, the offender is not under the influence of alcohol. One study of marital disputes which resulted in police intervention, for example, indicated that alcohol was not the primary reason for the assaultive behavior; rather, the presence of alcohol was associated with lessening violence.[153] (3) There is no direct "causal" relationship between alcohol use and violence. Alcohol use does not inevitably lead to aggression, and "only a very small proportion of alcohol use situations leads to violent crime."[154] (4) Of considerable importance is the social situation and the conditions in which the act of violence, as well as the drinking, take place and the person's previous experience with alcohol. It is probable that in most cases where alcohol is associated with criminal behavior the drug acted as a "depressant" and made the person temporarily less cognizant of the probable consequences of deviant behavior, or perhaps less able to respond in terms of his ordinary system of values and norms. In a sense it simply "released" behavior patterns already there instead of "causing" them. When murders and assaults are committed under the influence of alcohol they usually represent long-standing quarrels or difficulties in relations with others which may culminate in violence. (5) Even when crimes are committed under the influence of alcohol, no single pattern of criminality is seen as being associated with drinking. One study noted that the criminal alcoholic, like alcoholics generally, represents a heterogeneous group.[155]

Constantly increasing is the number of automobile accidents that involve drinking, as well as the number of deaths resulting. The proportion of auto accidents

---

[150]See, for example, Kai Pernanen, "Alcohol and Crimes of Violence," in Kassin and Begleiter, *Social Aspects of Alcoholism,* pp. 351–444; and Julian Roebuck and Ronald Johnson, "The Negro Drinker and Assaulter as a Criminal Type," *Crime and Delinquency,* 3 (1962), 21–33.

[151]Marvin E. Wolfgang, *Patterns in Criminal Homicide* (Philadelphia: University of Pennsylvania Press, 1958), p. 166.

[152]Kettil Bruun, "Alcohol Studies in Scandinavia," *Sociological Inquiry,* 31 (1961), 78–92.

[153]See Morton Bard and Joseph Zacker, "Assaultiveness and Alcohol Use in Family Disputes: Police Perceptions," *Criminology,* 12 (1974), 281–292.

[154]Pernanen, p. 388.

[155]Rolf Lindelius and Inna Salum, "Alcoholism and Crime: A Comparative Study of Three Groups of Alcoholics," *Journal of Studies on Alcohol,* 36 (1975), 1455.

involving alcohol has increased from 22 percent in the 1940s to 35 percent in the 1950s and 50 percent in the 1960s. Each year in the United States traffic deaths associated with significant amounts of alcohol, either in the driver or in the victim, account for about half of the 50,000 persons killed.[156] Between one and two million persons each year are seriously injured, and it is estimated that between 25 and 40 percent of these accidents involve the consumption of significant amounts of alcohol by the driver or the victim. Hundreds of millions of dollars in damages result from these accidents. In Wisconsin in 1975, 530 traffic deaths were tested for blood alcohol concentrations (BACs); a BAC of 0.05 percent or higher was found for 284 persons, with 85 percent of these persons having a level of 0.10 percent or higher, a level that constitutes *prima facie* evidence of intoxication. Although the BACs were twice as high for males as for females, figures for Wisconsin fatalities indicate that the female percentage of tested deaths has been steadily rising.[157] In San Antonio more than half the drivers and pedestrians killed in traffic accidents between 1957 and 1966 were drunk,[158] and a recent study of 300 fatal accidents in the Boston area revealed that 39 percent of the drivers responsible for these accidents were intoxicated from alcohol and 16 percent had used marijuana.[159]

A Harris public opinion poll in 1972 found that 87 percent of the American people felt that drunken driving is a "very serious problem" in the United States and that 79 percent were of the opinion that "the police and the courts should be tougher on drunken drivers than they are now." Drunken driving, however, is generally dealt with as a misdemeanor; if a person is injured as a result, in many states a sentence of up to five years can be given, and in case of death the person can be charged with negligent manslaughter. In 1975 nearly a million persons were arrested for driving while under the influence of alcohol in the United States. About 91 percent of them were males, and approximately three fourths of those arrested were over 25 years of age. Some studies indicate a marked recidivism rate among drunken drivers; three German studies indicated that between 51 and 72 percent had had previous convictions.[160]

Even though this situation is extremely serious, it is difficult to state positively that alcohol drinking causes the accidents. The situation is not a unitary one. More than 100 million Americans are licensed drivers, and some 90 million drink, constituting probably billions of occasions when alcohol is in the body of a person who is driving. It is therefore important to know about drinking-driving without accidents and about driving accidents that do not involve drinking. Bacon has stated that if, for example, in a given area 100 accidents occurred out of 10,000 driving occasions in a six-hour period, and if 10 of these accidents involved a driver with alcohol, "the total number of drivers with alcohol in that area at that time would have to be significantly less than

---

[156]Seldon D. Bacon, "Traffic Accidents Involving Alcohol in the U.S.A.: Second-stage Aspects of a Social Problem," *Quarterly Journal of Studies on Alcohol,* Supplement 4, 1968, p. 11.
[157]Data from *Blood Alcohol Testing for Motor Vehicle Deaths,* Division of Health, Wisconsin Department of Health and Social Services, Madison, issues 1970–1975.
[158]*The New York Times,* May 12, 1966.
[159]*The U.S. Journal of Drug and Alcohol Dependence,* 1 (April 1977), 1.
[160]Cited in Wolf Middendorff, *The Effectiveness of Punishment: Especially in Relation to Traffic Offenses* (South Hackensack, N.J.: Fred B. Rothman, 1968), p. 20.

1,000 if the usual claim that drinking-driving produces an excessive number of accidents is verified."[161]

The problem is further complicated by the definition of "drinking" in terms of alcohol amounts. An alcohol concentration of 0.10 percent in the blood is the usual standard for legal evidence of intoxication. Certainly effective driving must be impaired with high concentrations of blood alcohol (0.25 percent or even 0.15 percent), but the question is does 0.01 percent to 0.15 percent (one to five drinks) have generally enough effect to impair seriously a person's driving efficiency. One important and careful study, for example, found that persons whose blood alcohol content was 0.01 to 0.04 percent (one to two drinks in the previous half hour) had no greater record of accidents than those without alcohol.[162] Another report, however, concluded that driving skills deteriorate at relatively low blood alcohol levels, even less than 0.05 percent.[163] The nature of "driving" should also be clarified by any analysis of the relation of drunken driving to accidents. Granted that drinking had been sufficient to affect driver coordination, other factors would be the speed of the car, the time of day, the nature of the road and the traffic, and the condition of the automobile.

Sociocultural factors are also important in alcoholic patterns of driving behavior. Persons with higher education and in more prestigious occupations have been shown to be more likely to drive while under the influence of alcohol, yet lower-class persons are more likely to be arrested for it.[164] Middle- and upper-class persons are more likely to learn to behave "properly" after consuming alcohol and give the appearance of being in control even with the police, whereas lower-class persons may not care as much about attracting attention to their driving and drinking behavior. Middle- and upper-class persons appear to display more appropriate demeanor when stopped by the police, thus suggesting that not only is drinking behavior learned but also learned is the manner of dealing with social situations after alcohol has been consumed.

SOCIAL CONTROL OF ALCOHOL USE

Five modes of social control of alcohol use have been tried—prohibition, legal regulation, education about alcohol use and use of substitutes, and comprehensive programs to prevent alcohol abuse.[165]

---

[161]Bacon, "Traffic Accidents Involving Alcohol in the U.S.A.," p. 24.

[162]R. F. Borkenstein, R. F. Crother, R. P. Schumate, W. B. Ziel, and R. Zylman, in A. Dale, *The Drinking Driver in Traffic Accidents* (Bloomington, Ind.: University Department of Police Administration, 1964). For a comprehensive review of the literature on drinking, alcohol level, and injuries, see Julian A. Waller, "Alcohol and Unintentional Injury," in Kassin and Begleiter, *Social Aspects of Alcoholism*, pp. 307–349.

[163]*Alcohol, Drug Abuse/Highway Public Safety*, Task Force Report to the Council on Alcohol and Other Drug Abuse, Madison, Wisconsin, October 1976, p. 93.

[164]See Harvey Marshall and Ross Purdy, "Hidden Deviance and the Labeling Approach: The Case for Drinking and Driving," *Social Problems*, 19 (1972), 541–553. Also see MacAndrew and Edgerton; and Merton M. Hyman, "The Social Characteristics of Persons Arrested for Driving While Intoxicated," *Quarterly Journal of Studies on Alcohol*, 29 (1968), 138–177.

[165]The first four are derived from Edwin M. Lemert, "Alcohol, Values, and Social Control," in *Human Deviance, Social Problems and Social Control* (Englewood Cliffs, N.J.: Prentice-Hall, 1972), pp. 112–122.

Prohibition constitutes a system of laws and coercive measures that make it illegal to manufacture, distribute, or consume alcoholic beverages. This "prohibition" means of control has had a noteworthy history in the United States. The passage of the Eighteenth Amendment forbidding the manufacture and sale of alcoholic beverages resulted from the actions of various "reform" groups which identified abstinence as a middle-class symbol.[166] The Prohibition era began in January 1920 and lasted until the repeal of this legislation in 1933 with the passage of the Twenty-first Amendment. Any future prohibition movement in the United States seems highly unlikely in view of the failure of the earlier efforts and the increasingly permissive attitudes toward the moderate use of alcohol at all social levels.

A second model of social control is the *legal regulation* of the kinds of liquor consumed, monetary costs, methods of distribution, the time and place of drinking, and the availability of alcoholic beverages to consumers according to age, sex, and various socioeconomic characteristics. In this model of control the role of the law is one of regulation, establishing standards of control over the production and sale of alcohol short of prohibition. If there is any national policy in the United States in relation to alcohol, it is largely related to legal regulations. Through licensing and taxes, sales are limited, as is the age at which one may legally consume alcohol. Taxes make up about half the costs of hard liquor, a factor that does to some extent regulate its purchase by some people. Mass media in advertising is also regulative; hard spirits may not be advertised at all on television, and beer may be advertised only if it is never shown being consumed. Presumably these measures make alcohol somewhat less readily available to the public, or at least not as freely obtainable as if they did not exist.

A third control strategy is a system of *education* about the consequences of alcohol use, leading to more moderate drinking behavior or even to abstinence. This approach depends greatly on a program presenting factual information about the dangers of drinking for potentially heavy or problem drinkers. It is uncertain if these education programs can reach, and then convince, a public that derives most of its information and values about alcohol use from family and friends. As with formal programs designed for educating people about the use of other drugs, programs dealing with alcohol seem to be artificial in the sense that often they are divorced from drinking situations.

A fourth control model is a program of *alcohol substitution,* such as the use of beer with a reduced alcohol content, greater soft drink consumption, and even marijuana usage. Some people might justify the use of marijuana on the grounds that it is less harmful in the long run than either alcohol or cigarettes, but its proposal as a substitute would probably encounter great resistance even today on the part of the public.

Finally, there are *broad programs directed at the prevention of alcohol abuse* through changing attitudes toward the nature and amount of drinking alcoholic beverages. Historically, Americans have displayed ambivalence toward drinking: on

---

[166]See Joseph R. Gusfield, *Symbolic Crusade: Status Politics and the American Temperance Movement* (Urbana: University of Illinois Press, 1963).

the one hand, drinking is frowned upon as being inconsistent with certain religious doctrines and principles of abstinence, while on the other, alcohol serves an important function at many social gatherings, and abstinence may even be frowned upon on such occasions as a wedding celebration or New Year's Eve. Broad programs of alcohol education might recognize this ambivalence and programs of a comprehensive nature devised to channel drinking. It is only logical to try to prevent drunkenness and alcoholism, and a government report on excessive drinking has set up guidelines to change or to "channel" in the right direction the drinking of alcoholic beverages by pointing to drinking patterns which are associated with relatively low rates of drinking problems:

1. The children are exposed to alcohol early in life, within a strong family or religious group. Whatever the beverage, it is served in very diluted form and in small quantities, with consequent low blood-alcohol levels.

2. The [alcoholic] beverages commonly although not invariably used by the groups are those containing relatively large amounts of nonalcoholic components, which also give low blood-alcohol levels.

3. The beverage is considered mainly as a food and usually consumed with meals, again with consequent low blood-alcohol levels.

4. Parents present a constant example of moderate drinking.

5. No moral importance is attached to drinking. It is considered neither a virtue nor a sin.

6. Drinking is not viewed as a proof of adulthood or virility.

7. Abstinence is socially acceptable. It is no more rude or ungracious to decline a drink than to decline a piece of bread.

8. Excessive drinking or intoxication is not socially acceptable. It is not considered stylish, comical, or tolerable.

9. Finally, and perhaps most important, there is wide and usually complete agreement among members of the group on what might be called the ground rules of drinking.[167]

A program employing these patterns as objectives would require changes in the private organization of drinking practices, changes in the age levels for alcohol use, extensive education about alcohol, changes in commercial promotion, a different system of alcohol taxation, and adjustments in the regulations governing alcohol sales and the consumption of alcohol. Such a program at the personal level would involve a reorientation toward the use of alcohol as a natural part of life, primarily in the form of beer, wine, and less strong drinks in social gatherings with meals and in conjunction with other food rather than by itself. For example, it would be recognized that the host of a party has a responsibility to minimize excessive or irresponsible drinking, particularly where driving is involved. "Some Scandinavian hosts, for example, make it a practice to find out whether a guest is driving that evening before offering him an alcoholic drink. To develop such attitudes in America will not be easy since current practice generally requires the host to keep all guests full and often to push another drink on his guests before they are ready for it."[168] Programs of this type might include the following features:

[167]Department of Health, Education and Welfare, National Institute of Mental Health, *Alcohol and Alcoholism* (Washington, D.C.: Government Printing Office; 1967), p. 28.
[168]Plaut, p. 145.

1. Revision of minimum age laws permitting adolescents to buy alcohol and permitting parents to serve children alcohol in the home.
2. Public and classroom education that informs and debates rather than preaches, presents moderation in drinking rather than drinking per se as a sign of maturity, and suggests that the host and party-goer respect the abstainer.
3. Commercial advertising policies, encouraged by government regulation, to portray alcohol not as a lyrical or masculine symbol but as a moderate, if attractive, part of everyday living, taken with family and friends in circumstances of restraint. Women and children should be portrayed in or near drinking scenes in such a way to suggest restraint.
4. Tax changes and promotion that help shift consumption to lighter-proof drinks, associated with meals and snacks; licensing policies and promotion that associate alcohol definitely with meals in the home and in restaurants.
5. Licensing laws and other measures that move alcohol away from an emphasis on drinking only into settings and activities that can often be enjoyed by the whole family together: sports events, bowling alleys, theaters, certain resort facilities, and so on.

Some specific proposals may help to prevent or reduce the abuse of alcohol. (1) The federal alcohol-proof minimum for products labeled whiskey and gin could be lowered. (2) Since drinking is less in neighborhood taverns than under other circumstances, more taverns in neighborhoods could be established, particularly in newer residential areas. The specific prohibition on Sunday opening of taverns and other places serving liquor would be eliminated. (3) All grocery stores could be permitted to sell low-strength alcohol products, such as wine, most closely associated with eating occasions. (4) Frequent unannounced police road checks would be instituted to help deter those who drive while intoxicated, and stiffer penalties provided for driving under the influence of alcohol. This also involves "implied consent" legislation establishing the use of breath tests and other blood tests to check motorists who are suspected of having drunk too much. (5) Special "group discussion sessions" about the consequences of drinking and driving could be set up for convicted drivers in connection with the courts. (6) The suspension of driving licenses and other penalties of those who have been driving while intoxicated would be more widely publicized. Finally, (7) changes could be instituted in the monopolistic control in the sale of distilled spirits in the alcohol beverage industry. This business in the United States is dominated by four giants, Seagrams, National Distillers, Hiram Walker, and Schenley, and they, as well as other liquor interests at the national, state, and local levels, have operated in a fashion to control the industry and to keep out competition.[169] These business interests exploit for their own benefit and use government regulation—mandatory fair trade, licensing restrictions, curbs on advertising, and others.[170]

Although these proposals for changing alcohol-use patterns in order to prevent alcohol abuse may be logical to many persons, enormous problems remain in the United States in bringing about social change in alcohol use. Most of all, the very heterogeneity of the population makes any task of delineating a single norm of

---

[169]Expenditures by the alcohol beverage industry for all forms of national advertising in 1968 amounted to 250 million dollars, or 5 percent of all advertising revenue.
[170]Rupert Wilkinson, *The Prevention of Drinking Problems: Alcohol Control and Cultural Influences* (New York: Oxford University Press, 1970), p. 87. Also see Trice and Roman, pp. 11–12; and Denzin, "Notes on the Criminogenic Hypothesis: A Case Study of the American Liquor Industry," *American Sociological Review,* 42 (1977), 905–921.

drinking behavior practically impossible. Drinking customs and attitudes, as well as the drinking problems in our society, reflect the practices, beliefs, and values of many national, regional, ethnic, and social groups.

DEALING WITH PUBLIC DRUNKENNESS AND ALCOHOLISM

Individual drunkenness and alcoholism can be dealt with in a number of ways that might well alleviate the problems.[171] They include the decriminalization of public drunkenness, community-based treatment programs, and Alcoholics Anonymous.

Decriminalization

Changes in the criminal justice system to decriminalize public drunkenness would help to reduce the scope of the problem. There is little indication that the present system has been effective. A 1971 study done under the auspices of the American Bar Association recommended that alternatives be found to the repeated arresting of the chronic drunk.[172] A Presidential Commission also recommended that drunkenness in itself not be a criminal offense, although disorderly and other criminal conduct accompanied by drunkenness should remain punishable as separate offenses.[173] As alternatives, the Commission recommended the establishment of community civil detoxification units as part of a comprehensive treatment program.[174] By 1977, half the states had decriminalized public intoxication and replaced the police station as a place to detain inebriates initially and later jail confinement with civil treatment programs. Under the authority of civil legislation, drunken persons are brought to the public health facility, detained until they are sober, and then provided some after-care program. The American public appears to support such an alternative; a Harris public opinion survey in 1972 showed that the American people rejected, 52 percent to 25 percent, the idea of "the police arresting drunks" and believed that police instead should "take them to a hospital for treatment."

Community-Based Treatment Programs

In recent years in the United States, one has witnessed a substantial public health movement involving community-based referral and treatment centers for alcoholics,

[171]For a discussion of various methods used in the treatment of alcoholism, see *Alcohol and Health.*
[172]Nimmer.
[173]*The Challenge of Crime in a Free Society,* Report of the President's Commission on Law Enforcement and Administration of Justice (Washington, D.C.: Government Printing Office, 1967), "Drunkenness Offenses," p. 236.
[174]Richard J. Tatham, "Detoxification Center: A Public Health Alternative to the 'Drunk Tanks,'" *Federal Probation,* 33 (1969), 46–48. This method of dealing with public drunkenness has been adopted in England and Wales under the Criminal Justice Act of 1972. Also see Romine R. Deming, "Statutory Diversion of Drunkenness Offenders," *Journal of Criminal Justice,* 5 (1977), 29–39.

some providing counseling, some hospitalization. Concern over problem drinking resulted in the creation in 1971 of the National Institute on Alcohol Abuse and Alcoholism, and substantial funds are being appropriated to support training, education, and treatment programs. In 1977 in the United States there were 700 federally funded alcoholism service programs. They offer such services as counseling, psychiatric treatment in clinics and hospitals, behavior modification through the use of alcohol-aversion drugs, and others, including halfway houses.[175] Unfortunately, some programs have been individualistic, neglecting the group and social context of problem drinking. Often there is little success. Some programs, such as halfway houses, deal with the problem in a more natural social setting of group relations.[176]

Halfway houses have been used in attempting to rehabilitate the allegedly hopeless skid row type of alcoholic. They have been established on the premise that the deviant subculture of the skid row alcoholic and its meaning to him have to be considered if rehabilitation is to succeed. The halfway house is thus seen as a social milieu offering social support "half way" between the alcohol subculture and nonalcoholic groups. On entering, the alcoholic is expected to get a job, pay for his room and board, assist with maintenance, and stay sober. Frequently the staff consists of recovered alcoholics who conduct counseling sessions with new residents. The assumption is that group pressures operate to produce sobriety, whereas on skid row these pressures produce inebriety. Skid row alcoholics, however, are an extremely difficult group with which to deal, as was seen in a study of treatment programs for skid row drinkers in California. The program failed to reduce drinking among its clients, and it may even have produced more alcoholism in the community than it prevented, largely because it also recruited problem drinkers from outside the program area.[177]

Alcoholics Anonymous

Of all treatment methods, Alcoholics Anonymous (AA) is probably the most widely known and presumably the most successful approach to the social reintegration of the alcoholic. Its program is based on the principle that the alcoholic must be "delabeled" and accepted back into society. According to Trice and Roman, other efforts do not remove the stigmatic label nor do they replace it with one that is socially acceptable.[178]

Alcoholics Anonymous was founded in Cleveland about 50 years ago by two alcoholics who felt that their mutual fellowship had helped them with their drinking problems.[179] It is not an association or society in the generally accepted sense of that word, for it has no formal organization with officers or dues, although it maintains a

[175]Wilkinson.

[176]For a discussion of various treatment programs with reference particularly to alcohol problems in industry, see Trice and Roman, *Spirits and Demons at Work.*

[177]Lincoln J. Fry and Jon Miller, "Responding to Skid Row Alcoholism: Self-Defeating Arrangements in an Innovative Treatment Program," *Social Problems,* 22 (1975), 675–688.

[178]Trice and Roman, p. 219.

[179]For a history of this organization, see *Alcoholics Anonymous Comes of Age: A Brief History of A.A.* (New York: Alcoholics Anonymous Publishing, 1957). Also see Irving Peter Gellman, *The Sober Alcoholic* (New Haven, Conn.: College and University Press, 1964); and Harrison M. Trice, "Alcoholics Anonymous," in Harry Gold and Frank R. Scarpitti, eds., *Combatting Social Problems: Techniques of Intervention* (New York: Holt, Rinehart and Winston, 1967), pp. 503–511. Also see Edward Sagarin, *Odd Man In: Societies of Deviants in America* (Chicago: Quadrangle Books, 1969).

central office in New York City and publishes a journal called A.A. *Grapevine*.[180] It is a voluntary organization with more than 10,000 chapters or groups of recent alcoholics in the United States and many other countries. Total U.S. membership is about 300,000 in approximately 7,500 chapters.

First of all, each individual alcoholic, in order to become "delabeled," must accept for himself society's label of him as an "alcoholic." This is a crucial element in terms of the person's eventual ability to control the drinking behavior. This acceptance serves several purposes: (1) it forces an alcoholic to recognize and to resign himself to the reality of his own alcoholism; (2) it reinforces the negative feeling about the individual's undesirable drinking behavior; and (3) it shows an affirmation of, and solidarity with, the larger, more respectable, society of nondrinkers.[181] More specifically, the success of A.A. can be attributed to the following:

1. The program *breaks down the alcoholic's social isolation* that has resulted from the stigma of excessive drinking by drawing the person into a group in which he is accepted on face value as a past drunkard. This group is an intimate, primary one in which members can more easily orient themselves. An alcoholic feels at home with other alcoholics who, like himself, have known degradation and the stigma of being an alcoholic.[182]

2. The *life stories told at meetings* are helpful to the members. Frequent use is also made of a basic book, *Alcoholics Anonymous,* which contains well-known stories of successful members, particularly the founders of A.A., and which has been found to be effective over a long period of time. Two types of meetings are sponsored: open meetings, which family, friends, and other outsiders may attend; and closed meetings, attended only by A.A. members, which are more intimate, so that the former alcoholic feels free to speak more openly about problems and experiences.

3. Each, new member is *assigned to a sponsor,* perhaps an old friend or drinking companion, although more often a complete stranger, who refers to him as his "baby." The sponsor is someone who has been successfully coping with an alcohol problem and is ready at all times to give help. As soon as possible, the sponsor takes the "baby" to the meetings. The alcoholic's employer or spouse is often asked by the sponsor to support and understand the new member, and persons may also be contacted to whom the alcoholic has given worthless checks or from whom money has been borrowed, asking for continued support and understanding.[183]

4. *Reciprocal obligations of A.A. members* is particularly important; in fact, it is considered the most important therapeutic aspect of the program.[184] The relation of sponsor and "baby" and that of one member to another tends to create a reciprocal

[180]Gellman, pp. 172–173.
[181]Montanino, p. 356.
[182]John F. Lofland and Robert A. LeJeune, "Initial Interaction of Newcomers in Alcoholics Anonymous: A Field Experiment in Class Symbols and Socialization," *Social Problems,* 8 (1960), 102–111.
[183]See H. S. Ripley and J. K. Jackson, "Therapeutic Factors in A.A.," *American Journal of Psychiatry,* 116 (1959), 44–50, for a discussion of the roles of "sponsor" and "baby" and their importance. Sometimes the word "pigeon" is used in place of "baby."
[184]Robert F. Bales, "Types of Social Structure as Factors in 'Cures' of Alcohol Addiction," *Applied Anthropology,* 1 (1942), 8.

obligation network toward others which results in greater solidarity or identification with the group. Thus, in their prospective converts, members see themselves as they once were, and they become their own therapists by teaching the other.[185] This aspect of A.A. is quite similar to other self-help programs such as Addicts Anonymous and Recovery, Incorporated, for mental patients, all of which use "ex's" to help cure persons with conditions similar to their own. The process of using these persons as change agents and the general outcome of such efforts has been described as "retroflexive reformation" by Cressey.[186] Essentially, person A, the ex-deviant, in attempting to reform person B, the present deviant, is more apt to be rehabilitated than person B, because A had to learn and internalize rehabilitation values and attitudes in order to convey them to B. In this respect, perhaps the most therapeutic period in the program is that when a new member begins to bring others to A.A. meetings and to take some responsibility for their drinking behavior.

5. Each alcoholic takes up separately during the meetings the so-called *twelve steps,* which are discussed and interpreted by other alcoholics.[187] In the process he learns the common argot, such as "slip" to describe a person who has returned to drinking, "twelfth-stepping" for working with other alcoholics, and "dime therapy" for a member who uses the telephone to help someone avoid a "slip."

Although it is difficult to ascertain definitely the degree of success of A.A., there is considerable evidence that there has generally been a high rate of recovery among the members. According to one writer, A.A. claims it has a recovery rate of 75 percent for those who really try its methods.[188] Such statements are not easily verified, for A.A. has no complete set of records, many A.A. members have a number of "slips" during the program, and many persons associate themselves with A.A. who are totally unsuited for it. Actual evaluation studies of A.A. are also limited because of the anonymity of the relatives. A study of 393 members by another member of A.A. found that over a seven-year period, 47 percent had stayed sober at least a year, about 70 percent of those had stayed sober for two years, and 90 percent of those sober for two years continued to three.[189] There are also indications that those who associate themselves with the A.A. program had viewed previously their problems somewhat differently from those who had been exposed to A.A. but had not joined. In a study of A.A. members compared with nonmembers, a significant difference was found in that A.A. members tended to regard themselves, even before they attended a meeting, as persons who often shared their troubles with others. They tended less frequently to have known persons who they "believed" stopped drinking through will power. They had lost long-time drinking companions, and they had had exposure to favorable

[185]Joseph A. Cook and Gilbert Geis, "Forum Anonymous: The Techniques of Alcoholics Anonymous Applied to Prison Therapy," *Journal of Social Therapy,* 3 (1957), 9–13.

[186]Donald R. Cressey, "Changing Criminals: The Application of the Theory of Differential Association," *American Journal of Sociology,* 61 (1955), 116–120.

[187]*Alcoholics Anonymous* (New York: Works Publishing, 1950), pp. 71–72.

[188]H. M. Tiebout, "Therapeutic Mechanisms of Alcoholics Anonymous," *American Journal of Psychiatry,* 100 (1944), 468–473.

[189]Bill C., "The Growth and Effectiveness of Alcoholics Anonymous in a Southwestern City, 1945–1962," *Quarterly Journal of Studies on Alcohol,* 26 (1965), 279–284. (Bill C. is a pseudonym for an A.A. member.)

communications about A.A.[190] In a study of male alcoholics discharged from a hospital, success with A.A. was found to be associated with their need for affiliation, experience of intensive labeling as an alcoholic, physical stability previous to treatment, and proneness to feelings of guilt.[191]

The absence of sound empirical information on the effectiveness of A.A. has led both to praise and to criticism, based on grounds other than the eventual outcome of program participation. One problem associated with the program is the negative nature of A.A. therapy. The potential member must first accept a negative label of himself, condemn his former behavior, and vow not to repeat drinking in any form or at any time. Some observers claim that this public self-condemnation does little to alter the negative evaluation of A.A. members in the public's eyes.[192] A second problem is that according to A.A., alcoholism is a lifelong condition that is never really absent: "alcoholics remain alcoholics" even when they are sober over long periods of time. This assertion that "once an alcoholic, always an alcoholic" has not been empirically supported. In fact, recent research indicates that some alcoholics may eventually return to drinking without again becoming problem drinkers.[193] This research emphasizes, however, that not all, nor even most, alcoholics will be able to drink alcohol again, but that clearly some of them can do so without a repetition of their previous behavior patterns.

SELECTED REFERENCES

Beckman, Linda S. "Women Alcoholics: A Review of Social and Psychological Studies," *Journal of Studies on Alcohol,* 36 (1975), 797–824.

Beigel, Allan, and Stuart Ghertner. "Toward a Social Model: An Assessment of Social Factors Which Influence Problem Drinking and Its Treatment," in Benjamin Kassin and Henri Begleiter, eds., *Treatment and Rehabilitation of the Chronic Alcoholic.* New York: Plenum Press, 1977.

Cahalan, Don, and Ira H. Cisin. "Drinking Behavior and Drinking Problems in the United States," in Benjamin Kassin and Henri Begleiter, eds., *Social Aspects of Alcoholism.* New York: Plenum Press, 1976.

Cahalan, Don, Ira H. Cisin, and Helen M. Crossley. *American Drinking Practices: A National Survey of Drinking Behavior and Attitudes.* New Brunswick, N.J.: Rutgers Center for Alcohol Studies, 1969, Monograph 6.

Cahalan, Don, and Robin Room. *Problem Drinking among American Men.* New Brunswick, N.J.: Rutgers Center for Alcohol Studies, 1974.

---

[190]Harrison M. Trice, "The Affiliation Motive and Readiness To Join Alcoholics Anonymous," *Quarterly Journal of Studies on Alcohol,* 20 (1959), 313–321.

[191]Harrison M. Trice and Paul M. Roman, "Sociopsychological Predictions of Successful Affiliation with Alcoholics Anonymous," *Social Psychiatry,* 5 (1970), 51–59.

[192]See Harrison M. Trice and Paul M. Roman, "Delabeling, Relabeling and Alcoholics Anonymous," *Social Problems,* 17 (1970), 538–547; and Petrunik.

[193]Rand Corporation, *Alcoholism and Treatment* (Washington, D.C.: U.S. Public Health Service, Government Printing Office, 1976). See also in this regard Frank R. Funderbunk and Richard P. Allen, "Alcoholic's Disposition To Drink: Effects of Abstinence and Heavy Drinking," *Journal of Studies on Alcohol,* 38 (1977), 410–425.

Denzin, Norman K. "Notes on the Criminogenic Hypothesis: A Case Study of the American Liquor Industry." *American Sociological Review,* 42 (1977), 905–921.

Gellman, Irving Peter. *The Sober Alcoholic.* New Haven, Conn.: College and University Press, 1964.

Keller, Mark. "Problems of Epidemiology in Alcohol Studies," *Journal of Studies on Alcohol,* 36 (1975), 1442–1451.

LeMasters, E. E. *Blue-Collar Aristocrats: Life-Styles in a Working-Class Tavern.* Madison: University of Wisconsin Press, 1975.

MacAndrew, Craig, and Robert B. Edgerton. *Drunken Comportment: A Social Explanation.* Chicago: Aldine, 1969.

Pittman, David J., ed. *Alcoholism.* New York: Harper & Row, 1967.

Pittman, David J., and Charles R. Snyder, eds. *Alcohol, Culture and Drinking Patterns.* New York: Wiley, 1962.

Rand Corporation. *Alcoholism and Treatment.* Washington, D.C.: U.S. Public Health Service, Government Printing Office, 1976.

Room, Robin. "Ambivalence as a Sociological Explanation: The Case of Cultural Explanations of Alcohol Problems," *American Sociological Review,* 41 (1976), 1047–1065.

Snyder, Charles R. *Alcohol and the Jews.* New York: Free Press, 1958. (Reprinted in 1978 by Southern Illinois University Press, Carbondale, Ill.)

Spradley, James P. *You Owe Yourself a Drunk: An Ethnography of Urban Nomads.* Boston: Little, Brown, 1970.

Stivers, Richard. *The Hair of the Dog: Irish Drinking and American Stereotype.* University Park, Pa.: Pennsylvania State University Press, 1976.

Straus, Robert. "Alcoholism and Problem Drinking," in Robert K. Merton and Robert Nisbet, eds., *Contemporary Social Problems,* 4th ed. New York: Harcourt Brace Jovanovich, 1976.

Trice, Harrison M., and Paul M. Roman. *Spirits and Demons at Work: Alcohol and Other Drugs on the Job.* Ithaca, N.Y.: Industrial and Labor Relations Paperback Series, 1972.

Wuthrich, Peter. "Social Problems of Alcoholics," *Journal of Studies on Alcohol,* 38 (1977), 881–890.

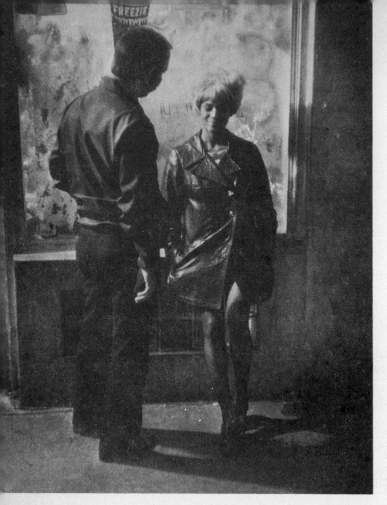

CHAPTER 11

Although prostitution has been approved in certain cultures, generally it has resulted in negative societal reaction. Some persons, particularly many in the Women's Rights Movement, believe that prostitution should be decriminalized and left to a woman's own choice. (Al Kaplan/DPI)

Heterosexual Deviance

PROBABLY more than any other form of human behavior, the sex act has in all societies been surrounded by all types of formalities and restrictions. This situation may well epitomize the famous remark that while man was born free everywhere, everywhere he is found in chains—in his culture and in his society, and his state having "enchained" his most basic desires. Throughout the history of humanity the sex act has constituted a natural part of human existence; in addition to its fundamental purpose of procreation, it is one of the most pleasurable sensations of all human experience. Sexual deviance, therefore, presents particularly difficult problems for definition and analysis. The recognized need of sexual behavior, according to Gagnon, makes the problem of establishing "cutoff points"—beyond which the interaction of persons, their acts, and the context of their behavior may be defined as being deviant—"even more obscure than it is in other areas of behavior."[1] While negative sanctions are frequently expressed for the vast majority of sexually deviant acts, only sporadically are they enforced by formal means such as the law.

SEXUAL NORMS

Sexual norms differ from other norms only by virtue of what they regulate; in other respects, they are the same. Sexual norms are learned from others by symbolic communication, direct interaction, and example; they elicit conformity through a complex system of rewards and punishments, and they specify what *ought* to take place in given situations. Like other forms of human activity, sexual behavior must be learned. Because the sexual drive is not essential for the individual's survival (like the alleviation of hunger and thirst), sexual taboos are not more stringent and absolute than food taboos, for example. Moreover, since sexuality can be stimulated by a variety of situational, visual, olfactory, and emotional conditions, there is an amazing variety of sexual behaviors to be regulated.[2] The problem is compounded when one considers that sexual intercourse is necessary for procreation (at least, until test-tube babies are feasible), and sexual norms, such as those concerning sexuality in the marriage relationship, have arisen to guarantee this necessary process for societal regeneration. But sexual gratification by any means is not the human preference; there is also the desire for intimate physical contact and communication, which places sexual activity outside, as well as inside, the marriage relationship. Like other relatively scarce conditions, sexual gratification, then, is not confined solely to those areas prescribed by sexual norms.

DEVIATING FROM SEXUAL NORMS

Sex deviations involve many different types of behavior, some of which are proscribed by law and some of which are negatively reacted to in other ways. They have in

---

[1]John H. Gagnon, "Sexual Deviation: Social Aspects," *International Encyclopedia of the Social Sciences* (New York: Crowell-Collier and Macmillan, 1968), Vol. 14, p. 216.
[2]Kingsley Davis, "Sexual Behavior," in Robert K. Merton and Robert Nisbet, eds., *Contemporary Social Problems,* 4th ed. (New York: Harcourt Brace Jovanovich, 1976), pp. 223–224.

common the fact that they may violate the formal norms of certain groups or legal codes, or both. Many of the offenses do little harm to other individuals and, in fact, the "victim" may have been a willing participant. If one is to ascertain what is sexually normal or deviant behavior in any given society one should look at it from the point of view of societal reaction to the behavior. Actually the term "sex deviant," however, is misleading; sex is but one and often a minor aspect of a person's total life. Although there are variations in different societies, most sex deviations and laws that control them involve these relations: the degree of consent to the act, such as forcible rape; the nature of the object, that is, restricting legitimate sex objects to human beings of the opposite sex, of a certain age, of a defined distance in kinship, and to the spouse; the nature of the sexual act to certain behavior in heterosexual intercourse; and, finally, the setting in which the sex act occurs.[3] What constitutes sexual deviance, of course, may be proscribed in legal codes, but this does not mean that various groups in a society necessarily consider the sexual acts deviant.

Innumerable written and unwritten prohibitions exist for the sex act, but these prohibitions are not uniform for societies or within them. They are forced sex relations (forcible rape); sex relations with members of one's own sex, through sodomy, fellatio, and mutual masturbation; sex relations with a member of one's own family (incest); sexual intercourse with a person under a certain age (statutory rape); sexual molestation of a child; adultery; sex relations between unmarried adults; co-marital sex relations between two or more married couples; abortion because of an unwanted pregnancy; deliberate exposure of one's sex organs (exhibitionism); watching persons who are undressed or in the act of sexual intercourse (voyeurism); and sexual intercourse with an animal (bestiality). There are also prohibitions on the display of the naked human body, presumably because this exposure involves display of the genital organs or women's breasts. The sale of pornographic and what is called indecent and obscene material is also often prohibited. Some of these acts are regarded more seriously in some societies than in others. Although all societies have some formal and informal controls over sexual behavior, there is a great diversity in emphasis in both the kinds of behavior controlled and the circumstances under which controls are imposed.[4] The Anglo-American criminal law of the seventeenth century did not include large areas of sexual behavior which are now considered to be crimes. In modern societies groups regard these acts in different ways; to some they are deviant and to others they are not.

It may be said that a sexual deviation is an act contrary to the sexual mores of the society in which it occurs. This has a number of limitations, however. Even here it is difficult to draw a line, for some acts are only slightly at variance with the mores. Moreover, sexual mores vary widely, for the society or culture in the United States, for example, consists of many subcultures, such as social and other class groups, with

---

[3]Stanton Wheeler, "Sex Offenses: A Sociological Critique," *Law and Contemporary Problems,* 25 (1960), 258–259. Also see Morris Ploscowe, "Sex Offenses: The American Legal Context," in *Law and Contemporary Problems,* 25 (1960), 217–225; and Morris Ploscowe, *Sex and the Law* (Englewood Cliffs, N.J.: Prentice-Hall, 1951).
[4]See Clellan S. Ford and Frank A. Beach, *Patterns of Sexual Behavior* (New York: Harper & Row, 1951), p. 130.

somewhat distinctive sexual norms. What is an accepted act with sexual connotations in one subcultural context may become a serious breach of law in another, as the following three situations illustrate.

1. A truck driver in a roadside cafe seats himself in a booth, gives the waitress his order, and, as she turns to depart, pats her on the buttocks. The other drivers who witness this are not offended, nor is the waitress, who is either inured to such behavior or interprets it as a slightly flattering pleasantry.

2. The same behavior occurs in a middle-class restaurant. The waitress feels that an indignity has been committed upon her person, and many of the waitresses consider it an offensive display of bad manners. The offender is reprimanded and asked to leave.

3. A man bestows the same pat upon an attractive but unknown woman on a city street. She summons a nearby policeman, some indignant witnesses gather to voice their versions of the offense, and the man is ultimately charged with a sexually motivated assault.[5]

Sexual deviance can be divided also into broader types according to the social dimensions of the activity into acts involving "normal deviance," "pathological deviance," and deviance that generates a specific form of social structure. Gagnon and Simon have analyzed these types of deviance in three groups, the first of which involves generally disapproved acts but those which serve socially useful purposes or which so often occur among a population and with such a low "social visibility" that only a small number of the participants in the behavior are actually sanctioned for it. Such behavior includes masturbation, premarital coitus, and heterosexual mouth-genital contact; all are acts engaged in by large numbers of people. "This type would correspond to the . . . pattern of relations between law, mores, and behavior, or what has been called 'normal deviance.'"[6] Second, certain sexual deviance corresponds to the general case where high correlations exist among law, mores, and behavior. One might call this type of deviance, which includes incest, exhibitionism, voyeurism, sexual contact with children, and aggressive or assaultive offenses, "pathological deviance." While the first type involves large numbers of persons, the latter involves few. Yet they resemble each other in that "pathological deviance does exist without supportive group structures that serve to recruit to the behavior, train participants in it, gather partners together for its performance, or provide social support for the actor."[7] The third type "involves precisely those kinds of behavior that generate specific forms of social structure. Clearly, among those to be included in this type of deviance are female prostitution and both male and female homosexuality."[8]

The examination of research on sex offenders increasingly reveals evidence of the effect of the cultural and social structure on individual deviation from sexual norms. Patterns of cultural learning seem to account for a great deal of sexual behavior that, to many persons, is a product of individual morals or some unique "personality disturbance." Some striking variations exist today in the norms of sex conduct,

[5]Paul H. Gebhard, John H. Gagnon, Wardell B. Pomeroy, and Cornelia V. Christenson, *Sex Offenders* (New York: Harper & Row, 1965), p. 2.
[6]John H. Gagnon and William Simon, *Sexual Deviance* (New York: Harper & Row, 1967), p. 8.
[7]Gagnon and Simon, *Sexual Deviance,* p. 9.
[8]Gagnon and Simon, *Sexual Deviance,* p. 9.

according to education, social class, race, religion, and region.[9] One study reported that when some southern rural families move north into more urban, middle-class areas, certain types of sexual behavior that previously had received little attention in the old permissive environment are looked upon as sex offenses.[10] Ethnic differences in rates of specific sex offenses show the effect of subcultural variables. Sutherland has referred to cultural influences in the etiology of sex offenses, pointing out that practically all of the present sex crimes have been approved behavior for adults in some society or other. "Similarly within our society deviant cultures with references to sex behavior prevail in sub-groups. The manner in which juveniles are inducted into the cultures of these sub-groups in the toilets of schools, playgrounds, and dormitories, as well as in other places, has been shown in many research reports on juvenile sex behavior."[11]

SOCIAL CHANGE AND SEXUAL BEHAVIOR

During the past three decades there has been a vast shift in U.S. society, as well as in some European societies, in both the importance of, and the interest in, sex as one of the dominant values in society. Gagnon and Simon have emphasized the significance of this evolutionary process, stating that few other topics occupy so much of the leisure time of the waking life, or even perhaps of the dreaming life, of large portions of society, either directly or indirectly. "Entire industries spend much of their time trying to organize presentations around sexual themes or try to hook products onto a potential sexual moment or success. That there has been a radical shift in the quantity and quality of sexual presentations in the society cannot be denied."[12]

Increasingly there is greater freedom in the mass media, and, in particular, the motion picture industry, in free discussions of sex and in the presentation of explicit sexual themes. The theme of homosexuality, for example, is being presented in an increasing number of plays, novels, and motion pictures. Previous bans on forms of sex prohibitions, such as those on premarital sex relations and homosexual behavior, are rapidly declining, and the naked body, with genitalia and pubic hair shown, even in color, is appearing in various forms of mass media. In addition, new forms of sexual relations are emerging such as co-marital or "group sex."

The increasing importance of the sexual theme, "the erotization of the society's environment," as well as more permissiveness in sex behavior, have encountered enthusiastic positive responses from some groups, strong negative reaction from

---

[9]Alfred C. Kinsey, Wardell B. Pomeroy, and Clyde E. Martin, *Sexual Behavior in the Human Male* (Philadelphia: Saunders, 1948); and Alfred C. Kinsey, Wardell B. Pomeroy, Clyde E. Martin, and Paul H. Gebhard, *Sexual Behavior in the Human Female* (Philadelphia: Saunders, 1953).

[10]*Report of the Governor's Study Commission on the Deviated Sex Offender* (Lansing: State of Michigan Printing Office, 1951), p. 31.

[11]Edwin H. Sutherland, "The Sexual Psychopath Laws," *Journal of Criminal Law and Criminology,* 40 (1950), 549.

[12]John H. Gagnon and William Simon, "Perspectives on the Sexual Scene," in John H. Gagnon and William Simon, eds., *The Sexual Scene* (Chicago: Aldine, 1970), p. 1.

others, and ambivalence from still others, as Gagnon and Simon view the situation. Those who are "joyous" believe that we now have "a rare opportunity" for the individual to grow and to mature as his sexual potential is "unleashed." Those who despair view the increased significance and importance of sex as a "portent of a disintegrating social order." "The vast majority in the society who do not have much of an ideological commitment one way or another on the sexual question are made uneasy by what they think is going on. There is general agreement, however, that there is profound change occurring and that this change will be of major consequence to the society."[13]

Many factors account for this change in the contemporary sexual scene. The growth of secularism and the decline of religion have caused both men and women to depart from traditional and authoritarian religious views about sex, most of which, including laws regulating many aspects of sex, have their origins in the Judeo-Christian religious traditions. The exceptionally strict, puritanical, and traditional sex views, which often encourage censorship of things sexual, are in sharp contrast to the desire to become more individualized and expressive in one's personal and private life. The growth of means of mass communication and education have also made it increasingly difficult for "traditional-conservative views of any type, including sexual views, to flourish unchallenged, unopposed, and unalloyed."[14] Another factor is that of the capitalist enterprise system wherein sex is viewed as "another commodity which can be profitably sold for public consumption and which therefore encourages highly salacious presentations in those media which are hospitable to them."[15] Still other factors include the increasing demand for equality by women (the women's movement); the shift in sex gender roles and performance, even in such matters as hair style, dress, and the use of cosmetics by heterosexual men; the wider recognition of the importance and necessity for women to experience orgasm; the introduction and wide use of contraceptive devices, which offer ever more security from unwanted pregnancies; and the greater tolerance by the young of variations and deviance in behavior. Still a further factor contributing to a much more relaxed sexual atmosphere has been an erosion of rigid gender differences. Gagnon and Simon point out that unisex clothing, hair styles, and nonsexual coeducational living arrangements are all outgrowths of a more permissive "early experience and the effects of increasing affluence and role flexibility."[16] As this role flexibility has increased a certain "casualness" about sexual matters has come about, making them more acceptable topics of conversation, interest, and participation.

All of these changes, and the erotic presentation of the mass media, have caused great conflict between the young and the old over sexual patterns, the older more likely to preach than to practice their beliefs, as can be seen in the subsequent discussion of pornography. Gagnon and Simon have stated that the older people,

---

[13]Gagnon and Simon, "Perspectives on the Sexual Scene," p. 3.
[14]Albert Ellis, "The Ambiguity of Contemporary Sex Attitudes," in Edward Sagarin and Donal E. J. MacNamara, eds., *Problems of Sex Behavior* (New York: Crowell, 1968), p. 18.
[15]Ellis, p. 18.
[16]John H. Gagnon and William Simon, *Sexual Conduct: The Social Sources of Human Sexuality* (Chicago: Aldine, 1973), p. 291.

who are most "invested with the theory of the power of the sexual drive and the perniciousness of pornography," are also inclined to believe "the more exotic descriptions of the sexual presented in the media." On the other hand, younger persons, "with their ahistorical arrogance, are more likely to find the current sexual landscape unexceptional and notice the repressive past only through the anxieties and incompletions of their parents."[17]

These changes point to what one observer has termed the "normalization of behavior" that had previously been frowned upon.[18]

> In 1963, Ralph Ginsburg was fined $42,000 and sentenced to five years in prison for publishing the magazine *Eros,* which a federal judge had found to be obscene. In 1976, Ginsburg found some copies of the magazine in a warehouse and donated all of them to the American Civil Liberties Union, which announced its intention to sell them at public auction. In 13 years what was once obscene had become tame; what had been deviant was now accepted.[19]

NUDITY

The human body is a part of everyone's normal experiences, devoid of normative judgments. From childhood everyone is accustomed to seeing his own body; occasionally he sees other human bodies, including those of the opposite sex. Yet the right to display one's naked human body, completely devoid of any clothing and with no sexual purpose, is negatively sanctioned by law ("lewd conduct") as well as by large numbers of persons in Western societies. While Western societies generally have placed tremendous emphasis on covering the human body in the presence of others, particularly members of the opposite sex, changes have been rapidly occurring toward nudity.

A significant legal case of this type developed in 1970 in Cambridge, Massachusetts, where five young adults who lived in a single rented house took naked sunbaths together on their own porch. One of the participants described what happened: "Some of the younger neighbors, catching wind of this irregularity next door, snatched the opportunity to test the values of their conventional parents by raising a great commotion when we became visible. This was what they had learned; that the naked body is shameful, that it must be covered in certain particulars in certain ways in certain places."[20] Two of the persons were arrested and charged with "open and gross lewdness and lascivious behavior." After court proceedings lasting nine months they were acquitted of the charge, but, as one participant wrote, "the *lewd* affair, in its modest origins, was a prototypical confrontation of American liberal theory and American illiberal fact, a confrontation of religious and secular mythologies, a conflict

---

[17]Gagnon and Simon, "Perspectives on the Sexual Scene," p. 9.
[18]Charles Winick, "From Deviant to Normative: Changes in the Social Acceptability of Sexually Explicit Material," in Edward Sagarin, ed., *Deviance and Social Change* (Beverly Hills, Calif.: Sage Publications, 1977), pp. 219–246.
[19]Winick, p. 219.
[20]*Lewd: The Inquisition of Seth and Carolyn* (Boston: Beacon Press, 1972), p. 3.

of democratic vs. authoritarian traditions, a tediously personal yet profoundly universal recapitulation of the struggle of awareness for open expression."[21]

In order to be free to be nude, considerable numbers of persons of both sexes, in
the United States and in Europe, have become associated with nudist colonies or
camps. One researcher on such camps views nudism as a deviant phenomenon, and
in 1964, before the growth of "hippie" nudism, he wrote that nudism is not accepted
in our culture, nudist camps being required to be located in an isolated area.

> Nudist values and practices, then, cannot be interpreted merely as a variation of
> American values; they are deviant. Outside of social nudism, every group in present-day
> American life enforces the inter-sex body taboo. With the exception of the marriage
> relationship, in American culture men and women simply are not allowed to associate
> together while in the nude.[22]

Yet the nudist does not view this behavior as being an immodest display of the body or
bodily functions. The ideology of the subculture of a nudist camp is a means of
providing a new definition of nudity, which, in effect, maintains that:

1. Nudism and sexuality are unrelated.
2. There is nothing shameful about exposing the human body.
3. The abandonment of clothes can lead to a feeling of freedom and natural pleasure.
4. Nude activities, especially full bodily exposure to the sun, lead to a feeling of physical,
   mental and spiritual well-being.[23]

Attitudes toward public nudity are such that charges are made, and people are
sometimes willing to pay high fees, for the privilege of seeing the public display of
women's bodies and, occasionally, the nude male body. It was estimated that in the
United States in 1967, about 7,000 women earned their living by removing their
clothing before paying audiences,[24] and this number has undoubtedly greatly
increased in the decade since then. This type of activity includes striptease dancing in
nightclubs and "go-go" establishments, working in massage parlors, and acting as
waitresses or bar girls in topless and bottomless bars and restaurants.[25] In many large
cities this behavior has been institutionalized in the form of burlesque shows for many
years, and those situations in which it may be proper to display the body have become
rapidly more liberalized during the past decade. In spite of such liberalization and the
changes toward nudity, the occupation of "stripping" has remained deviant or, at
best, a marginal occupation, according to Skipper and McCaghy.[26] Not only does the

---

[21]*Lewd,* p. 1.

[22]Fred Ilfeld, Jr., and Roger Lauer, *Social Nudism in America* (New Haven, Conn.: College and University Press, 1964), p. 195.

[23]Martin S. Weinberg, "Sexual Modesty and the Nudist Camp," in Earl Rubington and Martin S. Weinberg, eds., *Deviance: The Interactionist Perspective* (New York: Macmillan, 1968), p. 274. Also see Martin S. Weinberg, "Sexual Modesty, Social Meanings and the Nudist Camp," in Jack D. Douglas, ed., *Observations of Deviance* (New York: Random House, 1970), pp. 28–35.

[24]Libby Jones, *Striptease* (New York: Simon & Schuster, 1967).

[25]Richard G. Ames, Stephen W. Brown, and Norman L. Weinberg, "Breakfast with Topless Barmaids," in Douglas, pp. 35–54.

[26]James K. Skipper, Jr., and Charles H. McCaghy, "Stripteasers: The Anatomy and Career Contingencies of a Deviant Occupation," *Social Problems,* 17 (1970), 391–405.

general public consider it a low-status occupation, but they even regard it as a promiscuous one. In addition, almost *every* girl in their sample believed that it was "dirty" and "immoral." In turn, this belief has had its effect upon their behavior in public, many of the strippers not wishing to identify their work to outsiders. They prefer to call themselves dancers or entertainers, thus staying clear of a "pariah label."

PREMARITAL, EXTRAMARITAL, AND CO-MARITAL (SWINGING) SEX

Premarital sexual relations represent one area in which rapid changes have been occurring in the sexual norms. Not long ago such behavior would have carried with it relatively severe sanctions, primarily from one's own family and others. Today, however, premarital sex connotes deviance to a far less extent, not only among the more permissive members of society but also among the traditional, conservative segments.[27] Nonmarital cohabitation has become more and more "institutionalized" in U.S. society, not only among large segments of the young but among the middle-aged and the elderly. It remains unclear as to whether the incidence of premarital sex and cohabitation has actually increased or if the flouting of older sexual norms has merely become more open. One study obtained information from a sample of 2,510 young men concerning their experience with cohabitation.[28] Eighteen percent of the respondents had lived with a woman for six months or more without being married to her, but at the time of the interview only 5 percent were cohabiting. There was a sizable ethnic difference, with 29 percent of the blacks and 16 percent of the whites having cohabited for at least six months. It has now become increasingly clear that the norms governing such previously valued states as "virginity," sexual naivete, and noncohabitation without marriage are considered more and more acceptable and less and less likely to incur negative sanctions.

A Census Bureau report has estimated that almost one million unmarried couples were living together in 1977, an increase of 83 percent over the number in 1970.[29] This increase does not include the number of same-sex unrelated persons, including many homosexuals, which was estimated at 746,000 in 1977.

Less than two decades ago Reiss argued that premarital sex was deviant because it was viewed negatively by many persons who regarded it as going beyond the tolerance limit.[30] In a national sample of adults in 1967 he found that premarital sex

---

[27]Edward Sagarin, "Sex Deviance: A View from Middle America," in Edward Sagarin and Fred Montanino, eds., *Deviants: Voluntary Actors in a Hostile World* (Morristown, N.J.: General Learning Press, 1977), p. 437. See also John Gagnon, *Human Sexuality: An Age of Ambiguity* (Boston: Little, Brown, 1975); Arno Karlen, *Sexuality and Homosexuality: A New View* (New York: Norton, 1971); John Money and Patricia Tucker, *Sexual Signatures: On Being a Man or a Woman* (Boston: Little, Brown, 1975); and Paul Robinson, *The Modernization of Sex* (New York: Harper & Row, 1976).
[28]Richard R. Clayton and Harwin L. Voss, "Shacking Up: Cohabitation in the 1970s," *Journal of Marriage and the Family,* 39 (1977), 273–283.
[29]As reported in the *Los Angeles Times,* October 20, 1977, Part 1, p. 22.
[30]Ira L. Reiss, "Premarital Sex as Deviant Behavior: An Application of Current Approaches to Deviance," *American Sociological Review,* 35 (1970), 78–88.

was viewed as a norm violation by 77 percent of the sample, many of these adults expressing strong opinions against it. Those opposed to it felt that it results in unwanted pregnancies and unwanted marriage, guilt feelings, and venereal disease and that it often leads to unstable marriages.[31] Reiss reported that the "ancient double standard and abstinence classifications" had been replaced by "the permissiveness-with-affection standard."[32] Special characteristics of the courtship groups that promote acceptance of premarital sex were "high exposure to temptation via privacy, dancing and drinking, youth culture approval of adventure and hedonism, and approval of youth culture for the importance of affection as a basis for sexual relationships."[33]

A recent review of the literature, as well as a reformulation of the major hypotheses, on the social context of premarital sexual relations concludes that premarital sex occurs not merely as a function of the individual decision to engage in it; rather, it occurs as a function of one's position in the social structure (social class), the nature of participation in religious institutions in society, group membership patterns, and prior socialization experiences with the development of permissive attitudes toward premarital sexual behavior.[34] The authors present six propositions concerning the relationship between sexual permissiveness and social variables among females:

1. Females who perceive norms of sexual permissiveness in their peer group are more likely to engage in premarital sexual intercourse than females who do not perceive norms of sexual permissiveness in their peer group.

2. Females who are more permissive in their personal attitudes are more likely to engage in premarital sexual intercourse than females who are less permissive in their personal attitudes.

3. Females involved in an affectional relationship are more likely to engage in premarital sexual intercourse than females not involved in an affectional relationship.

4. There is a negative relationship between social class and participation in premarital sexual intercourse among females.

5. There is a negative relationship between religious orthodoxy and participation in premarital sexual intercourse among females.

6. There is a positive relationship between later maturation and having had premarital sexual relations among females.[35]

While there has been an ever-widening extension of the intimate sexual relationships to include cohabitation, a somewhat uneasy balance exists between the traditional or older ways and the innovative or newer ways of living together. In other words, the "sexual revolution" is not completely novel, as is the case in most social revolutions. Certain aspects of traditionalism still exist in the living-together-although-not-married situation.[36] One quite recent study of the division of labor among

---

[31]Ira L. Reiss, *The Social Context of Premarital Sexual Permissiveness* (New York: Holt, Rinehart and Winston, 1967).

[32]Reiss, *The Social Context of Premarital Sexual Permissiveness,* p. 176.

[33]Reiss, "Premarital Sex as Deviant Behavior," p. 83.

[34]J. Kenneth Davidson and Gerald R. Leslie, "Premarital Sexual Intercourse: An Application of Axiomative Theory Construction," *Journal of Marriage and the Family,* 39 (1977), 15–25.

[35]Davidson and Leslie, pp. 22–23.

[36]See Laura F. Henze and John W. Hudson, "Personal and Family Characteristics of Non-Cohabiting and Cohabiting College Students," *Journal of Marriage and the Family,* 36 (1975), 722–728; and Nancy Clatworthy, "Couples in Quasi-Marriage," in Nona Glazer-Malbin, ed., *Old Family/New Family: Interpersonal Relationships* (Princeton, N.J.: Van Nostrand, 1975), pp. 67–90.

cohabiting and married couples found that the women of both groups still were taking the major responsibility for, and performing most of, the routine household tasks, although married couples are significantly more traditional in their performance of these tasks than those who were cohabiting.[37] It is likely that it will be some time before older patterns of the division of labor in these relationships are overthrown, since the institutionalization of new norms that govern the behavior of the sexes in intimate relationships does not occur rapidly. The persistence of the more traditional division of labor among cohabiting couples appears not to be related to a power struggle between the man and the woman, or to the differential availability of time, since the male is more likely to be absent from the household for longer periods than is the female. There is, rather, an implicit ideology developed from parental modeling that preserves these more traditional roles. Even in the newer forms of sexual behavior and sexual contexts, therefore, elements of conventional norms and ties persist.

Co-Marital Sex

During the late 1950s and early 1960s a new form of nontraditional sexual relationship between individual married couples emerged, involving exchanges of partners among two or more couples and sometimes single persons in a threesome. A number of terms describe this behavior: "co-marital sex," "group sex," "swinging," "mate" or "wife swapping." It has been estimated that between several hundred thousand and several million couples in the United States engage in this type of sexual behavior and that the numbers are increasing. As of 1978, no reliable information had been presented as to its incidence, and it is quite possible that the numbers are exaggerated. It had been estimated by Kinsey in 1948, however, that 50 percent of husbands and 28 percent of wives engaged in extramarital sex by age 45, figures updated 20 years later by Gebhard, who estimated that 60 percent of husbands and 40 percent of wives engaged in extramarital sex by age 35.[38] It may thus be reasonably assumed that "probably not more than half of all marriages are monogamous," and many persons even base their extramarital sexual relationships "on the premise that intimate relationships outside the primary relationship are acceptable, or even desirable, attributes of the primary relationship."[39]

A sexually open relationship, in which partners agree to retain sexual freedom on an individual basis, can occur in a marriage or in any other type of primary relationship, such as a living-together arrangement involving two singles. Such an agreement is most often encountered in situations in which the couple is striving toward mutual personal growth

---

[37]Rebecca Stafford, Elaine Backman, and Pamela Dibona, "The Division of Labor among Cohabiting and Married Couples," *Journal of Marriage and the Family,* 38 (1977), 43–57.

[38]Kinsey *et al., Sexual Behavior in the Human Male;* Kinsey *et al., Sexual Behavior in the Human Female;* and Gebhard *et al.*

[39]James W. Ramey, "Alternative Life-Styles," *Society,* 14 (July/August 1977), 43. Also see Bernard I. Murstein, *Current and Future Intimate Lifestyles* (New York: Springer Publishing, 1977); James W. Ramey, *Intimate Friendships* (Englewood Cliffs, N.J.: Prentice-Hall, 1976); James R. Smith and Lynn G. Smith, *Beyond Monogamy: Recent Studies of Sexual Alternatives in Marriage* (Baltimore, Md.: Johns Hopkins Press, 1974); and Marvin B. Sussman, ed., *Variant Family Forms and Life Styles* (Minneapolis, Minn.: National Council on Family Relations, 1976).

and self-actualization within an egalitarian relationship. Such a relationship has been characterized as a "peer bond." The outside or secondary relationships are expected to involve lesser degrees of social, emotional, intellectual, family, career, and sexual intimacy than the primary relationship, but the mixture of these various types of intimacy will vary between secondary relationships. This situation is in marked contrast to "swinging," in which couples practice mate swapping but only in situations in which both mates are present and usually with distinct prohibitions against any kind of nonsexual intimacy.[40]

The distinctive feature of co-marital sex, or "swinging," is a behavior pattern involving agreement between husband and wife each to engage in sex relations with others at the same time and approximately at the same place. These relations, moreover, are to be conducted within an organized, institutionalized pattern; strenuous efforts are made to keep sex impersonal and free from all emotional attachments or jealousies. Sex is to be engaged in primarily for sheer enjoyment of the pleasurable act. Where sexual activities do take place, they are to be engaged in, to a greater or lesser extent, under the surveillance of each partner. In this way some control is exercised over the extramarital activity of the other partner, thus minimizing the possibility that the activity will take a romantic turn.[41] This disengagement from a jealousy-provoking relationship is, of course, the ideal picture that most swingers expect; in actuality, jealousies do develop and may even endanger the marriage.[42] Some couples do develop emotional involvement and long-term friendships within a swinging context.

Generally knowledge that persons are swinging is kept away from nonswingers because of the danger of social sanctions, but there is little fear of the police because the activity is not carried out in public, and it is usually restricted to private homes. "Fear of the police is not prevalent unless a party becomes very loud. A few people joke about being raided, but this is not based on substantial worry."[43]

Most swingers are white, they live in suburbia, and studies have shown that they are of the middle class, well educated, and largely politically conservative.[44] Both partners have had limited premarital sex experience, have tended to marry early, and have had few outside interests except those built around their marriage and home. As one couple described it, they did not fight, "because there was nothing to fight about. We just felt the inevitability of being together for the rest of our lives—something like brother and sister without the blood."[45] In such situations many couples claim to have found renewed interest in their own marital sex as a result of experiences with other couples. Some also claim that the common planning and preparation for co-marital

[40]Ramey, "Alternative Life-Styles," p. 44.
[41]Ronald M. Holmes, "Interview with Diane," in Ronald M. Holmes, *Sexual Behavior: Prostitution, Homosexuality, and Swinging* (Berkeley, Calif.: McCutchan, 1971), pp. 155–156. Also see Mary Lindenstein Walshok, "The Emergence of Middle-Class Deviant Subcultures: The Case of Swingers," *Social Problems,* 18 (1971), 488–495.
[42]Charles and Rebecca Palson, "Swinging in Wedlock," *Society,* 9 (1972), 28–37.
[43]Gilbert D. Bartell, *Group Sex* (New York: Peter H. Wyden, 1971), p. 183.
[44]Gilbert D. Bartell, "Group Sex among the Mid-Americans," *Journal of Sex Research,* 6 (1970), 113–130; and James R. Smith and Lynn G. Smith, "Co-Marital Sex and the Sexual Freedom Movement," *Journal of Sex Research,* 6 (1970), 131–142.
[45]Palson and Palson, p. 31.

sex relations and conversations afterward provide an exciting new common bond to marriage.

Becoming Involved

Persons willing to exchange marital partners are usually recruited through four methods: (1) advertisements in swinger publications, which is particularly useful for nonmetropolitan residents, (2) bars or clubs in metropolitan areas that are exclusively set up for swingers, (3) personal references from swinging couples, and (4) personal recruitment, including "seduction" of nonswingers. The most common method is the use of an anonymous advertisement in one of the national swinger newspapers, estimated in 1970 to number about 50. These ads describe location, age, physical assets, cultural and other interests, and certain preferences of a married couple and, particularly, of single men and women who may be interested in trial swinging. In many cases photographs are published with the ads. Typical ads read as follows:

> Attractive couple in late 30's. She 5'7", 145, 38-28-38. He 6', 180. Would like to hear from similar couples in Chicago area. Object: conversation, cocktails, and beginning of swinging interests. Photo of both a must.

> Discreet couple, late 40's desire to meet discreet, kind, broadminded couples of any age for fun and pleasure. Discretion an absolute must. Our first ad.

> Discreet, attractive couple 21 and 25 wish to meet couples and singles 21–35 for exciting and fun-loving adult relationships. Open-minded but not way out. No prejudices. Full length photo, address, and detailed letter assures same.[46]

These ads are not confined solely to sexually explicit publications nor to newsletters devoted exclusively to them; they appear regularly in "respectable" and otherwise intellectual publications, including *The New York Review of Books*. While the methods of introducing prospective partners to one another may change (*The New York Review* ads emphasize how cultured and educated the applicant should be), the desires do not; *The New York Review* ad writers may be more literate but no less "lustful." Answers are made to the newspaper, using the code numbers in the advertisement, furnishing details of the couple's qualifications, such as age and physical characteristics, and usually presenting their tastes, as in the case of the 50-year-old businessman and his wife:

> How stimulating it is to communicate with someone so obviously articulate, intellectual, and cosmopolitan. How gratifying to reach someone with reserve and discernment. We find you both most appealing. Would but that you could also find us attractive.
>
> Your taste for aesthetic does not parallel ours, but is not so divergent as to preclude understanding and perhaps rapport. Our preferences in the arts are nondifferentiated. With few exceptions, we enjoy all art and music forms. Our social activities are confined pretty much to bridge, the dinner party, dancing, and occasionally the theater.
>
> More importantly, however, we are interested in establishing (a) sexual liaison with another couple. We are interested, not in any metaphysical approach to gratification, but

---

[46]Bartell, *Group Sex.* Copyright © 1971 by Gilbert Bartell. Reprinted by permission of the David McKay Company, Inc.

in the physical components of the heterosexual sex act. We like coitus and mouth-genital contacts, but will entertain any nonpainful suggestion you care to make. We definitely do not enjoy receiving or administering corporal punishment; neither are we homosexual, nor do we use opiates, hallucinogens, or alcohol to excess. We do not wish to compete, impress, or instruct—we wish only to enjoy.

Please believe that we are ardent, willing, committed and technically competent.[47]

Swinger clubs and often bars are operated by persons interested in securing the business and encouraging swinging. Generally found in large cities, they become known to many swingers as places to go to become acquainted. This is the case also with most private clubs, most of whose ads sound little different from many others with common interests except that they appear in newspapers for swingers. After initial contacts through clubs and bars, or through ads, references from other couples are not difficult. Because of the group aspect of these sexual contacts, a few can create others. Seduction of another couple to the swinging life appears not to be common because of the possible severe negative response that may ensue.

Swinging may be done in private, closed swinging, or openly, involving as many couples as are present at any given time. Some may engage in sex relations in various combinations while others watch. Ordinary sex relations are indulged in as well as fellatio by the women and cunnilingus involving both men and women. Overtures are customarily made by the man, but no attempt is made either by the male or the female to force attention on anyone. In general, the following steps are common.

> At large parties, as on other swinging occasions, the man usually makes the first approach for swinging. Overtures are usually fairly casual and appear cool to the observer. He approaches the female, engages her in conversation, then perhaps holds her hand, puts his arm around her, places his hand on her thigh, and/or kisses her lightly. Any action is avoided that would bring a reaction of jealousy from a mate. A man then may say, "Let's swing," or "Let's go check on what's happening in the bedroom."
>
> In the meantime, the female indicates by her smile, tone of voice, conversation, and general friendliness whether she is receptive to his advances. The female may decide that she does not want to swing at that particular time or with this particular male. In that case she would be aloof, move away from him, not meet his eyes, move to someone else and start a conversation, or generally ignore his advances. The male then moves on to another female and begins again.[48]

The Process of Swinging

The course that swinging may take has been traced in a study of 136 cases.[49] It begins with considerable superficial curiosity and enthusiasm for a new and novel situation and relationship. While some experiment with swinging, others undoubtedly are influenced by the desires of the mate to try it. Much like the process described for initiating marijuana use, the potential swinger may feel that the spouse would like to try something different. The spouse agrees not out of personal curiosity but out of a

---

[47]Bartell, *Group Sex.* Copyright © 1971 by Gilbert Bartell. Reprinted by permission of the David McKay Company, Inc.
[48]Bartell, *Group Sex.* Copyright © 1971 by Gilbert Bartell. Reprinted by permission of the David McKay Company, Inc.
[49]Palson and Palson.

desire to fulfill the other's wishes. Given the traditional value put on sexual variety by the male, it is primarily the husband who initiates the idea, but the wife also finds the experience of being desired by others a pleasurable one. Two women have described their first experiences: "I got turned on, although I hadn't anticipated a thing up to that point. In fact, I still have a hard time accounting for my excitement that first time and the good time which I actually had." And another: "I *never* experienced anything like that in my whole life. I have never had an experience like that with quite so many. I think in the course of three hours I must have had 11 or 12 men, and one greater than the next. It just kept on getting better every time. It snowballed."[50]

This curiosity shortly declines for many, particularly the women, who have largely been raised to reject superficial sexual relations. This stage is followed by a stage of relative selectivity and increasing sexual individuation of self and others. The man has found frustrating difficulties, for example, in having an erection in group situations in which he assumed the presence of nude women would produce it. The woman, on the other hand, finding that she is generally sexually desired, wishes to return to sex relations on a more personal basis where she can choose and select. At this stage various changes begin to take place in marital relations, some being strengthened while others are torn with jealousies growing out of marital context in which these co-marital relations grew. Some try to avoid jealousies by not being so individuated and selective, by engaging only in open swinging to reduce emotional attachment and jealousies, and by the wife's experiencing more emotional attachment with other women than with men, which is more acceptable because it does not threaten the marriage relation. Finally, for various reasons couples may drop out of swinging altogether.

The Functional Aspects of Co-marital Sex

Several explanations for the emergence of this phenomenon, most of them functionally oriented to changes in the society, have been advanced. The changing role definitions of women, including the adoption of the view that sex is an end in itself and that women can enjoy sex as much as men, has a great deal to do with it. Widened sexual relations by married couples would still not have been possible without the present widely available contraceptive techniques, particularly the pill, which allows for spontaneous, unrestricted sex play with one's marital partner or with others.

Others have emphasized the fact that while sexual relations are stressed in U.S. society, they can become routine and boring within a consistently monogamous setting. To engage in extramarital relations, by one or both partners, is not a solution because of the possibility of emotional attachments that might endanger the marriage. Mate swapping is then a functional alternative to marriage. While it involves extramarital sex relations, it is less threatening and more compatible with the norms of a monogamous marital system.[51] It is a social mechanism that relieves sexual monotony in marriage without undermining the marriage itself. Bell states that

---

[50]Palson and Palson, pp. 30 and 35.
[51]Duane Denfield and Michael Gordon, "The Sociology of Mate Swapping: Or the Family That Swings Together Clings Together," *Journal of Sex Research,* 6 (1970), 85–100.

swinging does mean a single standard of sex for both the husband and wife. This single standard of participating sex implies important value changes for the wife and husband who accept it. For the wife it means that she has to separate sex from love, which she has been socialized to believe must go together. And her very ability to make this distinction may be the best indicator of her being able to swing without serious personal problems. For the husband it means that he must undo the socialization process that has conditioned him to believe that a wife is exclusively the sexual property of the husband. Not only are many swinging husbands able to do this, but some are even able to find that seeing their wives in sexual contact with others is a highly erotic experience.[52]

Some people feel this to be an insufficient explanation, primarily because as of the early 1970s swinging was a middle-class phenomenon or deviation, and the explanation must pertain largely to this group. Three components are involved in group sex in these terms. First, it is based on the high personal and social value put on sexuality in the middle class and the desire for personal competence in this area, as well as some sort of fulfillment which is lacking in everyday work and in routine living patterns. Closely related to this component is the prevalent view, particularly among the middle class, that much sex is "work," involving reading sex manuals, "working" to produce female orgasm, and using special techniques and equipment.[53] The "work" element in sex is the result of the need for many Americans to justify and dignify play and to resolve the contradictory values of work for work's sake and pleasure for pleasure's sake.[54] Whereas sex was repressed in the past, there is increasingly a feeling that personal freedom is achieved and that real happiness and self-affirmation are inextricably linked by one's sexual competence. "Only in a society where sex was once seen as the consummate evil could it become construed as a consummate good."[55] Consequently, it is those middle-class individuals, with a more restrictive sexual background, who invest sexuality with excess meaning. "The co-marital subculture provides the opportunity for both women and men from such backgrounds to discover adventure and sexuality while at the same time posing no basic threat to marriage or life style."[56] The third component involved is recently arrived suburban residents, many of whom are also new to the middle class. They wish to retain their status and not seriously to endanger it; they sustain a highly conventional life-style in every respect except sex. "The organized, routinized paths to sexual encounters, be they clubs, ads or cocktail parties, reinforce the impersonal quality of the sex and are consistent with the affectively neutral, segmented, and bureaucratized patterns of interaction to which technological man has become accustomed."[57]

Some evidence has been cited that swinging is related to other forms of sexual deviance in terms of the social processes that precede the swinging experience. One study, for example, found that married women who had engaged in mate swapping had had a higher rate of premarital sex, with more different men and more often with

---

[52]Robert R. Bell, *Social Deviance: A Substantive Analysis* (Homewood, Ill.: Dorsey Press, 1971), p. 78.
[53]Lionel S. Lewis and Dennis Brissett, "Sex as Work: A Study of Avocational Counseling," *Social Problems,* 15 (1967), 8–18.
[54]Lewis and Brissett.
[55]Walshok, p. 492.
[56]Walshok, p. 492.
[57]Walshok, p. 495.

each man, than had women without any mate-swapping experience.[58] The swinging woman also evidenced a higher level of sexual interest as reflected in a greater average monthly frequency of marital intercourse.

PROSTITUTION

Although prostitution is virtually universal, it is generally disapproved in most societies. The extent of prostitution and the reaction to it has fluctuated over many years, but its definition has remained the same. Prostitution is sexual intercourse on a promiscuous and mercenary basis, with emotional indifference. In some countries, as well as in many states of the United States, it is not prostitution that is legally a criminal offense; rather, soliciting is the offense for which a prostitute is punished.[59] The patron pays for this short-term intimacy, but the method of payment often clouds the definition of a true prostitute. "The reason for this lies in the broad gamut of female behavior in our culture containing elements of prostitution."[60] For example, when a customer "dates" a shopgirl for an evening dinner and show and later has sex relations with her, the relation is often on a mercenary, emotionally indifferent basis; yet the woman may not be considered, nor consider herself, a real prostitute. Such a woman may have a family and a job and may not make a practice of exchanging sex relations for an evening's entertainment. There are "semiprostitute" roles involving the commercialization of sex behavior. For example, taverns and bars may have "B-girls" who induce male customers to drink and for their "companionship" receive a return from the management.[61] Selling her sex "may be a part of the role she plays, but both the social and self-regulating attitudes differ in her case from those of a professional prostitute . . . where the ideal of a fair exchange for services rendered governs the relationship of the girl and the customer."[62]

Many women are promiscuous but are not prostitutes, for their sex relations have an element of affection, even if transitory. The prostitute "sells" her sex relations with an element of indifference. Although some prostitutes may be selective on the basis of race, age, economic status, or physical attractiveness of their customers, generally an act of intercourse may be carried out with almost anyone. With many prostitutes the sex act may be purchased in varied physical forms, other than the usual form of heterosexual relations, such as both oral and anal sex acts, as well as sadistic, masochistic, and exhibitionist acts of intercourse. So indifferent are most prostitutes to the emotional aspect of sex relations that they rarely experience an orgasm with a customer, although they frequently do with their "pimp" or male consort.

The very nature of prostitution links it to many of the values of "conventional" society. The general culture stimulates the importance of sexual values in life, and the

---

[58]Robert R. Bell and Dorthyann Peltz, "Extramarital Sex among Women," cited in Robert R. Bell, *Social Deviance: A Substantive Analysis,* rev. ed. (Homewood, Ill.: Dorsey Press, 1976), p. 74.
[59]See J. E. Hall Williams, "Sex Offenses: The British Experience," *Law and Contemporary Problems,* 25 (1960), 334–360.
[60]Edwin M. Lemert, *Social Pathology* (New York: McGraw-Hill, 1951), p. 238.
[61]See Sheri Cavan, "B-Girls and Prostitutes," in Douglas, pp. 55–64.
[62]Lemert, p. 239.

satisfaction of these values or desires may be difficult for many of the unmarried and some of the married. In his analysis of the basic appeal of prostitution, Kingsley Davis argues that the "advantage of prostitution is its impartiality, impersonality, and economy. Attracting and seducing a woman can be costly."[63] Prostitution and the impersonality of the sexual act with a prostitute make it especially attractive to strangers, the man away from his wife or girl friend or the man who has defined certain sexual acts as immoral even in his marriage relationship.[64] Prostitution thus becomes a needed commodity for which there is widespread demand with sometimes limited supply. The earnings of a prostitute may well exceed what the woman might earn legitimately, but Davis has pointed out that these earnings do not represent a "reward" for labor, skill, or capital but rather a reward for "loss of social standing."[65]

Extent

The true prostitute is one who makes her living primarily by selling, for money, sexual intercourse, but it is impossible to ascertain exactly how many women belong to this category. Some prostitutes have part- or full-time legitimate occupations that mask their real jobs as prostitutes. While arrest figures provide some statistical data, they are notoriously poor indicators of the number of prostitutes in the United States. Some prostitutes are arrested only once, others many times each year; when arrested they often are charged under a disorderly conduct or vagrancy statute. Without intimate knowledge of the jurisdiction and the prosecution policies, it is almost impossible to know how many of the persons are charged under these laws for sex violations and how many are charged for something else.

A 1971 study of 2,000 prostitutes estimated that prostitution involves between 100,000 and 500,000 women in the United States and that they gross over $1 billion.[66] With about three $10 "tricks" a day, six days a week, the average prostitute was found to gross about $9,300 per year or net from $5,000 to $6,000. With inflation, which affects the prostitute's prices as well as the price of coffee, this estimated income is even greater today.

In a 1948 study on prostitution it was estimated that prostitution accounted for less than 10 percent of the total nonmarital sexual outlet for males, and the figure is probably much lower now; not more than 1 percent of extramarital sexual intercourse is with prostitutes.[67] Although prostitution is extensive today, it appears to have declined steadily throughout the past four decades, except for periodic increases in wartime. Kinsey, in 1948, stated that the frequency of American male visits to prostitutes had been reduced by about one half of what it was prior to World War I.[68] Some have maintained that this decline has been due to organized drives against

---

[63]Davis, p. 248.

[64]Most patrons of prostitutes are married men. See Kinsey *et al.*, *Sexual Behavior in the Human Male*, p. 288.

[65] Davis, p. 249.

[66]Charles Winick and Paul M. Kinsie, *The Lively Commerce: Prostitution in the United States* (New York: Quadrangle Books, 1971).

[67]Kinsey *et al.*, *Sexual Behavior in the Human Male*, p. 597.

[68]Kinsey *et al.*, *Sexual Behavior in the Human Female*, p. 300.

prostitutes, elimination of "red-light" districts, and educational efforts regarding the control of venereal diseases and prostitution. Others insist, however, that the decrease in prostitution is the result not of these factors but of the increased sexual freedom of women. As young women have less restraint in their sexual relations, it is easier for men to have sex relations without recourse to prostitutes. Even with the decrease in activity, prostitution will probably always be around, for there will continue to be a group of men who are able to secure sexual satisfactions only if they pay for such services.

Societal Reaction

Attitudes toward prostitution have varied historically and today vary in different countries. The attitude toward, and the social status of, the prostitute, as Davis has suggested, varies according to three conditions: (1) if the prostitute practices a certain discrimination in her customers, (2) if the earnings are used for some socially desirable goal, and (3) if the prostitute combines with her sexual role others that are more acceptable.[69] In ancient Greece, for example, brothel prostitutes were given a different status from the hetaerae, who were educated in the arts and were often wealthy, powerful personages with great influence on many important leaders. Although prostitutes, they were generally highly respected. The devadasis, or dancing girls, were connected with the temples of India for centuries; besides singing and dancing, they engaged in temple prostitution. In general, these girls were the only Indian women who had learned to read. Because the devadasi was one of a social group of religious prostitutes attached to the temple, payment was given to the temple, and the act of intercourse was, to some extent, a religious ritual. In Japan special quarters were designated as sites for prostitution in the cities: in Tokyo this was one of the show places of the city. The Japanese courtesans were often prominently displayed in street cages, while in the more "genteel establishments their names and attributes were advertised on the equivalent of a marquee at the entrance."[70] The famous Japanese geishas, trained as they have always been in the arts like music, and in conversation and social entertaining, can be cited as examples of women who could often engage in prostitution yet still have high status in the society. While the geisha of modern times is more likely to be a mistress than a prostitute, some of them are actually prostitutes. There are organizations of geishas, and modern geisha girls still go through indoctrination courses, the training period varying by the class of the geisha house.[71]

Prostitution was widespread during the Middle Ages; it was not regarded as a criminal activity—rather, it was a necessary evil. The demand for it was great from all classes, and it was often not only tolerated but protected, regulated by law, and used as a revenue measure. Even the Catholic Church was involved in the maintenance of some houses of prostitution, particularly in France. With the Protestant Reformation, there was an upsurge of concern for personal morals and a reaction against any type of extramarital relations. There was also great concern for the rapid spread of syphilis,

[69]Davis, p. 245.
[70]See Lemert, p. 253.
[71]For an account of the situation of geishas in Japan in more modern times, see Boye de Mente, *Some Prefer Geisha: The Lively Art of Mistress-Keeping in Japan* (Rutland, Vt.: Charles R. Tuttle, 1966).

brought to Europe from the New World, and since many prostitutes were heavily infected, many statutes were enacted in the fifteenth and sixteenth centuries against prostitution. When prostitution passed from the domain of the ecclesiastical courts to the common law after 1640 in England it was regarded not as a criminal offense but as a public nuisance.

Since ancient times prostitutes have been identified with certain symbols, for example, certain styles of dress and of hair. In ancient Rome prostitutes generally dyed their hair red or yellow, and in some cultures "these appurtenances were guarded and perpetuated by sumptuary laws,"[72] In the late nineteenth and early twentieth centuries in the United States prostitutes were generally housed in red-light districts where they could easily be distinguished from the respectable women of the community "by their flamboyant clothes, abbreviated dresses, bobbed hair, rouged faces and lips, their use of tobacco, liquor, and profanity and generally bold mien in public," and Lemert has pointed out that "much of the behavior and morality" of the prostitute has "made its way upward and has been appropriated by the middle-class woman in her revolt against her traditional role."[73]

Prostitution, particularly soliciting, is strongly disapproved under Anglo-American criminal law.[74] Such stringent attitudes toward prostitution were largely derived from the Protestant Reformation. Even today, many Catholic countries, such as those in Latin America, have a rather tolerant view of it. To the middle class,

> sex was a disruptive factor in the orderly pursuit of business and capital accumulation, and from this conviction there developed the puritanical strictures upon sexual thought and practice which have pervaded middle-class morality of the past. Oddly enough, and this point has frequently been ignored, the sex compulsives of the puritanical middle class have centered around the disapproval of overt and indiscreet sex behavior rather than the fact of sex indulgence outside of marriage or prostitution per se. This is borne out by the fact that many states and communities have had no laws against prostitution itself but, rather, have legislated against such things as disorderly conduct, vagrancy, soliciting, and pandering in conjunction with sex indulgence and prostitution.[75]

Where it is illegal, prostitution represents an effort to control certain private moral behavior by punitive social control. Undoubtedly only a tiny proportion of acts of prostitution are ever apprehended. Where apprehended, prostitution—or, under some laws, the act of solicitation—is generally punished with a fine or with a jail sentence of less than a year. If repeated misdemeanor convictions occur, the prostitute may be convicted of a felony and sentenced to a longer term. Great Britain has provided for a graduated system of fines and jail terms.[76]

Prostitution is opposed on many grounds because (1) it involves a high degree

---

[72]Lemert, p. 253.
[73]Lemert, p. 253.
[74]For an account of attitudes toward prostitution in mid-Victorian England, see William Acton, *Prostitution* (New York: Holt, Rinehart and Winston, 1969; originally written in 1857).
[75]Lemert, pp. 257–258. Copyright © 1951 by McGraw-Hill, Inc. Used with permission of McGraw-Hill Book Company.
[76]*Wolfenden Report,* Report of the Committee on Homosexual Offenses and Prostitution (New York: Lancer Books, 1964).

of promiscuity, particularly with strangers, rather than being the exclusive possession of one man; (2) the prostitute is willing to sell and commercialize her sexual participation with emotional indifference outside of marriage, one participating for pleasure and the other for money; (3) the social effects on the women who engage in the profession are unwholesome; (4) it is a threat to public health in that it facilitates the spread of venereal diseases; (5) it needs police protection in order to operate and thus reduces the quality of general law enforcement; and (6) sexual acts with a prostitute are generally such that there is no possibility of marriage and procreation and for this reason are different from ordinary premarital sex relations. In Great Britain, the *Wolfenden Report* stated rather clearly the reasons for British public attitudes toward prostitution, many of which would also apply in the United States.

> If it were the law's intention to punish prostitution *per se*, on the ground that it is immoral conduct, then it would be right that it should provide for the punishment of the man as well as the woman. But that is not the function of the law. It should confine itself to those activities which offend against public order and decency or expose the ordinary citizen to what is offensive or injurious; and the simple fact is that prostitutes do parade themselves more habitually and openly than their prospective customers, and do by their continual presence, affront the sense of decency of the ordinary citizen. In doing so they create a nuisance which, in our view, the law is entitled to recognize and deal with.[77]

Types of Prostitutes

Prostitutes can generally be classified according to their methods of operation. There are the streetwalkers or common prostitutes operating alone, the inmate of an organized house of prostitution, the call girl, and the high-class independent professional prostitute. More specific types are streetwalkers, bar girls, masseuses working in massage parlors, photographic studio models, women provided by escort services, stag party workers, hotel and convention prostitutes, call girls, and circuit travelers or "road whores" who cater to working-class migrant labor camps.[78] These different types of prostitutes represent an adaptation to the characteristics of the available clientele. Trends in the organization and behavior systems of prostitutes should be interpreted in the light of the sexual requirements of the patrons of a class. "Variations in the patterns of prostitution may be related to the variability of the sociocultural characteristics of the clientele."[79]

The streetwalker procures her trade as best she can. She operates on the streets and in such places as bars and hotel lobbies, taking her customers to a prearranged cheap rooming house or hotel. Sometimes she has no connection with organized crime, but often she must pay for her own protection from arrest; occasionally she is part of a more organized operation. Some prostitution is not strictly organized as such, but is knowingly permitted and even encouraged through legitimate but often shady businesses, especially those in the commercial recreation industry such as burlesque

---

[77] *Wolfenden Report,* pp. 143–144.

[78] For a discussion of these types of prostitutes, see Jennifer James, "Prostitutes and Prostitution," in Sagarin and Montanino, pp. 368–428.

[79] Lemert, p. 245.

shows, night clubs, amusement parks, and the like. Through a variety of techniques some performers in strip tease shows, cabarets, or burlesque shows also recruit patrons for later dates.

Organized houses of prostitution, which used to flourish in the red-light districts, are not common today. Nevada is the only state with local county options for legalized houses of prostitution; all but three urban counties have legalized such prostitution. Customers drive out from town to trailers located in rural areas where the women work, paying from 50 to 60 percent of their earnings to the trailer owner. Wherever they are located, houses of prostitution vary greatly with respect to size, types of customers, and degree of respectability. New recruits are expected to learn the rules and regulations of the house, various sex techniques, how to handle large numbers of customers without running the risk of losing them as patrons, how to deal with different types of men, and how to protect themselves against venereal disease. They are often exploited by the house manager, for they have little chance to protect themselves, and a high percentage of their earnings, from 50 to 60 percent generally, is deducted by the "house" for linens, medical examinations, police protection, and the like. These houses are usually operated in conjunction with some type of organized crime, through which police protection is usually secured; likewise, they have close associations with taxicab drivers who receive commissions and with pimps who solicit for the women and live off their earnings.

Increasingly today the call girl is the more common type of prostitute, partly because police and health authorities have become more effective in doing away with street soliciting and with the more visible type of prostitution. This much-publicized woman in many ways is far more adapted to the mobility of the urban areas, responding as she does to phone calls and other contacts.[80] The client may come to her room or apartment, or she may go to his. This type of prostitution allows for greater individualization of operation and makes possible more part-time prostitution. It also depends upon some organization for patron recruitment, although the woman may have her own list of patrons who come to her directly. More frequently these patrons are secured through the intermediary services of a bellhop, a hotel desk clerk, a taxi driver, or other type of agent who, for a fee, will give her telephone number to the patron or arrange for her to come to his room or for him to go to hers. Call girls may work with lower-class hotels, but even some of the more expensive hotels allow this type of prostitute to operate on their premises. The call girl has become widely known, particularly through her role at conventions and in entertaining out-of-town businessmen. Generally the fee is between $50 and $100, but some patrons in New York City are reported to have paid large sums of money, reputedly as high as $500, for an evening's entertainment. A newer type of operation is provided by commercial escort services; by a phone call a customer can ask for a woman to accompany him for dinner and an evening, or even come directly to his room for prostitution. Because this type of prostitution is less visible than the "house" type, it gives the prostitute more concealment and the patron more anonymity. Frequently, however, the woman must pay the police or others for "protection from arrest."

---

[80]For details and case studies of call girls, see Harold Greenwald, *The Call Girl: A Social and Psychoanalytic Study* (New York: Ballantine, 1958).

The independent professional prostitute lives in her own apartment house, often in an expensive area of the city. She caters to middle- and upper-class patrons. Most of her clients are secured on an individual basis through referrals from customers.

Characteristics of Prostitutes

Inasmuch as physical attractiveness and youth are a necessity for the successful prostitute, she is usually between 17 and 24; the peak earning age is usually 22. Some prostitutes are older, but most of these have taken up the profession for special reasons, such as drug addiction or alcoholism, where their need for a continued supply of drugs or alcohol is expensive to support. Single women constitute the largest proportion of prostitutes, although some prostitutes are divorced or separated from their husbands. Many of those who give their marital status as married are living with or are married to pimps. On the whole, the professional common prostitute has less opportunity for marriage than the more "high-class" type of call-girl prostitute.

Other than the fact that prostitutes may primarily come from the lower socioeconomic groups and often from slum areas, there is no evidence that they enter this profession because of poverty even though they may desire to better their economic status. At one time there was probably a disproportionate number of prostitutes from various foreign-born groups; today there is a disproportionate percentage from racial minorities. The prevalence of slum living conditions among blacks appears related to the high proportion of black prostitutes.

The Process of Prostitution

At one time, perhaps 50 or 60 years ago, it was rather widely believed in the United States that the prostitute was often the victim of a "white slaver" who had induced a sexually inexperienced woman to enter the profession. The White-Slave-Traffic Act (the Mann Act) was aimed at eliminating this activity. It was believed that young women were "seduced" into a life of prostitution.

In general, studies of young women who make their living through prostitution in the United States and in most European countries indicate that the process of becoming a prostitute is quite different from these stereotyped means. In some cases these women have lived in local communities, such as slums, where sexual promiscuity has been approved or at least condoned. Although most have had considerable previous sexual experience, either with or without marriage, this fact in itself does not account for the prostitution. Gagnon and Simon have suggested that a sense of detachment from the family and/or community has often developed prior to entry into prostitution. It is not uncommon for the potential prostitute to experience geographical mobility, an unsatisfactory marriage, superficial interpersonal relationships, and a lack of contact with her family. While the transition to prostitution may be traumatic for some women, others may find a much more stabilizing life than they left behind.[81] An

---

[81]Gagnon and Simon, *Sexual Conduct,* Chap. 7.

important other factor is usually association with persons on the fringe of prostitution. An Israeli study of prostitutes found an important factor to be stigma within the family, largely growing out of the young woman's sexual promiscuity and leading to her expulsion from the family.[82] Processes of differential identification and association then led the girl into a career of prostitution, a process particularly seen in those girls coming from North African Orthodox homes. Picked up by pimps and other prostitutes, they are then inducted into the profession. The study concluded that a girl had become a prostitute, first, "because she is subconsciously favorably predisposed to this process by her stigmatization at home and her identification with images of deviant behavior, in this case sexual promiscuity; second, she is isolated and lonely in town, and any company, pimps and other prostitutes inclusive, would be quite welcome."[83]

Although modern prostitutes differ a great deal from their flamboyantly dressed and heavily made-up predecessors, they still have characteristics in common: often they have been indoctrinated into the profession by those closely associated with it. In the United States, contacts with persons in or on the fringes of prostitution are largely with women who themselves are practitioners; while some prostitutes are exploited by pimps, this is not usually the mode of entering the profession. Reckless claims it is rare in American prostitution to find a case of a woman who had never been a prostitute to be persuaded or forced into the business by a pimp.[84] Most women who acquire pimps do so after entering the profession.[85] A young woman relates how she got into prostitution at 18 after leaving home and going to live with the daughter of a friend who herself was engaged in prostitution.

> I thought that she was out of this world, and I really liked her. She fixed me up with this guy. Ginny was quite a bit older than me, and I still love her dearly. I said that I would go out with him, why not? I went out with him—and I hadn't slept with any more than three guys before in a period of a year because I was virgin until the time I was seventeen—and we had a good time, too many drinks, and I went to bed with him. About four o'clock in the morning he got up to leave and he gave me fifty dollars. I had no conception of the idea that he expected to pay me. I didn't expect any money. The guy could have kept his fifty dollars if he had any sense, I didn't known anything about it. So, Ginny said that this was something that she did every once in a while. I said, "Well, that's great because that was about what I was making in a week. So why not?" It just got to be a regular old habit. When I was too tired to go to work in the morning, I just would not go. I quit my job, I quit, they did not fire me. It got to where you could pick up three hundred to three hundred and fifty dollars a week. It was very nice. I had everything I wanted.[86]

The developmental career of a call girl includes three stages: the entrance into the career, the apprenticeship, and the development of contacts. The mere desire to

---

[82]Shlomo Shoham and Giora Rahav, "Social Stigma and Prostitution," *Annales Internationales de Criminologie,* 6 (1967), 479–513.
[83]Shoham and Rahav, p. 504.
[84]Walter C. Reckless, *The Crime Problem,* 5th ed. (New York: Appleton, 1972), pp. 170–171.
[85]In a study of a small sample of French prostitutes, 60 percent said that they had a pimp, although they had not entered the trade in this fashion. See Paul Le Moal, *Etude sur la Prostitution des Mineures: Problèmes Sociaux, Psychologiques et Psychiatriques Observés aupres de Cent Prostitutes Mineures* (Paris: Les Editions Sociales Françaises, 1969).
[86]Holmes, "Interview with Diane," p. 35.

become one is insufficient for the assumption of this role; there must be training and a systematic arrangement for contacts. One call girl said, "You cannot just say get an apartment and get a phone and everything and say, 'Well, I'm gonna start business,' because you gotta get clients from somewhere. There has to be a contact."[87] One study has concluded that "the selection of prostitution as an occupation from alternatives must be sought in the individual prostitute's interaction with others over a considerable time span."[88] After having entered through personal contact with someone actually involved in the profession, like a pimp or other call girls,[89] most call girls serve an apprenticeship. In a Los Angeles study of 33 call girls only one had not been brought in through these sources.[90] Half of the girls in this study had had initial contact with a call girl, some over a long period of time, others for shorter periods. Some were solicited by a pimp with offers of love and managerial experience. When a call girl has agreed to aid a novice she assumes responsibility for her training; women who are brought into prostitution by a pimp may either be trained by him or be referred to another call girl.

Once contact is made and the new person decides to be a prostitute the apprenticeship begins. The "classroom" is typically an apartment more or less like the future work place. Some women report spending up to eight months in training, but the average is two to three months. The trainer controls all referrals and opportunities. The content of the training consists of the development of the value structure of the profession of prostitution and the other interpersonal "dos" and "don'ts" in problematic situations. The acquisition of a set of values serves to create "in-group" solidarity and to alienate the apprentice from the "square society." It helps the trainer and the pimp to maintain a personal control and an economic advantage. Values that are transmitted include beliefs and justifications to support and maintain the behavior. Among these are that prostitution is simply a more honest behavior than that of most people, that most men are corrupt or exploitative, and that a well-trained call girl can, in turn, exploit a man. That men are often "cheating" on their wives, or will cheat a prostitute, is supporting evidence. Other values include fairness with other call or "working girls" and fidelity to the pimp. The rules governing interpersonal contacts with the customers include what to say on the phone during a solicitation—a "line" such as needing money to pay the rent, buy a car, or pay doctor bills; social interaction in obtaining the fees; the nature of specific customers' preferences and what types of customers to avoid; how to converse with a customer; caution in the use of alcohol; and knowledge of physical problems associated with prostitution. Although prostitutes may be taught some things, such as not experiencing sexual orgasm with customers in general, little instruction is given about sex techniques.

Not all call girls, however, accept all the training in either the values or the

[87]James H. Bryan, "Apprenticeships in Prostitution," *Social Problems,* 12 (1965), 289. For a discussion of the career prostitute in a house of prostitution, see Barbara S. Heyl, *The Madam as Entrepreneur: Political Economy of a House of Prostitution* (Rutgers University, New Brunswick, N.J.: Transaction, Inc., 1977).
[88]Norman R. Jackman, Richard O'Toole, and Gilbert Geis, "The Self-Image of the Prostitute," *The Sociological Quarterly,* 4 (1963), 160.
[89]For a discussion of the role of the pimp or male partner of the prostitute, see John M. Murtagh and Sara Harris, *Cast the First Stone* (New York: McGraw-Hill, 1957).
[90]Bryan, "Apprenticeships in Prostitution," p. 289.

techniques of interpersonal relations. One study showed that some "experience orgasms with the customer, some show considerable affect toward 'Johns,' others remain drunk or 'high' throughout the contact. While there seems to be general agreement as to what the rules of interpersonal conduct are, there seems to be considerable variation in the adoption of such rules."[91]

Since a call girl must have access to a clientele, an equally important aspect of training is the acquisition of contacts; this is done during the apprenticeship period. Books or "lists" can be purchased from other call girls or pimps, but some are unreliable. Most frequently, names are secured through contacts developed during the apprenticeship period. For an initial fee of 40 to 50 percent, the trainer call girl refers customers to the apprentice and oversees her. This fee becomes the pay of the "teacher," along with the convenience of having another woman available to meet the demand or to take care of her own contacts. On the other hand, the new recruit may have a rather high initial income because of the novelty of her newness to the business, and this may serve as an incentive for her to continue. For her pimp it is important that a new recruit develop a clientele.

The nonverbal skills acquired by a call girl, however, do not seem as developed or as complex as those demanded of the professional streetwalker. Most call girls look down on the streetwalker, perhaps because call work involves less physical effort and more verbalization. "The tasks of avoiding the police, soliciting among strangers for potential customers, and arrangements for the completion of the sexual contract not only require different skills on the part of the streetwalker, but are performances requiring a higher degree of professional 'know-how' than is generally required of the call girl."[92]

Prostitution requires a new monetary relation with males. Sexual talk in terms of preferences and of money come to replace dating and a degree of preliminary courtship before a sex act. This verbalization must become learned. The prostitute learns to speak about these matters that in the past have arisen and have taken place in "gestural and non-verbal contexts."[93] She then learns to tie the new talk to the pricing of the activity requested. While the "economic portion of the act must not be allowed to intervene in the nature of the sexual performance," the relation between the sexuality and money is what makes the act possible. Gagnon further analyzes this learning process as follows:

> The structure of talk, once learned, becomes highly ritualized and predictable, although it varies from one social level of customer to another and from one situation of prostitution to another. Thus the centrality of the cash exchange is high for the lower-class customer, the sexual activities preferred are limited, and the content of the sexual talk is small. On the other hand, in contacts with middle-class males the price is set and not referred to again (although there may be psychic gain for the male as a result of payment), the sexual interest may be wide, and there is a certain expectation of talk that transcends the immediate sexual character of the relationship. The capacity to meet all of these expecta-

---

[91]Bryan, "Apprenticeships in Prostitution," p. 293.
[92]Bryan, "Apprenticeships in Prostitution," p. 296.
[93]John H. Gagnon, "Prostitution," *International Encyclopedia of the Social Sciences* (New York: Crowell-Collier and Macmillan, 1968), Vol. 12, p. 594.

tions is a relatively uncommon skill, and this fact may account for the mobility problems of girls who enter the profession at various levels.[94]

Self-Concept

Prostitution requires a new conception of self, although it is somewhat difficult to discuss this development in a general sense because of the varied degrees of involvement in a career of prostitution. Societal reaction, arrests, and association with other prostitutes serve to increase the self-concept of the prostitute. On the other hand, if a prostitute's customers are more educated than she is and she moves in such a circle or she has another occupation, such as a secretary or a model, she is less likely to think of herself as a prostitute, particularly if such a concept refers to the "common prostitute" or streetwalker.

The self-image of the urban prostitute has been found to be related to the degree of social isolation, the more isolated women tending to define their behavior in a more acceptable light.[95] As with other deviant behavior, prostitutes are aware of the legal values involved in their sexual acts, but these are justified in three ways: (1) prostitutes are no worse than other people and often are less hypocritical; (2) prostitutes achieve certain of the dominant values in society such as financial success and the support of others who are dependent on them;[96] and (3) prostitutes perform an important and necessary social function. Research on the philosophies of 52 call girls with an average age of 22 and length of experience of 27 months found that virtually all respondents maintained that prostitution was important because of the varied and extensive sexual needs of men and the necessity to protect social institutions.[97] In their own views they serve sexually as outlets and therefore as protectors of society from more rapes, perversions, and broken marriages. Generally they also claimed that by furnishing friendship and giving physical comfort prostitutes help men who are embarrassed, lonely, or isolated. One prostitute stated that half of her work was what she called "social work."

> That is, say some friend of mine has someone come to London to visit his firm, and he gives him my number, I have connections with a lot of good firms. All right, he takes me out; dinner, a show, perhaps a party. I go down on his expense account, or something. It may lead to sex, it may not. Often it doesn't. I don't mind. In fact, I'm pleased.[98]

The favorable self-concept of the prostitute is supported particularly by the theory that clients should be exploited. In exploiting them, the prostitute regards herself as being no more immoral than her customers and the rest of the world. Another view is that in essence most interpersonal relations between the sexes are acts of prostitution. Wives and others use deception and sex to achieve other objectives, whereas prostitutes are at least honest. The sex act may play a part in premarital courtship and even in some marriages that is analogous to the commercial exploitation

---

[94]Gagnon, "Prostitution," p. 594.
[95]Jackman, O'Toole, and Geis, pp. 150–162.
[96]Jackman, O'Toole, and Geis, pp. 150–162.
[97]Bryan, "Apprenticeships in Prostitution," pp. 287–297.
[98]Wayland Young, "Prostitution," in Gagnon and Simon, *Sexual Deviance,* p. 121.

of sex in prostitution. Women may exploit their "femininity" to male customers for commercial gain without engaging in actual sex relations, as do many sales persons, hostesses, secretaries, waitresses, and models.

In actuality, however, such views are not held by many individual prostitutes, who know the ideology but do not support it. Prostitutes were asked to rate items on various ideological positions of themselves, other call girls, women in general, "johns," and men in general.[99] Correct individual predictions could not be deduced statistically from the accepted occupational ideology. For example, customers were evaluated by the call girl as being as worthwhile as herself and as significantly better than other call girls.

> Not infrequently, personal friendships with customers are reported: "Some of them are nice clients who become very good friends of mine." On the other hand, while friendships are formed with "squares," personal disputations with colleagues are frequent. Speaking of her colleagues, one call girl says that most "could cut your throat." Respondents frequently mentioned that they had been robbed, conned, or otherwise exploited by their call girl friends. Interpersonal distrust between call girls appears to be considerable.[100]

Reasons for this difference between the ideology of the deviants and their actual beliefs may be the relative lack of cohesiveness among prostitutes and possibly the fact that the stigma of the occupation is less than the ideology implies. However, in the first few months the ideology is important to the trainee, for she can counter a negative self-image and reduce moral conflicts by accepting the view that customers are exploitative, that other women are hypocrites, that prostitution provides a valuable social service, and that call girls' relations are close: "while the professional ideology is learned and perhaps serves a function during this apprenticeship period, it is doubtful that it remains of equal importance throughout the call girl's career."[101]

Primary and Secondary Prostitution

An individual who engages in sex relations for monetary reasons, promiscuously and without much emotion, may still be a "primary prostitute." The transition from primary deviation to professional or secondary deviation is accomplished as a person comes to acquire the self-conception, social role, ideology, and language of prostitution. It exists to the extent that the individual becomes identified with prostitution as a set of values and comes to accept the role definition accorded her by others. This can come about in a number of ways.

A young woman may enter the profession by engaging first in a series of quasi-prostituting sex experiences and later become associated with a trainer, usually an experienced prostitute. Instead of accepting gifts and entertainment in return for her "favors," she comes to perceive sex as a commercial act. When the prostitute sees the

---

[99]Bryan, "Apprenticeships in Prostitution," pp. 287–297. A "john" is slang for a customer of a prostitute.
[100]James H. Bryan, "Occupational Ideologies and Individual Attitudes of Call Girls," *Social Problems,* 13 (1966), 445.
[101]Bryan, "Occupational Ideologies and Individual Attitudes of Call Girls," p. 448.

functional values of her role, secondary deviation appears. Societal reaction is also important. It is the product of arrest and conviction; of a change to commercialized sex relations; of venereal infection and treatment with other prostitutes in a hospital or clinic; and of role-defining interpretations received from contacts with other prostitutes, pimps, and customers. The exploitation of prostitutes also aids the development of secondary deviation. The madam in the house, and the pimp, take a percentage of earnings, as do attorneys, physicians who treat prostitutes for venereal disease, policemen who are willing to look the other way, the bail bondsman, and even customers who may take some pleasure in inflicting physical abuse upon the prostitute.[102]

After going into prostitution, the women tend to develop attitudes and behavior patterns that are a part of the social role they play. In this connection they develop an argot, or special language, for their work, special acts and services, patterns of bartering with their customers and an impersonal relation with them, along with a large number of rationalizations for their activities. While many prostitutes are able to leave this occupation for marriage or for employment as waitresses, domestic servants, or sales persons, and a few others are able to achieve a high standard of living and to maintain it, for some of them age, venereal disease, alcoholism, or drug addiction result in a derelict life, punctuated more or less regularly by arrests and jail sentences.

Prostitution and Law Enforcement

Laws against prostitution discriminate against women. Logically, and increasingly the point of view of many women's equality groups as well as others, a woman should have the right to engage in intercourse for money if she so desires. A nation-wide organization of prostitutes in the United States (called COYOTE—Call Off Your Old Tired Ethics), along with one in France, attempts, through meetings, conventions, and speeches, to change public views and eventually to repeal laws dealing with prostitution. At present, however, it is the female prostitute (there are some male prostitutes, but they are seldom arrested) who is of primary concern to law-enforcement officials. Almost never are the clients regarded as offenders.

Arrests for prostitution usually fall under three headings: (1) arrest and prosecution for accosting and soliciting; (2) arrest and prosecution on a charge of "common prostitution," which may fall under disorderly conduct or vagrancy; and (3) arrest and detention under health regulations.[103] The enforcement of laws directed at prostitutes is sporadic, responding to public attitudes and police-prostitute relations. Most of it is simply to "contain" prostitution through police activity by exercising some control or "harassment."[104] Sometimes there is almost no enforcement, and at other times police conduct special drives which are more directed at streetwalkers in conspicuous places.

---

[102]See Lemert, pp. 263–264.
[103]Wayne R. LaFave, *Arrest: The Decision To Take a Suspect into Custody* (Boston: Little, Brown, 1965), pp. 457–463.
[104]For a discussion of police harrassment of prostitutes, see Paul Chevigny, *Police Power: Police Abuses in New York City* (New York: Random House, 1969).

The women arrested are more likely to be the inexperienced or those who make a mistake when high on alcohol or drugs.[105] The process of arresting a prostitute is not always easy for the police because of the legal problem of entrapment, as a member of a police vice squad has described:

> The broads are wisening up, getting real hanky. One of them told me she can always spot a cop because we never say, "Hey, baby, how would you like to turn a trick for ten bucks?" which is what a lot of these trollers say when one of these broads looks good to them. We got to wait for them to set the price, otherwise we don't stand a chance in court. It doesn't matter how many times a broad's been convicted for prostitution. If we set the price, we got no case. The law says we entrapped her.
>
> I was trolling one night and a broad walked over to the car and said, "Mister, I'm in trouble. I could use a little money."
>
> I said, "Well, I might be able to help you out, provided I get something for my money."
>
> She said, "You'll get something, but how much you givin'?"
>
> I said, "How much you asking?"
>
> She said, "How much you offerin' to pay?"
>
> "Well," I said, "How's about a dollar?"
>
> "Oh, mister," she said, "You must be a policeman"—and walked off.
>
> You see, Jerry, we got to get them to set the price and for what, straight date, half-and-half, French or Greek. Otherwise we're doing the soliciting.[106]

Law enforcement is often a sordid business in cases of prostitution. The demeanor of a prostitute to a police officer has a great deal to do with her vulnerability to arrest, and one who acts toward him in an offensive manner offends his sense of competence.[107] A prostitute is frequently arrested as the result of solicitation by the police or a "lure" provided by them, and sometimes informers are used to locate the rooms being used. In order to "buy" her way out of an arrest, she may offer to serve as an informant in the apprehension of her pimp or a narcotics peddler. Even the threat of a "quarantine hold" for venereal disease medical examination is used to control her behavior during arrest and to provide means for apprehending more serious criminals.

The revised penal codes of Illinois and Wisconsin, as well as a statute in New York, make the customers as well as the prostitute herself subject to prosecution. A study in New York City showed, however, that of 508 persons convicted, only 0.8 percent were for patronizing a prostitute.[108] The police generally ignored the patrons, whose names when arrested were rarely put into the newspapers. Most arrests were of streetwalkers, and the high-priced call girls and their patrons were ignored. It appears that streetwalkers and their customers rank lowest in social prestige; many call girls work individually and serve the upper classes, particularly corporate customers.

---

[105]Jerome H. Skolnick, *Justice without Trial: Law Enforcement in Democratic Society,* 2d ed. (New York: Wiley, 1975), p. 104.
[106]Skolnick, p. 103.
[107]Skolnick, p. 112.
[108]Pamela A. Roby, "Politics and Criminal Law: Revision of the New York State Penal Law on Prostitution," *Social Problems,* 17 (1969), 83–109.

"Because such behavior is generally not regarded as offensive, political groups do not exert pressure upon the police and city hall to 'clean it up.' "[109]

Laws against prostitution are, in effect, efforts to control private moral behavior through punitive social control measures; and in most countries these laws are only sporadically successful. The *Wolfenden Report* concluded that prostitution has persisted throughout many centuries in many civilizations, and the very failure of attempts to eradicate it by repressive legislation indicates that it cannot be stamped out through the criminal law. It is still true that without demand for such services the prostitute would not exist, and that there continue to be enough men who use the services of the prostitute to keep the trade alive. Since it is also true that there are women who choose this form of livelihood even when there is no economic necessity for it, the report concludes that as long as these factors remain true "no amount of legislation directed toward its abolition will abolish it."[110]

Massage Parlors

Largely beginning in the early 1970s, a new form of sex relations has developed in the form of "massage parlors." By 1978 they had become a booming business, with thousands of establishments in the United States. One study of a suburban West Coast community estimated one parlor for every 5,000 persons.[111] In Washington, D.C., more than 200 were listed in the 1976 classified telephone directory. Formerly a "massage" meant physical therapy for health reasons; today it has become synonymous with a world of sexual stimulation. This is explicit in the names of today's massage parlors: Bachelor Garden, This is Heaven, Jan's Health Studio, Genie's Magic Touch, Geisha House, and Cheri's Counseling Clinic. They range from "dives" to plush operations.

> Homes in unincorporated areas and low-rent, downtown storefronts have been converted into blue-collar massage parlors with the addition of partitions, curtains, a couch, a chair, massage tables and linen. Advertising is a necessity. Ads need only show a semi-nude girl with the caption "Your complete satisfaction on request." A few higher class parlors cater to wealthier businessmen and financially influential people, yet offer much the same services. These parlors advertise subtly, preferring to attract a select clientele. Customers are provided such comforts as plush carpets, soft couches, clean linen, piped-in music and soft lighting. All of this may demand a few thousand dollars extra, but as one manager said, "You wouldn't want to pay for a massage in a filthy place, would you?" Almost all parlors feature saunas and showers; the latter is required by law. Some even have their own laundry room for a constant supply of fresh linen.[112]

The women who work in these parlors may be described in advertisements as "beautiful playmates to serve you in plush stereophonic elegance," but on occasion they are referred to as "female counselors" to give a disguise of legitimacy. In either

---

[109]Roby, p. 99.
[110]*Wolfenden Report,* p. 132.
[111]Albert J. Velarde and Mark Warlick, "Massage Parlors: The Sensuality Business," *Society,* 11 (1973), 63–74.
[112]Velarde and Warlick, p. 64. Published by permission of Transaction, Inc., from *Society*, Vol. 11, No. 1. Copyright © 1973 by Transaction, Inc.

case a massage parlor may involve actual massage, a "half and half" (massage of the man who in turn massages the woman), sexual stimulation involving seminude or nude body display, or a "local" (hand masturbation or oral sex). In many cases, particularly in large cities, actual sexual intercourse takes place, sometimes with many sexual variations, cutting down on the massage and getting down to what the customer came for. One masseuse stated:

> It's $15 for an hour-long massage including a local. An extra $5 will get my top off and $5 more takes my bottom off. For $10 more he can bathe with me for a half hour. (This is a rare practice.) Anything after that is negotiable between me and the customer. I have to soak him for $35 before negotiating a blow-job or a lay.[113]

Oral sex is usually $30 or $40 and complete sexual intercourse between $40 and $60, although prices are lower in certain types of establishments. Not all is sex, however. One study showed that customers may come into a massage parlor simply to talk. After removing their clothes some customers are content to talk over some of their private problems.

> A lot of guys are just getting over the hangup of being nude and alone with a girl. We get things said to us that a customer would never dream of saying to someone he knows. Some things they say are just plain gross, but, more often we get dudes who rap about their personal relationships, homosexual tendencies or their sexual hangups. I guess they figure they're never gonna see us again if that's the way they want it.[114]

A 1977 investigation in New York City found that, at least there and probably in many other large cities, most of the so-called massage parlors are, in effect, brothels.[115] One type is the tawdry West Side or Midtown Manhattan parlor located in a run-down building and another the more expensively furnished parlor or spa on the East Side. The former charges $10 for a 10- to 15-minute session with a hostess in a cubicle hardly large enough for a cot. These places remain open 24 hours a day on Fridays and Saturdays, usually the busiest days; they employ 20 women during the day, another 20 on the night shift. According to former employees of such places, each woman is expected to "turn 20 tricks," or have sexual relations with 20 customers, on busy days. Thus the operators take in $8,000 a day from 800 male customers on an average Friday or Saturday. It has been estimated that one massage parlor charging $10 a session takes in more than a million dollars a year. The initial fee of $10 usually is split evenly between the hostess and the management, and the women earn tips on the side. Women who have worked in these parlors report being required to pay as much as $75 to $100 a week to the operators as a housekeeping charge.

New York's East Side establishments advertise in sex-oriented publications and distribute leaflets on the street. They usually employ about eight women on each shift and are believed to gross between $750,000 and $1 million in basic fees alone, according to IRS investigators and former employees. Hostesses in West Side parlors,

---

[113]Velarde and Warlick, p. 70. Published by permission of Transaction, Inc., from *Society*, Vol. 11, No. 1. Copyright © 1973 by Transaction, Inc.

[114]Velarde and Warlick, p. 70. Published by permission of Transaction, Inc., from *Society*, Vol. 11, No. 1. Copyright © 1973 by Transaction, Inc.

[115]Selwyn Raab and Nathaniel Sheppard, Jr., "Porno Business Reaps Huge Profits," *New York Times,* July 31, 1977.

who are usually recruited through advertisements for "models" or through "word of mouth," request tips from their customers and ask much higher for half-hour sessions, normally $30 to $50. According to New York City police, low- and middle-echelon racketeers associated with organized crime have increasingly taken over or attempted to take over many of these parlors since 1974. They "skim" profits through kickbacks from the establishments.

Customers According to one study of nine parlors in a suburban West Coast community, the largest group of customers are white men over 35.[116] Most of them are white-collar businessmen who claim curiosity and boredom with their daily urban routines as the main reasons for going. They seek attention, which they get from an attractive girl for one hour for a fee. The second largest group was found to be transients or persons encountering changes in their personal lives. They may have traveling positions, they may be new to the area, their wives may have left them, or, as one masseuse said, they may be young married men. "They've been married for, oh, two to five years and can't understand why their own sex lives have gone stale. I try to rap them about communication, you know, get 'em to tune into their old ladies. All they need, as far as I can see, is some confidence and a desire to work things out."[117] The third group of customers are men who are physically or mentally unattractive and who have difficulty securing personal attention from women, let alone actual sex. Some customers want to engage in unusual sexual practices, sometimes called a "dominant massage," for which large tips are commonplace.

Learning To Be Masseuses The women who work in these parlors, who must be attractive and personable, are for the most part young and without occupational skills. Advertisements state: "Masseuses needed—part-time or full-time—training included." Most of them seem to stay with the work even after they find out what it involves. Usually they receive some training in actual massage techniques. Particularly important is basic knowledge of solicitation laws, for women engaged in sexual acts must be certain that the customer does the soliciting. They must learn to discover undercover policemen by general appearance, mannerisms, type of language, and tone of voice. Some parlors even have tape recorders to present in court as to who solicited whom. The woman who handles the phone calls must learn how to handle them, taking extreme care that no mention is made of actual sex, taking care to emphasize that the service consists of "tenderness, sincerity, and loving care with another person." Despite the type of work done in these parlors, this emphasis does give the woman a self-image of not being a prostitute. "Even women who remain in the profession go to great lengths to protect themselves from the prostitute image": they regard themselves as masseuses or as people who work in an office.[118]

Problems of Legal Enforcement The sexual activities of massage parlors pose difficult legal problems. Since most of them are licensed, and many cities require the women to be licensed (including a police check and on occasion even training in a massage school),

---

[116]Velarde and Warlick.
[117]Velarde and Warlick, p. 69.
[118]Velarde and Warlick, p. 66.

their work is basically legitimate. Moreover, massage is an actual part of their activities; the difference lies in what the massage consists of and where it takes place. Street solicitation for sex is the illegal element in many prostitution arrests, and there is none of this. Generally the patron is expected to propose the type of sex relations he desires. Massage parlor owners or managers pretend to be unaware of any illicit sexual activity taking place between customers and masseuses. These arrangements are all in private, and the overtures for sex are supposedly made by the customer. The legal situation is further complicated by the parlors' occasional use of the term "female counselors" for their female employees. These complexities make prosecutions extremely difficult, particularly in smaller cities and suburban areas that have neither the funds nor the manpower for a vice squad. Investigations, arrests, and court proceedings become heavy financial burdens. "The most recent raids in this community saw five masseuses arrested on charges of solicitation to commit a lewd act. One manager estimated that this raid will ultimately cost the city $30,000. This is a high price to pay for putting five masseuses out of business for a day or two despite favorable publicity for the police."[119]

PORNOGRAPHY

During the last century or two some type of legal restriction has been placed on the publication and other forms of dissemination of erotic or sexually oriented materials. These items of what one might call "erotica" appear in the form of printed books, magazines, photographs, films, sound records, statuary, and sex "devices." While these materials are primarily for heterosexual persons, there is also "erotica" for the homosexual person. The President's Commission on Obscenity and Pornography reported in 1970 that the industries involved in traffic in the distribution of sexually oriented materials have an estimated gross sales amounting to $2,500,000,000.[120] This includes general release films, art and "stag" films, sexually oriented mass market books and periodicals, and various under-the-counter photos and sex gadgets. Pornographic films can be purchased in stores and through the mail, and they can be seen in thousands of stores offering "peep shows." These films portray women as playthings of the male—his toys, objects to be exploited and used for his pleasure. "There is no relating, only narcissistic groin-gazing, only the mechanical, ejaculation-obsessed male seeking to penetrate as many orifices as possible."[121] In New York City peep show customers pay 25 cents to view a two-minute section of a film or $1.25 for the entire 10-minute film. These same eight-millimeter films shown in the booths through the vending machines can usually be purchased there for approximately $15. These machines take in more than $100 a day in quarters, and even a relatively small store with 10 or 20 machines can make between $2,000 and $3,000 daily from the machines alone.[122]

---

[119]Velarde and Warlick, p. 73.
[120]*Report of the Commission on Obscenity and Pornography* (Washington, D.C.: Government Printing Office, 1970). This report has been published as a New York Times Book by Bantam Books (1970). All subsequent page references are to this latter edition.
[121]Robert T. Francoeur, "Sex Films," *Society,* 14 (1977), 36.
[122]Raab and Sheppard.

The Commission found that 85 percent of the men and 70 percent of the adult women have been exposed to such material, most of it voluntary. Depictions of nudity with sex organs exposed and of heterosexual intercourse are the most common, while depictions of homosexual activities and oral sex are less common. About a fifth to a fourth of the male population has regular experiences with such materials, only a fourth to one half, however, actually buying any of it themselves. Among adults, first experiences usually occur in adolescence. In a study of the Commission, about 80 percent of boys and 70 percent of girls reported having seen visual depictions or read textual descriptions of sexual intercourse by the time they were 18. On the other hand, studies report that the patrons of adult bookstores and of movie theaters where sexual materials are available or displayed are "predominantly white, middle class, middle aged, married males."[123]

Generally termed "obscene" (in the legal terminology) and "pornographic" (popular term), these materials are presumed to arouse a person sexually. Some people believe this leads to all kinds of negative consequences, such as premarital sexual relations, illegitimacy, and sex crimes. Typical of this viewpoint was a 1972 newsletter of a Presbyterian minister to his parishioners: "One cannot expect a city permitting dirty movies, lewd male shows in bars, outright filth passed as literature to experience anything other than rape and venereal disease."[124] The term "pornographic" in almost any form arouses extreme emotional reactions among certain groups, and many of these groups have had the political and social power to pass laws against it.

While obscenity laws are being modified or often not being enforced, all Western countries have regulatory laws of some degree. The only country that has completely abolished them is Denmark, which did so in 1966, except for juvenile and nonconsensual exposure. All the states in the United States have statutes that prohibit the distribution of "obscene" materials, and most of such violations are handled by the states rather than the federal government. There are also five federal laws regulating the distribution of obscene materials, including the mailing, importing, broadcasting, transporting in interstate commerce such material, and a recent law prohibits the mailing of it to persons who request that it not be mailed. Violations may carry a penalty of up to five years imprisonment and a $5,000 fine. The U.S. Supreme Court has held, as late as 1957, that these laws are constitutional and do not infringe on free speech, on the grounds that

> (1) the Framers of the Bill of Rights did not intend the free speech guarantee of the First Amendment to apply to all utterances and writings, (2) that "obscene" speech—like libel, profanity and blasphemy—was not intended to be protected by the Amendment, and (3) that a universal consensus had existed for many years that the distribution of obscenity should be legally prohibited.[125]

This ruling was modified in 1969 by the Supreme Court when it held that the constitutional guarantee of free speech protects the right of individuals to read or view

---

[123]*Report of the Commission on Obscenity and Pornography,* p. 25.
[124]As reported and reprinted in the *Wisconsin State Journal,* Madison, September 16, 1972.
[125]*Report of the Commission on Obscenity and Pornography,* pp. 43–44.

"obscene" material in their own homes. Other federal courts have held that the laws do not apply to the import of such materials for private use, the mailing of "obscene" material to those who request it, and to prohibitions applied to films or other materials exhibited to adults provided minors are not admitted. In 1972 the Supreme Court adopted the position, however, that state liquor commissions have the right to shut down taverns that feature bottomless dancers or sex acts or sex films on the grounds that they have the right to guard "public health welfare and morals."

The concern with pornography that led during the late 1960s and early 1970s to the formation of a national commission to study the issues also resulted in new Supreme Court decisions dealing with the regulation of obscene materials. The case of *Miller vs. California,* decided by the Supreme Court on June 21, 1973, set the most far-reaching precedent and carried with it the latest criteria for judging whether or not material is pornographic. Marvin Miller had been convicted of violating the Penal Code of the State of California in distributing obscene materials. Although Miller had conducted a mass mailing of advertisements offering for sale erotically illustrated books, he was specifically convicted for having sent some of these unsolicited advertisements to a restaurant in Newport Beach. The Supreme Court ruled in the Miller case that states can ban material that (1) appeals to "pruriency," (2) contains descriptions or depictions "patently offensive" to the community standards as specifically defined by the applicable state law as written or construed, and (3) lacks, as a whole, serious literary, artistic, political, or scientific value. All three criteria must "coalesce before material may be deemed 'obscene' for adults."[126]

An important aspect of the Supreme Court decision was putting back into the community the final decision as to what is obscene; local courts, using local community standards rather than national standards, were to be the final judges.[127] This may have been the result of the seemingly impossible task of deciding, on a national basis, what is pornographic and what is not. Obviously Las Vegas has different standards from those of Topeka, Kansas; what is unclear, however, is the best manner in which to gauge this community feeling. Some communities have relied upon the judgment of juries in pornography cases; others have felt that a public opinion poll is the better way. In 1977, for example, the city of Cleveland decided to survey the city inhabitants' views of pornography and obscenity through the distribution of questionnaires, distributed to about 100,000 households by garbage collectors who left one at each dwelling while making their pick-up rounds. The response was very small. In a 1978 decision, the Supreme Court decided that a juror sitting in judgment over a publication or film must "determine the collective view of the community as best it can be done." Moreover, the Supreme Court also declared that children's sensitivity was not to be taken into account when the publication or film was directed at adults only.

The Supreme Court decision has resulted in subjective interpretations. "Prurient" refers primarily to material that is sexually arousing: "arousingness" and "offensiveness" are difficult to define. The Commission found that material that is offensive may not be arousing, and material that is arousing may or may not be offensive. The judgment in these two areas varied:

---

[126]*Report of the Commission on Obscenity and Pornography,* pp. 44–45.
[127]See the discussion in Paul J. McGeady, "Obscenity Law and the Supreme Court," in Victor B. Cline, ed., *Where Do You Draw the Line?* (Provo, Utah: Brigham Young University Press, 1974), pp. 83–106.

for depictions of female nudity with genitals exposed, for explicit depictions of heterosexual sexual intercourse, and for graphic depictions of oral-genital intercourse. In addition, judgments differ among different groups: Males as a group differ from females as a group in their judgments of both "offensiveness" and "arousingness"; the young differ from the old; the college-educated differ from those with only a high school education; frequent church attenders differ from less frequent church attenders.[128]

The Commission found that the majority of American adults believe that they should be permitted to read or to see any sexual materials they wish to see; there is consensus among adults that young persons should be prohibited access to some sexual materials. Almost half feel that it is almost impossible to enforce laws against sexual materials.[129]

Advocacy of restrictions on the availability of explicit sexual materials is more likely to be found accompanying an orientation against freedom of expression generally. In addition, females tend to be more restrictive than males, older people more restrictive than younger people, those with a grade school education more restrictive than the high school-educated, who in turn tend to be more restrictive than the college educated, and people who attend church regularly tend to be more restrictive than those who attend less often.[130]

About 60 percent felt that either looking at or reading such materials would provide information about sex and would offer entertainment. Half felt that such material would improve sex relations of married couples. Moreover, the President's Commission on Obscenity and Pornography found that in research studies a substantial proportion of married couples reported more agreeable and enhanced marital communication and an increased willingness to discuss sexual matters with each other after seeing erotic materials.[131] While it may be thought that females are less stimulated by erotic materials than males due to cultural conditioning and traditional conceptions of sexuality and gender roles, this is not the case generally. Females have reported stimulation after exposure to erotic materials; some studies have confirmed this finding with measures of physiological states of women who have witnessed various sexual scenes, displays of nudity, and other stimulating sexual material.[132]

The Origin of Obscenity Laws

The crime of creating or distributing these sexual materials is of relatively recent origin in Anglo-American law. The first legislation in England authorizing the prosecution of obscene materials was enacted in 1824, and this covered public exposure of obscene books or prints; general legislation prohibiting a wider area was not enacted until

---

[128]*Report of the Commission on Obscenity and Pornography,* p. 46.
[129]*Report of the Commission on Obscenity and Pornography,* p. 49.
[130]*Report of the Commission on Obscenity and Pornography,* p. 49.
[131]*Report of the Commission on Obscenity and Pornography,* p. 49.
[132]See, for example, John P. Wincze, Peter Hoon, and Emily Franck Hoon, "Sexual Arousal in Women: A Comparison of Cognitive and Physiological Responses by Continuous Measurement," *Archives of Sexual Behavior,* 6 (1977), 121–133.

1857. In the United States Massachusetts in 1711 enacted a statute, and Vermont in 1821. The first federal statute prohibiting the importation of pictorial obscene material was enacted in 1842. Obscenity was first prohibited in 1865 in a federal statute forbidding its distribution in the mails.

It is important to recognize that the earliest prohibitions in England and the United States were not directed against explicit sexual materials as such. Obscenity *as a crime* began in both countries when sexual matters were incorporated into materials that directly attacked *religious* institutions and beliefs. The earliest prosecutions all pertained to sexual works that were condemned for their explicit antireligious content. It was not until after 1850 that a distinct offense of publishing explicit sexual material— unconnected with any expressed antireligious content—fully evolved in the United States and England. "The primary forces behind the ultimate creation of these prohibitions upon sexual materials appear, moreover, to have been religious ones."[133]

The proliferation of state obscenity statutes coincided with the decline in the direct influence of the church over community life, the beginnings of free universal education, and the increase in literacy. In the United States there was little enforcement of either state or federal obscenity laws until about 1870, after the passage in 1865 of the first mail obscenity act, and, in New York, after legislation enacted to prohibit the dissemination of obscene literature. Enforcement of existing statutes increased largely because of the efforts of one man, Anthony Comstock, who initially investigated violations of the 1865 act and later joined his efforts with the Young Men's Christian Association to work for legislation that would cover publishers as well as local dealers. After Congress broadened the federal mail act in 1873 to the form, essentially, in which it is today, this crusader became a special agent of the Post Office in charge of enforcing the law. States with no previous obscenity legislation passed their own laws, and by the end of the century some form of general prohibition on the dissemination of "obscene" materials was on the statute books of at least 30 states.

The Effects of Erotic Materials

Studies have been made by the President's Commission on Obscenity and Pornography to try to determine the effects of exposure to erotic materials and to determine whether these effects support sufficiently the presumed reasons for the existence of the obscenity laws. The conclusion was reached that exposure to erotic materials does produce sexual arousal in a substantial proportion of males and females, the extent of the arousal dependent on the particular characteristics of the viewer and on the materials. Younger persons are more likely to be aroused than older; those college educated, religiously inactive, and sexually experienced more often reported arousal than those with the opposite characteristics. For the most part, conventional sexual behavior arouses more than does homosexual behavior; petting and coitus themes stimulate more than oral sexuality. Great variations, however, were reported in the designation of "obscenity." Generally, older, less educated, religiously active, or

---

[133]*Report of the Commission on Obscenity and Pornography*, p. 349.

persons with less experience with erotic materials or those who have sexual guilt feelings were more likely to judge given materials as being "obscene."

While these findings referred only to sexual arousal and the definition of the "obscenity" of materials, a further matter of study was to what extent they resulted in increased sexual behavior. The majority of those studied reported no change in sexual behavior, although some did report increased masturbation and coital behavior, usually of short duration. Where there was an increase in behavior it occurred generally among those with a previous pattern of masturbation or other sexual experiences and with established and available sex partners. In one study, for example, middle-aged married couples reported increases in both the frequency and variety of coital responses during the 24-hour period after viewing erotic films. These materials generally also resulted in an increase in erotic dreams and fantasies, as well as increased conversations about sexual matters.

Exposure to erotic materials has little or no effect on already established attitudinal commitments either to sexuality or to sexual "morality." Experimental and survey studies suggest that persons who are *sexually* tolerant are less rejecting of sexual materials. On the other hand, studies show that persons who are unfamiliar with erotic materials may experience strong and conflicting emotional reactions when first exposed to sexual materials but that these responses are of short duration.

It has often been charged that erotic materials contribute to delinquency and crime. Actual studies of the President's Commission, however, led to the conclusion that there is "no evidence to date that explicit sexual material plays a significant role in the causation of the delinquent or criminal behavior among youth or adults."[134] Both delinquent and nondelinquent youth report generally similar experiences with explicit sex materials. Moreover, exposure is already widespread among both groups despite the laws. The age of first exposure, the kinds of materials, the amount and circumstances of the exposure are essentially the same for both groups when family and neighborhood are controlled. Peer group pressures are of great significance in regard to exposure to these materials.

For many persons, the crucial issue with respect to exposure to pornography is not sexual stimulation (this, in fact, is probably to be expected, though some exceptions are noted below), but physical sexual aggression. The general conclusion of the President's Commission is now well known: exposure to pornography does not result in increased sexually aggressive behavior, either in the form of interpersonal violence or in increased incidence of sexual crimes.[135] This conclusion, however, has received critically severe reactions; the main criticism points to the methodological defects of several of the studies used to support it.[136] Subsequent research into this issue has been conflicting. For example, in one experimental study it was found that male exposure to "mild erotic stimuli" (for example, pictures of seminude females) inhibited

---

[134]*Report of the Commission on Obscenity and Pornography*, p. 32.

[135]*Report of the Commission on Obscenity and Pornography*, p. 32.

[136]See Victor B. Cline, "Another View: Pornography Effects, the State of the Art," and Cline, "The Pornography Commission: A Case Study of Scientists and Social Policy Decision-Making," both in Cline, *Where Do You Draw the Line?* In Cline's concluding essay to this edited volume, he states: "A review of all the papers and evidences in this volume suggests the possibility of harms associated with exposure of humans to significant amounts of media violence as well as to certain kinds of pornography. Indeed, on the basis of a great deal of scientific evidence presented here, it would be difficult to deny such an assertion." Cline, "A Summing Up," in *Where Do You Draw the Line?*, p. 347.

later aggression, while exposure to more arousing sexual materials (for example, pictures of couples engaged in various acts of lovemaking or explicit erotic passages) neither facilitated nor inhibited such behavior.[137] In a follow-up study by the same investigator, this time with females, it was found that while mild erotic stimuli inhibited subsequent aggressiveness, exposure to more arousing stimuli actually facilitated aggressive behavior.[138] That is, the more arousing sexual materials increased the probability of sexual aggressiveness in females, while the same material inhibited aggressiveness in males. The explanation for this difference appears to rest in the label persons use to identify pornographic materials. While the males in Baron's first study found the more arousing sexual stimuli pleasant, the females did not. In fact, the females rated both the pictures of nudes and sexual acts in quite neutral terms; in short, while the males reacted positively to such materials, the females found them uninteresting or unpleasant. It would seem, then, that the sexes attached quite different labels to any sexual arousals they experienced as a result of exposure to erotic materials. This is not to say, however, that females are not sexually stimulated by pornographic materials, as we noted previously; rather, what constitutes stimulation in a sexual sense may differ for males and females.

The subject continues to be sharply debated in spite of the conclusions reached by the President's Commission. The debate centers primarily around which effects are "desirable" and which "undesirable." The Commission did *not* say that exposure to pornographic materials had no effects; it generally concluded that these effects were not clearly undesirable or, more precisely, dangerous to society. In fact, the Commission reported a number of findings from its own research and that of others which indicated that exposure to pornography did result in heightened sexual activity, although the connecting link between pornography and sexual crimes was not at all clear. One of the more troublesome issues faced by the Commission concerned the notion of "relationship," whether of a cause and effect or merely some other association.[139] Baron's research seems to point out the wisdom of also distinguishing between pornography (stimuli that produce pleasant, erotic feelings) and exposure to other materials (or the same materials differently interpreted).

The Functions of Pornography

One sociologist likened the function of pornography to that of prostitution, namely, that in a society which negatively labels impersonal nonmarital sex there are largely two roads, prostitution with a real sex object and pornography, which can lead to "masturbating, imagined intercourse with a fantasy object."[140] In fact, Polsky argues that only a fine line exists between sexual arousal by means of the so-called porno-

---

[137]Robert A. Baron and Paul A. Bell, "Sexual Arousal and Aggression by Males: Effects of Types of Erotic Stimuli and Prior Provocation," *Journal of Personality and Social Psychology*, 35 (1977), 79–87.

[138]Robert A. Baron, "Heightened Sexual Arousal and Physical Aggression: An Extension to Females," unpublished paper, Purdue University, West Lafayette, Indiana, 1977.

[139]See Weldon T. Johnson, "The Pornography Report: Epistomology, Methodology and Ideology," *Duquesne Law Review*, 10 (1971), 190–219. Johnson was one of the two full-time social scientists on the "Effects Panel" of the Commission.

[140]Ned Polsky, *Hustlers, Beats and Others* (Chicago: Aldine, 1967), p. 195. See also Polsky, "Pornography," in Sagarin and McNamara, pp. 268–285.

graphic materials and that by accepted literature and recognized art works; he calls "patently false" the assumption of the courts and the literary critics that pornography and art are mutually exclusive.

Similarly, the President's Commission, in explaining the reasons for the needed changes in the criminal law regulating erotic materials, pointed out that inhibitions on the free and open discussion of sexual matters in our society was, basically, the reason for its existence. In fact, the Commission also recommended a program of open and massive sex education in the United States, as the following passage from the report shows.

> The Commission believes that much of the "problem" regarding materials which depict explicit sexual activity stems from the inability or reluctance of people in our society to be open and direct in dealing with sexual matters. This most often manifests itself in the inhibition of talking openly and directly about sex. Professionals use highly technical language when they discuss sex; others of us escape by using euphemisms—or by not talking about sex at all. Direct and open conversation about sex between parent and child is too rare in our society. Failure to talk openly and directly about sex has several consequences. It overemphasizes sex, gives it a magical, nonnatural quality, making it more attractive and fascinating. It diverts the expression of sexual interest out of more legitimate channels. Such failure makes teaching children and adolescents to become fully and adequately functioning sexual adults a more difficult task. And it clogs legitimate channels for transmitting sexual information and forces people to use clandestine and unreliable sources.[141]

Some persons have pointed out the apparent contradiction between the Commission's conclusion of "no effect" with regard to exposure to pornographic materials and their recommendations for sex education programs which might well make use of such materials to influence the sexual development of youth. Thus on the one hand the Commission concludes that these materials will not affect the individual, while on the other it hopes that they will.[142] These approaches are not, however, as contradictory as might be supposed, because, as mentioned earlier, the Commission did not say that there were no effects at all. It states merely that no strong evidence was found that whatever effects did result (increased sexual stimulation, increased sexual activity, and so on) were not clearly detrimental. Before the use of erotic materials in sex education courses for adolescents can be strongly endorsed, therefore, more research is needed to isolate and identify the effects of these materials. Baron's research, for example, indicates the need to use different materials for each sex, as well as to monitor the effects more carefully, if the materials are to have the desired result.

The functions of pornography are probably outside the purview of the social scientist as scientist; probably they can be seen more reasonably in terms of social values. Great variations exist in the United States with reference to what is desirable or undesirable; what is functional is probably equally varied. For these reasons in the case of pornography it is unlikely that social science research can either show harmful

---

[141]*Report of the Commission on Obscenity and Pornography*, p. 53.
[142]See, for example, Ernest van den Haag, "Democracy and Pornography," in Cline, *Where Do You Draw the Line?*, pp. 269–270. Also see James Q. Wilson, "Violence, Pornography, and Social Science," *The Public Interest*, 22 (1971), 45–61.

effects or prove their absence. These are issues of a more moral nature that rest ultimately on political and philosophical considerations and criteria.

Still, it might be noted that sex-oriented materials in the form of books, magazines, and films could possibly serve informational, personal, and other needs.[143] (1) Sex-oriented material may offer an important avenue of sexual expression to those who have no partner for sexual activity. (2) Seeing a sexually explicit film may cut through defenses a patient has erected to verbal communication in a therapy session concerning sexual dysfunction. (3) Sexual material may provide one means of communicating sexual matters, through example, to supplement other, more traditional means. Sex therapy centers are presently exploring methods of using such materials in educational and therapy settings.

CONCLUSIONS

Space prohibits a discussion here of various other forms of heterosexual deviance. Chapter 12 presents an analysis of male and female homosexual behavior. Throughout the discussion in all of these areas the main concern has been with the nature of the behavior and its social context. So rapid have been the changes in the nature of sexual norms, particularly in the last decade or so, that conceptions of what is deviant have also undergone marked change. Violations of sexual norms are never clear-cut and absolute, and the situation is made even more complicated by the fact that it is difficult to know precisely what these sexual norms are—their content, the degree of their applicability, the corresponding sanctions associated with their violation, and the conditions under which the violations occur.

One point central to our discussion is that heterosexual deviance (and homosexual deviance) is behavior, not a condition. The medical model of deviance has exerted strong influence over our thinking about sexual matters and has traditionally pointed to the conclusion that sexual deviance is an illness to be treated and cured, much like any other illness, and that it represents a form of mental illness, perhaps coupled with hormonal imbalance. One need not, however (and particularly given the lack of evidence regarding the validity of the medical model), invoke a medical explanation for sexual deviance. Our discussion of social change and sexual behavior indicates that this behavior is to be expected with changes in the content of sexual norms and the increasing acceptance of alternative sexual activities. As noted with respect to premarital and extramarital behavior, sexual deviance—or disagreements about the nature of sexual deviance—is ultimately tied into the social context in which it occurs; it is patterned behavior which gives the appearance of being generated from the same general sources as other forms of deviance: the learning of deviant patterns, perhaps after experimenting with minor forms of the behavior previously. As such, sexual deviance, though more ambiguous perhaps than other forms of deviance, is amenable to the same overall explanatory scheme.

We have suggested (Chapter 1) that one manner in which we can discern the existence of norms is to examine the reactions of others to some behavior; that is, look

---

[143]Winick, pp. 241–242.

at the kinds of sanctions, if any, the act draws from its social audience. Sexual deviance and the examination of sexual norms are not exceptions. The important indication that sexual norms are changing lies not in whether there are more violations (that is, whether more persons are cohabiting today than five years ago, more persons are engaging in extramarital relations, and so on), but in the nature of the reactions, or sanctions, of others who are witnesses to or knowledgeable about the behavior. The forms of sexual deviance examined in this chapter, and the next, display considerable variance in terms of the severity and types of sanctions administered. While there has been a softening of sanctions with respect to premarital sex, stronger sanctions are still usually found with respect to adultery; while previously taboo homosexual practices among consenting adults are less likely to draw strong reactions today from most persons, child molesting is still strongly disapproved. But, regardless of the severity of the sanction to the particular form of deviance, that behavior which exceeds the community's tolerance (even though the amount of tolerance may change) and which draws a negative sanction can be considered deviant. And, as we shall see throughout our discussion, the same general social processes are able to "make sense" of sexual deviance in much the same way as nonsexual deviance.

SELECTED REFERENCES

Clayton, Richard R., and Harwin L. Voss. "Shacking Up: Cohabitation in the 1970s," *Journal of Marriage and the Family,* 39 (1977), 273–283.

Davidson, J. Kenneth, and Gerald R. Leslie. "Premarital Sexual Intercourse: An Application of Axiomatic Theory Construction," *Journal of Marriage and the Family,* 39 (1977), 15–25.

Davis, Kingsley. "Sexual Behavior," in Robert K. Merton and Robert Nisbet, eds., *Contemporary Social Problems,* 4th ed. New York: Harcourt Brace Jovanovich, 1976.

Gagnon, John H., and William Simon. "Perspectives on the Sexual Scene," in John H. Gagnon and William Simon, eds., *The Sexual Scene.* Chicago: Aldine, 1970.

Gagnon, John H., and William Simon. *Sexual Conduct: The Social Sources of Human Sexuality.* Chicago: Aldine, 1973.

Gebhard, Paul H., John H. Gagnon, Wardell B. Pomeroy, and Cornelia V. Christenson. *Sex Offenders.* New York: Harper & Row, 1965.

Holmes, Ronald M. *Sexual Behavior: Prostitution, Homosexuality and Swinging.* Berkeley, Calif.: McCutchan, 1971.

James, Jennifer. "Prostitutes and Prostitution," in Edward Sagarin and Fred L. Montanino, eds., *Deviants: Voluntary Actors in a Hostile World.* Morristown, N.J.: General Learning Press, 1977.

Packer, Herbert L. *The Limits of the Criminal Sanction.* Stanford, Calif.: Stanford University Press, 1968.

Palson, Charles and Rebecca, "Swinging in Wedlock," *Society,* 9 (1972), 28–37.

Polsky, Ned. *Hustlers, Beats and Others.* Chicago: Aldine, 1967.

Reiss, Ira L. *The Social Context of Premarital Sexual Permissiveness.* New York: Holt, Rinehart and Winston, 1967.

Report of the Commission on Obscenity and Pornography. Washington, D.C.: Government Printing Office, 1970.

Robinson, Paul. *The Modernization of Sex.* New York: Harper & Row, 1976.

Sagarin, Edward. "Sex Deviance: A View from Middle America," in Edward Sagarin and Fred L. Montanino, eds., *Deviants: Voluntary Actors in a Hostile World.* Morristown, N.J.: General Learning Press, 1977.

Velarde, Albert J., and Mark Warlick. "Massage Parlors: The Sensuality Business," *Society,* 11 (1973), 63–74.

Walshok, Mary Lindenstein. "The Emergence of Middle-Class Deviant Subcultures: The Case of Swingers," *Social Problems,* 18 (1971), 488–495.

Winick, Charles, and Paul M. Kinsie. *The Lively Commerce: Prostitution in the United States.* New York: Quadrangle Books, 1971.

Wolfenden Report. Report of the Committee on Homosexual Offenses and Prostitution. New York: Lancer Books, 1964.

OTHER
MAN
S NO
SIN!

GAYS
HAVE
VOTE
POWER!
...LET'S USE IT

The Gay Rights Movement to eliminate discrimination against homosexuals and to gain equality
with heterosexuals has become widespread in
the United States and in much of Europe. It often
takes the form of public demonstrations. (© Bettye
Lane/Photo Researchers, Inc.)

Homosexual Deviance

HOMOSEXUAL deviance represents sex relations with members of one's own sex, whether male or female. Between males sex can be carried out physically in a number of ways, sodomy (anal), fellatio (mouth-genital), and mutual masturbation. Homosexual relations between women can consist of oral stimulation of the clitoris (cunnilingus), mutual masturbation, and the use of objects like vibrators or an artificial penis. Such persons may regard these forms of sexual outlet as more satisfactory than heterosexual relations. Persons who engage in homosexual behavior, males or females, come from all social classes, have varying degrees of education, have a wide range of occupations and professions, have varied interests and avocations, and may be single or married.

More important sociologically is the concept of *homosexual identity,* which refers to a person's sexual self-concept; this is of more significance in the identification of a "homosexual" person than the type of behavior itself. Many persons prefer homosexual activities and consider themselves homosexuals even though they may occasionally engage in heterosexual relations.[1] A true homosexual is any adult who regards himself as a homosexual and who is prepared to say he is to another person.

MALE HOMOSEXUALITY

Male Homosexuality as Deviance

Most societies have what are termed sexually appropriate and sexually inappropriate roles according to a person's age, social status, and other criteria. In some societies homosexual roles and behavior are considered inappropriate for one's sex, and in others they are condoned or even approved. There is ample evidence that cultural attitudes toward homosexual or one-sex behavior have differed from one period in history to another. In Greek and Roman times this behavior was prevalent, and in some societies homosexual practices were related to certain religious rites. Ford and Beach studied 76 folk societies and found that among 49 of them, or 64 percent, "homosexual activities of one sort or another are considered normal and socially acceptable for certain members of the community."[2] But no known society has been generally accepting of persons who have, or wish to have, played a homosexual role indefinitely. That is, some societies have condoned homosexuality as a "phase" of development through which certain persons pass, but it has then been expected that they become heterosexual after a period of time.

In the United States the attribution of homosexuality may have great consequences for the individual. He may be treated as an object of avoidance or amusement; he may be dismissed from his employment and have difficulty in subsequent positions; the police may harass him, and he may even be confined in jail or prison.

---

[1]Barry Dank, "The Development of a Homosexual Identity: Antecedents and Consequences," unpublished Ph.D. dissertation, University of Wisconsin, Madison, 1972.
[2]Clellan S. Ford and Frank A. Beach, *Patterns of Sexual Behavior* (New York: Harper & Row, 1951), p. 130.

The author and journalist Merle Miller has described some of the negative experiences he has encountered as a homosexual.

A little while after the dance began a man whose face had been only vaguely familiar and whose name I would not have remembered if he had not earlier reminded me came up, an idiot grin on his face, his wrists limp, his voice falsetto, and said, "How about letting me have this dance, sweetie?" He said it loud enough for all to hear. . . . Later, several people apologized for what he had said, but I wondered (who would not?) how many of them had been tempted to say the same thing. Or would say something of the kind after I had gone. Fag, faggot, sissy, queer. A fag is a homosexual gentleman who has just left the room.

The fear of it simply will not go away, though. A man who was once a friend, maybe my best friend, the survivor of five marriages, the father of nine, not too long ago told me that his eldest son was coming to my house on Saturday: "Now please try not to make a pass at him." He laughed, I guess he meant it as a joke; I didn't ask.[3]

Normatively a number of objections to homosexual behavior have been raised. It cannot lead to reproduction or to a "normal" family situation. In a sense it distorts the general assignment of complementary sex roles to the members of a society. A 1976 study, for example, found that persons do *not* react negatively to homosexual acts *per se,* but they do react negatively to the sex role stereotypes associated with persons engaging in the acts.[4] People often find offensive the confusion of sex roles, that is, males who act feminine and women who act masculine, rather than homosexual behavior. Another basis for the negative attitudes toward homosexuals relates to the conception of what constitutes "normal" sexual functioning and development. While it is clear that the social and personal backgrounds of many homosexuals differ from those who identify with heterosexuality, as will be discussed presently, this does not mean that their behavior is "abnormal." With respect to sexuality, there is nothing inherently "normally sexual," but naming it makes it so. One theorist states that sexuality is a social construction "that has been learned in interaction with others."[5] It is not dictated by body chemistry but by the social situation. One learns to be aroused by some persons but not others. One learns at what age one is supposed to be capable of arousal and sexual intercourse. One learns which situations are appropriate for sexual arousal. The sex drive, in other words, "is neither powerful nor weak; it can be almost anything we make it."[6] The social meaning of sexuality, then, is one attained in the same manner as other social acts, as part of the overall socialization process of society. Sexuality is learned, not all at once but over a period of time and according to the principles of learning and social interaction that have been discussed in other contexts (see Chapter 2).[7] In the context of sexuality, orientation toward particular

---

[3]Merle Miller, "What It Means To Be a Homosexual," *New York Times Magazine,* January 17, 1971, p. 57.

[4]A. P. McDonald, "Homophobia: Its Roots and Meanings," *Homosexual Counseling Journal,* 3 (1976), 23–33.

[5]Kenneth Plummer, *Sexual Stigma: An Interactionist Account* (London: Routledge & Kegan Paul, 1975), p. 30.

[6]Erich Goode and Richard T. Troiden, eds., *Sexual Deviance and Sexual Deviants* (New York: Morrow, 1974), p. 15.

[7]The most explicit statements of the myth of the sexual drive and the social meaning of sexuality can be found in John H. Gagnon and William Simon, *Sexual Conduct: The Social Sources of Human Sexuality* (Chicago: Aldine, 1973); and John H. Gagnon, "Sexual Conduct and Crime," in Daniel Glaser, ed., *Handbook of Criminology* (Chicago: Rand McNally, 1974), pp. 238–243.

persons is similarly learned, and that learning can mean that a person can find sexual meaning in anything and in anybody, all depending upon the learning process.

The typical conception of sexuality, however, is quite different from this sociological portrait. Many people have become accustomed to thinking about sexuality as being innate and dependent on certain vague, biological determinants, loosely termed the "sex drive." Actually, there is no such thing, except in the imagination of persons who have been unable to conceive of sexual development in any terms other than biological. With this basic premise, and the failure to comprehend the basic learning process, many persons continue to believe that homosexuality is pathological in some sense, either moral or biological.

Male Homosexual Acts and the Law   Laws forbidding homosexual behavior come from the ancient Jewish sex codes which were formalized by the Christian church into the ecclesiastical laws that governed medieval Europe and later provided the basis for English common law.[8] The Emperor Justinian condemned homosexual offenders to the sword by edict in 538, and this Justinian Code prohibition constituted the foundation for the legal punishment of homosexuality in Europe for 1,300 years. For hundreds of years homosexual acts were punished by the ecclesiastical courts of the church, often with death or torture. By 1533, however, jurisdiction over the "vice of Buggery" in England was vested in the royal courts, and the English statute enacted by parliament during the reign of Henry VIII provided that on conviction the accused be put to death without benefit of clergy.[9] So the punishment remained until the nineteenth century when it was reduced to life imprisonment. Even the offenses against the person act of 1861, which remained in force until 1956, provided up to life imprisonment for sodomy by two men or by man and wife.

Under the British law of 1956 sodomy with a person under age was still life imprisonment, but the sentence for adults was reduced. Penalties of misdemeanor were also provided for certain public homosexual acts. After long Parliamentary commission studies and debates, penalties for homosexual acts in private between adults over 21 were removed in 1965. Penalties are maintained for acts with those younger and for those who procure for homosexual acts.

As late as the mid-eighteenth century homosexuals were burned at the stake in Paris. Liberalization of legal attitudes came in Europe with the French Revolution and the later Napoleonic Code, which left homosexual acts out of the legal structure, a fact that still exists in many European countries. These laws, however, were later changed to permit homosexual acts only between consenting adults over 21 years of age. While many societies seek to protect young persons from homosexual acts and to protect public decency, nearly all European countries, such as England, France, Spain, Italy, Denmark, and Finland, do not consider homosexual acts committed in private by adults to be criminal acts.[10]

The changes in laws in most European countries over the years have partially

---

[8]The best single source of historical material on homosexuality can be found in Jonathan Katz, ed., *Gay American History: Lesbians and Gay Men in the U.S.A.* (New York: Cromwell, 1976).
[9]J. M. Hyde, *The Love That Dare Not Speak Its Name: A Candid History of Homosexuality in Britain* (Boston: Little, Brown, 1970).
[10]For a discussion, see Gilbert Geis, *Not the Law's Business?* (Rockville, Md.: National Institute of Mental Health, 1972).

affected laws on homosexual acts in the United States. In 1977, these acts were still crimes under all circumstances, both public and private, in 36 states and the District of Columbia. Between 1961 and 1977, 14 states had changed the law, making homosexual acts a crime only if committed publicly (this is the same with heterosexual acts), exempting all homosexual acts done in private: Arkansas, California, Colorado, Connecticut, Delaware, Hawaii, Illinois, Maine, New Mexico, North Dakota, Ohio, Oregon, South Dakota, and Washington.

It must be remembered that in the United States and other countries it is never a crime to *be* a homosexual; the crimes are the homosexual *acts,* such as sodomy, fellatio, and mutual masturbation. Legally, the homosexual act is somewhat unusual in that the partner is likely to be a willing associate; for this reason, it has been called a victimless crime or a crime without a victim.[11]

Soliciting for such acts is also generally a crime. Practically the only homosexual acts that are punished are between males, for although homosexuality is by no means uncommon among women, it is generally not punished. In most states the penalty for male homosexual acts is five years imprisonment. A number of states still provide up to 10 years, and a few provide from 30 to 60 years. In addition, some states have sex deviate laws under which an offender can be committed for "treatment" in excess of the period provided by the criminal statutes. In actuality these criminal felony laws are seldom enforced; where there are arrests they are generally for solicitation, a misdemeanor with less than a one-year sentence.

Changing Public Attitudes   As knowledge about the learning process of sexual behavior increases, along with certain broad contemporary social changes such as greater equality for women and wider possibilities of heterosexual behavior, as well as the desire to have a lower birth rate, some people have wondered why homosexuality should continue to be strongly disapproved. The level of public disapproval of homosexuality, however, has declined markedly over the last decade; in fact, public reaction is much more liberal than the existence of the laws against it would indicate. To some degree this has also been due to changes in regard to homosexuality within the medical profession, specifically in the field of psychiatry. Homosexuality has been, and still is by some, viewed as a psychiatric disturbance of the individual. For years this approach was supported by psychiatrists, who listed homosexuality among the categories of mental illness.[12] In 1973, however, the American Psychiatric Association reversed itself and declared that by itself homosexuality does not "necessarily constitute a psychiatric disorder." This decision seems to have been the result of efforts to change the organization's perception of homosexuality on the part of certain activist groups within the association.[13] When an organization as prestigious as a psychiatric association "decriminalizes" homosexuality, informed persons tend to respect the decision. It is probably too soon to predict what eventual impact this decision might have on subsequent legislation; New York state, for example, has twice turned down a

---

[11]See Edwin M. Schur, *Crimes without Victims* (Englewood Cliffs, N.J.: Prentice-Hall, 1965).

[12]The American Psychiatric Association publishes the *Diagnostic and Statistical Manual of Mental Disorders,* which lists all psychiatric diagnostic categories, mainly used for convenience to standardize nomenclature and to aid in keeping consistent records.

[13]For an account of the dynamics involved in this decision, see Malcolm Spector, "Legitimizing Homosexuality," *Society,* 14 (1977), 52–56.

homosexual civil rights amendment since this decision, but this may well foreshadow changes in public opinion at the nonprofessional level.

Several cities in the 1970s adopted antidiscrimination laws to protect homosexual rights: San Francisco, for example, made it illegal to discriminate against a homosexual in employment, housing, and so on, and in 1977 Tucson's City Council unanimously adopted an ordinance against job discrimination on many grounds, including "sexual or affectional preference." It appears that these laws are widely supported in their respective communities. A 1977 Gallup national public opinion poll showed that 56 percent of Americans approve of equal employment rights for homosexuals. On the other hand, a large proportion of the sample disapproved of their employment in specific occupations such as elementary school teachers (75 percent) and the clergy (54 percent). The larger the city, the more likely is the public to have more tolerant attitudes toward homosexuals. The movement toward equal rights for homosexuals suffered a nationally publicized reversal in 1977 in Dade County (Miami, Florida) when an ordinance guaranteeing these rights was repealed. The repeal drive was spearheaded by a group called the Save Our Children crusade, whose leader, Anita Bryant, a well-known television and movie personality, also spoke to audiences nationally. She maintained that homosexuality is immoral, contrary to Christian religious doctrine and God's will, and that as teachers homosexuals would indoctrinate their students. It is impossible to predict what the nation-wide impact this reversal on homosexual rights may be, although the Tucson ordinance was adopted after the Florida repeal. The Florida campaign demonstrated, however, that homosexual males and females, and their sympathizers, are willing to display publicly their strong support for such laws on a massive basis.[14] In San Francisco, 200,000 persons marched in protest, partly precipitated by the fatal stabbing at about the same time of a homosexual boy by four young men shouting "faggot, faggot." Police estimated that this march, and the "Gay Pride Week" celebration that followed the march, were larger than any protest against the Vietnam war in the 1960s. In New York City, 25,000 marched, and in Seattle, the mayor proclaimed a Gay Pride Week, saying that it was consistent with the city's treatment of all as equals. Demonstrations were also held in Chicago, Atlanta, Amsterdam, and London, and influential nonhomosexual organizations condemned the repeal in Arkansas, Wichita, Austin, and Houston. On the other hand, this sentiment did not discourage Eugene, Oregon, for example, from repealing its homosexual rights ordinance in 1978.

Society's increasing tolerance of variations in sexual behavior, the freer circulation of information concerning homosexuality, and the militancy and openness of gay organizations are important trends now altering the stereotype of the homosexual. These developments have also facilitated self-identification of those inclined toward this behavior. The increased overt circulation of homosexual publications, such as magazines and newspapers, advertisements for gay movies, and books, articles, and movies about gay life, permits "the cognitive category of homosexuals to be known to a larger proportion of the population."[15] More important, more information can also be circulated that challenges the negative societal stereotype of a homosexual.

One study has attempted to isolate those conditions that are associated with

---

[14]"Gays March in U.S., Europe," *The Capital Times* (Madison, Wisc.), June 27, 1977.
[15]Barry Dank, "Coming Out in the Gay World," *Psychiatry*, 34 (1971), 194.

increased tolerance toward homosexuality and homosexuals.[16] Being female, having known homosexuals, and having parents who had an accepting attitude toward homosexuality were found to be associated with more tolerance. Moreover, while a father's occupation was unrelated, it was found that where the mother was employed outside the home, the respondent was more likely to accept less social distance between himself and homosexuals than when the mother was reported to be a housewife. Evidently, those persons who have had contact with homosexuals in the past and those from backgrounds that permit a diversity of social roles are more likely to have a chance to find homosexual stereotypes misleading or incorrect.

The Attribution of Homosexuality

A common myth is that male homosexuals can be readily recognized as physically effeminate persons and that women homosexuals are masculine in manners and appearance. Actually, most homosexuals are indistinguishable physically from heterosexuals. Where they are socially visible—and many are—it is because they play a homosexual role. An English study of male homosexuals found only 17 percent with slight or pronounced feminine characteristics, but two thirds said they could be recognized by other homosexuals. In order of importance were the glance of the eyes, the gestures, walk, voice, clothing, and vocabulary.[17] Another study maintained, however, that many male homosexuals display feminine traits because they believe they are "conforming to a stereotype." They feel impelled to "adopt what they consider feminine characteristics" because of the traditional division between the sex roles and because a male homosexual "construes his homosexual interest as evidence of a feminine component within himself."[18] Still, the study showed that some "obviousness" as a homosexual for males with extensive homosexual experience varied from 28 to 60 percent.[19] Sometimes subtle feminine mannerisms can be detected by a homosexual only as a part of a total syndrome. These subtleties are frequently associated with upper socioeconomic level tastes and behavior: "overmeticulous dress, too well-groomed fingernails, a gentle, modulated voice, an interest in aesthetics, etc."[20] In our culture, these characteristics have had some feminine significance, for example, women generally paying more attention to clothes than men. Since this particular study was made, however, these masculine-feminine distinctions in attitudes toward dress have become less marked.

Still, it is difficult to generalize about reversed sex roles because many exceptions can be found. Some indication of the great variations in the social and physical

---

[16]Barry Glassner and Carol Owen, "Variations in Attitudes toward Homosexuality," *Cornell Journal of Social Relations,* 11 (1976), 161–176.

[17]Gordon Westwood, *A Minority: A Report on the Life of the Male Homosexual in Great Britain* (London: Longmans, Green, 1960), p. 62.

[18]Paul H. Gebhard, John H. Gagnon, Wardell B. Pomeroy, and Cornelia V. Christenson, *Sex Offenders* (New York: Harper & Row, 1965), p. 348.

[19]Gebhard *et al.,* p. 652. The percentage of "some obviousness" has been added to the percentage of "obvious" in the figures given here.

[20]Gebhard *et al.,* p. 348.

characteristics can be seen in the long list of important historical figures throughout the centuries who were homosexuals—philosophers, military leaders, artists, musicians, and writers.

> Socrates and Plato made no bones about their homosexuality; Catullus wrote a love poem to a young man whose "honeysweet lips" he wanted to kiss; Virgil and Horace wrote erotic poems about men; Michelangelo's great love sonnets were addressed to a young man, and so were Shakespeare's. There seems to be evidence that Alexander the Great was homosexual, and Julius Caesar certainly was—the Roman Senator Curio called Caesar "every woman's man and every man's woman." So were Charles XII of Sweden and Frederick the Great. Several English monarchs have been homosexual. . . . About some individuals of widely differing kinds, from William of Orange to Lawrence of Arabia, there is running controversy which may never reach a definite conclusion. About others—Marlowe, Tchaikovsky, Whitman, Kitchener, Rimbaud, Verlaine, Proust, Gide, Wilde and many more—there is no reasonable doubt.[21]

Persons are often attributed or imputed to be homosexual as a result of how they are defined by others, whether they are or not. This definition does not necessarily follow from any specific behavior. One study of 75 persons who had "known" homosexuals indicated that the process of the attribution, or categorization, was indeed complex, based on both indirect and direct evidence.[22] Regardless of what evidence of homosexuality exists, it may become documented by retrospective interpretation of the person's behavior, a process that consists of a review of past interactions with the individual. In this review of these past interactions a search is made for those subtle cues and behavior that might provide the evidence to justify the attribution of homosexual. Indirect evidence includes rumor, general information about the person's behavior, associates, or sexual preferences, or the experiences an acquaintance might have had with the person even though it might not have been verified. Direct observation includes behavior that "everyone knows" as evidence of homosexuality or behavior that deviates from commonly held behaviors among members of the group to which the individual belongs, for example, effeminate appearance and manners. Finally, there are behavior-manners that the person interprets as overt sexual propositions; the person then interprets the so-called deviant's behavior as progressively inappropriate in the course of interaction with him.

Prevalence of Male Homosexuality

Various attempts have been made to estimate the size of the male homosexual population, particularly in the United States and in Great Britain. In his basic work on sex behavior 30 years ago, Kinsey reported that at some time between adolescence and old age about 37 percent of the white male population had had homosexual experiences (homosexual behavior), and to the point of orgasm. Only half as many

---

[21]Bryan Magee, *One in Twenty: A Study of Homosexuality in Men and Women* (New York: Stein and Day, 1966), p. 46.
[22]John I. Kitsuse, "Societal Reaction to Deviant Behavior: Problems of Theory and Method," in Howard S. Becker, ed., *The Other Side: Perspectives on Deviance* (New York: Free Press, 1964), pp. 87–102.

females as males had had homosexual experiences, but males had more frequent relations, continued their activities longer, and were more promiscuous.[23] Kinsey reported that 4 percent of his sample of males were career homosexuals. In 1963, Lindner stated that a conservative estimate of the extent of "genuine inversion" in the United States was roughly 4 to 6 percent of the total male population over 16, approximately 3 million persons.[24] A 1966 British study estimated that approximately 1 in every 20 persons, men and women, were homosexuals.[25] There is also ample evidence of extensive homosexual relations in prisons and in other one-sex communities.

To date, estimates as to the incidence, prevalence, and increase of homosexuality have been based on inadequate and unrepresentative data, often accompanied by fallacious reasoning. After examining the literature Schur stated that there were no satisfactory statistics regarding the prevalence of homosexuality. He claimed that estimates by individual homosexuals are not likely to be accurate, because many homosexuals "have a psychological stake in exaggerating their number."[26] Westwood reached a similar conclusion; he found the homosexual's estimate to be "biased" by the extent to which he could find sexual partners.[27] It is also impossible, he stated, to determine if the incidence has increased at different periods in Great Britain and in other European countries.[28] A similar conclusion was reported in a 1964 government study of homosexual behavior in Great Britain: the increased interest in studying homosexuality, as seen in the growing body of literature dealing entirely or incidentally with it, the report stated, does not necessarily mean that the behavior is more widespread than formerly.[29] There does appear to be some indication, however, that in the 1970s homosexual behavior has been increasing in the United States and in parts of Europe, although this may be a reflection of changes in the public's attitudes and the resulting more open expressions of individual homosexuality.

Varieties of Male Homosexuals

For male homosexuals who live together as partners in a more or less permanent union the homosexual relation may be quite stable, their sexuality having become integrated into long-standing affectional, personal, and social patterns. The majority of male homosexuals, however, are likely to have a widespread sexual life, their relations with other homosexuals confined generally to brief and relatively transitory sexual encounters. Permanent relationships for them are likely to be infrequent, but even less

---

[23]Alfred S. Kinsey, Wardell B. Pomeroy, and Clyde E. Martin, *Sexual Behavior in the Human Male* (Philadelphia: Saunders, 1948); and Alfred C. Kinsey, Wardell B. Pomeroy, Clyde E. Martin, and Paul H. Gebhard, *Sexual Behavior in the Human Female* (Philadelphia: Saunders, 1953).
[24]Robert Lindner, "Homosexuality and the Contemporary Scene," in Hendrix Ruitenbeek, ed., *The Problem of Homosexuality in Modern Society* (New York: Dutton, 1963), p. 61.
[25]Magee, pp. 43–46.
[26]Schur, p. 75.
[27]Westwood, *A Minority*, p. 62.
[28]Westwood, *A Minority*, p. 63.
[29]Report of the Committee on Homosexual Offenses and Prostitution, *Wolfenden Report* (New York: Lancer Books, 1964), pp. 40–41.

lengthy affectional-sexual ties in homosexual life are inclined to be overshadowed by the predominant pattern "of 'cruising' and relatively impersonal one-night stands."[30] Because of the relatively impersonal nature of such sex relations, certain male juveniles, who are likely not to be homosexuals themselves, offer their services on a monetary basis.[31] Transitory sex relations can also be arranged with the homosexual prostitute, the "hustler" for other homosexuals who provides, particularly for those who are less attractive physically and older, those services that might be difficult to obtain without great effort. The adult homosexual prostitute is a part of homosexual life; he learns his behavior role—such as gestures, vocabulary, clothing, and even makeup—in the same sense that heterosexual prostitutes become a part of heterosexual life.[32]

Many homosexuals become acquainted in such public places as toilets, bars, parks, clubs, cafes, baths, hotels, beaches, and movie theaters.[33] A large part of these sexual relations are highly impersonal and may even be carried out in a "tearoom," or "T-room,"[34] the homosexual name for a public toilet. These tearooms are readily accessible to the male population, being located near public gathering places— department stores, bus stations, libraries, hotels, YMCAs, and, particularly, in isolated parts of public parks. Usually a third person may act both as voyeur and lookout.

Persons who have studied the homosexual population have found that a substantial proportion of them have been at one time or another heterosexually married, the figure in one study being as high as one fourth.[35] It appears that in some cases the person may view his marriage to a woman as an act which will demonstrate to himself and others that he is very much like the "normal" person. Most of them did not conceive of themselves as homosexuals at the time they were married, in their twenties, even though they may have engaged in homosexual acts; only later did they develop this identity. Earlier, they thought that their homosexuality was only a passing thing. On the other hand, admitted homosexuals marry because of social pressures, a flight from homosexuality, or for commitment to a home-centered life.[36] A married homosexual described how he had discovered a men's room down on the beach and how he would make occasional sexual contacts there coming home from work in the afternoon, several times a week: "I stopped there on my way home to see what could be found, and I very frequently found something."[37]

Many such married persons who engage in impersonal sexual relations with other men cannot be called homosexuals sociologically in terms of a homosexual

---

[30]Schur, p. 89.

[31]Albert J. Reiss, Jr., "The Social Integration of Queers and Peers," *Social Problems,* 9 (1961), 102–120.

[32]John Rechy, *City of Night* (New York: Grove Press, 1963), p. 36.

[33]For a discussion of the role of public places in the lives of homosexuals, *see* Martin S. Weinberg and Colin J. Williams, "Gay Baths and the Social Organization of Impersonal Sex," *Social Problems,* 23 (1975), 124–136

[34]Laud Humphreys, *Tearoom Trade: Impersonal Sex in Public Places,* enlarged ed. (Chicago: Aldine, 1975).

[35]See, for example, Barry Dank, "Why Homosexuals Marry Women," *Medical Aspects of Human Sexuality,* 6 (1972), 14–23.

[36]H. Laurence Ross, "Modes of Adjustment of Married Homosexuals," *Social Problems,* 18 (1971), 385– 393.

[37]Dank, "Why Homosexuals Marry Women," p. 20.

identity. Their homosexual relations may serve them when the home situation is not satisfactory or their heterosexual relations are too infrequent. Humphreys' study of these tearoom participants showed that the largest group (38 percent) were married or were previously married men, largely truck drivers, machine operators, or clerical workers.[38] Most of them did not want a homosexual experience, but rather a quick orgasm, which was more satisfying than masturbation, less involved than a love affair, and less expensive than a prostitute. The second group were "ambisexuals," mostly better educated and socially members of the middle and upper classes, many of them married or otherwise heterosexual, who liked the "kicks" of such unusual sex experiences. The gay group of openly confessed homosexuals constituted only 14 percent, and the last group of "closet queens" made up an even smaller proportion of the tearoom trade. Closet queens are homosexuals, unmarried or married, who keep their homosexual acts secret. The term "closet queen" is a slang term used by many homosexuals, and the meaning of this term is variable. Usually it means a person who engages in homosexual acts and is homosexually attracted but does not admit to *himself* that he is homosexual.

Some evidence exists that homosexual behavior is more frequent in certain occupations, but the evidence is inconclusive: homosexuals are found in almost every occupation and among persons at all educational levels. Persons apprehended for the more overt homosexual acts in public places are more likely to come from lower occupations, whereas the secret homosexual is more likely to be a middle- or an upper-class person.[39] Some occupations may attract homosexuals because they need not conceal their behavior, other persons accepting the special nature of their occupational roles. Others once in the occupation may accept the definition of themselves by others as "effeminate." Schofield concludes that

> for whatever reason it is in fact now probable that there is a higher proportion of revealed homosexuality in certain job categories—such as interior decoration, ballet and chorus dancing, hairdressing, and fashion design—than in others. The adjective *revealed* is important, because the true proportions for those occupations in which greater concealment is necessary is not known.[40]

Learning Homosexual Behavior

Some important terms should be clarified before the learning context of homosexuality is examined. As has been pointed out, *homosexual behavior* refers to sexual practices with one's own sex. On the other hand, *homosexual attraction* refers to the subjective feelings that a person of the same sex is more sexually attractive than a person of the opposite sex. The distinction between these terms is subtle, but it is an important distinction because homosexuals may differ with respect to each of them. A

---

[38]Humphreys, *Tearoom Trade.*
[39]Maurice Leznoff and William Westley, "The Homosexual Community," *Social Problems,* 3 (1956), 257–263. Also see William J. Helmer, "New York's Middle-Class Homosexuals," *Harper's,* 226 (1963), 85–92.
[40]Michael Schofield, *Sociological Aspects of Homosexuality: A Comparative Study of Three Types of Homosexuals* (Boston: Little, Brown, 1965), p. 209.

person may engage in homosexual activities but still be primarily attracted to persons of the opposite sex.[41] On the other hand, many married homosexuals feel more attracted to persons of their own sex and find most of their sexual stimulation coming from them. The degree to which a person combines both a high level of homosexual attraction and a high level of homosexual behavior may be a product, as well as the function, of the homosexual subculture and the extent to which the person is a member of, identifies with, and has most of his social contacts with that subculture. For this reason, there is no such thing as *the* homosexual, but differing degrees of involvement with homosexuality at the levels of behavior and attraction.

In every culture there are present in varying degrees both adolescent and adult persons who define homosexual relations as pleasurable. Likewise, large numbers of children engage in experimental sex play of a homosexual nature, particularly when such experimentation is difficult to achieve with members of the opposite sex. The very first homosexual experience among a group of homosexuals studied in Great Britain was usually with a school boy of the same age and generally constituted sex play, often in a school situation.[42] These experiences, however, did not necessarily lead to homosexuality as a pattern of sex behavior because such sex behavior among boys may have little emotional feeling. The first "significant homosexual experience" can be defined as one carried out with an adult or repeated acts carried out with the same boy over a year or so. Over two thirds of such experiences were with another boy. Only one fifth were first introduced to homosexuality as boys by adults, and a further 11 percent had no experience of any sort until they were adults; and in all such cases the partner was an adult. Contrary to the popular view, seduction is not an important factor. With most homosexuals there was a long period during which they fought against their homosexual activity before recognizing it as permanent behavior and assuming a conception of themselves as being homosexuals. Another study, however, showed that homosexuals are likely to have had sexual experiences with adult males even before puberty; one third had been approached by men and one fourth had had physical contact with men.[43]

A British study involving six groups of 50 homosexuals each showed that by the time they were adults nearly all the homosexuals had had at least one exposure to sex.[44] Three fourths of the men in all three groups had had their first exposure before 16, and 16 percent had had it with an adult. As one put it, "At first I wanted to find out what it was all about, but when it happened I seemed to take it for granted. As far as I can recall, I liked it. It seemed to please me."[45] Another study found that approximately one half of all the homosexuals had had their first exposure before 15.[46]

It has been emphasized that sex roles are learned. Behavior patterns associated with masculinity and femininity are learned as part of one's sex role; they are not biologically inherited. Homosexuality and heterosexuality may thus be understood

[41]Reiss.
[42]Westwood, *A Minority*, pp. 24–39.
[43]Gebhard *et al.*, p. 329.
[44]Schofield.
[45]Schofield, p. 33.
[46]Gebhard *et al.*

within three concepts: (1) sex-role adoption; (2) sex-role preference; and (3) sex-role identification.[47] *Sex-role adoption* refers to the active adoption of the behavior characteristic of one sex or the other, not simply the desire to adopt such behavior. *Sex-role preference* is the desire to adopt behavior associated with one sex or the other, or the perception of this behavior as being preferable. Finally, *sex-role identification,* which is crucial in homosexuality, is the actual incorporation of a given sex role and the unconscious or unthinking reaction that is characteristic of that role. In this manner a person may thus be "identified with the opposite sex, but for expediency adopt much of the behavior characteristic of his own sex. He may even prefer the role of his own sex, although identified with the opposite sex role."[48]

On the basis of these concepts, *career homosexuals* are more likely to be those who have acquired inappropriate sex-role identification or sex-role assimilation in childhood.[49] Several studies have shown, for example, that the effectiveness of traditional sex-role learning in children is associated with the sex of the siblings, absence of father, and birth-order position in the family.[50] These points have been confirmed in a study which reported that most homosexuals in the sample came from backgrounds where the father was either physically or emotionally absent.[51] In a comparison study of a group of homosexuals and a group of heterosexuals, 84 percent of the homosexuals, and only 18 percent of the control group of heterosexuals, reported that their fathers were indifferent to them. Only 13 percent of the homosexuals, but two thirds of the controls, identified with their fathers; and while 18 percent of the homosexuals had what they would call a satisfactory relationship with their fathers, 82 percent of the heterosexuals reported a satisfactory relationship.[52]

Early childhood experiences, however, do not determine the individual's eventual sexual orientation; sexual learning continues through adolescence and into early adulthood with the learning of both appropriate and inappropriate sexual contexts, objects, and sentiments. Adolescence is particularly important because it is during this period that young persons are changing from "homosocial" contacts (contacts primarily with one's own sex) to "heterosocial" contacts (contacts with the opposite sex). Throughout adolescence young persons are exposed to sexual situations, and they learn to interpret these situations in the context of sexuality. By the end of adolescence they are fully aware of these contexts—which persons are sexually desirable, when and with whom it is appropriate to have sexual relations, and so on. By this period in their lives most have developed a sexual identity. As some individuals learn to define heterosexual acts as pleasurable, some also learn to define as pleasurable homosexual acts. The development process is the same; the content of what is learned is different.

---

[47]David B. Lynn, "A Note on Sex Differences in the Development of Masculine and Feminine Identification," *Psychological Review,* 66 (1959), 126–135.

[48]Lynn, p. 127.

[49]See Dank, "The Development of a Homosexual Identity"; and Gagnon and Simon, *Sexual Conduct.*

[50]See, for example, Orville Brim, "Family Structure and Sex Role Learning by Children," in Norman Bell and Ezra Vogel, *A Modern Introduction to the Family* (New York: Free Press, 1960), pp. 482–496.

[51]Marcel T. Saghir and Eli Robins, *Male and Female Homosexuality: A Comparative Investigation* (Baltimore, Md.: Williams and Wilkins, 1973).

[52]Saghir and Robins, pp. 144–145.

Primary and Secondary
Homosexual Deviance

It is important to distinguish between those secondary, or career, homosexuals who play a homosexual role under a variety of circumstances and those whose behavior is more likely to be the result of a particular situation. The behavior of the latter may be regarded as primary, or situational, and may occur, for example, in one-sex communities like prisons, isolated military posts, naval ships, and boarding schools. There are also those who have committed occasional homosexual acts, particularly in adolescence, and those who may commit homosexual acts for money. Most persons who commit homosexual acts are not homosexuals in a full sociological sense; they are not secondary or career deviants.

Secondary homosexual deviants tend to seek sexual gratification predominantly and continually with members of the same sex. They have developed a self-concept and play a homosexual role in connection with these acts. In fact, Goffman limits the term "homosexual" to "individuals who participate in a special community of understanding wherein members of one's own sex are defined as the most desirable sexual objects and sociability is energetically organized around the pursuit and entertainment of these objects."[53] An important aspect of secondary deviance is participation in those establishments, such as bars, that are primarily attended by homosexuals in the larger cities of western Europe and America. Depending on the size of the city, a great variety of homosexual bars serve as a necessary locus for the male homosexual community.[54] They allow the individual not only to meet other homosexuals but to get away from the concealment he may practice in the heterosexual world. There it is not necessary to hide one's sexual orientation; in fact, the nonhomosexual may be subjected to some stigma. It is likely that the positive attraction for such meeting places is that they provide the homosexual with a positive self-image in the face of the pressures of societal reaction.

Several studies have shown that there are homosexuals who, as secondary deviants, are fairly well adjusted to the homosexual role and experience little conflict. One study, in which half the cases had a high degree of psychological adjustment, concluded that homosexuality "may be a deviation in sexual patterns which is within the normal range psychologically."[55] Such individuals have developed their own identities. Rationalizations, the attitude of partners, and the homosexual subculture help. In fact, one writer maintains that "those who accept their homosexual impulses are less likely to get into trouble with the law and are more likely to be capable of establishing an emotional relationship with another man."[56]

Few studies attempt to indicate the stages through which a person moves from primary to secondary homosexuality. Schofield's study involved six samples of 50 each: convicted homosexuals, homosexuals who had received psychiatric care, and

---

[53]Erving Goffman, *Stigma: Notes on the Management of Spoiled Identity* (Englewood Cliffs, N.J.: Prentice-Hall, 1963), pp. 143–144.
[54]Carol A. B. Warren, *Identity and Community in the Gay World* (New York: Wiley, 1974), pp. 21–29.
[55]Evelyn Hooker, "The Adjustment of the Male Overt Homosexual," in Ruitenbeek, p. 160.
[56]Schofield, p. 210.

homosexuals who had not been convicted nor had received psychiatric care.[57] The other groups were made up of those convicted of relations with boys under the age of 16 and two groups of nonhomosexuals. A homosexual was defined as a male over 21 but under 61 who "regarded himself as a homosexual and was prepared to say so to the interviewers." Most of the convicted homosexuals and those who were in psychiatric treatment remained to a degree primary deviants in that they never seemed to accept their behavior as constituting a socially acceptable role; consequently, they expressed guilt feelings. This may have been a result of limiting their activities to occasional acts and therefore increasing the likelihood of getting into trouble. Those who had not been convicted and were not under treatment were more likely than the others to have close homosexual friends, to mix socially with other homosexuals, and to have a current affair, but less likely to have promiscuous relations. Their relations with their partners were more likely to be a permanent liaison.

Definite conclusions on the adjustment problems of older career homosexuals are difficult to reach. One study of over 1,500 male homosexuals found that the older ones, those over 45 years of age, were better adjusted to their homosexual role than were those younger.[58] While there was, with aging, less association with homosexuals and with the gay world, as well as a lower frequency of homosexual sex, the older homosexual did not appear to be more lonely or depressed. Part of this is due to the process of aging more than to homosexuality. Others feel that with aging the lack of permanent personal sexual ties and loss of physical attractiveness appear to be common difficulties.

Developing a Homosexual Identity—The Coming Out

Homosexuals may identify with other homosexuals, but few of them regard themselves as criminals or deviants, as being "sick" or immoral. On the other hand, the negative reaction of heterosexual society affects the homosexual in many ways. He often feels it necessary to conceal his homosexuality. Concealment from nonhomosexual colleagues and friends becomes important because of the fear of forfeiting membership in the group.[59] There is also the need to conceal activities from the police, depending largely upon where the person lives and his social status. In spite of all the rationalizations provided by the subculture, the individual often feels guilt and even religious conflict, although as participation in the subculture continues these feelings seem gradually to diminish. Possibly of more importance than any of these, however, is the negative effect of homosexuality on personal ties such as family and close friends, the people to whom one generally remains close throughout life.

---

[57]Schofield. See also Saghir and Robins, Chap. 14.

[58]Martin S. Weinberg, "The Male Homosexual: Age-Related Variations in Social and Psychological Characteristics," *Social Problems*, 17 (1970), 527–537. Also see Dank, "The Development of a Homosexual Identity," pp. 155, 158, 160, and 162.

[59]For two excellent accounts of these problems, see Merle Miller, *On Being Different: What It Means To Be a Homosexual* (New York: Random House, 1971); and Howard Brown, *Familiar Faces, Hidden Lives* (New York: Harcourt Brace Jovanovich, 1976).

Several crucial factors are related to the development of a *homosexual identity*—in other words, how the individual has come to define homosexual acts as both more pleasurable and more significant than heterosexual relations and how he then learns to define himself as a homosexual. Involved in this process are the expectations of others, the degree of identity with the role models available, and the reactions of others—the attribution or imputation of homosexuality to him. Generally, homosexual identity grows out of continued participation in one-sex activities and environments rather than out of public labeling. Occasionally persons who are classified by others as homosexuals react to this classification by accepting it in their own self-concept. On the other hand, official negative definitions of the person as a homosexual by medical doctors, psychiatrists, or the police may serve to inhibit or even to change the development of the homosexual identity.[60] One study found that the development of a homosexual identity depends on the extent and type of information about homosexuals and homosexuality available to one who has sexual desires toward persons of the same sex.[61]

Before a person can identify himself as a homosexual he must be aware of the homosexual category and he must be able to identify within himself those evaluative meanings that are associated with this category.[62] Contrary to the process that occurs in the development of heterosexual roles, there is often little or no anticipatory socialization for the homosexual category. One homosexual expressed it in this way: "After I met gay society I found an awful lot of myself. In almost everyone I met, I found a part of me."[63] When a person says to himself that "I am a homosexual" it is quite different from his actually engaging in a homosexual act. A person can engage in a homosexual act and think of himself as homosexual, heterosexual, or bisexual, just as one who engages in a heterosexual act thinks of himself as heterosexual, homosexual, or bisexual. One may also engage in no sexual acts and still have a sexual identity of a heterosexual, homosexual, or bisexual person.[64] The recognition of a homosexual identity is extremely important, and when the person does fully change to this homosexual identity he is said by many to have "come out."

In a study of 368 homosexuals Dank found the mean age for the development of a homosexual identity, or "coming out," to be 21.[65] In urban areas a homosexual identity is likely to be developed at an earlier age.[66]

Generally, the social contexts for coming out are the presence of other homosexuals. One-sex situations are also conducive to this process of recognizing one's homosexual identity, as are seeing a professional person or reading literature that explains homosexuality (see Table 12.1). As an example of coming out in the context of gay bars, a man of 23 who had been predominantly homosexual for a number of years spoke of his experience.

---

[60]Dank, "Coming Out in the Gay World."
[61]Dank, "Coming Out in the Gay World."
[62]See Peter Fisher, *The Gay Mystique: The Myth and Reality of Male Homosexuality* (New York: Stein and Day, 1972), pp. 22–24.
[63]Dank, "The Development of a Homosexual Identity," p. 64.
[64]Dank, "Coming Out in the Gay World," p. 180.
[65]Barry M. Dank, "The Homosexual," in Goode and Troiden, pp. 174–210.
[66]Dank, "The Development of a Homosexual Identity."

I knew that there were homosexuals, queers and what not; I had read some books, and I was resigned to the fact that I was a foul, dirty person, but I wasn't actually calling myself a homosexual yet. . . . I went to this guy's house and there was nothing going on, and I asked him, "Where is some action?" and he said, "There is a bar down the way." And the time I really caught myself coming out is the time I walked into this bar and saw a whole crowd of groovy, groovy guys. And I said to myself, there was the realization that not all gay men are dirty old men or idiots, silly queens, but there are some just normal-looking and acting people, as far as I could see. I saw gay society and I said, "Wow, I'm home!"[67]

A distinction is often made by the gay community between a *homosexual identity* and a *gay identity,* but this distinction is not usually made by the general society. "A homosexual identity simply describes one's sexual orientation, whereas a gay identity implies affiliation with the gay community in a cultural and sociable sense."[68] Thus a homosexual is a person who practices homosexuality and will admit to being a homosexual, while a gay person is someone who in addition to all this also identifies and interacts with the gay world. While a person cannot develop a gay identity without having first developed a homosexual identity, the development of a homosexual identity does not mean that the person will eventually and inevitably develop a gay identity. This gay identity means membership and participation in the subculture of the homosexual community.

TABLE 12.1

Social Contexts in Which Respondents Came Out

Social Contexts	N^a	%
Frequenting gay bars	35	(19)
Frequenting gay parties and other gatherings	46	(26)
Frequenting parks	43	(24)
Frequenting men's rooms	37	(21)
Having a love affair with a homosexual man	54	(30)
Having a love affair with a heterosexual man	21	(12)
In the military	34	(19)
Living in a YMCA	2	(1)
Living in all-male quarters at a boarding school or college	12	(7)
In prison	2	(1)
Patient in a mental hospital	3	(2)
Seeing a psychiatrist or professional counselor	11	(6)
Read for the first time about homosexuals and/or homosexuality	27	(15)
Just fired from a job because of homosexual behavior	2	(1)
Just arrested on a charge involving homosexuality	7	(4)
Was not having any homosexual relations	36	(20)

^{a}Total N of social contexts is greater than 180 (number of respondents) because there was overlap of contexts.
Source: Barry M. Dank, "Coming Out in the Gay World," *Psychiatry,* 34 (May 1971), 184.

---

[67]Dank, "The Homosexual," p. 181.
[68]Warren, p. 149.

The Homosexual Subculture

Social and sometimes legal pressures may lead to participation in the homosexual subculture. Quite possibly the law in a homosexual's community may be strictly enforced, he might have experienced occupational discrimination, and he may feel that only another homosexual can fully understand his problems and his life-style. Over a period of time the social ties that have become important to the individual relate to his associations with other homosexuals; he learns to speak their language and to accept their status system. This does not mean that his only friends and companions are other homosexuals, for homosexuals also have contacts with the "straight" world, many of them rewarding and socially satisfying. A study concluded that the homosexual is not confronted by two highly distinct lives and that only on certain occasions does he differentiate his life into two worlds.[69] Contacts with family and employers constitute only two of the more frequent nonhomosexual relations maintained by homosexuals.

Individuals who belong to the subcultural world or community of homosexuals become socialized into a special role now termed gay: they have become secondary deviants. In this subcultural world a special language makes the subculture more cohesive and also serves to keep the members' secret from the out group when desired. Their special argot is similar in some respects to that of the underworld, in others to that of the theater.[70] Recognition by other homosexuals appears to involve particularly these terms, but of importance also are gestures, walk, clothes, and other membership indicators.

There is no one homosexual subculture or gay community; their actual number depends upon the region and the outside community's tolerance of homosexuality. New York City and San Francisco have well-developed gay communities: other cities have gay subcultures but they are less visible to outsiders. Similar subcultures exist in the cities of other countries, and one study has compared these different gay communities.[71] Homosexuals in the United States were found to rely more on subcultures than do those in, for example, the Netherlands or Denmark. The gay communities in the latter countries were found to be more diffused and less well organized, particularly in light of the lower level of legal repression and negative attitudes toward homosexuality.[72] The development of gay communities seems to be related to the lack of tolerance for homosexuality and the necessity for the community to reduce the stigmatization of homosexuals by the outside society. In this sense the gay community is functional, performing a number of services for its members. In many communities homosexuals can gather in special meeting places, usually at street corners or in parks, taverns, coffee houses, clubs, baths, churches, and lavatories.[73] In a large Canadian

---

[69]Martin S. Weinberg and Colin J. Williams, *Male Homosexuals: Their Problems and Adaptations* (New York: Oxford University Press, 1974), p. 385.
[70]Donald W. Cory, *The Homosexual in America* (New York: Greenberg, 1951), p. 90.
[71]Weinberg and Williams, *Male Homosexuals*.
[72]Weinberg and Williams, *Male Homosexuals*, pp. 382–384.
[73]For a discussion, see Dank, "The Homosexual"; and Gordon Westwood, *Society and the Homosexual* (New York: Dutton, 1953), Chaps. 19–21.

city it was found that the homosexual community or subculture provides for its members what other communities do: a training ground for norms and values, a milieu in which people may live every day, and social support as well as an information medium for members.[74] Large numbers of distinctive groups participate in the homosexual community, and within these groups the members are bound together in a "strong and relatively enduring bond and between which the members are linked by tenuous but repeated sexual contacts."[75] In turn, there are links with other, similar communities, in Canada and the United States in this particular study, primarily through the mobility of the members.

The diversity of gay communities, as noted earlier, depends upon the locale. No one can seal himself off completely from the influences and contacts with the larger social order, and homosexuals are no exception. Within the gay community members vary in the degree of their involvement. At one extreme a person may spend most of his time with other homosexuals at work, frequenting gay bars and other social functions with gays at night, while at the other extreme a married homosexual may rarely go to gay bars and other meeting places, displaying minimal contact with other gay community members.[76] In this sense, then, there is no ideal type of gay community, simply variations on a common theme—the protection and facilitation of homosexual relations through the common bonding of like others around the homosexual role. In a local homosexual community secret ("closet queens") and overt homosexuals may be linked through sex and friendship, and these groups, which often cut across class and occupational lines, serve to relieve anxiety and to furnish social acceptance. Within these groups narration of individual sexual experiences and talk about the sexual exploits of others may furnish gossip and give some unity to the group.

A particularly important group mechanism of the homosexual world is the gay bar, associated with larger cities and communities where homosexuals are numerous.[77] Gay bars serve a function for the homosexual community; here clusters of friends gather to exchange gossip and enjoy a social evening. These bars serve as communication centers; they provide sexual markets where agreements are made for the exchange of sexual services without commitment—"the one-night stand." They also serve for induction and training and for integration into the homosexual community; here a homosexual learns a body of knowledge and a set of common understandings about sexual activities, including the language, the legal aspects of homosexuality, and how if necessary to recognize vice squad officers, as well as varieties of sexual acts.[78]

A loosely knit extended series of overlapping networks of friends operates within the homosexual network outside of bars, but linked with it by members common to both. These networks vary greatly in form. The three most common forms are (1) tightly knit clique structures formed from pairs of homosexually "married" persons, or

---

[74]Leznoff and Westley.
[75]Leznoff and Westley, p. 263.
[76]See Plummer, pp. 155–157.
[77]See Nancy Achilles, "The Development of the Homosexual Bar as an Institution," in John H. Gagnon and William Simon, eds., *Sexual Deviance* (New York: Harper & Row, 1967), pp. 228–244.
[78]Warren, pp. 55–61 and 148–149.

singles, many of whom are heterosexually married; (2) larger groups with one or more loose clique structures as sociometrically central and a number of peripheral members; and (3) loose networks of friends who may meet only on the occasion of a party. These clique structures and pairs, as well as loose networks of friends, cut across both occupational and socioeconomic levels, although particular professions or occupations may form in-groups with their own social gatherings. These occasions range from the simplest to the most elaborate and from the most intimate to the large, spur-of-the-moment affairs, much as is the case in the heterosexual world. Some groups make special efforts to maintain social relations with heterosexual couples, usually those who are aware of, and at least partially accept, their homosexuality.[79]

Organization   Other subcultural aspects of homosexuality are the increasingly significant homosexual organizations and gay clubs in many parts of the world. The homosexual or "homophile" movement in the United States began on the West Coast after World War II. The first major organization was the Mattachine Foundation, originally established in 1950 in Los Angeles as a secret club to promote discussion and educational efforts regarding homosexuality. The society was chartered in 1954 with the title of Mattachine Society, Inc., with headquarters in San Francisco. Mattachine societies have been organized in other areas of the United States, but they are not currently coordinated by the San Francisco chapter.[80] National organization of homophile societies approached reality in 1966 with the establishment of the North American Conference of Homophile Organizations, which, among other things, organized annual meetings for clubs and societies. During the 1970s the homosexual movement, like other movements, had become more militant, with many local associations proclaiming the still popular slogans "gay is good" and "out of the closets and into the streets." Foremost among these militant organizations was the relatively short-lived New York Gay Liberation Front, and the Gay Activist Alliance, also in New York.[81] As of 1974 it was estimated that there were probably more than 1,000 grass roots gay liberation groups in the United States.[82]

Contrary to other organizations of deviants, such as Alcoholics Anonymous and Synanon for drug addicts, homosexual organizations espouse no desire to change the behavior of their members; they wish to ease some of the social and legal stigma surrounding homosexuality, and in this sense they wish to reinforce and legitimize homosexual behavior. These organizations engage in a number of activities: they furnish speakers, distribute literature, and publish magazines that deal with any subject which might concern homosexuals. Some of them take cases to court and demand changes in federal regulations governing employment and security classifications.[83] Homosexual organizations reject vigorously any idea that homosexual behavior

---

[79]Evelyn Hooker, "The Homosexual Community," in Gagnon and Simon, *Sexual Deviance,* pp. 180–181.
[80]Weinberg and Williams, *Male Homosexuals,* p. 41.
[81]For a description of these activities, see Laud Humphreys, *Out of the Closets: The Sociology of Homosexual Liberation* (Englewood Cliffs, N.J.: Prentice-Hall, 1972).
[82]Weinberg and Williams, *Male Homosexuals,* p. 44.
[83]A publication out of Los Angeles, the *Sexual Law Reporter,* is devoted exclusively to legal changes that affect sexual behavior, including homosexuality.

represents a "sickness" or pathology; in fact, many homosexuals maintain that there is a homosexual component in everyone, and some maintain that all persons are potentially if not actually bisexual. Many of the local organizations provide public information about homosexuality. One representative publication discusses such topics as what constitutes a homosexual experience, the implications of that experience for subsequent homosexual behavior, attitudes toward homosexuality on the part of religious organizations, the content of specific laws relating to homosexuality, venereal disease, and the problems that gay persons have.[84] More important for their purposes, perhaps, is that they also provide specific counseling services for persons who believe that they may be homosexual but who fear the effects of this discovery for both themselves and others.

Decriminalization of Male Homosexual Behavior

In 1977, 36 states provided criminal penalties for adults who commit homosexual acts in either public or private places. They are subject to arrest, but the likelihood of arrest, conviction, and prison sentence is probably not great at present and is continually diminishing. Most arrests for homosexuality are for solicitation, a misdemeanor, which does not carry a prison sentence. Where they do occur, the arrest and the trial may be as damaging as conviction and sentencing in that they constitute a public degradation ceremony for the homosexual person. Public hysteria bordering almost on a "witch hunt" occurred a few years ago, for example, at the discovery of and arrest for homosexual acts of a considerable number of middle-class males in Boise, Idaho.[85] Enforcement may be strict in cases involving minors or particularly flagrant public acts. There may be irregular harassment through entrapment by police in such places as public toilets or by raids on gay bars. In some large U.S. cities police have accepted large bribes from homosexuals for protection, and the threat of exposure has also been a source of frequent blackmail.

Actually the possibility of arrest or the much lower likelihood of conviction if arrested is much less feared than the possible civil disabilities that can be imposed on homosexuals who become known. Consequently, homosexuals are sensitive to the possibility or threat of investigation into their private affairs. They may be ineligible for government service, and they may be dismissed when discovered because of their vulnerability to extortion and because of what is termed their "moral unsuitability." These possibilities vary considerably and are undergoing rapid changes.

Efforts are increasingly being made in the United States to remove homosexual acts from the category of crimes, particularly private acts, provided that the persons involved are above a certain age and that the act does not take place in public. It is considered that such laws represent unwarranted attempts to regulate personal sexual morality. A 1969 federal government report in the United States recommended the

---

[84]Operation Socrates Handbook, "Male Homosexuality," in Benjamin Schlesinger, ed., *Sexual Behavior in Canada: Patterns and Problems* (Toronto: University of Toronto Press, 1977), pp. 148–161.
[85]See John Gervassi, *The Boys of Boise: Furor, Vice and Folly in an American City* (New York: Macmillan, 1966).

decriminalization of homosexuality and an end to its being viewed as a condition requiring treatment.[86] Already 14 states have decriminalized private homosexual acts (see p. 426). Earlier a government report in Great Britain had recommended decriminalization, stating that private sexual acts, such as homosexual behavior between consenting adults, were not within the purview of the law if they did not interfere with public order and decency, if the protection of citizens from what is offensive or injurious was assured, and if they did not exploit others, particularly younger groups.[87] The main arguments against the use of criminal law against homosexuality have been summarized as follows:

1. The law discriminates irrationally against private male homosexuality, while leaving untouched female homosexuality.

2. The social consequences of the law are almost wholly bad. Many cases of blackmail and suicides have undoubtedly resulted from it, while it tends to increase rather than diminish homosexual promiscuity, instability and public misbehavior by denying homosexuals the legitimate chance of establishing discreet permanent relationships.

3. Many homosexuals could be helped to a better adjustment if they felt freer to seek advice without incriminating themselves by doing so.

4. The law does much to ensure that adolescents and young men who once become involved in homosexual practices will feel it far harder to escape than would otherwise be the case.

5. The lack of any distinction between homosexual behavior committed in public or in private, or between those above or below an "age of consent," decreases the protection of the youth.[88]

It is unrealistic to believe that the U.S. penal system can have a rehabilitative effect upon a homosexual. Even under optimal conditions it is questionable that the homosexual orientation can be changed. Moreover, in the prison's sexually segregated social environment homosexuality, as well as homosexual rape, is prevalent.[89] It has been estimated that between 30 and 45 percent of male inmates have homosexual contacts during their periods of confinement.[90] Two chief reasons for this extensive homosexuality in prison can be cited. First, prison environments are largely devoid of situations in which legitimate affectional ties with others can be established. Homosexual liaisons, even though of short duration, serve as substitutes for these ties, especially for men serving long sentences and who have consequently lost many, if not all, of their contacts with persons in free society. Second, prisons offer inmates few if any opportunities to demonstrate their masculinity by physical prowess, and homosexual relations can serve this purpose.[91] For these reasons it is unlikely that conjugal visits can "solve" the basic problem of prison homosexuality; these visits are reserved for

---

[86]Evelyn Hooker, Chair, *Final Report of the Task Force on Homosexuality: National Institute of Mental Health* (Bethesda, Md.: National Institute of Mental Health, 1969).

[87]*Wolfenden Report,* p. 48.

[88]Schofield, p. 193. See also R. O. D. Benson, *In Defense of Homosexuality: Male and Female* (New York: Julian Press, 1965); and Fisher.

[89]Clyde B. Vedder and Patricia G. King, *Problems of Homosexuality in Corrections* (Springfield, Ill.: Charles C Thomas, 1967).

[90]Gagnon and Simon, *Sexual Conduct,* p. 244.

[91]Gagnon and Simon, *Sexual Conduct,* p. 257. The reader will notice the irony—ironic only because of popular stereotype—that homosexuality can represent an expression of masculinity.

men with families on the outside, inmates who are less likely to engage in homosexuality in any case.

Some evidence for considering prison homosexuality as a means of demonstrating masculinity comes from Sagarin's recent study, based on a very small sample, of the postprison sexual adjustment of inmates.[92] He concluded that among those inmates who had sought out a homosexual experience actively, not only entering into it willingly but also inflicting it on others, "all returned to heterosexuality." "On the contrary, all of those who had been forced and subdued into homosexuality, who insisted that it had hurt and disgusted them and that they had entered it most unwillingly, continued the pattern and pursued it in their postprison years."[93]

FEMALE HOMOSEXUALITY (LESBIANISM)

Relatively little research has been done on female homosexuality, or lesbianism,[94] in comparison to that done in the area of male homosexuality. In many ways female homosexual activities seem to resemble those of males, but in certain areas there are differences.

Lesbianism as Deviance

Unlike male homosexuals, lesbians seldom fear the law; the sexual acts usually are not specifically designated as illegal, and where they might be brought under other laws, this is rarely done. Most arrests for homosexual behavior among male homosexuals are made for its occurrence in public, in and around public toilets, for example, actions rarely carried out by women homosexuals. In fact, according to Kinsey, not a single case of a female convicted of homosexual activity was recorded in the United States from 1696 to 1952. In his large sample of women who had had a homosexual experience, only four had had any difficulties with the police.[95] Still, for many female homosexuals some fear of disclosure is always present when they are on the job and even when they are among their nonhomosexual friends. One lesbian has described her situation:

> Some [friends] may suspect, I don't know. Normally I just don't tell people unless there is a reason for it. You know, where the question comes up, where I might have to explain some peculiar behavior. Once or twice it came out when I had too much to drink. I try to watch it, but you can't be on your guard all the time. Normally, my practice is not to tell people unless I'm pretty sure what the reaction will be.[96]

---

[92]Edward Sagarin, "Prison Homosexuality and Its Effect on Post-Prison Sexual Behavior," *Psychiatry,* 39 (1976), 245–257.

[93]Sagarin, p. 254.

[94]The term "lesbianism" is derived from the Greek island of Lesbos where the Greek poetess Sappho (600 B.C.) made herself the leader of a group of women whose relations were characterized by homosexual feelings and behavior.

[95]Kinsey *et al., Sexual Behavior in the Human Female,* p. 484.

[96]Quoted in William Simon and John H. Gagnon, "The Lesbians: A Preliminary Overview," in Gagnon and Simon, *Sexual Deviance,* p. 274.

The two worlds, the "straight" and the lesbian, present a particular problem for lesbians who work, and most of them have to work. In fact, many female homosexuals appear to be more committed to their jobs than most women because they cannot depend upon a male for financial support. One attractive young lesbian described the problem of keeping in the two worlds in the job situation where all the other persons were "straight." "I have to put on this big scene of being heterosexual. And I don't like putting on fronts. But the men who come in like to flirt and expect me to flirt back. If I could just tell everyone that I'm homosexual, I wouldn't have to put on this big front, but everyone won't accept it."[97]

Lesbians are not, however, as often identifiable, and any adverse public opinion against them usually becomes manifest only when they proclaim a unique style of dress or associations. Close relations and a certain amount of limited physical demonstration are common among close women acquaintances, and the line between that demonstrative behavior and deviant lesbian relations is more difficult to draw than in male homosexual relations. Females are more likely to be more bisexual and inconsistent in their sexual behavior than male homosexuals.[98] Some women who identify with heterosexuality have performed homosexual acts with other females. Some women may regard themselves as bisexual, but they do not identify with lesbianism. One of these women has said: "I fell in love with a woman, but I didn't really meet other Lesbians and was not part of the Lesbian subculture at all. I would, in fact, definitely consider myself not like them, and I would actively reject the label."[99] Some who do identify with lesbianism sometimes engage in heterosexual as well as homosexual acts. In other words, lesbians display the same range of behavior and identity as do male homosexuals.

Extent

It is far more difficult to estimate the number of lesbians than male homosexuals, largely because the lesbian subculture is much less definite and less open. Female homosexuals more frequently maintain a seeming front of heterosexuality, so their identification is extremely difficult. Thirty years ago Kinsey estimated that one fifth of single women and 5 percent of all women, at the time of marriage, had had a homosexual relation leading to orgasm, a figure which was lower than that for men.[100] Most sexual studies do not even attempt to estimate the prevalence of lesbianism. Lesbianism is difficult to identify because it is not visible in most women, and most lesbians maintain a low profile.[101] Perhaps the only agreement about the extent of female homosexuality has been the popular speculation that it is more widespread than has been commonly thought, and may even be more prevalent than male homosexuality.

---

[97]Simon and Gagnon, p. 266.
[98]See, for example, Philip W. Blumstein and Pepper Schwartz, "Lesbianism and Bisexuality," in Goode and Troiden, pp. 278–295.
[99]Blumstein and Schwartz, p. 283.
[100]Kinsey *et al., Sexual Behavior in the Human Female,* p. 512.
[101]Susan Hanley, Benjamin Schlesinger, and Paul Steinberg, "Lesbianism: Knowns and Unknowns," in Schlesinger, p. 145.

Learning Lesbian Behavior

It is important to understand how certain values and norms might be conducive to female sexual experimentation, although they might not lead to female homosexuality. Everywhere women have, to varying degrees, valued themselves as heterosexually desirable, because it is in this manner that they are extensively portrayed in the mass media, and it is on this basis that the expectations of men are developed. Sexuality, therefore, becomes a part of a woman's self-evaluation, and women recognize sexuality, both their own and others', in strongly emotional terms. Traditionally women have become, in part, "sexual objects" for males, and this attitude may also shift to other females. A further sociological consideration is the set of norms, which differs from that for men, that permits women to touch one another physically and to become emotionally related to one another. Although intimacy is usually defined exclusively in social terms, it is both more accepted and more common among women than among men in our society. In some cases shared discussions of sex and sexual fantasies may lead to experimentation. The situation of two adult females living together is seldom disapproved, although the reverse may be the case for males. In this sense differences in society's expectations for each sex may help to conceal female homosexuality.

Women more often "drift" into homosexuality than men, starting with vague romantic attachments with other women. Physical contacts with other women generally occur before the age of 20, and a large percentage of them before 15; then more actual involvement occurs in the early twenties. One lesbian has described her "romantic drift" into lesbianism:

> The fall after graduation from high school I started at [residential school]. I met a girl there who was extremely attractive. She had a good sense of humor and I was drawn to her because I liked to laugh. Many of the girls used to sit around in the evenings and talk. As our friendship grew, our circle narrowed and narrowed until it got to be three or four of us who would get together at night and talk. Then there was only three. Then two—us. And maybe after a couple of months of this our relationship developed into something more. Started out by simply kissing. Later petting. That type of thing. It didn't actually involve overt sexuality (genital contact) until February.[102]

A study of one group of lesbians indicated that while the nature of the first sexual contact varied, in the majority of cases only manual stimulation was involved. Almost a third of the women studied said that oral sex was part of their first contact, but it was unrelated to the achievement of orgasm at that time.[103] This study compared such activities to those of young heterosexuals who often engage in manual stimulation rather than "going all the way." Despite clear-cut boundaries between the homosexual and the heterosexual worlds, nearly two thirds of the lesbians had had sexual relations with men, a third of them within the previous year.

The sexual-role behavior patterns of lesbians tend to resemble closely those of heterosexual females.[104] The sexual learning of both homosexual and heterosexual

---

[102]Simon and Gagnon, pp. 251–252.
[103]Jack H. Hedblom, "The Female Homosexual: Social and Attitudinal Dimensions," in James A. McCaffrey, ed., *The Homosexual Dialectic* (Englewood Cliffs, N.J.: Prentice-Hall, 1972), p. 56.
[104]Gagnon and Simon, *Sexual Conduct,* p. 180.

females is quite parallel because the cultural expectations of the female role in our society are generally consistent. This does not mean, however, that the early experiences of the two are always the same. Saghir and Robins found that a significant number of the homosexual females they studied displayed "tomboy" attitudes as young girls and behaved as boys.[105] They found that "boy-like behavior in girls seems to be much more prevalent than girl-like behavior in boys" when they compared male and female homosexual backgrounds.[106] Lesbians also seem to have had more male than female friends as youths, thereby perhaps predisposing them toward more masculine behavior and attitudes.

Most of the lesbians studied by Gagnon and Simon discovered their homosexual feelings in late adolescence, often even in young adulthood, and overt homosexual behavior frequently developed as a late stage of an intense emotional relationship.[107] Experimentation and curiosity seem to be the major reasons given by females who identify with heterosexuality but who have experienced lesbian relations. One research team reported that it was common for such women to have had their first experiences as a result of "male orchestration," that is, situations in which they were part of a "spontaneous threesome," with the male encouraging the two females to engage in sexual intimacies.[108]

Only limited studies have been made of the role of occupation in the development of lesbianism, although some occupations are known to have high rates of lesbian activity. A study of stripteasers found that one fourth of them engaged privately in homosexuality.[109] Moreover, the study estimated that the bisexual activities common among this group ranged from 50 to 75 percent. Several factors were thought to contribute to this high percentage. The limited opportunity stripteasers have for stable sexual relations with males and the negative attitudes they have developed toward men because of the way they see them at sex shows lead many of them to prefer to associate primarily with other women. Much the same situational involvement in homosexual activities is found in women's prisons as is found among male prison inmates.[110]

Identity

A major difference between male and female homosexuals is that the lesbian tends to view herself as being less promiscuous than does the male homosexual.[111] She is much less likely to "cruise" for sex partners, even in bars, and generally she is more likely to "go with someone" or to be "married" in the homosexual sense, with long-term, more emotional bonds. Again, this difference has been attributed to the female role in which sexual gratification is woven more into an emotional or romantic

---

[105]Saghir and Robins, pp. 192–194.
[106]Saghir and Robins, p. 201.
[107]Gagnon and Simon, *Sexual Conduct,* p. 184.
[108]Blumstein and Schwartz, p. 282.
[109]Charles H. McCaghy and James K. Skipper, Jr., "Lesbian Behavior as an Adaptation to the Occupation of Stripping," *Social Problems* 17 (1969), 262–270.
[110]See Rose Giallombardo, *Society of Women: A Study of a Woman's Prison* (New York: Wiley, 1966), Chap. 9; and Esther Heffernan, *Making It in Prison: The Square, the Cool, and the Life* (New York: Wiley, 1972).
[111]Hedblom, p. 55.

involvement with women than with men. One writer has stated that initial lesbian relations tend to be more romantic, more affectionate, relatively long-lasting, and monogamous.[112] The close relationship that forms the basis for a lesbian encounter is crucial in the development of a lesbian identity. "The majority pattern appears to be one in which self-identification as a lesbian develops before or during genital contact itself, and as a late stage of a close, affectionate relationship."[113] In her search to establish such a close relationship the lesbian can have extremely traumatic experiences in the breakup of a love affair, as one woman has reported:

> Maybe it will pass, but right now love is very important to me. Being near someone all the time. Wanting to love them and having them love you back. It's like being on a high and not wanting to come down. Maybe it's my fault. Maybe I've just had bad luck in the lovers I've known. They seem to come down too quickly and then it becomes ugly and sordid.[114]

Lesbians are often stereotyped as masculine in aggressiveness, dress, and manners: in the lesbian world this is termed the "butch" role. Only a minority of lesbians are actually committed to such a role, even though some may experiment with it, particularly during the "identity crisis" period that takes place at the time of their own self-admission "of a deviant sexual commitment" or when they enter into the subculture.[115] Nearly all the women interviewed by Simon and Gagnon wanted to become emotionally and sexually attached to another woman who would respond to them as women.[116] Still, when they abandon the world of men and a heterosexual life, lesbians must take on many social and often economic responsibilities carried out by men.

It is difficult for the homosexual female to develop an acceptable self-concept and identity. The emergence of the women's movement and the women's gay lib movement may be helpful in this respect. The most important variable in attempts to understand the lesbian's adjustment is the process by which, or the degree to which, she accepts herself or learns to manage her own feelings about her preferences and emotions. In the process she develops some balance of what she is and wants to be, as well as an ability to "like herself." Much depends on the outcome of many factors—her family relationships, how many and how close her friendships are, her role and her utilization of it in a lesbian community, her adjustment in her work, and her success in her search for love.[117]

The Lesbian Subculture

Lesbians do not utilize the gay world or become involved in its subculture as much as do male homosexuals. For one thing, the role of the female homosexual is less alienating than that of the male, and for another, lesbians can mask their sexual

---

[112]Denise M. Cronin, "Coming Out among Lesbians," in Goode and Troiden, pp. 268–277.
[113]Cronin, p. 273.
[114]Simon and Gagnon, p. 276.
[115]Simon and Gagnon, p. 265.
[116]Simon and Gagnon, p. 265.
[117]Simon and Gagnon, p. 277.

deviance behind an assumed asexual response to women to a much greater extent than can men, who are assumed to be more sexually active and aggressive. Moreover, lesbianism tends to be of a more private nature. Many lesbians form semipermanent relationships with other females, and the social lives of these women are centered in more private places like apartments and houses than in the more public arena of gay bars and other lesbian meeting places. The longer-lasting relationships suggest less of a turnover of partners for lesbians and thus less need to "make the gay scene" to search for partners.

While many of the functions performed by the homosexual community are not as necessary for lesbians as for male homosexuals, for some women they are important. Particularly in large cities, some lesbians on occasion tend to congregate in certain bars, usually those patronized by male homosexuals, and these places facilitate sexual relationships. The community can also provide contacts for females who have no ongoing relationships. While both male and, to some extent, female homosexuals "cruise" the physical locales of the gay community, there is a dramatic difference between the nature of the male and female alliances that result from these activities. The homosexual woman, in her search for sex, looks first for a relationship, and she usually establishes one prior to any sexual activity. With the male homosexual sex generally precedes such a relationship, and sex is most often practiced casually with no intent to form a relationship.[118] While this pattern does not indicate the frequency of lesbian relations resulting from the lesbian subculture, many people believe that male homosexuals obtain many more sexual contacts than lesbians do.[119] The gay community also provides a source of social support. In this milieu the lesbian can express herself fully and openly with persons who have had feelings and experiences much like her own. As with the male homosexual subculture, a special language and ideology are also provided, and these help to provide members with attitudes and rationalizations with which to resist negative social attitudes and stigma.

Organization Because they are less stigmatized, female homosexuals have less need of an organized subculture than do male homosexuals. The lesbian subcultures that do exist are often less organized in comparison to those of males. Male homosexual organizations, for example, are more numerous, few female groups have been organized on a national level, and only one—the Daughters of Bilitis—has any claim to national representation. A number of lesbian organizations, however, are currently coming into existence, although for the most part they are local organizations whose main functions are educational and counseling.[120]

The affiliation of gay women with the women's movement in the 1970s was probably inevitable, and this affiliation has further reduced the need for a distinct, well-developed female homosexual subculture. As the women's movement helps to carry forward the political interests of lesbians with those of heterosexual females, the need

---

[118]Saghir and Robins, p. 313.
[119]Saghir and Robins. A recent study, however, has suggested that the opposite might be true. See Kenneth J. Nyberg, "Sexual Aspirations and Sexual Behaviors among Homosexually Behaving Males and Females," *Journal of Homosexuality,* 2 (1976), 29–38.
[120]For a general discussion, see Ruth Simpson, *From the Closet to the Courts: The Lesbian Tradition* (Baltimore, Md.: Penguin Books, 1976).

for separate organizations to perform this function is greatly reduced. Both lesbians and their heterosexual counterparts have rejected the long-established status of women as second-class citizens, and they give only secondary consideration to differences in sexual-object choice. Members of both groups identify themselves first and foremost as women. "All strive to develop self-respect and self-worth, which necessitates withdrawing themselves from the potentially oppressive influence of any relationships with chauvinistic, heterosexual males; lesbian love and sexuality is as distinctly feminine as that of her heterosexual sister."[121]

It has been speculated that the women's movement has already had, or may have, a more direct role in the increasingly favorable attitudes toward lesbianism than merely an affinity of political goals.[122] This movement has attacked the very basis of sex roles and female socialization in our society. By stressing alternatives to conventional sexual roles and institutions, it has increasingly made legitimate the number and the kinds of options available to women, not only with respect to educational and occupational opportunities but to sexuality as well. This movement seems to have been "born" out of the necessity for alternatives for women. A recent account of it has claimed that when the Industrial Revolution transferred productive relations and functions outside the family it reduced the woman's productive function to one of custodial care and domestic service. As demands for labor increased women were drawn into the labor market and eventually were competing with males. Only after married women had entered the labor market on a long-term basis did the women's movement develop into a force that could not be reversed.[123] While this movement was originally tied to economic matters, it soon touched women's lives in all other respects—religious, familial, and sexual.

The women's movement has provided important sources of ideas about female sexuality; among other things it has suggested that female-female associations may be a welcome alternative to unsatisfactory heterosexual relationships. Sexual experimentation between females may even result from membership and commitment to the movement's ideology. In fact, some women may feel that it is important to have at least one sexual experience with another woman in order to widen sexual and political liberation. One woman reported: "I went to bed with a radical lesbian; I just had to know what it was like."[124] Some of the more militant members have even suggested that heterosexual relations are politically incompatible with the ideology of the movement. It has been said that

> the purpose of feminist analysis is to provide women with an awareness of their servitude as a class so that they can unite and rise up against it. The problem now for strictly heterosexually conditioned women is how to obtain the sexual gratification they think they need from the sex who remains their institutional oppressor.[125]

[121]Goode and Troiden, p. 236.
[122]Blumstein and Schwartz.
[123]John Huber, "Toward a Sociotechnological Theory of the Women's Movement," *Social Problems,* 23 (1976), 371–388.
[124]Blumstein and Schwartz, p. 287.
[125]Jill Johnston, *Lesbian Nation: The Feminist Solution* (New York: Simon & Schuster, 1973), pp. 275–276.

It is the lesbian who unites the personal and political in the struggle to become freed of the oppressive institution.[126]

CONCLUSIONS

Throughout this chapter the changing sexual norms and values of U.S. society have been examined. Although homosexual behavior cannot be said to be common or to be accepted by most persons at present, it is evident that neither the behavior nor the individuals who engage in it elicit the same degree of disapproval, or from as many persons, as has been true in the past. Changes in the content of sexual norms have resulted basically from three factors. First has been the increased interest in sexual matters on the part of the scientific community. With the pioneering work of Kinsey and his associates in the 1940s and 1950s, and continuing with the widely known work during the 1960s and 1970s of Masters and Johnson related to the physiology of sex and sex therapy, the scientific community has come to regard orientations in sexual behavior as more acceptable and legitimate areas of investigation.[127] Second, noticeable changes have occurred in the sexual life-styles of many persons, primarily in the area of cohabitation.[128] Changes in heterosexuality, which has been the most preferred type of sexual context, have shown that there are alternatives to our conventional stereotypes about sexuality as a whole. Third, increasingly, the freedom of the individual to adopt his or her own life-style has been recognized, primarily as a result of the revolutions in the youth life-styles of the 1960s.

The future of homosexuality as an enduring and accepted pattern of behavior cannot be predicted, but it is certain that important changes are now occurring in the sexual norms governing homosexuality. As a result many persons more fully accept homosexuality; others oppose homosexuality as strongly as ever, or even more strongly. Changes will continue to occur, and more conflicts may be expected between gay organizations and groups of persons with opposing views about homosexuality as more active attempts are made to influence legislation and public opinion. The nature of these conflicts will not center on eradicating homosexuality but on the most appropriate means of dealing with it both in terms of the individual homosexuals and all of society.

SELECTED REFERENCES

Blumstein, Philip W., and Pepper Schwartz. "Lesbianism and Bisexuality," in Erich Goode and Richard T. Troiden, eds., *Sexual Deviance and Sexual Deviants*. New York: Morrow, 1974.

---

[126]Johnston, p. 276.
[127]William H. Masters and Virginia Johnson, *Human Sexual Inadequacy* (Boston: Little, Brown, 1970). For a recent compendium of this work, see John Money and Herman Musaph, eds., *Handbook of Sexology* (New York: Elsevier, 1977).
[128]David A. Schulz, "Sex and Society in the Seventies," *Society*, 14 (1977), 20–25.

Dank, Barry M. "Coming Out in the Gay World," *Psychiatry,* 34 (1971), 192–198.

Fisher, Peter. *The Gay Mystique: The Myth and Reality of Male Homosexuality.* New York: Stein and Day, 1972.

Gagnon, John H., and William Simon. *Sexual Conduct: The Social Sources of Human Sexuality.* Chicago: Aldine, 1973.

Glassner, Barry, and Carol Owen. "Variations in Attitudes toward Homosexuality," *Cornell Journal of Social Relations,* 11 (1976), 161–176.

Goode, Erich, and Richard T. Troiden, eds. *Sexual Deviance and Sexual Deviants.* New York: Morrow, 1974.

Hedblom, Jack H. "The Female Homosexual: Social and Attitudinal Dimensions," in James A. McCaffrey, ed., *The Homosexual Dialectic.* Englewood Cliffs, N.J.: Prentice-Hall, 1972.

Humphreys, Laud. *Tearoom Trade: Impersonal Sex in Public Places,* enlarged ed. Chicago: Aldine, 1975.

Katz, Jonathan, ed. *Gay American History: Lesbians and Gay Men in the U.S.A.* New York: Cromwell, 1976.

Money, John, and Herman Musaph, eds. *Handbook of Sexuality.* New York: Elsevier, 1977.

Plummer, Kenneth. *Sexual Stigma: An Interactionist Account.* London: Routledge & Kegan Paul, 1975.

Saghir, Marcel T., and Eli Robins. *Male and Female Homosexuality: A Comparative Investigation.* Baltimore, Md.: Williams and Wilkins, 1973.

Schur, Edwin M. *Crimes without Victims.* Englewood Cliffs, N.J.: Prentice-Hall, 1965.

Simpson, Ruth. *From the Closet to the Courts: The Lesbian Tradition.* Baltimore, Md.: Penguin Books, 1976.

Spector, Malcolm. "Legitimizing Homosexuality," *Society,* 14 (1977), 52–56.

Warren, Carol A. B. *Identity and Community in the Gay World.* New York: Wiley, 1974.

Weinberg, Martin S., and Colin J. Williams. *Male Homosexuals: Their Problems and Adaptations.* New York: Oxford University Press, 1974.

CHAPTER 13

A young married woman, the victim of acute mental illness (schizophrenia) in a state of complete social withdrawal, is unable or unwilling to communicate verbally and socially with her husband due to her condition.

Mental Disorder

S OCIETY, both collectively and as individual members, reacts differently to the mentally ill—those with mental disorders—than to physically ill persons. People are generally sympathetic toward someone with a physical illness because it is often better understood or more visible, or because their own past experiences make it possible for them to identify with it. Mental illness, on the other hand, involves many intangible feelings and ideas that others often cannot comprehend or that may even make them fearful; attitudes toward the mentally ill may range from avoidance to ridicule and revulsion. The different reactions to physical illness on the one hand and mental illness on the other lie basically in the behavioral aspects of mental disorders, as will be indicated in this chapter.

Persons tend to think that mentally ill persons are somehow more responsible for their conditions than the physically ill. Mechanic points out that this explains at least in part the stigma associated with psychiatric disturbances.[1] Mentally ill persons are also stigmatized because their behavior is often socially disruptive and unpredictable, even threatening or frightening to other persons. Mechanic states that while physical illnesses occasionally are associated with similar serious problems, in general, persons who are physically ill "do not threaten the community in the same way as do many psychiatric patients."[2] While it is not difficult for persons to identify with a physically ill person, most people having experienced physical illness of various types, they cannot identify with mentally ill persons and usually do not accept the fact that they themselves might become mentally ill.

The behavior exhibited by a person with a mental disorder is inappropriate to the situation and may even be bizarre. A mentally disturbed person cannot meet normal expectations, and for this reason the individual is a "source of deviance."[3] These social expectations, or norms, form the base of the assessment of deviance and the subsequent administration of sanctions. Persons with mental disorders are often sanctioned, either being labeled mentally ill, insane, "crazy," or, in more extreme cases, mental hospital patients.

Increasingly, sociologists and social anthropologists are giving their attention to the role played by social and cultural factors in the development and treatment, as well as the prevention, of mental disorder. Of particular interest have been the extremely difficult problem of socially defining mental disorder, the effects of societal reaction to mental disorder, and the status and role of the mentally ill person. In order to understand more fully the broad sociological approaches to this form of deviance, it is important to examine the various types of mental disorder as they are generally classified at present.

PSYCHIATRIC TYPES OF MENTAL DISORDERS

There are many criticisms of the psychiatric definitions of mental disorder which will be discussed later in detail. Because of such criticisms, one might well question the

---

[1]David Mechanic, *Mental Health and Social Policy* (Englewood Cliffs, N.J.: Prentice-Hall, 1969), p. 25.
[2]Mechanic, *Mental Health and Social Policy,* p. 25.
[3]John A. Clausen, "Mental Disorders," in Robert K. Merton and Robert Nisbet, eds., *Contemporary Social Problems,* 4th ed. (New York: Harcourt Brace Jovanovich, 1976), p. 105.

relevance of including in the sections that follow a description of the various psychiatric types of mental disorder. First, they are terms widely used by psychiatrists, who are after all the persons chiefly responsible for the treatment of mental disorders. Second, they are terms used by others, including, frequently, sociologists. It is therefore necessary to become familiar with the terms and their use. Again, however, it should be understood that there is much ambiguity in the terms; they are not clear-cut in the sense, for example, that the term "cancer" is. In fact, many "normal" persons exhibit the behavior described in each type, although in all probability to a lesser extent and in a manner that does not provoke much societal reaction. Probably all persons have to some degree exhibited such behavior as hallucinations, phobias, persecution complexes, and emotional extremes of elation and depression. Almost everyone at one time or another has had irrational fears, daydreams, flights of ideas, and disorders of memory. A sociologist has pointed out the many characteristics that operate to varying degrees in minds considered to be normal, as well as in minds so disordered that a diagnosis of insanity has been made:

> sense of inferiority, sublimation, imperception, illusion, hallucinations, delusions, disorders of judgment, disturbance of the train of thought, flight of ideas, nonessential ideas and thoughts, incoherence, retardation or inhibition of thought, disorders of orientation, disturbance of consciousness, clouding of consciousness, confusion, dream states, negativism, inaccessibility, obsession, fears, phobias, disorders of attention, disorders of memory, conflict, complexes, compensation, symbolization, etc.[4]

According to the *conventional classification of psychiatry,* there are two basic types of mental illness, those with an organic basis and the functional, or nonorganic, disorders. The *organic types* are usually caused by some organism, by a brain injury, by some other physiological disorder, or, in certain rare types of mental disorder, possibly by some hereditary factors. The *functional disorders,* on the other hand, are less specifically broken down into categories, being broadly divided into the neuroses and the psychoses. The *neuroses* are considered to be the mildest and the most common type, and the essential feature of these disorders is that they involve behaviors which deviate less markedly from societal norms than do the *psychoses.* They are for this reason considered to be "less serious," and they generally are more tolerated by society. Psychotic behavior, on the other hand, is more often characterized by a loss of contact with reality. Before turning to the functional disorders we need to examine the disorders brought on by certain organic, or physiological, processes.

Organic Mental Disorders

The three most important organic mental disorders, none of which is really hereditary, are the senile psychoses, paresis, and the alcoholic psychoses. The *senile (or old age) psychoses* are generally classified as organic on the assumption that they are produced by certain physiological processes of aging. They account for about one fourth of all state hospital admissions. Some of these cases are due to arteriosclerosis and thus result from changes in the circulatory system which affects the brain, but others are not. Senile psychoses are characterized by a loss of memory, particularly for recent events, inability to concentrate, or certain delusional thoughts. There is increasing

---

[4]Lawrence Guy Brown, *Social Pathology* (New York: Appleton, 1946), p. 62.

evidence that many of the psychoses brought on by aging are products of nonorganic conditions that arise from interpersonal relations, such as social isolation and loss of status. There is considerable evidence, moreover, that the higher rates of commitment of older persons to mental hospitals in recent years are related to structural changes in society, among them changes affecting family organization, housing conditions, and concepts of family responsibility. Persons today are more willing to deal with the mental problems of older parents by placing them in nursing homes or having them committed to mental hospitals.

Paresis, or dementia paralytica, is caused by syphilis. It develops at least 10 years after the initial syphilitic infection, and there is often progressive brain degeneration in those who go untreated. Although the paresis symptoms may not differ from those of many functional psychoses, the condition may be relatively easy to diagnose through positive Wasserman and Kahn reactions. There may also be tremors, convulsive seizures, and a lack of coordination in bodily movements. The mental symptoms are often a complete alteration in personality traits—for example, a neat, well-dressed individual becomes careless and slovenly. Eventually, memory about time and place may become defective, and in some cases there is depression. As a rule, paretics do not live long. The elimination of syphilis would end paresis, and advances have been made toward this goal.

The *psychoses resulting from alcoholism* are not as definitely organic as paresis, although they are usually classified as the same type. Relatively few alcoholics develop psychoses. Some doubt exists as to how much mental disorder is organically produced by the alcohol and what proportion results from certain sociopsychological conditions. The prolonged existence of chronic alcoholism, associated with vitamin and nutritional deficiencies, may in some cases produce such deterioration in physical and psychological behavior that alcoholic psychoses result. Some patients develop terrifying hallucinations, others have tremors, often referred to as delirium tremens, or "DT's," and still others show general progressive deterioration. Not all cases of DT's indicate a psychosis, however, for many of these symptoms may be short-lived.

Functional Mental Disorders

The disorders of primary interest to the social scientist are the functional disorders, which have been conventionally labeled as the neuroses, schizophrenia, the manic depressive psychoses, and paranoia. These functional disorders will be referred to as mental disorder in the sections that follow.

According to many psychiatrists, the functional, or nonorganic, mental disorders "function" to adjust the individual to his particular difficulties; hence the term "functional." The idea that such mental disorders are necessarily an adaptation to stress is difficult to prove, although in many cases this adaptation may play an important role. As yet no one has been able to demonstrate *conclusively* that any functional disorder results from heredity, physiological disorders, or other organic deficiency. Although numerous studies have reported hereditary factors in schizophrenia, the issue is still controversial, as will be discussed later.

The general tendency in psychiatry is to regard functional disorders as clinical entities, as constituting a type of "sickness." Because of their medical training, psychiatrists obviously look for disease entities and think in terms of a medical diagnosis, or the medical model.[5] In the case of mental disorder these diagnoses have come to be known as neuroses and psychoses; the latter, in turn, have been divided into schizophrenia, manic-depressive disorders, paranoia, and other categories. There is actually a great deal of confusion in the psychiatric profession as to whether mental disorder is primarily a disease in which biological factors play an important part, whether it is a disturbance in the functioning of the personality pattern deeply rooted in childhood development, or whether it arises from problems of social living.[6]

These diagnostic categories themselves, and the adequacy of the diagnosis by psychiatrists, have been severely criticized by many writers, who believe that rather than being disease entities, they actually are *descriptions* of certain behavior. Hollingshead, for example, has written that psychiatry currently has no standard test which researchers may use to diagnose any of the functional mental disorders. "A standardized, valid, diagnostic test would enable a researcher to determine the presence or absence of functional mental illness in individuals."[7] Thus, research into functional mental disorders will continue to be hampered until this problem is solved. The labeling or identification of mental disorders does not result simply or directly because of "symptoms," even in the same cultural context. In the absence of a chemical or physical test for diagnosing a functional mental disorder, the diagnosis must depend upon the clinician's judgment: this, in turn, is affected by his own conception of mental disorder and the explanation for its origins that he holds, as well as the values and attitudes of the patient. Other factors, such as age, sex, race, religion, and social status of the patient may also influence the diagnostic consideration. These factors all affect the kind of treatment and the therapist-patient relationship that follows the diagnosis. Professionals generally prefer to work with patients from middle-class backgrounds similar to their own and are more optimistic about their ability to help patients with higher levels of education and occupational status.[8]

The lack of reliability and validity of psychiatric diagnosis[9] has been shown in a number of studies. A review of six studies comparing the agreement rate of diagnosis varied between 56 and 88 percent.[10] In one mental hospital significant differences were found from one ward to another in diagnostic classifications of patients with functional psychoses.[11] For example, on one ward the diagnoses changed with the change in the ward administrator. Whereas these data were based on reports of

[5]For a critical discussion of the implications of medical training for psychiatric treatment, see Erving Goffman, *Asylums* (New York: Doubleday Anchor Books, 1961), pp. 320–386.

[6]See the discussion in Mechanic, *Mental Health and Social Policy,* pp. 4–6.

[7]August B. Hollingshead, "The Epidemiology of Schizophrenia," *American Sociological Review,* 26 (1961), 10.

[8]Alexander Askenasy, *Attitudes toward Mental Patients: A Study across Cultures* (The Hague: Mouton, 1974), pp. 102–104, 125, and 148.

[9]David Mechanic, "Problems and Prospects in Psychiatric Epidemiology," in E. H. Hare and J. K. Wing, eds., *Psychiatric Epidemiology* (New York: Oxford University Press, 1970), pp. 3–22.

[10]Donald Conover, "Psychiatric Distinctions: New and Old Approaches," *Journal of Health and Social Behavior,* 13 (1972), 167–180.

[11]Benjamin Pasamanick, in "Work Conference in the Mental Disorders," mimeographed, New York, February 1959, pp. 143–145.

hospitalized patients, Leighton did research in which he attempted to assess the mental status of a nonpatient group. In his study six psychiatrists were asked to read the field protocols on 50 adult white males and were instructed to assess whether each man was mentally "ill" or "well." Fifteen were placed in an uncertain category, and five were thought to be "well," although the five men diagnosed as "well" differed for each of the six psychiatrists. In fact, one psychiatrist's five "wells" had been placed in another's "sickest" group.[12]

One of the major difficulties in using psychiatric descriptions of mental disorders is that people do not necessarily reject a person who has such characteristics. It is necessary to distinguish those who are *publicly* defined as mentally ill and those who are *psychiatrically* defined. The severity of a psychiatrically determined mental disorder may not be the reason for the rejection by others but, rather, the social visibility of the symptoms. Serious psychiatrically determined symptoms may be present without much social visibility. One study has reported, for example, that men are rejected more strongly than are women for deviations from role expectations.[13] In the case of former mental patients, it was found that rejection was not so much a result of the label as of the labeling, in addition to the visibility of the deviating behavior.

The Neuroses

Some neurotic symptoms can be classified as dissociated behavior and others as compulsive disorders. In all of them the societal reaction to the behavior is not as great as with the psychoses. Hysteria, amnesia, and disturbances of speech, hearing, and sight are examples of dissociated behavior. In addition to hysterical fainting, there may often be facial tics or uncontrolled movements. Ingenious tests have been devised, for example, to separate the person who is "hysterically blind" in one eye from the truly blind.[14]

A person with compulsive neurotic behavior feels "compelled" to do, say, or think something in a specific manner, a force that often cannot be repressed in spite of strong contrary tendencies. As a result of the difficulty in repressing these tendencies, the person develops anxiety reactions which continue and intensify only to be relieved when the person indulges in the behavior.[15] *Compulsive behavior* includes stepping on, or avoiding, cracks in the sidewalk, excessive hand-washing or bathing, counting telephone poles or other objects, dressing in a set manner, and insisting on certain meticulous order, such as all drawers carefully closed or shoes and other objects lined up in order. The behavior is often not of a physical nature but consists of *obsessions,* or persistent ideas, representing emotional fears of objects, acts, or situations. Some

---

[12]Alexander H. Leighton, in Pasamanick, pp. 147–148.

[13]Derek L. Phillips, "Rejection of the Mentally Ill: The Influence of Behavior and Sex," *American Sociological Review,* 29 (1964), 679–687. Interestingly, professionals seem to prefer to work with male mental patients than females. See Askenasy, p. 148.

[14]Red and green letters are put on a card so that the letters are alternatively colored. On one there may be the red letters JHSOKN and the green letters ONHPIS. The subject is given glasses, through one lens of which can be seen only the red letters, through the other only the green. If the subject reads "Johns Hopkins," it is apparent that both eyes are being used even if the person reports having vision in only one eye.

[15]Norman Cameron, *The Psychology of Behavior Disorders* (Boston: Houghton Mifflin, 1947), p. 12.

obsessions may be a more or less constant fear of death, of losing one's mind, or of losing one's friends, prestige, or job. A fairly common neurotic fear is anxiety about one's health—hypochondria—which may involve fear about one's general health or about nonexistent heart conditions or cancer. Neurotic *phobias* are often of a general nature such as fear of confinement (claustrophobia) or its opposite, fear of open places, and fear of high places. Persons suffering from these fears are generally not only ashamed of this behavior but may become perplexed and resentful of it as being absurd and burdensome.

Among psychiatrists and others there is little agreement on the definition of a neurosis. This fact is shown by estimates of the number of neurotics in the general population, some as high as 40 percent, others about 5 percent. Some have gone so far as to suggest that nearly everyone in a modern urban society is neurotic. When used in this way the concept becomes almost meaningless. There are indications that psychiatrists, however, are often more likely to give members of the middle and upper social classes the more acceptable label neurotic than the less acceptable label psychotic.

The Psychoses

The functional psychoses are generally divided by psychiatrists into three main types: schizophrenia, the manic-depressive psychoses, and paranoia. The social reaction in all of these categories tends to be more intense than it is in the case of the neuroses. Schizophrenic conditions account for about one fourth of all first admissions to mental hospitals and from one half to three fifths of persons occupying hospital beds at a given time.[16] This disorder is sometimes referred to as dementia praecox; it develops primarily between the ages of 15 and 30, with few persons developing it after 50. Manic-depressive psychotics constitute about 15 percent of all institutionalized patients, women making up roughly three quarters of all the cases. Only about 1 percent of all new admissions to state mental hospitals each year has a diagnosis of true paranoia.

Schizophrenic Behavior Partly because of its extent and nature, social science research and writing on mental disorder are probably more concerned with schizophrenia than with any other disorder. This condition is said to involve a detachment of the emotional self from the intellectual self, and it is for this reason the term "schizophrenia"—or "split personality" as it is sometimes called—is used. Psychiatrists sometimes attempt to classify schizophrenia into simple, hebephrenic, catatonic, and paranoiac schizophrenia, but these classifications are highly unreliable. The most characteristic symptom of a schizophrenic is withdrawal from contact with the world and an inability to play expected roles. These processes may be so disturbed that an imaginary world is built up, including false perceptions and hallucinations of all kinds, such as ideas, voices,

---

[16]Babegian estimates that roughly three fifths of all patients occupying beds in mental hospitals in the United States are diagnosed schizophrenics. See H. M. Babegian, "Schizophrenia: Epidemiology," in Alfred M. Freedman, ed., *Comprehensive Textbook of Psychiatry* (Baltimore, Md.: William and Wilkins, 1975), Vol. 2.

and forces which enter daily living and which cannot be controlled. Some schizophrenics show increasing tendencies to withdraw, to daydream, and to be unable to concentrate. They become exceedingly careless of their personal appearance, manners, and speech, are listless and apathetic, and lose their interests and ambitions. Sometimes their behavior involves pronounced silliness with a great deal of situationally unwarranted smiling, giggling, odd mannerisms, gesturing, and incoherent speech and thought. Some have suggested that the more bizarre reactions of hospitalized patients may, in fact, be reactions to their institutionalization and deprivation of civil rights.[17] This might apply to other types of patients as well. Schizophrenics also may have delusions of persecution, as illustrated by the following case:

> A 46-year-old laborer admitted to the state hospital with complaint of feeling weak, mixed up, unable to work. Following admission to hospital he appeared shy, mixed poorly, and complained that someone was following him and wanted to get rid of him. He improved spontaneously, was discharged to his family, then readmitted seven years later. On readmission he had a crutch and cane, claimed he had not been working for several years because of a spinal injury. He offered various ideas of persecution and strange expressions, i.e., that he was surrounded by detectives who were trying to "run a secret world." He was being bothered by "radio tones." After a course of 23 electric shock treatments he discarded his cane and crutch and gave up his ideas about not being able to walk. He has remained chronic with persistent delusions, some persecutory and other grandiose, e.g., identifying himself with Roosevelt and Truman, thinks he has done important "government work" in the past and that he is entitled to a large pension. He was well adjusted in the hospital.[18]

Many researchers have claimed that because of certain hereditary genes, schizophrenics are persons who are vulnerable to certain social situations.[19] If the environment is favorable, the genetic predisposition may not have an effect. In this connection geneticists have attempted to demonstrate that heredity plays a leading role in schizophrenic disorders.[20] Kallman was the leading proponent of the theory that schizophrenia is inherited, and the conclusions from his studies, even though done over 40 years ago, are often still cited as proof that genetic factors predispose certain persons to schizophrenic behavior.[21] He found that two thirds of the children whose parents were both schizophrenic developed schizophrenia. Where there was one such parent, the chances were about 1 in 6; with schizophrenic siblings, 1 in 10; nephews and nieces, 1 in 25; and grandchildren, 1 in 20. He further concluded that the more distant the relationship, the less likelihood of schizophrenia and that the "the predisposition to schizophrenia—that is, the ability to respond to certain stimuli with a

---

[17]*Action for Mental Health,* Final Report of the Joint Commission on Mental Illness and Health (New York: Basic Books, 1961).

[18]From a case record collected by the senior author.

[19]See I. I. Gottesman and James Shields, *Shizophrenia and Genetics: A Twin Study Vantage Point* (New York: Academic Press, 1972); and Lenord Heston, "The Genetics of Schizophrenia and Schizoid Disease," *Science,* 167 (1970), 249–256.

[20]David Rosenthal, *Genetic Theory and Abnormal Behavior* (New York: McGraw-Hill, 1970).

[21]Franz Kallman, *The Genetics of Schizophrenia* (Locust Valley, N.Y.: J. J. Augustine, 1938). Also see Frans J. Kallman, "The Genetic Theory of Schizophrenia," *American Journal of Psychiatry,* 103 (1946), 309–322.

schizophrenic type of reaction—depends on the presence of a specific genetic factor which is probably recessive and autosomal."[22] Although Kallman's is the leading study, others have tried to show that schizophrenia is hereditary.

A British researcher compared the adjustment of 47 adults born to mothers diagnosed as schizophrenics with a matched control group of adults born to nonmentally ill mothers.[23] The subjects in both groups of adults had been separated from their natural mothers in the first few days of life and reared in foster homes. The investigator found a higher incidence of schizophrenia and other pathologies among the group born to the schizophrenic mothers than among the matched control group. According to Mechanic, this type of study supports a hereditary etiology of schizophrenia: since the subjects studied had been removed from their schizophrenic mothers not long after birth, their higher rate of pathology could not have been due to interaction with a schizophrenic mother. He indicated that this general theory depends mostly, however, on studies of twins, and for this reason further consideration of the real implications of such studies is needed.[24]

Various attempts have been made to link environmental factors to the so-called genetic predisposition to schizophrenia. Generally they have not been sufficiently precise, although it does appear that severe stressful situations preceding the onset of the illness are involved. Mechanic has well summarized the three types of theories that attempt to explain the biological link of schizophrenia to environment.

> One view is that those genetically predisposed to schizophrenia have nervous systems particularly vulnerable to the intense stimulation which social changes can bring. In this view a breakdown reflects the inability of the patient to tolerate a high level of stimulation. A second explanation for the increased vulnerability of schizophrenics to major changes and intense emotions involves the assumption that these conditions are threatening to persons who lack the ability to handle problems. Because of biological incapacities of inadequate social training, schizophrenics do not develop a repertoire of interpersonal techniques which allow them to face and deal with new and challenging situations. Therefore, they are more likely to suffer a breakdown in such circumstances. A third position is that schizophrenia is an adaptive attempt to meeting social adversity and difficulty, and although this approach has certain advantages, it results in disruptions as well.[25]

Criticisms of Inheritance of Schizophrenia All of these efforts to establish a genetic link to schizophrenia have been severely criticized. Some indication of the present confusion about this question of heredity and schizophrenia is seen in a government report on the question. This report concluded that heredity is important but that many basic questions remain unanswered. Various questions are raised:

> Is it an enzyme defect, a biochemical abnormality, a minor neurologic deficit, or any one of a seemingly infinite number of factors? If a predisposition is inherited, what is it? How

---

[22]Kallman, "The Genetic Theory of Schizophrenia," p. 321.
[23]L. Heston, "Psychiatric Disorders in Foster Home Reared Children of Schizophrenic Mothers," *British Journal of Psychiatry,* 112 (1966), 819–825.
[24]Mechanic, *Mental Health and Social Policy,* p. 36.
[25]Mechanic, *Mental Health and Social Policy,* © 1969, p. 37. Reprinted by permission of Prentice-Hall, Inc., Englewood Cliffs, New Jersey.

does it operate? What is the nature and course of the spiraling feedback mechanism set up in the individual, his family, and the social system?[26]

Without answers to these questions it would appear that the establishment of a hereditary basis for schizophrenia cannot be presumed.

1.   The problem of diagnosis of schizophrenia itself is the greatest obstacle in the genetic study of the disorder. In actuality, the criteria used to diagnose this illness vary so widely that they are not always reliable.[27] Diagnostic difficulties are not surprising because there is no clear, fundamental definition of schizophrenia, and marked differences are seen in international psychiatry as to exactly what the term means. Two leading authorities have stated that this diagnosis is either easy or difficult: "The typical cases, and there are very many such, can be recognized by the layman and the beginner; but some cases offer such difficulties that the most qualified experts in the field cannot come to any agreement."[28] The diagnosis is so unreliable, in fact, that one psychiatrist has even suggested that the only meaning of the term resides in the vague conceptions within psychiatrists themselves.[29] Moreover, once attached, the label of schizophrenia is difficult to remove, even from persons to whom it does not apply.[30]

2.   Cultural factors appear to play a role even in the symptoms of schizophrenia. Differences in the nature of schizophrenic symptoms have been found, for example, between persons from Irish and Italian subcultures, the former favoring fantasy and withdrawal to the extent of paranoid reactions, while the Italian patients suffered from poor emotional and impulse control.[31] Among the Hutterites, a tightly knit religious sect living in western United States and Canada, manic-depressive behavior is much more common than schizophrenia, which is a rare illness.[32] Hindus, Chinese, and Malayans in Singapore have different amounts and types of disorders, including schizophrenia, depending upon their cultural experiences.[33] Pronounced differences in the extent and nature of mental disorders were found among Spanish-Americans and Anglo-Americans in Texas.[34]

3.   The fact that schizophrenia may appear in a family line does not prove that it is inherited. Diseases or physical illnesses of various types may run in families without their necessarily having a genetic basis. For example, beriberi does run in families, but

---

[26]Loren R. Mosher and David Feinsilver, "Special Report on Schizophrenia," National Institute of Mental Health, U.S. Department of Health, Education and Welfare, April 1970, p. 16.
[27]F. C. Redlich and D. X. Freedman, *The Theory and Practice of Psychiatry* (New York: Basic Books, 1966).
[28]Redlich and Freedman, p. 507.
[29]See Thomas Szasz, *Schizophrenia: The Sacred Symbol of Psychiatry* (New York: Basic Books, 1976).
[30]See D. L. Rosenhan, "On Being Sane in Insane Places," *Science,* 179 (1973), 250–258.
[31]Marvin K. Opler, "Cultural Differences in Mental Disorders: An Italian and Irish Contrast in the Schizophrenics—USA," in Marvin K. Opler, ed., *Culture and Mental Health* (New York: Macmillan, 1959), pp. 425–442. Also see the review in Nancy E. Waxler, "Culture and Mental Illness: A Social Labeling Perspective," *Journal of Nervous and Mental Disease,* 159 (1974), 379–395.
[32]Joseph W. Eaton and Robert J. Weil, *Culture and Mental Disorders* (New York: Free Press, 1955).
[33]H. B. M. Murphey, "Culture and Mental Disorder in Singapore," in Opler, *Culture and Mental Health,* pp. 291–316.
[34]E. Gartly Jaco, "Mental Health of the Spanish-American in Texas," in Opler, *Culture and Mental Health,* pp. 467–489.

what is inherited actually is "the pattern of preference for vitamin-poor foods which children pick up from their parents."[35]

4. Most genetic studies need to take into account the effects on children of being reared in a family where one or both parents are "mentally disturbed" without genetic factors being present.

5. A joint study by a sociologist and a psychiatrist who made a comprehensive survey of 847 schizophrenic cases under treatment in the Greater New Haven area found that only 25 percent had schizophrenic relatives.[36]

6. Although it is doubtful, genetic factors may conceivably be necessary attributes of schizophrenia; they are certainly not a sufficient condition, nor an explanation, for its etiology.[37] Even if evidence of a genetic component in the etiology of schizophrenia were found to exist, it would not rule out the importance of environmental, psychological, and sociological influences. In fact, the difficulties noted here in diagnosing schizophrenia point to the interpretation of the variable nature of this condition, depending upon its social and psychological context.

Manic-Depressive Behavior As the name implies, manic-depressive behavior may be extreme elation, in the manic stage, or depression, although manic-depressives do not necessarily pass through cyclical stages of mania and depression. In the manic stage the patient is agitated and excited, elated and aggressive. The person rapidly shifts from one topic, object, or activity to another, and there is a constant flow of manic talk, which, although continuous, is socially understandable. This method of talking is often filled with quips, rhymes, poems, and other witticisms, many with personal references. The extreme manic person sings or whistles, shouts, dances, walks, teases, or clowns. Often the individual disregards such bodily needs as food and rest.

In the depressed phase there is much brooding and unpleasantness but little serious mental deterioration. Agitated depression involves restless overactivity and despair, whereas activity is minimized and stupor is not uncommon in retarded depression. This disturbance is generally characterized by feelings of dejection, sadness, and self-depreciation. The patient seems to have lost friends, home, family, and all purpose in life. He feels guilty about acts committed or omitted, and he believes he has grievously wronged or been wronged. Contact with reality is nonetheless maintained, as are memory and place-time orientation. Not all depressed behavior is psychiatrically symptomatic of a manic-depressive psychosis, for neurotics may display secondary depression. Involutional melancholia is another fairly common mental disorder characterized largely by depression. This condition may occur among women during the menopause and among men at a slightly older age.

Paranoia and Paranoid Behavior At one time a large proportion of persons with mental disorders were diagnosed as suffering from a single entity, paranoia, but today

---

[35]Don D. Jackson, "A Critique of the Literature on the Genetics of Schizophrenia," in Don D. Jackson, ed., *The Etiology of Schizophrenia* (New York: Basic Books, 1960), p. 44.

[36]August B. Hollingshead and Frederick Redlich, *Social Class and Mental Illness* (New York: Wiley, 1958); also a private communication from A. B. Hollingshead.

[37]See the discussion in Clausen, pp. 124–126.

paranoia is not widely used as a diagnostic category. Most persons suffering from paranoid disorders are now considered to exhibit a form of schizophrenic behavior. Paranoids are thought to be extremely suspicious and to have ideas of persecution, with an intellectual defense that often appears to have bases. Their delusions are usually limited to a few areas and may even be centered on a single person. The behavior of most people who are paranoid, however, does not seriously interfere with most of their life activities; their personalities do not deteriorate, nor do they have hallucinations.

PROBLEMS OF DEFINITION

It is difficult to assess the deviant nature of mental disorder because what is meant both by mental health and, consequently, mental disorder, has not been adequately defined. Mechanic points out that attempts to define mental illness in some precise fashion continue to be disappointing.[38] While usually defined in terms of some deviation from normality, it is not a simple matter to define normality. Certainly some individuals behave in strange or inappropriate ways, or they verbalize bizarre thoughts or rationales for their actions; but they are frequently judged to be mentally ill by subjective standards. Actions that may be normal in some situations may not be normal in others. For example, an individual might wash his hands 50 times or more during the day, which might be appropriate and necessary for an automobile mechanic or a dentist but would be considered extremely odd and "compulsive" activity for an office worker or business executive.

There is, then, no one way to define mental illness. A number of broad approaches have been utilized to define both mental health and mental disorder. The methods of definition presented here are statistical, clinical, and operational in terms of residual norms and societal reaction.

Statistical

Although mental health is not the same as the statistically normal in terms of averages, if it were to be viewed in this statistical perspective, it might be said that the "mental health" of those persons in the "middle" would represent what might be termed normality. It is impossible to measure the mental health of the average citizen, however, in such average statistical measures as the mean, the median, or the mode, because there is no satisfactory frequency curve of mental health as is attempted in the case of intelligence test curves.

Clinical

In clinical medicine the problem of defining the "normality" of health is often difficult and complicated, but it cannot compare with the complexities in clinically defining

---

[38]Mechanic, *Mental Health and Social Policy,* p. 2.

"mental health." There are problems connected with normative definitions and value judgments.

Disregard of Normative Definitions   From a clinical point of view, mental disorder often is regarded as behavior that digresses from clinically "normal" behavior.[39] Redlich presented three criteria that must be met before behavior can be clinically labeled normal or abnormal.[40] (1) The motivation of the behavior must be taken into account, such as "normal" washing of the hands and a neurotic washing compulsion. (2) The context or situation in which the behavior occurs must also be considered. Wearing swimming trunks on a New England street in winter is one thing; on a summer bathing beach, another. (3) By whom is the judgment made that the behavior is clinically abnormal—the experts, such as the psychiatrist, or the general public? Since there are no universal clinical criteria, many propositions regarding the normality of behavior are perceptibly lacking in both reliability and validity and are subject to challenge by the public, particularly if they are lacking in strong scientific evidence or contrary to current public opinion.[41]

The very behavior that may be contrary to the ideal values of "mental health" may often be considered normal in another society. Comparative studies of so-called mental disorders in a number of cultures have a bearing on the clinical definition of mental health and mental disorder.[42] Distinctions between beliefs in witchcraft and mental disorder are confusing, for example, in West Africa.[43] The Berens River Ojibwa in northern Canada have fears about encounters with animals, as well as phobias about snakes and huge imaginary animals such as toads.[44] The belief also exists that personal transgressions are related to disease. The most pronounced fear of these people concerns beliefs about the "Windigo," or cannibals. Human beings can, they believe, be transformed into cannibals, and this belief may be perceived by certain phenomena exhibited by individuals. To an outsider these fears appear to be "neurotic" mental disorder, in the sense that there is no real danger and that they arise from sheer fantasies. One must, therefore, distinguish between individual fears and such culturally induced fears. This problem is prevalent in the clinical diagnosis of mental disorder in more complex societies with numerous and varied subcultures and social classes, where people may play roles that are normal in their own group but that are considered clinically abnormal to a psychiatrist.

After reviewing the relation of cultural definitions of mental disorder and the

---

[39]Psychoanalysts, for example, often regard "mental health" as freedom from anxiety and as a condition in which the rational replaces the irrational.

[40]Frederick C. Redlich, "The Concept of Health in Psychiatry," in Alexander H. Leighton, John A. Clausen, and Robert N. Wilson, eds., *Explorations in Social Psychiatry* (New York: Basic Books, 1957), pp. 145–146.

[41]Redlich, p. 146. Also see H. Warren Dunham, *Sociological Theory and Mental Disorder* (Detroit: Wayne State University Press, 1959).

[42]Jane M. Murphey and Alexander H. Leighton, eds., *Approaches to Cross-Cultural Psychiatry* (Ithaca, N.Y.: Cornell University Press, 1965).

[43]S. Kirson Weinberg, "'Mental Healing' and Social Change in West Africa," *Social Problems,* 11 (1964), 157–169. Also see S. Kirson Weinberg, "Cultural Aspects of Manic-Depression in West Africa," *Journal of Health and Human Behavior,* 6 (1965), 247–253.

[44]A. Irving Hallowell, "Fear and Anxiety as Cultural and Individual Variables in a Primitive Society: Ojibwa," in Opler, *Culture and Mental Health,* pp. 41–62.

varied definitions of what is considered mental disorder even within a society, a French social scientist has commented on the artificial line between mental normality and mental disorder.

> The dividing line between the two realms varies, as we shall see, from group to group within the same society. Thus it is never entirely possible to escape from relativity. The function of the psychiatrist is to search for the "causes," to report on the "whys" of the illness, but society decides who his patients will be. There is a subtle play of influences between the doctor and the public. The doctor, through the mass media or other agencies, tends to enlarge the field of mental illness, to make the public more aware of disturbances that are minor and have been until then attributed to "oddness" or "eccentricity." On the other hand, he accepts the lay definition of mental illness, and his work is limited to refining or making more explicit this definition by introducing categories of "insanity" (schizophrenia, manic-depressive psychosis, confusional states, and so on). But these categories never extend beyond the boundaries of insanity as defined by public opinion.[45]

Value Judgments   The clinical definition of "mental health" leads into the area of value judgments. Mental health is defined according to certain traits, capacities, and relations which are considered to be "normal," and many criteria can be found for what "normal" activity is. Among the definitions used by leading psychiatric writers are the striving for happiness, effectiveness, and sensitive social relations, freedom from symptoms and unhampered by conflict, the capacity to love a person other than oneself, the successful integration of one's personality, and a proper balance of instinctual and ego forces. Karl Menninger's still widely quoted definition states:

> Let us define mental health as the adjustment of human beings to the world and to each other with a maximum of effectiveness and happiness. Not just efficiency, or just contentment, or the grace of obeying the rules of the game cheerfully. It is all of these together. It is the ability to maintain an even temper, an alert intelligence, socially considerate behavior, and a happy disposition. This, I think, is a healthy mind.[46]

With such criteria it is often difficult to see how anyone can be regarded as normal. A state of emotional health is thus regarded as par, if one can use the golf term, for the upper levels of health attainment.[47] They are ideals, and they are often contradictory. These contradictions are evident in the widely varying estimates of the prevalence of "mental disorder" in the general population with the use of clinical definitions. A review of the 25 studies of the prevalence of mental disorder has shown percentages ranging from 1 to 64.[48] Moreover, the median rate of disorder for studies after 1950 was seven times higher than for studies before 1950, a difference not likely to have been due to a real difference in the trends but rather to the nature of the

---

[45]Roger Bastide, *The Sociology of Mental Disorder*, Jean McNeil, trans. (New York: David McKay, 1972), p. 60.

[46]Karl Menninger, *The Human Mind* (New York: Knopf, 1946), p. 1.

[47]Leslie A. Osborn, *Psychiatry and Medicine* (New York: McGraw-Hill, 1952), p. 211. For a critique of ideal definitions of mental health, see Marie Jahoda, *Current Concepts of Positive Mental Health* (New York: Basic Books, 1958), pp. 5–9 and 65–80.

[48]Bruce P. Dohrenwend and Barbara Snell Dohrenwend, *Social Status and Psychological Disorder* (New York: Wiley-Interscience, 1969).

criteria used to define mental disorder. The validity of these studies depends upon the criteria used to determine degrees of mental disorder, and these criteria, as well as the methodology, have been severely criticized.[49] In the Midtown Manhattan survey, for example, questions were asked in the interviews about psychiatric disorders, or feelings of "nervousness" and "restlessness," and difficulties in interpersonal relations.[50] This information was then abstracted and given to a team of psychiatrists who rated the person and the amount of "impairment" in psychiatric terms. Numerous problems are associated with such epidemiological studies, including deficiencies in case identification, the inadequacies of the scales used to measure mental disorder, and the fuzziness of diagnostic categories.[51] Mechanic states that the estimates of mental illness are conservative if it is viewed as the presence of a clearly established disabling condition, but if it is also defined "as the presence of psychosomatic conditions, anxiety, or any of a wide variety of problems in living, then we can characterize a large proportion of the population as having some form of mental illness."[52] In fact, the Midtown Manhattan study and a study of Nova Scotia[53] showed such high estimates of mental disorder—four fifths and two thirds of the general population—that many people concluded that either the research techniques were wrong or the results were meaningless.

Residual Norms and Societal Reaction

Perhaps the most satisfactory definitions of mental disorder can be stated in terms of norms and societal reactions. Groups tend to have norms that designate as deviant behavior acts that are termed crime, sexual deviations, drunkenness, bad manners, and other more specific behavior. Mental disorder can be viewed as residual rule breaking or residual deviance in that it covers deviant normative behavior that is left over, what is termed various forms of "mental disorder."[54] The latter includes such behavior as withdrawal, hallucinations, muttering, posturing, depression, excited behavior, compulsions, obsessions, and auditory states. Such residual deviance must, however, be viewed as normative behavior not only in and of itself but also in terms of

---

[49]See, for example, Derek L. Phillips and Kevin J. Clancy, "Response Biases in Field Studies of Mental Illness," *American Sociological Review,* 35 (1970), 503–514; Kevin J. Clancy and Walter R. Gove, "Sex Differences in Mental Illness: An Analysis of Response Bias in Self-Reports," *American Journal of Sociology,* 80 (1974), 205–216; Frank E. Hartung, "Manhattan Madness: The Social Movement of Mental Illness," *Sociological Quarterly,* 4 (1963), 261–272; and Bruce P. Dohrenwend, "Social Status and Psychological Disorder: An Issue of Substance and an Issue of Method," *American Sociological Review,* 31 (1966), 14–34.

[50]Leo Srole, Thomas S. Langner, Stanley T. Michael, Marvin K. Opler, and Thomas A. C. Rennie, *Mental Health in the Metropolis: The Midtown Manhattan Study* (New York: McGraw-Hill, 1962).

[51]Mechanic, "Problems and Prospects in Psychiatric Epidemiology." See also Richard J. Plunkett and John E. Gordon, *Epidemiology and Mental Illness* (New York: Basic Books, 1960).

[52]Mechanic, *Mental Health and Social Policy,* p. 65.

[53]Alexander Leighton, *My Name is Legion* (New York: Basic Books, 1959); and Dorethea Leighton, John S. Harding, David B. Macklin, Allister MacMillan, and Alexander Leighton, *The Character of Disorder* (New York: Basic Books, 1963).

[54]Thomas J. Scheff, *Being Mentally Ill: A Sociological Theory* (Chicago: Aldine, 1966). Also see Henry B. Adams, "'Mental Illness' or Interpersonal Behavior?" *American Psychologist,* 19 (1964), 191–197; and Thomas J. Scheff, *Labeling Madness* (Englewood Cliffs, N.J.: Prentice-Hall, 1975).

the social context in which it occurs. Talking to spirits within the religious context of spiritualism, for example, would not be considered residual deviance. Imputations of rule breaking in a social context may come from various sources, such as the family, school, or factory. The normative violations called mental disorders are therefore not within the individual but within the context in which they occur.

An operational definition of "mental normality" in terms of social reactions means "normal for what" and "normal for whom."[55] This definition seems to be helpful in any adequate definition of "mental disorder." The extent to which behavior, for example, can be tolerated by others may be different for a business executive and a person employed in a minor capacity in an industrial plant, both in terms of what is presumed to be normal and what is the societal reaction of others.

It is therefore very difficult to draw a sharp, operational line between mental health and mental ill health or mental disorder except in terms of norms. What we really have is the problem of the social limits of "eccentricity." An English writer stated that there appears to be no clear-cut criterion of what actually constitutes a psychiatric case, for whether the person is thought to need medical treatment is always "a function of his behavior *and* the attitude of his fellows in society."[56] The person may be slightly, moderately, or severely impaired, depending upon the way his behavior is evaluated by others.[57] One prominent psychiatrist has even gone so far as to deny that mental disorder is an "illness" but rather that it merely represents defective strategies for handling life situations which the individual finds difficult.[58]

The more closely a person's behavior conforms to the expectations of other persons, the more favorably he is evaluated by those around him. On the other hand, when his behavior is not within the expected range, he is likely to be evaluated negatively. Thus it is not necessarily the severity of the disorder or the pathology of the behavior from a clinical viewpoint that leads to the rejection of mentally ill individuals but rather the social visibility of the behavior. Indeed, it is generally agreed that persons who are grossly disturbed and even overtly psychotic by clinical standards may remain for long periods of time in the community without ever being "recognized" as "mentally ill." Researchers have similarly found that the public does not necessarily recognize certain clinical symptoms as seriously disturbed behavior.[59]

Collective action, then, on the part of a family, neighborhood, or community to hospitalize (that is, to label formally) an individual as being mentally disordered will always be a product of interaction between the nature of the behavior and the

---

[55]Redlich.

[56]G. M. Carstairs, "The Social Limits of Eccentricity: An English Study," in Opler, *Culture and Mental Health,* p. 337. He shows historically how people have reacted in different ways to eccentricities. For a history of the norms and societal reaction involved in Europe during the seventeenth and eighteenth centuries, see Michael Foucault, *Madness and Civilization: A History of Insanity in the Age of Reason* (New York: Pantheon, 1965).

[57]See Hollingshead and Redlich, Chaps. 1, 2, and 6.

[58]Thomas S. Szasz, *The Myth of Mental Illness,* rev. ed. (New York: Harper & Row, 1974). Also see E. Fuller Torrey, *The Death of Psychiatry* (Radnor, Pa.: Chilton Books, 1974).

[59]See, for example, Elaine Cumming and John Cumming, *Closed Ranks: An Experiment in Mental Health Education* (Cambridge, Mass.: Harvard University Press, 1957); and Bruce P. Dohrenwend and Edwin Chin-Shong, "Social Status and Attitudes toward Psychological Disorder: The Problem of Tolerance of Deviance," *American Sociological Review,* 32 (1967), 417–432.

tolerance of the group for the behavior. In addition to the variable of visibility of symptoms, other area characteristics affect tolerance differentials, such as the percentage of a given population living in family groups, the type of housing in an area, and other physical features of the neighborhood. Also affecting group tolerance for certain behaviors are characteristics of the individual deviant, such as age, sex, marital status, and the presence or absence of children in the families in which they live, as well as certain characteristics of the surrounding "society."[60] Ethnic background, socioeconomic status, educational level, and size of community all affect the tolerance quotient, resulting in a measure of either high group receptivity or limited group tolerance. One reason for this is that in a complex society there is differential access to existing "professional" knowledge of "mental disorder symptoms" and, therefore, awareness of it.

An operational definition depends also upon the societal reaction. Mechanic gives an excellent discussion of the processes involved.

> In evaluating the criteria by which visible symptoms might be judged, one practical basis is the extent to which the person failed to fulfill adequately expectations in performing his primary social roles (especially his familial and occupational roles), and the extent to which he violated legal and moral norms and highly important values of the group. Whether a definition of deviancy is made and acted upon will depend, largely, on how serious the consequences of this deviation are for the social group. Some deviant behaviors are rewarded and tolerated, others have some idiosyncratic function for the group as is often the case with the "comic," or the deviant may be thought of as "eccentric," "queer," or "strange" but not sufficiently so to merit a definition of illness. On the other hand, should the deviancy begin to have serious consequences, either in that it is damaging or harmful to the individual, a group, or both, or becomes so visible to external groups that the family suffers status loss, it might be redefined as "mental illness" and the person sent for treatment. In some groups, of course, the stigma attached to a definition of mental illness is sufficiently great to bring about group resistance to such a definition.[61]

One study reported on a group of wives, for example, who went through a "process of recognition" of what they defined as mental disorder symptoms in their husbands sufficient to call for hospitalization.[62] Initially their interpretations of their husbands' behavior were not those of mental disorder, then progressing from "nothing really wrong" to "character weakness" and "controllable" behavior (lazy, mean, and so on); physical problems; normal response to a crisis; mildly emotionally disturbed: "something" seriously wrong; and a serious emotional or mental problem. The process in which the wife comes to define the behavior as constituting a problem and requiring hospitalization is a highly individualistic matter:

---

[60]Gerald Gurin, Joseph Veroff, and Sheila Feld, *Americans View Their Mental Health* (New York: Basic Books, 1960), p. 209; Phillips; and Jack P. Gibbs, "Rates of Mental Hospitalization: A Study of Societal Reaction to Deviant Behavior," *American Sociological Review,* 27 (1962), 788.

[61]David Mechanic, "Some Factors in Identifying and Defining Mental Illness," in Thomas J. Scheff, ed., *Mental Illness and Social Processes* (New York: Harper & Row, 1967), pp. 28–29.

[62]Marian Radke Yarrow, Charlotte Green Schwartz, Harriet S. Murphey, and Leila Calhoun Deasy, "The Psychological Meaning of Mental Illness in the Family," in Scheff, *Mental Illness and Social Processes,* pp. 32–48.

in some instances, it is when the wife can no longer manage her husband (he will no longer respond to her usual prods); in others, when his behavior destroys the status quo (when her goals and living routines are disorganized); and, in still others, when she cannot explain his behavior. One can speculate that her level of tolerance for his behavior is a function of her specific personality needs and vulnerabilities, her personal and family value system and the social supports and prohibitions regarding the husband's symptomatic behavior.[63]

It was concluded that the social pressures and expectations serve to keep not only behavior in line but also to a great extent the perceptions of mental disorder.[64]

MENTAL DISORDER AND SOCIAL ROLES

Mental disorder has been explained in terms of biological, personality-type, and behavioristic factors related to the sociocultural setting.[65] Currently, there are three general, theoretical perspectives from which it is possible to examine the nature of mental disorder. First, one can regard it, both specifically and generally, as resulting from some biological defect or genetically based deficit, but because of the limitations already noted the studies done in this particular area will not concern us here. Attention has been called to their existence because of the tendency among sociologists to rule out biological considerations when they interpret their own findings. Second, mental disorder is regarded as the outcome of certain types of personalities that have been formed from conditioning and learning experiences. Such types display behavior that is inappropriate to situations, and they are triggered into social recognition by the impact of various kinds of interpersonal relations and cultural patterns upon them. This perspective represents a dualism wherein personality becomes an entity separated from its biophysiological base. A third possibility is to view mental disorder largely in behavioristic terms, seeing it as a kind of behavior that has become defined as deviant and unacceptable by the significant others that surround the person. Here, mental disorder as such becomes tied to the values and social preferences operating in a given cultural system. From this perspective it can easily be seen that what is considered mental disorder in a society is extremely changeable, for it will tend to vary as cultural values, expectations, and preferences vary.[66]

Mental disorder may also be perceived sociologically in terms of social roles, primarily in terms of an inability to shift roles, as playing the role of the mentally ill, and as self-reactions and social roles. As was pointed out in Chapter 2, the adequate

---

[63]Yarrow *et al.,* pp. 38–39.

[64]Yarrow *et al.,* p. 47.

[65]For a discussion of various theoretical approaches, see Franz Alexander and Sheldon T. Selesnick, *The History of Psychiatry: An Evaluation of Psychiatric Thought and Practice from Prehistoric Times to the Present* (New York: Harper & Row, 1966); Dunham, *Sociological Theory and Mental Disorder;* Weinberg, and Don Martindale and Edith Martindale, *The Social Dimensions of Mental Illness, Alcoholism and Drug Dependence* (Westport, Conn.: Greenwood Press, 1971), especially pp. 132–136.

[66]H. Warren Dunham, "Anomie and Mental Disorder," in Marshall B. Clinard, ed., *Anomie and Deviant Behavior: A Discussion and Critique* (New York: Free Press, 1964), pp. 130–131.

performance of social roles is basic to the assessment of deviance. Inadequate role performance violates normative expectations, thus increasing the probability that a negative sanction will be imposed. Like other forms of deviance, mental disorders elicit negative sanctions from a number of sources, including family, friends, employers, and relatives, as well as from such outside sources as the police or mental health professionals. Moreover, as has just been explained, self-reactions are also likely, depending upon the person's cultural background, the stereotype of mental illness to which one subscribes, and the degree to which others sanction the individual.

Inability To Shift Roles

Many persons who develop mental disorders appear to be unable to shift from one social role to another. As has been indicated, everyone normally plays many roles, even in a single day, depending upon the situation and the expectations of others. An individual's inability to shift roles means that when "insurmountable personal difficulties arise [he] cannot abandon the non-adaptive perspective by shifting through roles to one that might offer a different solution."[67]

Some people view schizophrenics as individuals who find it difficult to play the roles expected of them in normal social relations and therefore tend to be socially isolated. Under stress they are unable to change their role in social situations. They are unable to establish intimate and informal relationships and, consequently, by withdrawing they avoid the evaluation of others.[68] One study of the social aspects of the childhood and adolescence of schizophrenics and a matched control group of so-called normal persons found, however, that only about one third of the schizophrenics were isolated from their peers early in adolescence.[69]

According to Cameron's well-known theory, paranoid behavior appears to be a product of inappropriate role-playing and role-taking.[70] Such persons look at things in an inflexible way; they cannot shift roles or see alternative explanations for the behavior of others. Gradually a private world is built up in which the self as a social object becomes central and in which slights and discriminations, some real, some imagined, from the outside world are interpreted to fit the paranoid's preconceptions. The person develops a "pseudocommunity" which is a product of his unique interpretation of "persecution" in the ordinary behavior of others toward him. He is unable to interpret accurately the roles of others and is therefore not socially competent to interpret their motives and intentions. The reactions of the real community in the form of restraint or retaliation for any of his vengeful or defensive overt behaviors make him convinced that the interpretations of his paranoid pseudocommunity are correct. This interpretation of a "pseudocommunity" has been challenged by Lemert, however, who maintains, after studying a number of cases of paranoia, that the

---

[67]Cameron, *The Psychology of Behavior Disorders,* p. 94.
[68]See H. Warren Dunham, "The Social Personality of the Catatonic Schizophrenic," *American Journal of Sociology,* 49 (1944), 508–518.
[69]M. L. Kohn and John A. Clausen, "Social Isolation and Schizophrenia," *American Sociological Review,* 20 (1955), 265–273.
[70]Cameron, *The Psychology of Behavior Disorders,* pp. 466–467. Also see Norman Cameron, "The Paranoid Pseudocommunity Revisited," *American Journal of Sociology,* 65 (1959), 52–58.

community to which the paranoid reacts is real and not a pseudo or symbolic fabrication.[71] He found that "while the paranoid person reacts differentially to his social environment, it is also true that 'others' react differentially to him and this reaction commonly if not typically involves covertly organized action and conspiratorial behavior in a very real sense."[72] Moreover, the reactions of the potential paranoid and those of "others" are reciprocal and result in exclusion. The delusion and associated behavior that develop must be understood in the context of a process of exclusion which disrupts his social communication with others.

Playing the Role of a Mentally Disordered Person

A sociological theory of mental disorder in terms of playing the role of the mentally ill and labeling of the behavior has been set forth by Scheff.[73] Normative violations that characterize mental disorder such as withdrawal, depression, compulsions, obsessions, and hallucinations are common, and Scheff terms such norm violations "residual rule breaking" to distinguish them from the violations of the criminal law or social conventions such as etiquette. They may arise from diverse sources, such as organic difficulties, psychological problems, external stress, or willful acts of defiance against some person or situation; consequently, the nature of the origin is of little consequence. Residual rule breaking is very common, goes largely unnoticed, is of transitory significance, and constitutes primary deviance. Most residual rule breaking, for the average person, is not recognized by others or even by the individual, or there is a tendency to explain or rationalize it. The average person may have an illusion or hear odd sounds or voices and simply forget it. Scheff states that the evidence shows that gross violations of rules often go unnoticed, or if they are noticed they are excused as personal eccentricities. Many ordinary individuals who are withdrawn, who "fly off the handle" for periods of time, who now and then imagine fantastic events or occasionally hear an odd sound or voice, or who may see odd sights are generally not labeled as being insane either by themselves or by others. "Their rule breaking, rather, is unrecognized, ignored, or rationalized."[74]

The explicit identification and labeling of such residual behavior by others, however, helps to organize the behavior into a "role of being mentally ill" that has been defined by, and therefore learned from, the culture. Many societies, such as that of the United States, popularly define certain behavior as "crazy": people have shared conceptions of what is meant by insanity, or what Scheff has termed the "social institution of insanity."[75] Popular conceptions of mental illness or being insane are

[71]Edwin M. Lemert, *Human Deviance, Social Problems and Social Control,* 2d ed. (Englewood Cliffs, N.J.: Prentice-Hall, 1972), pp. 246–264.

[72]Lemert, p. 247.

[73]Scheff, *On Being Mentally Ill.*

[74]Scheff, *On Being Mentally Ill,* p. 48.

[75]See Thomas J. Scheff, "The Societal Reaction to Deviance: Ascriptive Elements in the Psychiatric Screening of Mental Patients in a Midwestern State," in Stephen P. Spitzer and Norman K. Denzin, eds., *The Mental Patient: Studies in the Sociology of Deviance* (New York: McGraw-Hill, 1968), pp. 276–293. Also see Thomas J. Scheff, "The Labeling Theory of Mental Illness," *American Sociological Review,* 39 (1974), 444–452.

perpetuated and reaffirmed in everyday conversations and in such forms of mass media as comic strips, television, newspapers, books and songs, and even advertising. One can learn from the culture the stereotyped imagery associated with being "insane," "off one's rocker," or "crazy in the head," even in childhood, and children often play at being "crazy."[76] All adult persons probably know how to "act crazy."

Like the typecasting of actors, the playing of the role of a mentally disordered person can become stabilized because of the labeling expectations and role-taking received from others. Where professional "treatment" by psychiatrists, psychologists, counselors, and others tends to attach the label of mental disorder to a person, it may enhance the stability of the mentally ill role to the person. In fact, labeled deviants under treatment may be "rewarded" by professional persons for "accepting" the fact that they are mentally ill. Moreover, labeled deviants may have difficulty in turning to another role and come to accept their deviant role as the only one available. This well-known sociological theory has been summarized in this way.

> Role imagery of insanity is learned early in childhood and is reaffirmed in social interaction. In a crisis, when the deviance of an individual becomes a public issue, the traditional stereotype of insanity becomes the guiding imagery for action, both for those reacting to the deviant and, at times, for the deviant himself. When societal agents and persons around the deviant react to him uniformly in terms of the traditional stereotypes of insanity, his amorphous and unstructured rule-breaking tends to crystallize in conformity to these expectations, thus becoming similar to the behavior of other deviants classified as mentally ill, and stable over time. The process of becoming uniform and stable is completed when the traditional imagery becomes a part of the deviant's orientation for guiding his own behavior.[77]

Much sound reasoning is evident in this definition of mental disorder: (1) the normative definition in terms of residual norms, (2) persons becoming more aware of the relation of their behavior to these norms, and (3) the idea of mental disorder as a role-playing of the behavior expected of the mentally ill. The theory as set forth by Scheff, however, tends to make labeling by others a necessary condition for the explanation. This view has had some support. For example, one study showed that on the whole people tend to reject a person as having a "mental disorder" according to the source of the "help" to which he turns. The rejection scores given for identical descriptive cases of mental disorder by a sample of persons interviewed were found to be lowest for those who sought no help, followed by those who received help from a clergyman, a physician, and a psychiatrist, and then finally by going to a mental hospital.[78] Another study indicated that the fairly positive or negative views toward the patient were positively related to the length of hospitalization.[79]

Unfortunately, the labeling perspective on mental disorder has been exagger-

---

[76]See A. C. Cain, "On the Meaning of 'Playing Crazy' in Borderline Children," *Psychiatry,* 27 (1964), 278–289.

[77]Scheff, *On Being Mentally Ill,* p. 82. A study of schizophrenia among lower-class persons in Puerto Rico seems also to support the role of cultural stereotypes in a person's definition of himself as "crazy" or "loco." See Lloyd R. Rogler and August B. Hollingshead, *Trapped* (New York: Wiley, 1965).

[78]Derek L. Phillips, "Rejection: A Possible Consequence of Seeking Help for Mental Disorders," in Spitzer and Denzin, pp. 213–226.

[79]James Greenley, "The Psychiatric Patient's Family and Length of Hospitalization," *Journal of Health and Social Behavior,* 13 (1972), 25–37.

ated by Scheff and by others who take the position that the public automatically applies a negative stereotype of mental disorder to individuals and that pronounced mental disorder or secondary deviance results from this labeling.[80] Gove asserts, however, that the vast majority of people who become psychiatric patients have serious disturbances, but they are not arbitrarily labeled as mentally ill, since most families tend to deny mental illness until its recognition is unavoidable.[81] In fact, the nature of the psychiatric symptoms were found to be more important than the attitude of the patient's family. Contrary to the labeling view, secondary deviance is not a necessary consequence of being labeled mentally ill and being hospitalized: in fact, Gove maintains that such secondary deviance can be avoided if hospitalization is short term. He concludes that, in general, the evidence on stigma, while it is far from being conclusive, suggests that for most ex-patients stigma does not present a serious problem, and that when it is a problem it is related more directly to the person's current psychiatric status or to his general ineffectiveness than to his having been a patient in a mental hospital.[82] Another study indicated that the behavior of the individual, rather than the label, is of greater significance in determining the reactions of others, especially when that behavior is tied into a situational context that permits more accurate judgments of both mental illness and subsequent social competence in terms of role performance.[83] Labels may play an important role, however, in helping others to judge the social competence of the mentally ill person.[84] Moreover, in a comparative study no support was found for the labeling hypothesis that popular stereotypes of mental disorders are primary determinants of symptomatology.[85] Mechanic has summarized the limitations of the labeling perspective of mental disorder (also see p. 78):

> No one would deny that social labels can have powerful effects on individuals, but little evidence suggests that such labeling processes are sufficiently powerful to be major influences in producing chronic mental illness. Obviously, the labeling process is not sufficient in itself to produce mental illness, yet existing theories of societal reaction are extremely vague in defining clearly the conditions under which labeling will or will not produce deviant behavior. Some patients get well rather quickly and stay well, while

[80]Scheff, *On Being Mentally Ill;* Scheff, *Labeling Madness;* and Scheff, "The Labeling Theory of Mental Illness." Also see Greenley.
[81]Walter R. Gove, "Societal Reaction as an Explanation of Mental Illness: An Evaluation," *American Sociological Review,* 35 (1970), 873–884. Also see Richard J. Bord, "Rejection of the Mentally Ill: Continuities and Further Developments," *Social Problems,* 18 (1971), 496–510. An extended critique of the labeling approach to mental disorders can be found in Walter R. Gove, "Labeling and Mental Illness: A Critique," in Walter R. Gove, ed., *The Labeling of Deviance: Evaluating a Perspective* (New York: Sage/Halsted, 1975), pp. 35–81.
[82]Gove, "Societal Reaction as an Explanation of Mental Illness," p. 881. Also see Walter R. Gove and Terry Fain, "The Length of Psychiatric Hospitalization," *Social Problems,* 22 (1975), 407–419; and Walter R. Gove and Patrick Howell, "Individual Resources and Mental Hospitalization: A Comparison and Evaluation of the Societal Reaction and Psychiatric Perspectives," *American Sociological Review,* 39 (1974), 86–100.
[83]See, for example, Stuart A. Kirk, "The Impact of Labeling on Rejection of the Mentally Ill: An Experimental Study," *Journal of Health and Social Behavior,* 15 (1974), 108–117.
[84]L. Anthony Loman and William E. Larkin, "Rejection of the Mentally Ill: An Experiment in Labeling," *The Sociological Quarterly,* 17 (1976), 555–560.
[85]J. Marshall Townsend, "Cultural Conceptions, Mental Disorders and Social Roles: A Comparison of Germany and America," *American Sociological Review,* 40 (1975), 739–752.

others, such as schizophrenics, tend to be chronically ill; the theory of labeling does not explain why such differences occur.[86]

Self-Reactions and Social Roles

All persons have a self-reaction to their appearance, status, and conduct. They come to conceive of themselves not only as physical objects but as social objects as well. Likewise, human beings learn to express approval of themselves and are able to reproach themselves. This capacity of self-conception, which all persons have, plays an important part in mental disorder. Mentally disordered persons may develop distorted self-conceptions or self-images that are reflections of difficulties in interpersonal relations and continuing anxiety. Other persons may come to think of them as "odd," "crazy," or "difficult." Some may become less confident and more preoccupied with themselves. Without logical reasons, they may adopt egocentric ideas of being either a great success or a great failure. Where interpersonal relations have been difficult, the mentally disordered person may learn to use self-reactions in fantasy. Such persons may dream of themselves as people they are not in order to overcome conflicts. The paranoid's self-reaction is one of conceit and suspicion, which affects that individual's relations with others. The self-delusions of grandeur that develop out of this glorified self-conception are seen in extreme form in the paranoids who claim that they "own the entire world." The schizophrenic's continued preoccupation with self and lessened ability to share experiences with others intensifies self-centeredness. Self-centered reactions obstruct the capacity to communicate and to relate to others, and this consequently magnifies the person's own concern about symptoms and conflicts, so that there is less ability to act with emotional feeling.

What a person does can result in self-approval or self-reproach. The person can praise himself for what he has said or done, or he may be disturbed by what he has done and rebuke himself, producing frustration and conflict. For adults with a depressive psychosis, this self-punishment, representing an internalization of difficulties with their outside social situations, can become a "tragic melodrama, where the depressed self-accused lashes himself so mercilessly in talk and fantasy that death seems the one promise of penance and relief."[87] If the depressed person feels guilty, self-hostility may result in such a loss of self-respect and so much self-reproach that suicide may result. In such mental disorders the self may become so detached from the individual that it becomes not a social object but a physical object to be mutilated and punished for "sin." In certain forms of neurotic behavior involving dissociation, the person may even be able to forget his own identity. In some cases of hysteria and amnesia the person may even identify with a past role or with another self; here one attempts to get away from one's conflicts by changing oneself. The new selves may be alternating or co-existing, and one self may not be aware of the other.

Disturbances in language and in meaningful communication, which are often symptoms in schizophrenia, indicate rather clearly their connection with interpersonal

---

[86]Mechanic, *Mental Health and Social Policy,* © 1969, p. 47. Reprinted by permission of Prentice-Hall, Inc., Englewood Cliffs, New Jersey.
[87]Cameron, *The Psychology of Behavior Disorders,* p. 101.

relations.[88] A schizophrenic may be viewed as a person who is unable to discriminate the subtleties in an accurate sense in the communications from others and therefore is unable to respond adequately to others.[89] Verbal imagination is perfectly normal, for without it books, poems, or great music could not be written, but a person with a mental disorder, being socially isolated, may verbalize thoughts and then become afraid of what has been created. The mentally disordered person is able to invent a world of his own through his thought processes with language. With language, the neurotic is able to conjure up all types of evil thoughts of which he is afraid. The depressed person is able to talk himself into self-depreciation; the manic, into a frenzy. The schizophrenic is able to invent a world of private fantasy which lifts him in his own estimation. This expansion of fantasy, growing out of inadequate response to shared social situations, continues until it no longer responds to the role-taking of others in the culture. One interesting experiment that resulted in the modification of beliefs involved bringing together in group interaction three schizophrenic persons, each of whom believed he was Christ.[90] The disorders in thought processes are eventually expressed through his language; the fact that the schizophrenic lives in a world of his own making, through verbal imagery, not only reflects and influences his thought processes but distorts his verbal reactions until they swing completely away from socially adequate responses. Language becomes private and not social; whether the other person understands it is immaterial. The schizophrenic patient, living in his private world, invents his own common words and links them in such a fashion as to make his speech seem incoherent to others. In response to the question, "Why are you in the hospital?" one patient replied:

> I'm a cut donator, donated by double sacrifice. I get two days for every one. That's known as double sacrifice: in other words, standard cut donator. You know, we considered it. He couldn't have anything for the cut, or for these patients. All of them are double sacrifice because it's unlawful for it to be donated any more. (Well, what do you do here?) I do what is known as the double criminal treatment.
>
> Something that he badly wanted, he gets that, and seven days criminal protection. That's all he gets, and the rest I do for my friend. (Who is the other person who gets all this?) That's the way the asylum cut is donated. (But who is the other person?) He's a criminal. He gets so much. He gets twenty years' criminal treatment, would make forty years: and he gets seven days' criminal protection and that makes fourteen days. That's all he gets.[91]

Cultural factors influence the nature of self-reactions: these factors include religion, the degree to which material success is emphasized in the society, and the amount of control one perceives oneself to exercise over events in the world. One study reported that mental patients of Asiatic origin were more likely to perceive of the

---

[88]See Julius Laffal, *Pathological and Normal Language* (New York: Atherton, 1965). One study has indicated that part of what is called disturbances in language or meaningful conversation of the mentally ill is often actually a reflection of social class. See Lloyd R. Rogler and August B. Hollingshead, "Class and Disordered Speech in the Mentally Ill," *Journal of Health and Human Behavior,* 2 (1961), 178–185.
[89]William R. Rosengren, "The Self in the Emotionally Disturbed," *American Journal of Sociology,* 66 (1961), 454–462.
[90]Milton Rokeach, *The Three Christs of Ypsilanti* (New York: Vintage Books, 1965).
[91]Cameron, *The Psychology of Behavior Disorders,* pp. 466–467.

label of mentally ill in more magical terms, reacting more to the "power" of the label and how that "power" is transferred to the individual.[92] Patients with Western cultural backgrounds, on the other hand, were more likely to react to the label as indicating some sign of "differentness" from their group or their self-concept; the Western patients had a self-concept of being "sick."

SOCIAL STRATIFICATION AND MENTAL DISORDER

Mental disorder, either as a whole or by type of disorder, has not been found to be distributed randomly in the population. The evidence indicates that certain *diagnosed* mental disorders are related to differences in social class and occupation. The highest rates of severe psychiatric disorders have been found disproportionately concentrated in the lowest social classes.[93] A 15-year study of a rural county in maritime Canada reported that the prevalence of symptoms of mental disorder increased as social status declined.[94] A midtown Manhattan survey found that one third of those in the higher socioeconomic status groups were rated "well" while less than 5 percent of the lowest strata were so rated. In the highest group only 12.5 percent were considered "impaired," while nearly one half of the lowest strata were so rated.[95] A study of nearly all persons in New Haven, Connecticut, who were patients either of a psychiatrist or a psychiatric clinic, or who were in psychiatric institutions, revealed rather decided class differences.[96] The group of 1,891 patients was compared with a 5 percent random sample of the normal population, or 11,522 persons. When both groups were divided into five classes and compared, Class I at the top and Class V at the bottom, it was found that the lower the socioeconomic class, the more prevalent the diagnosis of disorder. Class I contained 3.1 percent of the population and only 1.0 percent of the mental patients, whereas the lowest group, with 17.8 percent of the population, had almost twice as many mental patients. When sex, age, race, religion, and marital status were analyzed, social class was still found to be the most important factor. Diagnoses of neuroses were found to be more prevalent at the upper-class levels, however.

---

[92]Mordechai Rotenberg, "Self-Labelling Theory: Preliminary Findings among Mental Patients," *British Journal of Criminology,* 15 (1975), 360–375.

[93]See Marc Fried, "Social Differences in Mental Health," in John Kosa, Aaron Antonovsky, and Irving Kenneth Zola, eds., *Poverty and Health: A Sociological Analysis* (Cambridge, Mass.: Harvard University Press, 1969), pp. 113–167.

[94]Leighton, *The Character of Disorder.*

[95]Srole *et al.,* p. 138.

[96]Hollingshead and Redlich. Part of this difference was undoubtedly due to differential diagnosis on the part of the psychiatrists. Moreover, a number of Class I patients were not included in the study because some private psychiatrists refused to cooperate. Some studies have challenged the relation of schizophrenia to social class on the ground that there is little difference between classes if the cases are distributed not by the patient's class but by that of his father's. See H. Warren Dunham, *Community and Schizophrenia: An Epidemiological Analysis* (Detroit: Wayne State University Press, 1965); and H. Warren Dunham, Patricia Phillips, and Barbara Srinivasan, "A Research Note on Diagnosed Mental Illness and Social Class," *American Sociological Review,* 31 (1966), 223–236.

Schizophrenic behavior appears to be most common among the lowest socio-economic groups and communities, those who are in unskilled and semiskilled occupations, and among the unemployed.[97] On the basis of a survey of 41 studies reporting the incidence of schizophrenia in various parts of the world, it was concluded that there is a disproportionate number of cases in the lower class.[98] Using a different measure, others have found that the relative incidence of schizophrenia is directly related to the size of the discrepancy between education and occupational status.[99]

Why a disproportionate number of schizophrenics are found in the lower class is still undetermined. Some emphasize the importance of genetic factors combined with environmental factors, while others explain it in terms of downward mobility or the childhood socialization patterns and conflicts of lower-class life itself. Some writers (for example, Mechanic) suggest that this disproportionate incidence of schizophrenia is the result of genetic selection and either downward social mobility or a person's failure to move upward with his peers as a result of the debilitating consequences of the disorder.[100] The Dohrenwends made a controversial, far from conclusive study, due to many other variables, to determine whether genetic factors are involved in lower-class mental disorder, particularly schizophrenia.[101] As a result of their analysis of 41 studies in various developed and less developed countries, they concluded that if "we find symptoms that persist in the absence of secondary gain, we must infer some cause other than the social environment. . . . We posit, therefore, that symptoms that persist in the absence of stress situations or secondary gain in everyday life are genetic in origin."[102] This conclusion is implausible; rather, one could more likely explain the differences as being due to the nature and the stresses of lower-class living, differential socialization, social mobility, differential psychiatric diagnoses, and the differential treatment of mental disorder.[103] Moreover, this comparative study assumed that the diagnosis of schizophrenia in various countries is not only an accurate one but also that

---

[97]See Dohrenwend and Dohrenwend, *Social Status and Psychological Disorder;* Dunham, *Community and Schizophrenia;* David Mechanic, "Social Class and Schizophrenia: Some Requirements for a Plausible Theory of Social Influence." *Social Forces,* 50 (1972), 305–309; R. Jay Turner and M. Wagenfeld, "Occupational Mobility and Schizophrenia: An Assessment of Social Causation and Social Selection Hypotheses," *American Sociological Review,* 32 (1967), 104–113; Melvin Kohn, "Social Class and Schizophrenia: A Critical Review," in D. Rosenthal and S. Ketty, eds., *The Transmission of Schizophrenia* (New York: Pergamon Press, 1967), pp. 155–173; and Paul M. Roman and Harrison M. Trice, *Schizophrenia and the Poor* (Ithaca, N.Y.: Cayuga Press, 1967), pp. 18–47. Mechanic, "Social Class and Schizophrenia," questions this relationship and suggests that more research is required to demonstrate the precise linkage.

[98]See Dohrenwend and Dohrenwend, *Social Status and Psychological Disorder,* p. 166.

[99]Jacob Tuckman and Robert J. Kleiner, "Discrepancy between Aspirations and Achievement as a Predictor of Schizophrenia," *Behavioral Science,* 7 (1962), 443–447. Another study, however, found this discrepancy to be lower in some persons than in their fathers. See Dunham, Phillips, and Srinivasan, pp. 223–227.

[100]Mechanic, "Social Class and Schizophrenia."

[101]Dohrenwend and Dohrenwend, *Social Status and Psychological Disorder.*

[102]Dohrenwend and Dohrenwend, *Social Status and Psychological Disorder.* p. 173.

[103]One study of the relation of economic factors to mental disorders tends to support this view. In the large-scale study in which several indicators of the state of the economy were used as predictors, it was found that "mental hospitalization will increase during economic turndowns and decrease during upturns." More specifically (1) economic downturns cause increases in certain psychiatric symptoms, and (2) economic downturns cause increases in the intolerance of mental illness, but the study did not specify the intervening mechanisms that account for this relationship. See M. Harvey Brenner, *Mental Illness and the Economy* (Cambridge, Mass.: Harvard University Press, 1973).

psychiatrists are not more likely to make this diagnosis for lower-class persons. In those developing countries that were included, the number of psychiatrists is small, and their values reflect the type of training they received, most of it abroad.

Stresses of lower-class life resulting from downward mobility have been found associated with the development of schizophrenia, as in the case of a study of schizophrenic males that showed downward mobility accounting for these symptoms.[104] In an attempt to determine the source of lower-class occupational overrepresentation, it was found that the fathers of patients were also overrepresented at the lowest prestige level, although to a lesser degree. A detailed analysis of the occupational movement of patients relative to the position of their fathers indicated that the overrepresentation of schizophrenics resulted primarily from downward mobility. Another study, on the other hand, has suggested that lower-class life itself is related to schizophrenia, and offers as an explanation the high valuation of conformity to external authority that occurs in lower-class life, as well as the fact that lower-class individuals have more difficulty in coping with stress.[105] Another survey attempted a somewhat similar explanation by combining the patterns of childhood socialization in the lowest socioeconomic stratum with the patterns of environmental stress, particularly occupational insecurity, and disorganization among this group.[106] Regardless of etiological factors, there is no question that being in the lower class has much effect upon the course of schizophrenia, because persons in this group are exposed to delays in receiving professional advice and because the types of treatment offered by public agencies tend to increase the severity of the disorder.[107]

Not only do mental disorders vary with social class, but the nature and frequency of mental disorders differ by sex. Rates of mental disorder in general are consistently higher for males.[108] There appear to be no consistent sex differences in rates of functional psychoses in general, or for schizophrenia, but females generally have higher rates of manic-depressive psychoses and neuroses. Explanations for these differences in the rates of certain mental disorders have usually been phrased in terms of the greater status pressures on women, particularly their tendency to find marriage less satisfying than do males.[109] A recent study of this issue suggests that while marital status is not as important as was previously thought, the fact that a person is a female does seem to be significant in the likelihood of the person's becoming mentally disturbed and seeking treatment for the condition.[110] Moreover, it appears that it is not marital status *per se* that accounts for this relationship but rather *changes* in marital

---

[104]Turner and Wagenfeld. Also see Elliott G. Mishler and Norman S. Scotch, "Sociocultural Factors in the Epidemiology of Schizophrenia," *International Journal of Psychiatry,* 1 (1965), 258–305; and E. M. Goldberg and S. L. Morrison, "Schizophrenia and Social Class," *British Journal of Psychiatry,* 109 (1963), 785–802.

[105]Kohn, p. 159.

[106]Roman and Trice, Schizophrenia and the Poor, pp. 42–78.

[107]Hollingshead and Redlich.

[108]Bruce P. Dohrenwend and Barbara Snell Dohrenwend, "Sex Differences and Psychiatric Disorders," *American Journal of Sociology,* 81 (1976), 1147–1154.

[109]See, for example, Walter R. Gove, "The Relationship between Sex Roles, Marital Status and Mental Illness," *Social Forces,* 51 (1972), 34–44; and Walter R. Gove and J. F. Tudor, "Adult Sex Roles and Mental Illness," *American Journal of Sociology,* 78 (1973), 812–835.

[110]George J. Warheit, Charles E. Holzer, III, Roger A. Bell, and Sandra A. Arey, "Sex, Marital Status, and Mental Health: A Reappraisal," *Social Forces,* 55 (1976), 459–470.

status that produce symptoms of mental disorder. Those females whose marriages had been disrupted, particularly those who had been separated, were found to be more likely to develop stress than those who were single or who had been married only once. It is to this issue of *stress* that we now turn.

SOCIAL STRESS AND MENTAL DISORDER

Normal emotional stress is useful in many ways to the individual; in contrast to healthy stress, however, intense and persistent stress of a social nature, associated with anger, fear, frustration, worry, and so forth, can threaten health. In the field of medicine, for example, much interest has long been shown in the relation between excessive social stress and such physical conditions as hypertension and digestive disorders. Our concern here is directed at the relation of social stress to mental disorder. The evidence is not yet conclusive, but it appears that social stress is directly related to behavior that is socioculturally defined as mental disorder. Such stressful situations in life as marriage, divorce, the illness or death of a close relative or friend, as well as more minor but still stressful events such as marital disputes, coping with troublesome children, or even minor but annoying conflicts with other persons, have been used to predict mental disorder. These various situations and others like them have been incorporated into a scale and weighted according to the degree of stress that each is likely to generate. A review of studies in which these scales have been used has led to the conclusion that they clearly indicate that certain stressful "life events tend to occur to an extent greater than chance expectation before a variety of psychiatric disorders."[111] Certain types of disorders are the result of a higher proportion, while others are the result of a lower number, of stressful life events. Thus, persons who attempt suicide report the greatest number of these events, depressives the next highest, and then schizophrenics.[112] The relationship between life events and psychological disorders appears to be highest with depressives, but substantially lower with other forms of disorder. Among neurotics, there appears to be a direct relationship between the amount of stress and the severity of the symptoms.[113]

Stress and Anxiety

In social interaction persons frequently encounter conflict situations which may produce stress, particularly if the situation threatens the person's self-image, roles, or values. Stress factors tend to produce a certain amount of *anxiety*. Anxiety resembles fear in many ways; like fear, it is an emotional reaction produced by stimulation with

---

[111]E. S. Paykel, "Life Stress and Psychiatric Disorder: Applications of the Clinical Approach," in Barbara Snell Dohrenwend and Bruce P. Dohrenwend, eds., *Stressful Life Events: Their Nature and Effects* (New York: Wiley, 1974), p. 147.

[112]Paykel, p. 148. Also see Robert E. Markush and Rachel V. Favero, "Epidemiologic Assessment of Stressful Life Events," in Dohrenwend and Dohrenwend, *Stressful Life Events*, pp. 171–190.

[113]Joseph E. McGrath, ed., *Social and Psychological Factors in Stress* (New York: Holt, Rinehart and Winston, 1970).

which one is unable to deal. Unlike fear reactions that call forth avoidance and even flight from a real danger when it appears or seems possible, however, the emotional reaction in anxiety does not go on to completion. Fear is overt; anxiety is covert. It leaves the person in an undefined emotional state with which he would like to cope but cannot. He is afraid, but since he cannot identify what he fears, he cannot eliminate the anxiety. As contrasted with overt fear reactions, which can be identified, anxiety reactions created by stress are less visible and are often inaccessible to both the individual and others. If stress develops beyond the limits of the individual, chronic anxiety reactions and even acute anxiety attacks may occur. Not only do the symptoms of anxiety continue for a long time but the individual may have extremely pronounced attacks of anxiety, even panic reactions.

Stress is seen in neurotic compulsive behavior, such as orderliness and obsessional ideas that help to relieve anxiety. The acts, words, and thoughts involved in the compulsive relief of stress and anxiety may include preoccupation with certain obsessions, tapping, counting, or saying set words. In hypochondria, for example, the individual's constant preoccupation with his health simply constitutes solutions in which this preoccupation diverts and releases anxiety. It has been said that the "fruit" of resisting the compulsion is mounting anxiety, while the "reward" of indulging the compulsion provides only a temporary respite.[114] Tendencies to compulsive neurotic behavior are irritating and are fought against, but the feelings of stress and anxiety are relieved. The relief is always temporary, for eventually with stress the anxiety begins to mount again, and in order to reduce it the person has to give in to the compulsive behavior. Moreover, the societal reaction of others to certain noticeable forms of neurotic behavior may tend to increase stress and anxiety. In the schizophrenic and depressive disorders individuals may withdraw and thus find the stress diminished as they retreat from conflicts.

Stress and Social Situations

Mental disorders appear to arise out of a continuous series of events, often over a long period of time, but stress situations often act as precipitants, bringing the process to a climax. The effect of an immediate stress situation is particularly important in the manic-depressive disorders. A study of a group of manic-depressive cases, for example, revealed that in nearly four fifths of them the conditions were precipitated by some particularly disturbing stress situation—a marital disagreement, a death, a career crisis, or a feeling of personal failure induced by harsh criticism.[115] In most cases anxiety and the conflict had been built up over a period of one to six months.

The hypothesis has been advanced, particularly in connection with the neuroses, that the intense striving for material goods and the competitive emphasis in present-day industrial urban society lead many persons to irreconcilable conflicts. In a well-known and still widely respected study, Horney characterized life in modern

---

[114]Cameron, *The Psychology of Behavior Disorders,* p. 277.
[115]Thomas Rennie, "Prognosis in Manic-Depressive Psychoses," *American Journal of Psychiatry,* 98 (1942), 801–818.

Western societies as being highly individualistic, with great competitive striving for achievement and social status.[116] This leads to conflicts between materialistic desires and their possible fulfillment and between competitive striving and the desire for the affection of others, all of which tend to produce stress and neuroses, particularly in urban males.[117] Another study reported that neuroses resulted from the struggle for achievement that produced feelings of hostility in some, while in others the culturally prescribed standards of success and prestige presented goals impossible to achieve and thus augmented already existing conflicts.

Other situations furnish illustrations of the role in mental disorder of tension arising from conflicts in a society. The conclusion of a study of mental disorders in different societies was that the variation and the fact that there is less mental disorder are due to the amount of stability and integrated cultural traits, consistent role expectations, and close interpersonal, family, and community ties.[118] Many Andean Indians who migrate to coastal urban centers of Peru have pronounced psychiatric problems, in part because of the migration but also because of the "extreme differences between the cultures of the Sierran Indians and the coastal urban populations which magnify the dimensions of change required of the Indian."[119] Mental disorders were increased among the Ifaluk of Micronesia as a result of culture conflict arising from the Japanese occupation during World War II.[120] Tensions arising from lack of cultural integration have been found to account for the highest incidence of schizophrenia among two groups of Japanese who migrated to Hawaii.[121]

Even the psychiatric symptoms of depersonalization, disordered thought, and delusions of psychotics have been said to be a natural product of sleep deprivation produced by stress.[122] Experimental psychological studies in sleep deprivation have produced similar phenomena in persons without mental disorder who have been deprived of sleep. But as contrasted with the rational explanation that normal persons may give to these phenomena, the psychotic person becomes sure he is "losing his mind" and accepts the psychotic experiences as real. He experiences such phenomena while agitated and awake and without a ready explanation for them.

Psychological stress affecting mental disorder appears to be linked to social class. Lower-class persons experience more unpleasant events and also experience the most difficulty in dealing with them.[123] Interpersonal relationships are more fragile and provide relatively minimal social support for persons facing crises. In the midtown

---

[116]Karen Horney, *The Neurotic Personality of Our Time* (New York: Norton, 1937).

[117]Stanley A. Leavy and Lawrence Z. Freedman, "Psychoneurosis and Economic Life," *Social Problems,* 4 (1956), 55–67.

[118]Eaton and Weil; Opler, *Culture and Social Psychiatry,* and *Culture and Mental Health;* Waxler; and Saxon Graham, "Sociological Aspects of Health and Illness," in Robert E. L. Faris, ed., *Handbook of Modern Sociology* (Chicago: Rand McNally, 1964).

[119]Jacob Fried, "Acculturation and Mental Health among Indian Migrants in Peru," in Opler, *Culture and Mental Health,* p. 136.

[120]Melford E. Spiro, "Cultural Heritage, Personal Tensions, and Mental Illness in a South Sea Culture," in Opler, *Culture and Mental Health,* pp. 141–171.

[121]Kiyoshi Ikeda, Harry V. Ball, and Douglas S. Yamamura, "Ethnocultural Factors in Schizophrenia: The Japanese in Hawaii," *American Journal of Sociology,* 68 (1962), 242–248.

[122]Walter R. Gove, "Sleep Deprivation: A Cause of Psychotic Disorganization," *American Journal of Sociology,* 75 (1970), 782–799.

[123]Jerome K. Myers, Jacob J. Lindenthal, and Max P. Pepper, "Social Class, Life Events, and Psychiatric Symptoms: A Longitudinal Study," in Dohrenwend and Dohrenwend, *Stressful Life Events,* pp. 191–205.

Manhattan study the number of stressful factors, but not their nature, was found to be associated with mental disorder, and low-status groups were found to encounter the most stress.[124] The development of neurotic symptoms was found to be related, in yet another study, to the stress produced by the sharp and even moderate inconsistency between high ascribed status based on racial or ethnic rank and low achieved status.[125] A study of the relation of mental disorder among blacks to goal-striving stress found that mentally disordered persons set higher goals than they could achieve and experienced high levels of self-imposed goal-striving stress.[126] On the other hand, physical illness and injury, regardless of their seriousness, appear to be among the more stressful situations that generally do not lead to psychological disorders.[127] Such events are generally not perceived by individuals as being within their control.

The importance of stress produced by role conflict has been shown in a study of a group of schizophrenic married women; the conclusion was that these women had repeatedly experienced severe difficulties over the years in their marital situations.[128] In fact, husbands or wives who were schizophrenic presented "no evidence that they were exposed to greater hardships, more economic deprivation, more physical illnesses, or personal dilemmas from birth until they entered their present marriage than do the mentally healthy men and women."[129] The intensive study of schizophrenics and nonschizophrenics in this representative sample of lower-class husbands and wives, between the ages of 20 and 39, in the slum and housing projects (*caserios*) of San Juan, Puerto Rico, showed that such disorders could not be explained by childhood experiences, social isolation, or occupational history. Rather, they were due to the stress created by conflicts and problems associated with lower-class life and neighborhood situations. The schizophrenics had many more, as well as more severe, problems than the nonschizophrenics. The culture and their low socioeconomic status in the society present some persons with tension points. Such problems in this Spanish culture of Puerto Rico include courtship, women's adjustment to sexual and other roles in marriage, the disparity between achieved and desired levels of living, conflict with neighbors, and the absence of privacy in the housing projects as well as various problems of role fulfillment and performance. These stress problems continue to mount, imposing contradictory claims and leading to conflict, mutual withdrawal, and alienation of neighbors, until individuals reach a breaking point in which they are "trapped."

---

[124] Thomas S. Langner and Stanley T. Michael, *Life Stress and Mental Health* (New York: Free Press, 1963), pp. 147–157. Mechanic has criticized this study on the grounds that it found only small differences in average scores on stress index relative to socioeconomic status. See Mechanic, "Social Class and Schizophrenia." When the amount of stress was controlled, low socioeconomic status was associated with mental health risk for all but the lowest stress group.

[125] Elton F. Jackson and Peter J. Burke, "Status and Symptoms of Stress: Additive and Interaction Effects," *American Sociological Review*, 30 (1965), 556–564.

[126] Seymour Parker and Robert J. Kleiner, *Mental Illness in the Urban Negro Community* (New York: The Free Press, 1966); and Morris Rosenberg, "The Dissonant Religious Context and Emotional Disturbance," *American Journal of Sociology*, 68 (1963), 1–10.

[127] David Mechanic, "Discussion of Research Programs on Relations between Stressful Life Events and Episodes of Physical Illness," in Dohrenwend and Dohrenwend, *Stressful Life Events*, pp. 87–97. Also see Barbara Snell Dohrenwend and Bruce P. Dohrenwend, "Overview and Prospects for Research on Stressful Life Events," in *Stressful Life Events*, pp. 313–331.

[128] See Rogler and Hollingshead, *Trapped*.

[129] Rogler and Hollingshead, *Trapped*, p. 404.

The person who decompensates into a schizophrenic solution to his personal difficulties, metaphorically speaking, is caught in a trap with two compartments; one is the inter-meshed series of insoluble dilemmas he encounters in his failure to fulfill the role requirements of his society; the other is the culturally defined role of the *loco*. The sick man or woman fears, as he searches for a way out of his personal maze of problems, that he may spring the catch on the trap that will make him a *loco*. [130]

Depressions among senile patients appear to result from excessive brooding over the stress created by lowered status, functions, and roles imposed upon them by the society and from the lack of satisfying outlets. [131] In some cases, the aged person may retreat into a world of neurotic behavior, fantasies, and even psychoses, wherein the self is satisfied by memories of past beauty or success in business or on the job. Some develop psychotic behavior but not all such behavior is actually psychotic. Havighurst explains why some old people escape from stress through hallucinations:

Sometimes a woman who has lost her husband or a man who has lost his wife will go on talking to the absent loved one. Why not? It is a pleasure to have someone to talk to. So why not go on talking to the people one loved? If one listens carefully, one may hear them reply; and so a person living alone may converse a great deal with absent persons. Then when someone—a son or daughter—notices this, that person becomes disturbed and goes to a doctor and says, "My old mother (father) is having hallucinations." Yet when a child discovers what we call an imaginary playmate, which often happens with only children or first children, and carries on long conversations with that imaginary person, the parents are often quite proud, and they say, "My, what a good imagination that child has!" [132]

In conclusion, the evidence is considerable that stress is linked with much mental disorder, particularly the neuroses. It is not known, however, how different people respond to stress and in what manner stress-fed situations are perceived or reacted to by the individual. Stress in itself, often even of a severe nature, does not inevitably produce mental disorder, as is seen in studies of the effects of stressful modern living, of the stress of wartime civilian bombings, and of the stress situations of soldiers under combat, prisoners in Nazi concentration camps, and persons with severe physical illnesses or injuries. Still, there is much evidence that stressful conditions of living do increase the nervousness and the anxiety that play a definite part in mental illness.

THE SOCIAL CONTROL
OF MENTAL DISORDER

Persons who have mental disorders may voluntarily seek help, or they may have this help forced upon them involuntarily. In either case the assistance may be in the form of outpatient treatment with an individual psychiatrist, psychologist, or social worker;

---

[130]Rogler and Hollingshead, *Trapped,* p. 412.

[131]Robert J. Havighurst, "Social and Psychological Needs of the Aging," *The Annals,* 279 (1952), 16. Also see H. Warren Dunham, "Sociological Aspects of Mental Disorders in Later Life," in Oscar Kaplan, ed., *Mental Disorders in Later Life* (Stanford, Calif.: Stanford University Press, 1956); and Marjorie Fiske Lowenthal, "Some Social Dimensions on Psychiatric Disorders in Old Age," in Richard H. Williams, Clark Tibbitts, and Wilma Donahue, ed., *Processes of Aging* (New York: Atherton, 1963), Vol. II, pp. 224–246.

[132]Havighurst, p. 16.

treatment at a community psychiatric clinic; or residential care in a local hospital or a mental hospital. Involuntary treatment most frequently is given in a mental hospital. The former widespread use of large mental hospitals has shifted to the general development in recent years of local voluntary outpatient community facilities for persons with mental disorders.

The situations and the underlying reasons that motivate a person to seek help for their symptoms and the problems associated with their disorder differ widely. In one study of applicants to psychiatric clinics in New York several stages were found to occur in the decision to consult a psychiatrist: (1) realization of the problems; (2) discussion of the problem with friends and relatives; (3) choosing to go to a psychiatrist; and (4) selection of the particular practitioner.[133] Friends and others who supported psychotherapy were important, for membership in such a reference group makes it easier to enter therapy and to choose a clinician. This type of support makes it easier to recognize one's problems and to seek advice; friends and supporters provide information and define a wide variety of problems, for example, "lack of self-fulfillment," as sufficient reason for therapy. Mechanic has well summarized the range of factors that influence individuals' going to others to seek help for their symptoms.

1. The visibility, recognizability, or perceptual salience of deviant signs and symptoms.
2. The extent to which the person perceives the symptoms as serious (that is, the person's estimate of the present and future probabilities of danger).
3. The extent to which symptoms disrupt family, work, and other social activities.
4. The frequency of the appearance of deviant signs and symptoms, or their persistence.
5. The tolerance threshold of those who are exposed to and evaluate the deviant signs and symptoms.
6. The information available to, the knowledge of, and the cultural assumptions and understandings of the evaluator.
7. The degree to which autistic psychological processes (i.e., perceptual processes that distort reality) are present.
8. The presence of needs that conflict with the recognition of illness or the assumption of the sick role.
9. The possibility that competing interpretations can be assigned to the symptoms once they are recognized.
10. The availability of treatment resources, their physical proximity and the psychological and monetary costs of taking action (included are not only physical distance and costs of time, money, and effort, but also such costs as stigmatization, resulting social distance, and feelings of humiliation resulting from a particular illness definition).[134]

Involuntary Commitment and Violation of Civil Rights

A mentally ill person may voluntarily commit himself to a mental hospital, or he may be committed by the courts. Involuntary commitment depends upon the responses of others to his behavior and their willingness to take legal action. The complainant may

---

[133]Charles Kadushin, *Why People Go to Psychiatrists* (New York: Atherton Press, 1969).
[134]David Mechanic, *Medical Sociology: A Selective View* (New York: Free Press, 1968), pp. 128–157.

be a next of kin such as husband or wife, a neighbor, employer, or some other person such as a psychiatrist, family physician, clergyman, or the police.[135] On an emergency basis the police have considerable discretion in arresting and taking persons to mental hospitals, particularly if they have annoyed others or acted strangely or suspiciously in public places.[136] Emergency apprehensions occur under five conditions: (1) when the signs of serious psychological disorder are evidenced by particularly agitated behavior or indications of violence; (2) when signs of serious disorder are shown by incongruous behavior in physical appearance like odd posturing, nudity, and extreme uncleanliness; (3) when there is evidence that a person has attempted or is attempting suicide, whether or not the individual is mentally disoriented; (4) where persons whose behavior is disoriented create a nuisance in public; and (5) where the police have been summoned by a complainant.[137]

After apprehension, the courts or the hospital staff decide whether to keep or to release the person. It is at this point that the person's civil rights may be seriously endangered.

1. Many judges do not take sufficient time to determine adequately whether the person should actually be admitted, simply accepting the statement of medical examiners and thus making it a predetermined event.[138] In a study of involuntary commitments in a Florida county, it was found that 79 percent of the cases were declared to be mentally incompetent, and that in 39 percent of the cases the examining committees had not met legal requirements.[139]

2. Since the person is seldom represented by counsel, he often cannot interrogate either his "accusers" or the medical examiner. This is now being raised as a possible violation of the individual's civil rights.

3. Moreover, many states have such loosely defined commitment laws that there is no precise determination of whether the individual should be hospitalized. This is an important consideration, particularly since psychiatrists have been unable to determine with any objective certainty how potentially dangerous most mentally ill persons are.[140]

4. Most difficulties may stem from the lack of agreement on what constitutes "dangerousness," either to the person himself or to others. One observer has noted that "dangerousness, like beauty, is to some extent in the eye of the beholder."[141] For

---

[135]See, for example, Thomas S. Szasz, "Crime, Punishment and Psychiatry," in Abraham S. Blumberg, ed., *Current Perspectives on Criminal Behavior* (New York: Knopf, 1974).

[136]Egon Bittner, "Police Discretion in Apprehending the Mentally Ill," *Social Problems,* 14 (1967), 278–292.

[137]Bittner, pp. 282–285.

[138]See Thomas S. Szasz, *Law, Liberty and Psychiatry: An Inquiry into the Social Uses of Mental Health Practices* (New York: Macmillan, 1963). Also see Szasz, "Crime, Punishment and Psychiatry"; Bruce J. Ennis, *Prisoners of Psychiatry: Mental Patients, Psychiatrists and the Law* (New York: Harcourt Brace Jovanovich, 1972).

[139]Sara Fein and Kent S. Miller, "Legal Processes and Adjudication in Mental Incompetency Proceedings," *Social Problems,* 20 (1972), 57–64.

[140]See John Monahan, "The Prevention of Violence," in John Monahan, ed., *Community Mental Health and the Criminal Justice System* (New York: Pergamon Press, 1976), pp. 13–34; and John Monahan and Gilbert Geis, "Controlling 'Dangerous' People," *The Annals,* 423 (1976), 142–151.

[141]Alan A. Stone, *Mental Health and the Law: A System in Transition* (Rockville, Md.: National Institute of Mental Health, 1975), p. 26.

example, which behavior is more dangerous, the acts of a disturbed mental patient, the actions of a mugger, or the practices of a corporation that systematically, deliberately, and continuously pollutes the air that people breathe?

5. Further significant considerations concerning violating civil rights in involuntary commitment for "treatment" are the availability of treatment and its effectiveness. Psychiatric treatment is often little more than custodial care. In a 1971 Alabama court decision, *Wyatt v. Stickney,* the federal judge found that the state mental hospital in Tuscaloosa, Alabama, had only one certified psychiatrist among 16 physicians caring for 3,800 patients. He ordered that patients could not be involuntarily committed until arrangements were made to provide more adequate treatment, including not only the professional personnel but such physical plant facilities as more toilets and air conditioners and better provision for the patient's privacy.[142] This case opened the door for court actions in other states based on the right of patients to have adequate treatment and hospitals' responsibilities to provide this treatment.

Perhaps the most dramatic case of the right of mental patients to receive treatment was decided by the Supreme Court in 1975 in the case of *Donaldson v. O'Connor.* Donaldson had been committed to the Florida state mental hospital in 1957 by his father, who thought him to be suffering from "delusions." During the following 18 years several organizations had petitioned the hospital for his release. Each request had been denied, even though there was no evidence that Donaldson was dangerous either to himself or to others. The confinement consisted simply of custodial care, and the court found that the patient's constitutional rights were being denied by this confinement without treatment. A further legal position was the claim that commitment of an involuntary nature is a deprivation of liberty to which the state cannot be a party without due process of law, in which case the commitment must be justified in the name of the treatment the individual requires and must receive. Mere custodial care in an institution is not sufficient basis for continued confinement.

Mental Hospitals

It is important now to examine the hospitals in which persons are treated for mental disorders either on a voluntary or involuntary commitment basis. They are institutions of fairly recent origin; for centuries the traditional method of dealing with pronounced mental disorder was punishment or isolation of the person, or both. Beginning in the eighteenth century persons were confined in institutions referred to as lunatic or insane asylums, which were later more politely called mental hospitals.[143] In the United States confinement in large public mental hospitals was the usual method until the early 1960s, but since then a large-scale shift has been made to smaller treatment institutions and to community-based outpatient facilities. This shift in treatment methods, plus the use of sedatives to keep patients more "manageable," has resulted in a dramatic decline in inmate populations in the typical large mental hospital. On June

---

[142]See William J. Fremouw, "A New Right to Treatment," *The Journal of Psychiatry and Law,* 2 (1974), 7–31; and Stuart Golann and William J. Fremouw, eds., *The Right to Treatment for Mental Patients* (New York: Irvington Publishers, 1976), pp. 29–46.
[143]See David Rothman, *The Discovery of the Asylum: Social Order and Disorder in the New Republic* (Boston: Little, Brown, 1971).

30, 1973, there were approximately 248,562 patients in state and county mental hospitals, a decrease of 26.4 percent since 1970. During 1971, 87 percent of the patients were discharged within six months of admission. Of the total 1,755,916 patients *admitted* for treatment in 1971, 745,259 were in state and county mental hospitals, 542,642 in psychiatric wards of general hospitals, 176,800 in Veterans Hospitals, 130,088 in community mental health centers, 97,963 in private mental hospitals, 28,637 in residential treatment centers for emotionally disturbed children, and 34,427 in other multiservice facilities.[144] Since large mental hospitals still exist, although their numbers are declining, and since various alternatives must be evaluated, it is important to understand the sociological nature of these institutions. In 1978 this is a difficult task, however, because of the pronounced changes that have been made and are currently taking place in many hospitals, while at the same time there have been few changes in many large and custodial-type mental hospitals.

Mental hospitals appear to have had two main functions, the treatment of patients to enable them to return to normal society and to provide "protection" for both patients and society. The more historical function has been to protect the interests of society, groups, or families by removing persons whose behavior is disruptive from their normal social environment—the custodial function taking precedence over the treatment function.[145] Characteristically, a state hospital is forbidding in appearance, and it contains large numbers of patients whose daily lives are scheduled to fit certain institutional routines. It often provides inadequate care even in terms of such bare necessities as food and clothing, and the general atmosphere is one of custody with a repressive atmosphere generated by various measures of restraint, solitary confinement, and barred doors and windows.[146] The custodial atmosphere has partly been due to sheer size of the inmate populations, and the hospitals have often been little more than dumping grounds for the aged, the chronically ill, and the mentally disordered of the lower class. Some have claimed that state mental hospitals are nothing more than warehouses which process people, offering little in the way of constructive help. They serve the function of being able to maintain persons who might otherwise prove to be enormous burdens to their friends and families. It has been said that persons "are not in the hospital because they are mad, but because they have been rejected by society and have no suitable place in it."[147]

In view of these conditions it has been almost impossible for most state hospitals to provide much effective psychotherapeutic treatment. The majority of the patients receive either no treatment or are given somatic treatment, usually in the form of tranquilizers and antidepressant drugs or such shock therapies as insulin and electric shock. This type of treatment can be administered to large numbers of patients in a minimum of time and with little effort. While the therapy helps reduce anxiety and relieve symptoms, it rarely deals with the disorder itself, and thus the relapse rate is

---

[144]Stone, pp. 41–42.

[145]This historical context is developed in Andrew T. Scull, *Decarceration: Community Treatment and the Deviant—A Radical View* (Englewood Cliffs, N.J.: Prentice-Hall, 1977), pp. 15–40.

[146]Morris S. Schwartz and Charlotte G. Schwartz, *Social Approaches to Mental Patient Care* (New York: Columbia University Press, 1964), pp. 102–103.

[147]Robert Perucci, *Circle of Madness: On Being Insane and Institutionalized in America* (Englewood Cliffs, N.J.: Prentice-Hall, 1974), p. 30.

high. It has been found that upper-class patients are much more likely to receive psychotherapy.[148] Even where psychotherapy is available, its effectiveness cannot easily be determined.[149] On its own merits psychotherapy is hard to assess, but the mental hospital setting makes it unusually difficult. Generally, inmates are poorer-risk patients, because the others are "selected" for residential or outpatient therapy settings.

Social Structure of the Mental Hospital

As in most total institutions—prisons, for example—mental hospitals represent unique communities with special social structures in terms of status and decision-making powers. Patients make up the "lowest" status group, below attendants and clerical staff. At the top of the prestige hierarchy are superintendents and professional staffs, including psychiatrists, psychologists, occupational therapists, and social workers. A major difficulty of this social system of status and power has been that in the treatment of the mentally disordered persons there has often been a breakdown in formal and informal communication between staff members and between staff and patients.[150] Status distance between nurse and patient occurs frequently, particularly where patients are of relatively low social standing.[151] This breakdown in the communication of information leads to misunderstanding and interferes with the patient's recovery.

Patients in large public mental hospitals generally do not have quite the same attitude toward the professional staffs as have patients under care in private hospitals; the contacts between the patients and the staff are quite different in character when one physician, for example, has as many as a hundred or more patients under his care. Here the patient-doctor relation may be highly impersonal and superficial, even if the doctors would like more personal relations. As one patient said: "The doctor just comes through one door and goes out the other. He spends no time with the patients."[152] Other patients have felt that because doctors can shorten or prolong an inmate's stay, they can in a sense exercise great control over their future; thus, patients try to cultivate the friendship of doctors and even learn to feign symptoms of recovery. Patients from the upper class are more highly motivated and in general more cooperative than those from the lower socioeconomic groups. The latter have less scientific knowledge about mental disorders and tend to consider them as physical

---

[148]See, for example, Enrico Jones, "Social Class and Psychotherapy: A Critical Review of Research," *Psychiatry*, 37 (1974), 307–320.

[149]For a discussion of some of the research problems, see Ralph K. Schwitzgebel and David A. Kolb, *Changing Human Behavior: Principles of Planned Intervention* (New York: McGraw-Hill, 1974), pp. 206–226. Also see Paul M. Roman and Harrison M. Trice, eds., *The Sociology of Psychotherapy* (New York: Jason Aronson, 1974).

[150]Alfred H. Stanton and Morris S. Schwartz, *The Mental Hospital* (New York: Basic Books, 1954), pp. 193–243.

[151]Leonard J. Pearlin and Morris Rosenberg, "Nurse-Patient Social Distance and the Structural Context of a Mental Hospital," *American Sociological Review*, 27 (1962), 56–65.

[152]S. Kirson Weinberg and H. Warren Dunham, *The Culture of the State Mental Hospital* (Detroit: Wayne State University Press, 1960), p. 41. Also see Robert Perrucci, "Social Distance Strategies and Intra-Organizational Stratification: A Study of the Status System on a Psychiatric Ward," *American Sociological Review*, 28 (1963), 951–962.

illnesses that require not therapy, but "pills and needles." They are also more secretive in giving information about mental illness in the family, attributing it to "bad blood," "a bump on the head," "too much booze," or some physical defect. When lower-class patients fail to cooperate, they are regarded as "bad" patients, particularly if they display the violence characteristics of many lower-class persons.[153] Upper-class patients, on the other hand, stress fatigue and overwork, and this tends to make them more amenable to treatment.

Although the situation generally is improving, some public mental hospitals are inadequately staffed, and there is a high attendant staff turnover. Frequently the attendant staff lack proper motivation, and they receive insufficient training for their work with disturbed persons. It is with these attendant staff members that patients have the greatest contacts, even though their role is still largely custodial.[154] A study of staff-patient interaction on a schizophrenic ward found that attendants were more likely than other personnel to respond favorably to those patients whom they defined as the least self-sufficient and determined.[155] In another study it was found that ward attendants were more authoritarian than other staff members in their attitudes toward mental illness and the patients' treatment.[156]

The 24-hour experience of being viewed and labeled as a mental patient encourages the acceptance of the "sick role."[157] This process of role assignment and role-playing increases the likelihood that a mental patient will develop a more or less stabilized identity as a mental patient, what Goffman and others refer to as the "career" of a mental patient.[158] "Patienthood" becomes a form of organizational role and career of an entering "inmate." Regardless of their path of entering a mental hospital, the patient learns to adjust to the regime, the restricted movement, communal living, and the imposition of authority in terms of his "helplessness"—all humbling experiences that affect his self-perception and attack his self-image. He himself is the "reason" for it, a failure; he is constantly reminded that he is there because he is "sick" and that he "must 'insightfully' come to take, or pretend to take, the hospital's view of himself."[159] In order to leave the mental hospital he must accept the hospital ideology and adopt the patient role it has designed for him. Some resent the subordinate role in the hospital, the aimless boredom in the wards, and the performance of menial tasks, but others become so habituated to it that they become

---

[153]Jones, pp. 313–315.

[154] B. E. Segal, "Nurses and Patients: Time, Place and Distance," *Social Problems,* 9 (1962), 257–264.

[155]J. Cohler and L. Shapiro, "Avoidance Patterns in Staff-Patient Interaction on a Chronic Schizophrenic Ward," *Psychiatry,* 27 (1964), 377–388.

[156]See J. H. Williams and M. H. Williams, "Attitudes toward Mental Illness, Anomia and Authoritarianism among State Hospital Nursing Students and Attendants," *Mental Hygiene,* 45 (1961), 418–424. Also see Thomas J. Scheff, "Control over Policy by Attendants in a Mental Hospital," *Journal of Health and Human Behavior,* 2 (1961), 93–105.

[157]Schwartz and Schwartz, p. 201.

[158]Goffman, pp. 125–169. The concept of a mental patient career has been questioned in one study in which no increased dependency was found on the part of the patient toward the institution and there was no evidence that playing the "sick role" was reinforced by hospital staff. See William W. Eaton, "Mental Hospitalization as a Reinforcement Process," *American Sociological Review,* 39 (1974), 252–260. Another study found that the career is closely tied to the symptomology of the patient and the response of the staff. See Gove, "Labeling and Mental Illness," pp. 35–81.

[159]Goffman, p. 155.

increasingly incapacitated for the outside world. Trial home visits before a patient's release are crucial experiences for most of them, but the readjustments necessary because of institutional living and the stigma of having been in a mental hospital often become too much for the patient. The longer schizophrenics, for example, remain in the hospital, the more difficult they are to discharge.[160] With prolonged hospitalization, furthermore, the less likely many mental patients are to have visitors, and thus continued contacts with family and relatives are restricted.

The Community Mental Health Approach

As the large mental hospitals have increasingly been found to be of limited value in treating patients, new methods have been developed. A significant advance has been the extension of outpatient care in the local community. Early diagnosis and treatment have been emphasized, with efforts being made to arrest the development of further disorders, along with the increased use of either general local hospital facilities or small regional treatment hospitals. Community psychiatric facilities have greatly increased in number since the 1960s, and increasing efforts are being made to integrate community health facilities and to maximize the number of patients remaining in the community. This form of treatment received its greatest impetus from the proposals of the Joint Commission for Mental Health in 1961 and from President Kennedy's proposals to Congress in 1963.[161] The Commission recommended that treatment should be primarily directed at helping persons with mental disorders to sustain themselves in the community and that most persons in mental hospitals should be returned to the community as quickly as possible to avoid the isolating effects of hospitalization. The main responsibility for persons with mental disorders should remain in the local community. Congress subsequently initiated a program that involved the establishment, with federal aid, of comprehensive community mental health centers, along with other treatment improvements. These centers, located in the patient's own community, are expected to emphasize prevention as well as treatment. The preventive aspects of the program are directed at dealing with stress situations and the stress perspectives on the etiology of mental disorder and are thus particularly suited to community psychology.[162] In Europe, programs like community psychiatry in Amsterdam, the open-door hospitals in England, and the auxiliary psychiatric units in hospitals and rehabilitative houses have broken the conventional and traditional concepts of mental illness as necessarily requiring social isolation, thus paving the way for a new approach to treatment.

Outpatients, those who have and those who have not previously been hospitalized, are offered a variety of services through these local clinics. They are staffed by psychiatrists, psychologists, social workers, and nonprofessional workers; the pro-

---

[160]J. K. Wing and G. W. Brown, *Institutionalism and Schizophrenia: A Comparative Study of Three Mental Hospitals, 1960–1968* (New York: Cambridge University Press, 1970).

[161]*Action for Mental Health;* and John F. Kennedy, "The Role of the Federal Government in the Prevention and Treatment of Mental Disorders," in S. Kirson Weinberg, ed., *The Sociology of Mental Disorders: Analyses and Readings in Psychiatric Sociology* (Chicago: Aldine, 1967), pp. 297–300.

[162]Mechanic, *Mental Health and Social Policy,* p. 44.

grams offer individual counseling and group therapy. Where necessary, antidepressant drugs are used. Local communities also offer day-care centers for those in need of job training, occupational therapy, and workshops. Special halfway houses for ex-mental patients are often operated, and there are also such related community ex-patient clubs as Recovery Incorporated. Should a patient require hospitalization, a local general hospital is usually used where the individual can receive various therapies for extreme depression and be given some occupational therapy.

Individual and group therapy are offered.[163] In the more usual group method a professionally trained person and from 5 to 20 patients hold frequent discussions, the patients participating and sharing their experiences with the group. In some cases lectures deal with difficulties of adjustment and personality problems, and these lectures are often followed by discussions. Other group therapy sessions are offered for close relatives of patients. These sessions, held for about an hour or two once or twice a week, are limited to approximately 10 persons. Since relatives often harbor feelings of isolation, disgrace, hopelessness, and even guilt, the purpose of these sessions is to discuss these feelings openly and to offer a more positive approach to the patient and his difficulties. In the patients' group therapy sessions, the mentally disturbed person often appears to develop an identification with others who have similar problems, and a degree of group integration emerges. Each member is given the opportunity to play new roles and to acquire a new self-conception. In the light of others' problems, it is possible for individuals to see their own difficulties. The evaluation of psychotherapy is extremely difficult, however, as we have pointed out earlier, and some people believe that in spite of extensive research efforts little conclusive knowledge has been produced about the efficacy of different forms.[164] Yet, as one author has stated, "the enduring popularity of psychotherapies is strong evidence that they do some good."[165]

Increasingly in the United States mentally disordered persons are being cared for either in their own homes or in foster homes. An important experiment has shown that hospitalization of schizophrenics, considered to be one of the most difficult groups to treat, can be avoided through a program that combines medication and public health nursing with home care. In a study of women mental patients who had returned to their homes after short terms in mental hospitals, it was found that 85 percent had succeeded in remaining in the community at least six months and that they were performing at higher levels than were those who were hospitalized.[166] A careful evaluation of this home-care program, involving schizophrenic patients and a hospital control group, revealed that three fourths of the home-care patients remained outside the hospital over a period of from 6 to 30 months.[167] The study concluded that if there is no marked deterioration or if no acute episodes or grossly exaggerated symptoms

---

[163]See Jerome D. Frank, *Persuasion and Healing: A Comparative Study of Psychotherapy,* rev. ed. (Baltimore, Md.: Johns Hopkins Press, 1973).
[164]Frank. For an analytic and critical discussion, see Roman and Trice, *The Sociology of Psychotherapy.*
[165]Frank, p. 23.
[166]Shirley S. Angrist, Mark Lefton, Simon Dinitz, and Benjamin Pasamanick, *Women after Treatment: A Study of Former Mental Patients and Their Normal Neighbors* (New York: Appleton, 1968).
[167]Benjamin Pasamanick, Frank R. Scarpitti, and Simon Dinitz, *Schizophrenics in the Community: An Experimental Study in the Prevention of Hospitalization* (New York: Appleton, 1967).

are in evidence, there is no special need to keep these patients hospitalized. Home care was also found to reduce costs and to spread limited psychiatric and other professional personnel. The study further indicated that community mental health centers are a more effective approach to the problem than mental hospitals. This community intervention program and the extensive use of drug therapy, however, was later found to have relatively short-range benefits. In a follow-up five years after the experiment and community therapy had ended, the investigators concluded that while the continued use of home-nursing contacts, referrals to psychiatrists when necessary, and particularly medication were quite effective in keeping patients out of the hospital, there were, unfortunately, no long-term differences in the rate of rehospitalization after the experiment was suspended. In the five-year follow-up approximately two thirds of each group, the control as well as the experimental, were rehospitalized, a finding that demonstrated the necessity for continued after-care.[168]

The development of community mental health programs has not been without its critics. Dunham, for example, has questioned the medical background and general lack of social science knowledge of the community and its implications for treatment of most psychiatrists.[169] Others have felt that persons at the community level may quite possibly become apathetic to the needs of the mentally disordered person and hope that the individual will recover simply by remaining in the community without being hospitalized.[170] Still others point out that stigma and rejection by the community and family remain serious problems, although it is the hope that eventually local community programs will change this. In 1972 a study group under Ralph Nader found that some programs using federal funds were not reaching the poorer sections of the community but rather the middle class, and that doctors were using these public facilities to treat private patients.[171] Some programs in 1972 were not giving persons recently released from state mental hospitals adequate after-care such as board and lodging, regular psychiatric counseling, or help in finding work. On the whole, the greatest problem is that in shifting to a new milieu older conceptions of the mentally disordered will be continued both by professional personnel and the community, as Mechanic has pointed out.

> In the long run, of course, little is achieved by changing the labels we use without changing our practices. Obviously, the proper organization of an educationally oriented rehabilitation program depends on the attitudes and approaches of mental health workers. To the extent that they nurture the patient's dependency responses, encourage sick-role reactions, and serve the patient rather than motivate him to serve himself, educational efforts are limited. An educational approach must start with the assumption that mental patients either have or can develop the capacities to meet their own needs; through sympathetic attention, encouragement of motivation, and scheduling and rein-

---

[168]Ann E. Davis, Simon Dinitz, and Benjamin Pasamanick, *Schizophrenics in the New Custodial Community: Five Years after the Experiment* (Columbus: Ohio State University Press, 1974).

[169]H. Warren Dunham, "Community Psychology: The Newest Therapeutic Bandwagon," *International Journal of Psychiatry,* 1 (1965), 562.

[170]Leopold Bellak, *Handbook of Community Psychiatry and Community Health.* (New York: Grune and Stratton, 1964), p. 7. Also see Harry Gottesfeld, ed., *The Critical Issues in Community Mental Health* (New York: Behavioral Publications, 1972).

[171]*New York Times,* Sunday, July 30, 1972, p. 36.

forcement of mastery experience, we may be able to set the stage for the patient's improvement in social and psychological functioning.[172]

It should also be recognized that part of the criticism directed at public mental hospitals has been that they are large and impersonal, with high patient-staff ratios. The evidence indicates that small mental hospitals where these criticisms do not apply have been performing, for the most part, more effectively.[173] Mechanic has pointed out that neither the construction nor the modification of effective environments for mental patient care is a community or hospital venture exclusively, because some patients with severe psychiatric conditions "may achieve a higher quality of life within a sheltered institution than outside one; and in condemning bad institutions we need not abandon the institutional idea entirely since some persons probably function best in them."[174]

SELECTED REFERENCES

Bellak, Leopold. *Handbook of Community Psychiatry and Community Health.* New York: Grune and Stratton, 1964.

Cameron, Norman. *The Psychology of Behavior Disorders.* Boston: Houghton Mifflin, 1947.

Dohrenwend, Bruce P., and Barbara Snell Dohrenwend. "Sex Differences and Psychiatric Disorders," *American Journal of Sociology,* 81 (1976), 1147–1154.

Dohrenwend, Bruce P., and Barbara Snell Dohrenwend. *Social Status and Psychological Disorder.* New York: Wiley, 1969.

Dohrenwend, Bruce P., and Barbara Snell Dohrenwend, eds. *Stressful Life Events: Their Nature and Effects.* New York: Wiley, 1974.

Eaton, William W. "Mental Hospitalization as a Reinforcement Process," *American Sociological Review,* 39 (1974), 253–260.

Frank, Jerome D. *Persuasion and Healing: A Comparative Study of Psychotherapy,* rev. ed. Baltimore, Md.: Johns Hopkins Press, 1973.

Goffman, Erving. *Asylums.* New York: Doubleday Anchor Books, 1961.

Gove, Walter R. "Labeling and Mental Illness: A Critique," in Walter R. Gove, ed., *The Labeling of Deviance: Evaluating a Perspective.* New York: Sage/Halsted, 1975.

Hollingshead, August B., and Frederick C. Redlich. *Social Class and Mental Illness.* New York: Wiley, 1958.

Jones, Enrico. "Social Class and Psychotherapy: A Critical Review of Research," *Psychiatry,* 37 (1974), 307–320.

Mechanic, David. *Mental Health and Social Policy.* Englewood Cliffs, N.J.: Prentice-Hall, 1969.

Perrucci, Robert. *Circle of Madness: On Being Insane and Institutionalized in America.* Englewood Cliffs, N.J.: Prentice-Hall, 1974.

Roman, Paul M., and Harrison M. Trice, eds. *The Sociology of Psychotherapy.* New York: Jason Aronson, 1974.

Rothman, David J. *The Discovery of the Asylum: Social Order and Disorder in the New Republic.* Boston: Little, Brown, 1971.

---

[172]Mechanic, *Mental Health and Social Policy,* © 1969, p. 116. Reprinted by permission of Prentice-Hall, Inc., Englewood Cliffs, New Jersey.

[173]See L. P. Ullman, *Institution and Outcome: A Comparative Study of Psychiatric Hospitals* (New York: Pergamon Press, 1967).

[174]Mechanic, *Mental Health and Social Policy,* p. 95.

Scheff, Thomas J. *On Being Mentally Ill: A Sociological Theory.* Chicago: Aldine, 1966.

Scheff, Thomas J., ed. *Labeling Madness.* Englewood Cliffs, N. J.: Prentice-Hall, 1975.

Scull, Andrew T. *Decarceration: Community Treatment and the Deviant—A Radical View.* Englewood Cliffs, N.J.: Prentice-Hall, 1977.

Stone, Alan A. *Mental Health and the Law: A System in Transition.* Rockville, Md.: National Institute of Mental Health, 1975.

Szasz, Thomas S. *Schizophrenia: The Sacred Symbol of Psychiatry.* New York: Basic Books, 1976.

Waxler, Nancy E. "Culture and Mental Illness: A Social Labeling Perspective," *Journal of Nervous and Mental Disease,* 159 (1974), 379–395.

CHAPTER 14

Persons who commit suicide take different means to terminate their lives. A variety of motivations and social meanings underlie suicides. They can be understood and explained in sociological terms. Only rarely are they related to mental disorder. (Wide World Photos)

Suicide

S UICIDE is the destruction of oneself—self-killing, or self-murder in the legal sense. It can be intentional or it may result from a person's failure to prevent death when it is threatened. Durkheim included such acts of altruism as religious martyrs, defining suicide as "all cases of death resulting directly or indirectly from a positive or negative act of the victim himself, which he knows will produce [suicide]."[1] The terms "suicide" and "suicidal" are somewhat ambiguous, however, in view of the wide range of situations to which they can be applied. In some situations life-taking may actually be obligatory rather than voluntary, as in the old traditional practice of hara-kiri among Japanese nobility and samurai warriors, and in instances where a person directs another to kill himself—as when Nero ordered an attendant to kill him so that his death would not be by his own hand.[2]

SUICIDE AS DEVIANT BEHAVIOR

So strongly is suicide condemned by Western European peoples that one might assume this attitude to be universal. Both today and in the past, however, attitudes toward self-destruction have varied widely. Mohammedan countries strongly condemn suicide; the Koran expressly condemns it, and in actuality it rarely occurs there. The people of the Orient, however, did not normally disapprove of suicide. In fact, suttee, or the suicide of a widow on her husband's death, was common in India until well into the last century.[3] Priests taught that such a voluntary death would be a passport to heaven, atone for the sins of the husband, and give social distinction to the relatives and children. Other aspects of Hindu philosophy encouraged suicide for religious reasons, particularly the tendency to disregard the physical body. Suicide was regarded as acceptable in China; when committed for revenge it was considered a particularly useful device against an enemy because it not only embarrassed him but enabled the dead man to haunt him from the spirit world. Voluntary death has been given an honorable place in Buddhist countries, but for devout Buddhists, there is neither birth nor death, the individual being expected to be prepared to meet any fate with stoical indifference.

For many centuries suicide was even favorably regarded in Japan. Among all classes, but particularly among the nobility and the military, it was traditionally taught that one must surrender to the demands of duty and honor. Hara-kiri, originally a ceremonial form of suicide to avoid capture after military defeat and later to avoid disgrace or other punishment, was practiced during World War II. The suicide pact of

[1]Emile Durkheim, *Suicide,* John A. Spaulding and George Simpson, trans. (New York: Free Press, 1951), p. 44.

[2]For a discussion of the terms "suicide" and "suicidal," as well as some of the situations these terms might suit, see Norman L. Farberow, "Suicide," in Edward Sagarin and Fred Montanino, eds., *Deviants: Voluntary Actors in a Hostile World* (Morristown, N.J.: General Learning Press, 1977), especially pp. 503–505.

[3]Upendra Thakur, *The History of Suicide in India* (Delhi: Munshi Ram Manohar Lal, Publishers, 1963). Also see the discussion in Robert Nisbet and Robert G. Perrin, *The Social Bond,* 2d ed. (New York: Knopf, 1977), p. 250.

lovers who wish to terminate their existence in this world and go to another is still not unknown in Japan, nor is suicide for revenge to protest the actions of an enemy.

The attitude of contemporary Western European peoples toward suicide originated mainly in the philosophies of the Jewish and later the Christian religions. The Talmudic law of the Jewish religion takes a strong position against suicide: respect should not be paid the memory of the suicide, although comfort should be given to the individual's family. Suicide and infanticide had been prevalent in ancient Rome, but with the spread and acceptance of Christianity came a change in the attitude toward human life. Basic to the Christian condemnation of suicide were the concepts that human life is sacred, that the individual is subordinate to God, and that death should be considered an entrance to a new life in which one's behavior in the old is important. Moreover, death was followed by purgatory, in which an individual suffered in order to expiate some types of sins, but those who had committed such a sin as suicide were banished eternally to the torments of hell. Death, to the Christians, unlike the pagans of Rome, was not something to look forward to without some misgivings. This concept of life after death strengthened the position of the Church. In addition, Christian doctrine looked upon life as an opportunity for moral discipline and resignation in the presence of pain and suffering endured in the hope of another and happier world.

Although at first Christians sanctioned suicide connected with martyrdom or the protection of virginity, eventually they disapproved of it for any reason, and it became not only a sin in Christian countries but a crime against the state.[4] The property of a suicide might, for example, be confiscated and the corpse subjected to various mutilations. The laws of some European countries provided that the body of a suicide could be removed from a house only through a special hole in the wall, could be dragged through the streets, might be hung on the gallows, thrown into a sewer, burned, or even transfixed by a stake on a public highway as a sign of disrespect.

In the Middle Ages Church leaders denounced suicide, particularly Augustine, who stated in the *City of God* that suicide is never justifiable. He maintained that suicide precludes the possibility of repentance, that it is a form of murder prohibited by the sixth commandment, and that a person who kills himself has done nothing worthy of death. Similarly, Thomas Aquinas opposed it on the grounds that it was unnatural and an offense against the community. Above all, he considered it a usurpation of God's power to grant life and death. Generally, in both England and Scotland, as well as on the Continent, laws provided for special treatment of the bodies of suicides, often outside regular graveyards. Throughout the Middle Ages and well into modern times the strong religious opposition, the force of condemnatory public opinion, and the severe legal penalties were so effective that few had the temerity to take their lives, despite infrequent sporadic outbreaks of mass suicide on certain occasions, such as epidemics, religious fanaticism to gain martyrdom, or crises.[5]

These views did not go unnoticed or unopposed by later philosophers, particularly those of the Age of Enlightenment, who challenged many existing institutions and discussed the importance of individual choice, even of life and death. David Hume, in his *Essay on Suicide,* argued that persons have the right to dispose of their lives

---

[4]Donald McCormick, *The Unseen Killer: A Study of Suicide, Its History, Causes and Cures* (London: Frederick Mueller, 1964), pp. 36–51.
[5]Louis I. Dublin, *Suicide: A Sociological and Statistical Study* (New York: Ronald Press, 1963).

TABLE 14.1	Suicide Rates per 100,000 Population for Selected Countries, 1972	
	Country	*Rate*
	Hungary	36.9
	Czechoslovakia	24.6
	Finland	24.0
	Denmark	23.9
	Austria	23.4
	Sweden	20.3
	Federal Republic of Germany	19.9
	Switzerland	19.5
	Japan	16.8
	France	16.1
	Belgium	15.4
	Luxembourg	14.9
	Canada	12.2
	United States	12.0
	Poland	12.0
	Hong Kong	11.4
	Bulgaria	11.4
	Norway	9.0
	Iceland	8.6
	Portugal	8.2
	Netherlands	8.2
	Scotland	8.1
	England and Wales	7.7
	Israel	7.5
	Italy	5.8
	Chile	5.5
	Spain	4.4
	Ireland	3.0
	Mexico	0.7

Source: *World Health Statistics Annual,* 1972, Vol. 1. *Vital Statistics and Causes of Death.* Geneva: World Health Organization, 1975.

without the act's being sinful. Other writers, such as Montesquieu, Voltaire, and Rousseau in France, challenged the laws on suicide and the denial of individual choice about life and death. In Germany, however, the philosopher Kant opposed such views and said that suicide was contrary to reason. Today, from a theological point of view both Catholics and Protestants are opposed to suicide, although the Catholic position is a stronger one, and the rates of suicide in Catholic countries are generally lower; they are very low in Mexico, Spain, and Ireland (see Table 14.1).

Suicide was punished as a felony or crime in England for centuries, and the suicide's property was forfeited to the Crown. In fact, these provisions were not abolished until 1870, although they had been largely in disuse since the eighteenth century. In his famous *Commentaries* on the law, Blackstone had given these reasons for forefeiture: "The suicide is guilty of a double offense; one spiritual, in evading the prerogative of the Almighty and rushing into his immediate presence uncalled for; the temporal, against the King, who hath an interest in the preservation of all his subjects."[6] To a certain extent this concept, but without the law of forfeiture, was carried to America. In 1660 the Massachusetts law forbade burial of a suicide in the common burying place of Christians. Instead, burial was in some common highway, with a cartload of stones laid upon the grave, as a brand of infamy, and as a warning to others to beware of similar "damnable practices." This law was repealed in 1823, but it helped shape the attitude toward attempted suicide in America.

Studies show strong negative attitudes toward suicide attempters. These negative attitudes are most likely to be elicited by attempters who appear to be less serious in their attempts to die, for example, those who did it "only for a gesture."[7] Such negative reactions may prompt the attempter to engage in further suicidal behavior.

Until the 1950s attempted suicide was a crime in New Jersey and both North and South Dakota. Attempted suicides did raise interesting legal problems, since by definition "a suicidal act is not punishable as an attempt unless it was intended to result in suicide."[8] Some cases are genuine attempts; others are suicidal demonstrations where what is done is not really a serious attempt; finally, there are probably cases that fall in between. Many attempters, whether serious or not, may endanger the lives of other persons or rescuers, as do those who resort to carbon monoxide gas in rooms or garages, who try to drown themselves, or who use firearms. Sometimes persons are prosecuted under other statutes. For example, in Oregon a woman jumped off a bridge in a definite suicide attempt, and a soldier jumped to save her. He found himself in trouble in a current, and a third person who jumped in saved the woman while the soldier was drowned. The woman was held under the misdemeanor-manslaughter law since attempted suicide was not against the law of that state.

Attempted suicide is not illegal in any European country, including the Soviet Union. England had such a law from 1854 until its repeal in 1961. Prior to World War II in England, most attempted suicides were punished by a short period of imprisonment; for a second attempt, up to six months. From then until 1961, the law was largely applied only in those cases where there had been repeated attempts or where the would-be suicide threatened to try it again, refused treatment, or became an unnecessary nuisance.[9] Actually, in 1955, only about 1 in 10 attempted suicides were brought before the courts, and only a small percentage of these persons were sentenced to prison. Nearly all, however, were found guilty, resulting in a criminal record.[10] There was no evidence that the law was preventing suicide and, as a result, it was repealed in 1961.[11] Because it was thought that repeal might encourage suicide pacts, the act made it a crime to aid, abet, counsel, or procure the suicide of another person. As in England, there is a general rule in the United States, under common law, that in the case of a suicide the life insurance policy is not recoverable. Several states, however, have statutes providing that a suicide does not affect the policy if it occurs after a certain period of time, unless it can be proved that the insured intended to commit suicide at the time the policy was taken out.

---

[6]William Blackstone, *Commentaries on the Laws of England,* IV (1765–1769), p. 188.
[7]See Edward L. Ansel and Richard K. McGee, "Attitudes toward Suicide Attempters," *Bulletin of Suicidology,* 8 (1971), 22–29.
[8]G. L. Williams, *The Sanctity of Life and the Criminal Law* (New York: Knopf, 1957), p. 283.
[9]Williams, p. 280.
[10]Kenneth Robinson, "Suicide and the Law," *The Spectator,* March 14 (1958), p. 317.
[11]Erwin Stengel, *Suicide and Attempted Suicide* (Baltimore, Md.: Penguin Books, 1964).

SOCIOLOGICAL THEORIES OF SUICIDE

Several attempts have been made to formulate a general theoretical explanation of suicide: social integration, degrees of social constraint, status integration, and status frustration. In his classic study Durkheim stated that the suicide rate in any population could be explained not by the attributes of the individuals in the population but by the varying degrees of social cohesion or *social integration*.[12] This view is still widely accepted today. Durkheim believed that suicide was related inversely to the stability and integration of social relations among people, whether religious, familial, or other. Many examples were cited by Durkheim as evidence for this conclusion, including the lower suicide rates among Catholics as compared with Protestants, of married persons as compared with the single, divorced, or widowed, all of which he attributed to greater social integration. While he demonstrated his thesis in many ways, Durkheim has been criticized for not establishing a set of rigorous criteria for measuring "social integration."[13] Maris has proposed a modification of Durkheim's thesis in terms of suicide varying inversely with the *degree of social constraint* on the individual.[14] External constraint is low when an individual is not regulated either by other people or by shared ideas; an example is the higher probability of suicide when there is social isolation or role failure in the work situation of men, particularly older men.

Somewhat related to Durkheim's theory of social integration is another sociological theory which has attempted, through the use of suicide differentials in the United States, to link suicide to a particular pattern of status occupancy or the degree of integration in a society.[15] Suicide varies inversely with the degree of *status integration* in the population. Fewer suicides occur in populations in which one status position is closely associated with other status positions; as a result, the members are less likely to experience role conflict and are more capable of conforming to the demands and expectations of others. In these situations they are also more capable of maintaining stable and durable social relations. This theory has been challenged on both logical and empirical grounds.[16]

Several persons have tried to link suicide and homicide within a framework of different adjustments to *status frustrations* which produce aggression. According to Henry and Short's theory of suicide, the aggression is directed at the self, whereas in homicides it is directed at others. They have said that suicide is thus

---

[12]Durkheim. See also Steven Lukes, *Emile Durkheim: His Life and Work* (Baltimore, Md.: Penguin Books, 1977), Chap. 9.

[13]See Ronald Maris, *Social Forces in Urban Suicide* (Homewood, Ill.: Dorsey Press, 1969); and Jack D. Douglas, *The Social Meanings of Suicide* (Princeton, N.J.: Princeton University Press, 1967), for a number of other criticisms of Durkheim. Whitney Pope, *Durkheim's Suicide: A Classic Analyzed* (Chicago: University of Chicago Press, 1976), provides one of the best critiques of Durkheim's theory and the evidence he provides in support of the theory.

[14]Maris.

[15]Jack P. Gibbs and Walter T. Martin, *Status Integration and Suicide: A Sociological Study* (Eugene: University of Oregon Books, 1964); and Jack P. Gibbs and Walter T. Martin, "Theory of Status Integration and Its Relationship to Suicide," *American Sociological Review*, 23 (1958), 140–147.

[16]William J. Chambliss and Marion F. Steele, "Status Integration and Suicide: An Assessment," *American Sociological Review*, 31 (1966), 531. See also the reply by Gibbs and Martin, "On Assessing the Theory of Status Integration and Suicide," *American Sociological Review*, 31 (1966), 533–541; and Robert Hagedorn and Sanford Labovitz, "A Note on Status Integration and Suicide," *Social Problems*, 14 (1966), 84.

a form of aggression against the self aroused by some frustration, the cause of which is perceived by the person as lying within the self. Failure to maintain a constant or rising position in the status hierarchy relative to others in the same status reference system is one—but by no means the only—important frustration arousing aggression.[17]

As evidence of this relation they explain the lower suicide rate of married persons as compared with that of the nonmarried (divorced, widowed, or single) as being due to the fact that married persons are involved in a stronger relational system in which they must conform more to the demands and expectations of others. The degree of involvement with other persons also explains the lower rates of rural areas, the high rates in the central areas of a city, and the general tendency for rates to increase as persons age and have fewer close relations with others. This general explanation of suicide in terms of status frustration is intriguing, but it is largely a theory read into certain broad statistical findings and does not seem to be proved by the evidence.

In the final analysis, the validity of all these theories of social integration, the degree of social constraint, and status frustration rests on the accuracy of official suicide rates. The use of such statistics to draw meaningful theoretical conclusions has been criticized particularly by Douglas, because coroners use different operational definitions of suicide and different investigative and search procedures in their attempts to obtain evidence for their decisions.[18] Variations also arise from changes in officials entrusted with suicide certification and changes in reporting causes of death, all of which have great bearing on the validity of suicide theories from Durkheim on. It appears that the most significant error made in the use of official statistics has been the same error made in the theories themselves, and this is the assumption that suicidal actions carry the same meaning throughout Western societies, with officials and theorists using the same definitions and with the officials among themselves using similar definitions; in other words, some uniformity is assumed when actually "an *official* categorization of the cause of death is as much the end result of an *argument* as such a categorization by any other member of society."[19]

Consequently, the view has been taken by two researchers that suicide notes have more significance for explaining why people commit suicide than do the official statistical analyses.[20] One in every 16 suicides leaves a note.[21] These notes can be

---

[17]Andrew F. Henry and James F. Short, Jr., "The Sociology of Suicide," in Edwin S. Schneidman and Norman L. Farbarow, eds., *Clues to Suicide* (New York: McGraw-Hill, 1957), p. 68. See also Henry and Short, *Suicide and Homicide* (New York: Free Press, 1954). Suicide and homicide are related in that both respond to changes in the business cycle and therefore are, they claim, not common responses to frustration.

[18]See Douglas, *The Social Meanings of Suicide.* For a discussion of suicide demography in the United States and problems of accurate information, see Leonard L. Linden and Warren Breed, "The Demographic Epidemiology of Suicide," in Edwin S. Schneidman, ed., *Suicidology: Contemporary Developments* (New York: Grune and Stratton, 1976), pp. 77–98.

[19]Douglas, *The Social Meanings of Suicide,* p. 229.

[20]Douglas, *The Social Meanings of Suicide;* and Jerry Jacobs, "A Phenomenological Study of Suicide Notes," *Social Problems,* 15 (1967), 60–73. Schneidman has challenged the use of suicide notes. He observes that "that special state of mind necessary to perform a suicidal act is one which is essentially incompatible with an insightful recitation of what was going on in one's mind that led to the act itself. . . . In order to commit suicide, one cannot write a meaningful note; conversely, if one could write a meaningful note, he would not have to commit suicide." Edwin S. Schneidman, "Suicide Notes Reconsidered," in Schneidman, *Suicidology,* p. 266.

[21]Schneidman, "Suicide Notes Reconsidered."

analyzed in terms of the perspective of the suicide, what had been experienced and how these experiences were viewed, the social constraints that had restrained the individual from suicide, and how successfully or unsuccessfully they had been overcome. These notes obviously cover a wider and more meaningful aspect than has been implied in this analysis of the meanings of suicide. In one phenomenological study they have been classified as "so sorry" illness notes, "not sorry" illness notes, notes of direction accusation, last wills and testaments, and notes dealing simply with instructions.[22]

Suicide is a social process representing substantial social meanings and antecedents. As is true in other types of behavior, suicidal behavior can be learned, and certain social rewards or advantages can be associated with the behavior. In their notes suicides often have a substantive advantage in being able to point out to others that "you were wrong about me," or that "see, I really do love you," thus portraying a presentation of self in the most dramatic manner possible. Studies of attempted suicide have often noted that the attempt may bring forth helpful reactions from others, reactions more readily obtained in a suicidal situation and most helpful once obtained.[23] One reason for this, of course, is that most persons acknowledge that the voluntary taking of one's own life is deviant conduct. Since this norm is widely held, the normal reaction when someone attempts to violate the norm is to help the person with the problems that "obviously" drove the individual to attempt suicide. In applying the concept of social learning to suicide, Akers has stressed the importance of receiving social reinforcement and of perceiving attempted suicide as a means of seeking help in relieving the problems. Moreover, the suicidal process may be seen as a means of communicating with others to obtain such help.[24]

EXTENT OF SUICIDE

Many persons commit suicide each year, but the number is small compared with the numbers involved in other forms of deviant behavior such as property crimes, mental disorder, illicit drug use, or problem drinking. Still, more than 20,000 persons commit suicide each year in the United States, a total that surpasses homicides. Suicide figures are estimated to be underreported by as much as one fourth to one third, largely because of the stigma attached to suicidal death.[25] Relatives and others may deliberately conceal the true circumstances of death out of embarrassment and shame. Death certificates may also be altered to protect the feelings of survivors.

Since absolute numbers can be misleading, suicide figures are usually reported in terms of rates, that is, the number of suicides per 100,000 population. The 1974 suicide rate in the United States was 12.0.[26] Over a long time span these rates fluctuate markedly, being particularly responsive to economic changes, generally higher during

---

[22]Jacobs, "A Phenomenological Study of Suicide Notes."
[23]*See* Stengel, p. 37.
[24]Ronald L. Akers, *Deviant Behavior: A Social Learning Approach* 2d ed. (Belmont, Calif.: Wadsworth Publishing, 1977), Chap. 24.
[25]See "Suicide among Youth," Special Supplement, *Bulletin of Suicidology,* 1971, p. 2. Also see Dublin.
[26]Farberow, "Suicide," pp. 532–533.

periods of depression and lower during periods of prosperity. The highest suicide rate in the United States was 17.4 in 1932; the lowest, 9.8 in 1957. The rates decline noticeably during wartime, as noted almost 80 years ago by Durkheim.[27] From 1938 to 1944, during the period of World War II involvement, rates declined from 20 to 50 percent in all the nations that were at war.[28] In the United States the rate per 100,000 declined by about one third, from 15.3 in 1938 to 11.2 in 1945. In other words, possibly as many as 25,000 persons failed to take their lives during the war years. There was a steady decline from year to year until the postwar years when the rates increased. Several factors may have accounted for the decline. The feeling of unity that prevails during most wars is the opposite of the social isolation of the typical suicide. Wars also bring increased economic opportunities, and it has already been indicated that the suicide rate is related to the business cycle.

ATTEMPTED SUICIDE

Suicidal attempts in the United States and in the United Kingdom, particularly in urban areas, appear to be at least six to eight times the total of actual suicide,[29] bringing attempts to as high as 140,000 cases in the United States. A 1970 Los Angeles study estimated that 4 out of every 100 adults there, about 75,000 persons, have tried to kill themselves at least once.[30] Most suicide attempts are carried out in a setting that often makes intervention to prevent the suicide possible or probable, the person remaining near others and thus allowing for the possibility of prevention.[31] Whether people will always intervene is another matter.

One study of 5,906 attempted suicides in Los Angeles, as compared with 768 persons who actually did commit suicide, found that the typical (modal) suicide attempter was a female, white, in her twenties or thirties, either married or single (not divorced or separated), a housewife, native-born, who attempted suicide by barbiturates and gave as a reason marital difficulties or depression.[32] In contrast, the typical person who did commit suicide was a male, white, in his forties or older, married, a skilled or unskilled worker, native-born, who committed suicide by gunshot, hanging, or carbon monoxide poisoning and who gave as a reason ill health, depression, or marital difficulties. An earlier study in Detroit had reported that women generally attempt suicide twice as often as men.[33] This fact invites at least two interpretations:

[27]Durkheim. Also see Fred Dubitscher, *Der Suicid* (Stuttgart: Georg Thieme, Verlag, 1957), pp. 80–115.
[28]See Peter Sainsbury, "Social and Epidemiological Aspects of Suicide with Special Reference to the Aged," in Richard H. Williams, Clark Tibbitts, and Wilma Donahue, eds., *Processes of Aging* (New York: Atherton Press, 1963), Vol. II, p. 166.
[29]Stengel, p. 75.
[30]R. S. Mintz, "Prevalence of Persons in the City of Los Angeles Who Have Attempted Suicide," *Bulletin of Suicidology,* 7 (1970), 9–16. Also see J. Wilkins, "Suicidal Behavior," *American Sociological Review,* 32 (1967), 286–298.
[31]Stengel.
[32]Edwin S. Schneidman and Norman L. Farberow, "Statistical Comparisons between Attempted and Committed Suicide," in Norman L. Farberow and Edwin S. Schneidman, eds., *The Cry for Help* (New York: McGraw-Hill, 1961), pp. 19–47.
[33]F. C. Lendrum, "A Thousand Cases of Attempted Suicide," *American Journal of Psychiatry,* 13 (1933), 479–500.

women are less successful in committing suicide, or, more likely, women more frequently use threats of suicide to accomplish a certain goal. Threats of, or attempts at, suicide must, however, be taken more seriously, at least when made by men. Three fourths of a group of Los Angeles County male suicides had previously threatened or attempted to take their own lives.[34] It is reported that 12 percent of all suicide attempts in the United States are made by adolescents and that 90 percent of these attempts are made by adolescent girls.[35]

VARIATIONS BY COUNTRY

For many years Japan had the highest suicide rate in the world, but in recent years this dubious distinction has gone to Hungary, with Czechoslovakia second (see Table 14.1). The United States, with a rate of 12.0 in 1972, has an almost middle position among 28 countries. Comparisons of rates of different countries indicate such great variations exist that it is almost impossible to establish firm uniformities or patterns. International comparisons are further complicated by the vast differences in reporting suicide information and the manner in which they are detected. In countries like Sweden, for example, autopsies are routine, and few moral inhibitions interfere with a formal finding of suicide; in other countries where moral reservations about suicide are strong there is greater likelihood that many suicides will be classified as due to other causes.

In general, predominantly Catholic countries have lower suicide rates, yet Austria, a Catholic country, has the fifth highest rate in the world. Among the Scandinavian countries, Finland, Denmark, and Sweden rank among the top six, yet Norway's rate is quite low.[36] One explanation for differences among Scandinavian countries typically relates to differences in childrearing patterns in the countries. It has been claimed that the Norwegian unbringing stresses more openness of emotion and aggressive feelings on the part of children, thereby resulting in less "pent-up" hostility later in life.[37] More likely, the greater strength of the primary group in Norway may contribute to relations unconducive to suicide.[38]

SOCIAL DIFFERENTIALS IN SUICIDE RATES

Two authorities have said that where customs and traditions have accepted or condoned suicide, many individuals will take their own lives, but where it is severely

---

[34]Schneidman and Farberow, "Clues to Suicide," in Schneidman and Farberow, *Clues to Suicide,* p. 9.
[35]"Suicide among Youth," p. 8.
[36]For a general discussion of this fact, see Nils Retterstol, "Suicide in Norway," in Norman L. Farberow, ed., *Suicide in Different Cultures* (Baltimore, Md.: University Park Press, 1975), pp. 77–94.
[37]Herbert Hendin, *Suicide in Scandinavia* (New York: Grune and Stratton, 1964).
[38]M. L. Farber, *Theory of Suicide* (New York: Funk & Wagnalls, 1968).

condemned by the state or by the church it will not often occur.[39] Such a generalization about the reaction to suicide, however, cannot easily be related to the variations seen within a country by sex, race, marital status, and so forth. For example, there is no reason to believe that the lower suicide rates among blacks and the young indicate that suicide is more severely disapproved by them. Moreover, there is no evidence that all the increases or decreases in the rates of the various countries reflect corresponding changes in the differing norms that pertain to suicide.[40]

Few forms of deviant behavior, in fact, exhibit as pronounced differences in rates among various segments of the population as does suicide. Such differences in social factors have generally been found not only in Western societies but in Asiatic societies, as has been shown in the studies of suicide in the Philippines, Ceylon, Singapore, and Hong Kong.[41] Many of these factors operate in the same fashion in these cultures. One must keep in mind, however, that differentials in suicide rates are extremely variable. It has been said that there is no social status or condition that generates a constant rate in all populations, and the example has been given of how "an occupation with a high suicide rate in one community may have a low rate in another; and rates for countries or religious groups change substantially over time."[42]

Sex

Suicide is much more common among men than among women in Western European civilization, generally three to four times higher: in the United States nearly three times as many men as women commit suicide. In Finland almost four times as many men as women commit suicide; in Norway, South Africa, and France the ratio is three to one. In Hungary and Austria, two countries with very high rates, it is only slightly over two to one. In the older age group the ratio of male to female suicides is even greater. On the other hand, the difference among adolescents is generally not as great.

Women in Asia commit suicide much more frequently than do women in Western Europe and America; thus the difference in the ratios is much less. In Japan the ratio of males to females is about 1.5 to 1. In some areas of India the suicide rate for women is greater than that of men; in a large study of suicide in the state of Gujarat, the rate was twice as great.[43] This appears to be due to the conflicting roles and subordinate status of women in the Indian family and society. Nearly all marriages in India are still arranged, and girls from poor homes may suffer taunts, humiliation, and persecution for not bringing a good dowry. Even when the parents learn of a daughter's unhappiness in the husband's family they hesitate to take her back into their own homes because of the loss of social prestige. The realization of their often

---

[39]Louis I. Dublin and Bessie Bunzel, *To Be or Not To Be* (New York: Harrison Smith and Robert Haas, 1933), p. 15.

[40]Jack P. Gibbs, "Suicide," in Robert K. Merton and Robert Nisbet, eds., *Contemporary Social Problems,* 3d ed. (New York: Harcourt Brace Jovanovich, 1971), p. 302.

[41]P. M. Yap, *Suicide in Hong Kong* (Hong Kong: Cathay Press, 1958).

[42]Sanford Labovitz, "Variations in Suicide Rates," in Jack P. Gibbs, ed., *Suicide* (New York: Harper & Row, 1968), p. 72.

[43]Jyotsna H. Shah, "Causes and Prevention of Suicides," paper presented at the Indian Conference of Social Work, Hyderabad, December 1959.

difficult family role has also become greater as freedom for women in India has increased.

Race

Previous research on the distribution of suicide by race concluded that whites have a substantially higher rate than blacks. In a 1969 Chicago study, rates for white suicides were found to be twice as high as those for nonwhites.[44] One significant exception was seen: young nonwhite females had a higher rate than a comparable white female age group. This was thought to be due to the greater role pressures and role conflicts on the nonwhite females who are more likely to be employed than the white. Explanations for the difference between white and nonwhite suicide rates relate to the fact that nonwhites are more likely to come from more rural backgrounds, even though many of them live in the cities, and this has probably tended to inhibit suicide. Furthermore, only recently have blacks had higher status opportunities, and as a result there have been, in the past, fewer competitive status pressures on blacks.

Beginning in the early 1970s, however, suicide rates began to rise among black youths; at present the rate is almost equal to that of whites. Suicide rates among young black women in this same period has risen from being three times less than that for black men to a rate that nearly equals theirs.[45] Whether this trend will continue is not clear, but with advances in the socioeconomic status of blacks it would not be surprising if the black suicide rate stabilizes near that of the white rate.

Age

Generally, suicide rates increase with age; the rate for those aged 25–34, for example, is twice as great as for those aged 15–24. A Chicago study confirmed these rates, concluding that the older a person is, the more the individual is socially and physically isolated, with a greater wish to die.[46] The rate for persons over 65 in the United States was almost twice as high as for those between 25 and 34. A study of a group of patients in a high-suicide-risk age range of 45–60 concluded that five variables are associated with suicidal thoughts or actions: isolation, knowledge of other suicides, pride, belief in an after life, and a history of depression.[47] They "were more socially isolated; more knew others who had committed suicide; more felt no pride in aging and predicted poor treatment from relatives when they became even older; more approved suicide in some circumstances and did not believe in an after life; more had

[44]Maris, pp. 100–107.

[45]See M. Peck and R. E. Litman, "Current Trends in Youthful Homicides," *Medical Tribune,* 14 (1973), 13–17; E. Reingold, "Black Suicide in San Francisco," in *Mini Consultation on Mental and Physical Health Problems of Black Women* (Washington, D.C.: Black Women's Community Development Foundation, 1974); F. Wylie, "Suicide among Black Females: A Case Study," in *Mini Consultation on Mental and Physical Health Problems of Black Women;* and James S. Bush, "Suicide and Blacks: A Conceptual Framework," *Suicide and Life-Threatening Behavior,* 6 (1976), 216–222.

[46]Maris, p. 15. Similar rates prevail in England and Wales. See Sainsbury, pp. 153–175. Conversely, in Japan the age group with the highest suicide rate is generally 15–44.

[47]Lee N. Robins, Patricia A. West, and George E. Murphey, "The High Rate of Suicide in Older White Men: A Study Testing Ten Hypotheses," *Social Psychiatry,* 12 (1977), 1–20.

been depressed severely and/or frequently and had a family history of depression."[48] The fact that they were more socially isolated is not surprising in light of the previous discussion of Durkheim's theory that the lack of social integration removes the person from social support, which may be crucial as the person ages, particularly if the person fears the aging process and is easily depressed.

Suicides among adolescents and youth receive much publicity, and thus their numbers have been exaggerated in the popular mind. In 1972 the suicide rate in the age group 15–24 was 9.4. The number of suicides of children and adolescents, however, is probably underestimated by an even greater amount than is the number of adult suicides.[49] Children under the age of 10 practically never commit suicide, and only occasionally are there suicides between the ages of 10 and 14. In the United States in 1972 the suicide rate between 5 and 14 was 0.3 compared with the national rate of 12.0. These figures do not mean that many children, as they grow up, do not on occasion, when encountering extremely frustrating situations, "wish they were dead," as studies have shown. This is particularly the case following certain punishment situations. That these do not end in suicide seems partly the result of an incomplete formation of self-identity, status, and social roles which are endangered by certain situations. Moreover, childhood crises are usually temporary, and there is seldom the long-range "brooding" that accompanies comparable adult crises. Studies of college and university students, both in the United States and England, have generally concluded that their suicide rates are about twice the expected rate for this same age group.[50]

Marital Status

In general, the close personal relationships that exist in marriage seem to provide one of the best protections against the desire to commit suicide, even though some situations produced by an unsatisfactory or a broken marriage may be conducive to it. Married persons have a much lower rate than the single, the divorced, or the widowed. If age is not taken into account, variations sometimes occur. In general, for those over 20 the pattern is the same, although there is a much greater difference in the older age categories. Further evidence for this is the fact that in each age grouping over 20, the suicide rate is lower for married persons than for single persons of the same age group. About three times as many widowers and five times as many divorced men take their lives as do married men. Yet these comparisons should not minimize the fact that many married persons do commit suicide.

Another indication of the important relation of the family to suicide is the fact that suicide appears to be greater among couples without children than among couples with children, who naturally have greater personal ties and feelings of responsibility that act as inhibiting factors. In fact, a Chicago study concluded that the highest rate of male suicides occurs among those who live alone, are unmarried or divorced, and who have no children.[51]

---

[48]Robins, West, and Murphey, p. 14.
[49]"Suicide among Youth," p. 2.
[50]"Suicide among Youth," p. 37.
[51]Maris, p. 98.

Religion

Suicide rates among the main religious groups in Western European civilizations vary greatly. In general, in both Europe and the United States, Catholic rates are much lower than Protestant. Formerly, the Jewish rate appears to have been lower than the Catholic, except that, on occasion, when persecutions made their situation particularly difficult or hopeless, waves of suicides occurred. Within recent years, the Jewish suicide rate has risen considerably, perhaps reflecting changes in religious influence and greater participation in the general society. Both Catholic and Protestant rates have increased during the past century.

Religious differences in suicide rates have been interpreted as meaning in part the degree of integration of the various religious groups. Protestant religious groups tend to be more individualistic than Catholic. The Catholic position on suicide is more specific than that of most Protestant groups, at least in regard to the effect of suicide on the individual's after life and on the right to burial in consecrated ground. Analyses of data from countries with large Catholic and Protestant populations, such as Germany and Switzerland, show that even when all other factors are similar, fewer Catholics commit suicide.

It is difficult, however, to place too much emphasis on the factor of religious affiliation alone. The rate of suicide in northern Italy was almost exactly twice as great as in the south of the country where economic conditions are poorer, there is much less education, and adherence to Catholicism seems greater.[52] Most of the conclusions about the relation of religion, moreover, are based on large statistical categories and not on the effect of Catholicism at the individual level. Ferracuti has emphasized the possible role the Catholic confession may play in furnishing a mechanism that might reduce the number of suicides.[53]

While strong religious feeling appears to discourage suicide, one study of suicide notes and diaries found evidence that in actuality religion is often used in constructing a moral justification of suicide.[54] Mention was often made of meeting someone in the "hereafter," "a happy reunion," the freedom of being released from worldly problems and off "to the final rest." Suicides may use religion to convince themselves that they are blameless and without sin and that this represents their only choice in dealing with their lives. The following two notes are typical of this type:[55]

> I am sad and lonely. Oh God, how lonely. I am starving. Oh God, I am ready for the last, last chance. I have taken two already, they were not right. Life was the first chance, marriage the second, and *now I am ready for death, the last chance. It cannot be worse than it is here.*

> My dearest darling Rose: *By the time you read this I will have crossed the divide to wait for you. Don't hurry.* Wait until sickness overtakes you, but don't wait until you become senile. *I and your other loved ones will have prepared a happy welcome for you.*

---

[52]Franco Ferracuti, "Suicide in a Catholic Country," in Schneidman and Farberow, *Clues to Suicide,* p. 74.
[53]Ferracuti, pp. 76–77.
[54]Jerry Jacobs, "The Use of Religion in Constructing the Moral Justification of Suicide," in Jack D. Douglas, ed., *Deviance and Respectability: The Social Construction of Moral Meanings* (New York: Basic Books, 1970), pp. 229–252.
[55]Both quoted in Jacobs, "The Use of Religion in Constructing the Moral Justification of Suicide."

Occupational Status

In his classic study of suicide Durkheim found that occupational status is linked to suicide, occurring more frequently in the upper ranks of various occupations as well as in positions of higher status.[56] Since that time, however, most research has strongly suggested that suicide is more likely to occur in the lower social classes. One study, for example, found that professionals as a whole have one of the lowest suicide rates while laborers have the highest.[57] Similar results have been reported in Hong Kong[58] and in New Orleans.[59] Some occupations offer exceptions to this generalization: police, farmers, and fishermen in one study, for example, while of lower class, had quite low suicide rates.[60] At the upper range of status, pharmacists have been found to have a suicide rate 24 times that of carpenters.[61]

One of the most comprehensive studies of differential mortality in the United States reached a similar conclusion. At least for white males (data for other groups were incomplete), suicide and education are inversely related.[62] That is, the higher the educational level, the lower the suicide rate. In fact, the least educated group had twice the suicide rate as did the highest group. Another study, also using level of education, found almost precisely the same relationship: the higher the educational level, the lower the suicide rate.[63]

Suicide rates may be higher in occupations in which there is a great deal of uncertainty and economic insecurity, as well as a less cohesive atmosphere. Those workers who enjoy security of employment and support from other workers generally have a lower suicide rate. In this sense, suicide may have an important subcultural component which operates much like other forms of deviance, though here the inhibition of deviance (suicide) is the likely outcome rather than the perpetuation of the deviance, which is often the case in subcultures for homosexuals, addicts, and criminals.

TYPES OF SUICIDE

Suicide is related to the type of society, being more common in urban societies. Self-destruction is reported as not occurring among some folk societies. One observer who asked Australian aborigines about suicide stated that whenever he interrogated them

---

[56]Durkheim, p. 257.
[57]Maris.
[58]Yap.
[59]Warren Breed, "Occupational Mobility and Suicide among White Males," *American Sociological Review,* 28 (1963), 179–188.
[60]Yap, pp. 33–36.
[61]Elwin H. Powell, "Occupation, Status and Suicide: Toward a Redefinition of Anomie," *American Sociological Review,* 23 (1958), 131–139.
[62]Evelyn M. Kitagawa and Philip M. Hauser, *Differential Mortality in the United States: A Study in Socio-Economic Epidemiology* (Cambridge, Mass.: Harvard University Press, 1973).
[63]Wen L. Li, "Suicide and Educational Attainment in a Transitional Society," *The Sociological Quarterly,* 13 (1972), 253–258. This relationship is discussed in N. J. Demerath, III, and Gerald Marwell, *Sociology: Perspectives and Applications* (New York: Harper & Row, 1976), pp. 410–411.

on this point they invariably laughed at him, treating it as a joke.[64] A similar response was reported from natives of the Caroline Islands. A survey of some 20 sources dealing with the Bushmen and Hottentots of South Africa revealed no references to suicide among these people.[65] The Andaman Islanders in the Indian Ocean appear to have had no knowledge of suicide prior to their association with people from India and Europe, nor was suicide reported among such folk societies as the Indians of Tierra del Fuego and the Zuñi of the southwestern United States.

It would be simple to analyze the problem of suicide in folk societies if other data were as consistent as those just cited. Suicide occurs among some folk societies, however, some having a much higher rate than others. Suicides have been reported among the natives of Borneo, the Eskimos, and many African tribes. It is also said to have been fairly common among the Dakota, Creek, Cherokee, Mohave, Ojibwa, and Kwakiutl Indians and the Fiji Islanders, the Chuckchee, and the Dobu Islanders.

Durkheim was particularly interested in the problem of suicide among folk societies because they are generally well integrated. As a result of his studies, he classified suicides by type into *altruistic, egoistic,* and *anomic;* he then examined the different motives underlying each type of suicide.[66] On the whole, according to Durkheim, suicide occurring among a folk people is considerably different from that in modern society. To him, the extent of suicide was a measure of the degree of social integration and regulation in a society, the amount of group unity, and the strength of ties binding people together. Suicide was not an individual phenomenon but was related to certain features of the social organization. A high or a low rate of suicide in a group may be related to the degree of its integration. Societies with a low rate of integration have a high rate of suicide. Suicide occurring in Western European countries is generally either egoistic or anomic, whereas nearly all suicide among folk people is of an altruistic nature. Another type of suicide, fatalistic, was mentioned by Durkheim, but he made little of it, and those who have commented on his theories have generally ignored it. Suicides of this nature result from excessive regulation in which futures are "pitilessly blocked and passions violently choked by oppressive discipline." A good example of fatalistic suicides would be the suicide of slaves. A recent article has maintained that altruistic and fatalistic suicides do not belong in Durkheim's scheme and that egoistic and anomic suicides are identical in that both deal with the level of integration. Consequently, there is only one cause of suicide.[67]

Altruistic Suicide

Among folk societies suicides tend to be altruistic in that a person takes his life with the idea that by doing so he will benefit others. The individual in such societies thinks

[64]Edward A. Westermark, *Origin and Development of the Moral Ideas* (London: Macmillan, 1908), Vol. II, p. 220.
[65]Robert E. L. Faris, *Social Disorganization* (New York: Ronald Press, 1948), p. 148.
[66]Durkheim.
[67]See Barclay D. Johnson, "Durkheim's One Cause of Suicide," *American Sociological Review,* 30 (1965), 875–886. See also Bruce P. Dohrenwend, "Egoism, Altruism, Anomie and Fatalism: A Conceptual Analysis of Durkheim's Types," *American Sociological Review,* 24 (1959), 466–473.

primarily of the group welfare. When his actions or his continued living hurts the group, he may turn to suicide so that the group will have one less mouth to feed or so that he may protect it from the gods. Suicides among folk peoples that may be classified as altruistic are those arising from physical infirmities, or connected with religious rites or with warfare, or in expiation for the violation of certain mores, such as tabus. Under such conditions suicide does not constitute a deviation; in fact, it would be considered a transgression to refrain from the act. It would be a mistake, however, to assume that all suicides among these groups are altruistic in nature. One study of suicide found little or no egoistic suicide among certain African tribal groups, but it did find a moderate amount of anomic suicide, the suicides committed by Africans who are not satisfactorily integrated into operating institutions.[68]

Suicides occur in certain primitive societies where limited food supplies make an old or infirm person a burden to the tribe. Among the Eskimos and the Chuckchee, for example, old people who could no longer hunt or work killed themselves so that they would not use food needed by other adults in the community who produce it. On the death of certain persons in some folk societies, it is customary to commit suicide as part of a religious observance; women, for example, commit suicide on the death of their husbands, and relatives may kill themselves in order to propitiate the souls of the dead. Some suicide occurs in warfare when persons kill themselves to avoid capture and slavery or because of the disgrace of their failure as warriors. Probably the most common form of altruistic suicides among folk societies is the suicide committed as expiation for a violation of the mores, such as a taboo. In these cases the society itself feels that since it has been made unclean, the only recourse for the offender is death by execution or by his own hand to avoid public disgrace. Individuals who fail to commit suicide in atonement for these wrongs risk the imposition of other sanctions, such as perpetual public disgrace. The Trobriand Islanders, for example, having violated taboos, generally committed suicide by climbing a palm tree, from which they gave a speech before jumping to their deaths.[69]

In modern societies an elderly person or an incurably sick person may sometimes end his life in order not to become a burden on others, but this type of altruistic suicide is generally not approved. Also a man may commit suicide so that insurance benefits will go to his family. Occasionally in peacetime, but more frequently during war, individuals may give their lives in order to accomplish some goal involving group values. Sometimes this behavior is approved as being heroic. These suicides in modern society resemble the altruistic type found among folk people. In peacetime people will sometimes give their lives to save others, as in danger or during a fire. Soldiers volunteer for dangerous missions knowing there is no chance of returning alive. The Japanese on many occasions during World War II engaged in what was termed suicidal behavior; faced with certain death, large numbers of Japanese troops died to a man in suicidal banzai charges. In the latter days of that war Japanese kamikaze pilots became legendary for their disregard for their own lives. Loading their

[68]Paul Bohannan, "Patterns of Murder and Suicide," in Paul Bohannan, ed., *African Homicide and Suicide* (Princeton, N.J.: Princeton University Press, 1960), pp. 262–264.
[69]See Bronislaw Malinowski, *Crime and Custom in Savage Society* (London: Routledge & Kegan Paul, 1926), p. 97.

planes with explosives, they dived into Allied warships in order to make sure of destroying them completely.[70] Because of the peculiar settings in which such altruistic types of suicide take place in modern society, however, many of them cannot be classed with typical altruistic suicides in folk societies. Group attitudes and pressures in a military unit under battle conditions and the emotional nature of a peacetime crisis situation involving the saving of a human life are not found in most ordinary situations giving rise to suicide.

Egoistic Suicide

The egoistic and anomic types of suicide found in modern Western European society must be clearly distinguished from the group-oriented, altruistic type common among folk societies. Egoistic suicides are not products of a tightly integrated society, but of one in which interpersonal relations are neither close nor group oriented. These suicides, the most common in modern societies, are a measure of identity with others or a lack of group orientation. In such societies individualistic motives for suicide are not unusual and are associated with such personal problems as financial difficulties. Durkheim cited the higher suicide rate among Protestant and single persons as evidence that weakened group ties create the likelihood of higher rates of this type of suicide.

The Anomic Suicide

The anomic type of suicide occurs when the individual feels "lost" or normless in the face of situations in which the values of a society or group become confused or break down.[71] They also occur where the person is downwardly mobile, or where the individual has achieved everything, so that life has little meaning left. An example of a suicide of this latter type was a wealthy, middle-aged businessman with no apparent financial, health, or marital problems. He had devoted his life to building up his company to achieve something he had always wanted, namely, a merger with a larger company. In this merger he retained the presidency of his own concern and became the vice-president of the larger company, but after the agreement was concluded he immediately went into a depression. The coroner commented that this was the reaction of a man who had built his business, made the deal he had wanted, and then realized that he no longer was the single, direct owner of the business he spent his life building. Another example of anomic suicide was found in a study of white male suicides in New Orleans.[72] Such suicides were associated with substantial work-related problems, as seen in downward mobility, reduced income, unemployment, and other job and business difficulties.

---

[70]For a discussion of suicide in Japan, see Mamoru Iga and Kickinosuke Tatai, "Characteristics of Suicides and Attitudes toward Suicide in Japan," in Faberow, *Suicide in Different Cultures,* pp. 255–280.
[71]This is a different use of anomie from Merton's in Chapter 3. See Marshall B. Clinard, "The Theoretical Implications of Anomie and Deviant Behavior," in Marshall B. Clinard, ed., *Anomie and Deviant Behavior: A Discussion and Critique* (New York: Free Press, 1964), pp. 1–56.
[72]See Warren Breed, "Suicide and Particular Social Statuses or Conditions," in Jack P. Gibbs, ed., *Suicide* (New York: Harper & Row, 1968), pp. 209–227.

In some instances suicides arise when the equilibrium of society has been severely disturbed. A social void exists in which the social order cannot adequately satisfy the desires of the person, and the individual does not know which way to turn. Commonly such anomic suicides occur in modern society as an aftermath of severe and sudden economic crashes or depressions, such as the stock market crash in the United States in 1929, which was followed by a large number of suicides. A similar situation confronts people after a severe political crisis or a defeat in war. In Hong Kong the suicide rate for post-World War II immigrants, who were mainly refugees, was five times greater than the combined rate for prewar immigrants and those born in Hong Kong.[73] Similarly, sudden, abrupt changes in the standard of living of the wealthy, or the sudden breakup of a marriage by divorce or separation, may produce a sense of normlessness and account for the higher rates of suicide among these two groups.

THE SUICIDE PROCESS

Certainly most people in modern society are aware of the alternative to meeting (or solving) life's problems in the form of personal death. While only a relatively few persons actually commit suicide, one writer has claimed that over half the people of the United States have contemplated it.[74] Death wishes are expressed in a variety of ways. One is the vague wish "never to have been born." Others occur in daydreams of death in which the person is likely to imagine himself dead and to speculate on the reaction of others to his death. By doing so the person lives out an experience which he desires but which he probably wishes will not occur.

Prolonged frustrations and crises by no means always result in suicide, and it is not clear as yet just why some persons do kill themselves. People face innumerable unpleasant crises in different ways; some become drunk, some seek religion, some make light of the situation, and others evade the issue or even consciously try to avoid it. The person who commits suicide is generally unable to find a satisfactory alternative solution.

The suicide process involves the search for possible alternatives to deal with problems and then the final decision on death as being the only possible solution. Ringel has identified three principle components of the suicide syndrome: (1) constriction, or a narrowing of alternatives where problems are all-consuming and the person feels there is "no way out" except suicide; (2) a certain aggression which is directed toward the self, perhaps in the form of blaming oneself for an unfortunate accident or some other trauma in one's life; and (3) the presence of suicidal fantasies where the person constructs and mentally plays out suicidal acts.[75] Pinpointing these conditions, and then acting constructively on them, is a crucial dimension for the worker in the

---

[73]Yap, p. 76.
[74]Ruth S. Cavan, *Suicide* (Chicago: University of Chicago Press, 1928), p. 178.
[75] Erwin Ringel, "The Presuicidal Syndrome," *Suicide and Life-Threatening Behavior,* 6 (1977), 131–149.

suicide-prevention center. This process has been summarized in more detail as follows:

> 1. A long-standing history of problems.
> 2. A more recent escalation of problems; that is, the inability to resolve old problems at the same time that many new ones have been added.
> 3. The progressive failure of available adaptive techniques for coping with old and increasing problems, which leads the individual to feel a progressive isolation from meaningful social relationships.
> 4. The final stage—the days and weeks immediately preceding the suicide—at which time the individual feels he has experienced an abrupt and unanticipated dissolution of any remaining meaningful relationships and the prospects of ever establishing them in the future. He experiences, in short, "the end of hope."[76]

Several factors may play a significant role in the *final stage* of a suicide. First, the desired goal may become so *dominant* that in many cases it becomes almost an obsession. For example, a person whose engagement has been broken may feel that nothing else—parents, career, or other interests—is of any consequence. Second, there is a *fixity* in the interest so that nothing else can satisfy it. Once having become determined to satisfy this fixed idea no alternative solution seems possible. This nonadaptability is unusually prominent in the suicide. If the person has determined upon a certain way to satisfy it, no alternative can be considered.[77] Third, a particular *lack of objectivity* on the part of those who commit suicide makes them see the difficulty only from their own point of view. A fourth factor is the *interpretation of the difficulty* by the person. Circumstances such as economic losses or other difficulties that may seriously disturb one person may have little effect on another. The need for the object desired or the loss of status may be interpreted by a suicide as destroying all future hope. A prosperous businessman who has lost his fortune and commits suicide may have felt that because of the loss of money his previous social status is irrevocably ended. Satisfaction and material comforts, the future of his family, and the plans for his old age have all come tumbling down at once and he has no desire to try to rebuild his life. Sometimes persons commit suicide for some provocation that might not seem to be sufficiently serious to warrant suicide in the eyes of others but which to the suicide has assumed tremendous proportions.[78] Interpersonal elements, particularly disruptive social relations, are crucial etiological factors in suicide.[79] Some suicides, such as those of adolescents, are often impulsive actions that follow a broken romance, the denial of some privilege, or a severe rebuke. These situations may be of minor importance to an adult, but to the adolescent suicide seems the only solution. Conversely, some persons, such as old people or a person who has lost a marital partner, may shrewdly calculate the balance between the difficulties of continued living and "escape" through suicide. Situations of ill health may also lead to suicide.

Suicides may on occasion be definitely planned without being carried to completion. Some persons may even have planned to kill themselves on a number of

---

[76]Jacobs, "The Use of Religion in Constructing the Moral Justification of Suicide," p. 23.
[77]Cavan, p. 173.
[78]Cavan.
[79]See William A. Rushing, "Individual Behavior and Suicide," in Gibbs, *Suicide,* pp. 96–121.

occasions, the final act being prevented by the removal of the original cause, an alternative solution, or the reinforcement of some attitude, particularly a strong religious one, opposed to self-destruction. Other persons may play a role in the potential suicide's definition of the situation.

> An individual comes to feel that his future is devoid of hope: he, or someone else, brings the alternative of suicide into his field. He attempts to communicate his conviction of hopelessness to others, in an effort to gain their assurance that some hope still exists for him. The character of the response at this point is crucial in determining whether or not suicide will take place. For actual suicide to occur, a necessary (although not sufficient) aspect of the field is a response characterized by helplessness and hopelessness.[80]

SOCIAL MEANINGS OF SUICIDE

Suicidal actions are meaningful in the sense that something is fundamentally wrong with the situations of the actor. The real *meaning* of a suicide is not necessarily that reached by friends, family, or the coroner. Outsiders may regard the suicide as "senseless" and "irrational," because the person was "distraught," "lost," or "depressed." In actuality, studies of suicide notes and diaries, as well as interviews with those who have attempted suicide, indicate suicidal actions through death and the dying process are means of transforming the essential "substantial" self of the actor in many ways.[81] Suicides generally have a number of patterns of social meanings which they have constructed for themselves and in relation to others, according to Douglas.

> 1. *Suicide as a means of transforming the soul from this world to another.* Such individuals are motivated to die in order to live, and in this sense "'life' is treated as a thing or an entity outside the speaker. It is spoken of as a property of the person or subject of the statement, not as part of the person, as some essential or substantial quality of person which is necessary before one can even speak of a person as existing." [287] Suicide notes indicate that these individuals conceive of returning to God, to a new world.
> 2. *Other suicides seek to transform the substantial self in this world or another world.* In the suicide the individual seeks to show that he is something quite different and that people were mistaken with past identifications. By killing himself a person can show, for example, how serious, committed, and sincere he actually was. One is giving what is of highest value, namely, one's life. He, for example, may give his life for what he has done and in a sense atone for his errors.
>
> But the power to convince significant others that one's substantial self is other than what they thought it was, frequently because you can show them by your suicidal action that you are not the *type* of person who would do such a thing, is only partly the result of sacrificing what is considered to have the highest value. One must,

---

[80]Arthur L. Kobler and Ezra Stotland, *The End of Hope: A Socio-Clinical Study of Suicide* (New York: Free Press, 1964), p. 252.
[81]Douglas, *The Social Meanings of Suicide,* pp. 284–319. Reprinted by permission of Princeton University Press. The following first four patterns and quotations are from Douglas, five and six by the authors.

generally, combine the sacrifice with certain other fundamental meanings that must be imputed to him if his communicative work is to be successful. [p. 302]

3. *Suicidal actions may serve as means of achieving fellow feeling.* In such suicidal action individuals seek to gain some sort of sympathy or pity for themselves and in so doing come to share themselves with others.

4. *Suicidal actions may have the social meaning of blaming others for one's death and are, therefore, means of getting revenge.* In such suicides it is important to point to the person one feels to be blamed and whom one intends to hold responsible for the suicidal actions. In one case a husband wrote his reactions while taking gas because his wife had fallen in love with his brother.

A young clerk 22 years old killed himself because his bride of four months was not in love with him but with his elder brother and wanted a divorce so that she could marry the brother. The letters he left showed plainly the suicide's desire to bring unpleasant notoriety upon his brother and his wife, and to attract attention to himself. In them he described his shattered romance and advised reporters to see a friend to whom he had forwarded diaries for further details. The first sentence in a special message to his wife read: "I used to love you; but I die hating you and my brother, too." This was written in a firm hand: but as his suicide diary progressed, the handwriting became erratic and then almost unintelligible as he lapsed into unconsciousness. Some time after turning on the gas he wrote: "Took my 'panacea' for all human ills. It won't be long now. I'll bet Florence and Ed are having uneasy dreams now." An hour later he continues: "Still the same, hope I pass out by 2 a.m. Gee, I love you so much, Florence. I feel very tired and a bit dizzy. My brain is very clear. I can see that my hand is shaking—it is hard to die when one is young. Now I wish oblivion would hurry"—the note ended there.[82]

5. *Suicides may also represent escape patterns from the responsibilities of continued life.* In such cases there is a high degree of restlessness, although the nature of this dissatisfaction is often not specified. The person feels "disgusted with life," or "useless." A married woman of 24, for example, left this note: "I've proved to be a miserable wife, mother and homemaker—not even a decent companion. Johnny and Jane deserve much more than I can ever offer. I can't take it any longer. . . . This is a terrible thing for me to do, but perhaps in the end it will be all for the best."[83] A divorced man of 50 left this suicide note.

To the Police—

This is a very simple case of suicide. I owe nothing to anyone, including the World; and I ask nothing from anyone. I'm fifty years old, have lived violently but never committed a crime.

I've just had enough. Since no one depends upon me, I don't see why I shouldn't do as I please. I've done my duty to my Country in both World Wars, and also I've served well in industry. My papers are in the brown leather wallet in my gray bag.

If you would be so good as to send these papers to my brother, his address is: John Smith, 100 Main Street.

I enclose five dollars to cover cost of mailing. Perhaps some of you who belong to the American Legion will honor my request.

---

[82]Dublin and Bunzel, p. 294.
[83]Schneidman and Farbarow, *Clues to Suicide,* pp. 43–44.

I haven't a thing against anybody. But I've been in three major wars and another little insurrection, and I'm pretty tired.

This note is in the same large envelope with several other letters—all stamped. Will you please mail them for me? There are no secrets in them. However, if you open them, please seal them up again and send them on. They are to the people I love and who love me. Thanks.

George Smith[84]

6. *Another suicide pattern is exemplified by those persons who, after killing another person, for example, commit suicide.* In a Philadelphia study about 4 percent of those who committed homicide took their own lives. Other studies in the United States have shown an incidence of 2–9 percent in such suicides[85] In England and Wales the proportion is much greater: each year about one third of all murders are followed by suicide, one in every 100 suicides being of this nature.[86] Other crimes where there is a major element of personal disgrace, for example, embezzlement, are also occasionally followed by suicide.

A major problem in a suicide is its effect, in the term of *guilt feelings,* on significant others—family, friends, employers, and so forth. One study has attempted to classify people's reactions to a suicide, examining the various techniques of "guilt neutralization." It was concluded that if the following techniques of neutralization are utilized successfully, guilt feelings will be eliminated.

1. *He defines other persons and/or impersonal factors as the causal agents that led to the suicide.* In his view there is neither anything that he did nor anything that he neglected to do that led to the suicide. In addition, he defines his own acts toward the person who committed suicide as good.

2. *He defines the suicide as inevitable.* He views the suicide as having been impossible to stop, looking on himself as having been powerless in the face of this crushing inevitability. He had neither the knowledge nor the power to stop the suicide.

3. *He defines the suicide in positive terms.* He minimizes the suicide event itself and or emphasizes certain consequences of the suicide as good. He can, for example, view the deceased as now being in a better state than previously, defining suicide as the means by which God took the individual to Himself. He also defines altruism as the motive for the suicide: the suicide was not seeking to escape from him, but rather he suicided out of love and concern, attempting to spare him some hurt or pain.[87]

SUICIDE AND MENTAL DISORDER

Persons who commit suicide are not generally "mentally deranged" or suffering from "temporary insanity." A government report on suicide has stated categorically that "there are no modern writers who contend that mental disorder is either a necessary

---

[84]From Schneidman and Farberow, *Clues to Suicide,* p. 44.

[85]Marvin E. Wolfgang, *Patterns in Criminal Homicide* (Philadelphia: University of Pennsylvania Press, 1958), p. 274.

[86]Donald J. West, *Murder Followed by Suicide* (London: William Heinemann, 1965).

[87]James M. Henslin, "Guilt and Guilt Neutralization: Response and Adjustment to Suicide," in Douglas, *Deviance and Respectability,* p. 222. Italics are Henslin's.

or sufficient cause of suicide."[88] This idea developed from the notion that "no one in his right mind" would take his own life. To be considered a suicide resulting from a psychosis, the patient must generally have been under treatment or there must be some other demonstrable evidence of psychosis. Hearsay evidence from relatives cannot be accepted. Approximately only 20 percent of 22,000 suicides among industrial policyholders of a large life insurance company were found to have a recognized mental illness.[89] Severe depression, either involutional melancholia or manic-depressive psychosis, seems to be the most common form of psychosis associated with suicide. The percentage of psychotic disturbances, although not large, is great enough to account for concern, in most cases of attempted suicide, since there may be present some severe mental disorder which will lead to a repetition of the attempt unless the disturbance is discovered and treated. Likewise, psychiatrists must be on guard for such possibilities in patients suffering from severe depression. Actually, most suicides are rationally planned and carried out with no more evidence of mental disorder than would be found in the so-called normal person. The goals sought by most suicides, no matter how exaggerated, generally are real goals; the personal losses suffered are real losses and are usually not the product of psychotic hallucinations or delusions having little or no basis in reality.

In spite of the state of mind necessary prior to the act of suicide, the suicide process is essentially a social one brought about in patterned ways from a number of influences that appear to affect some groups more than others. The different rates of suicide among countries with differing cultural traditions and beliefs, the differences in rates among different subgroups in the population in the same country, and the social psychological meaning of the act all point to the importance of a social explanation of suicide. This suggests that it may represent a form of learned behavior, as has been previously indicated, although the learning obviously is not one of personal experience with the completed act. Part of this process can be noticed by observing that well-publicized cases of suicides by public figures, such as Marilyn Monroe, seem to trigger a chain reaction of successful imitations. With data from the United States and Great Britain between 1947 and 1968, one study found a direct relationship between the amount of publicity given suicide in the newspapers and the suicide rate in those communities where the news stories were carried.[90] This study found the largest increases in Britain and the United States following the death of Marilyn Monroe. In the month after Marilyn Monroe's suicide, suicides in the United States increased by 12 percent, and in England and Wales by 10 percent. "In the two-month period following Miss Monroe's death, there were 303 excess suicides in the U.S. and 60 excess suicides in England and Wales."[91] The suggestion of suicide appears to call into consciousness the option of suicide, giving it a certain legitimacy. This process occurs not only with the deaths of well-known persons but may also operate with the suicides of friends, family, or neighbors.[92]

Everyone has learned that one way to gain attention or to solicit help for some

---

[88]"Suicide among Youth," p. 22.
[89]Dublin and Bunzel, p. 300.
[90]David P. Phillips, "The Influence of Suggestion on Suicide: Substantive and Theoretical Implications of the Werther Effect," *American Sociological Review,* 39 (1974), 340–354.
[91]Phillips, pp. 350–351.
[92]Demerath and Marwell, p. 394.

problem is to be sick or hurt. Techniques for gaining sympathy are learned early in life in experiences with parents and friends, and those techniques that prove to be the most successful—that is, those that receive the most social attention and reward—are retained by the individual. The progressive use of certain techniques, such as deliberately injuring oneself or feigning illness, or even actually producing illness through a controlled but nonaccidental taking of drugs, may produce suicide. Obviously, the process is complicated, it involves learning techniques and rationales for using them, and it takes place over a long period of time. There is no need to invoke a mental illness explanation for suicide when others, such as social learnings, are probably more sound.

PREVENTING SUICIDE

The identification of the social forces that ultimately produce suicide may eventually point to preventive remedies, largely through changes in society. If suicide is "caused" by the conditions of modern life and the stresses placed on individuals in complex, industrialized societies, perhaps broader remedies can be adopted. In the meantime, most preventive efforts continue on an individualistic basis without necessarily a coherent and valid sociological theory to guide them.

A large number of community agencies have been set up in the United States and various other countries to prevent suicides by counseling and offering other assistance. Much of this work was pioneered after World War II. In Vienna, Austria, most of the suicide-prevention work is carried out through Caritas, a Catholic organization, which also works with a preventive clinic for attempted suicides at the Vienna hospitals. A special suicide-prevention telephone service is maintained which a person comtemplating suicide, or a relative or neighbor, may call to speak to someone about his problems. If he so desires, a social worker will visit him in his home, or he may come for a visit. Great Britain has an effective volunteer organization, The Good Samaritans, established in 1953, whose program combines religion and psychotherapy.[93] Its 28 centers dealt with over 1,000 cases in the first 10 months of existence.

In the United States, the best-known organizations are the National Save-a-Life League, Inc., established in 1906, and the Suicide Prevention Centers, the first of which was founded in 1958 in Los Angeles.[94] Numerous such organizations are now found in most states, dealing with suicide prevention under a variety of names such as Suicide Prevention Service, Call-for-Help Clinics, Crisis Clinics, Crisis Call Centers, Rescue, Inc., Dial-a-Friend, and Suicides Anonymous. A Center for Studies of Suicide Prevention was established by the National Institute of Mental Health in 1967 and that same year began publication of the *Bulletin of Suicidology*. This bulletin contains much information on various preventive programs and techniques.

Los Angeles has the oldest suicide-prevention center in the United States. Each year about 6,000 cases are contacted out of an estimated annual potential of 50,000 suicides in the total Los Angeles metropolitan area population of 7 million persons. "In Los Angeles, where there are approximately 1,200 suicides a year, one would need to

---

[93]See McCormick, pp. 157–170.
[94]Farberow, "Suicide," p. 543.

prevent about 300 suicides in order to establish an obvious and significant decrease in the suicide rate. For this, the Suicide Prevention Center would have to contact about 35,000 suicidal persons a year."[95]

Much of the initial work of the suicide-prevention centers is carried out on the telephone. In fact, over 99 percent of it was done by phone in a Los Angeles study. Most large cities have the telephone numbers of these prevention centers prominently listed in their directories and also through other publicity means. Efforts are made to encourage the suicidal person to talk, to offer him help, and to get him to come to the center.

The formalization of suicide prevention through these centers constitutes an example of how formal social controls serve as a back-up to informal controls. Most persons refrain from committing suicide, if they consider it seriously, because of their strong moral or religious convictions opposed to self-killing. Some persons attempt suicide for reasons other than self-death, for example to get attention for some problem that might otherwise pass unnoticed. Still others are serious in their suicidal behavior but do not have available to them preventive resources to which they can turn. Suicide-prevention centers offer an alternative to the person who does not know where else to turn for help with serious problem.

Suicide-prevention centers serve as crisis-intervention points; that is, the services they offer are geared toward the individual's immediate rather than long-term needs, which may require more intensive counseling and advice. In other words, they provide short-term services 24 hours a day, usually in the form of telephone counseling directed at the situation. As part of this effort, the worker answering the phone takes the following steps:

1. Establishes rapport and maintains contact with the caller.
2. Clarifies the caller's immediate need and less urgent problems.
3. Evaluates suicide or danger potential. That is, an assessment must be made of how close the caller is to committing suicide so that action can be taken.
4. Evaluates resources available to the caller which may help in this situation.
5. Sets up a treatment plan. This portion of the call, usually at the end of the interview, explores the caller's situation in light of the needs of the person and organizes these needs in some coherent plan for future action.[96]

Persons who call suicide-prevention centers fit no convenient stereotype: they present a variety of problems, and they are troubled by a number of conflicts, all of which may require different alternatives. As one might expect, they represent higher risks than the population at large. In contrast to the national suicide rate of about 12 per 100,000 population, the suicide rate for center cases has been estimated to be about 1,000 per 100,000.[97] Studies of prevention centers in Los Angeles,[98] Chicago,[99]

[95]Robert E. Litman, "Suicide Prevention Center Patients: A Follow-Up Study," *Bulletin of Suicidology,* 6 (1970), 17.
[96]Farberow, "Suicide," pp. 546–547.
[97]Robert E. Litman, "Experiences in a Suicide Prevention Center," in Jan Waldenstrom, Tage Larsson, and Nils Ljungstedt, eds., *Suicide and Attempted Suicide* (Stockholm: Nordiska Bokhandelns Forlag, 1972), pp. 217–230.
[98]Litman, "Suicide Prevention Center Patients."
[99]James Wilkins, "A Follow-up Study of Those Who Called A Suicide Prevention Center," *American Journal of Psychiatry,* 127 (1970), 155–161.

and Cleveland[100] have estimated a suicide rate of between 1 and 2 percent for the first and second year after contact with the centers. Another study conducted a call-back campaign and found that workers evaluated the suicide potential as lower in 70 percent of the cases that cooperated with the study, higher in 12 percent of the cases, and the same in 18 percent.[101]

One study of callers to the Los Angeles Suicide Prevention Center showed that most of them were depressed, and about two thirds of them were contemplating suicide, while the others were in the act of suicide when they called.[102] Two thirds of the callers were women, and about half had a history of suicide attempts. More than half of them called the center themselves, while the others were represented over the phone by family members, friends, or professional persons. The study reported that the ratings of suicidal potential were high for about 20 percent of the callers, moderate for 40 percent, and low for the remaining 40 percent. In comparing this sample with a group who actually committed suicide even though they had contact with the center (many of those who call are prevented from their acts), it was found that the profiles differed in a number of important respects. The proportion of men and women was reversed: two thirds were male, one third female, and depression was more marked in those who actually committed suicide.

It is difficult to evaluate precisely the effectiveness of suicide-prevention centers, since many callers who do not commit suicide are not found after their call. Still, some attempts have been made to study this issue. One of the most comprehensive studies analyzed data in North Carolina comparing counties who did and who did not have suicide-prevention centers. It was concluded that the centers had a minimal effect on suicide rates based on a before-center and after-center comparison of suicide rates.[103] There are those, however, who feel that even if one person is prevented from suicide, the services are important and valuable.

SELECTED REFERENCES

Bridge, T. Peter, Steven G. Potkin, William W. K. Zung, and Beth J. Soldo. "Suicide Prevention Centers: Ecological Study of Effectiveness," *Journal of Nervous and Mental Disease,* 164 (1977), 18–24.

Douglas, Jack D. *The Social Meanings of Suicide.* Princeton, N.J.: Princeton University Press, 1967.

Dublin, Louis I. *Suicide: A Sociological and Statistical Study.* New York: Ronald, 1963.

Durkheim, Emile. *Suicide,* John A. Spaulding and George Simpson, trans. New York: Free Press, 1951.

Farberow, Norman L. "Suicide," in Edward Sagarin and Fred L. Montanino, eds,. *Deviants: Voluntary Actors in a Hostile World.* Morristown, N.J.: General Learning Press, 1977.

---

[100]Charles H. Browning, Robert L. Tyson, and Sheldon I. Miller, "A Study of Psychiatric Emergencies. II: Suicide," *Psychiatry in Medicine,* 1 (1970), 359–366.

[101]Farberow, "Suicide," pp. 560–561.

[102]Carl I. Wold, "Characteristics of 26,000 Suicide Prevention Center Patients," *Bulletin of Suicidology,* (1970), 24–28.

[103]T. Peter Bridge, Steven G. Potkin, William W. K. Zung, and Beth J. Soldo, "Suicide Prevention Centers: Ecological Study of Effectiveness," *The Journal of Nervous and Mental Disease,* 164 (1977), 18–24.

Farberow, Norman L. ed. *Suicide in Different Cultures.* Baltimore, Md.: University Park Press, 1975.

Gibbs, Jack P. "Suicide," in Robert K. Merton and Robert Nisbet, eds., *Contemporary Social Problems,* 3d ed. New York: Harcourt Brace Jovanovich, 1971.

Gibbs, Jack P., and Walter T. Martin. *Status Integration and Suicide: A Sociological Study.* Eugene: University of Oregon Books, 1964.

Jacobs, Jerry. "A Phenomenological Study of Suicide Notes," *Social Problems,* 15 (1967), 60–73.

Maris, Ronald W. *Social Forces in Urban Suicide.* Homewood, Ill.: Dorsey Press, 1969.

McCormick, Donald. *The Unseen Killer: A Study of Suicide, Its History, Causes and Cures.* London: Frederick Mueller, 1964.

Phillips, David P. "The Influence of Suggestion on Suicide: Substantive and Theoretical Implications of the Werther Effect," *American Sociological Review,* 39 (1974), 340–354.

Robins, Lee N. Patricia S. West, and George E. Murphey, "The High Rate of Suicide in Older, White Men: A Study Testing Ten Hypotheses," *Social Psychiatry,* 12 (1977), 1–20.

Schneidman, Edwin S., ed. *Suicidology: Contemporary Developments.* New York: Grune and Stratton, 1976.

Stengel, Erwin. *Suicide and Attempted Suicide.* Baltimore, Md.: Pelican Books, 1964.

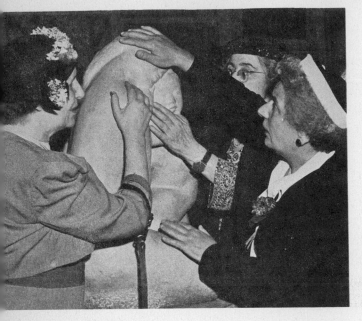

CHAPTER 15

Persons with pronounced physical disabilities, such as these blind persons exploring a statue, frequently encounter severe social stigma and discrimination because of ascribed rather than achieved deviance. They are often forced into a deviant social role that affects their self-conception.

Physical Disabilities

A WIDE range of physical disabilities and impairments results in such severe stigma and discrimination that they may be regarded, and are so regarded here, as being deviant in many, if not in most, societies. Goffman has referred to the blind, the deaf, the mute, the epileptic, the crippled, and the deformed as classic examples of stigma.[1] There are also others—the mentally retarded, the obese, those afflicted with cerebral palsy, and those who stutter. Goffman points out that society fails to accord the person "the respect and regard which the uncontaminated aspects of his social identity have led them to anticipate extending, and have led him to anticipate receiving; he echoes this denial by finding that some of his own attributes warrant it.[2] A large number of persons in the United States have these severe physical disabilities. It has been estimated, for example, that there are over six million mentally retarded persons,[3] over four million deaf and hard of hearing, more than three million with orthopedic impairments, 1,500,000 epileptics, about 550,000 suffering from cerebral palsy, and over 600,000 blind and partially sightless persons.[4] The total population of these disabled or impaired persons is at least 15 million.

Physical disability is a "pattern of behavior emergent from incapacity—the loss of ability to perform expected role activities because of a chronic physical or mental impairment."[5] The emphasis is on the behavioral effects of impairment which constitute disability, namely, the imputation, through the societal labeling process, of disability onto the individual. Moreover, the disabled condition is generally considered in most cases to be permanent and irreversible: once the stigmatizing process is complete, the individual can expect to face a life of adjustment to his physical disability.

Disability must be distinguished from illness. Mechanic has pointed out that the sick are exempt from social role responsibilities: they are exempt from responsibility for their conditions. The patient is expected to want to get well, and he is expected to seek competent help. In these respects sickness has quite different attributes from the more permanent aspects of disability. Another writer has distinguished between the two in these terms: "The label of sickness, although it may imply severity, also implies a temporary condition which can, through some kind of intervention (usually medical), be made to disappear. It is only the label of disability that carried the connotation of permanency and irreversibility regardless of the degree of severity of the condition.[6]

There are, of course, degrees of physical disability and impairment; in all probability, the more extreme cases are more likely to be reacted to in a negative manner fitting the cultural stereotype. For example, there is great variation in the

---

[1]Erving Goffman, *Stigma: Notes on the Management of Spoiled Identity* (Englewood Cliffs, N.J.: Prentice Hall, 1963).

[2]Goffman, pp. 8–9.

[3]See Robert B. Edgerton, *The Cloak of Competence: Stigma in the Lives of the Mentally Retarded* (Berkeley: University of California Press, 1967), p. 1.

[4]Robert A. Scott, *The Making of Blind Men: A Study of Adult Socialization* (New York: Russell Sage, 1969), p. 42.

[5]David Mechanic, *Medical Sociology: A Selective View* (New York: Free Press, 1968), p. 173. Also see David Mechanic, "Illness and Social Disability: Some Problems of Analysis," *Pacific Sociological Review*, 2 (1959), 37–41.

[6]Constantina Safilios-Rothschild, *The Sociology and Social Psychology of Disability and Rehabilitation* (New York: Random House, 1970), p. 71.

extent of the blindness, the seriousness of the crippling or facial disfigurement, and the severity of mental retardation. While the legal definition of blindness has been put at a 20/200 vision level, Scott severely criticizes what he terms this arbitrary level as being insensitive to most of the important determinants of the person's functional vision, excluding as it does those with nearly similar levels of visual acuity. It also "lumps together people who are totally blind and people who have a substantial amount of vision."[7] For this reason people labeled as blind are extremely diversified, and the "blindness population" is a heterogeneous one. Deafness is a matter of degree ranging from those who are only partially impaired to those who are totally deaf. Pronounced obesity is also a matter of degree: in one study it has been defined, arbitrarily, as 30–40 percent beyond "normal" weight.[8] Persons can be overweight in varying degrees, but it is a highly visible fat person who is usually termed "obese."[9] Likewise, a stutterer may have severe and constant speech impairment, or he may stutter only under certain conditions. With respect to mental retardates, the range is extremely varied: the American Association on Mental Deficiency lists classifications, based on a "normal" IQ (intelligence quotient) of 90–110, of borderline as 70–84, and of various degrees of retardation below 70. About 85 percent of the retardates fall in the category of "mildly retarded" with IQs between 55 and 70.[10] Moreover, physical impairments in given cases may differ according to when they occurred, the type of onset, the degree of pain, the degree of limitation, the degree of visibility, the treatment, the state of progression, and the prognosis. Impairments differ, then, according to such characteristics as:

> (1) the point in the life cycle at which onset occurs; (2) the type of onset—either gradual and progressive, allowing early warning in signs and symptoms, or sudden or accidental, allowing no warning; (3) the degree of pain, trauma, and threat to life; (4) the nature and degree of limitations imposed upon the individual's capacities and level of functioning; (5) the degree of visibility, disfigurement, or associated stigma; (6) the type of treatment and care required and received; (7) the state of the underlying pathology—either eliminated or arrested with fixed residual limitations, or slowly or rapidly progressive, with or without recurring acute episodes, and (8) the prognosis for the condition, that is, prospects for recovery, prosthetic compensation, adaptive and restorative training, and potential for other forms of rehabilitation.[11]

PHYSICAL DISABILITIES AS DEVIANCE

Disability can be regarded as being deviant from a number of perspectives. According to one writer, the presence of a physical disability at the social level, partly due to the

---

[7]Scott, p. 42.

[8]Werner J. Cahnman, "The Stigma of Obesity," *The Sociological Quarterly,* 9 (1968), 283–299.

[9]Jean Mayer, *Overweight: Causes, Cost, and Control* (Englewood Cliffs, N.J.: Prentice-Hall, 1968).

[10]See Edgerton, pp. 4–5. Also see R. Heber, "Modifications in the Manual on Terminology and Classification in Mental Retardation," *American Journal of Mental Deficiency,* 66 (1961), 499–500.

[11]Saad Z. Nagi, *Disability and Rehabilitation: Legal, Clinical, and Self-Concepts and Measurement* (Columbus: Ohio State University Press, 1969), p. 11.

limitations imposed on the disabled person's range of activities and his behavior, but chiefly because of his reaction to his disability, renders him a "deviant."[12] Freidson states that a handicap is "an imputation of difference from others, more particularly, imputation of an *undesirable* difference. By definition, then, a person said to be handicapped is so defined because he deviates from what he himself or others believe to be normal or appropriate."[13] Many of the disabled violate the norm of physical well-being and "wholeness." They are "not intrinsically deviant because of their disability, but because those around them label them 'deviant' since they impute to them an undesirable difference."[14] It should be recognized, however, that not everyone in a society labels those with physical disabilities as deviant and the reaction varies with the type, the extent of the physical disability, and the particular group situation.

Disability as Deviant Status

Disability is a socially defined category of behavior that groups label; it is a master status, and as such it overrides all other statuses. Those with physical disabilities often experience "a personally discreditable departure from a group's expectations."[15] Groups in general expect a person to have two legs and two arms, ears and eyes that function, and to be able to carry on daily activities in normal fashion. The amputee, the deaf, blind, or the paralyzed, for example, do not fit the normative expectations of society. The situation is also personally discreditable; the disabled finds that his identity is defined in terms of his handicap. He no longer is an individual but a "cripple," a "deaf-mute": he becomes discredited and stigmatized. Such disability impairment as facial disfigurement attaches "visible signs of moral inferiority to persons."[16] They find it difficult to secure jobs, they have trouble dating, and they may be excluded from many social gatherings; some may even have to pay for companionship in the form of prostitutes, bar girls, and hostesses in dance halls.

Some persons argue, however, that deviance and disability, like sickness, differ primarily in the extent of responsibility imputed to the individual for his condition. The crucial difference in this distinction between deviance and disability with regard to imputed responsibility is that deviants can choose to enter the deviant role: the disabled cannot choose his disability. These persons argue that deviance is willful and subject thus to the individual's control and that disability does not fit this model.[17] Thus while researchers claim that the drug user or the homosexual chooses to commit the deviant act, this option is not available to the blind, the deaf, or the crippled. The

---

[12]Safilios-Rothschild.

[13]Eliot Freidson, "Disability as Social Deviance," in Marvin B. Sussman, ed., *Sociology and Rehabilitation* (Washington, D.C.: American Sociological Association, 1965), p. 72. Freidson also includes illness in general as social deviance. See Eliot Freidson, *Profession of Medicine: A Study of the Sociology of Applied Knowledge* (New York: Dodd, Mead, 1970), Chap. 10, "Illness as Social Deviance," pp. 205–223.

[14]Safilios-Rothschild, p. 115.

[15]Howard S. Becker, *Outsiders: Studies in the Sociology of Deviance,* enlarged ed. (New York: Free Press, 1973), p. 33.

[16]Edwin M. Lemert, *Human Deviance, Social Problems and Social Control* (Englewood Cliffs, N.J.: Prentice-Hall, 1967), p. 42.

[17]See Lawrence D. Haber and Richard T. Smith, "Disability and Deviance: Normative Adaptations of Role Behavior," *American Sociological Review,* 36 (1971), 87–97.

disabled are more clearly labeled "victims" of unforeseen circumstances, while the deviant is motivated in his deviant behavior. Freidson convincingly maintains, however, that while there is no general desire to be handicapped or to seek out the deviant role, the behavior of the disabled "may be said to consist in large part in an attempt to avoid the role."[18] Moreover, these distinctions may be ideal but varying in reality. Some disabled (for example, car accident victims who were at fault or incurably ill persons whose procrastination in seeking medical care has aggravated their conditions) may be viewed as being more responsible for their own misfortunes. The obese are rather universally judged as being responsible for their condition; little sympathy is given them, as in the case of the blind or paraplegics. The obese, moreover, tend to internalize that viewpoint, as one of them indicated: "Although I have felt anger and embarrassment at being called fat, I have always felt that they were right, and guilt about not being able to lose weight was my predominant feeling."[19]

One must recognize that the views of many people toward physical disabilities are ambivalent in that, along with stigma, positive factors are also seen in the disabled: they may be regarded as being kinder, more courteous, less selfish, more tolerant and sensitive, more trustworthy, and more courageous.[20] People often cite the use of stories of individual success in terms of status achievement of physically handicapped people as indicative of the fact that physical disability means little to others. Physique has become subordinated to other characteristics that provide the person with status.[21] Actually, this approach carries its own defeat inasmuch as it actually connotes a devaluation of the average person who has a disability.

The Sick Role

The ambivalence that many persons display toward forms of disability relates to their conceptions of the "sick role." According to Parsons, the sick role consists of two interrelated sets of exemptions.[22] An individual who is defined as ill is freed from certain obligations and responsibilities due to illness. The illness is not considered his "fault," nor is he expected to improve through his own motivation alone. He is viewed as someone whose capacity to function normally is impaired, and he is usually relieved of his normal familial, occupational, and other duties. In exchange for these exemptions, however, there are certain expectations of the individual occupying the sick role. For example, the person is expected to define for himself the sick role as "undesirable" and to do everything within his power to facilitate recovery; in the case of illness, the person should obtain and cooperate with medical help, usually a physician. Following doctor's "orders" means precisely that: the advice of a physician on medical matters reflects not only the recommendation of one supposed to know these conditions but also society's expectation that the ill person will try to move to more conventional roles. The ambivalence of many persons about physical disabilities thus reflects their views that the disabling condition is both unavoidable and at the same

---

[18]Freidson, "Disability as Social Deviance," p. 89.
[19]Werner J. Cahnman, "The Stigma of Overweight—Six Autobiographies," unpublished paper, p. 16.
[20]Beatrice A. Wright, *Physical Disability—A Psychological View* (New York: Harper & Row, 1960), pp. 57–59.
[21]Wright, p. 83.
[22]Talcott Parsons, *The Social System* (New York: Free Press, 1951), pp. 428–479.

time undesirable. One authority states that while illness is defined as deviance from the normal and the desirable, it is not regarded reprehensible in the same way as is either sin or crime, the sick person neither being blamed nor punished as are those considered to be "sinful or criminal." "So long as he does not abandon himself to illness or eagerly embrace it, but works actively on his own and with medical professionals to improve his condition, he is considered to be responding appropriately, even admirably, to an unfortunate occurrence. Under these conditions, illness is accepted as legitimate deviance."[23]

It is this voluntary nature of the deviance, then, that differentiates the physically disabled from other deviants. Deviance is generally considered undesirable, so much so that negative sanctions are applied to those who violate the social norm at issue; but the degree to which it is voluntary is one variable that affects the degree of tolerance of the social audience to a deviant act. The various forms of disability considered here fit this general framework to different extents. The totally blind who have no reasonable hope of recovery, the crippled, and the mentally retarded fit best. The obese and the stutterers fit to a lesser extent, because there is at least a reasonable chance for them to move from the sick role to other, more conventional roles, even though the cause of the disability or condition may be outside the individual's control.

The issue of responsibility becomes important not only in assigning one to the sick role but also in administering, or withholding, sanctions to the deviant. The less responsible the person is for his deviant status, the less likely social groups are to show their disapproval of the deviance in administering negative sanctions. Although the issue of individual responsibility is clear in most cases of physical conditions, during the last decade U.S. society has witnessed a general movement toward defining other forms of deviance in these terms. One example has been the "political prisoner" label that has developed recently and been applied to inmates in correctional institutions. The view that inmates are unfortunate victims of larger economic, social, and political forces, particularly in the control of the criminal justice system by the more powerful, has had the effect of removing some of the individual responsibility from these persons, transferring it to some larger unit, either the political system or the economy. Similarly, as has been seen with alcoholics, the movement to make problem drinking a medical rather than a law-enforcement problem, even though it does not conform entirely to the social reality of alcoholism, has had the effect of making the dimensions of the sick role applicable to these individuals. Much of what is done about any problem is the result of the manner in which the problem is conceived and the implications that this conception has for action. If alcoholics are "sick," then police lockups are inappropriate; hospital beds and medications are.

SOCIAL CONTROL AND THE AMBIVALENCE OF DEVIANCE

In order to understand the crucial role of sanctioning for these disabilities one must consider the culture-bound character of disability. Not all impaired persons are

---

[23]Renée Fox, "The Medicalization and Demedicalization of American Society," *Daedalus,* 106 (1977), 15.

regarded as disabled; images of disability vary from culture to culture and from age to age. A facial disfigurement in one country results in stigmatization of the individual; in another, it may be regarded as a sign of beauty or even supernatural powers. American adolescents with some physical blemishes may be rejected by their peers, but in some societies scarring marks or tattoos are done for "beauty." Obesity is often scorned in contemporary Western society, yet formerly the institution of the "fattening house" among chieftains and royal families in parts of Africa was considered important in producing more beautiful women. Whereas the physical accompaniments of old age may be dreaded and scorned in one society, advanced age is viewed as the ultimate stage of human wisdom and power in another. In old China the feet of a Chinese noblewoman were so bound that she could not walk, but she was not considered to be physically handicapped because this was regarded positively.

Clearly, then, disability is a social rather than a mere behavioral or biological fact, and it is defined by societal reaction. One study traced the historical development of the idea that "a sound mind is in a sound body," and it was found that the physically disabled have been rejected throughout human history and in almost all cultures.[24] Another study showed that on a scale of 1 to 21, ex-prisoners and the mentally ill were placed at positions 18 and 21, respectively, in social acceptance, the high numbers connoting low acceptance in this range scale.[25] What may be perhaps even more enlightening is that the respondents were willing to put blindness (7), deafness (8), old age (11), and cerebral palsy (15) near the more conventional deviant categories in undesirability.

The role of societal reaction in the definition of deviance can be illustrated with the blind, the mentally retarded, the visibly physically handicapped, the obese, and stutterers. In each of these categories the role of cultural definition or socialization in the societal reaction to what is basically a physical or physiological problem is quite clear.

The Blind

As with all physical disabilities, the task of estimating the number of blind persons in the United States is complicated because of the widely divergent definitions of blindness, the problem of locating and identifying blind individuals, and the complex social factors associated with the meaning of blindness to the handicapped themselves. For these reasons estimates of the number of blind persons range from somewhat less than a half a million to more than a million and a half, including persons whose vision is sufficiently impaired to be classified as legally blind, although many included in the higher figure are not so classified.[26] Some of this discrepancy in the estimates is due to the confusing and sometimes arbitrary definition of blindness. Three categories of blindness are used: (1) totally blind—the total absence of any light

---

[24]Lee Meyerson, "Physical Disability as a Social Psychological Problem," in Edward Sagarin, ed., *The Other Minorities* (Boston: Ginn, 1971), pp. 205–210.

[25]"The Undesirables," *Human Behavior,* story No. 26, January–February 1972.

[26]Frances A. Koestler, *The Unseen Minority: A Social History of Blindness in the United States* (New York: David McKay, 1976), p. 46.

or image perception; (2) legal blindness—central visual acuity of 20/200 in the better eye with corrective lenses and the central visual field so restricted that the individual can see only objects within a 20 degree arc; and (3) functional blindness—inability to read ordinary newspaper print even with perfectly fitted glasses.[27] Because of these rather technical distinctions, most persons refer to "blind" persons as those who are totally or nearly totally blind, that is, the absence of any light, and the "visually impaired," or those with some lesser but serious visual deficiency.[28]

The blind have long been one of the most conspicuous groups of disabled persons. As much of human expressive behavior centers on the eyes, it is extremely disturbing to others when they do not function properly. Various behavior mannerisms increase this visibility, for example,

> odd postures, rocking, moving the head rhythmically, poking and rubbing the eyes, exploring bodily appendages and orifices, feeling and snapping objects, groping and fluttering the hands in front of the eyes. Dark glasses and thick lenses which magnify the eyes, canes, seeing-eye and guide dogs, and other mechanical aids also make the blind more noticeable in public places.[29]

Historically the blind have traditionally been relegated to inferior roles as outcasts and beggars; often giving alms to blind beggars was treated as a means of gaining religious merit, the begging blind even saying prayers for the givers. In Europe under Queen Elizabeth I attempts were made to work out a more systematic poor relief system and to repress the numerous beggars of various types, including the blind. The blind were grouped with paupers, orphan children, and mentally disordered persons and remained so until the specialization of welfare services which developed in the eighteenth and nineteenth centuries for different types of dependents.[30] With the urbanization and industrialization of the nineteenth century the blind assumed a different type of stigmatized reaction.

> The humanitarianism and organized philanthropy of the second half of the century in England and the United States introduced the conception of character defect as a middle-class explanation of pauperism, which had the concomitant result of associating physical defect with personality weakness and lack of self-resolution. This became the contemporary variant of the ancient idea of the origins of blindness in sin. At the same time the humanitarian movement was responsible for the special regard for the blind which gave them a more secure relief status than other dependent groups. It was also middle-class interest and concern with methods of restoring the self-reliance of the individual which led to the creation of special schools for the blind and to the generalized convictions of their educability and employability.[31]

Today there are various public stereotypes of the blind, which include beliefs of "helplessness, docility, dependency, melancholia, aestheticism, and serious-mindedness."[32] More than anything, however, is the general stigma associated with blindness.

---

[27]Koestler, pp. 45–46.
[28]Koestler, p. 52.
[29]From *Social Pathology* by Edwin Lemert. Copyright © 1951 by McGraw-Hill, Inc. Used with permission of McGraw-Hill Book Company.
[30]Lemert, *Social Pathology,* p. 113. See also Koestler.
[31]Lemert, *Social Pathology,* p. 114. Copyright © 1951 by McGraw-Hill, Inc. Used with permission of McGraw-Hill Book Company.
[32]Scott, p. 21. Also see Koestler, pp. 1–12.

Blindness is a stigma, carrying with it a series of moral imputations about character and personality. The stereotypical beliefs I have discussed lead normal people to feel that the blind are different: the fact that blindness is a stigma leads them to regard blind men as their physical, psychological, moral, and emotional inferiors. Blindness is therefore a trait that discredits a man by spoiling both his identity and his respectability. When a person with a stigma encounters a normal person, barriers are created between them. These barriers, though symbolic, are often impenetrable. They produce a kind of "moving away," much like the action of two magnetized particles of metal whose similar poles have been matched. These avoidance reactions are often induced by a fear that direct contact with a blind person may be contaminating, or that the stigmatized person will somehow inflict physical or psychic damage. . . . The effects of these reactions on a blind man are profound. Even though he thinks of himself as a normal person, he recognizes that most others do not really accept him, nor are they willing or ready to deal with him on a equal footing. . . . The stigma of blindness makes problematic the integrity of the blind man as an acceptable human being. Because those who see impute inferiority, the blind man cannot ignore this and is forced to defend himself.[33]

The definition of a person as "blind" can lead to the individual's being segregated from others. This sense of being segregated is indicated by the reactions of a newly blinded girl who visited the Lighthouse, an institution for the blind, on leaving the hospital.

My questions about a guide dog were politely turned aside. Another sighted worker took me in tow to show me around. We visited the Braille library; the classrooms; the clubrooms where the blind members of the music and dramatic groups meet; the recreation hall where on festive occasions the blind dance with the blind; the bowling alleys where the blind play together; the cafeteria, where all the blind gather to eat together; the huge workshops where the blind earn a subsistence income by making mops and brooms, weaving rugs, caning chairs. As we moved from room to room, I could hear the shuffling of feet, the muted voices, the tap-tap-tapping of canes. Here was the safe, segregated world of the sightless—a completely different world, I was assured by the social worker, from the one I had just left. . . . I was expected to join this world. To give up my profession and to earn my living making mops. The Lighthouse would be happy to teach me how to make mops. I was to spend the rest of my life making mops with other blind people, eating with other blind people, dancing with other blind people. I became nauseated with fear, as the picture grew in my mind. Never had I come upon such destructive segregation.[34]

The Mentally Retarded

The exact number of mentally retarded persons in the United States is not known, nor is it possible to determine exactly which persons could be so classified in view of the wide variations in the meaning of intelligence and how it is currently measured. There is an enormous amount of literature on both these questions, and while reliance for the most part is put on the determination of the IQ, it is commonly agreed that these

---

[33]Scott, pp. 24–25, © 1969 by Russell Sage Foundation, New York.
[34]T. Keitlen and N. Lobsenz, *Farewell to Fear* (New York: Avon Books, 1962), pp. 37–38, as quoted by Goffman, p. 37.

tests are both "relative" and "fallible." While some cases are obvious, difficulties arise in those cases that are not severe. The President's Panel on Mental Retardation in 1961 concluded that approximately 3 percent of the total population is mentally retarded, with 150,000 mental retardates being born each year.[35] The study did estimate, however, that most of these persons are not "profoundly, severely, or even moderately" retarded, but only mildly so, with IQ's between 55 and 70.

Of all human assets, the ability to think (plan and arrange one's life, manage one's affairs) is probably the greatest, as well as the most cherished. Those who are found wanting in these attributes because they lack the mental capacity for them experience one of the most devastating of all stigmata, at least in modern Western cultures. While a general lack of intellectual competence is not immediately evident in many cases, that is, for persons who are not severely retarded, their stigma is great and their efforts to deny their conditions are endless and elaborate.

> No other stigma is as basic as mental retardation in the sense that a person so labeled is thought to be so completely lacking in basic competence. Other stigmatized persons typically retain some competencies, limited though they may be, but the retarded person has none left to him. He is, by definition, incompetent to manage *any* of his affairs. And, unlike the psychotic, who at times may be considered (and, in fact, may be) competent to manage his practical affairs, the mental retardate is *forever* doomed to his condition. As everyone "knows," including the ex-patients, mental retardation is irremediable. There is no cure, no hope, no future. If you are once a mental retardate, you remain one always.[36]

The nature of the deviation of mental retardation and the societal reaction to this deviation is related to Goffman's distinction between stigma that has the character of "evidentness" or visibility as contrasted with "obtrusiveness" which interferes with social interaction.[37] In this frame of reference Edgerton has commented about mental retardates in his study of those who had been patients in an institution for the feeble-minded.

> The incompetence of these former patients should not be particularly evident, at least not "at a glance." Their physcial appearance is not distinctive and they appear to be able to move through most public places without revealing any telltale signs of their stigma. In this sense, then, their incompetence is not "evident." They remain "unknown about" in most of their superficial, casual, and brief appearances in the normal world. However, they do not escape detection when their public exposure becomes face-to-face, when it is prolonged, or when they must deal with problematic social situations. In such instances the former patient is found out; his incompetence becomes quite evident.
>
> Once this incompetence is recognized, it becomes obtrusive in Goffman's sense of interfering with the flow of interaction. It almost inevitably results in reduction of all subsequent interaction to a less complex level than the normal person would otherwise have attempted. For example, the normal person who becomes aware of the incompetence of the former patient regularly switches his mode of speech to a condescending tone and a simplified content. The normal person "talks down" and sometimes even attempts

[35]Edgerton, p. 5.

[36]Edgerton, p. 207. Copyright 1967 by The Regents of the University of California; reprinted by permission of the University of California Press. Also see Jane R. Mercer, *Labeling the Retarded* (Berkeley: University of California Press, 1973).

[37]Goffman, pp. 48–49.

a form of "baby talk" as might a colonial Englishman in talking to "native" servants. There is also a tendency for the normal person to speak both more slowly and more loudly than he ordinarily would. Interaction is reduced to a plane upon which the normal person asks few questions, utilizes the simplest possible vocabulary, avoids complexities of humor, and assumes that the former patient has almost no knowledge of what is commonplace, much less what is intricate, in the world. Furthermore, since the normal person generally wishes not to embarrass the retardate, he exercises conspicuous tact. The result is a slowing down of interaction to the point of virtual cessation. . . . the most conspicuous incompetence of these former patients occurs where space and time, and the numbers that relate to these matters, are concerned. As was demonstrated again and again in the course of this study, the ex-patients were most incompetent when required to deal with spatial, temporal, and numerical relationships.

It is in this sense that we must evaluate the words of the ex-patient: "Most of us people that was at the colony just can't figure. . . . Outside you gotta learn to figure or you'll go down the old pot. Seems like most of us go down the pot."[38]

To be regarded by others as a mentally retarded person is such an extreme stigma that there are many consequences. One writer pointed out that when a person of low intellectual capacity gets into trouble it is rather automatically attributed to his "mental defect," while those of "normal intelligence" are not regarded as having acted because of anything special when they get into similar difficulties.[39] The comments of former inmates of a hospital for the mentally retarded express this as follows:[40]

When I got out of that place it was horrible. I knew everybody was looking at me and thinking that it was true what they thought I was. I couldn't stand for people to think that about me. That's a terrible thing for people to think. Nobody could stand to have people thinking about them like that.

I don't believe that anyone from the hospital has it easy outside. There's problems from being in that place. I mean with people you meet. They take me as if I'm not a smart person. That's what makes me so provoked. And I mean they act like I don't understand things, which I do understand things. That's a terrible thing; I'd never do that to anybody. I don't know why I have to suffer like this. Sometimes I'd rather be dead than have people act like I'm not a smart person.

The Visibly Physically Handicapped

Persons who have visible physical handicaps from birth or by accident or illness include individuals born with a physical deformity, persons who have lost a limb through illness or accident, burn victims, or individuals who have become partially or totally paralyzed in some manner. Depending upon the severity of the handicap and

[38]Edgerton, pp. 215–217. Copyright 1967 by The Regents of the University of California; reprinted by permission of the University of California Press.
[39]L. A. Dexter, "A Social Theory of Mental Deficiency," *American Journal of Mental Deficiency,* 62 (1968), 923.
[40]Case material from Edgerton, p. 206. Copyright 1967 by The Regents of the University of California; reprinted by permission of the University of California Press.

the individual's or society's reaction to it, this person is likely to be regarded as a deviant, particularly in a society that tends to put great emphasis on physical health and attractiveness. In this sense, "someone who perceives himself/herself and is perceived by others as unable to meet the demands or expectations of a particular situation because of some physical impairment—i.e., an anatomical and/or a physiological abnormality" is considered a physically handicapped person.[41]

Societies have commonly separated the pronounced cripple from "normal" persons, and this has resulted in varying degrees of isolation, persecution, and ridicule. The blind, the crippled, the lepers traditionally have been the beggars. Among many preliterate societies newborn crippled infants were commonly exposed to the elements to perish. In ancient Sparta deformed children were eliminated from the society in order that the perfection of the state might be achieved. In general, the attitude of many societies has been to treat a physical deformity as a blight sent by God or as a punishment for having sinned. According to Hebraic law, for example, physical abnormalities were signs of physical degradation, and cripples were specifically prohibited from going near the temple. The Bible contains many specific passages:

> For whatsoever man he be that hath a blemish, he shall not approach: A blind man, or a lame, or he that hath a flat nose, or anything superfluous, or a man that is broken-footed, or broken-handed, or crookback, or a dwarf: or that hath a blemish in his eye, or be scurvy or scabbed, or hath his stones broken: No man that hath a blemish of the seed of Aaron the priest shall come nigh to offer the offerings of the Lord made by fire; he hath a blemish; he shall not come nigh to offer the bread of his God. He shall eat the bread of his God, both of the most holy, and of the holy: Only he shall not go in unto the vail, nor come nigh unto the altar, because he hath a blemish: that he profane not my sanctuaries: for I the Lord do sanctify them.[42]

Cripples were often regarded with ridicule during the Middle Ages, and they frequently served as court jesters. During the sixteenth and seventeenth centuries it was thought that cripples had an evil spirit which had deformed their bodies, and many cripples were burned as witches: others became beggars. Some reflection of the attitudes at that time toward the evil nature of cripples is reflected in Shakespeare's plays. These views were later reflected in other literary works which linked the body and mind, as Victor Hugo did in *The Hunchback of Notre Dame*.

Even today, the individual with a visibly deformed body is regarded, to a certain degree, as being apart from other human beings and is often looked at with pity or repulsion. In a 1972 study the amputee, the paraplegic, and the hunchback were ranked high as undesirables.[43] Regardless of his desire to take part in the activities of a larger community, the cripple learns that he has been offered "a particular role that society expects him to play."[44] Cripples face problems in connection with their occupations, their courtship, and their general social participation. Seldom, for example, are crippled persons found as sales personnel in stores or in similar positions

---

[41]Teresa E. Levitin, "Deviants as Active Participants in the Labeling Process: The Visibly Handicapped," *Social Problems,* 22 (1975), 549.
[42]Leviticus 21:16–23.
[43]"The Undesirables."
[44]Leonard Kriegel, "Uncle Tom and Tiny Tim: Some Reflections in the Cripple as Negro," in Sagarin, pp. 165–183.

where the public might become prejudiced because of their external appearance. In reference to a polio victim, one researcher notes that "society is made somewhat uncomfortable by his presence. It treats him as if he were an errant, rather ugly little schoolboy."[45] A crippled girl has written:

> When . . . I began to walk out alone in the streets of our town . . . I found then that wherever I had to pass three or four children together on the sidewalk, if I happened to be alone, they would shout at me. . . . Sometimes they even ran after me, shouting and jeering. This was something I didn't know how to face, and it seemed as if I couldn't bear it. . . . For awhile those encounters in the street filled me with a cold dread of all unknown children. . . . One day I suddenly realized that I had become so self-conscious and afraid of all strange children that, like animals, they knew I was afraid, so that even the mildest and most amiable of them were automatically prompted to derision by my own shrinking and dread.[46]

The Obese

Generally speaking, in the Western world whenever obese "people have existed and whenever a literature has reflected aspects of the lives and values of the period, a record has been left of the low regard usually held for the obese by the thinner and clearly more virtuous observer."[47] Highly visible obese persons are frequently perceived as deviants, encountering strong societal reaction.[48] "People who are not fat have attitudes, mostly hostile, toward those who are. People who are fat have attitudes, mostly self-deprecatory, toward themselves."[49] They often suffer great social stigma because they make other members of a group feel "contaminated" by association with them. This combination may produce a "formidable barrier to acceptance."[50] "Visible contact with stigmatized persons is marked by contamination although the same person may be appreciated—at a price—if witnesses are excluded. For example, an overweight boy may be kept out of a ball game but asked over the phone for the solution to a mathematical problem."[51]

Attitudes of rejection of obese persons are built into the culture and they are formed at an early age. When various drawings of children with deformities of various types were shown, in one study, to 10- and 11-year-old children who were then asked to indicate their preferences in selecting these children as friends, the majority selected the obese child as their last choice.[52] The drawings also depicted a normal child, a child with crutches and a brace on one leg, one confined to a wheelchair, one with an

---

[45]Kriegel, p. 170.
[46]Quoted in Goffman, p. 17.
[47]Mayer, p. 84.
[48]George L. Maddox, Kurt W. Back, and Veronica R. Liederman, "Overweight as Social Deviance and Social Disability," *Journal of Health and Social Behavior,* 9 (1968), 287–298.
[49]Mayer, p. 91.
[50]See Cahnman, "The Stigma of Obesity."
[51]Cahnman, "The Stigma of Obesity," p. 297.
[52]Stephen A. Richardson, Norman Goodman, Albert H. Hastorf, and Sanford M. Dornbush, "Cultural Uniformity in Reaction to Physical Disabilities," *American Sociological Review,* 26 (1961), 241–247; and by the same authors, "Variant Reactions to Physical Disabilities," *American Sociological Review,* 28 (1963), 429—435.

amputated forearm, and one with a facial disfigurement. "However, there was a significant difference among the sexes: boys were somewhat more wary of the amputated child than of the obese child, while girls consistently ranked the obese child last."[53] Obese persons have made the following comments about societal reactions to them:

> I feel that this was one of the main reasons why I detested school and couldn't wait to get home after classes. I realized that to be "fat" was considered weak and ugly by many of my classmates. I was unable to interact with my classmates because of this barrier that stood in my way, and thus, I was not part of "the group" in school even though I wanted to be.

> The kids who didn't know me yelled out "fatty" when I passed. People either laughed at me or pitied me.

> When I applied for a job at the A & P Tea Company, the interviewer told me I would have to lose weight. He said it won't look right for the company to have a lot of overweight people as checkers. I felt that he was discriminating against me as my weight wasn't related to my ability to work as a checker. I did get the job, though, and this is when I began to feel guilty about my size.[54]

At one time it was the case that in addition to interfering with a girl's employment and marriage possibilities, obesity may have also interfered with her admission to a more socially prestigious college. A study done in the high schools of a middle-class suburban community in New England and in the first year class of students in one of the Ivy League or Seven Sister colleges in 1964 found that there were twice as many obese persons in the high school female population as in the college female population, with a smaller but still considerable difference for the boys.[55] Correspondingly, two thirds more of the girls who were not obese went to college following high school graduation than the obese, and only three fifths as many nonobese girls than obese went to work without further training following high school.

> There was no significant difference for females as well as for males regarding motivation to attend high-ranking colleges, academic performance, and social class, whether they were obese or non-obese. The New England School Study permits the conclusion that obesity, especially as far as girls are concerned, is not so much a mark of low SES (socioeconomic status) as a condemnation of it.[56]

The attitude toward obesity has a moral connotation, the individual being presented as "gluttonous" and unwilling to control his behavior regardless of the consequences. Many people feel that in a way they are getting what is coming to them, that they could have prevented the problem. "The obese teenager is thus doubly and trebly disadvantaged: (1) because he is discriminated against; (2) because he is made to understand that he deserves it; and (3) because he comes to accept his treatment as

---

[53]Cahnman, "The Stigma of Obesity," pp. 295–296, with reference to studies by Richardson *et al.*
[54]Excerpts from Cahnman, "The Stigma of Obesity," © *The Sociological Quarterly.*
[55]*See* Helen Channing and Jean Mayer, "Obesity—Its Possible Effect on College Acceptance," *New England Journal of Medicine*, 275 (1966), 1172–1174.
[56]Cahnman, "The Stigma of Obesity," p. 290, © *The Sociological Quarterly.*

just.''[57] The result is that he learns to live with it, being unable to escape it. ''He becomes timidly withdrawn, or eager to please, or tolerant of abuse. He may escape into intellectual pursuits, assume the role of a funny character, resort to empty boasting, or submit to spells of despondency.''[58]

The Stutterer

Stuttering is one form of speech disorder, along with other speech disorders which includes lisping, cleft palate speech, stammering, and atypical pitch.[59] These disorders involve problems of articulation, rhythm, and phonation. Stuttering is flow of speech which is abnormally interrupted by a prolongation of sounds, interjection of sounds or words, and unduly prolonged pauses.[60] From the standpoint of others, the stutterer does not measure up to normative definitions of proper speech in the communication process. While nearly all stutterers can communicate what they have in mind they do not do so in the normal manner. Consequently, societal reaction to those who stutter may be strong, and this reaction in turn enhances the stutterer's insecurity, which itself then tends to increase the stuttering. One writer described the stutterer's problem:

> We who stutter speak only when we must. We hide our defect, often so successfully that our intimates are surprised when in an unguarded moment, a word suddenly runs away with our tongues and we blunt and blat and grimace and choke until finally the spasm is over and we open our eyes to view the wreckage.[61]

In addition to being subjected to ridicule and laughter, the stutterer may become the butt of crude practical jokes. Lemert points out that laughter and amusement are more often provoked by the stutterer than is hostility or deep sympathy, but that added to these is ''a degree of embarrassment and irritation, prevalent among those who empathize the reactions of the stutterer. This is perceived overtly in the impulsive tendency of a stutterer's auditors to supply words and finish sentences for him, or in other cases looking away and breaking eye contact with the person as he speaks.''[62] The stutterer may have difficulty in finding employment, as even the job interview may be a great hazard for him. The child who stutters has difficulties with his peer group and with those teachers who find the situation so frustrating that they may even excuse the child from performing in class.

> The experiences of the stuttering child in his peer age group are much more likely to be traumatic ones, in contrast to the sheltering he receives in the family. Small children at best are only partially socialized. Their reactions to deviants in their group are simple, direct, and uninhibited, and they are capable of great cruelty to handicapped play-mates—especially in the absence of supervision. In play situations they mock and mimic

---

[57]Cahnman, ''The Stigma of Obesity,'' p. 294.

[58]Cahnman, ''The Stigma of Obesity,'' pp. 294–295.

[59]C. van Riper, *Speech Correction: Principles and Methods,* 4th ed. (Englewood Cliffs, N.J.: Prentice-Hall 1963).

[60]Wendell Johnson, *Speech Handicapped Children,* 3d ed. (New York: Harper & Row, 1967); and Wendell Johnson, *Stuttering in Children and Adults* (Minneapolis: University of Minnesota Press, 1955).

[61]C. van Riper, *Do You Stutter?* (New York: Harper & Row, 1939), p. 601.

[62]Lemert, *Social Pathology,* p. 153.

the child with a speech handicap and use him as the object of their aggressions in many other ways. It is in the play group that nicknames and trait labels are invented and applied to its members, and it is there that sharply invidious distinctions are drawn between the deviant and the rest of the group.[63]

SELF-REACTION OF THE PHYSICALLY DISABLED

Basically there are three ways in which an individual may react to the public labeling of his disability.[64] He can deny its existence, he can accept it, or he can seek indirect benefits from the situation. Those individuals who have always put a singularly high value on their appearances tend to view physical handicaps as misfortunes or even personal disasters. The most likely reaction to an incurred disability in this case is denial of its existence. Some persons desperately attempt to deny the situation and to remain "normal" and nondisabled, a practice common among the mentally retarded.[65] Deaf persons may pretend to hear, and the stutterer often tries to "mask" his speech behavior. The masking of a disability, for example, the wearing of an artificial leg or arm by a handicapped person, does not hide the fact from the person himself that he is disabled, nor does it hide it from certain significant others. The married person with an artificial leg is always aware that his wife knows he is not a "whole person."

Some may view their incapacitated state as acceptable although not ideal. They are able to accept their disabilities without being plunged into hopelessness and despair. Such individuals feel that they are worthwhile persons who can go on living a full life by capitalizing on their unchanged abilities and minimizing what they can no longer do. Often it is not an immediate response to labeling but rather one that occurs after the individual has passed through the denial or despairing period. Kriegel maintains that such acceptance is the only "socially rewarding" attitude:

> For no matter how limited his functioning in the society of normals may be, there are certain definitive guidelines that he is offered. Once he has accepted being pigeonholed by society, he finds that he is safe as long as he is willing to live within the boundaries of his categorization. To break out of its confines calls for an act of will of which he may already be incapable. Should he choose to resist, he will probably discover that he has inflamed those who see themselves as kind and tolerant.[66]

A third category of disabled persons consists of those who appear to adapt to the changes of disability all too eagerly and painlessly and seek benefits that accrue from it. Physical limitations and restrictions that could be overcome are maximized: remaining capacities are minimized. Though this disabled person has been legitimately

---

[63]Lemert, *Social Pathology,* p. 157. Copyright © 1951 by McGraw-Hill, Inc. Used with permission of McGraw-Hill Book Company.
[64]Safilios-Rothschild.
[65]See John G. Cull and Richard E. Hardy, "The Meaning of Disability," in Richard E. Hardy and John G. Cull, eds., *Mental Retardation and Physical Disability* (Springfield, Ill.: Charles C Thomas, 1974), p. 11.
[66]Kriegel, p. 182.

labeled, he tends to cultivate secondary and "illegitimate" gains from his status. Obese people may win affection by fawning for attention. One obese girl said: "I felt my weight was not the real problem, that I just used it to cover some kind of horrible, basic flaw, which if uncovered, would be too unsightly to view and would prove people right in not accepting me. As a result, I have always demanded that people liked me, no matter how disgusted they may have been by my moaning for attention."[67] In other cases, disabled persons may even be motivated to resist medical treatment or rehabilitation therapy if they perceive that this care could bring about a sufficient improvement in their conditions that they could be required to return to their undesirable predisability status.

Stereotyping simplifies interaction for the nondisabled when they meet disabled persons and assessment of the disabled tends to stop at the other's perception of his disability. From then on communication tends to be shaped on that basis. This has great effect on the individual, for example, in the case of the blind, for "people who can see come to behave as though they cannot, and from so heterogeneous a population such homogeneity is eventually created."[68] The blind must defend the self from imputations of moral, psychological, and social uniformity.

> The norms that govern the conduct of the ordinary relationship of everyday life depend enormously on vision. When one of the actors in an encounter is blind, the situation is infused with ambiguity and uncertainty. Tensions arise over how to proceed, how to project a self-image, and how to evaluate the image projected by the other. The idiosyncratic responses of the seeing to this situation contribute to the blind man's socialization by reinforcing his conviction that he is different. Furthermore, his blindness denies him the honest, direct feedback essential to the development of a realistic self-concept.[69]

Members of different social class and cultural subgroups may vary in their reactions to types of disability according to functional considerations. Societal labels and reactions may be a function of a group's needs and values. Lower-class children have been found to rate physical disabilities as most damaging, for these children depend upon physical prowess in order to survive.[70] Middle-class children feel that cosmetic disabilities are more traumatic: they are not as dependent on physical prowess, but appearance is an important attribute to them.

Legitimation of the disability of a family member may help to hold a family together. The inclusion of a disabled person exerts both positive and negative effects on the functioning of the family group. Members may be united in their care and concern for the disabled person. When that person dies or leaves the home, other family relationships may be significantly altered also. In some cases, however, an aged member of the family or a mentally retarded child may act as a scapegoat for other family problems. Instead of expressing rage and frustration against each other, the scapegoat may receive it and thereby enable a modicum of stability to pervade the other family relationships.

---

[67]Cahnman, "The Stigma of Overweight—Six Autobiographies," p. 16.
[68]Scott, p. 43.
[69]Scott, p. 118, © 1969 by Russell Sage Foundation, New York.
[70]E. Chigier and Mary Chigier, "Attitude to Disability of Children in the Multicultural Society of Israel," *Journal of Health and Social Behavior,* 9 (1968), 310–317.

SECONDARY OR "CAREER" DISABILITY

The disabled person, once he is labeled, is constantly made aware of his status of being "different." In essence, he becomes signified, registered, and derogated just as any other recognized deviant.[71] Career disability or secondary deviance is role adaptation rather than a new role formation. Once the disability is legitimated or labeled by social control agents and others, an individual's role expectations may change to correspond with the judged extremity or seriousness of impairment. Societal reaction is crucial in the process of forming a stable or secondary deviance pattern of disabled behavior, and this social process can be instrumental in the creation of a new self-concept. One obese boy explained how he felt: "I was about ten or eleven. A boy in my class called me a name. He was saying something but it ended with 'fatty.' It was really a gradual process. Slowly it accumulated until the full realization that I was different occurred."[72] Once formed, it is difficult for persons so stereotyped to break away from the label.

The labeling process is often subtle in nature. It is often not what people say that disturbs, but rather "what is subtly, though dramatically, communicated to them through facial expression and behavior."[73] The labeling reaction of others may take the form of being deviant through the kindnesses and concerns of those around him.[74] On the other hand, the labeling may occur when the disabled person realizes that he cannot complete certain tasks by himself and that he must ask those around him for help.[75] A polio victim elaborates: "Almost everyone *did* things for me—except, of course, to see me. For to see me as a individual *me,* that kind of personal encounter that results in a stripping away of stereotype and symbol and a willingness to accept the humanity of the other, at whatever the personal cost. . . ."[76]

Professionals and Agencies

Interactions with professional persons such as doctors, counselors, and social workers are extremely significant in the shaping of a disabled person's self-concept and his movement to secondary deviance. Doctors, for example, have the responsibility of revealing the extent of the disability to a patient, speech therapists may remove stutterers from regular school groups and put them into special classes, and the social worker may advise the person with "poor" eyesight that he is blind. One study of the mentally retarded points out the dangers of psychologists socially diagnosing children as mentally retarded based on IQ tests that are constructed in such a way—or in any case have the effect—that children who are white and usually from the middle class

---

[71]David Matza, *Becoming Deviant* (Englewood Cliffs, N.J.: Prentice-Hall, 1969).
[72]Cahnman, "The Stigma of Overweight—Six Autobiographies," p. 5.
[73]Jules Barron, "Physical Handicap and Personality: A Study of the Seen vs. the Unseen Disabilities," *Archives of Physical Medicine and Rehabilitation,* 36 (1955), 639.
[74]Marvin Hyman, "Disability and Patient's Perceptions of Preferential Treatment: Some Preliminary Findings, " *Journal of Chronic Diseases,* 24 (1971), 329–342.
[75]Myerson, pp. 205–210.
[76]Kriegel, p. 175.

tend to score higher.[77] If the average scores of the white children are socially defined as "normal," many children from minority groups automatically fall into a lower than normal category, thereby increasing their chances of being identified as retarded. Mercer claims that the testing process itself is the most important structural factor contributing to the disproportionate labeling of children as mentally retarded. While the intelligence test may be the diagnostic tool with which to identify retardation, since most operational definitions of retardation select some relatively arbitrary IQ as a cutoff, the detection of the condition should not be confused with the condition itself.

Such discretionary power and action on the part of formal agents and agencies are especially significant in the case of those disabilities for which monetary compensation or support is provided. The legitimated disabled person acquires a new status of marginality and new standards for future role performance as the "price" that must be paid for income maintenance or other benefits. These agents may accept or reject the claim for exemption from conventional vocational demands.

> The accredited disabled individual is excused from his role failure by legitimization and may be provided with alternative patterns of behavior for meeting the organizational requirements for care, rehabilitation, employment, or income maintenance. His behavior will also be organized into a pattern of secondary deviations, relative to the general norms, but based on alternative patterns of expected behavior.[78]

Interactions with these professional groups are critical to the disabled person's future role status and self-conception, and the sheer chance selection of the agents may be important in the career of the person, as well as the actions of these agents "to report or not, to put it in the books or not, to refer here or there."[79] Scott has emphasized how such rehabilitative agencies are often significant in "making" men or women "blind."

> When those who have been screened into blindness agencies enter them, they may not be able to see at all or they may have serious difficulties with their vision. When they have been rehabilitated, they are all blind men. They have learned the attitudes and behavior patterns that professional blindness workers believe blind people should have. In the intensive face-to-face relationships between blindness workers and clients that make up the rehabilitation process, the blind person is rewarded for adopting a view of himself that is consistent with his rehabilitators' view of him and punished for clinging to other self-conceptions. He is told that he is "insightful" when he comes to describe his problems and his personality as his rehabilitators view them, and he is said to be "blocking" or "resisting" when he does not. Indeed, passage through the blindness system is determined in part by his willingness to adopt the experts' views about self.
> Gradually, over time, the behavior of blind men comes to correspond with the assumptions and beliefs that blindness workers hold about blindness, whether these beliefs follow the restorative or the accommodative approach. The restorative approach assumes that blind people can lead independent and fulfilled lives in the outside world, but only if they first recognize and accept as final the fact that they are blind. The accommodative approach regards these objectives as noble but unrealistic for most blind

---

[77]Mercer.
[78]Haber and Smith, p. 92.
[79]Freidson, "Disability as Social Deviance," p. 90.

people. It holds that a more realistic objective is to provide environments to which blind people can accommodate with a minimum of effort. Such environments are created and sustained in many blindness agencies and in most sheltered workshops as well. Those of the blind who live in them can function well there, but in the process they become seriously maladjusted to the outside world.[80]

Many rehabilitation and other agencies involved in the prevention, treatment, and control of disabilities contribute much to the individuals themselves and to the community. Agency support, however, often depends upon the extent of the disabilities they serve: thus, increased numbers of accreditied disabled persons strengthen agency requests for additional staff and resources. A combination of such relative and arbitrary factors becomes extremely significant in engineering life-style changes in those individuals who are involved. Freidson points out that agencies for the physically handicapped, as well as prisons and mental hospitals, have been observed "to organize and stabilize deviant behavior into special roles, rather than eradicate it."[81] He concludes that many handicaps exist because they are defined as such by treatment personnel. "It is an imputed condition, and the imputation may or may not rest on the physical reality. Not all handicapped people are called handicapped or act like handicapped people."[82]

Subcultures and Groups

The formation and growth of subcultures are important for the maintenance of patterns of career deviance. Subcultures institutionalize customs, recruit new members, and provide support to members; as a result, they aid in the management of the deviant identity. Some groups are formal, such as those of the blind, the mute, and those with specific physical disabilities. They may hold regular meetings and conventions, and the groups generally serve as quasi-interest groups for their constituent members, those persons who commonly experience discrimination and prejudice in their dealings with the "normal" majority. Freidson maintains that groups of the disabled are formed as a result of their needs for self-defense because, like members of minority groups, they are not allowed to participate in the larger society.[83] Some specific functions of disability subcultures are to provide social and recreational outlets, to educate the public about the nature of particular disabilities, and to offer help in finding marriage partners and jobs.[84] In addition, these groups may lobby for protective legislation or equal rights, and they may solicit funds for research. In general, the emphasis is on changing the disabled themselves rather than on changing the society which has labeled and discriminated against them. Other informal groups arise spontaneously among patients who share a common waiting room in doctors' offices where they share information and offer mutual support.

Some research studies have shown that participation in a subculture enables an

[80]Scott, p. 119, © 1969 by Russell Sage Foundation, New York. Also see Koestler.
[81]Freidson, "Disability as Social Deviance," p. 87.
[82]Freidson, "Disability as Social Deviance," p. 74.
[83]Freidson, "Disability as Social Deviance," p. 74.
[84]Dee Wood Harper, Jr., "Socialization for the Aged Status among the Negro, French and non-French Subcultures of Louisiana," unpublished Ph.D. dissertation, Baton Rogue, Louisiana State University, 1967.

individual better to manage his disability. In some categories of disability, however, the options and psychological support associated with subcultural involvement are not open to the individual. Stutterers and obese individuals may on occasion belong to an organization with others like themselves, but they often do not closely associate with them and thus are much less likely to form specific subcultures. Despite the advantages associated with membership in subcultural groups, some individuals may choose to decline recruitment. There are certain disadvantages to subcultural participation which some people may wish to avoid. They include the admission that one is disabled, acknowledgment of the loss of former status, and the problem of learning new patterns of self-management.

Explanation of Disabilities

Some disabled persons are motivated to progress into a stabilized or secondary disabled status. Certain advantages may be attached to this status. An individual with slightly crippled limbs may sustain the identity of a cripple, despite his ability to ambulate on his own. As a cripple the individual is removed from his traditional responsibilities and has become dependent on others. Stuttering behavior may enable a person to avoid stressful social interaction situations. Hyman has described the functional side of accepting the deviant label: he states, "the hint of belongingness in the sick role implicit in preferential treatment by his associates leaves an especially strong mark on the patient and may persuade him that his physical state mandates a certain amount of disability."[85] It is probably true, however, that most individuals try to avoid being stereotyped as disabled persons if it is at all possible to do so.

Some disabled persons live off their disabilities and are also secondary or career deviants. They include, particularly, the blind and the crippled and, in many less developed countries in Asia, the leper. Begging is often lucrative, and many beggars are able to earn more than they would by working in a workshop for disabled persons. The beggar deliberately exploits the dependency role in order to profit from playing the role of a disabled person. Most of these persons have often received what rehabilitation and other services are available, have rejected continued programs, and have set out on their own as beggars. "They are held in great disdain by almost all workers for the blind and many blind people as well, who say they do great harm to the cause of bettering the position of the blind in society because they exploit, and thereby reinforce, stereotypic ideas about blindness."[86] Scott concludes:

> It is essential to recognize that the causes of this adaptation to blindness lie not only in the psychology of marginal individuals but in general reactions to blindness as well. If sighted persons did not pity the blind, or cut them off from the mainstream of society, or force them into positions of helplessness, or patronize them, begging could not exist. There would be no motivation to beg, and there would be no market for the beggar's product. In this sense, judgments about the seemingly immoral actions of beggars are incongruent with the responses to and treatment of blind persons by the sighted.[87]

[85]Hyman, "Disability and Patient's Perceptions of Preferential Treatment," p. 334.
[86]Scott, p. 110.
[87]Scott, p. 112, © 1969 by Russell Sage Foundation, New York. Also see M. V. Moorthy, ed., *Beggar Problems in Greater Bombay* (Bombay: Indian Conference of Social Work, 1959), p. 44, and M. V. Moorthy, ed., *The Beggar Problem in Metropolitan Delhi* (Delhi: Delhi School of Social Work, 1959).

Negative and Positive
Effects of Labeling

The evidence points to no invariate career path of deviance for the physically disabled any more than for those who have no disabilities but who are considered deviant in their behavior. Yet the labels used to denote the physically impaired are pejorative; the mockery of the disabled young by other children, the less active social life of obese adolescents, the myths and the stereotypes about the blind, the ridicule or shunning by others of the stutterer, and the occupational discrimination of the mentally retarded are but a few of the consequences of their conditions for these persons. The evidence points to still another result of the labeling process, one that can move some of them away from the sick role to other, conventional roles. A recent study of several groups that aid obese persons lose weight found that the use of labels encouraged them in their "normalization" processes. Specifically, "groups who used ex's [ex-obese persons, in this case] as change agents, all used strategies of identity stigmatization in order to facilitate normalization of members' behavior."[88] The use of labels in this context were therapeutic and did not have the effect of pushing the persons further into a deviant career path. Another study dealing with the visibly physically handicapped found that they were active participants in the labeling process and that they were able, through their behavior and verbalization, to negotiate the deviant label. Such disabled adults recognized the disvalued status that had resulted from their injuries or illnesses, but

> they vigorously and systematically tried to influence the content of their deviant label and role in ways most favorable to themselves. A major social problem for the handicapped is that normals tend to organize their perceptions and evaluations around the disability and to ignore the handicapped's many valued aspects and identities. These handicapped actively resisted such a social fate, but their preferred definitions and strategies varied with the duration of the disability (temporary or more permanent) and the type of encounter (sociable encounters and encounters with agents of social control).[89]

Perhaps more clearly than other forms of deviance, the physically handicapped are not considered to be deviant only from the actions of formal or informal labels. The labels alone do not create the physically handicapped individual; an objective reality does, whether it is blindness, obesity, or a crippling condition or disease. Informal labeling may have a more important effect with these persons than with other forms of deviance. Abundant evidence is found among cardiac patients, for example, that informal support and higher levels of integration of the deviant and his family and peers, following labeling, leads to a greater chance of recovery from, or more successful adaptation to, the physical condition.[90] Conversely, it might be argued that

---

[88]Barbara Laslett and Carol A. B. Warren "Losing Weight: The Organizational Promotion of Behavior Change," *Social Problems,* 23 (1975), 79. See also Carol A. B. Warren, "The Use of Stigmatized Labels in Conventionalizing Deviant Behavior," *Sociology and Social Research,* 58 (1974), 303–311.
[89]Levitin, p. 556.
[90]See, with cardiac patients in particular, Sydney Croog, Alberta Lipson, and Sol Levine, "Help Patterns in Severe Illness: The Roles of Kin Network, Non-Family Resources and Institutions," *Journal of Marriage and the Family,* 34 (1968), 32–41; Marvin Hyman, "Social Isolation and Performance in Rehabilitation," *Journal of Chronic Diseases,* 25 (1972), 85–97; and Thomas F. Garrity, "Vocational Adjustment after First Myocardial Infarction: Comparative Assessment of Several Variables Suggested in the Literature," *Social Science and Medicine,* 7 (1973), 705–717.

if this support is lacking, or, worse, if negative labels are attached to the individual, adaptation becomes increasingly difficult, even impossible under some circumstances. This support may be crucial in generating or reinforcing the deviant's motivation to move from the sick role into conventional, nondeviant, roles.[91]

The ambivalence with which most persons regard the physically and mentally handicapped thus tempers the conception persons have of these individuals as deviants and their conditions as deviance. They are, alternatively, loved and hated, pitied and scorned, feared and accepted, and found attractive and repelling. Freidson may be correct in claiming that deviance in disability is viewed as "conduct which violates sufficiently valued norms,"[92] but it must be recognized that most persons are willing to grant exemptions from the deviant label, particularly when the conduct in question (or the condition under review) is conceived in nonvoluntaristic terms. The sanctions imposed by society on the physically and mentally disabled are quite variable, and many are imposed in the context of therapy or help. Certain sanctions, such as the labeling discussed above, may provide effective measures of social control rather than mechanisms that insure the perpetuation of a deviant career. The question, of course, is under what conditions does the imposition of such labels lead to beneficial results, and when does it not.[93]

THE MANAGEMENT OF DISABILITY

The reactions of significant others like family and friends may engender so much stress in an individual that he is often required to develop management techniques. Riffenburgh has observed that "the problem of the blind individual in dealing with the sighted may be greater than the problem of dealing with the blindness itself."[94] The visibly disabled person may select from a variety of coping techniques.[95] He may be hypersensitive about his condition, deny his status, "normalize" his condition, withdraw from the world, identify with the dominant group and hate himself, become prejudiced against others with the same disability, become militant, attempt to make up for deficiencies by striving in other areas, or may retreat into a mental disorder. He may forget, conceal, or idolize normal standards, seek or reject group identification, or compensate for his disability as Lord Byron did for his clubfoot by becoming an illustrious poet and lover of some distinction.[96] This range of responses is similar to that which is available to anyone who is stigmatized.

---

[91]See G. Frank Lawlis, "Motivation: The Greatest Challenge to Rehabilitation," in A. Beatrix Cobb, ed., *Special Problems in Rehabilitation* (Springfield, Ill.: Charles C Thomas, 1974), pp. 346–366.

[92]Freidson, "Disability as Social Deviance," p. 73. See also Richard T. Smith, "Societal Reaction and Physical Disability: Contrasting Perspectives," in Walter R. Gove, ed., *The Labelling of Deviance: Evaluating a Perspective* (New York: Sage/Halsted, 1975), pp. 147–156.

[93]See, for example, Carol K. Whalen and Barbara Henker, "The Pitfalls of Politicalization: A Response to Conrad's 'The Discovery of Hyperkinesis: Notes on the Medicalization of Deviant Behavior,'" *Social Problems,* 24 (1977), 590–595.

[94]Ralph S. Riffenburgh, "The Psychology of Blindness," *Geriatrics,* 22 (1967), 127.

[95]Safilios-Rothschild.

[96]Wright, pp. 20–56.

Two problems emerge when one examines the question of disability management: first, when does disability become a problem for the individual, and, more important, how does the disabled manage his stigma? Goffman dealt with the first issue when he differentiated the "discredited" from the "discreditable."[97] The former refers to individuals whose disability is apparent or already known. The latter designates those disabled whose condition is neither known nor immediately visible. The more visible one's disability, the greater the management problem it presents for the individual; for example, a slight limp is less visible than an amputated limb. The person who limps experiences less discriminaton, for he is discreditable but not discredited.

The disabled employ a large variety of management techniques. They can attempt to pass and thus avoid "playing the deviant role entirely."[98] Thus they try to be accepted according to standards applied to normal persons; in order to be judged as normal they try to disguise their deviance.[99] Goffman has suggested another method, "covering," such as, for example, the wearing of dark glasses by blind persons. Covering differs from passing, since it requires that the individual acknowledge the existence of his stigma. Covering draws attention away from the disability, easing matters for people who know about it and concealing it from others.

Passing

There are many ways to pass, but the success of this technique depends upon the visibility of the stigma. A study of the mentally retarded, for example, concluded that without exception the mental retardate finds the label of his condition a "humiliating, frustrating, and discrediting stigma" and his own self-esteem so lowered that he would not be able to face life were he not able to build up strong defenses to his condition.[100] He must deny the implication of this public defamation. This defense includes, first, a complete denial of his condition and an acceptable number of "excuses" for his inadequacies: for example, his period of stay in an institution for the mentally retarded "prevented" him from going to school, he had been "put there" by persons of evil intent, and so on. In addition to hs denial of his condition, he builds up numerous means of passing. He cannot, and he does not, accept the official "fact" that he is or was retarded; he is totally unable to accept the self-knowledge of mental retardation. The mentally retarded cannot think that and maintain self-esteem which is vital to them, and thus passing and denial are vital.[101] While others, as Goffman has shown, are often able to face stigma with a laugh, the situation is far too serious for the mental retardate; he must make serious efforts to evade stigma through the deceptions of passing and denial which must proceed despite his defective brain.

> The ex-patient *must* take his intelligence very seriously, for he has been accused and found guilty of being so stupid that he was considered incompetent to manage his own life. As a consequence, he has been confined in an institution for the mentally incompe-

[97]Goffman.
[98]Freidson, "Disability as Social Deviance," p. 94.
[99]Fred Davis, *Passage through Crisis* (Indianapolis: Bobbs-Merrill, 1963).
[100]Edgerton.
[101]Edgerton, p. 205.

tent. . . . The stigma of having been adjudged a mental retardate is one which the ex-patients in this study reject as totally unacceptable. Hence, their lives are directed toward the fundamental purpose of denying that they are in fact mentally incompetent.[102]

Normalizing

Disabled persons can also normalize their deviance. This process requires that disabilities be explained in some manner. For instance, the physically handicapped person tells normal persons that he lives a "normal" life, or he may interject taboo words like "cripple" into the conversation. He may be especially attentive to the normal person's conversation, portray himself as comical or gifted, or surround himself with normal persons. Some, like the blind, for example, may work as respresentatives of organizations of disabled persons to explain their problems to others. The use of management techniques among lepers, for example, has often resulted in some patients becoming "public relations" persons who then help to educate the public on the truth about leprosy.[103] They minimize its crippling effects and generally disavow their deviant status. Despite the fact that they often can pass and thus avoid negative societal reaction, they may refuse to do so. This tactic is not without its difficulties, as has been pointed out:

> In "breaking through" many of the handicapped are confronted by a delicate paradox, particularly in those of their relationships which continue beyond the immediate occasion. Having disavowed deviance and induced the other to respond to him as he would to a normal, the problem then becomes one of sustaining the normalized definition in the face of many small amendments and qualifications that must frequently be made to it.[104]

One could cite many instances in which society recognizes physical disabilities among those who are interested in moving out of the sick role and into the conventional roles. Special physical arrangements are often made to help the physically handicapped students in a university, for example, but, once admitted, they are expected to perform on the same intellectual level as the nonhandicapped students and not to excuse poor performances due to their handicaps. Exceptions are made, of course, to this expectation depending upon the nature of the handicap and the sympathy of the university faculty and the administration, although the range of tolerance is less than might be supposed.

Coping

Persons with physical disabilities who repeatedly encounter the staring and questioning of normal persons develop various specific ways of coping with this situation. Wright has outlined three general categories of situations in which the "normal" person is thought by the disabled one to be an intruder.[105] First, the

---

[102]Edgerton, p. 145. Copyright 1967 by The Regents of the University of California; reprinted by permission of the University of California Press.
[103]Zachary Gusson and George S. Tracy, "Status Ideology and Adaptation to Stigmatized Illness: A Study of Leprosy," in Sagarin, pp. 242–262.
[104]Fred Davis, "Deviance Disavowal: The Management of Strained Interaction by the Visibly Handicapped," *Social Problems,* 9 (1961), 120–132.
[105]Wright, pp. 212–217.

recipient feels that the intruder, who is usually a stranger, is interested only in his disability, and he wishes to retaliate in a matter which will make the intruder feel foolish. He accomplishes this with biting sarcasm or through a dramatic prevarication. Second, the disabled person excludes the disability from the situation either through the "ostrich reaction" of completely running away (as children do) or pretending it does not exist or by redirecting the interaction course, for example, turning the conversation suddenly. In the third type of situation, the disabled manages to exclude the condition and preserve the relationship either through good-natured levity or by embarking upon a superficial conversation. In none of these situations does the person wish to talk about the deeper and more personal meanings of his condition; he simply wants to get out of the dilemma as best he can.

Disassociation

Another technique of deviance management has been termed "disassociation."[106] Davis defines disassociation as a retreat and a passive acceptance of the deviant role, a rejection of conventional roles and activities, which increases the likelihood of interacting with nondeviants. Handicapped children, for example, learn quickly that interaction with other children may be painful and is thus to be avoided if at all possible, if only to escape the stares and jokes; obese persons may reduce their social activities because they appear conspicuous to others. As a result, some physically handicapped persons may become angry and resent the nonhandicapped.[107] All of these reactions have as their purpose the desire to "avoid or remove the sting from the often negative, condescending, and deprecating attitudes of 'normals.'"[108]

Employment

Disability may be incurred before one enters the labor force, or it might develop after work patterns have been established. In some ways the person who has been disabled early in life is worse off; often he is discriminated against so that despite education and skill he may never find work which is commensurate with these abilities. Early disability thus often restricts one's entry into the labor force. When manpower needs are low it is particularly difficult for the disabled to find jobs. Partly for this reason, unemployment rates among the disabled tend to be higher than among the nondisabled. While the unemployment rate among the general population in the United States in the early 1970s was 5–6 percent, blind adults had a 30 percent unemployment rate, and rates for the deaf and epileptics ranged from 15 to 25 percent.[109] One study of 47 stutterers, mostly college educated, none of whom were over 34 years, revealed a concentration of job experiences in the unskilled and clerical categories.[110] A woman who has been handicapped from birth may have less chance

---

[106]Fred Davis, *Illness, Interaction and the Self* (Belmont, Calif.: Wadsworth, 1972), p. 107.
[107]For the importance of the "normal standard" in handicapped-normal relations, see D. L. Adler and T. Dembo, "Studies in Adjustment to Visible Injuries: Social Acceptance of the Injured," *Journal of Social Issues,* 4 (1948), 55–61.
[108]Davis, p. 107.
[109]*A Long, Long Way: A Program Guide for 1971–72,* President's Committee on Employment of the Handicapped. (Washington, D.C.: Government Printing Office, 1972), p. 15.
[110]Lemert, *Human Deviance, Social Problems and Social Control,* p. 165.

of marriage, partly because potential suitors doubt her ability to run a household satisfactorily.

On the other hand, the degree and effects of a disability which is incurred after initial entry into the labor force may be highly specific to the type of job. It appears that there are different probabilities of becoming disabled according to the type of job one holds. A greater proportion of accidents occurs among blue collar workers, more than half of these accidents occurring at work. In addition, postdisability participation depends upon the scarcity of one's skills and the general economic conditions. Men who are skilled, blue collar, middle aged, and white are more likely, therefore, to be able to adjust their disabilities to job requirements than are unskilled, older, lower-class minority group members or women. Moreover, the type of job may also determine how seriously a person defines his impairment and to what degree his job performance is affected by it. For example, what is a vocational handicap for one person may be a mere inconvenience for another. The loss of a left arm may incapacitate an assembly line worker, while it is of less long-term significance to a professor, who would be quite seriously handicapped, however, if something should happen to his speech.

"Hire the handicapped" campaigns are increasingly carried on as a means of opening up new job opportunities for those with physical disabilities. There is considerable evidence that failure to hire the aged and the physically and mentally handicapped represents a considerable loss for the business community and the larger economy. The retarded, for example, are often better able to perform repetitive and unskilled tasks on a more reliable basis than are other workers. Moreover, one study reported that 1 percent of retarded laundry workers were absent three days or more in a year, as compared with 30 percent of nonretarded workers.[111] While it may be true that individual disabled persons can be placed and that employers' attitudes may be changed, the bulk of the disabled will continue to suffer discrimination in employment. This is largely due to the fact that they will be competing with younger, nonhandicapped, normal people for scarce job resources in an age of automation, overpopulation, and general impersonality.

CONCLUSIONS

The central difference between physical disabilities and other forms of deviance is that a disability is not a behavior; it is a condition, and one over which the individual has no control. While criminals and drug addicts are said to choose these forms of deviance, the handicapped, the physiologically obese, and the mentally retarded are accorded a deviant status by factors outside their immediate control. Their statuses are ascribed, not achieved. However, the same general processes of deviance management are evidenced with these persons as are seen with criminal offenders, homosexuals, and the survivors of unsuccessful suicides—techniques designed to minimize the stigma and the negative sanctions that might otherwise result. In this chapter, too, as with prior chapters, the importance of the social role of the deviant, as well as the behavior, are noted. The role of being deviant differs from the commitment of a deviant act. The

---

[111]*A Long, Long Way,* p. 13.

latter denotes a behavior; the former, an organization of behavior and accompanying attitudes and values.

The study of physical disabilities is further instructive in illustrating an important conceptual matter in the study of deviance generally. As was seen in Chapter 1, the concept of deviance is best understood by reference to a set of rules (norms) whose violation is called deviance. The discussion of physical disabilities, however, indicates why it is often difficult to know exactly what the norms are. It is for this reason, in fact, that there is considerable ambivalence with respect to physical disabilities. It is known, however, that physical disabilities frequently elicit negative sanctions. Some of these sanctions are directed at the condition itself (for example, the ridicule of children of the obese), and some may be directed at the person's inability to redirect his action outside of the sick role (for example, the stutterer who rejects trained speech therapy). The study of the physically disabled shows how important the social control process is in determining what is and what is not deviant. Through the sanctioning process, social groups make known that one or another norm is being violated. If the particular norm is too subtle or too obscure to be identified, the sanctioning process itself indicates that something is deviant. Taylor has put it more strongly: "Deviance may only be spoken of when actual sanctions are seen to be administered by the group following certain behavior."[112] This statement may seem extreme, however, when one considers that some deviant acts and conditions are "well managed" and hidden from view from potential sanctioning agents.

The social control process may be helpful in determining what certain groups regard as deviant, but it is not the sanctioning process that creates the deviance in the first place. Rather, the deviance creates the social control, which in turn identifies the deviance for the group. The importance of the sanctioning, as pointed out in previous chapters, is that it may influence the deviant, the subsequent conduct, and the reactions of others to this conduct. It may facilitate the person's ability to play a particular role, a deviant role. The particularly sociological concept of deviance rests in its social qualities. "As a significant social entity, the 'deviant' is the occupant of a special role which is recognized and ordered in a process of interaction. If a person is not assigned to this role and not treated as deviant, he cannot be regarded sociologically as a deviant."[113] It is the social control process that defines this role. It is the role of a deviant that many of the physically handicapped play. They do so by virtue of their conditions and the reactions of others to these conditions. The fact that these occupants of the deviant role may be unwitting agents in the process makes both the role assignment and the deviant nature of the status more tenuous.

SELECTED REFERENCES

Cahnman, Werner J. "The Stigma of Obesity," *The Sociological Quarterly*, 9 (1968), 283–299.

Edgerton, Robert B. *The Cloak of Competence: Stigma in the Lives of the Mentally Retarded.* Berkeley: University of California Press, 1967.

---

[112]Laurie Taylor, *Deviance and Society* (London: Michael Joseph, 1971), p. 51.
[113]Paul Rock, *Deviant Behavior* (London: Hutchinson University Library, 1973), p. 19.

Freidson, Eliot. "Disability ao Social Deviance," in Marvin B. Sussman, ed., *Sociology and Rehabilitation.* Washington, D.C.: American Sociological Association, 1965.

Fox, Renée. "The Medicalization and Demedicalization of American Society," *Daedelus,* 106 (1977), 9–22.

Haber, Lawrence D., and Richard T. Smith. "Disability and Deviance: Normative Adaptations of Role Behavior," *American Sociological Review,* 36 (1971), 87–97.

Koestler, Frances A. *The Unseen Minority: A Social History of Blindness in the United States.* New York: David McKay, 1976.

Laslett, Barbara, and Carol A. B. Warren. "Losing Weight: The Organizational Promotion of Behavior Change," *Social Problems,* 23 (1975), 69–80.

Levitin, Teresa E. "Deviants as Active Participants in the Labeling Process: The Visibly Handicapped," *Social Problems,* 22 (1975), 548–557.

Mechanic, David. *Medical Sociology: A Selective View.* New York: Free Press, 1968.

Mercer, Jane R. *Labeling the Mentally Retarded.* Berkeley: University of California Press, 1973.

Myerson, Lee. "Physical Disability as a Social Psychological Problem," in Edward Sagarin, ed., *The Other Minorities.* Boston: Ginn, 1971.

Nagi, Saad Z. *Disability and Rehabilitation: Legal, Clinical, and Self-Concepts and Measurements.* Columbus: Ohio State University Press, 1969.

Safilios-Rothschild, Constantina. *The Sociology and Social Psychology of Disability and Rehabilitation.* New York: Random House, 1970.

Scott, Robert A. *The Making of Blind Men: A Study of Adult Socialization.* New York: Russell Sage, 1969.

Smith, Richard T. "Societal Reaction and Physical Disability: Contrasting Perspectives," in Walter R. Gove, ed., *The Labelling of Deviance: Evaluating a Perspective.* New York: Sage/Halsted, 1975.

PART THREE

SOME
CONCLUSIONS

It probably will never be possible to estimate the indirect effects of major crimes in high places on general law obedience in America, or to ascertain to what extent Watergate was a product of existing forces in American society. (Wide World Photos)

The Social Nature of Deviance

MANY persons still tend to regard deviance as a problem of the individual; it is the individual's problem that is to be studied, explained, and controlled in dealing with deviance. A completely different approach has been adopted here. The explanation of deviance, even the meaning of deviance, must be sought in the social context in which it occurs—social groups and society. In summarizing this perspective of deviance, we hope to make our approach somewhat more explicit. In doing so, a number of facets of deviance will again be more closely examined, in an attempt to tie them together in a comprehensive manner.

THE MEANING OF DEVIANCE

Social deviance refers to the process whereby norms are created, tolerance of norm-conforming and norm-violating behavior is maintained, and social control efforts are mobilized against the behavior. What constitutes deviance is dependent upon a given society (or social group), its group composition, and the particular time period under consideration. Deviance is behavior that violates a norm beyond the tolerance of a particular group, in such a way that there is a probability that a sanction will be applied (see pp. 14–16). As Durkheim has said, even in a society of saints there would still be deviance.[1] What Durkheim meant, of course, is that even in a crimeless society small differences in behavior that had no moral significance would take on new and larger meaning. Small breaches of manners and minor violations of good taste, for example, would become violations of a greater degree. In other words, "there cannot be a society of saints because a process of social redefinition operates continuously to insure that all the positions on the scale from wickedness to virtue will always be filled and that some will always be holier than others."[2] Such a process is completely natural and inevitable.

Social Norms

The definition of deviance is itself dependent upon social norms, which are expectations that govern the limits of variation in social behavior. These social norms are derived from subcultures, countercultures, or the general culture; some of them may be transmitted from generation to generation.[3] Norms are crucial to the maintenance of order, whether they are proscriptive or prescriptive. They have varying degrees of strength, depending on the willingness of the group to tolerate violations (which will be discussed shortly) or to suppress them. Identifying what deviance is, and who is deviant, necessitates specifying which groups define certain normative behavior as deviant and which groups do not.

---

[1]Emile Durkheim, *The Rules of Sociological Method* (Chicago: University of Chicago Press, 1938; originally published in 1895), pp. 67–71.
[2]Albert K. Cohen, *The Elasticity of Evil: Changes in the Social Definition of Deviance* (Oxford, England: Oxford University Penal Research Unit; Basil Blackwell, 1974), p. 5.
[3]For a general discussion, see J. Milton Yinger, "Countercultures and Social Change," *American Sociological Review,* 42 (1977), 833–853.

Norms are not just rules—they are social rules, the result of a social process. The process by which some norms come to be defined as legal norms (or laws), for example, reflects the importance of the social processes of conflict, compromise, cooperation, and accommodation.[4] For this reason norms are relative to the group that defines them. Analyses of the creation of vagrancy statutes,[5] laws pertaining to violations of financial trust,[6] Prohibition,[7] and tobacco smoking[8] all point to the importance of social influences in defining certain actions as deviant through the creation of norms, some of which are legal, others of which are extralegal and informal. Norms change as the composition and interests of social groups change.

The norms of a social group may change as a result of a number of conditions. Yinger has identified several possible sources of normative change: drastic reorganization of the way people make their living; changes in the size, location, age distribution, and sex ratio of a population; rapid importation of new ideas, techniques, goods, and values from alien societies or from earlier periods; sharp increase in life's possibilites, hopes, dreams, and actualities, followed by a plateau, actual loss, or serious threat of loss; less participation in intimate and supporting social circles; and a loss of meaning in the deepest symbols and rituals of society.[9]

In a sense, norms are "outside" groups in that they are idealizations; they express what "ought" to occur in given situations. This feature makes them difficult to study since many norms are implied in social situations rather than being explicit. While legal norms are written for all to see, many other norms are not, though they appear to direct people's behavior just as effectively. Moral inhibitions of a religious person may be just as effective, or even more so, in keeping such persons "in line" as the fact that some behavior is against the law and subject to criminal penalties.[10]

Tolerating Deviance

Just as social norms are relative to a particular social group, so too is the tolerance of deviance. A group's tolerance is not something either there or not there; it is the product of the social forces within the group that make some norms more important than others. The amount of group tolerance of various forms of deviance is reflected by a number of indicators. The degree of tolerance may be related to the "costs " of not having something be deviant. White-collar crime, for example, may be an integral

---

[4]For an account that stresses conflict, see Richard Quinney, *Class, State and Crime: On the Theory and Practice of Criminal Justice* (New York: David McKay, 1977). For an account that stresses compromise and accomodation, see Edwin M. Lemert, *Legal Action and Social Change* (Chicago: Aldine, 1970).
[5]William J. Chambliss, "The State, the Law, and the Definition of Behavior as Criminal or Delinquent," in Daniel Glaser, ed., *Handbook of Criminology* (Chicago: Rand McNally, 1974), pp. 7–44.
[6]Jerome Hall, *Theft, Law and Society,* 2d ed. (Indianapolis: Bobbs Merrill, 1952), pp. 4–33.
[7]Joseph R. Gusfield, *Symbolic Crusade* (Urbana: University of Illinois Press, 1963); and Gusfield, "On Legislating Morals: The Symbolic Process of Designating Deviance," *California Law Review,* 56 (1968), 54–73.
[8]Elane Nuehring and Gerald E. Markle, "Nicotine and Norms: The Re-Emergence of a Deviant Behavior," *Social Problems,* 21 (1974), 513–526.
[9]Yinger, p. 847.
[10]Arnold Birenbaum and Edward Sagarin, *Norms and Human Behavior* (New York: Holt, Rinehart and Winston, 1976); and Robert F. Meier and Weldon T. Johnson, "Deterrence as Social Control: Legal and Extralegal Factors in the Production of Conformity," *American Sociological Review,* 42 (1977), 292–304.

feature of capitalistic economies. If one prefers capitalism to alternative forms of government, then one must tolerate a certain amount and kind of white-collar crime. This form of deviance is tolerated (which is not the same thing as desired) because it is an accompaniment of something that is desired.

Some idea of the tolerance within the United States of various crimes has been estimated by public opinion surveys in which persons have been asked to rate the seriousness of criminal acts. These surveys have shown rather consistently that persons tend to rank crimes with respect to their seriousness in a uniform manner, regardless of their age, sex, race, and socioeconomic status: crimes of personal violence are generally rated as most serious, followed in degree of seriousness by crimes against property, occupational offenses, and public order crimes.[11] This does not mean that sociologists who study deviance necessarily agree with the amount of tolerance displayed by the general public. One survey of crime seriousness found, for example, that persons tended to rate the use of heroin as more serious than "killing spouse's lover after catching them together," or than killing someone in a barroom brawl.[12] The appropriate sociological response to such a finding is not to pass judgment on the public for misplaced values, but to inquire into the conditions surrounding such a valuation. Sociologists may lament the fact that drug use is considered by some people to be more deviant than homicide, or that white-collar crimes are considered less serious than petty burglaries, but these ratings are important data: they tell us that some acts of deviance are more tolerated than others.

Still another indicator of a group's tolerance of certain forms of deviance is the severity of sanctions administered or applied to them. The more strongly disapproved the deviance, the more severe the sanction. The fact that premeditated homicide carries the potential for life imprisonment, or even death, reflects how strongly the community feels about it; jaywalking, on the other hand, is sanctioned by only a small fine. The use of a drug such as heroin is heavily sanctioned, while the use of alcohol, nicotine, or caffeine in coffee is not. Sanctions are applied differentially even within the same form of deviance. In a study of homicide in Houston, one investigator found that the penalties for murder between intimates (for example, husband and wife) were less severe than those for murder between strangers.[13] The sociological task becomes one of exploring the reasons for such differences. Why, for example, is the use of one kind of drug more strongly reacted to than the use of another? One cannot assume that there is something intrinsically "evil" about heroin but not caffeine or nicotine; nor is the reaction of most persons toward the use of these substances an individualistic one. Were this the case, there would not be much agreement concerning the deviant nature of heroin use and the nondeviant nature of caffeine use in coffee.

---

[11]See Elizabeth A. Rooney and Don C. Gibbons, "Social Reactions to 'Crimes without Victims,'" *Social Problems*, 13 (1966), 400–413; and Peter H. Rossi, Emily Waite, Christine E. Bose, and Richard E. Berk, "The Seriousness of Crimes: Normative Structure and Individual Differences," *American Sociological Review*, 39 (1974), 224–237.

[12]Rossi *et al.*

[13]Henry P. Lundsgaarde, *Murder in Space City: A Cultural Analysis of Houston Homicide Patterns* (New York: Oxford University Press, 1977).

Social Control

Agents that exercise the social control of various forms of deviance—the criminal justice system with respect to crime, psychiatrists and mental hospitals with respect to mental disorder, clergy and morally influential citizens with respect to sexual deviance, physicians with respect to physical disabilities, and so on—do not react negatively merely because a norm violation has occurred; rather, their response has to do with the social importance of the violation. Social control agents would not react to each instance of deviance, even if it were known to them, unless the deviance exceeded at least one person's expectations of desirable behavior and those expectations were conveyed to them. Sanctions are socially organized; they are not automatic.

Even violations of the criminal law, where one might expect reactions independent of social pressures to enforce compliance, are not acted upon without someone's expectations being known and conveyed to the police. The police on their own detect crime and apprehend criminals in only a small proportion of cases; they must rely on citizen complaints to inform them that a crime has occurred and for information leading to the arrest of a suspect.[14] In instances where the police observe a crime firsthand, there is no guarantee that they will take action. The police may decide that, for a number of reasons, an arrest should not be made.[15]

Similarly, psychiatrists do not actively seek patients who have mental disorders. The patients must first be referred to them, usually through some complaint. Like other formal agents of social control, they are reactive and respond only after someone else has brought the deviance to their attention. Psychiatrists may be active, however, in perpetrating certain "images" of deviance.[16] They may give the public conceptions of what mental disorder is and help the public identify persons and behavior that is consistent with those images.

Because the application of sanctions is not automatic, social control is perhaps best thought of in terms of probabilities. A norm violation must have occurred (or thought to have occurred), and it must have exceeded the group's tolerance of that behavior. Finally, the behavior is deviant "if it falls within a class of behavior for which there is a probability of negative sanctions subsequent to its detection."[17] The probability is increased if the norm being violated is strongly supported by the group, if the group's tolerance of its violation is low, and if there are pressures on social control agents to take action.

Labeling theorists (see pp. 73–81) have concentrated on the importance of social control in defining deviance. As one classic statement has put it, "the deviant is one to whom that label has successfully been applied; deviant behavior is behavior

---

[14]Peter K. Manning, *Police Work: The Social Organization of Policing* (Cambridge, Mass.: MIT Press, 1977); and Albert J. Reiss, Jr., *The Police and the Public* (New Haven, Conn.: Yale University Press, 1971).
[15]Herman Goldstein, *Policing a Free Society* (Cambridge, Mass.: Ballinger, 1977). Chap. 5; and Kenneth Culp Davis, *Police Discretion* (St. Paul: West Publishing, 1975).
[16]See Thomas J. Scheff, "The Labeling Theory of Mental Illness," *American Sociological Review,* 39 (1974), 444–452.
[17]Donald J. Black and Albert J. Reiss, Jr., "Police Control of Juveniles," *American Sociological Review,* 35 (1970), 63.

that people so label.[18] Although it is an important element of deviance, the application of sanctions, or labels, is only part of the social process, the component that appears to come last in the temporal sequence of norm violation, beyond group tolerance and social control.[19] Social control efforts are helpful to the sociologist in identifying norms by determining what kinds of behavior elicit sanctions.

What makes deviance "social" is the social nature of norms, group tolerance, and other people's reactions to behavior that violates norms. Deviance refers to something that is disvalued by the social group. This valuation is reflected in the content of the group's norms and its tolerance for certain behavior, as well as in the group's efforts to control the disvalued behavior. In fact, one theorist has argued that valuation on the part of social control agents "is a central concept in the explanation of deviation."[20]

Deviance and Relativity

Because norms, tolerance, and the application of sanctions are relative, the concept of deviance is also relative. There are, however, dangers with respect to a relativistic view of deviance. "Taken literally, the 'everything is relative' vulgarization implies that almost any behavior is deviant—to some people. And that no behavior is deviant— that is, to absolutely everyone."[21] But to say that deviance is relative is not to say that it is in reality "in the eye of the beholder," as is often thought. Were this the case, what constitutes deviance would depend exclusively on individual preferences, tolerances, and valuations of conduct. But the concept of deviance is more than merely individual preferences and valuations—it is a social entity, not an individualistic one. It is social because the rules that define it, the tolerance of certain violations of these rules, and the reactions to the violations are social, not individualisitic.

It appears that some forms of behavior in a given social system are necessarily deviant in the sense that most members of that system cannot "be free to applaud or even to ignore them."[22] In this sense deviance is not relative from person to person but from system to system. Moreover, depending on the circumstances, some forms of deviance may be supported by most members of a system. Such events as Halloween,

---

[18]Howard S. Becker, *Outsiders: Studies in the Sociology of Deviance,* enlarged ed. (New York: Free Press, 1973), p. 9.

[19]A common term that denotes what social control efforts are directed *to* is "putative," a word used to mean "alleged." See Prudence Rains, "Imputations of Deviance: A Retrospective Essay on the Labeling Perspective," *Social Problems,* 23 (1975), 1–11. See also Eliot Freidson, *Profession of Medicine: A Study of the Sociology of Applied Knowledge* (New York: Dodd, Mead, 1970), p. 219.

[20]Edward M. Lemert, "Social Structure, Social Control, and Deviation," in Marshall B. Clinard, ed., *Anomie and Deviant Behavior* (New York: Free Press, 1964). p. 127.

[21]Erich Goode, "On Behalf of Labeling Theory," *Social Problems* 22 (1975), 579. See also Erich Goode, *Deviant Behavior: An Interactionist Approach* (Englewood Cliffs, N.J.: Prentice-Hall, 1978), pp. 32–36.

[22]Travis Hirschi, "Procedural Rules and the Study of Deviant Behavior," *Social Problems,* 21 (1973), 169. Also see Judith Blake and Kingsley Davis, "Norms, Values and Sanctions," in Robert E. L. Faris, ed., *Handbook of Modern Sociology* (Chicago: Rand McNally, 1964), pp. 456–484; and John Finley Scott, *Internalization of Norms: A Sociological Theory of Moral Commitment* (Englewood Cliffs, N.J.: Prentice-Hall, 1971).

football weekends, Mardi Gras, New Year's Eve, and 24-hour rock concerts are now common features in the United States.[23]

The Context of Deviant Behavior

The very existence of urban life and the great growth of urbanization probably best exemplify how deviant behavior can be related to broader social forces. As a product of the urbanization process, the mass society has developed. With the mass society has come increased social differentiation, the clash of norms and social roles, and the inevitable breakdown or interruption in interpersonal relationships. Urbanization brings about pronounced changes in the way of life, the patterns of population distribution, contacts with ever-wider circles of people with subsequent increases in impersonal relationships, differences in leisure-time pursuits, and the great diversity of subcultures and countercultures. Increased urbanization has meant extensive conflicts of norms and values, rapid social change, increased mobility of the population, emphasis on material goods, and individualism. It has also brought about greater release from informal social controls. Urbanization has frequently been accompanied by the development of areas with a slum way of life; it is particularly the slum way of life that has been associated with high rates of youth criminality, adult crime, drug usage, alcoholism, prostitution, mental disorder, and suicide. One cannot properly regard the background of a deviant without considering whether or not the individual has come from a predominantly urban, as opposed to a rural, background. One cannot regard the activities of a slum gang, for example, as a collection of discrete individuals; rather, their behavior must be interpreted in terms of a youth group operating in a social setting.

Not all forms of deviance, of course, are found in inner-city areas. White-collar and corporate criminality, for example, are upper-class forms of deviance.[24] The upper and middle classes also have many of the other forms of deviance found in the lower classes, although they are generally not to the same extent. Similarly, rural areas are also characterized by many forms of deviance, although they are not as common as in urban areas.

The terms "urban" and "rural" do not refer exclusively to the relative size of a community but to the social accompaniments of the development process. One study, that compared delinquents from urban and rural areas, for example, found that the differences in self-reported delinquency between urban and small town males were few and quite small.[25] However, that area which contained the highest rate of self-reported delinquents was a small mining town which might be considered "rural"-

---

[23]Yinger, p. 844.

[24]See John M. Johnson and Jack D. Douglas, eds., *Crime at the Top: Deviance in Business and the Professions* (Philadelphia: Lippincott, 1978).

[25]Maynard L. Erickson and Gary F. Jensen, "'Delinquency Is Still Group Behavior!': Toward Revitalizing the Group Premise in the Sociology of Deviance," *Journal of Criminal Law and Criminology*, 68 (1977), 262–273.

based on population size, but which could be characterized as displaying many of the features of urbanism mentioned above. It is not the absolute number of people in a community that leads to predictions about the extent of deviance but the social dynamics among those persons.

Mass Media and the Image of Deviance

In Western societies generally the public has great interest in stories about crime, drug addiction, and other forms of deviance. This is seen in both the amount of space and the prominent location given these stories in newspapers and other mass media, and in public and private conversations. The concept of free enterprise condones the emphasis on stories that deal with deviance as a valuable vehicle for increasing circulation and thus the sale of advertisements. On the other hand, the concept of social responsibility suggests that the mass media re-evaluate their role in society. Newspapers are particularly important in making our society a crime-centered culture, since they devote much space, and give front-page treatment to, crime stories. As a result of the detailed coverage given to murders and killings in connection with muggings and robberies, the public has developed the impression that these crimes are more prevalent than they actually are.[26] In addition, there is a marked difference between the reporting of a crime in factual, verifiable statements, as is often done in many countries, and "loading" a long, detailed crime story with emotionally charged descriptions.

Contrary to the emphasis put on conventional crimes, the public as a whole is often not made aware through the mass media of occupational and corporate criminality and of the great importance that these types of crime have for society. These offenses simply do not provide the often exciting drama of armed robbery or muggings.[27] There is nothing particularly dramatic about common frauds, investigations of the trade practices of large corporations, or the complicated illegal reporting of individual tax returns or those by businesses and corporations.[28] Furthermore, these activities do not provoke the same fears and personal identification for an ordinary citizen unfamiliar with complicated financial and legal terminology. There is, in fact, some indication that large corporations may set the limits within which public debate on issues relating to them are discussed in the mass media by means of the corporation's influence in purchasing advertising.[29] It is highly unlikely that a corporation would sponsor the advertising presented on a special television documentary or a weekly program dealing with corporate crime such as is done with ordinary crimes.

---

[26]Stories dealing with criminals tend to emphasize the offender's personal circumstances and background, thus leading the public to evaluate the "causes" of crime in those terms. See Hazel Erskine, "The Polls: Causes of Crime," *Public Opinion Quarterly,* 38 (1974), 288–298.

[27]Jeffrey C. Hubbard, Melvin L. DeFleur, and Lois B. DeFleur, "Mass Media Influences on Public Conceptions of Social Problems," *Social Problems,* 23 (1975), 22–34.

[28]For an account of one such offender, see Michael Hellerman with Thomas C. Renner, *Wall Street Swindler* (New York: Doubleday, 1977).

[29]David L. Sallach, "Class Domination and Ideological Hegemony," *The Sociological Quarterly,* 15 (1974), 38–50. Also see Richard Bunce, *Television in the Corporate Interest* (New York: Praeger, 1976).

The media thus do influence public thinking about crime and various forms of deviance, and through their presentation of that material the public develops a certain consensus about its nature, frequency, and seriousness.[30] What is "deviant" and who is the "deviant" then becomes a product of what the mass media stereotype as deviance.

FORMS OF SOCIAL DEVIANCE

The social nature of deviance, its relative meaning, its context, and mass media accounts of what constitutes deviance provide the background against which certain aspects of deviance can be looked at again. In this further discussion, the social nature rather than the individualistic nature of deviance will be emphasized. We will then conclude by contrasting two social systems with differing amounts of one form of deviance (crime): the United States and Switzerland.

Mental Disorder

Mental disorder is not easily defined. Inasmuch as it is primarily a problem of relativity, its definition poses questions not easily resolved. For the most part, mental illnesses are actually related to society's tolerance of eccentricity. Howard Hughes, the U.S. billionaire who died in 1976, ran his business empire for years as a recluse completely isolated from public view and private contacts, with only a few immediate business associates around him. For months he lay for the most part naked in his bedroom, the windows sealed from all light, and for months his hair, beard, finger- and toenails were allowed to go uncut. He once paid $1,000 for a haircut. He was obsessed by a fear of germs, he would not shake hands, and articles had to be handed to him wrapped in Kleenex; large amounts of paper kitchen towels were used to assure he had no contact with the unclean world. "Handling inanimate objects had developed into a complicated ritual. When you were going to bring him a spoon, for example, the spoon handle had to be wrapped in Kleenex and Scotch-taped. Then you would take another piece of Kleenex to hold the Kleenex wrapping, so the wrapping wouldn't get contaminated. He would lift the wrapped spoon off the piece of Kleenex you were holding it with."[31] His biographer said about this strange case: "In the everyday world, a recluse who cowers naked amid self-neglect in his bedroom is called insane. A billionaire who thus flees the world is termed eccentric."[32]

Certainly a more permissive and tolerant society would have less difficulty with a rule-breaker who is customarily labeled "nuts," "insane," "off his rocker," and so on. A good example of society's tolerance of behavior is that of the "Manhattan Drummer Boy," a midtown Manhattan resident who frequently each day stops in the middle of

---

[30]See Stanley Cohen and Jock Young, eds., *The Manufacture of News* (Beverly Hills, Calif.: Sage Publications, 1973).
[31]James Phelan, *Howard Hughes: The Hidden Years* (New York: Warner Books, 1976), p. 224.
[32]Phelan, p. 21.

the street and pounds his drumsticks on the road while cars, taxis, and pedestrians get out of his way. His home is an alcove in the center of the city, under a window and beside a hot air vent, where he eats, sleeps, and holds court with window washers and passersby. When asked why he lives and plays in the street he responds that it is cheaper there, and the tone on the alphalt is "nice." He collects bottle caps and imaginary insects; he does not beg, nor does he drink or curse others. He says little, and what he does say is often disconnected. What is significant is that his behavior is tolerated by others; he is not confined to a mental hospital or other institution. Rather, people look after him in a number of ways:

> People give money, food, clothes, leaving them in his little cave. Sometimes he accepts them. Sometimes he takes the money to the corner newstand for safekeeping, or puts it in the mailbox. Up and down the block, Walter is looked after by the cops, by the window washers, by the salesmen in the clothing store. And there's the clerk at the deli, the cashier at the coffee shop, and "Pop" at the corner newstand.
>
> Officer Lou D'Ambrosio, the cop on the Rockefeller Center beat, is fond of Walter, chiding him, washing his drumsticks, urging him to take a bath and not to pick lice off himself on busy Sixth Avenue. "Walter is not a bad guy, he's like a child. He just gave up on the world," says D'Ambrosio. "If you clean him up, put a business suit on him and cut his hair, there's not much difference between Walter and a lot of other people on the street," he says. "People walk down the street all the time, clapping, singing, shouting, jumping and doing lots of weird things," he says. "We walk in traffic, we get killed. Walter plays in traffic day after day and nothing happens. The taxi drivers give him change. He seems happier than a lot of us. Maybe he found his utopia," says the philosopher cop.[33]

From these examples we see that the reactions of others to behavior reflects the degree to which rules are being broken and the amount of tolerance afforded the violations. People do act strangely, but mental disorder as an entity is elusive, influencing some writers to abandon the concept altogether.[34] Persons behave "strangely" only because our expectations of "normal" behavior are violated; what is thus "mad" depends on our conceptions of appropriate behavior.

Sex and Society

It is difficult to say what is proper or improper, what is moral or immoral, in sexual standards because normative standards of sexual behavior vary by society and over time. What are "natural" sex practices, and what practices are right or wrong, is relative to time and culture. Some would try to enforce their own sexual standards, which are usually those of the group to which they belong, on the community as a whole.[35] Continuous questions arise over homosexual behavior, the nature of heterosexual relations, the legal age of sexual intercourse, prostitution, and the example to be discussed here, pornography.

---

[33]*The Wisconsin State Journal* (Madison), September 11, 1977, Section 7, p. 12.
[34]See, for example, Thomas J. Scheff, ed., *Labeling Madness* (Englewood Cliffs, N.J.: Prentice-Hall, 1975); and Thomas Szasz, *The Manufacture of Madness* (New York: Harper & Row, 1970).
[35]Some communities are more diffuse than others, and some feel more strongly about certain conduct than others. A large national survey reported, for example, that 93.5 percent of conservative Christians supported Anita Bryant's stand against the gay rights bill. *Los Angeles Times,* December 31, 1977, Section 2, p. 1.

As sex has moved into the mass media, it has taken on a new relevance, which has meant that it has entered the area of political relevance, a situation that has drastically altered the relation between sex and the law.[36]

The social control of pornography, for example, raises fundamental issues about the relation of sexuality to the general society. Pornography is a commodity, an illegal commodity in many communities depending upon the content, which is sought by certain segments of the community. Like alcohol and drugs, the issue is not whether it can be completely eliminated but rather whether it can be controlled within acceptable community limits. The sociological study of pornography has included the possible effects it might have, the process by which legislation has been enacted, and the most appropriate national policy for pornography. On the basis of their own studies, as well as their estimates of public attitudes generally and the studies of other social scientists, the President's Commission recommended in 1970 the repeal of all federal, state, and local legislation prohibiting the sale, exhibition, or distribution of sexual materials to consenting adults.[37] The Commission recommended, on the other hand, special legislation to prohibit the commercial distribution or display for sale of certain sexual materials to juveniles. This would, for example, include nudity only when the genitalia are exposed or emphasized.

Studies indicated, in 1971, that antipornographic or "public decency" campaigns are likely to occur in smaller communities and cities of less than 250,000, areas where there is a more recent rural orientation, a generally religious outlook, either dogmatic or fundamentalist, and a politically conservative approach.[38] Here the populations are largely middle class and relatively traditional, and they will be experiencing threats to the prestige of their traditional life-style. Above all, in these communities potential leadership will be available for the "symbolic crusade," persons formerly engaged in "decency" activities or in religiously or patriotically oriented voluntary associations. "That leadership will be able to establish a small cadre whose members are influential in the community and from whom and with whom leaders can call upon for additional expertise and assistance."[39] These groups have experienced structural strain in the form of their perception of loss of status, prestige, or wealth, a situation in which the precipitating factor may be a media event that calls attention to the growing "problem" of pornography in a community. When this occurs the potential crusaders will be convinced that their generalized beliefs about pornography are correct. Perceiving that they do have reason to fear the threat to their conservative and traditional life-style, they feel they must act to defend it.[40] Thus it matters not if the threat is real; it is enough that it is thought to be real.

The issue of the decriminalization of pornography, for many persons, concerns primarily the effect of pornography and the possibility that exposure to such material

[36]See Donal E. J. MacNamara and Edward Sagarin, eds., *Sex, Crime and the Law* (New York: Free Press, 1977).
[37]*Report of the Commission on Obscenity and Pornography* (Washington, D.C.: Government Printing Office, 1970).
[38]Louis A. Zurcher, Jr., R. George Kirkpatrick, Robert G. Cushing, and Charles K. Bowman, "The Anti-Pornography Campaign: A Symbolic Crusade," *Social Problems,* 19 (1971), 217–238.
[39]Zurcher *et al.,* p. 235.
[40]Louis A. Zucher, Jr., and R. George Kirkpatrick, *Citizens for Decency: Anti-Pornographic Crusades as Status Defense* (Austin: University of Texas Press, 1976), p. 322.

will increase the probability of aggressive behavior toward the opposite sex, in particular with respect to the incidence of sexual crimes such as forcible rape. As has already been pointed out (Chapter 11), the evidence for such an increase is not conclusive one way or the other, even though most observers have associated themselves with the position that there is no negative effect. There is little evidence that erotica causes antisocial acts or individual pathologies in isolation.[41] Obviously, this lack of evidence is not of concern to crusaders in antipornography campaigns, inasmuch as they view the law as the very last bastion of defense against moral decay. It does not matter to activists, in these crusades at least, whether pornographic matter is in some way harmful to those exposed to it: the issue is more properly a moral one related to fundamental elements of social status and life-styles.

There is an increasing openness in speaking of and seeing sexual materials, changes that are likely to continue, though this change to openness appears to vary by sex. Women, for example, continue to advocate stricter controls on pornography than do men, but this may not be because women are not aroused by these materials and do not find them pleasurable. Rather, it may because they do find them often stimulating.[42] This increased willingness to speak about sexual matters and to incorporate sexual materials into school curricula does not mean that pornography will continue in much the same form as today. Legal regulations for pornography are likely to continue, although the precise form of the regulations remains in doubt. There is evidence, for example, that the public favors some kind of legal regulation, in spite of the fact that it has been shown that this type of control has not performed the prohibitionist task originally envisaged for it.[43] Legal regulation leads to the underground marketing for pornography and the suppression of sex information, or the association of sexual matters with certain attitudes of "dirtiness" may lead to confusion and guilt feelings that may result in problems of sexual adjustment.[44] It is generally agreed that early exposure to sexual information is important in normal sexual development, but the problem fundamentally is who is to take charge of this sexual education and how appropriate is the role of the law in the process.

Society and Drugs

Our society has sometimes been referred to as the "drugged society" in that legal drugs are widely used. In this sense, the distinction between the use of legal and illegal drugs often becomes tenuous. Alcohol and cigarettes are widely used legal drugs, but marijuana is still largely not legal. Two specialists who have studied the overall drug scene have written about the significant role of the widespread use of a broad spectrum of "remedies" in modern society:

---

[41]See the *Report of the Commission on Obscenity and Pornography;* and Robert R. Bell, *Social Deviance,* rev. ed. (Homewood, Ill.: Dorsey Press, 1976), pp. 146–150.
[42]See Paula Johnson and Jacqueline D. Goodchilds, "Pornography, Sexuality, and Social Psychology," *Journal of Social Issues,* 29 (1973), 236.
[43]A. B. Smith and Harriet Pollack, *Some Sins Are Not Crimes* (New York: Franklin Watts, 1975), p. 162.
[44]George D. Muedeking, "Pornography and Society," in Edward Sagarin and Fred Montanino, eds., *Deviants: Voluntary Actors in a Hostile World* (Morristown, N.J.: General Learning Press, 1977), p. 493.

The promotion of such over-the-counter drugs has contributed to the convincing of large sections of the public that there is a pill for every ill, and that there is—in fact, there *must* be—a chemical answer to every physical, emotional, and sociological discomfort of mankind. In addition, widespread medication by modern "pill-popping" parents may have played a role in inducing young people to avoid unpleasant aspects of life by turning to marijuana, the amphetamines, the barbiturates, mescaline, and LSD.[45]

The so-called psychoactive drugs such as sedatives, tranquilizers, stimulants, and antidepressants have presented a confusing and difficult problem in modern medicine, and their use by the medical profession has increased dramatically within the last decade or so. These prescribed psychoactive drugs account for more than 200 million prescriptions per year, dispensed at community pharmacies at a retail cost of nearly a billion dollars. For these drugs usage increased by 44 percent from 1964 to 1970, with an increase of around 78 percent for minor tranquilizers alone.[46] Silberman and Lee explain that whereas relatively little criticism has been voiced about major tranquilizer usage for treating several schizophrenic or other serious psychotic patients, the use of minor tranquilizers, such as antianxiety drugs like meprobamate, diazepam (Valium), and others given persons with anxieties or depression, has come under attack largely because they are widely prescribed by general practitioners who are under pressure to alleviate the problems of their patients. The situation has been described in these terms:

> It has been estimated that 60 percent of the patients who appear in a general practitioner's office or clinic do so for largely nonmedical reasons. They come because they are lonely, depressed, anxious, dissatisfied, or unhappy. They are troubled because they are finding it difficult or impossible to measure up to prevailing social prescriptions as to what one ought to get out of life. They are not as popular, successful, sweet-smelling, thin, vigorous, or beautiful as they have been led to believe (by the advertising arms of industry and the media) they ought and deserve to be.[47]

Society with a High Crime Rate

Criminality involves the learning of norms and attitudes conducive to law violation, whether it is a matter of burglary, an income tax violation, or false advertising. Some of these norms and attitudes are derived from the general society, and they may lead either to criminality itself or to the development of attitudes favorable to various types of criminality under certain circumstances. Barron lists six values that are related to the high crime rate in the United States:[48]

---

[45]Milton Silberman and Philip R. Lee, *Pills, Profits, and Politics* (Berkeley: University of California Press, 1974), p. 22.

[46]Silberman and Lee, p. 293.

[47]Statement of Henry L. Lennard and Mitchell Rosenthal in U.S. Senate, *Advertising of Proprietary Medicines*, 2 (1971), 801, as quoted in Silberman and Lee, *Pills, Profits and Politics*, pp. 293–294.

[48]Milton L. Barron, "The Criminogenic Society: Social Values and Deviance," in Abraham S. Blumberg, ed., *Current Perspectives on Criminal Behavior* (New York: Knopf, 1974), pp. 68–86. Quotes are from pages 74 and 76.

1. *Success.* Success is undoubtedly one of the prime values in the culture, whether it is defined in terms of occupational goals or a boy's or girl's ability to hit .300 in Little League. "When people come to the realization that they cannot attain success by conventional hard work and thrift, many are apt to turn to delinquency and crime."

2. *Status and power ascendance.* Americans have traditionally been status conscious, and the struggle for higher status marks the history of most of the immigrant groups coming into this country. When status and power desires are thwarted, they may be obtained through illegal means.

3. *Pecuniary and material wealth.* Money and the desire for success and status are closely interrelated, but money as much as any single symbol has come to denote "worthiness." "It is often not what a person is that matters, but rather what he has." Most of the crimes that are eventually punished through the courts are theft-related.

4. *Resistance to authority.* The "rugged individualism" and the "pioneer spirit" are still valued in U.S. society, many years after their function in settling the country has waned. Americans tend to resist rules, and they prefer to be free from too many controls. In fact, complete conformity to rules is often ridiculed in our society, because it indicates a person's failure to show an independent spirit.

5. *Toughness.* This value is particularly important to males, but females are also expected to demonstrate this virtue in psychological ways. Males are often defined in terms of toughness, and on specific occasions they are expected to show others how tough they are.

6. *Dupery.* The ability to manipulate people is an important value; it is prevalent, for example, in the sometimes indistinguishable line between white-collar crime and "good, hard business." Perhaps the best examples of dupery relate to consumer fraud. One study of a number of occupations showed that false repairs were made on merchandise actually in working order. This study reported that watch repairmen were the most honest of those surveyed, though they too were dishonest to some extent. For the watch repairmen, "the test . . . was made by loosening the little screw that fastens the winding wheel in the watch. Of the 462 watch repairmen investigated throughout the nation, only 49 percent [a lower percentage than other occupations] lied, overcharged, gave false diagnoses, or suggested expensive and unnecessary repairs. A bare majority, 51 percent, were honest, only 8 of them charging nothing at all.[49]

A commonly held belief in U.S. society is that "everyone has a racket," and a good example of this is common misrepresentation in advertising in newspapers, periodicals, and on television. Many people believe that white-collar crime is extensive—and it is. Two thirds (64 percent) of the American people, as reported in a 1972 Harris national opinion poll, for example, felt that "tax laws are written to help the rich and not the average man." A 1977 Gallup survey of a national sample of teenagers aged 13–18 found that only one third felt that the ethical standards of business executives and labor union leaders ranked very high or high and only one fifth of advertising executives.[50] As an example of rackets, a well-known case (during the

---

[49]Cited in Barron, p. 79.
[50]George Gallup, "Teens Rate Doctors, Clergy Most Ethical" *The Wisconsin State Journal (Madison), August 17, 1977, Section 1, p. 12.*

1950s) involved a number of television quiz programs which were found to have been rigged by feeding the contestants answers in advance.[51] On this basis one contestant, whose father and uncle had each won a Pulitzer Prize in literature, defeated 13 opponents and thereby won $129,000. Others confessed to winning large amounts fraudulently, as much as $237,500 in one case and $98,500 in another. Altogether, 10 contestants were brought before the courts on charges of perjury, since they had denied the charges under oath before a grand jury. They were given suspended sentences but were allowed to keep their "earnings." A racket on a higher level in 1975 was the connivance of New York City Mayor Beame and six major banks to sell $4 billion of New York City municipal bonds to an unsuspecting public, even though they knew that the city was on the verge of financial collapse. According to the Securities and Exchange Commission (SEC) report to Congress in 1977, the misleading information was contained in the annual budget reports in which the city used budgetary, accounting, and financial practices known to distort the city's true financial picture. One misleading tactic used was the listing of city-owned property on tax rolls for income purposes even though the city gets no taxes from its own property. In addition, operating expenses were paid from the capital budget, which caused decreased city assets, and public investors were led to believe that the city was in far better condition financially than it really was.[52]

General Disobedience of Law The U.S. culture professes obedience to law, yet there is extensive flaunting of laws. There are indications that disobedience to law is far more widespread than reports of the crimes committed actually show. Throughout the United States merchants suffer from a plague of shoplifting and employee theft that hurts not only the businesses themselves but the consumer as well, even though little of it comes to the attention of the police. Despite the about 11 million serious crimes such as assault and burglary that are reported annually in the country, more precise crime victimization studies show that only about a third to a half of them are reported to the police. Moreover, only a small part of the white-collar and corporate crimes even come to the attention of the authorities. Studies of self-reported criminality and delinquency in the general population have shown that in general it is extensive, but that much variation exists in the frequency and seriousness of the behavior.[53] Most persons have committed some criminal act during their lifetimes, even of a relatively minor nature. A well-known self-report study of the criminal behavior among the general adult population in metropolitan New York, for example, found that 64 percent of the men and 29 percent of the women could have been convicted of

---

[51]For an account of the rigging of television quiz shows during the 1950s, see Richard S. Tedlow, "Intellect on Television: The Quiz Show Scandals of the 1950s," *American Quarterly*, 14 (1977), 483–495.

[52]"N.Y. Bond Deception Charged," *The Wisconsin State Journal* (Madison), August 27, 1977, Section 1, p. 1.

[53]See the review of these studies in Travis Hirschi, "Labelling Theory and Juvenile Delinquency: An Assessment of the Evidence," in Walter Gove, ed., *The Labelling of Deviance: Evaluating a Perspective* (New York: Sage/Halsted, 1975), pp. 188–191. Also see Albert J. Reiss, Jr., "Inappropriate Theories and Inadequate Methods as Policy Plagues: Self-Reported Delinquency and the Law," in N. J. Demerath III, Otto Larsen, and Karl F. Schuessler, eds., *Social Policy and Sociology* (New York: Academic Press, 1975), pp. 211–222.

felonies.[54] The mean number of offenses committed by the men in adult life (over 16 years of age) was 18, ranging from 8 percent for ministers to 20 percent for laborers. Between 8 and 9 of every 10 men and women had stolen something; 1 in 4 of the men admitted stealing an automobile, and 1 in 10 of this group had robbed someone. Reported criminality ranges from persons who have committed no criminal acts (probably few in number) to those who have committed frequent and serious acts (also probably few).[55]

It has been estimated by the U.S. Department of Commerce that losses in the service industries total $9.2 billion a year, largely due to dishonest employees.[56] Doctors steal stethoscopes from hospitals, nurses take home supplies, hospital staff members steal narcotics, lawyers and doctors connive to swindle insurance companies. Most of the losses in the hotel and motel businesses, which total about $1.5 billion annually, are the result of pilfering by employees, although one survey indicated that one in every three guests steal something from the place of lodging. The largest losses to crime, amounting to $2.5 billion, are in cargo transport, with truck losses alone accounting for about half the total loss. Although there is some hijacking of cargo, it is only a small percentage of theft-related claims, the employees with access to the shipments being the chief culprits. In banks, employees tap accounts, rig computers to siphon off money into accounts for themselves, and otherwise enrich themselves at the expense of the bank and its customers. In the insurance area, 1 out of 10 claims are said to be fraudulent, with losses annually of $1.5 billion, thus raising premiums to the public by at least 15 percent. Persons stage accidents with damaged, stolen, or rented cars, phantom accidents are contrived, and body shop frauds are particularly insidious. Arson for profit defrauds insurance companies easily because it is the least detectable of all crimes. The fire itself usually destroys the evidence, arrest rates do not exceed 1 percent, and prosecution for this imperceptible percentage does not exceed 1 percent.

Lawlessness even extends into U.S. high schools where a national survey in 1977 of high school youth found that one in five feared for their safety while in school.[57] As one student put it, "It's not safe to walk in the corridors." Moreover, the levels of victimization reported in the survey did not differ greatly by size of community or by region of the country. One out of three students reported that they had money or property stolen at school or had personal property damaged or destroyed. As many as one parent in four fears for their children's physical safety.

Fraud may be the most prevalent crime in the United States today. Some studies

---

[54]James S. Wallerstein and Clement J. Wyle, "Our Law-Abiding Law-Breakers," *Federal Probation,* 25 (1947), 107–112.

[55]This is not to say that all persons have committed a serious crime, or even that many have. One study found that most of the delinquencies committed by a large group of youth in Philadelphia were concentrated in a relatively small subgroup of them. See Marvin E. Wolfgang, Robert M. Figlio, and Thorsten Sellin, *Delinquency in a Birth Cohort* (Chicago: University of Chicago Press, 1972).

[56]*Los Angeles Times,* December 4, 1977, Section 1, p. 22.

[57]Gallup poll, reported in the *Wisconsin State Journal* (Madison), December 15, 1977, Section 4, p. 6. Another study showed that each month 282,000 students are attacked and 5,200 teachers assaulted, based on investigations by David Bayless and associates at the Research Triangle Institute in Triangle Park, North Carolina. Reported in *The Wisconsin State Journal,* April 19, 1978.

indicate that as many as one income tax return in five is fraudulent.[58] Over two million returns in 1966, for example, were found to have underreported tax liability by an average of $1,250. Although this figure includes computational and deduction errors, it also includes much fraud. Fraudulent reports of taxes on income property are common. A study of rental income found that one half of this type of income was unreported to the tax authorities.[59] Fraud is particularly extensive in private insurance claims. "Chiseling" occurs with considerable frequency in unemployment compensation.[60] It also occurs in various types of welfare cases and within the medical profession where the number of fraudulent Medicare medical claims grows each year. Defects in commodities are often concealed in all types of merchandising: there is misrepresentation in labeling, various "fillers" are used in clothing, and "list" prices are not what they are claimed to be. Corruption is extensive in private business. Persons making large-scale purchases for department stores, hotels, and many other concerns accept, and even demand, gifts or payments of money, and in so doing, they violate the trust given them even though it is not necessarily in a criminal manner. It is the consumer who eventually pays for such gifts because the costs are added to that of the merchandise being sold.

Many of the large corporations in the United States have been the subject of charges of social irresponsibility, unethical practices, and illegal behavior.[61] Such actions have included (1) paying off or bribing foreign purchasers and officials; (2) allowing the paying of kickbacks or "Christmas gifts" to purchasing agents; (3) hiring away of employees of other corporations or government regulatory agencies in order to gain trade secrets and even on occasion stealing them; (4) operating the corporation to gain personal benefits for corporate management at the expense of the stockholders; (5) fraudulent advertising, unwarranted claims for, or misrepresentation of, their products; (6) selling virtually worthless products—for example, cereals lacking in adequate nutrition or drugs with no medically proven effects; (7) selling harmful or unsafe products such as drugs, foods, autos, tires, and appliances; (8) refraining from developing or manufacturing a cheaper product, withholding more efficient products from the market, or building obsolesence into the products; (9) disregarding the physical environment and exploiting natural resources without regard for future generations; (10) deliberately building a false image of the social consciousness of a corporation; and (11) making illegal political contributions to gain influence over government. After investigating the extensive illegal corporate contributions to the 1972 Nixon presidential campaign, the Special Watergate Prosecutor concluded:

[58]*New York Times*, April 16, 1972.

[59]Harold M. Groves, "An Empirical Study of Income-Tax Compliance," in Gilbert Geis and Robert F. Meier, eds., *White-Collar Crime: Offenses in Business, Politics and the Professions* (New York: Free Press, 1977), pp. 197–205.

[60]Erwin O. Smigel, "Public Attitudes toward 'Chiseling' with Reference to Unemployment Compensation," in Erwin O. Smigel and H. Laurence Ross, eds., *Crimes against Bureaucracy* (New York: Van Nostrand Reinhold, 1970), pp. 29–46.

[61]See, for example, M. David Ermann and Richard J. Lundman, eds., *Corporate and Governmental Deviance: Problems of Organizational Behavior in Contemporary Society* (New York: Oxford University Press, 1978). Also see the discussions of corporate crime in Chapter 7 and the citations.

It was clear that, even though relatively few major federal prosecutions had been brought in the past, almost all corporate officials were well aware of the illegality of contributing corporate money to candidates for federal office. As a result, most did not make such contributions, motivated, if not by principle, at least by fear of being caught. As a device to remain within the letter of the law, a number of major corporations simply "encouraged" their officers to contribute from personal funds. . . . Even where the amount of money contributed by an officer bore a suspiciously direct relationship to salary level, the corporate officers denied any express understanding of "ear-marking" a percentage of salary for political contributions. In a number of instances, corporate officials resorted to more transparent devices, such as reimbursement of corporate official contributors by phony "bonuses" or "expense accounts."[62]

The very pervasiveness of corruption and usurpation seems to vary from one society to another, and within a single society over time public concern about it rises and falls correspondingly. "But the problems and the resulting concerns seem to be an inherent part of the governing process."[63]

Political corruption in the United States is a serious problem. Within recent years, it has involved presidents, particularly President Nixon, Cabinet officers, senators, representatives, governors, and mayors of our largest cities, as well as important government employees. Maryland, geographically in proximity to the nation's capital, furnishes an apt illustration of how entrenched political corruption can become established in a society. In 1977, Governor Marvin Mandel was convicted of accepting bribes (exceeding $350,000) and was sentenced to serve a prison term of four years. The man whom Mandel had succeeded, Spiro Agnew, resigned as Vice President of the United States in 1973 after pleading no contest to federal tax evasion charges that he had failed to report $29,500 received in 1967 when he was governor of Maryland. He was also accused of other violations, including accepting bribes. The man who had followed Agnew as Baltimore County executive was convicted in 1974 by a federal jury on 32 counts of income tax evasion and extorting kickbacks. Corruption charges in Maryland also extended into the prosecutorial ranks when Baltimore County prosecutor Samuel Green was convicted in 1974 of obstructing justice, conspiring to obstruct justice, misconduct in office, and encouraging perjury. In recent years in Maryland, a congressman and a speaker of the state house of delegates have been convicted on criminal charges. Both convictions involved a scandal in the savings and loan industry. The highest-ranking Maryland official after Agnew and Mandel to become involved in criminal actions was former U.S. Senator Daniel Brewster, who was convicted of accepting an unlawful payment in connection with pending legislation dealing with third-class mail rates. The prosecuting attorney of Agnew and Mandel has claimed that Maryland has an extensive political boss system which fosters corrupt

---

[62]From *The Right and the Power* by Leon Jaworski. Copyright © 1976 by The Leon Jaworski Foundation. Used with permission. All rights reserved.

[63]Jack D. Douglas and John M. Johnson, eds., *Official Deviance: Readings in Malfeasance, Misfeasance, and Other Forms of Corruption* (Philadelphia: Lippincott, 1977), p. 2. Corruption is also widespread in many other countries, including the developing countries. See Marshall B. Clinard and Daniel J. Abbott, *Crime in Developing Countries* (New York: Wiley, 1973), pp. 51–57.

practices.[64] "There is a fine line between a campaign check and bribery. Over the passage of time, the line becomes hazy and soon it disappears," he says, making the pursuit of political corruption a first priority in restoring public faith in government. It would be difficult to convince many of the state's ordinary criminals, particularly those in prison, to respect the law under these circumstances.

Selective Disobedience of Law   In modern U.S. society persons tend to obey laws on a selective basis. Instead of obeying all laws, an individual disregards certain laws directly affecting that person's own life and activities. Some laws are obeyed, others are not, according to personal beliefs. Persons who are otherwise law-abiding may steal objects from hotels and restaurants. Towels, pillowcases, draperies, even television sets, are taken by guests from all types of lodging facilities, and in restaurants people help themselves to silverware, vases, plates, ashtrays, salt and pepper shakers, potted plants, and even restroom fixtures. To the individual, they are often "souvenirs"; to the law, they are thefts.

Many business persons and corporations believe that laws which regulate securities and banking procedures, tax collections, restraint of trade, labor relations, and the like, are not as binding on the individual as, for example, burglary and robbery laws. One study has concluded that one reason for the attitude that certain economic offenses are permissible is the lack of enforcement efforts directed at violations of these laws.[65] By failing to enforce antitrust laws, for example, the impression is given that not only are these violations permissible but that they may even be necessary at times. Some labor leaders see no reason for obeying laws that prohibit labor "racketeering" or laws affecting the conduct of labor relations and strikes, if it is to their advantage to break them. Farmers have been known, too, to disobey the law selectively; examples include their failure to pay proper income taxes, interference with forced farm auctions, and their dumping of milk trucks to keep up the price of milk. Government officials operate in situations where bribes and favors are on occasion offered by persons in business. Policemen are bribed by citizens, business persons, and organized criminals. Politicians, including congressmen, exert influence on behalf of special interests for a financial or other payment.

There is no better example of how selective obedience to law may have tremendous repercussions on U.S. society than the 1973 Watergate scandal. Here a President of the United States, in association with a group of colleagues, set himself above the law in order to win an election and to keep the political party in power. The defense was that the presidential office gave certain powers to the chief executive which must be safeguarded; that what was done was done to protect the security of the nation, which carried the implication that it was important to keep in power a conservative political leadership which was allied to many businesses and corporations and in this capacity was carrying out the electoral "mandate" and the goal of a

---

[64]"Boss System Seen as Cause of Corruption," *The Washington Post,* December 8, 1977, Section B, pp. 1 and 2.
[65]Albert E. McCormick, Jr., "Rule Enforcement and Moral Indignation: Some Observations on the Effects of Criminal Antitrust Convictions upon Societal Reaction Processes," *Social Problems,* 25 (1977), 30–39.

"proper American way of life." The Watergate Special Prosecutor, Leon Jaworski, after a thorough investigation, summed up the criminal charges against President Nixon (according to sections of the U.S. Criminal Code):

> There was evidence that the President conspired with others to violate 18 U.S.C. 1503—obstruction of justice—via the means set out in the cover-up indictment. This included paying of funds and offers of clemency and other benefits in order to influence the testimony of witnesses, making and facilitating the making of false statements and declarations, obtaining information about the ongoing investigation from the Justice Department for the purpose of diverting or thwarting the investigation.
>
> There was evidence that the President conspired with others to violate 18 U.S.C. 1623—perjury—which included the President's direct and personal efforts to encourage and facilitate the giving of misleading and false testimony by aides.
>
> There was evidence that the President conspired with others to violate 18 U.S.C. 201 (d)—bribery—by directly and indirectly suggesting and implicitly offering something of value—money and clemency in the case of Howard Hunt, clemency and/or pardon in the case of some aides—with the intent to influence their testimony before grand juries, courts and congressional committees.
>
> There was evidence that the President conspired with others to violate 18 U.S.C. 1505—obstruction of a congressional committee—by corruptly endeavoring to influence testimony of various persons before the Senate Watergate Committee.
>
> And there was evidence that the President conspired with others to violate 18 U.S.C. 1510—obstruction of a criminal investigation.[66]

Nixon repeatedly committed perjury: he lied to the congressional committees and to the American public for two years. He misused and obstructed the various government agencies such as the CIA and the FBI in order to conceal the offenses, and he used the tax powers of the Internal Revenue Service to punish enemies of the Administration and to reward its friends.[67] Political funds were solicited from businesses and corporations in order to obtain favors or under fear of retaliatory actions. Published reports appeared that ITT (International Telephone and Telegraph Corporation, one of the largest U.S. corporations) had promised to provide $400,000 for the 1972 Republican National Convention in order to suppress a Justice Department antitrust suit against it under presidential pressure, a suit subsequently dropped.[68] Moreover, the President engaged in a series of tax activities that were either illegal or, at the minimum, highly unethical. He took a tax deduction of $482,018 on the gift of his Vice Presidential papers to the National Archives, a deed that was delivered nine months after the effective date of a 1969 law that prohibited such gifts, a deed that was never accepted by the Archives as a formal written document. The President paid a total income tax of $789 in 1970 and $878 in 1971. Large sums of public money were spent on Nixon's large, private residences in Key Biscayne and San Clemente, much of which was spent not to improve the security of the residences but to increase the value of the properties. At about the time that these revelations were coming out, the President gave a speech on television in which he stated: "I've made mistakes, but in

---

[66]Jaworski, p. 213. Copyright © 1976 by The Leon Jaworski Foundation. Used with permission. All rights reserved.
[67]Jaworski, pp. 116 and 84.
[68]Jaworski, pp. 177–178.

all my years of public life I have never profited from public service. I have earned every cent. And in all of my years of public life I have never obstructed justice. People have got to know whether or not their President is a crook. Well, I'm not a crook. I earned everything I've got."[69]

The payoffs to those who were involved in the Watergate burglary—$75,000 to one—of the National Democratic Headquarters, primarily to keep them quiet, were made in great secrecy. "Communications were made from phone booths to phone booths. Code names were used and coded messages were sent. Cash, that nonfundable commodity, was always used. The bundles of cash were left in phone booths, in lockers at airports, on ledges in hotels, and in the dead of night in mail boxes out in Potomac, Maryland."[70]

In all, 25 persons were imprisoned and many more convicted as a result of Watergate, which conceivably might never have been discovered or, if discovered, might not have resulted in justice except for a tough-minded Federal judge, John Sirica. Three of Nixon's top lieutenants, his presidential assistants, and the attorney-general were sentenced to two and a half years (which was later reduced). The former deputy director of the 1972 presidential campaign served seven months in prison and the general-counsel more than four years. Most of them, however, received short sentences or were put on probation. Nixon received a presidential pardon, and later he earned $600,000, plus a percentage of the profits, from a series of nationally televised interviews, and his memoirs are expected to earn for him about $2 million. Many of the participants each received sums ranging from $50,000 to $100,000 from book royalties, lectures, and interviews, and there are indications that these sums will greatly increase. Over 300 corporations made illegal contributions, and several of their officers were convicted of making illegal campaign contributions, but few received substantial penalties. Despite these convictions and penalties, perhaps someone will be able at some time to estimate the indirect effect of such a major crime in high places on the belief in the importance of law obedience among the youth and adults of the nation.[71]

The implications of selective obedience to law can also be seen if ordinary crimes are considered. Unemployed and sometimes poor persons, particularly youth, excuse or rationalize theft on the basis of their situations. This excuse is often given for crime by slum people and was the rationalization offered, for example, for the extensive looting in the New York City slums during a 1977 power blackout when hundreds of stores were looted, with losses totaling hundreds of millions of dollars.[72] Many persons who engage in theft and robbery believe the legal penalties are unjust and overly severe, and they often have a number of rationalizations for these activities. They point to the general dishonesty of the public, the brutality of the police, and the

---

[69]Jaworski, p. 66.

[70]Jaworski, p. 326.

[71]For an insightful comparison between the criminal nature of both power-hungry and heroin-hungry persons, see Talcott Parsons and Dean R. Gerstein, "Two Cases of Social Deviance: Addiction to Heroin, Addiction to Power," in Edward Sagarin, ed., *Deviance and Social Change* (Beverly Hills, Calif.: Sage Publications, 1977), pp. 19–57.

[72]Later it was found that approximately 40 percent of those apprehended were employed. Two of the main targets of the looters were liquor and appliance stores.

corruption of public officials, including those in the courts. A professional confidence man who is smart enough to out-trick a "sucker" may contend that the law should not punish him, or in any event not as severely as it does. A man with a prison record who has a dependent family, whose wages are low, and whose record interferes with employment possibilities may advance such arguments as rationalizations for his crimes. Certainly ordinary criminals are acquainted with the effects of this selective obedience to law, and this attitude presents a major problem in the rehabilitation work of correctional institutions.

In his 1978 Harvard University Commencement address, Alexander Solzhenitsyn, winner of the Nobel Prize in literature and staunch critic of, and exile from, the Soviet Union, pointed out the weaknesses of American society. Among them were the materialistic goals of the society, the use of laws by the rich and powerful to gain more power and wealth, and the irresponsible press. He stated that the human soul longs for things higher, warmer, and purer than those offered by today's mass living habits and "TV stupor."

A Low-Crime-Rate Society

Generally, high rates of conventional crime accompany a high degree of urbanization, industrialization, and affluence, as in U.S. society. Switzerland, however, represents an exception to this general rule. In terms of per capita wealth, it is the richest industrial country in the world, yet its crime problem is far less serious than it is in the next most affluent Western countries (Sweden, the United States, and the Federal Republic of Germany head the list in order of affluence). The crime problem in Switzerland is much lower than that in the three most affluent countries, as measured by studies of public concern about crime, official crime rates, crime victimization surveys, insurance rates for burglary, theft and auto theft, and the extent of crime news in newspapers.[73]

One cannot explain this phenomenon on an individual basis; instead, one must turn to the nature of the Swiss society. Due to the unique government and political structure of the country, as well as to its historical development, the process of urbanization has been slow and the cities have never become too large (the largest Swiss city has a population of about 425,000 as compared with, for example, Stockholm with nearly a million). No areas of any Swiss city are characterized by a slum way of life such as is found in most larger cities in the United States or in, for example, Hamburg, Paris, Marseilles, or London. As a result, norms favorable to the growth of criminal patterns have not been established in specific areas of Swiss cities.

Swiss citizens dislike the delegation of much responsibility to the federal government, as is the case in most European countries. Instead, the average Swiss citizen assumes great responsibility in a highly decentralized political system. The six million people are divided into 25 semiautonomous cantons and half cantons and these, in turn, are divided into 3,000 political units termed communes. Each canton has its own legislative body, its own educational system, and even the administration of its own

---

[73]Marshall B. Clinard, *Cities with Little Crime: The Case of Switzerland* (Cambridge, England: Cambridge University Press, 1978).

courts and its police. The small communes deal with the collection of taxes, elections, selection of teachers, relief funds, maintenance of public buildings, and many other affairs. The Swiss citizen's widespread sense of responsibility and active participation in community affairs affects each individual's behavior and that of others, including compliance not only with the generally accepted social norms but also with the law. It is commonly said, for example, that in Switzerland "everyone is his own policeman." The people are conscious of the judgment that others make of behavior that violates laws and regulations and thus risks public censure. The possibility of public censure restrains many from getting into trouble; in fact, the desire to avoid public censure is more conducive to conformity than fear of a police reprimand.

Property crimes, which constitute the bulk of all serious offenses, are generally committed by youth under the age of 18, or at most under 20. One of the major explanations of Switzerland's lower crime rate is that it has a considerably lower percentage of offenders among the youth. Moreover, Swiss offenders are in general older than are offenders in other Western countries. If the younger age groups, for example, from 14 to 17, do not engage in crime in Switzerland in the same proportion as they do in other countries, the total crime rate is reduced. In addition, there is little organized youth gang behavior.

Several factors play a role in this reduced youth crime. The urbanization process in industrialized societies is usually associated with and, in fact, aids in bringing about, a breakdown of social controls over youth. As the process develops and peer groups are formed, communication between the groups diminishes and the youth become increasingly alienated from the adult generation and from their families. This process appears to have been limited in Switzerland, although it is developing, and this has had an important bearing on the lower crime rate found among the youth. There appear to have been more opportunities to bridge the generation gap, and, as a result, the youth are less separated from their elders. This does not mean that there is not some youth unrest or that they do not seek a degree of independence: they are just not as often alienated as they are in many Western European societies. Of great significance is the fact that some studies indicate that young Swiss persons, unlike many adolescents elsewhere, do not necessarily prefer their peers to adults as significant others. Support for the view that Swiss youth continue to be more integrated into the general society than they are in most similar societies is perhaps better shown in a study made in 1973 of a representative sample of Zurich canton young persons between 15 and 25.[74] About three fourths (77 percent) of the youth preferred to participate in a group that is heterogeneous with respect to age. In another study only 1 percent of a stratified nonrepresentative sample drawn from the larger study indicated popularity among the peer group as the most important of five given items.[75]

---

[74]Robert Blancpain and Erich Hauselmann, *Zur Unrast der Jugend. Eine sociologische Untersuchung Uber Einstellungen, politische Verhaltensweisen und irhe gesellschaftlichen Determinanten* (Frauenfeld and Stuttgart: Verlag Huber, 1974), p. 54.

[75]Claudio Casparis, *Zur Unrast der Jugen: Eine socialpsychologische Untersuchung der Deziehungen zwischen Erwachsenen und Jugendlichen in Familie Bildung und Beruf* (Frauenfeld and Stuttgart: Verlag Huber, 1975).

In addition to the general social structure, with strong family ties even in urban areas and a more disciplined school system, both of which tend to strengthen the status quo, other factors are important in maintaining more family solidarity and contacts between age groups and more conformity in the family. Although care must be exercised in overemphasizing one aspect of Swiss life, certain traditions act to bridge the gaps between age groups. The long and important tradition of out-of-doors activities that begins early and continues into the older years has resulted in joint activities of all kinds throughout life. Teenaged, and even older youth, often travel with their parents and other adults to hike and ski in the mountains, and they participate in nonsports-related endeavors as well. Traditionally, in rural Switzerland, annual Alpen-festes of sports and singing that involve all age groups are still held. Regardless of age, the Swiss often participate in gymnastics, hiking, skiing, and various individual competitions like wrestling and group singing.

Another factor of significance in the maintenance of more open lines of communication between generations is the greater tendency for youth in their early twenties to continue to live with their parents in the cities while they go to school or work. They are accustomed to associate with older persons, and Swiss youth are frequently seen drinking beer and wine in association with older men in cafes, taverns, and other public gathering places. Of even greater significance is Switzerland's long tradition of a largely citizen army. All males between the ages of 20 and 50 (previously it was 55, and this age remains now only for officers) are supposed to serve as members of the army unless they are exempted. This produces a great deal of interaction between the youth and the adult men. Target installations are located in communities of all sizes, and they are used regularly each week, particularly on the weekends. Premilitary age groups—those from 16 to 19—often participate in target practice under the direction of older persons. Restaurant and drinking places display community awards and team trophies for target shooting and other activities, particularly sports events. All of this, together with the other varied activities carried out in Switzerland across age lines, serves to inhibit the age separation, alienation, and growth of a separate youth culture that has increasingly become characteristic of the United States, Sweden, and many other highly developed countries. Although these factors represent only one aspect of a total Swiss way of life, they play an important role in the low crime rate and the crime trend.

The nature of the Swiss criminal justice system has also helped to reduce ordinary crime. In the German-speaking area, offenders are seldom arrested; citations are usually given instead. No plea bargaining is available for a reduction in the charge; most sentences to prison are suspended, dependent upon no further violation of law; and prison sentences are of a very short duration, generally less than one year, and usually only one person in six receives a sentence of more than six months. Even short prison sentences are not always served to completion. Swiss inmates thus are not incarcerated over long periods of time that might permit the acquisition of additional criminal sophistication. As indicated by the general crime situation, few offenders appear to develop secondary criminal careers that involve a criminal self-concept, the acquisition of advanced criminal techniques, and rationalizations for crime, all of which are likely to lead them into careers in armed robbery, burglary, or other crimes of a serious nature. Since it appears that few sophisticated criminals are developed in the system, few other persons in the society become "infected" with such criminal norms. All of this tends to reduce both the volume and the seriousness of conventional crime.

Unfortunately, while the nature of Swiss society tends to inhibit conventional crime, other aspects of it appear to make for a crime problem in certain businesses and banking, primarily at the international level. This includes such forms as swindles in stocks, bonds, and real estate, the misuse of bills of exchange, and the "laundering of dirty money" from abroad through the Swiss banking facilities. Although Swiss banking enjoys high prestige, the federal government has only weak controls over commercial and banking transactions, and the cantons are far too numerous—and many of them are also too small—for any practical control over large-scale financial dealings. This is due to the fact that the country is an international center for business and finance. It is also the result of the economic power differentials in what is defined as real crime, the tolerance of the Swiss public of these illegal activities (as contrasted with other kinds of crime), bank secrecy laws, and the inability of the cantons to deal with the national and international complexities of white-collar crime.

The smaller size of a country like Switzerland need not preclude the applicability of the lessons learned to much larger countries. There are a number of practical implications of a study of the nature of Swiss society for the United States and for other societies. Some of these are:

1. Large urban concentrations can be controlled by the dispersal of industry and the development of satellite cities, which would help to decentralize the size and population densities of the large cities. With rare exceptions, optimum city population should not exceed 250,000 to 500,000.

2. Communities or cities that wish to prevent crime should encourage greater political decentralization by developing small governmental units and encouraging citizen responsibility for law obedience and crime control. The increased delegation of responsibility for crime control to the police and to governmental agencies, as well as the tendency to blame them for the crime problem, should probably be reversed.[76] This is particularly true in the large urban areas. In order to stimulate a reversed trend, urban, and particularly slum, areas could well be broken down into semipolitical units of approximately 5,000 persons, who would be encouraged to assume more active participation in crime control along with involvement in other acute urban problems. As local leadership is encouraged, as well as greater individual initiative and broader-based citizen organization, a situation could be developed more closely parallel to the general local citizen responsibility found in Switzerland.

3. The close relationship between conventional crime and youth demands the development of broader integration of youth and adults in common activities and purposes. The common method of dealing with youth problems by means of special youth programs, rather than through the integration of youth with adult groups, has tended to maximize, rather than diminish, the alienation of youth from the adult world. Such a goal can be accomplished partly by more interage social and sports groups and

---

[76]One writer has argued that the reluctance of the people to make crime a matter of concern for the state has contributed heavily to the apparently low crime rate in China. See Harold Pepinsky, "Despotism in the Quest for Valid Crime Statistics: Historical and Comparative Perspectives," in Robert F. Meier, ed., *Theory in Criminology: Contemporary Views* (Beverly Hills, Calif.: Sage Publications, 1977), pp. 69–82.

by the appointment and election of youth to political office and to national and local boards and committees. The lowering of the voting age from 21 in national and local elections to 18, both in the United States and in several European countries, may gradually result in more youth participation in the general society. Younger persons in the United States have been increasingly elected to local political office. Several states have even granted full adult privileges to those who are 18.

4. Many aspects of the Swiss criminal justice system might well be adopted, including the substitution of the issuance of citations for many arrests, the elimination of bargaining for a reduction in the offense charged, and the reduction in the severe length of sentences now given in the United States, the longest in the world. The recommendations of a recent U.S. Commission for a reduction in the length of prison sentences might well be adopted, though probably not to the extent of those in Switzerland given the more serious nature of the crime problem in the United States.[77]

CONCLUDING REMARKS

The nature and control of deviance must be sought in features of social structure and interpersonal interaction. Social groups "create" deviance by making rules (norms), by displaying valuations about behavior (tolerance), and by reacting against behavior that violates the rules beyond the group's tolerance (sanctions). Because norms, tolerance, and sanctions are intrinsic components of all social groups, deviance is an inevitable feature of all social systems.

Deviance is more prevalent in some social contexts than in others. Urban settings, particularly inner-city or slum areas, provide a number of social pressures conducive to deviance. Deviance is not a random phenomenon in terms of the distribution of the forms of deviance discussed here. Systematic differences between social groups are based on age, race, occupation, and socioeconomic status. Moreover, there are group aspects to these forms of deviance; some forms are more group related than others. Crime and delinquency, for example, are group forms of deviance with distinctive subcultural elements. Suicide and physical disabilities have less distinct group properties, though even here the meaning of these forms of deviance is best seen on the sociological level.

The problem of explaining social order, particularly in social groups characterized by a sophisticated division of labor and a multiplicity of social roles and statuses, constitutes one of the core problems of sociology. As such, the study of deviance represents a central sociological concern; in fact, one could argue that it stands at the center of sociological inquiry.

SELECTED REFERENCES

Barron, Milton L. "The Criminogenic Society: Social Values and Deviance," in Abraham S. Blumberg, ed., *Current Perspectives on Criminal Behavior.* New York: Knopf, 1974.

---

[77]National Advisory Commission on Criminal Justice, Standards, and Goals, *Corrections* (Washington, D.C.: U.S. Department of Justice, 1973).

Becker, Howard S. *Outsiders: Studies in the Sociology of Deviance,* enlarged ed. New York: Free Press, 1973.

Clinard, Marshall B. *Cities with Little Crime.* Cambridge: Cambridge University Press, 1978.

Cohen, Albert K. *The Elasticity of Evil: Changes in the Social Definition of Deviance.* Oxford: Oxford University Penal Research Unit, Basil Blackwell, 1974.

Erickson, Maynard L., and Gary F. Jensen. "'Delinquency Is Still Group Behavior!': Toward Revitalizing the Group Premise in the Sociology of Deviance," *Journal of Criminal Law and Criminology,* 68 (1977), 262–273.

Goode, Erich. "On Behalf of Labeling Theory," *Social Problems,* 22 (1975), 570–583.

Hirschi, Travis. "Procedural Rules and the Study of Deviant Behavior," *Social Problems,* 21 (1973), 159–173.

Jaworski, Leon. *The Right and the Power: The Prosecution of Watergate.* New York: Pocket Books, 1977.

Johnson, John M., and Jack D. Douglas, eds. *Crime at the Top: Deviance in Business and the Professions.* Philadelphia: Lippincott, 1978.

MacNamara, Donal E. J., and Edward Sagarin, eds. *Sex, Crime and the Law.* New York: Free Press, 1977.

Manning, Peter K. *Police Work: The Social Organization of Policing.* Cambridge, Mass.: MIT Press, 1977.

Sallach, David L. "Class Domination and Ideological Hegemony," *The Sociological Quarterly,* 15 (1974), 38–50.

Silberman, Milton, and Philip R. Lee. *Pills, Profits and Politics.* Berkeley: University of California Press, 1974.

Yinger, J. Milton. "Countercultures and Social Change," *American Sociological Review,* 42 (1977), 833–853.

NAME INDEX

SUBJECT INDEX

A

Absolutist definition of deviance, 12–13
Abstinence syndrome, 294
Addiction (*see* Drug addiction)
Adolescence
  roles acquired in, 38
  See also Delinquency; Youth; Youth crime
Adolescent violations, 170
  See also Delinquency; Youth crime
Advertising
  of alcoholic beverages, 371
  deceptive (false and misleading), 214; by corporations, 220–221
  drug use and, 290–291
Age
  classification of criminals by, 186–188
  marijuana use and, 299–300
  of opiate addicts, 303–304
  suicide rate and, 507–508
  violent crimes and, 199
  See also Youth
Aggressiveness (aggression)
  mass media and, 172–173
  pornography and, 416
  suicide as, 501–502
Alcohol (alcoholic beverages)
  physiological and psychological aspects of, 334–337
  prevention of abuse of, 369, 371
  social control of, 368–372
  See also Alcoholics; Drinking; Drunkenness
Alcoholics (alcoholism)
  argot of, 375
  chronic, 348
  community-based treatment programs for, 372–373
  costs of, 351–352
  definition of, 25, 347–348
  drinking patterns of, 348–349
  extent of, 349–354
  group and subcultural factors in, 354–365; companions, 356; ethnic groups, 365; occupation, 358–359; sex differences, 361; skid row drinking, 357–358
  halfway houses for, 373
  labeling of, 353–354
  medical model and, 352–353
  personality traits of, 112
  psychoses resulting from, 26, 456
  skid row type, 373
  societal reaction to, 353
  women, 350–351

Alcoholics Anonymous, 8, 373–376
Alcohol substitution, 369
Altruistic suicide, 511–513
Ambulance chasing by lawyers, 216
American Indians, drinking patterns of, 364
Amphetamines, legal use of, 287–289, 291
Anomic suicide, 513–514
Anomie, 67–73
  class bias of, 70–71
  conflict and, 81
  definition of, 67
  drug addiction and, 322–323
  simplicity of, 71–72
  universality assumed by, 70
Anonymity, urbanism and, 137
Anxiety, mental disorder and, 480–481
Apathy of slum dwellers, 154, 158
Approval of deviations from norms, 10
Argot
  of alcoholics, 375
  of drug addicts, 317, 319
  of professional criminals, 237
  skid row, 357–358
  See also Language
Arrest rates
  by age, 186–188
  for violent crimes, by race, 198
Arrests
  for drunkenness, 340–342
  for prostitution, 406
Assault (aggravated assault), 196
  alcohol-related, 365–366
  victims of (*see* Victims, of violent crimes; Violent crimes)
Attachment, definition of, 89
Attitudes
  changes in, 34
  criminal (*see* Criminals, attitudes and criminal behavior of)
  motives and, 34–35
Audience, relative deviance and, 15–16
Automobile accidents, drinking involved in, 366–368
Automobiles, manufacture of unsafe, 221
Automobile theft, 206

B

Barbiturates
  illegal use of, 297
  legal use of, 286–288, 291
Bars, 343–345
  gay, 440

599